Admiralty Manual
of Seamanship

VOLUME I
B.R. 67(1)

LONDON
HER MAJESTY'S STATIONERY OFFICE
1972

Consolidated Edition 1972
Incorporating Change 1

© *Crown copyright 1972*

HER MAJESTY'S STATIONERY OFFICE

Government Bookshops

49 High Holborn, London WC1V 6HB
13a Castle Street, Edinburgh EH2 3AR
109 St Mary Street, Cardiff CF1 1JW
Brazennose Street, Manchester M60 8AS
50 Fairfax Street, Bristol BS1 3DE
258 Broad Street, Birmingham B1 2HE
80 Chichester Street, Belfast BT1 4JY

Government publications are also available
through booksellers

Produced in England for Her Majesty's Stationery Office
by Page Bros (Norwich) Ltd., Norwich
Dd 506024 K400 5/72
SBN 11 770973 5

ADMIRALTY, S.W.1

1st January 1964

D.N.D.54/61

B.R. 67(1), *Admiralty Manual of Seamanship, Volume I*, 1964, having been approved by My Lords Commissioners of the Admiralty, is hereby promulgated.

B.R. 67(1) dated 1951 is hereby superseded.

By Command of Their Lordships,

PREFACE

The *Admiralty Manual of Seamanship* is in three volumes. *Volume I* is the basic book of seamanship for officers and men joining the Royal Navy. *Volume II* contains more technical detail and is a general textbook and reference book for ratings seeking advancement and for junior officers. *Volume III* is intended mainly for officers. It covers such essential seamanship knowledge as the handling of ships and also information on a variety of subjects that could be classed as advanced seamanship, such as aid to ships in distress.

The chapters in each volume are arranged in the following four Parts, dealing generally with the subjects shown.

PART I: *Ship Knowledge and Safety.* Types of ship and their construction; firefighting; stability; control of damage; lifesaving.

PART II: *Seamanship.* The uses of rope; rigging; sailing boats and power boats; anchors and cables; evolutions such as towing, salvage and lifting or moving heavy loads.

PART III: *Ship Organisation.* General organisation of a ship; naval communications; ceremonial; ship upkeep and ship husbandry.

PART IV: *Shiphandling and Navigation.* Steering; elementary navigation and pilotage; handling of ships in different conditions; the Rule of the Road.

Questions on the information given in each chapter of Volume I are included as an Appendix to that volume, in order to give candidates for oral examinations some idea of what they may be asked.

It is hoped that the volumes may also prove useful outside the Royal Navy, to all who put to sea in ships or boats.

CONTENTS

Part II. SEAMANSHIP

CONTENTS

Part IV. SHIPHANDLING AND NAVIGATION

PART I

SHIP KNOWLEDGE AND SAFETY

CHAPTER 1

General Sea Terms

Every profession and trade uses its own technical terms to describe the more specialised parts of its work; nowhere is this more evident than in the language of the seaman. Many terms used by the British seaman have, in the course of time, become part of the English language. This is because so many of the inhabitants of our small island kingdom have been born and bred near the sea, and because no other country has for so long been dependent for its existence and prosperity on its Royal and Merchant Navies.

To learn seamanship the young seaman must first learn the more general nautical terms and expressions which are explained in this chapter. Others, more technical, are included in the chapters on the different aspects of seamanship to which they are applied.

Appendix 1 is a glossary of terms used by the experienced seaman; it includes the various phrases by which he expresses himself and, in some cases, their origins. Such expressions, rich in vigour, vividness and humour, characteristically portray the typical British seaman.

TERMS RELATING TO A SHIP

PARTS OF A SHIP

The hull

The main body of a ship is called the hull. It is divided approximately into three—the *fore* part, the *midship* part and the *after* part. The fore part ends in the *stem**, the after part in the *stern* (fig. 1–1). When standing anywhere inside

Fig. 1–1. Parts of the hull

the hull a man is facing *forward* when he faces the stem and facing *aft* when he faces the stern.

Any line which runs lengthways in the ship is said to run *fore-and-aft* and the line joining the middle of the stem to the middle of the stern is called the

---

* The stem is really the upright or inclined (raked) continuation of the keel at the fore end of the ship and the word is seldom used at sea. It is more usual to speak of the *bow*.

fore-and-aft centre line (middle line or centre line in ship's plans and drawings) (fig. 1–2).

FIG. 1–2. Parts of the hull

The vertical plane (surface) passing through the fore-and-aft centre line divides the ship into two halves. When facing the bow the *starboard* side is on the right hand and the *port* side is on the left (fig. 1–3). It is a custom to give

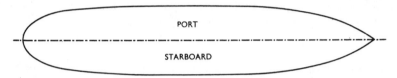

FIG. 1–3. Parts of the hull

equipment, such as ship's boats, odd numbers on the starboard side and even numbers on the port side.

Hull surfaces (fig. 1–4)

The sides of a hull can be described generally as starboard or port, meeting under the bottom of the ship at the *keel*. The curved surface of the fore part is called the bow (port or starboard) and the curved surface of the after part is called the quarter (port or starboard); the centre part is referred to as *amidships*.

When a ship is *afloat* or *water-borne* the *waterline* divides the sides into *ship's side* above the waterline and *bottom* below it. These terms are used in a general sense, for example, painting ship's side or scraping the bottom. A more precise definition of an area can be achieved by referring to the side, the part and the waterline, for example—'the ship was holed on the starboard bow four feet below the waterline'.

The continuous horizontal surfaces of a ship are called *decks*; if exposed they are called *weather decks*. Those that are not continuous are called *flats* or *platforms*.

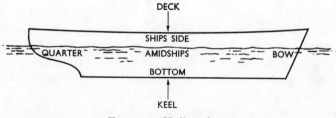

FIG. 1–4. Hull surfaces

Terms applied to the hull (fig. 1–5)

Freeboard. The height of the highest continuous watertight deck (usually known as the upper deck) above the waterline at any point along the hull.

Draught. The depth of the keel below the waterline at any point along the hull.

Beam. The greatest width of the hull.

Camber. The curve given to the surface of a deck so that water will drain away to the ship's side. It is also known as *round of beam.*

Bilge. The nearly flat part of the bottom of the hull both inside and out. 'Bilge' is also the foul water that collects inside the ship in the *bilges.*

Bilge keel. A long projecting fin designed to decrease the rolling of a ship. It is normally secured to the hull at the *turn of the bilge.*

Tumble home. When the ship's sides slope or curve inwards above the waterline they are said to tumble home.

Flare. When the ship's sides curve outwards above the waterline they are said to be flared.

Flush deck. When the uppermost deck of a ship is continuous from stem to stern, unbroken by any raised or sunken portion (except upper works or superstructure), the ship is said to be flush-decked.

Decks

Whatever the arrangement of decks in different ships may be, it is useful and instructive to know their origin.

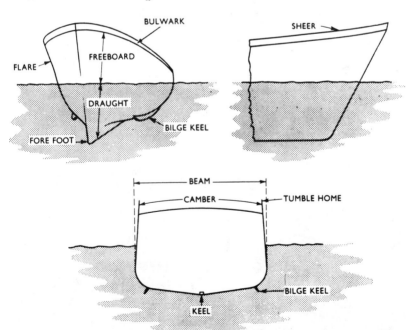

FIG. 1–5. Hull terms

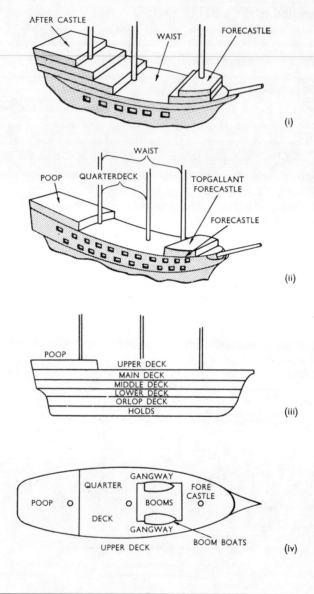

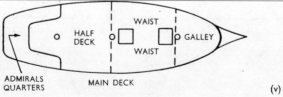

FIG. 1–6. Arrangement of decks in a sailing man-of-war

At the time of the Armada the ends of the upper deck were built up in tiers of decks to form castles from which the soldiers could fight. They were called the *forecastle* and *aftercastle*. The lower part between the castles was called the *waist* (fig. 1–6 (i)). By the end of the eighteenth century the level of the upper deck had been raised to make room for additional gun decks. Naval warfare had developed, but castles still existed. They were then called the *topgallant forecastle* and the *poop*. The forecastle was that part of the upper deck before the foremast, and the quarter deck was that part of the upper deck between the mainmast and the poop (fig. 1–6 (ii)).

In a large ship of Nelson's days the waist between the topgallant forecastle and the poop was covered by an extra deck, which became the upper deck, and the poop was stepped up to make room for the admiral's quarters. The decks below the upper deck were then named *main, middle, lower* and *orlop*, and the space below the orlop deck was known as the *hold* (fig. 1–6 (iii)). On the upper deck were the *booms* amidships over the *main hatch*; as the name implies, they constituted the stowage for spare spars and the ship's boats (fig. 1–6 (iv)). Right aft on the main deck were the admiral's cabin and cabins for his staff, and the space between them and the mainmast was called the *half deck*; the space between the mainmast and foremast was the waist, and the space between the foremast and the bows, which housed the kitchens, was known as the *galley* (fig. 1–6 (v)).

Most of these terms have been retained in naming the decks of a modern ship, and adapted to suit changes in construction and design. However, in men-of-war the decks are now also numbered in sequence from the uppermost weather deck downwards, e.g. No. 1, 2, 3, etc. deck. The traditional and the modern systems of nomenclature are both shown in fig. 1–7. The super-structure is numbered upwards (01, 02, 03, etc.).

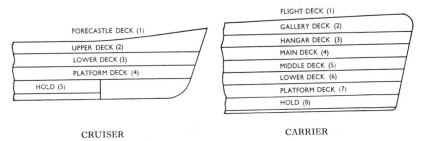

FIG. 1–7. Arrangement of decks in a modern warship

The highest complete deck (except in aircraft carriers) is known as the upper deck, the lowest the hold. The names of intermediate decks vary in accordance with their number.

In an aircraft carrier the hangar deck corresponds to the upper deck, but the numbering of decks starts from the weather (flight) deck.

Parts of decks. Certain parts of any of these decks may also have special names. Below the upper deck a *flat* is a platform that does not run the length and breadth of a ship; a *lobby* is a space giving access to one or more compart-ments. These flats or lobbies may be named according to the principal adjacent compartments or equipment installed, e.g. Wardroom flat, Captain's lobby, Capstan Machinery flat, or they may be referred to by deck numbers and positions in the ship relative to the bow and the centre line (Chapter 4).

The arrangement of the weather decks and superstructure of a ship is shown in fig. 1–8.

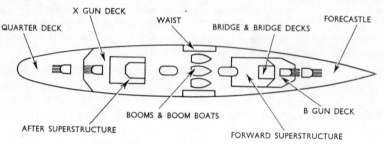

FIG. 1–8. Arrangement of weather decks and superstructure of a ship

TERMS DEFINING POSITION AND DIRECTION IN A SHIP

Position in general

A landsman lives *in* a house, therefore a seaman speaks of living *in* a ship—not *on* a ship. Let us now describe the movements of a seaman who is returning to his ship, the ship in which he is *borne*. If he arrives by boat he goes up an *accommodation ladder* which is secured *outboard* (board is the old name for a ship's side), he comes over the *side* and he is then *on board*. If the ship is lying against a dock wall it is *alongside* and the seaman crosses a *brow* from the dock to the ship and he is then on board and *on deck*, or on board and *between decks* if the brow leads into the ship below the weather deck; in either case he is *inboard* the moment he comes over the side.

Having reported his return, he then goes *below* by a *ladder* which gives access to the deck below through an opening in the deck called a *hatch*. He then reaches his living quarter (*mess*) which is in a space of the ship called a *messdeck* of which the walls are called *bulkheads*, the ceiling is called *the deck head* and the floor is the *deck*.

Position fore and aft

In fig. 1–9 the mast is *forward* (pronounced 'forrard') and the funnel is *aft*.

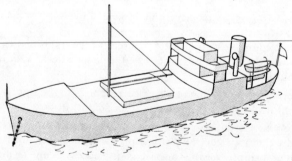

FIG. 1–9

The ensign staff is right aft and the jackstaff right forward. A hatch is *amidships*.

Amidships describes the position roughly in the middle of the ship; it also describes any position on the fore-and-aft line. *Midships* is used when defining an object: for example, the midship hatch is either the one that is in the middle of the ship, or if there are two or more hatches, that which is nearest the middle.

Comparing positions of objects with one another, the funnel is *abaft* (aft of) the bridge, the bridge is abaft the hatch but *before* or *forward of* the funnel.

Position athwartships

A position athwart or across the ship can be described relatively to either the centre line or to the sides. The centre line divides the ship into port and starboard, while the ship's sides give an *inboard* and *outboard* position. In fig. 1–10,

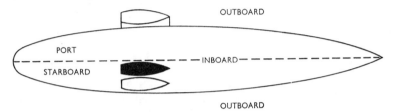

FIG. 1–10

for example, a ship is carrying three boats; one is swung outboard to port, the other two are stowed inboard to starboard. When comparing the position of the two boats stowed on the starboard side, the black boat can be described as lying inboard of the white boat, or the white boat outboard of the black. The white boat can also be described as the ship's side boat and the black boat as the midship boat.

The position of an object can be clearly described by combining the two methods, as shown in fig. 1–11.

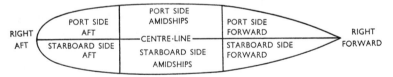

FIG. 1–11

Movements of objects on board

A seaman speaks of going forward, aft, below, on deck and aloft (i.e. anywhere in the rigging of a mast). He uses the same expressions for shifting an object; thus he may shift something aft, or further forward, to port or starboard, or nearer the ship's side. (The terms inboard and outboard should not be used to describe the movement athwartships.)

The following terms are used to describe how an object is moved:

To *launch* is to drag or heave an object along.

To *lift and launch* is to lift an object and then to heave it along.

To *fleet* is to shift an object a short distance.

To *ship* is to place an object in its proper position.

To *unship* is to remove an object from its proper position.

TERMS DEFINING THE MOVEMENT OF A SHIP

A vessel is *under way* when she is neither anchored nor secured to a buoy, nor made fast to the shore, nor aground. When actually moving through the water, a vessel has *way* on her; if she is moving too fast she is said to have *too much way on.*

When moving ahead a vessel is said to be *going ahead* or *making headway*; when moving astern a vessel is said to be *going astern* or *making sternway* or *making a stern board.* A vessel *gathers way* when she begins to move through the water, and she has *steerage way* when her speed is sufficient for steering (i.e. the rudder is effective).

A vessel moving sideways is said to be moving *broadside-on* (to port or starboard); if she is making headway and at the same time being blown sideways by the wind, she is said to be making *leeway.* When the wind is blowing from one side of the vessel, that side is called the *weather side*; the other, sheltered, side is called the *lee side.*

A ship is said to be *adrift* when broken away from her moorings and without means of propulsion.

A ship is steered by compass in a direction called the *compass course* or simply the *course.* The question *How is the ship's head?* means in what direction by the compass is she heading (pointing).

TERMS DEFINING DIRECTION AND POSITION OUTSIDE A SHIP

Relative bearings (figs. 1–12 and 1–13)

Ahead, astern and *abeam* are relative bearings. In addition, when an object is midway between ahead and abeam it is said to bear *on the bow*, and when midway between abeam and astern it is said to bear *on the quarter.* The expressions *fine* and *broad* may also be used relative to ahead or astern; for example, an object may be fine on the port bow, broad on the starboard quarter (or abaft the starboard beam).

A greater degree of accuracy in relative bearings is obtained by expressing them in terms of degrees from ahead on each side of the ship. The horizon is divided in degrees from zero right ahead to 180 right astern, those on the starboard side are called green and those on the port side red. Thus, in fig. 1–13,

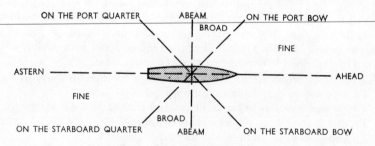

FIG. 1–12. General relative bearings

the sailing vessel bears *red* 40 and the steamship bears *green* 130 (the word 'degrees' is always omitted).

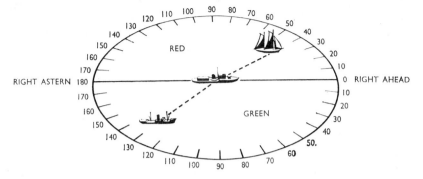

FIG. 1–13. Red and green relative bearings

When one ship is lying next to another or on a dock wall it is said to be *alongside* the other ship or wall. When two ships are on the same course and level with each other they are said to be *abreast*.

Compass bearings

The bearing of an object from the ship may be given relative to True or Magnetic North. If it is a gyro-compass the horizon is divided into 360 degrees from true North (the meridian). If it is a magnetic compass the horizon is divided into 360 degrees from magnetic North.

The *magnetic compass card* (fig. 1–14) is divided into 360 degrees from North

FIG. 1–14. A compass card

(0°), through East (090°), South (180°), West (270°), and so back to North. The card may be divided into 32 points of 11¼ degrees. The principal points, North, South, East and West are called *cardinal points*; the *intercardinal points* are North-east, South-east, South-west and North-west; and the *intermediate points* are North-north-east, East-north-east, East-south-east, South-south-east, South-south-west, West-south-west, West-north-west and North-north-west. The remaining 16 points are known as *by-points* (see Chapter 15).

Distances

The distance of an object from the ship may be expressed in nautical miles (one nautical mile is roughly equal to 2,000 yards), cables (one cable is one-tenth of a nautical mile), or in thousands of yards.

Inclination

Having established the bearing and distance of another ship, it is also possible to give an indication of her course by inclination. The inclination is the angle between the line of sight from the observer and the other ship's course, measured in degrees from 0 to 180 right or left, as illustrated in fig. 1–15.

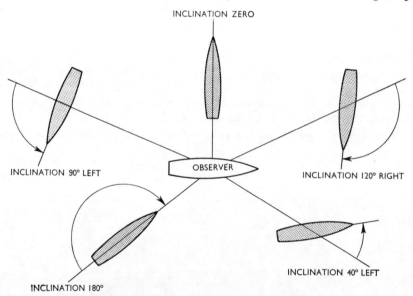

INCLINATION ZERO

INCLINATION 90° LEFT

OBSERVER

INCLINATION 120° RIGHT

INCLINATION 180°

INCLINATION 40° LEFT

FIG. 1–15. Inclination

TERMS RELATING TO SHIPPING, HARBOURS AND DOCKS

DRAUGHT AND LOADING MARKS
TONNAGE MEASUREMENTS

Draught marks

These show the draught of a ship, usually at the bows and stern and (in larger ships) amidships. They are scribed in and then painted, usually in roman numerals six inches high and six inches apart; or they may be metal figures of the same size welded to the hull and then painted (see fig. 1–16).

23 ft 6 in. – – – – – **XXIII**

23 ft – – – – – – – –

22 ft 6 in. – – – – – **XXII**

22 ft – – – – – – – –

21 ft 6 in. – – – – – **XXI**

21 ft – – – – – – – –

F IG. 1–16. Draught marks

When a ship is drawing 22 ft forward and 23 ft 3 in. aft, the waterline at the bows touches the lower edge of the numeral XXII and reaches halfway up numeral XXIII at the stern.

Plimsoll mark and load lines (fig. 1–17)

These are marks on the sides of merchant ships to denote the greatest depth to which they may be safely loaded under various conditions, in accordance with the Ministry of Transport regulations. They are named after Samuel Plimsoll, a Member of Parliament, who rendered a great service to seamen by introducing these regulations to Parliament; they were ratified under the Merchant Shipping Acts of 1876 and 1890.

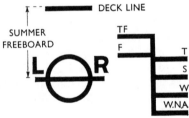

TF   tropical fresh water   WNA   winter, North Atlantic, for vessels under
F   fresh water   330 ft in length
T   tropical sea water   LR   These letters indicate the registration
S   summer, sea water   society, in this case Lloyd's Register.
W   winter, sea water

F IG. 1–17. Plimsoll mark and load line

Load waterline

This is a term chiefly used in H.M. ships to denote the position of the waterline when the ship is fully loaded with crew, stores, water, fuel, etc. The ship is then said to be in the *deep condition*.

Tonnage measurements

The tonnage of a ship can be expressed in terms of weight or of volume. When expressed by weight the unit of measurement in Great Britain is the 'avoirdupois' ton of 2,240 pounds, and when expressed by volume the unit is a ton of 100 cubic feet. The tonnage can be measured in a variety of ways, of which the following are the more usual:

Displacement. This is the actual weight of the vessel represented by the number of tons of water she displaces when loaded with fuel, water, stores and crew on board. It is seldom used for merchant ships because of the great difference in their displacements when fully and lightly loaded. It is, however, the usual method of describing the tonnage of warships.

Gross tonnage. This is the measure of the total internal volume of a ship reckoned in tons of cubic capacity, and is the usual method of expressing the tonnage of merchant ships.

Net Register tonnage. This represents the earning capacity of a merchant ship. It is a measure, in tons of cubic capacity, of that part of her internal volume which can be used for carrying cargo or passengers. In other words it is her gross tonnage less the spaces occupied by such items as machinery, crew, bridges and cable lockers. This measurement is usually employed when assessing costs, such as harbour and port dues and canal tolls.

Dead Weight tonnage. This is the measurement in weight of the cargo, passengers, crew, stores, fuel and water which a vessel can carry when floating at her load draught. In other words it is the weight of the removable or expendible items which a ship can carry.

SHIPBUILDING AND LAUNCHING

A ship is built on a *slipway*, which is a sloping platform erected on the foreshore of a deep river or estuary and extending well beyond and below the water's edge. The ship is launched in a *cradle*, which slides down the slipway until the ship becomes waterborne (fig. 1–18). Usually the ship is launched stern first, but in some shipyards the tideway (river or canal) is not sufficiently broad to allow this and the ship has to be launched sideways.

All the main structure of the hull up to the upper deck is completed before launching. In some cases the main machinery and other large equipment may be installed and some parts of the bridge and other superstructures may be erected.

After launching the ship is taken to a *fitting-out* berth in a *basin* where machinery not already fitted, internal fittings, armament, radar equipment, funnels, masts and external fittings are secured in position and the rest of the superstructure completed. Finally the ship is ready for equipment trials and then to proceed to sea for sea trials.

DOCKS AND SLIPS

Periodically during a ship's life it is necessary to inspect her hull below the waterline, to clean the bottom, change propellers, etc.; for this special docks or slips are built and the process is called *docking* or *slipping*, followed by *undocking* or *unslipping*.

Dry dock or graving dock (fig. 1–19)

This is an excavation faced with solid masonry, which is connected with a harbour, river or basin. The entrance is closed by a sliding *caisson* (pronounced

FIG. 1-18. Launching a ship from a slipway

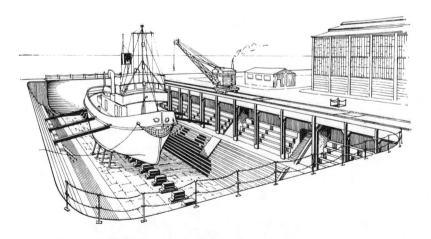

FIG. 1-19. Dry dock or graving dock

'cassoon'), a floating caisson, or *dock gates*. Water is admitted through valves (*penstocks*) until the level in the dock is the same as that outside; the entrance is then opened and the ship floated in. The entrance is then closed and the water pumped out, thus leaving the ship resting on *keel blocks* and supported by *breast shores* from the side of the dock to the ship's side, and by *bilge shores* to give additional support. Side keel blocks, and sometimes *cradles* in the wake of (below) concentrated weights, are also used for heavier ships.

Some small dry docks depend on the tide for flooding and draining. The vessel is floated in at high water, the gates are closed and, as the tide falls, the water is drained out through valves, which are shut when the dock is dry.

Floating dock (fig. 1–20)

This is a floating watertight structure which can be submerged sufficiently to receive a ship by flooding the *pontoon tanks* which form the bottom of the dock. When the ship has been floated into the dock and secured, the pontoon tanks are pumped out until the pontoon deck and the ship are dry. The ship rests on a line of blocks under the keel and in some cases blocks are positioned under the bilges. A floating dock being a live structure, it is essential that the ship be supported by breast shores placed between the ship and the side of the dock. The pressure of the shores also resists the tendency for the walls of the dock to deflect inwards when the ship is resting on the blocks.

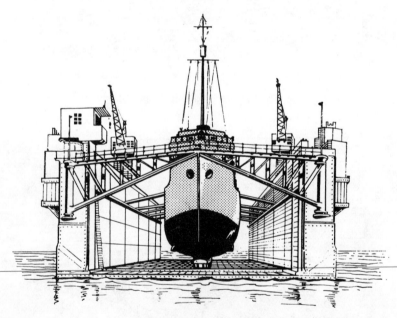

F I G. 1–20. Floating dock

Patent slip (fig. 1–21)

This consists of a sloping runway of masonry or concrete, extending some distance below the low water mark, on which rails are laid. A cradle, fitted with a wheeled carriage, is run out to receive the vessel when there is sufficient water. The vessel and cradle are hauled up the runway by winch or capstan until they are clear of the water.

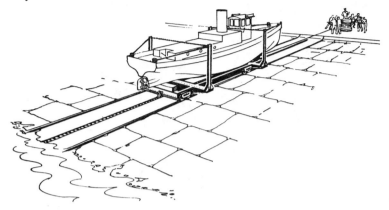

FIG. 1–21. Patent slip

Marine railway

This is the term usually applied in Canada and the United States of America to a patent slip.

Gridiron (or grid)

This is a platform, usually sited against a tidal wall of a dockyard, on which a vessel is berthed at high water for underwater inspection at low water. The grid is normally constructed of parallel baulks of timber secured to the wall.

BASINS

When a ship is loading, unloading, being repaired or fitted out (after launching) it is safer and more convenient for her to be berthed in non-tidal waters.

Basin or wet dock (fig. 1–22)

This is an area of water which, except for its entrance, is enclosed with walls of masonry and excavated to a sufficient depth to take floating ships. The water is shut in by caissons or gates, and is kept at a level sufficient to ensure that ships remain afloat. The entrance is usually through a *lock*.

Lock (fig. 1–22)

This is an excavated channel or approach to a basin or wet dock, faced with masonry and fitted at each end with a caisson or gates. Ships may then be moved to or from tidal waters at certain states of the tide without appreciably altering the level of the water in the basin or wet dock. Some locks are designed for use as dry docks.

Camber

This is a made-up strip of sloping foreshore from above high water level to well below low water level used for hauling boats clear of the water. The term is also applied to a small *dock* or *tidal basin* which has an open entrance and may dry out at low water.

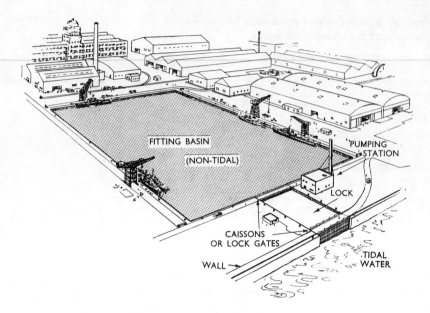

FIG. 1–22. Basin or wet dock

JETTIES, PIERS AND SIMILAR STRUCTURES

Jetty. A platform built out from the shore on piles so that there is sufficient depth alongside it to berth ships.

Pier. A narrow jetty built of masonry or on piles usually extending seaward at right angles to the line of the shore. It may be used as a breakwater or as berths for shipping.

Pens. These are bays, formed by a series of jetties or piers, for accommodating a number of small ships in berths alongside.

Mole or breakwater. A long pier of heavy masonry built on the seaward side of a harbour for protection. It may be designed for berthing ships on its shore-ward side, either alongside or with anchors down and wires from the stern to bollards (mooring posts) firmly embedded in it.

Groins. Timber and board constructions between high and low water marks to prevent coast erosion by the scouring action of the sea.

MISCELLANEOUS

Brow. A narrow platform placed between ship and shore for embarkation and disembarkation, sometimes called a gangway.

Between wind and water. The term used to describe that part of a ship's side near the waterline which is alternately submerged and exposed by the move-ment of the waves and the rolling of the ship. It is also used to describe that part of a sea wall, pile, etc. which is uncovered between high and low water.

Careening. A vessel is careened when she is heeled over on one side, by shifting weights across the decks, or by hauling her mast over by tackle, or by grounding her in shoal water on a falling tide so that part of the ship's bottom is exposed for cleaning or repairs.

Catamaran. A stoutly constructed wooden or steel raft placed between ships or between ship and jetty to avoid damage to the ship or jetty.

Cove. A small bay, the greater part of which is land-locked.

Creek. A narrow inlet or arm of the sea.

Dolphins. Mooring posts, usually composed of groups of piles, driven into the bottom of a harbour (fig. 1–23).

DOLPHINS

FIG. 1–23. Dolphins

Dumb lighter. A lighter without means of self-propulsion (see *Lighter*).

Floating bridge. A form of ferry which is warped from shore to shore by hauling on chains or wires laid across the bed of a channel or river.

Gang-plank. A narrow platform placed between one ship and another for embarkation and disembarkation.

Gangway. The opening in the bulwarks or position in the ship's side by which the ship is entered or left. The term is also used to describe a passage in a ship, and sometimes used to describe the platform between ship and shore (see *Brow*).

Hard. A made-up strip of foreshore used as a landing place for boats at low water.

Lighter. A vessel used for transporting cargo or stores to or from a ship.

Piles. Baulks of steel-pointed timber or lengths of ferro-concrete which are driven into the harbour bottom and used as the foundations for the platforms of piers and jetties. Some wooden piles are used for facing the sides of stone or concrete wharves. Some piles are made of steel sections which are embedded in rock and reinforced concrete.

Pontoon. This may be any floating structure used as a buoyant support. It may be used in salvage work to buoy up a damaged vessel, or it may be used to support a bridge across water. In tidal waters a flat-topped pontoon is used as a landing place for boats and ferries on a muddy foreshore, or alongside piers and jetties where the range of tide is considerable; such pontoons are usually connected to the shore or jetty by a hinged bridge.

Stream. The 'stream' is a general term to describe the navigable channels and anchorages in the tidal waters of an estuary or river.

Trot. A line of moored buoys between which a number of small ships can be secured *head and stern.*

Turnaround. The interval between arrival and departure of a merchant ship at her *terminal ports.*

Warp. A rope extending between ship and shore, for moving (warping) the ship without using her engines.

Winding. The action of turning a ship the other way round in her berth (turning *end for end*).

SEA MEASURES

Fathom

One fathom is equal to 6 ft. The fathom is the general unit of measurement for ropes, hawsers, depths of water and soundings.

Cable

One cable is equal to one-tenth of a nautical mile (sea mile) and measures 608 ft, or roughly 200 yd. It is the unit for measuring short distances. (The length of a ship's anchor cable was once 101 fathoms (606 ft); the length of a modern ship's anchor cable varies with the type and size of the ship and bears no relation to the cable measure.)

Nautical mile or sea mile

One nautical or sea mile is equal to 6,080 ft, or roughly 2,000 yd. It is the unit of measurement for long distances.

Knot

A knot is a unit of speed equal to one nautical mile per hour. For example, a ship may be *steaming at 15 knots.* (The expression 'knots per hour' is incorrect and should never be used to describe speed.) The term is derived from a method of measuring speed in the days of sail, when a piece of wood attached to a line was thrown overboard; the number of equally-spaced knots in the line that passed over the taffrail in a fixed time gave the speed of the ship in *knots.*

Questions on this chapter will be found in Appendix 2.

CHAPTER 2

Types of Ship

Men-of-war can be classified broadly under *type* and *class*. The term *type* is used to distinguish between ships built for different purposes, e.g. aircraft carriers and frigates. The term *class* is used to distinguish between different ships of the same type, e.g. Leopard class frigates. But some frigates have also been given type numbers in addition to the class name.

Merchant ships can be classified by their type, e.g. liners, tankers.

Different types of ship can be recognised by certain distinctive features in their general appearance because the design of a ship depends mainly on the work she is required to perform. For example, the chief considerations in the design of a freighter are maximum carrying capacity, easy handling of cargo and low running costs whereas speed, manoeuvrability and armament govern the design of any man-of-war, and so they differ widely in appearance.

In this chapter the distinctive features of various types of man-of-war, merchant ship, vessel and craft are described, and a glossary of the more common terms applied to the structure and equipment of a ship is included to assist the novice in recognising the general features of a ship. *Many of these terms are applicable to several types of ship, and they should therefore not be read as referring only to the particular type of ship illustrated.*

MEN-OF-WAR

Aircraft carrier (fig. 2–1)

Aircraft carriers provide offensive power at very long ranges by using their aircraft to attack with guided weapons, bombs, rockets, torpedoes and mines. Their aircraft also intercept and destroy enemy attacking and reconnaissance aircraft, and provide long-range reconnaissance for their own Fleet. Carriers have defensive armament, but rely on other types of ship and anti-submarine (A/S) helicopters for close protection against submarines. They are easily

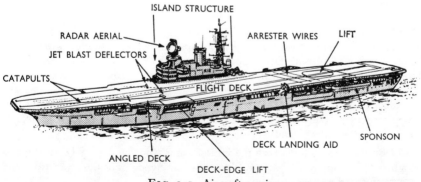

FIG. 2–1. Aircraft carrier

recognised by the *flat top* flight deck. They displace between 20,000 and 50,000 tons, and are from 700 to 1,000 ft in length.

Flight deck. Long, flush, uppermost deck used by aircraft for assembly, take-off (usually by catapult) and landing. Modern carrier flight decks are angled so that landing operations are safer and do not interfere with the ranging of serviced aircraft and their catapult take-off.

Island superstructure. Compact structure, which includes funnel, radar masts and aerials, bridges and operations rooms, built on the starboard side of the flight deck.

Sponson. A platform projecting from the ship's side on which guns and other equipment are mounted.

Aircraft lifts. Power-operated platforms for carrying aircraft up and down between the flight deck and the hangars below. Usually placed in the centre line of the ship, but sometimes at the deck edge.

Hangar. Accommodation for aircraft below the flight deck where maintenance is done.

Catapults. Most modern aircraft require a greater length of deck for take-off than can conveniently be provided afloat, therefore steam-operated catapults are fitted at the fore end of the flight deck for short, boosted take-off.

Jet blast deflectors. Hinged screens fitted abaft the catapults to protect the rest of the flight deck when jet aircraft are being catapulted.

Deck landing aid. Mirror or projector deck landing sights are fitted at the edge of the flight deck to enable the pilot of an incoming aircraft to fly on a predetermined path and into the arrester wires.

Arrester gear. Modern aircraft require a greater length of deck for landing than can conveniently be provided afloat. This is overcome by fitting arrester wires athwart the flight deck which, when hooked by the landing aircraft, bring it to rest in a short distance.

Radar aerial. These are rotating directional aerials used with radar sets for the detection of air or surface targets.

Commando ship

Some carriers have been converted to carry commando troops and helicopters for transferring them from ship to shore.

Cruiser (fig. 2–2)

Cruisers are general-purpose fighting ships whose main function is to provide close cover and anti-aircraft support to convoys or carrier task groups. They combine hitting power with speed, manœuvrability and endurance. Their turrets mount medium-calibre guns capable of a high rate of fire and are automatically controlled. They can be recognised by their turrets and extensive superstructure. They displace from 12,000 to 14,500 tons, and have an overall length of between 555 and 613 ft.

Jackstaff. The staff at which the Union flag is worn by day by H.M. ships at anchor and when *dressed* at sea. The forward anchor light is shown from the top of the staff at night.

FIG. 2–2. Cruiser

Breakwater. A low raked barrier built across the forecastle to stop heavy seas from sweeping aft.

Turret. A revolving box-like armoured structure housing guns (usually two or three) and known as a twin or triple turret. A turret is *superimposed* when it is mounted above and behind another over which it can fire.

Barbette. A cylindrical armoured structure protecting the circular roller path and turret-turning gear beneath a turret.

Funnel. A streamlined casing containing the cylindrical duct built to carry the exhaust gases from boilers or diesel engines above the superstructure. Generally fitted with a cowl top to help lift the gases clear of the ship.

Armour. Thick, special quality steel plating fitted to the hull around engines, magazines and steering gear or used to construct turrets, barbettes and main electric cable trunks to protect those vital parts of a ship from enemy shells, bombs, etc.

Armament. Guns, guided weapons, anti-submarine mortars, torpedoes or other weapons carried by a warship.

Protective plating. Special quality steel plating used in the construction of a ship to protect important radar, gun direction installations, etc. from bomb and shell splinters.

Crane. Lifting apparatus for handling boats, stores, etc.

Lattice mast. Steel pylons built to carry rotating radar aerials, fixed radio aerials and visual signalling arrangements. They are generally fitted with aerial spurs and pole topmasts.

Raked. Inclined to the vertical. The stem is usually raked and occasionally the funnels and masts.

Ensign staff. Staff at which the white ensign is worn. At sea it is usually shifted to the gaff (a short spar on the mainmast).

Guided missile destroyer (fig. 2–3)

These modern ships of the County class are equipped with guns, ship-to-air guided missiles, anti-submarine (A/S) homing torpedoes and an A/S helicopter. They displace over 5,000 tons, are 520 ft in length and have steam and gas turbine engines.

Enclosed bridge. The modern warship's bridge is enclosed to give protection from radioactive fall-out. In the guided missile destroyer the enclosed bridge is a special type known as a 'turret' bridge.

2+M.S.—I

Liferafts. The inflatable liferaft is the main lifesaving equipment in surface warships where it is neither practical nor desirable to carry sufficient lifeboats for all the ship's company.

Whip aerials. These are the transmitting and receiving aerials for short-range radio communications.

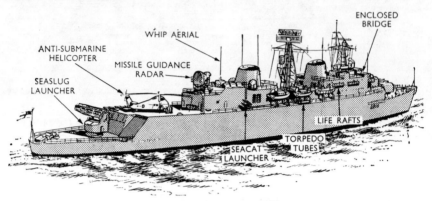

FIG. 2–3. Guided missile destroyer

Seacat launcher. For close range ship-to-air guided missiles.

Seaslug launcher. For medium range ship-to-air guided missiles.

Flagship. A ship of a fleet, task force, task group, squadron, etc. which flies an admiral's flag or the broad pendant of a commodore.

Squadron. A number of warships, usually of the same type, grouped into one unit under one command.

Destroyer

Before the advent of special types of frigate the destroyer was the versatile small ship for A/S protection of the fleet, naval gunfire support of the Army, offensive operations with gun and torpedo and limited minesweeping and mine-layinig Some destroyers of the Daring, Weapon, Battle and 'C' classes are still operational, modernised to fulfil many special functions (1963).

Torpedo tubes. These may be single, twin, triple, quadruple or side-dropping mountings for firing anti-ship torpedoes.

Fast minelayers

These fast ships were designed for offensive minelaying in enemy waters.

Frigates

There are four main types of frigate:
1. The General Purpose frigate for escort work, giving A/S and A/A protection and capable of limited direction of aircraft.
2. The A/S frigate, whose main function is the destruction of submarines.
3. The A/A frigate for the protection of convoys against aircraft.

4. The Air Defence (A.D.) frigate for the direction of carrier-borne or shore-based aircraft.

Both (3) and (4) have limited gun power for offensive operations.

General Purpose frigate, Type 81 (fig. 2–4)

These frigates (destroyer type) of the Tribal class are designed for A/S and A/A protection of the fleet, having also limited aircraft direction facilities. They have the same versatility as the destroyer. They displace 2,300 tons, have a length of 360 ft and are driven by combined steam and gas turbines.

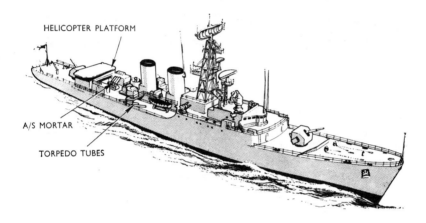

FIG. 2–4. General Purpose frigate

A/S frigate

A/S frigates include the Leander, Rothesay and Whitby (fig. 2–5) classes of the Type 12 with a displacement of 2,150 tons, and ex-destroyers of about 2,200 tons, also the Blackwood class of the Type 14 with a displacement of 1,020 tons.

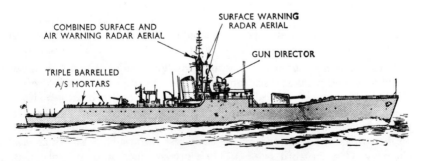

FIG. 2–5. A/S frigate

A/A frigate (fig. 2–6)

The A/A frigate of the Leopard class, Type 41, has a displacement of 2,250 tons, is 340 ft in length, and is diesel-engined. It is designed for the protection of convoys against aircraft and for offensive operations.

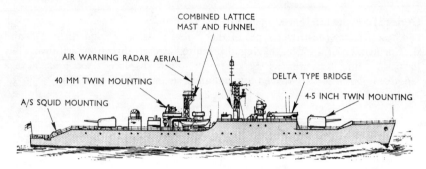

FIG. 2–6. A/A frigate

A.D. frigate (fig. 2–7)

The A.D. frigate of the Salisbury class, Type 61, has a displacement of 2,090 tons, is 340 ft in length, and is diesel-engined. It has additional radar equipment for aircraft direction.

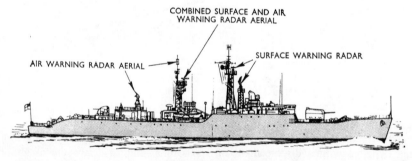

FIG. 2–7. A.D. frigate

Submarine (fig. 2–8)

Submarines attack the enemy's submarines, surface warships and supply ships. They usually patrol by themselves in enemy waters far in advance of the fleet. Their main armament may consist of ballistic missiles and torpedoes, but they can also lay mines and some can mount a gun. Submarines rely on stealth to achieve success, and emphasis in their construction is placed on quietness.

Nuclear-powered submarines are immensely versatile; they are designed to spend very long periods at sea completely submerged. Their speed is very high and their endurance practically unlimited. Conventional submarines also have a long endurance compared with other types of warships, but they are not so fast as nuclear submarines. They can propel themselves by their diesel engines on the surface or submerged; in the latter case the system is known as *snorting* (from the German word *snorkel*). Their primary method of propulsion when submerged, however, is by electric motor.

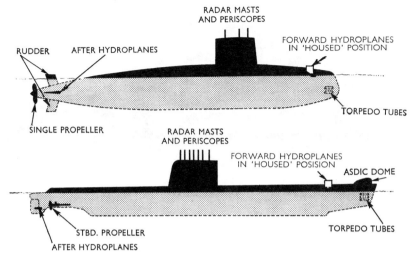

RADAR MASTS
AND PERISCOPES

FORWARD HYDROPLANES
IN 'HOUSED' POSITION

RUDDER   AFTER HYDROPLANES

TORPEDO TUBES

SINGLE PROPELLER

RADAR MASTS
AND PERISCOPES

FORWARD HYDROPLANES
IN 'HOUSED' POSISION

ASDIC DOME

STBD. PROPELLER

TORPEDO TUBES

AFTER HYDROPLANES

FIG. 2–8. (i) Nuclear submarine; (ii) conventional submarine

Submarines vary in length from 250 to 350 ft. Conventional types usually displace from 1,000 to 2,500 tons, nuclear-powered ones considerably more.

Bridge fin. A prominent streamlined superstructure projecting above the main hull and embracing completely the surface directing position, the supports to the periscopes, snort mast, wireless and radar masts.

Periscope. Long vertical tube which can be raised or lowered at will by means of a hydraulic hoist. It encloses a system of lenses and mirrors which gives an observer in a submerged submarine a view over the surface of the sea. Usually two periscopes are fitted.

Pressure hull. The inner hull of a submarine, which is constructed to withstand the pressure of water at the greatest depth for which the submarine is designed.

Snort mast. A breathing tube, with automatic valve on top, which can be raised or lowered by hydraulic gear. When the mast is raised the submarine can replenish air and run diesel engines whilst still submerged, the valve stopping water from entering should the upper end of the tube happen to go under.

Radio and radar masts. Long vertical telescopic tubes on which the necessary aerials are mounted so that a submarine can operate radio or radar when submerged at periscope depth.

Conning tower. A narrow cylindrical extension of the pressure hull inside the fin, which gives access to the bridge.

Main ballast tanks. Large blister-like tanks running along the sides of the pressure hull which are full of air when the submarine is on the surface and which can be filled with water to make the submarine dive.

Hydroplanes. Horizontal rudders at each end of the submarine which control the depth.

Casing. A light steel or aluminium framework external to the pressure hull, usually extending the length of the submarine, which provides a support for sonar installations, anchor and cable, bollards, etc., and is a working platform for personnel when the submarine is on the surface.

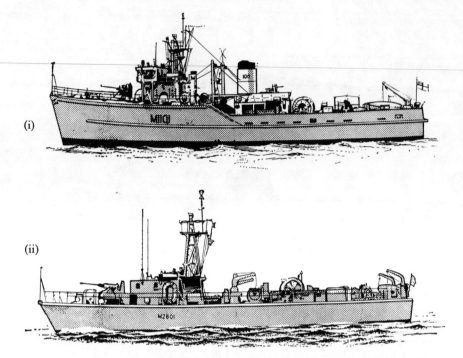

FIG. 2–9. Minesweepers—(i) coastal (C.M.S.); (ii) inshore (I.M.S.)

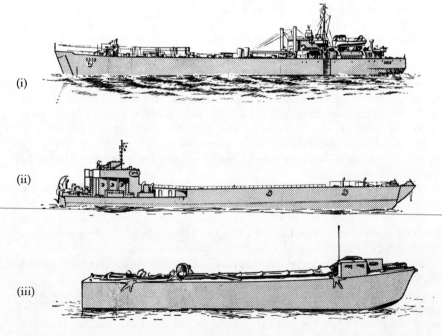

FIG. 2–10. Landing ships and craft—(i) L.S.T.; (ii) L.C.T.; (iii) L.C.A.

Minesweepers (fig. 2–9)

There are two types of minesweeper, the Coastal (C.M.S.) of about 450 tons which is equipped to sweep moored, magnetic and acoustic mines, and the Inshore (I.M.S.) of about 150 tons which can sweep for moored and acoustic mines.

Landing ships and craft (fig. 2–10)

These are special ships and craft for landing assault troops, guns, tanks, equipment and stores on beaches.

The L.S.T. (Landing Ship Tank) of about 4,000 tons is designed to carry the L.C.A.s (Landing Craft Assault) at davits. On reaching the lowering position they are lowered and the assault troops embarked. The L.S.T. then opens hinged bow doors, beaches and lowers a ramp, down which specially waterproofed track or wheeled vehicles can be driven on to the beach.

The L.C.T. (Landing Craft Tank) of about 800 tons is designed specifically for carrying tanks when required in immediate support of infantry.

The L.C.A. is the infantry assault craft of about 10 tons hoisted in assault ships, L.S.T.s and other specially-designed ships.

The L.C.R. (Landing Craft Raiding) is a fast craft used for special landing operations.

Coastal forces (fig. 2–11)

These consist of very fast small craft equipped with guns or torpedoes or mines for operations in coastal waters off our own or the enemy's coast.

FIG. 2–11. Fast patrol boat

Port Auxiliary Service (P.A.S.)

All vessels operating within a port, such as harbour tugs, mooring vessels, lighters and harbour launches and coastal store carriers are included in this service.

Fleet auxiliaries (fig. 2–12)

In ocean warfare the fleet may remain at sea for long periods working many thousands of miles from its main bases. Fleet auxiliaries, which include depot and repair ships, tankers, store ships, hospital ships and ocean-going tugs, are equipped to supply the needs of the fleet at advanced anchorages and bases; the tankers and store ships are specially equipped for replenishing at sea. These ships can be distinguished from merchant ships by their grey colour, by their ensigns and in some cases special equipment and fittings. When a number of auxiliaries are concentrated for the purpose of supplying a fleet they are known collectively as the *fleet train*.

FIG. 2–12. Fleet auxiliaries—(i) tanker; (ii) storeship

MERCHANT SHIPS

Merchant ships are more difficult to classify by type than warships because one type of ship may often be used for many different purposes. Generally speaking, however, they belong to one of the following main types.

A typical merchant ship (fig. 2–13)

Hull form. The type and shape of the hull.

Forecastle. The raised part of the hull at the fore end of the merchant ship.

Aftercastle or poop. A raised part of the hull at the after end of a merchant ship.

Centrecastle. A raised part of the hull in the centre of a merchant ship, sometimes known generally as the bridge.

Well deck. That part of a merchant ship's upper deck between the forecastle and centrecastle, or the poop and centrecastle.

Hatches. Openings in the decks above the holds through which cargo is hoisted or lowered. When at sea they are covered with hatchboards supported

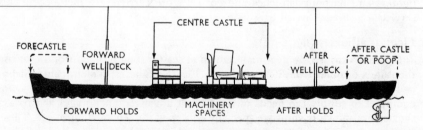

FIG. 2–13. A typical merchant ship

on steel beams and covered with *tarpaulins* (sheets of tarred canvas). Steel hatch covers are usually fitted in modern ships.

Cargo. Any goods that a ship carries in her holds or tanks. Cargoes of loose grain, coal, coke, oil and mineral ores are called *bulk cargo*. Miscellaneous goods are called *general cargo*. Cargo occasionally carried on deck is called *deck cargo*.

Ballast. Water, sand, etc., carried in the bottom of a ship to make her seaworthy when carrying little or no cargo. The majority of vessels carry water ballast in tanks constructed under the flooring of the holds.

In ballast. Term applied to a ship which has little or no cargo in her hold and is ballasted with water to give a reasonable draught and trim.

Passenger liner (fig. 2–14)

Passenger liners are designed for carrying passengers between the major ports of the world. They vary in size from about 10,000 tons gross to 84,000 tons gross, and carry comparatively little cargo because most of their capacity is devoted to the accommodation for passengers and their baggage, food, stores and a large crew. Their speed varies from about 14 to 30 knots or more, and for this reason they usually carry mails. They can be distinguished by their size and long, high upperworks, and, at night in peacetime, by the blaze of lights from their hulls and superstructures.

FIG. 2–14. Passenger liner

Superstructure or upperworks. Structures or deck houses built above the main hull of the ship.

Promenade deck. An upper deck used mainly by passengers in the larger passenger liners.

Boat deck. The deck on which the lifeboats of a merchant ship are stowed, usually the highest deck.

Lifeboats. Boats carried by all merchant ships for saving life. They are slung from davits.

Oil-burning. Descriptive of vessels in which oil fuel is used for the boiler furnaces.

Cargo liner (fig. 2–15)

Cargo liners are designed chiefly for carrying cargo, but they have accommodation for a small number of passengers. They vary in size from about 5,000 to 15,000 tons gross, with speeds from 12 to 19 knots. They can be distinguished

2*

by the number of derricks for working cargo, by the superstructure, which is larger than that of the normal cargo vessel, and by the number of lifeboats.

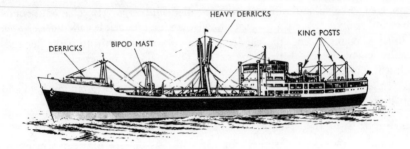

FIG. 2–15. Cargo liner

Liner. Any ship which sails on a regular route with fixed ports of call.

Navigating bridge. The raised structure from which a vessel is steered and navigated. All navigating instruments, controls, radar, signal flags and lamps are situated here.

Docking bridge. A raised platform erected across the after part of a vessel for use when manœuvring a ship into or out of her berth.

Ensign. The national flag displayed by all vessels on a flagstaff well aft or at the gaff on the mainmast.

Cargo ship (fig. 2–16)

These vessels are of many classes and varieties; their gross tonnage varies from about 2,000 to 10,000 and their speed from about 10 to 15 knots. They are designed to carry all types of general cargo. They ply between all ports of the world, and as they do not follow a regular route they are often known by the term *tramps.* They can usually be distinguished by their small upperworks and their numerous masts, posts and derricks.

FIG. 2–16. Cargo ship

Derrick. A long spar (usually of tubular steel) hinged to the foot of a mast or kingpost and used like the jib of a crane to load and discharge cargo from the hold beneath it.

Heavy or jumbo derrick. Larger and heavier type of derrick which is usually clamped against its mast at sea.

Goal-post mast. Two vertical tubular structures joined athwartships by a platform (so that they resemble goal-posts when seen from ahead or astern). The topmast is stepped into the centre of the platform.

Kingpost. A vertical tubular structure placed in the vicinity of a hatchway. Such posts erected in pairs athwartships are described as *twin kingposts.*

Whistle. Every ship must have some sound-making apparatus to give warning of its presence at sea in a fog and to indicate the direction of its movement to other ships that can see it. It is usually fitted on the fore side of the funnel and is operated from the bridge. It is called the *siren* in H.M. ships.

Tanker (fig. 2–17)

Tankers, as their name implies, are built to carry liquids such as petrol, crude oil, refined oil or molasses. Their gross tonnage varies from 2,000 to over 100,000 and their speed from 10 to 20 knots. They can be easily recognised because they have few or no derricks and their machinery is right aft. The bridge structure may be amidships or aft.

FIG. 2–17. Tanker

Motor vessel (M.V.). A vessel driven by internal combustion engines, usually diesel.

Fore-and-aft bridge or catwalk. A raised gangway running fore-and-aft in a low freeboard ship for the safety of personnel.

Signal letters. A group of four letters allocated to every registered merchant ship for identification.

Bow wave. The wave created by the vessel's bows when moving ahead in the water.

Wake. The disturbed water astern of a vessel caused partly by the turning propeller and partly by the movement of the hull through the water.

Bulk freighter (fig. 2–18)

These freighters are designed to carry cargoes such as coal, ore and grain in bulk. Like the tankers, which sometimes they resemble, they are a specialised type of ship usually trading only between certain ports. Their speed varies from 10 to 15 knots.

Ventilator. Funnel-like fitting with a cowl-shaped top through which air is drawn to, or expelled from, machinery and other spaces.

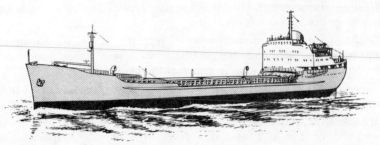

FIG. 2–18. Bulk freighter

Steamship. A vessel in which the propelling machinery is driven by steam.

Coal-burning. Descriptive of vessels in which the fuel for boiler furnaces is coal.

Laden. A ship is laden when she has cargo on board.

Coaster (fig. 2–19)

Coasters are small cargo vessels, usually under 2,000 tons gross and of slow speed, employed on coastal trade. They are not built for ocean trade and have a limited radius of action. They have similar features to their larger sisters, and often can only be distinguished from them by their size.

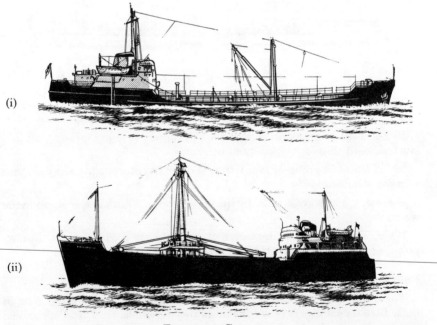

(i)

(ii)

FIG. 2–19. Coasters

Rubbing strake. A heavy wooden guard, fitted permanently along the hull close above the waterline to protect a ship's plating when going alongside a wharf. Fitted in coasters, cross-Channel passenger vessels, tugs, etc.

Auxiliary sailing vessel. A sailing vessel fitted also with propelling machinery, usually motor.

Bulwark. The ship's side that is above the upper deck, affording protection to crew and deck fittings.

Freeing ports. Hinged ports in the bulwarks through which water on deck can escape but the sea cannot enter.

Taffrail. The rail round the stern of a vessel; it may be a continuation of the bulwarks.

Fishing vessels (fig. 2–20)

These vessels may be encountered in large numbers in northern waters, on the fishing grounds, around the coasts, and in the open sea. Their size varies from about 70 to 1,000 tons. Their speed may be as much as 15 knots on passage.

GALLOWS GALLOWS

FIG. 2–20. Fishing trawler

Trawler. An ocean-going vessel which fishes by towing a trawl on the sea bed astern.

Whaler. A vessel similar to a trawler, very manœuvrable, and equipped with a harpoon gun on the forecastle for whaling.

Drifter. A vessel which fishes by drifting with a long line of float-supported nets ahead.

Pareja. A vessel similar to a trawler seen in the Atlantic off the coasts of Spain and Portugal.

Gallows. A steel framework (shaped like an inverted U) fitted in trawlers and used for 'shooting' and hauling the trawl.

SAILING VESSELS

Until recently the prime test of a good seaman was his ability to handle a vessel under sail—because he had to pit his skill and wits against every vagary of weather, wind and sea, entirely unaided by mechanical propulsive power. Sailing vessels no longer provide a commercially profitable means of transporting passengers or cargoes across the oceans, but many types of small sailing vessel are still to be found in coastal trade throughout the world, and in sufficient numbers to warrant a professional interest being taken in them by the modern seaman. Sailing, moreover, still provides the best medium for training a seaman to be alert, handy and observant, and has few equals as a sport.

Classification

Sailing vessels are classified by their *rig*, which is a term covering masts, yards, booms, gaffs, standing and running rigging, and sails. There are two main types of rig: *square rig* in which sails are bent to yards carried athwart the mast, and *fore-and-aft rig* in which the sails are bent to masts, booms and gaffs in the fore-and-aft line of the ship. Fore-and-aft rig has superseded square rig, which is seldom seen nowadays except in topsail schooners.

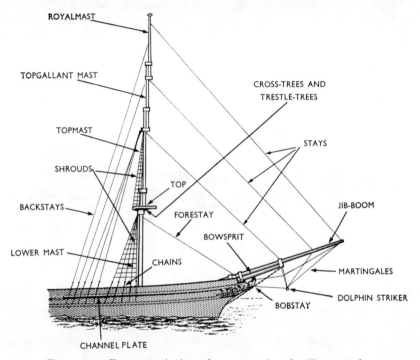

FIG. 2–21. Foremast rigging of a square-rigged sailing vessel

Before it is possible to identify the different types of sailing vessel it is necessary to know the principal features of their rigging.

Masts

A mast (fig. 2–21) is stayed athwartships by *shrouds* and forward and aft by *forestays* and *backstays*. When a mast is too tall to be made of one timber, there may be two, three or four sections stepped one above the other and they are called successively the lower mast, topmast, topgallant mast and royal mast. On the top of each mast is a mast cap, and the platform at the foot of each upper mast section is called a *top*. *Trestle-trees* are the heavy fore-and-aft timbers which support the tops, and *cross-trees* are the athwartship timbers to which are secured the shrouds of the upper masts.

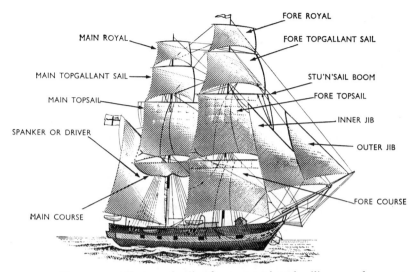

F IG. 2–22. Masts and sails of a square-rigged sailing vessel

When a ship has only one mast it is always called the mainmast. If there are two masts their names are determined by their size and position: if the foremost mast is the larger it is called the mainmast and the other is called the mizzenmast; if the aftermost mast is the larger it becomes the mainmast and

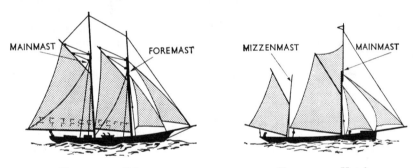

F IG. 2–23. Schooner   F IG. 2–24. Ketch

the foremost mast is the foremast (figs. 2–23 and 2–24). When there are more than two masts they are called successively fore, main, mizzen and jigger masts.

Sails

Sails are *bent* to yards, booms and gaffs, and they are *spread* or *unfurled* when *making sail*. When *taking in* or *shortening* sail they are *furled* or *handed*, and they are *reefed down* when their area is reduced by gathering in and securing a portion of the sail. Masts are *stepped* into a ship, or one upon another, and yards are hoisted into position by *halyards* (haulyards) and *crossed* on the masts. When uppermasts or yards are lowered to the deck they are *struck* or *sent down*, but when only lowered a short distance they are *housed* by *settling* or easing away on the halyards or mast ropes.

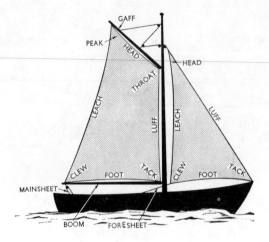

FIG. 2–25. Parts of a foresail and a mainsail

The names for the parts of a foresail and a mainsail are shown in fig: 2–25.

Types and rigs of coastal sailing vessels

Figs. 2–26 and 2–27 illustrate typical coastal sailing craft of today.

Lateen and lug. Confusion frequently arises between the lateen sail and the lug sail; the true difference is that the lateen sail is triangular, whereas the lug sail is usually four-sided. The yard of the lateen sail is supported near its middle, the tack is attached to the end of the yard, and the sail is not dipped round the mast when the vessel goes about from one tack to the other. On the other hand, the lug sail is supported at a point about one-third of the distance along the yard, the tack is attached to the tack of the sail and not to the yard, and in some rigs the yard and sail are dipped round the mast when the vessel goes about from one tack to another.

Bermudian and gunter. The Bermudian and gunter rigs are also similar. In the former the luff of the triangular mainsail is bent throughout its length to the mast by means of rings or slides in a mast track. In the latter the upper part of the luff of the triangular mainsail is laced to a gaff, which is triced nearly in line with the mast and slides up and down it; the lower part of the luff is laced to the mast itself.

Cutter. In the cutter rig the head of the mainsail is bent to a gaff, the foot is bent to a boom, and a gaff-topsail can be set between the gaff and the upper part of the mast. A cutter carries a foresail, and sometimes a jib which is set on a bowsprit.

Sloop. Sloop rig is very similar to cutter rig, the difference being that the mainsail is rigged as a standing lug instead of being bent to a gaff. The mainsail is sometimes *loose-footed* (i.e. not laced to a boom), and its yard lies closer to the mast than does the gaff of a cutter.

Sprit. In the sprit rig the mainsail has neither gaff nor boom, but is spread by means of a spar called a sprit, which runs diagonally from the foot of the mast to the peak of the sail.

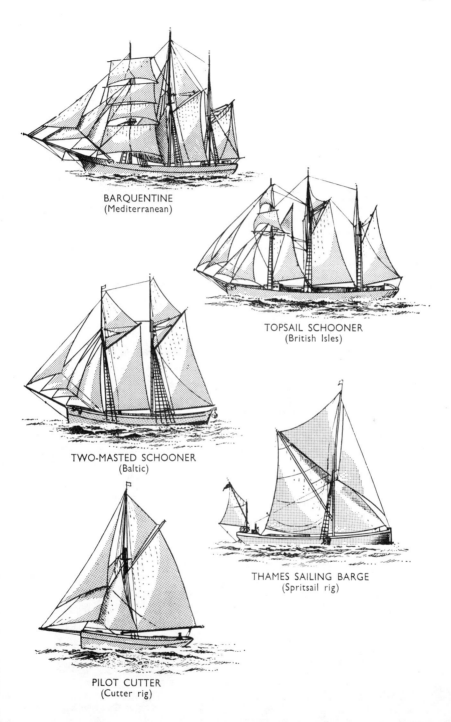

BARQUENTINE
(Mediterranean)

TOPSAIL SCHOONER
(British Isles)

TWO-MASTED SCHOONER
(Baltic)

THAMES SAILING BARGE
(Spritsail rig)

PILOT CUTTER
(Cutter rig)

FIG. 2–26. Types of sailing vessels

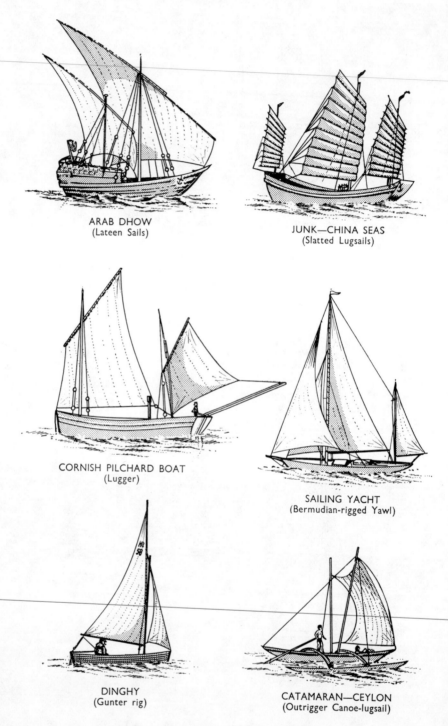

ARAB DHOW
(Lateen Sails)

JUNK—CHINA SEAS
(Slatted Lugsails)

CORNISH PILCHARD BOAT
(Lugger)

SAILING YACHT
(Bermudian-rigged Yawl)

DINGHY
(Gunter rig)

CATAMARAN—CEYLON
(Outrigger Canoe-lugsail)

FIG. 2-27. Types of sailing vessels

Yawl and ketch. The difference between the yawl and ketch rigs is that the mizzenmast of a ketch is larger and stepped before the rudder post, whereas the mizzenmast of a yawl is stepped abaft the rudder post and the mizzen boom projects beyond the stern of the vessel. Generally speaking, the ketch rig is used for larger vessels than the yawl rig.

Topsail schooner. Topsail schooners are the last survivors from the days of square rig, and are rarely encountered nowadays. The topsails of the schooner are useful when running before the wind.

Junk. Junks are virtually lugger-rigged, their sails being bent to yards which are slung fore-and-aft. Across the sails are rigged wooden slats, and the sails are furled and unfurled in a similar way to a venetian blind, which greatly simplifies reefing. Junks vary considerably in their build and rig; the one in fig. 2–27 is a sea-going junk of the south China coast.

Outrigger or catamaran. The outrigger canoe or catamaran is used as a fishing vessel off the coasts of Ceylon and southern India.

Other rigs. Many other variations in rig and construction are still in use in various parts of the world, and the study of small sailing craft affords an interesting and instructive hobby for seamen.

Some sailing terms

The act of getting under way by spreading sails on the masts is called *setting sail*, and a vessel under way is said to have so many sails *set*. They are said to set well or badly according to their appearance. After a sail is spread it is *sheeted home* to the required angle with the wind by means of its *sheets*. Sails are *loosed* if the sheets are eased away, or *let fly* until the sails flap, and they are *spilled* when not fully filled by the wind.

A vessel is *running* when the wind is abaft her beam, and *close hauled* when sailing as near as possible into the direction from which the wind is blowing. Most sailing vessels cannot sail closer than 4 points (45°) off the wind. When it is desired to *make good* a course which is closer to the wind than the ship can sail, she *beats* to windward by steering on a series of zigzag courses called *tacks*, and at the moment when she alters course from one tack to another she is said to *go about*. When a vessel is running with the wind on one quarter and she alters course so as to bring the wind on her other quarter she is said to *gybe*. When she goes about from one tack to another by turning away from the wind instead of turning through the wind she is said to *wear*.

Questions on this chapter will be found in Appendix 2.

CHAPTER 3

Design and Construction of Warships

INTERNAL FITTINGS

Not all the fittings in the hull of a warship are described in this chapter, only the more common fittings which the seaman has to maintain in an efficient condition. A more detailed description of the fittings and structure of warships is to be found in B.R.569, *Practical Construction of Warships*.

The structural components and fittings found in a typical *living space* of a warship are illustrated in fig. 3–1. Underfoot is the *deck* and overhead is the *deck head*; the landsman's terms of 'floor' and 'ceiling' are not used because in a ship each describes something quite different, as is explained in the section headed 'Elementary Ship Construction' (page 63). A wall of a compartment is called a *bulkhead*, except where it is formed by the side of the hull, when it is known as the *ship's side*. Bulkheads can be watertight or non-watertight, and strict rules govern the opening and closing of the doors in a watertight bulkhead. Decks within the hull are always watertight, and strict rules govern the opening and closing of their hatches. *Frames* and *stringers* form parts of the hull structure (see pages 66 and 67), and they support and strengthen the ship's side plating.

Ventilation of compartments is provided by electric fans and trunking, and heating and cooling arrangements are fitted in the ventilation systems.

The firemain runs throughout the length of the ship, and connections for hoses, called *hydrants*, are fitted in most of the main compartments.

Other fittings illustrated are described below.

Watertight hatches (fig. 3–2)

Decks are pierced by rectangular or circular openings, called *hatches*, to allow access to the compartments below. A hatch is fitted with a *coaming* to prevent flood water from flowing below, and a lid called a *hatch cover* is hinged to it. The hatch cover has a rubber sealing strip let into its inner side where it bears on the edge of the coaming, so that, when clamped down by means of wing nuts working on threaded bolts hinged to the coaming, the hatch cover makes a watertight joint with the coaming.

Special attention should be paid to the maintenance of a good bearing surface between hatch cover and coaming; neither the edge of the coaming nor the rubber should ever be painted, and the latter should be kept in good condition by cleaning it with a damp cloth and dusting it with French chalk. The hatch cover should always be lowered in position, never let fall, and the wing nuts should be screwed home hand-tight, not hammered home. The threads of the wing nuts should be kept lightly greased and never be painted.

Some hatch covers have watertight escape manholes, fitted with double clips to enable them to be opened from either side. Ladders with hand chains or

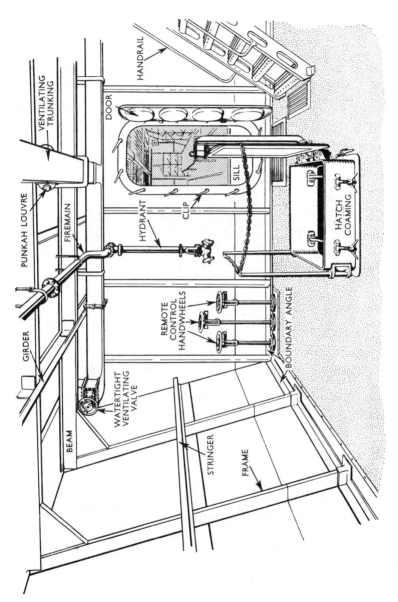

FIG. 3–1. A typical compartment

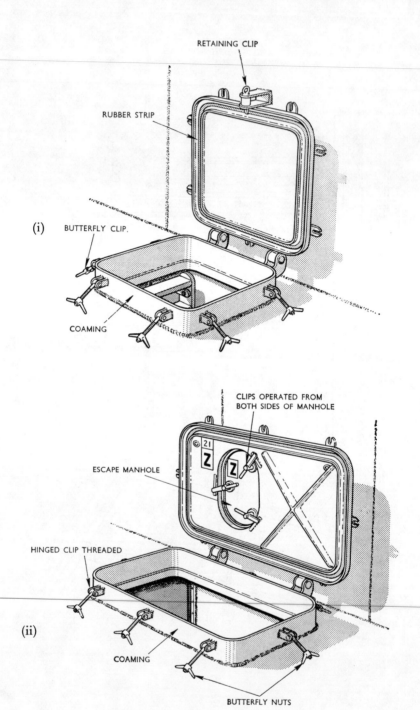

FIG. 3-2. Hatches

handrails are provided and these should always be correctly secured in position before the hatchway is used. Guard chains and stanchions, or handrails, are provided round the tops of hatchways, and these should always be set up correctly; for obvious reasons, it is dangerous to sit upon or lean against the guard chains or handrails. Before descending a hatchway always make sure that the hatch cover is securely clipped back in the open position. Heavy hatch covers are held in the open position by preventer chains and chain blocks shackled to the cover. Each hatchway should be provided with a Jacob's ladder for use if the main ladder is displaced by the shock of an explosion.

Hatch covers are fitted with an air test plug the purpose of which is to ascertain before opening the hatch whether the compartment below is flooded; it is also used when doing the routine test for the watertightness of the compartment below, by pumping air into the compartment and seeing whether the air pressure is maintained.

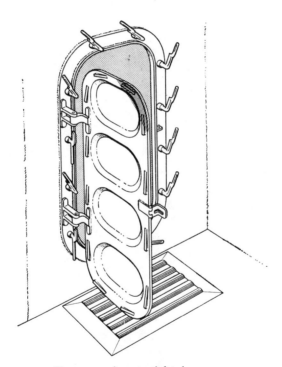

FIG. 3–3. A watertight door

Doors (fig. 3–3)

The openings in bulkheads are called *doorways*, and they are closed by hinged watertight doors. These doorways are made watertight by means of a rubber strip in the door, similar to that in a hatch cover, but the door is clamped shut by double clips and wedges, operable from either side, instead of by winged nuts and bolts. The same care should be taken of doors as of hatches to maintain them in a watertight condition. The clips and wedges should be kept clean and dry, but the clips should not be removed for cleaning as their reassembly is a skilled job. Clips should be clamped hand-tight, not hammered home. Grease nipples are fitted for lubricating the spindles of clip hatches.

Sidelights, side scuttles and windows

Above number 1 deck circular fixed *sidelights* are fitted to provide natural light to compartments, with lightweight metal covers for darkening ship. These sidelights are 'fixed' in modern warships, i.e. they do not open, because the air conditioning and ventilation work more efficiently without such openings. Older ships are still fitted with *side scuttles*, which can be opened, but only if the damage control state of the ship permits. The side scuttle (fig. 3–4) has a hinged

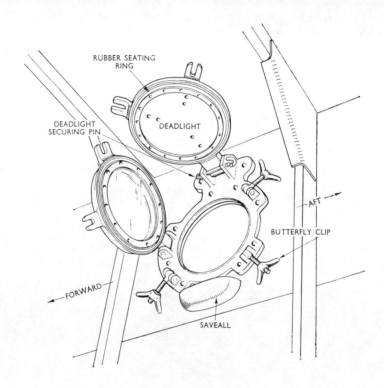

FIG. 3–4. A side scuttle

thick glass *light* (also sometimes called a *sidelight*) which, when closed by butterfly nuts, makes a watertight joint with the frame; and has a hinged *deadlight* which is lowered and clamped over the light to darken ship.

Rectangular windows are usually fitted to enclosed bridges, with heating arrangements to prevent icing up, and with wipers on some of the windows.

The same care should be given to the maintenance in a watertight condition of sidelights, side scuttles and windows as is given to doors and hatches.

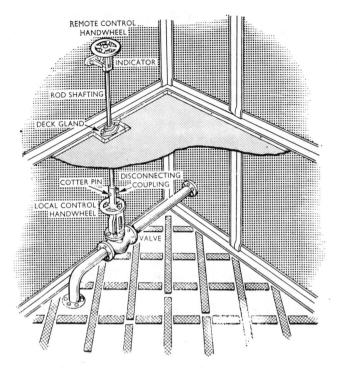

REMOTE CONTROL HANDWHEEL

INDICATOR

ROD SHAFTING

DECK GLAND

COTTER PIN

DISCONNECTING COUPLING

LOCAL CONTROL HANDWHEEL

VALVE

FIG. 3-5. Remote and local control of valves

Remotely-controlled valves (fig. 3–5)

There are many valves which, because of their importance to the safety of the ship, can be operated from one or more places in addition to the compartment in which they are situated; those of the magazine flooding arrangements are examples. In older vessels remote control is usually transmitted by rod gearing, which may pass through several compartments and decks and is operated by a handwheel at each position. In modern ships hydraulic or pneumatic control is fitted to valves that would otherwise require long and tortuous runs of rod gearing.

The system is designed for use in emergency, and must be ready to function at a moment's notice. No gear should ever be hung on the handwheels or rod gearing; and the joints, crown wheels and deck glands should be kept lightly greased and never be painted over; the tallies on the handwheels should be kept clean so that they are easily legible.

ELECTRICAL EQUIPMENT

A warship's electrical equipment is as important to her fighting and navigational efficiency as are her main engines, and the ship's safety and the comfort of her crew are largely dependent upon its correct functioning. The care and maintenance of the electrical equipment is the responsibility of the Electrical Branch, and in no circumstances should others interfere with it. Any defects should be reported at once to the Electrical Office, where the necessary steps will be taken for their repair. Notes on certain electrical equipment are given below.

Telephones

A description of the various telephone systems is given in Volume II. Telephones and broadcast transmitters, including handsets, headphones, transmitters and microphones, are delicate instruments and must therefore be handled with care. Flexible leads of such instruments should be kept free of turns and not be pulled forcibly; this applies particularly to the long leads fitted to telephone headsets. When a flexible lead has to be plugged into a socket, care must be taken to ensure that the plug is properly engaged and held firmly in it. Water or liquid of any description must be kept away from all telephone and broadcasting apparatus.

Radio

A warship carries numerous radio installations, including wireless telegraphy, radio telephony and radar. They are placed as far as possible in offices to protect them from the weather, dirt and shock, but certain parts of them may be in exposed positions about the ship.

The three greatest enemies of radio equipment are water, dirt and ill-usage; remarks on these are given below.

Water. Most of these radio installations use high voltages (from about 400 to 20,000 volts). Protection against these high voltages by adequate insulation is a great difficulty. Water, especially salt water, conducts electricity, and if it reaches radio equipment the insulators will be rendered useless and the high voltages will *flash over*, causing burning and serious damage throughout the equipment. Even when salt water is dried out the difficulties are not overcome, because the grains of salt remain, absorb moisture from the air and start the trouble all over again. The following precautions should therefore be taken:

1. Hoses should not be used near radio equipment, or near the ventilation to radio rooms.
2. As little water as possible should be used when scrubbing decks near radio equipment; it should not be splashed about, and the deck should be wiped dry with a cloth.
3. Ventilation to radio rooms should be kept running.

Dirt. Dust and dirt, like water, will conduct electricity. Dust in a ship usually consists of tiny particles of metal, carbon and other conductors of electricity, and a film of such dust over insulators will allow the high voltage to discharge through them. In the vicinity of radio equipment, tobacco ash, cigarette ends, pipe dottle and other refuse should therefore always be placed in a closed tin, and a moist cloth should be used for dusting because a dry duster merely scatters or disturbs the dust instead of removing it.

Ill-usage. Radio equipment is extremely delicate and may easily be seriously damaged; no unauthorised person is therefore allowed to interfere with or alter the setting of any radio equipment.

Care should be taken not to break, crush, dent, bend or chafe the leads to and from the aerials.

Electrical dangers

The operation of all electrical devices depends on electrical power, which is transmitted through the conducting wires and cables which run through most compartments. To prevent leakage of power, all conductors have to be insulated from the metal parts of the ship, and this insulation is provided by layers of non-conductive material between the current-carrying conductor and the protective watertight cover of the cable. If this insulating material is damaged in any way, or rendered ineffective by water or damp, the resultant leakage of electric power may be dangerous. For this reason the cap of any plug socket which is no longer in use should always be replaced; cables must never be chipped or scraped, and nothing must be hung from them or the cable plating overhead.

Just as hoses are more likely to leak than the ship's firemains, so flexible electric cables on portable apparatus are more likely to leak than the ship's permanent wiring, and a leak of electricity can easily cause death. Because the steel hull of a ship is a good conductor and men are often working in a state of sweat, when body resistance is reduced, the conditions aboard ship are more hazardous from the standpoint of electric shock than those normally encountered ashore. For this reason better and safer electrical equipment is needed afloat and more attention must be paid to safety precautions.

No attempt should be made to repair electric irons, portable drills, electric scaling machines, wandering leads, or any other portable electric apparatus, because such repairs of equipment by inexpert persons may lead to serious injury or loss of life.

INTERNAL ARRANGEMENTS

The internal arrangements of a warship vary according to the type and size of the vessel and the constantly changing requirements of sea warfare, but there is a certain similarity in the general layout of most warships. In fig. 3–6 is

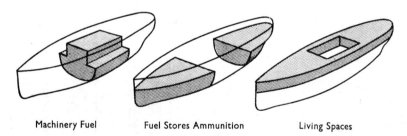

Machinery Fuel   Fuel Stores Ammunition   Living Spaces

FIG. 3–6. General allocation of space in the hull of a warship

shown a typical allocation of space in the interior of a warship's hull for machinery, stores and ammunition, and living quarters; this allocation, together with that for the armament, is one of the basic factors of warship design.

The main and auxiliary machinery is usually situated midway between bow and stern, and, together with its fuel, is kept for protection as far as possible below the waterline. Stores and ammunition are situated before and abaft the machinery space, and as far as possible below the waterline. Living spaces are usually arranged above the waterline and near the ship's side. More detailed descriptions of the interior arrangements of a warship are given in the following pages and illustrated by the sectional drawings of a cruiser (figs. 3–7 and 3–8). These illustrations should be taken only as a general guide to the text.

In aircraft carriers the internal arrangements below the level of the upper deck are very similar to those of other warships of the same size, but above this deck they are very different; a short description of the layout of an aircraft carrier is therefore given on page 58 and illustrated in fig. 3–11.

Watertight sub-division (figs. 3–7 and 3–8)

The decks and main bulkheads divide the hull into a number of main watertight spaces, and these are sub-divided into smaller watertight compartments which house the various items of the ship's equipment. This watertight sub-division is of vital importance to the safety of the ship if her hull is damaged below the waterline, because it confines any ingress of water to the immediate vicinity of the damage instead of allowing it to flow unchecked throughout the ship.

Watertight decks and bulkheads have to be pierced by hatches and doorways to allow access to the various compartments, and they have also to be pierced for electrical leads, piping, ventilating trunking, shafting, etc., led into or through the compartments. Wherever this occurs each opening is made watertight by special fittings, and it is essential to the safety of the ship that the watertightness of each fitting should be maintained in an efficient condition, and that doors, valves and hatches are opened only when necessary. Special rules are laid down for the opening and closing of all doors, hatches, valves and other watertight openings situated near or below the waterline.

Ventilation and air conditioning (fig. 3–9)

Most compartments in the ship must be supplied, either continuously or intermittently, with fresh air so that the crew may live and work in them and stores and provisions may remain in good condition. This air is provided in one of two ways, known as *natural* or *forced* ventilation, each of which introduces fresh air into the compartment through an *inlet* and allows the foul air to escape through an *exhaust*.

Natural ventilation is provided through side scuttles, through skylights, ventilators and cowls in the weather decks, and through doorways and hatches. It is only provided to compartments which have direct access to the air, and are well above the waterline, and then only when considerations of watertight integrity permit.

Forced ventilation. Most compartments have no direct access to the air, so they have to be supplied by a system of forced ventilation in which fresh air is drawn by electric fans from various positions above the weather decks and forced through trunking to the various compartments. The foul air is exhausted back to the weather deck through trunking, either naturally or by exhaust fans.

One fan can supply several compartments, and the system is designed to change the air in each compartment every few minutes. To do this the air must circulate freely inside each compartment and along the whole length of the supply system; consequently, stopping or slowing down a fan which is

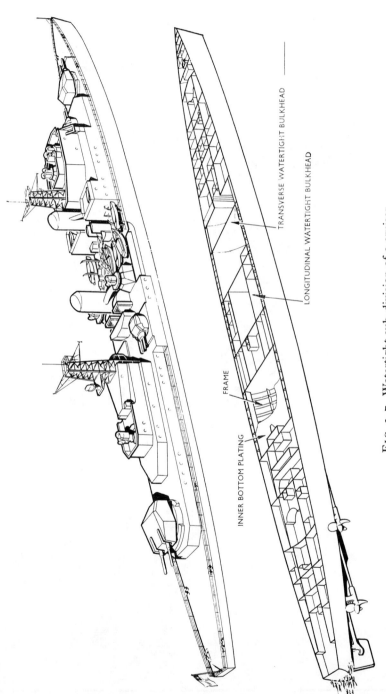

TRANSVERSE WATERTIGHT BULKHEAD

LONGITUDINAL WATERTIGHT BULKHEAD

FRAME

INNER BOTTOM PLATING

FIG. 3–7. Watertight sub-division of a cruiser

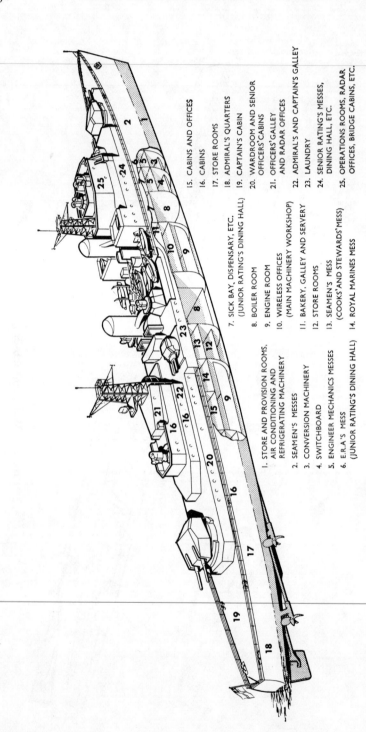

FIG. 3–8. Internal arrangement of a cruiser

1. STORE AND PROVISION ROOMS, AIR CONDITIONING AND REFRIGERATING MACHINERY

2. SEAMEN'S MESSES

3. CONVERSION MACHINERY

4. SWITCHBOARD

5. ENGINEER MECHANICS MESSES

6. E.R.A'S MESS (JUNIOR RATING'S DINING HALL)

7. SICK BAY, DISPENSARY, ETC. (JUNIOR RATING'S DINING HALL)

8. BOILER ROOM

9. ENGINE ROOM

10. WIRELESS OFFICES (MAIN MACHINERY WORKSHOP)

11. BAKERY, GALLEY AND SERVERY

12. STORE ROOMS

13. SEAMEN'S MESS (COOKS' AND STEWARDS' MESS)

14. ROYAL MARINES MESS

15. CABINS AND OFFICES

16. CABINS

17. STORE ROOMS

18. ADMIRAL'S QUARTERS

19. CAPTAIN'S CABIN

20. WARDROOM AND SENIOR OFFICERS' CABINS

21. OFFICERS' GALLEY AND RADAR OFFICES

22. ADMIRAL'S AND CAPTAIN'S GALLEY

23. LAUNDRY

24. SENIOR RATING'S MESSES, DINING HALL. ETC.

25. OPERATIONS ROOMS, RADAR OFFICES, BRIDGE CABINS, ETC.

apparently supplying too much air to one compartment may have the effect of entirely depriving other compartments of their fresh air. The same effect may result if valves or louvres are interfered with to give a compartment more than its fair share of air.

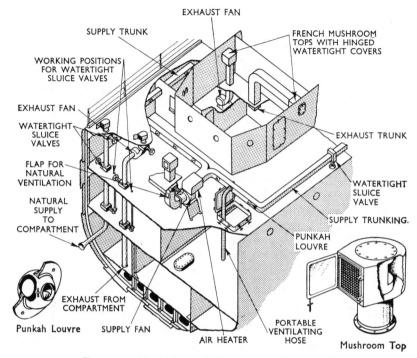

FIG. 3–9. Typical ventilation system of a warship

Ventilation trunking can be the means of spreading water from a flooded compartment to another compartment unless the trunking is made sufficiently strong to resist damage or fitted with valves where it passes through watertight decks or bulkheads.

Air conditioning is a modified form of forced ventilation in which mechanical cooling equipment automatically extracts moisture from a mixture of re-circulated and fresh air. The drier air renders conditions within the ship more comfortable especially when in tropical climates. Apart from adjusting the *punkah louvres* to give the best direction of air stream, the system should not be tampered with in any way. If the system appears to be operating incorrectly or conditions within the compartments show signs of deterioration over a period, the matter must be reported to the Engineering, Electrical or Shipwright Departments.

Punkah louvres must not be painted, or they will become stiff and impossible to adjust.

Fans are designed to operate at full speed, and it is most important that they are not run at half speed if proper ventilation or air conditioning is to be maintained.

Baffles are adjusted before the ship is commissioned to give the correct distribution of air; they must never be touched.

Armament (fig. 3–10)

This term includes all offensive weapons such as guns, guided missiles, torpedoes and anti-submarine mortars. There are many types of armament and the following descriptions are only intended to be read in a very general sense.

Guns. Cruisers carry their main armament guns in armoured revolving turrets, mounting two or three guns in each. The turrets are usually on the centre line, before or abaft the main superstructure, and sited to command the clearest field of fire. In smaller ships the guns are similarly placed, but they are mounted singly or in pairs in lightly-armoured turrets or in gun shields. Although turret guns can be laid (elevated) and fired independently, they are trained on the target by the movement of the turret itself, which revolves on top of a ring bulkhead which is inside an armoured tube called the *barbette*. This armour extends from the deck on which the turret is situated to below the armoured deck of the ship. Below this are the magazines and shell rooms. The ammunition is brought to the guns in mechanical hoists.

Guided weapons. In order to provide adequate defence against modern high-speed aircraft, guided weapons are being fitted in many new ships.

Torpedoes. The torpedo is the weapon of submarines against surface ships, small surface ships against larger surface ships and anti-submarine ships against submarines. It is fired from a tube by compressed air or explosive charge. These tubes may be mounted singly or in threes and fours on a rotatable turn-table. In submarines they are part of the structure. The torpedo is such a heavy and cumbersome weapon to handle that reloading a tube, except in submarines, is a lengthy operation and not normally undertaken at sea.

Anti-submarine mortars. The mortar is the primary weapon of anti-submarine frigates. The mounting can be trained in any direction and a salvo of projectiles fired at a submarine that has been detected by underwater listening equipment or by other means.

Armour

In larger ships the machinery spaces, magazines and certain other vital equipment are usually protected by armour plating secured to the adjacent part of the hull. On account of its weight the amount of armour must be kept to a minimum; all vital equipment is therefore grouped in as short a length of the ship as possible, and then protected by a box-like citadel of armour plating which extends from below the waterline on each side, across the deck (armoured deck), and over the bulkheads at each end. Some protection is also afforded to vital equipment by placing it below the waterline.

Propellers

A warship may have one, two, three or four propellers which are keyed to shafts driven by the *main engines*. The shafts lead through watertight shaft tunnels, and are supported at intervals by bearings known as *plummer blocks*; they emerge from the hull through a shaft tube fitted with a watertight gland. Where shafts are not on the centre line of the ship, a supporting bearing is fitted close to the propeller, and is secured to the hull by a bracket known as the *A bracket* or *shaft bracket*.

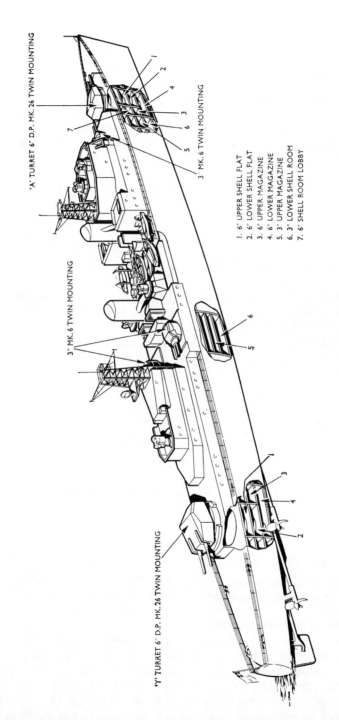

'A' TURRET 6" D.P. MK. 26 TWIN MOUNTING

3" MK. 6 TWIN MOUNTING

3" MK. 6 TWIN MOUNTING

'Y' TURRET 6" D.P. MK. 26 TWIN MOUNTING

1. 6" UPPER SHELL FLAT
2. 6" LOWER SHELL FLAT
3. 6" UPPER MAGAZINE
4. 6" LOWER MAGAZINE
5. 3" UPPER MAGAZINE
6. 3" LOWER SHELL ROOM
7. 6" SHELL ROOM LOBBY

FIG. 3–10. Typical armament layout of a cruiser

Main engines

Steam-driven turbines. A warship is usually propelled by steam-driven turbines, the steam being generated in oil-fired boilers. Usually one set of turbines drives each propeller shaft. The main engines and boilers are situated in watertight compartments known as *engine rooms* and *boiler rooms*, and in larger ships there may be two or more of each to guard against complete immobilisation of the main machinery by one hit from a torpedo or mine. In fig. 3–8, for example, it will be seen that the cruiser has four propellers, two engine rooms and two boiler rooms; the forward boiler room and engine room form an isolated group driving the outer shafts, while the after group drives the inner shafts.

Supplies of fuel and water for the boilers are stored in tanks built into the bottom of the hull.

Diesel engines. Some small ships and submarines have diesel main engines arranged in groups or banks on each shaft and clutched in according to the speed required. The advantages of diesel over steam turbines are saving of weight and space and rapid starting (a few minutes as compared with two or three hours from cold).

Gas turbines. These also develop full power from cold within a few minutes, and are fitted in some warships to supplement the steam turbines for high speed work and to get quickly under way in harbour.

Nuclear power. In nuclear-powered ships the nuclear reactor provides the source of power instead of the conventional ship's boilers, and hence there is no requirement for oil fuel stowage.

Auxiliary machinery

All other machinery associated with the main engines and boilers, the supply of electricity, salt water in firemains or any other ship service whether steam, diesel or electrically-driven is called auxiliary machinery.

Steering gear

Ships are steered by the movement of one or more rudders in the wake of the propellers. Each rudder is operated by hydraulic and electric steering gear which is controlled from the steering position by the telemotor system (Chapter 16).

Living spaces

These include the messes, mess decks, cabins, bathrooms, galleys, canteens, recreation spaces and the ship's administrative and technical offices.

Store and provision rooms

Sufficient stores are normally carried by a warship to enable her to maintain all her equipment in running order for periods varying between three and six months without recourse to supply bases or dockyards, and their number and type is therefore very considerable. For the most part they are stowed in store rooms situated low down in the hull, before and abaft the machinery spaces.

A sufficient quantity of provisions is normally carried by a ship to feed her crew for a period of three months, and these are augmented as opportunity occurs by fresh provisions, such as meat, fruit and vegetables. The *dry* provisions are stowed in well-ventilated *provision rooms* in the vicinity of the living spaces. Fresh meat is stowed in *cold rooms* which are maintained at the required temperature by refrigerating machinery. Fresh vegetables may be stowed in cold rooms, or in well-ventilated stowages on or near the upper deck.

Fresh water tanks and supply system

Water for drinking, cooking and washing is carried in tanks situated forward and aft in the hull. From these tanks it is pumped to the fresh water mains, from which branches are fed to the various drinking-water tanks, pantries, galleys and bathrooms throughout the ship. Storage of sufficient fresh water to provide for the domestic purposes of a warship's crew throughout any but a very short voyage would constitute an uneconomical use of weight and space; fresh water is therefore distilled on board from the surrounding sea water by means of *evaporators*, in which the sea water is boiled by steam from the boilers and the resulting steam condensed into fresh water, which is pumped into the storage tanks. The evaporators have also to provide a sufficient supply of fresh water for the boilers, and, because their output is limited, strict economy in the use of fresh water must be observed on board a ship.

Production of steam and electric power

The chief forms of power in a warship are steam and electricity. Steam pipes are more vulnerable than electric cables and more difficult to repair or replace, and for this reason the use of steam to drive machinery is usually confined to the main machinery spaces and to other parts of the ship behind armour. Electricity is produced by generators, situated either in the engine and boiler rooms, where they are driven by steam turbines, or in *generator rooms* situated outside the main machinery spaces, where they are driven by diesels or by gas turbines. This differentiation guards against complete failure of electric power should the boilers be put out of action.

Distribution of electric power

In modern ships electricity is generated at 440 volts a.c., three-phase, 60 c/s. Power from these generators is supplied to independent switchboards which can be interconnected when required.

Power is distributed from the switchboards via switch-fuses or feeder breakers at 440 volts by a three-phase three-wire unearthed main supply system.

Power for the lighting system and miscellaneous small services is distributed at 115 volts by a 60 c/s, two-wire, unearthed, single-phase system supplied from the main supply system through three-phase 440/115 volt transformers.

Voltages and frequencies different from those given above are supplied to radio, armament and other services through transformers, rectifiers, or rotating conversion machinery. Alternative and emergency sources of supply are available for all important services.

In older ships and most small ships electricity is produced at 220 volts d.c. In small ships the supply of power is distributed from one or more centralised switchboards, but in large ships it is distributed from a *ring-main* system, which consists of heavy armoured cables which are led around inside the armoured part of the ship in the form of a ring and fed through special switchgear by all the generators. By means of various switches this ring can be sectionalised to isolate damaged sections so that supplies are maintained to the other sections via branch breakers.

Electric power at any voltage other than 220 volts d.c. is supplied from conversion machinery.

Pumping and flooding

A ship can be flooded as a result of damage, firefighting or deliberate action. Certain compartments of greater fire hazard than others, such as the magazines and spirit room, can be flooded direct from the sea by opening *sea cocks* in the ship's bottom. Other compartments can be flooded through the *firemain*, which is a system of pipes running throughout a ship and fed with salt water under pressure by steam- or electrically-driven pumps. The firemain is painted bright red and has hydrants with hose connections at frequent intervals so that all parts of the ship may be reached by hose.

The firemain also provides water for the spraying systems in magazines for drenching ammunition when there is risk of fire; for pre-wetting as a safeguard against nuclear fall-out; for the sanitary services; for scrubbing decks and cleaning anchors and cables when weighing anchor.

Flood water can be removed by fixed steam- or electrically-driven pumping equipment through a system of pipes, or by portable pumps and flexible hoses, or by scuppers and drains.

AIRCRAFT CARRIERS

Aircraft carriers are usually armoured and have a speed of over 23 knots. They carry the maximum anti-aircraft armament that is possible without obstructing the flight deck and other flying arrangements. Their hangar capacity is at least 20 aircraft.

Layout and general arrangements (fig. 3–11)

The uppermost deck is called the *flight deck* and is flush from bow to stern, without a break except for the lifts. At each end the flight deck curves downwards to form what is known as the *round down*. The landing area of the flight deck is angled between 5° and 9° to port of the centre line to allow an aircraft to take off again if it fails to connect with the arrester wires.

On the starboard side of the flight deck are the funnel, masts, bridge and various flying and armament control positions, grouped together in a superstructure known as the *island*. At the forward and after ends of the flight deck, on each side, are the *safety nets* or *walkways* where members of the deck handling party are stationed when aircraft are taking off or landing on. Various flight deck control positions are built into the *walkways*. The equipment of a carrier includes a mobile crane, tractors for towing aircraft, and fork trucks for lifting and transporting light stores or equipment.

Across the after part of the flight deck run a number of *arrester wires*, which are raised a few inches off the deck when aircraft are landing on, but otherwise

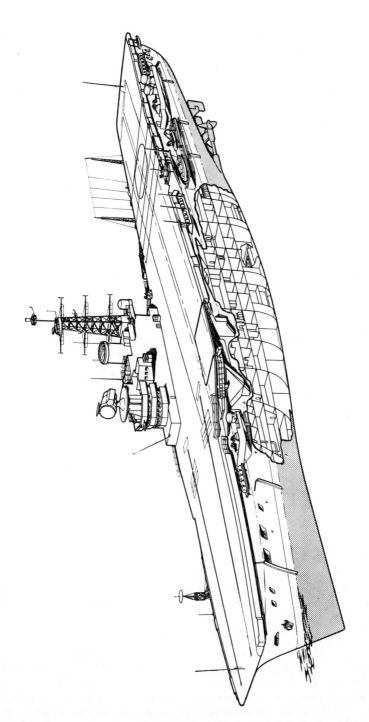

Fig. 3–11. Layout and general arrangement of an aircraft carrier

lie flat on the deck. These wires render when caught by the arrester hook with which deck landing aircraft are fitted, but are hydraulically braked and controlled so as to bring the aircraft to a standstill within a short distance of its touchdown.

In cases of emergency, i.e. when an aircraft is damaged and unable to lower its arrester hook or undercarriage, or if an aircraft has insufficient reserve of fuel to allow retake off and attempt another landing, an emergency barrier is rigged across the flight deck just aft of the island structure. The aircraft is brought to rest by engaging this net, which envelops the aircraft, dissipating its energy in the extension of lengths of undrawn nylon rope which are connected to the end of the net and pulled out from packs sited in pre-determined positions on the flight deck.

Two *catapults* are fitted, one each side at the forward end of the flight deck, to enable aircraft to be launched from the carrier.

Two deck landing projector or mirror sights are fitted at suitable positions on the port and starboard sides of the flight deck. These sights can be set to indicate a projected or reflected beam of light which determines the flight path into the arrester wires required to be followed by the pilot of the particular type of aircraft to be landed.

Below the greater part of the flight deck are situated the hangars, which are divided by fire curtains into sections. On each side of the hangars and before and abaft them are the workshops, offices, and stowages for stores and equipment. Living spaces are usually before and abaft the hangars and on the decks below. Below the *hangar deck*, which corresponds to the upper deck of other vessels, the internal arrangements are very similar to those of other major warships.

Operation of aircraft

Modern aircraft have a high landing speed. Since the deck of a carrier cannot be as long as an airfield, the carrier first steams into the wind to reduce the relative speed of the oncoming aircraft, then the aircraft is brought to a standstill by hooking one of the arrester wires. After each aircraft has landed the arrester wire is disengaged from the aircraft's arrester hook automatically and hove taut ready for the next one.

The present generation of aircraft are unable to reach the required take-off speed unaided and with few exceptions are always catapulted. Each aircraft taxies up to the loading base at the after end of the catapult track, where it is connected by a wire strop to a catapult towing shuttle and is subsequently launched. The catapults are fired in rapid succession.

While the carrier is steaming head to wind at a constant speed for landing on or flying off her aircraft, she presents a very vulnerable target, especially for submarine attacks. These operations therefore require a special organisation and method of control so that they can be carried out as quickly as possible. The flying organisation, internal administration and routine of an aircraft carrier are not, however, within the scope of this book.

IDENTIFICATION OF COMPARTMENTS

Before 1950 a compartment could be identified by its name—for example, No. 2 diesel generator room—and its position in the ship could be described by giving the deck name, the *stations* between which it was situated, and whether it lay to port, starboard or in the middle of the ship. The frames of a ship are numbered consecutively from forward to aft and known as *stations*. This system proved inadequate in the more complicated design of ship, such as an aircraft carrier, and the 1950 system of markings was introduced for all warships.

THE 1950 SYSTEM

This system can be applied to any ship regardless of its size and the number of compartment sub-divisions (in practice it is applied to frigates and above).

Compartments and openings

The basic unit is the compartment. Doors, hatches, manholes, etc. are then identified by the compartment in which they are sited or to which they give access. The position, and hence the marking, of a compartment is defined by a combination of letters and figures. First the deck number establishes the deck on which the compartment stands: then the fore-and-aft sub-division letter establishes the section between main transverse bulkheads between which it lies; for example, 4D indicates the shaded part of fig. 3–12.

Sub-division fore and aft. When the main section is sub-divided by transverse bulkheads, the compartments are given the suffix A, B or C starting from forward, or Z, Y or X starting from aft (the suffix letters are smaller capitals than the main section letters and deck figures, as shown in fig. 3–13).

Sub-division athwartships. When fore-and-aft bulkheads divide the main section, the figures 1, 3, 5, etc. after the deck figure and section letter or letters are used to indicate compartments to starboard of the centre line and 2, 4, 6, etc., for those to port of the centre line, numbering *from* the centre. Compartments on the centre line are numbered 0. This is illustrated in fig. 3–14.

Compartments more than one deck high. These compartments are given the marking for the deck on which they stand.

Nomenclature of compartments. Since every compartment in a ship is given a marking by the 1950 system, it is both convenient and desirable to refer to many compartments and fittings by the deck number and section letter rather than by an arbitrary number, for example '3N flour store' and '4K hull and fire pump'. In fact it may be found an advantage to refer to living spaces in the same way, so that the ship's company become rapidly accustomed to the system.

Doors. In general, doors bear the markings of the compartment to which they give access. When two or more doors give access to the same compartment they are distinguished by the words PORT (or STARBOARD) and/or FORWARD (or AFT) written in abbreviated form after the marking.

Hatches. A hatch bears the number of the deck in which it is cut followed by the letters (and number) of the compartment to which it gives access.

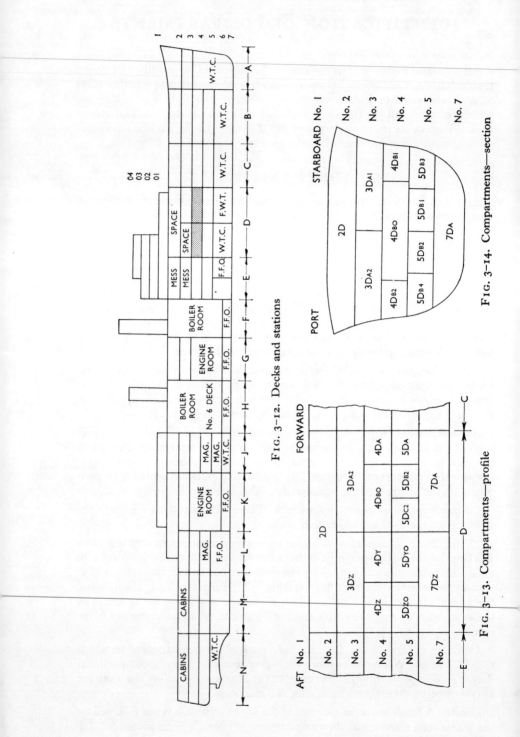

Fig. 3–12. Decks and stations

Fig. 3–13. Compartments—profile

Fig. 3–14. Compartments—section

Other markings. Some other special markings and further details of the system are given in B.R.2170, *Ship A.B.C.D. Manual, Vol. I.*

ELEMENTARY SHIP CONSTRUCTION

Hull stresses

The hull of a ship must be strong enough to withstand all the stresses imposed upon it by encountering heavy seas, or by resting on the blocks in a dry dock; it must also be sufficiently strong to withstand damage in the event of collision or grounding. The most important requirement of a warship's hull is that it should withstand damage in action.

The stresses to which a ship may be subjected are illustrated in fig. 3–15. The most important are the *hogging* and *sagging* stresses, caused by pitching head-on into heavy seas, which tend to break her back. When a ship rolls heavily in a sea-way she is subjected to *racking* stresses which tend to distort her sides and upper deck, and a combination of both pitching and rolling subjects her to *torsional* stresses which tend to twist her hull about its fore-and-aft axis. In addition, the pressure of the water against the underwater surface of the hull tends to bend the hull plating inwards. A concentration of weight between decks along the middle line of a ship tends to draw the top sides of her hull inwards. The opposite effect is produced when the ship rests on her keel in a dry dock; also her sides then tend to sag outwards and have to be supported by bilge and breast shores.

Hull form

The hull of a ship can be compared with a box, the ends of which are *faired off* to form the bows and stern, and the underwater portion of which is shaped to reduce its resistance to the water when moved through it. The bottom is rounded to meet the sides, at the turn of the bilge, and the degree of rounding varies with the type and size of the vessel. Most merchant ships have a nearly rectangular cross-section for the greater part of their length, the bottom being flat, the sides vertical, and the bilges sharply rounded; but high-speed vessels such as cruisers and destroyers have rising bottoms and less sharply rounded bilges.

The gradual broadening of the underwater part of the hull under the bows from the stem to the main body of the hull is called the *entry*, and the corresponding narrowing under the quarters towards the stern is called the *run*. Cruisers, destroyers and other high-speed vessels have a *fine entry* and a *fine run*, while ships designed essentially for large carrying capacity, such as freighters, have a comparatively *bluff entry* and *bluff run*.

Hull plating (fig. 3–16)

The outer surface of the hull is built of steel plates, which are welded or riveted to each other and to the main internal structural members of the hull. The plating covering the bottom is known as the *outer bottom plating*, and that covering the sides is generally known as the *side plating*. The thickness of the plates varies with their position in the hull, the thickest or heaviest being usually found over the bottom and at the deck edges amidships. In the larger warships,

3*

armour plating made of thick slabs of specially toughened and hardened steel is secured to the side plating of those parts of the hull within which are situated the more vital items of her equipment.

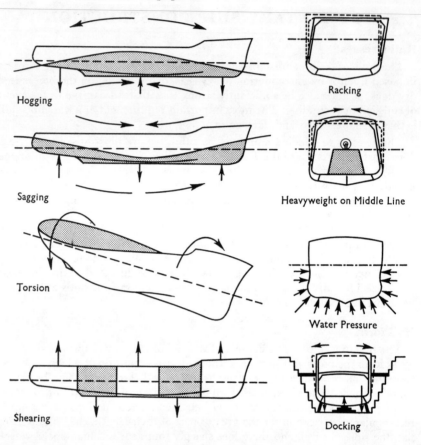

Hogging

Racking

Sagging

Heavyweight on Middle Line

Torsion

Water Pressure

Shearing

Docking

FIG. 3–15. Hull stresses

The short sides of each plate are called the *ends*, and the long sides the *edges*. Plates are joined end to end to form a panel of plating which runs forward and aft and is known as a *strake*. The joint between the ends of any two plates in a strake is known as a *butt*, and that between two strakes is known as a *seam*. Some strakes run continuously throughout the length of the hull, but others, particularly those around the turn of the bilge, may run only for a short distance amidships. The heaviest and most important strakes are the *garboard strakes* which run each side of the keel, and the *sheer strakes* which are the topmost strakes next below the upper deck; the sheer strakes run continuously throughout the length of the hull and give considerable longitudinal support to its structure. The strakes each side are usually lettered alphabetically from the keel outward and upward, the garboard strake being known as the 'A' strake and the next strake as the 'B' strake, and so on up to the sheer strake. In cross-Channel steamers and other vessels which frequently berth alongside

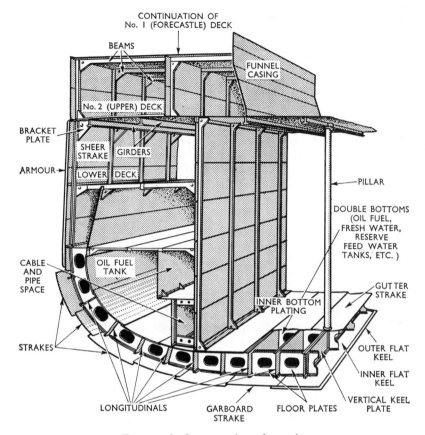

FIG. 3–16. Cross-section of a cruiser

jetties the strake just above the waterline is reinforced and protected with a baulk of timber, which is faced with steel and known as the *rubbing strake.*

MAIN MEMBERS OF THE HULL STRUCTURE

The main members of the internal structure of the hull (fig. 3–16) are the *keel,* the *stem* and *stern post,* the *frames,* the *longitudinals,* the *beams* and *girders,* the *decks* and the *bulkheads.* These all combine to support and strengthen the shell of the hull and enable it to withstand the various stresses to which it may be subjected.

The keel, stem and stern post

The most important structural member of the hull is the keel, which forms the backbone of the ship. It is constructed of horizontal and vertical keel plates and runs throughout the length of the hull, to the stem at its fore end and to the stern post at its after end. In small vessels the vertical keel may project a few inches from the bottom to form a *bar keel,* which helps to counteract the tendency of the vessel to roll.

The lower plate of the keel, called the *flat keel plate*, forms the centre strake of the outer bottom plating and is frequently fitted in two thicknesses. On this is built the *centre vertical keel*, which is constructed of plates to form a continuous girder of 'I' cross-section and whose height usually determines the depth of the *double bottoms*. On the top of the vertical keel is built the *gutter strake*, which forms the centre strake of the inner bottom plating. At either end of the midships section the cross-section of the lower keel plate begins to take the shape of a 'V', which becomes progressively sharper to conform to the finer lines of the hull at its entry and run.

The stem can be a single casting or forging, or, like the keel, can be built up of shaped plating and sections. The stern post is more complex, and in most ships has to take the weight of the rudder. It may consist of a single casting or forging, continued with shaped plating and sections. The stem and the stern post provide the anchorages for the extremities of the strakes of the outer plating.

Frames

The frames of a ship can be likened to the ribs of a skeleton. Their lower ends are secured to the keel, whence they extend outwards and upwards to the upper deck, and, with the longitudinals, form the main support of the shell plating. The frames conform to the shape of the hull and are closely spaced at intervals throughout its length. The spacing between the frames varies with the method of construction of the ship and with the position of the frames in the ship; generally speaking, they are spaced closer together at the bows and quarters and in the wake of heavy side armour. In large ships the intervals may be as much as from 4 to 6 ft amidships, and from 2 ft 6 in. to 3 ft at the bows and stern, while in small ships the intervals may be as small as from 1 ft 9 in. to 2 ft 6 in.

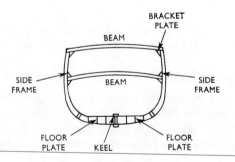

FIG. 3–17. Frame

Where the frames join the keel they are of the same depth as the vertical keel, but their depth tapers progressively from the turn of the bilge to their extremities at the upper or forecastle decks. The lower part of a frame which runs across the bottom of the ship is usually called the *floor plate* or, more shortly, the *floor*, and it forms part of the double bottom structure of the hull.

Longitudinals

These main structural members run forward and aft and provide longitudinal strength to the hull. Together with the frames they provide the support for the hull plating, and with the floors they support the plating of the double bottoms. The main longitudinals are usually numbered outwards from the keel, those next to it being known, respectively, as *No. 1 longitudinal port* and *No. 1 longitudinal starboard*. Smaller longitudinals may be placed along the ship's side where extra strength above the double bottoms is required, particularly at the bows and stern, and these are usually known as *stringers*.

Double bottoms

The keel, with the floors of the frames and the bottom longitudinals, form the cellular structure extending about two-thirds the length of the hull known as the double bottoms. They are covered by the layer of watertight plating called the *inner bottom* or *tank top*, and thus prevent the ship becoming flooded should the outer bottom plating be holed. The double bottoms, in addition to contributing greatly to the strength of the hull, provide storage space for oil fuel and fresh water. In some merchant ships they enclose the ballast tanks, which can be filled with sea water to give additional stability to the ship when she is lightly loaded; when in this condition the ship is said to be *in ballast*.

The double bottoms of most merchant ships and some warships extend across the bilges to their turns, and the inner bottom or tank top is flat and forms the deck of the engine rooms, boiler rooms, cargo holds and store rooms. In cruisers and some larger warships the double bottoms may extend up to the waterline and thus form part of the underwater protection of the ship against mine or torpedo.

The bottom and sides of the holds of merchant ships are usually sheathed with a layer of wooden planks as a protection for the cargo, this sheathing being known as the *ceiling*.

Bulkheads

The term *bulkhead* is used by the seaman to describe any wall of a compartment which is not formed by the ship's side. Bulkheads can therefore be watertight or non-watertight, and transverse or longitudinal, and they may either serve as partitions between compartments or form part of the main structure of the ship.

The hull is divided vertically and athwartships, by *main structural bulkheads*, into a number of watertight sections. These bulkheads usually extend between the frames from the bottom of the hull to the main deck above the waterline, but in places they may be continued up to the upper and forecastle decks. In addition to dividing the ship into watertight sections these bulkheads appreciably contribute to the transverse and longitudinal strength of the hull.

The interval between transverse bulkheads is determined by the type of ship and her manner of construction; generally speaking, they are spaced closer together at the forward and after ends of the hull than amidships. The forward bulkheads help the bows to withstand the impact of the waves and form a barrier against the ingress of water in the event of collision; the after bulkheads help to strengthen the hull against the thrust of the propellers and the stresses of pitching and rolling. The positions of the bulkheads in the main body of the hull are largely determined by the spaces required for boiler rooms, engine rooms, cargo holds, magazines, shell rooms and other main features of the ship's equipment. In a freighter the main structural bulkheads may provide the only watertight division of the hull, but in warships and passenger liners, where a tier of decks runs almost continuously forward and aft, the hull is sub-divided by watertight decks and longitudinal and transverse watertight bulkheads into what is virtually a honeycomb of watertight compartments. This watertight compartmentation provides a great measure of safety to the ship should her hull be holed below the waterline, as it enables the resultant flooding to be confined to a small portion of the hull.

Decks, beams and pillars

The hull is divided horizontally by decks, which in a warship run continuously from stem to stern except where they are broken by the main machinery spaces; in a freighter their continuity is further broken by the holds. Non-continuous decks may be found in many ships, and these are usually called *flats* or *platforms*. The number and names of the decks vary with the type and size of the ship. In warships, decks up to and including the upper deck are made watertight wherever possible, and with the bulkheads they thus complete the watertight compartmentation of the ship; in addition, they lend consider-able transverse and longitudinal strength to the hull.

A deck is formed of strakes of steel plates which extend forward and aft and are joined together in the same way as the hull plating. The plates forming the outer strakes are heavier than the remainder and are known as the *stringer plates*, and the edges where they join the side plating are known as the *boundary angles*. Decks above the waterline are usually *cambered* (i.e. arched) to aid the drainage of any surface water to the gutters, called *waterways*, which extend fore and aft at the sides of the decks. From these waterways the water is drained over the ship's side by pipes called *scuppers*. A *spurn water*, which is a wooden or metal beading, prevents water spilling over the side. Weather decks are frequently covered with a layer of wooden planking which, in addition to affording a safe foothold for the crew in wet weather, helps to insulate the spaces below them against heat and cold. The edge where the upper deck meets the ship's side is known as the *gunwale*; this term survives from the early days of wooden ships when the hull was strengthened longitudinally by one or more heavy strakes called *wales*, the one supporting the main gun-deck being then known as the gunwale. In many ships, particularly merchant ships, the ship's side abreast the waist and well-decks is built up several feet above the upper deck by a strake of plating joined to the gunwale and known as the *bulwarks*; these form a protecting breakwater against heavy seas, and prevent the crew from being washed overboard or falling overboard, and they are pierced at intervals with openings fitted with hinged flaps called *freeing ports*, to allow the escape of any water shipped in a sea-way.

Decks are supported by beams which extend athwartships between the frames, and by girders which extend forward and aft between the beams. The beams are usually joined to the frames by *brackets* or *knee plates*, which thus unite the beams, frames and decks in contributing to the transverse strength of the hull. *Pillars* assist the beams and girders in supporting the decks over large compartments, around large hatchways, and below heavy equipment.

Bilge keels

These take the form of two long, narrow, fore-and-aft girders, which are built out from the hull at the turn of the bilge on each side of the ship to check her rolling in a sea-way.

SUBMARINES

A submarine dives by flooding her *main tanks*. She then maintains her fore-and-aft trim by adjusting the levels of water in her *trim tanks*, and by the use of *torpedo operating tanks* to compensate for the loss of weight when torpedoes are fired. *Compensating tanks* are fitted so that the weight of the submarine can be adjusted during a patrol to allow for the change of density of sea water, the compression of the hull when dived, and for the consumption of stores, provisions and fuel.

The submarine surfaces by blowing water out of her main tanks by compressed air.

Design and construction

These differ in several important respects from those of surface ships, as is shown in figs. 3–18 and 3–19, which show the general layout and a midship cross-section of a typical submarine. The framework of the *pressure hull* has no longitudinal girdering except that required to support main engines and motors, and the main frames are transverse and welded direct to the hull. The increase in diving depth necessitated by improved anti-submarine detection required that the pressure hull should be circular throughout its length, having specially-shaped *domed* ends, and be constructed of special quality steel. Any discontinuity in this main hull, such as the torpedo hatch and shaft recesses, requires much heavier compensation for the loss of strength than is needed in a surface ship. Electric welding, now adopted for the entire pressure hull, has greatly facilitated the symmetrical and economical disposition of the material, with a consequent improvement in diving depth. The use of radiography to search out defective welding enables full reliability to be placed upon the completed hull.

The *outer hull*, which accommodates the main ballast tanks and external fuel tanks, and fines off the form of the vessel forward and aft, is built outside the pressure hull. Light casings are built around the capstan gear, battery ventilation pipes and other such excrescences outside the hull to provide a streamlined form and so reduce the frictional drag of the hull. The same applies to the fin which encompasses the conning tower, periscope brackets, the bridge and other fittings, and this structure has to be sufficiently high and spacious to permit navigation on the surface in adverse weather. The reserve buoyancy of a submarine when on the surface, measured by the capacity of the main ballast tanks, is much smaller in proportion to the surface displacement than in surface ships. Broadly speaking, the outer hull is shaped to obtain as streamlined a form as possible. The main tanks and external fuel tanks are usually built in the form of *saddles* on the pressure hull, or as a light outer skin circumscribing the

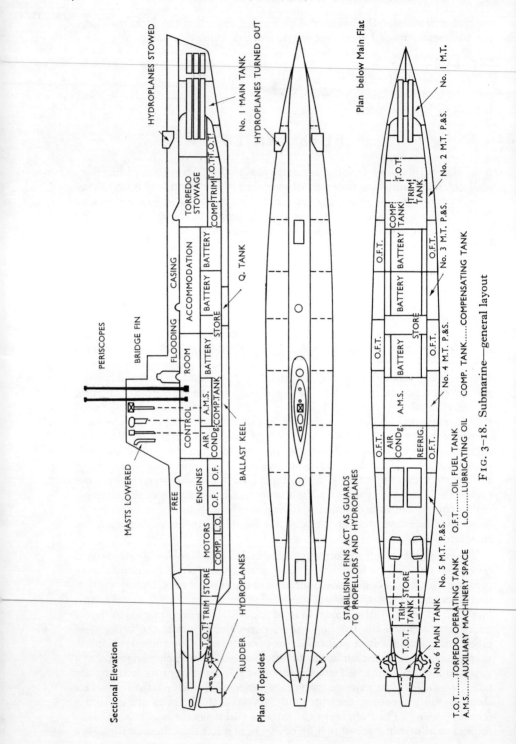

Sectional Elevation

PERISCOPES

BRIDGE FIN

MASTS LOWERED

HYDROPLANES STOWED

No. 1 MAIN TANK

HYDROPLANES TURNED OUT

TORPEDO STOWAGE

COMP | TRIM | O.T. | O.T.

CASING

FLOODING

ACCOMMODATION

ROOM

BATTERY

BATTERY

STORE

Q. TANK

CONTROL

COMP | TANK

A.M.S.

AIR | COND&

BATTERY

BALLAST KEEL

ENGINES

O.F. | O.F.

FREE

MOTORS

COMP | L.O.

STORE | TRIM

T.O.T.

HYDROPLANES

RUDDER

Plan of Topsides

STABILISING FINS ACT AS GUARDS
TO PROPELLORS AND HYDROPLANES

Plan below Main Flat

No. 1 M.T.

No. 2 M.T. P.&S.

T.O.T.

TRIM
TANK

COMP.
TANK

No. 3 M.T. P.&S.

O.F.T.

BATTERY

BATTERY

O.F.T.

O.F.T.

STORE

O.F.T.

No. 4 M.T. P.&S.

A.M.S.

BATTERY

O.F.T.

AIR
CONDg.

REFRIG.

O.F.T.

No. 5 M.T. P.&S.

T.O.T.

TRIM
TANK

STORE

No. 6 MAIN TANK   No. 5 M.T. P.&S.

T.O.T......TORPEDO OPERATING TANK   O.F.T......OIL FUEL TANK
A.M.S......AUXILIARY MACHINERY SPACE   L.O......LUBRICATING OIL   COMP. TANK......COMPENSATING TANK

Fig. 3-18. Submarine—general layout

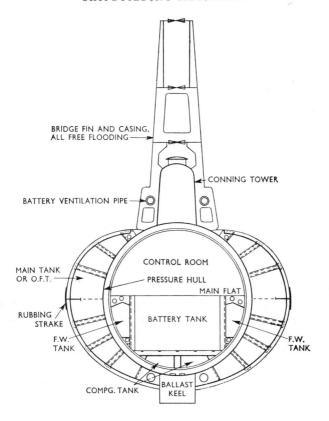

BRIDGE FIN AND CASING,
ALL FREE FLOODING

CONNING TOWER

BATTERY VENTILATION PIPE

MAIN TANK
OR O.F.T.

CONTROL ROOM

PRESSURE HULL

MAIN FLAT

RUBBING
STRAKE

F.W.
TANK

BATTERY TANK

F.W.
TANK

COMPG. TANK

BALLAST
KEEL

FIG. 3–19. Submarine—midship section

pressure hull. Submarines constructed in the latter manner are known as the *double hull* type.

In all designs adequate stability, both when on the surface and submerged, can usually be achieved only by the provision of special ballast low down in the ship, usually packed in a strongly constructed *ballast keel* which facilitates docking and *bottoming* on the sea bed. Some of the ballast is arranged to be readily portable so that adjustments can be made to the vessel's trim to compensate for changes in weight and moment arising from modifications during refit.

SHIPBUILDING MATERIALS

Every ship carries a statement or drawing showing where the various different materials are used in the ship's structure, as it is necessary to know the type of material when painting, chipping or welding, in order to avoid the wrong treatment.

Steel

Mild steel is the general-purpose steel used throughout the hull structure. Medium-tensile steels such as 'A' and 'B' quality steel, and high-tensile steels such as Q.T.28 and Q.T.35, are usually only used for particular parts of the structure where a steel stronger than mild steel is required.

Plating is generally specified in terms of its weight per square foot, e.g. steel plate 1 in. thick would be described as a 40 lb plate. Angle bars and other sections are denoted by the size of the section and the weight per foot run, e.g. an angle bar might be 3 in. × 3½ in. × 10 lb.

Cast steel is used for structural castings such as hawsepipes and stern castings, but the number of castings used nowadays is less than formerly, as it is often possible to produce a lighter and cheaper fitting by fabricating it from mild steel, using welding. Forged steel is also used for this kind of work, e.g. shaft brackets, rudder frames, and in particular for anchor chain cable.

Aluminium

Aluminium alloys are now used extensively for hull structure, such as minor bulkheads and deck houses. They are also used for furniture and non-watertight doors.

Copper alloys

These are not used for the structure of the ship, but they are used extensively for fittings, pipes, bearings, etc., e.g. naval brass for fittings, gun-metal for valves, aluminium bronze for small castings and corosion-resistant fastenings, phosphor bronze for bearings and sleeves, copper–nickel–iron for salt water piping.

Non-metallic materials

In addition to the conventional materials such as wood and linoleum, a large and ever-increasing number of materials is now available for such purposes as deck coverings, insulation, decorative linings, sound-proofing, protective coatings, etc. from the range of materials known as 'plastics'.

Methods of connection

Welding is the method now most commonly employed for joining the structural members, both steel and aluminium. Riveting is limited to particular applications. The shipbuilder has many different automatic welding processes at his disposal, and uses carefully-controlled welding procedures when welding the high-strength and other special steels. These facilities are not available to ship's staff, and it is for this reason that welding by ship's staff is only permitted under certain specified conditions.

When steel and aluminium are riveted together, an insulating material is required at the joint, as corrosion occurs between any two dissimilar metals which are in contact, because of what is known as electrolytic action. As an additional precaution, the steel is galvanized or zinc-sprayed.

Questions on this chapter will be found in Appendix 2.

CHAPTER 4

Ship Safety

The term 'ship safety' is used here to describe the normal precautions which are taken in a warship to guard against fire, flooding, general damage, and casualties to personnel, whether caused by accident or by the enemy, and to minimise their effects. These precautions, together with the action necessary to repair damage to the ship and her services, are known collectively as 'ABCD', which stands for *A*tomic, *B*iological and *C*hemical Defence and *D*amage Control (including firefighting). Detailed information and instructions on ABCD are contained in the *Ship ABCD Manual*, Volumes 1 and 2. This chapter is intended only to introduce the seaman to the more important aspects of damage control, namely, precautions against flooding, damage and casualties, and to give some general rules for the maintenance of ship safety. Also included are some general remarks on abandoning ship in the event of the ultimate disaster. Precautions against fire and descriptions of the simpler firefighting equipment are given in Chapter 5, more details being included in Volume II.

There is in every ship an organisation to fulfil the functions of ABCD and an officer responsible for directing the organisation and co-ordinating the necessary training. The organisation has as *its nucleus* a small team of officers and men drawn from different departments. In its broad sense, however, ABCD concerns the whole ship and *every man in it* and has a definite application to all divisions, departments and quarters. Every member of the ship's company is a potential link in the organisation and the action taken by him, whether as a matter of routine or emergency, may prove decisive to the safety of the ship. Thus every person on board must have some understanding of:

1. The effects of damage and how they can be minimised.
2. The layout of the ship and the whereabouts and use of equipment provided for firefighting, emergency repair, ABC monitoring, and decontamination.
3. The function of ABCD control positions and organisation.
4. The method of passing quick and accurate reports.
5. The necessity for watertight and gastight integrity and the meanings of risk and control markings.
6. The care and use of personal equipment in self-defence and a knowledge of first aid.
7. The need for careful stowage of store rooms, offices and personal belongings, to reduce the risk of fire and to avoid hampering repair operations or the pumping of compartments.

ORGANISATION

The ABCD organisation varies with the size and type of ship; at one end of the scale are such craft as minesweepers, with an extremely simple organisation; at the other the largest aircraft carrier, with very complex arrangements. It must be remembered that the organisation is so framed that the required degree of control can be exercised under all the differing circumstances possible in peace and war, and can transfer smoothly from one set of conditions to another.

Headquarters and sections

For ABCD purposes, every ship larger than a destroyer is divided into ABCD sections, each of which extends from the keel to the weather deck between certain transverse bulkheads. Damage control is dealt with in each section from its own *section base*. Hangars in carriers are regarded as additional separate sections and the Hangar Control Position does duty as section base. Destroyers and smaller ships are treated as 'one-section' ships, but the available men and materials are divided between sub-sections or repair positions forward and aft. Overall assessment and central control is exercised from ABCD Headquarters (generally called H.Q.1), which is sited centrally in the ship. In ships larger than destroyers, if H.Q.1 is put out of action its functions are taken over by either a Secondary Headquarters (H.Q.2) or one of the section bases suitably equipped.

Communications

In ships larger than destroyers certain positions in each section are connected to the section base by telephone. The bases are similarly connected with each other and with H.Q.1 (and H.Q.2). Certain other positions in the ship are connected directly with H.Q.1 (and H.Q.2), including the principal electrical control positions, which also usually have communications with the section bases. There are three telephone systems—one with its hand-sets and boxes coloured *red* for matters concerning fire and general damage; one coloured *green* for electrical equipment and circuits; and one *yellow* for pumping and flooding. There is also a special broadcast system controlled from H.Q.1 (and H.Q.2).

In all smaller ships there is an ABCD telephone system centred in H.Q.1 with connections to all important positions in the ship.

Control and manning

In ships larger than destroyers the organisation is controlled from H.Q.1 unless the possibility of enemy action is very remote, or in harbour in peace-time, when it may be controlled by the Officer of the Watch. In smaller ships the organisation is controlled from H.Q.1 only when action is imminent or highly probable, H.Q.1 being normally used for some other purpose.

The extent to which damage control stations are manned depends on the probability of enemy action or the risk of damage (e.g. from mines or in fog). When it is imminent or highly probable the stations are fully manned with special parties. In H.Q.1 there is a team of officers and men trained and equipped to assess the effects, to organise the repair of all types of damage which may occur, and to take such other measures as are necessary to ensure the safety of the ship. In small ships under similar conditions H.Q.1 may be under the charge of an officer or responsible senior rating. In large ships, in each section there is a composite team of ratings who are trained and equipped to take immediate and appropriate action to deal with any type of damage in the section as soon as it occurs; an officer stationed at the section base controls the section team, which includes 'fire and repair parties', 'pumping and flooding parties', 'supply', 'first aid' and 'electrical repair' parties and 'W.T. integrity patrols'. Each team works as a unit within the limits of its section, but H.Q.1 may order one section to be reinforced by men from other sections. In small ships the repair parties in the forward and after sub-sections will usually be under the charge of the senior rating of the party, unless an officer is available to take charge of the work.

When action or damage is less probable, stations are only manned with skeleton teams in large ships, and not at all in small ships. When the possibility is remote, as in harbour in peace, stations may not be manned and damage control requirements would then be met by the 'part of the watch' or the duty emergency party.

PRECAUTIONS AGAINST FLOODING

Watertight sub-division and openings

Ships are divided by watertight decks and bulkheads into a number of watertight spaces and compartments, as explained in Chapter 3. Any flooding resulting from damage to the hull below the waterline can thus be confined to a small part of the ship. Each compartment, however, has to be provided with a door or hatch for access, and means of ventilation (trunks, side scuttles, ports); in addition, electric cables, pipes, trunks and rod gearing may pass through it. These fittings and the places where they penetrate the decks and bulkheads must be made watertight, and rules must be laid down for the opening and closing of such openings, the rules being adapted to the use made of each compartment and to its liability to flooding. By keeping these watertight openings shut, especially in the higher parts of the ship, the spread of blast and fire can be prevented.

Gastightness and gastight openings

Besides the necessity to maintain watertightness (generally known as *watertight integrity*), there is a need to keep out of the ship radioactive material, and biological and chemical agents (all included under the general name 'gas'). Much of the external shell of the ship, including bridges and superstructures, can be made gastight. All interconnecting compartments which can be grouped together with unbroken gastight boundaries form what is called a *citadel*. Other spaces can be made gastight but for geographical or other reasons cannot be included in a citadel; these are called *gas-free spaces*. Openings in the boundaries of citadels and gas-free spaces must be controlled in a similar way to watertight openings. Some openings must fulfil both functions, watertightness having prior claim on some occasions and gastightness on others.

Ventilating systems

Ventilation is required to provide fresh air for health and alertness and to maintain tolerable temperatures; to provide combustion air for machinery; and to remove hot or foul air, noxious gases and inflammable vapours. Compartments may be ventilated by natural or forced ventilating systems. The former is little used nowadays except high in the ship, where scuttles and ports assist the ventilation. Forced ventilation is by a system of fans and airtight trunking: fresh air is drawn by a fan through an inlet on a weather deck and forced through trunking to the compartments served; foul air is similarly exhausted.

Ventilation trunking pierces decks and bulkheads and can therefore prejudice watertight and gastight integrity. To meet ABCD requirements, the following principles are observed as far as possible in design and fitting:

1. Systems are grouped so that the number of weather-deck openings is kept to a minimum to allow rapid closing down of the ship.
2. The weather-deck openings of trunks are fitted with watertight or gastight covers.
3. Gas flaps (gastight valves) are fitted as necessary in the trunking to allow uncontaminated air to be recirculated in the citadels.
4. When the ship is closed down, air in the citadel is augmented by fresh supplies drawn into the ship through air filtration units and recirculated in the citadel. This allows a small positive pressure to be built up in the citadel which helps to exclude gas.
5. *Main* watertight bulkheads are not usually pierced by trunking below a point where this would be dangerous to watertight integrity. Where they must be pierced, the trunk is kept as high as possible and the opening in the bulkhead is fitted with a watertight slide valve. Low in the ship, as much trunking as possible is made watertight and slide valves are fitted as necessary to restrict interflooding between compartments after damage. Many of the valves are operated from higher decks by rod gearing.

Unventilated compartments. Many compartments, such as double bottom spaces, have no fitted ventilation and can only be ventilated by portable fans and hoses. As these may therefore contain poisonous, inflammable or explosive gases, or may lack sufficient oxygen to support life, certain precautions, described under the heading 'Precautions Against Casualties' (page 83), must be taken before anyone is allowed to enter or work in them.

CONTROL OF OPENINGS

The control of openings (including ventilation openings and fans) is achieved by using *watertight* and *gastight conditions*. To maintain these conditions, risk and control markings are required on openings affecting watertight or gastight integrity. There are three watertight conditions, XRAY (X), YANKEE (Y) and ZULU (Z); and two gastight conditions, ALFA (A) and BRAVO (B). The circumstances under which these are used will be described later.

Risk markings

Red. If a ship sustains hull damage at or below the waterline, compartments in the vicinity will flood immediately. Because of possible heel and trim after damage, this area extends above the waterline, especially at the ends and sides of a big ship. Openings to all compartments within this zone (the extent of which is decided by Admiralty) are deemed to be, when open, an *immediate risk* to watertight integrity (i.e. immediate risk of flooding). All such openings are marked with a red disc or triangular flash and are known as *red openings*. In an emergency (e.g. after damage with flooding, or when collision is obviously

imminent) these can be shut by order. The order is 'Close all red openings'—
it is an emergency—speed is vital—*the order overrides any permission which may
be in force for a red opening to be open.* The object, of course, is to restrict the
spread of flooding.

Blue. After damage, during a long trip to harbour or under adverse weather
conditions, it may be necessary to exercise a rigid control over some openings
just above the red zone, overriding the normal rules for openings. These
openings are given a blue marking, which denotes this lesser risk but is not an
emergency mark in the same way as the red.

Orange. Openings in the boundaries of citadels and gas-free spaces constitute,
when open, a risk to gastight integrity and are similarly marked in orange. This
again has not quite the significance of the red marking. It *can* be used to shut
the openings in an emergency, but it is seldom likely to be so needed.

Control markings

For control purposes, openings must be classified in accordance with the use
to which they are put and their position in the ship. The basic principles of this
must be to ensure:

1. The safety of the ship.
2. The maintenance of habitability and the free flow of traffic; access for
   inspection, routine and other purposes; complete closing down of the ship
   against A, B or C agents while maintaining reasonable circulation of air.

The control markings, with their meanings and rules, are shown in the table
on page 78. It will be seen that whereas there are five 'conditions' there are
seven control markings. In machinery spaces and some radar offices it is
necessary, in order to safeguard personnel and equipment, for the 'user'
department to control fans and openings in gastight conditions; air filtration
units must be similarly controlled. To allow this, 'M' is placed on such fittings
(in addition to any watertight control already on them) and indicates that the
'user' must exercise control *in gastight conditions only.* At all other times, any
watertight control marking on the door must take precedence. In no other case
may an opening bear two control marks.

The other control letter 'R' is used on certain fittings which *must* remain
open or running for efficient recirculation. This includes recirculation fans,
W.T. slide valves in recirculation systems and, in some ships, certain openings
specially fitted for recirculation.

WATERTIGHT AND GASTIGHT CONDITIONS

Watertight

In Peace

Harbour and normal cruising	Condition X (X openings closed)
Dangerous circumstances (e.g. navigational hazards, mines)	Condition Y (X and Y closed)
Exercises	As required

In War

Defended harbour, refitting, etc.	Condition X (X closed)
Undefended harbour, cruising	Condition Y (X and Y closed)
Action or relaxed action	Condition Z (X, Y and Z closed)

Gastight

Gastight conditions are imposed on watertight conditions as required.

In Peace	Required only for exercises
In War	
Preparedness for ABC attack	Condition B (B closed)
ABC attack imminent	Condition A (A and B closed)

Condition B is that from which condition A (the fully closed-down condition) can be attained in *5 minutes* or less. In a few ships a third gastight condition and

BASIC RULES FOR WATERTIGHT AND GASTIGHT OPENINGS

Control marking on opening, valve or fan	Colour	Signification
X	BLACK	Watertight control. Opened only by permission. If required to be kept open, a sentry must be posted or adequate arrangements made for instant closing. To be reported when closed. Red zone only.
Y	BLACK	Watertight control. In condition X may remain open; closed in Y and Z. When closed, may be opened for passage or use and shut again. If required to be kept open, the rules as for X openings apply (see Note i). Red zone only.
Z	BLACK	Watertight control. In conditions X and Y may remain open; closed in Z. When closed, rules for Y openings apply (see Note i). Used, almost without exception, above the red zone only.
B	ORANGE	Gastight control. Closed in condition B. When closed, not to be opened without permission. Openings which affect gastight integrity, except doors and hatches.
A	ORANGE	Gastight control. Closed in condition A—open in B. When closed, not to be opened without permission (except as in Note ii). Openings which affect gastight integrity, except doors and hatches.
M	ORANGE	In *gastight conditions only*, under control of 'user' department. At all other times, controlled by watertight marking if so marked. On some openings to machinery spaces, on air filtration units and ventilation to some radar offices.
R	ORANGE	Gastight control. Fan must continue to run or opening must remain open for recirculation. On any opening requiring it—mainly fans and slide valves.

Notes:

(i) In condition A, any Y or Z opening with an orange risk mark must not be opened without permission (except as in Note ii).

(ii) Doors or hatches to be used for 'citadel in', 'citadel out' or for gaining 'shelter' *may* be opened in condition A for the purpose indicated, but must be shut again and fully clipped. When closed down in condition A, but *before* the ship is contaminated, citadel in/out doors must be used. *After* the ship is contaminated, ENTRANCE must be only through a cleansing station, the outer access door or hatch being marked CLEANSING STATION.

QUALIFYING SYMBOLS

Symbol	Applicable Opening	Signification
2 CLIPS	Y or Z door or hatch	Used where the volume of traffic makes full clipping impracticable. The two clips used are opposite to the hinged side and are marked by double black lines on the door. In an emergency, all clips must be used.
VENT 2 CLIPS or VENT NO CLIPS	X, Y or Z hatches	Hatches so marked are to be clipped as indicated when magazines are ordered to be in the venting condition. In emergency, all clips are to be used.
CITADEL IN or CITADEL OUT	Y or Z door	Used on doors or hatches selected for getting in and out of the citadel via an airlock when in condition A.

marking (C) may be met. This would be found where a very large number of ventilation systems and openings necessitated some being more or less permanently shut down.

Thus a ship can be in any one of the following six conditions: X, Y, YB, Z, ZB, ZA. *No other conditions are normally possible or required.* As an exception, in war when carrying out essential maintenance in a defended harbour, the ship may be in condition X while needing to retain some measure of gastight control in condition B.

'May be left Open' discs

There are four uses for these. The wording on the disc (which is in red on a white ground) indicates the use for which it is intended.

1. On openings (as few as possible) which may need to be open in one or more watertight conditions without having to post a sentry. They bear the words 'May be left Open', the identification marking of the opening, and the condition(s) for which permission is given. The disc is hung on a screw and covers the control marking. *At all times*, other than when so authorised, the disc is to be returned to the issuing authority and the opening controlled according to its normal marking.

2. On openings which may need to be opened and possibly remain open (in spite of the control mark) for action purposes. Bears the words 'May be open in ACTION'. Is screwed on the door *not* covering the control. Applied by officers of quarters in accordance with ship's orders—at all other times, controlled by normal marking.

3. In some ships on a very few doors or hatches which would normally be governed by a watertight control marking but which must be open for

recirculation of air. Bears the marking 'May be left open for RECIRCULA-TION'; screwed on the door; permissive in the 'closed-down' condition only.

4. When series of hatches are visited frequently and regularly (e.g. once or twice a watch) a disc bearing the words 'May be left open—MAN BELOW' is hung on the topmost hatch of the series. The disc is to be removed when the hatches are closed. At all other times, governed by the normal control mark. Used for such spaces as gland and plummer block compartments.

STATES OF READINESS

ABCD states of readiness are required to ensure that the ship is always pre-pared to resist the effects of damage and flooding, whether from attack or accident. There is *always* some risk present, so there is always a need for some state of readiness. The ship and her crew cannot be keyed up to the highest pitch at all times because maintenance, habitability and morale would suffer; nor, in fact, is there need for this. The state adopted at any time will depend on the calculated risk existing at that time, the warning time which can be ex-pected and the speed with which the highest state can be assumed. The state of readiness governs ABCD personnel requirements and many material measures such as control of services and machinery. The watertight and gas-tight conditions, although not tied to the states of readiness (since one can be changed without the other), can be related, as shown in the table on page 81.

Comparison with 'degree of readiness'

The ABCD states of readiness will not necessarily coincide with the 'degrees of readiness' which may be assumed by the armament organisation, because the latter are controlled by active offence or defence requirements. For example, if the ship were steaming in waters where air or surface attack was improbable but mines might well be encountered, the ABCD organisation would be in State 2, or even State 1 relaxed, whereas the armament would be in the Third or Fourth Degree. Another reason for this difference is that the change from one *state* of readiness to another may take as long as half-an-hour because considerable changes in the state of the ship's machinery and equipment may be involved, whereas the change from one *degree* of readiness of the armament to another can be effected in a few minutes.

STATES OF READINESS USED

STATE 1	Attack imminent	Highest state of ABCD preparedness; all positions fully manned.
STATE 1 relaxed	Attack likely but not imminent	All positions manned, but up to 50 per cent personnel may be relaxed for meals, etc.
STATE 2	Attack possible, or dangerous waters	War seagoing state; watch system. In peace, passage through mined waters, navigational hazards, etc.
STATE 3	Attack unlikely without adequate warning	Defended harbour in war; normal cruising in peace.
STATE 4		Normal peace routine in harbour.

STATES AND CONDITIONS

The following table shows the relationship between states and conditions under most normal circumstances.

Possible conditions	Circumstances	Possible states
X	*Peace*—harbour; normal cruising	4 (harbour) 3 (cruising)
	War—defended harbour when refitting, etc.	3
Y	*Peace*—dangerous circumstances, e.g. fog, or mines	3 or 2
	War—undefended harbour and normal cruising	2
YB	*Peace*—as required for exercises	2
	War—cruising or undefended harbour and prepared for ABC attack	2
Z	*Peace*—exercises	1 or 1 relaxed
	War—action or relaxed action	1 or 1 relaxed
ZB	*Peace*—exercises	1 or 1 relaxed
	War—as Z but prepared for ABC attack	1 or 1 relaxed
ZA	*Peace*—exercises	1
	War—as Z but ABC attack imminent	1

A gastight condition *cannot* be used alone; if required, it must be superimposed on a watertight condition. It should also be noted that a high gastight condition requires the assumption of at least as high a watertight condition.

Executive orders

The proper method of setting the states and conditions is by pipe broadcast. The condition or the state can be changed independently, e.g. without changing the state, change condition X to Y, or Y to YB; or in condition Y, change state from 3 to 2. The condition and state can also be assumed or changed together, e.g. 'Assume State 3 condition Yankee Bravo', or 'State 2 condition Zulu' or 'State 1 condition Zulu Alfa'.

PUMPING AND DRAINING SYSTEMS

Older ships

Older ships are provided with one or more pumping systems by which flooded compartments low down in the ship can be pumped out when the flow of water into them has been checked. Flooded compartments higher up in the ship can be similarly pumped out by portable pumps. Some compartments situated above the level of the main suction systems may be provided with drain pipes to enable flood water to be drained to the bilges, or to a lower compartment, whence it can be pumped overboard by the main pumping system. Some compartments above the waterline, such as bathrooms and galleys, are provided with scupper pipes to drain off sullage and waste water; these pipes, and those of the weather-deck scuppers, usually lead close within the ship's side to a position just above the waterline.

Suction pipes, drain pipes and scupper pipes may constitute a serious flooding risk if they are damaged or if the compartment in which they are situated is flooded. Watertight valves are fitted as required where suction or drain pipes pass through decks, bulkheads or the ship's side. Scupper pipes have positive closing arrangements fitted at their ship's side outlets, excepting those in upper hangars of large aircraft carriers, which are open throughout their length. Any valve controlling a sea inlet or an outlet to the sea is given a watertight risk marking.

Modern ships

In modern ships flood water is pumped out by means of portable pumps and eductors. No fixed pumping system is fitted for removing flood water, except in machinery spaces where circulating pumps and emergency bilge pumps, although fitted for other work, can be used for this purpose. Eductors are operated by high-pressure water from the firemain. The firemain, therefore, is assuming much greater importance in the field of salvage, and fire pumps are fitted in these ships solely for supplying the firemain and salt water services.

PRECAUTIONS AGAINST GENERAL DAMAGE

Dispersal of machinery and alternative power supplies

Where possible main machinery is divided into self-contained units, each unit (boilers, engine and ancillary equipment) driving one shaft. Important items of auxiliary machinery, such as pumps, air compressors and electrical generators, are dispersed in the ship so that any single hit will cause the least possible loss of their services. Important equipment which depends on electric power is supplied from two or more widely-separated sources, any one of which can be brought into use if the others fail. Examples of this are armament and steering gear. Lighting in important spaces is supplied in halves from two sources. The firemain, main suction (if fitted), compressed air lines and hydraulic mains can be divided into self-contained sections by closing valves.

Provision of damage control equipment

Equipment for firefighting, repairing the ship's structure and stopping leaks is provided in special stowage at various focal positions throughout the ship. Battery-operated floodlights, headlamps and torches are also included. In addition there are lengths of flexible electric cable which can be connected up to provide emergency power supplies and emergency lighting when permanent runs of wiring are damaged. To ensure the immediate availability of such equipment it is essential that it should be maintained in a serviceable condition, kept in its correct stowage, and not tampered with or used for purposes other than damage control.

Automatic emergency lanterns are hung in main gangways and other key positions. They are battery-operated and connected to the mains supply by plug and socket. They are automatically switched on when the mains supply fails. Since the battery life is limited, and men's lives may depend on their functioning in an emergency, the lamps must never be unplugged by unauthorised persons.

Duplication and dispersal of stores

The most important stores are distributed between two or more widely-separated store rooms to ensure, as far as possible, that a proportion of such stores will be available if the ship is damaged. In addition, when the ship is liable to go into action, emergency dumps of rations are provided in different sections of the ship.

PRECAUTIONS AGAINST CASUALTIES

First aid

Everyone should possess a thorough knowledge of first aid and be trained in its practice. This is a duty and a service to one's shipmates.

Entering unventilated compartments

Should it be necessary to enter an unventilated suspect compartment before first testing the air in it—to rescue someone inside, for example—a breathing apparatus which provides its own oxygen or air should always be worn. The Service anti-gas respirator is useless for this purpose because the noxious gases in an unventilated compartment usually lack oxygen, and the respirator does not provide oxygen but merely acts as a filter.

Precautions in action

Observations on some of the main causes of casualties in action, and the precautions which should be taken to guard against them, are given below.

Flash from explosion. This spreads much further than do splinters, and it can travel through pipes or trunking to a considerable distance from the actual scene of the explosion. Flash is of very short duration, and even thin clothing will afford some protection. In action, or when action is imminent, it is therefore most important that everyone should be completely covered with clothing and that anti-flash gear should be worn.

Shock from violent explosion. Shock from mine or torpedo hits, for example, may be so severe that men are thrown upwards with such force that their heads or necks are broken on the deck above, or their ankles are broken when they come down again. In action every man not actually employed should therefore lie down on his back with his hands behind his head.

Splinters. These travel horizontally rather than vertically, so lying down athwartships with the feet outboard affords the best protection.

Nuclear explosion. An airburst nuclear weapon emits immediately light, heat, nuclear radiations and blast. The first indication will probably be the flash of light. Anyone caught in the open must take immediate shelter behind any convenient bulkhead, turret or screen. Speed is vital and no time must be wasted in trying to gain greater shelter at a distance. Men should throw themselves to the deck, face down, eyes shut, arms round the back of the neck, staying in this position until the blast wave has passed. Never look at the flash or follow the course of a falling object—temporary or even permanent blindness may result.

Poisonous fumes. Anti-gas respirators provide a certain degree of protection from poisonous fumes, so they should always be at hand in action. It should be remembered, however, that a respirator only acts as a filter and does not provide oxygen, and that when attacking a fire (which consumes oxygen) one of the special breathing apparatuses supplied should therefore be worn if the fire is between decks or otherwise enclosed.

RULES FOR SHIP SAFETY

The following general rules, and rules for the care and maintenance of fittings and equipment, should be observed by everyone.

General rules

1. Report flooding, fire, or any other dangerous incident immediately to ABCD Headquarters when at sea, and to the Officer of the Watch when in harbour (or ABCD Headquarters, if functioning).

2. Tackle flooding immediately and stop it spreading by closing all watertight openings in the vicinity.

3. Observe the rules for opening and closing watertight openings. Ensure that closed doors and hatches are securely fastened.

4. Tackle a fire immediately and close all ventilation in its vicinity. Study the methods of firefighting and learn thoroughly the correct use of all fire-fighting appliances. Ensure that especially inflammable articles, such as paint pots, are returned to their correct stowage immediately after use.

5. Know your ship thoroughly, from stem to stern and from truck to keel; you should be able to find your way to any part of her in the dark.

6. Keep your personal kit correctly and securely stowed and your locker door securely shut. Don't hang gear on valves, rod gearing or clips, and don't leave gear in the wake of doors or operating gear.

7. See that all stores and equipment are kept correctly and securely stowed. Before leaving a store room or compartment see that any radiators (or other heating appliances) and the lights are switched off. See that the ventilation and watertight openings are closed, and that those which by regulations should be left open are left correctly adjusted. Ensure that no litter or unstowed gear is left in the compartment.

8. Never allow any damage control equipment—particularly secondary lighting lamps, torches and special tools—to be used for any other purpose than damage control. Keep damage control equipment in good order, and learn the maintenance rules and routine.

9. Ensure that all lifelines, and ladders at hatchways, are correctly rigged.

10. When at sea under war conditions do not allow any unauthorised lights or smoking above decks between the times of 'darkening' and 'undarkening' ship. A lighted match can be seen in the dark from a distance of 3 miles, and a burning cigarette from one mile.

11. When at sea under war conditions do not throw anything overboard except at the times ordered; a trail of 'gash' in the wake of a ship will give away her position and course.

12. You must be able to swim, otherwise you will be a burden to your shipmates if you have to abandon ship. At sea in war always wear your lifejacket and test it daily. Have your anti-flash gear and respirator always handy for action stations. At sea in war sleep with your clothes on or near you so that you can be ready at a moment's notice for any emergency.

Rules for maintenance of fittings and equipment

1. Report any defects at once.

2. Keep the bearing surfaces of watertight fittings and their rubber sealing strips clean and free from paint. Keep door clips, hatch nuts and hinges and the moving parts of valve rod-operating gear clean, greased and free from paint.

3. Lower hatch covers, and close doors, gently; careless handling may distort them and render them ineffective. Don't hammer door clips or hatch nuts into place; securing them hand-tight is sufficient.

4. Don't remove door clips for cleaning; their re-assembly and refitting is a skilled job.

5. Keep the lettering of tallies readable; never paint over them. When necessary to paint over directions, symbols and markings, ensure that they are re-painted with the least possible delay.

6. Fire hoses should always be stowed ready for running out. Ensure that the rubbers in the hose hydrant connections are in place, and inspect the hoses carefully for cracks or tears. Handle hoses with care, especially over decks with sharp projections. Handle carefully hose connections, nozzles and branch pipes, and ensure that they function correctly.

7. Never put a fire extinguisher back in its stowage if it is empty, and make sure that all those in place are loaded and ready for functioning. Never paint over fire extinguishers.

EMERGENCY STATIONS

The object of the order 'Hands to Emergency Stations' is to clear the ship between decks of all hands not employed on damage control duties. This will ensure the maintenance of watertight integrity, and at the same time give the damage control parties room to carry out their work. At this order, all hands not employed with the damage control parties should partially inflate their lifejackets, fall in on the upper deck at their appointed emergency stations and keep silence. They will then be available when needed to assist the damage control parties or for any work on deck.

No one should leave his post until ordered to do so, e.g. watchkeepers remain on watch until relieved or ordered to leave. Before abandoning a compartment all watertight openings in it should be closed, all machinery stopped, and electric current switched off. After leaving, the hatch or doorway of the compartment should be closed and clipped. After abandoning a compartment report the fact to ABCD Headquarters and then go to the upper deck and report to the nearest officer for orders.

ABANDON SHIP

If, after being seriously damaged, all measures taken to save the ship are un-successful, preparations will be made to abandon her in an orderly manner and with the least possible loss of life. Remembering the object of emergency stations, it will be obvious that in many cases hands will already be at emergency stations when the necessity to abandon ship becomes apparent. They are then in the best position to clear away the inflatable liferafts and carry out any other preparations for a successful evolution.

When it is known that the ship will be abandoned the inflatable liferafts are cleared away, slipped into the water and inflated; lifejackets are fully inflated; manropes, lifelines, scramble nets or hose pipes are lowered to the waterline to enable men to board the liferafts without getting too wet. If time permits extra clothing should be put on and the trousers tucked inside socks. Do not remove your shoes.

To abandon ship in a heavy sea or when the ship is on fire, for example, will be a severe test of good training and discipline which will call for coolness, steadiness and sometimes self-sacrifice. Strict obedience to orders is essential and strict silence must be maintained. Any signs of panic or loss of self-control must be suppressed.

At the order 'Abandon Ship' the result of discipline and training in the individual will be apparent. Board the rafts as quickly as possible; the ship's organisation will include adequate arrangements for evacuating the sick and wounded, together with the medical staff; if you can board the raft dry shod so much the better, but if you have to jump into the water this can be done quite safely from any height when wearing a fully inflated Naval inflatable lifejacket. You should jump feet first, keeping the feet together, placing one arm over the front of the lifejacket and pinching the nostrils with the thumb and forefinger of the other hand. This will ensure a safe drop into the water, prevent any undue movement of the lifejacket and stop water being forced up the nose.

Each raft when fully manned (if circumstances merit keeping the raft along-side) should be cast off from the ship by cutting its retaining painter.

Conduct in the water

If men have been unable to reach a raft or have abandoned ship after the rafts have been cast off, they should swim at least 100 yards clear of the ship to avoid being sucked down or entangled in the rigging as the ship founders. The only efficient way to swim whilst wearing an inflatable lifejacket is on the back.

Avoid any oil fuel, if possible. Keep together and rope together by means of the toggle and line on the lifejackets, preferably in a circle facing outwards. Avoid undue exertion. A group of swimmers stands a better chance of being rescued than do individuals. Nevertheless, always endeavour to reach a liferaft, if one is in sight and not too far distant.

In strong winds it may be difficult to keep rafts clear of the ship's side. On the windward side they will be blown against the ship, and on the leeward side the ship will tend to drift on to the rafts. If difficulty is experienced in getting clear, the rafts should be pushed along the ship's side towards the bow or stern. When rafts are clear of the ship they should secure to each other in groups by their painters. This facilitates the adjustment of crews, transfer of wounded and stores, and enables orders to be passed easily from the senior officer or rating to the person in charge of each raft.

Detailed instructions on Abandoning Ship, Survival, and Rescue are given in Volume II.

Questions on this chapter will be found in Appendix 2.

CHAPTER 5

Fire Precautions

It is essential to the safety of his ship that every seaman should have a working knowledge of the causes of accidental fires, and of how to prevent, control and extinguish them. More detailed information and instructions are contained in B.R.1257 *Ship Firefighting Manual*, B.R.1754 *Regulations for Storing and Handling Gasoline and other Inflammable Stores*, B.R.4 *Naval Storekeeping Manual* and in Vol. II. These publications should be studied by the specialists directly concerned. This chapter contains general information with which every officer and rating should be familiar.

Fire is dependent upon three elements, namely:
1. *Inflammable material*, such as gasoline, oil, paint, paper and wood
2. *Heat*
3. *Oxygen* which, together with heat, ignites the fuel.

These three elements may be represented by the three sides of a triangle (fig. 5–1); the triangle is only complete, and fire will only occur or continue, while

FIG. 5–1. Fire triangle

all three are present. Fire prevention consists of keeping these three elements separated by paying careful attention to the stowage of inflammable substances and liquids and to their protection from sparks, and by observing the necessary precautions in the disposal of burning material such as smouldering cigarette ends and matches.

Firefighting consists of the elimination of one or more of these three elements. This is done by removing the inflammable material or preventing more of it from becoming ignited, or by cooling the inflammable material and the air in its vicinity to a temperature below ignition point, or by preventing oxygen from reaching the fire by smothering or blanketing the flames or shutting off all ventilation in the vicinity.

FIRE PREVENTION

With the exception of those caused by enemy action, most fires on board ship can be prevented by keeping things in their proper places, maintaining cleanliness and tidiness, and obeying the relevant regulations. The following notes on fire prevention are dealt with under the three headings of inflammable materials, heat and oxygen.

Inflammable material

These have been eliminated from H.M. ships as much as possible, but ships which have to steam, fight, and yet be habitable must carry and incorporate liquids and materials which will burn or explode. The precautions which must be taken for the stowage and handling of such matter are given here.

Gasoline. This constitutes one of the greatest fire dangers on board ships and every effort has been made to reduce the amount carried. Its use, however, is essential in aircraft carriers and in small gasoline-driven craft. Gasoline should always be kept in the authorised stowages. No unauthorised stocks such as cigarette lighter fuel should be allowed on board.

Stringent precautions are laid down and must be observed when gasoline is being embarked or transferred; the most important are:

1. No smoking or burning of naked lights is allowed in the vicinity.
2. Fires such as galley and incinerator fires must be extinguished.
3. Radio transmission is not permitted because of the danger of sparking.
4. Ports in the ship's side adjacent to gasoline tanks must be kept closed.
5. Sentries must be posted.
6. Ships must fly the approved danger signals.

Avpin, a helicopter starter fuel, is subject to the same precautions as Avgas (Aviation gasoline), and is usually stored in two-gallon cans either in a specially designed compartment where large quantities are required, or, in the case of small quantities, on the weather deck where they can be easily jettisoned.

Avcat, which is carried in aircraft carriers for use of aircraft, is a comparatively safe fuel and is normally stored in the same manner as furnace fuel or diesel oil.

Furnace fuel and diesel oil. While every precaution is taken in designing the ship to confine these inflammable liquids to positions of safety, there is always the possibility of leakage, especially when the ship is damaged. Every man must look out for such leaks and report them immediately. Any escaped oil must be cleaned up at once, and the cause of the leak dealt with; cotton rag used for this purpose is particularly inflammable and must not be left lying about.

Wood. Woodwork has been replaced in ships by metal wherever possible, but some is still necessary. Timber should not be stowed near hot surfaces, or where it can become saturated with inflammable liquids.

Paint. Paint pots and brushes, as well as paint, should be stowed in the paint store; keeping pots of paint in other parts of the ship for *touching up* constitutes a highly dangerous fire risk. Coats of paint, especially of oil paints, should be kept to a minimum. Paint stores in large warships are fitted with spraying arrangements.

Clothing and bedding. These must be stowed in their correct places. Kit lockers must be clipped shut to prevent their contents from falling out and thus being exposed to the danger of a fire in the event of action damage.

Cooking fat. This must be stowed in a cool place, and when being used in the galley must not be left unattended owing to the danger of its catching fire.

Paper. All paper must be stowed where it cannot be spread about the ship by an explosion. Scrap paper must be kept collected and disposed of. Books and papers must be stowed away, and not tucked overhead near sleeping billets.

Cotton rags. When supplied for cleaning purposes, cotton rags must not be left lying about; they must be placed in metal bins and disposed of regularly. Such materials are particularly dangerous when soaked with oil or gasoline and may well be a source of spontaneous combustion.

Explosives and fireworks. All explosives, including fireworks, obviously constitute a grave risk, and regulations for their safety are the result of other people's unpleasant and unfortunate experience. These regulations are contained in *Naval Magazine and Explosives Regulations*, and are also published in the ship's orders and prominently displayed as posters in danger areas. Every man on board must observe these regulations concerning explosives.

Heat

Where heat is expected, in galleys and boiler rooms for example, extra care must be taken to keep everything clean and to avoid collections of grease or rubbish. A typical example is afforded by galley hoods, where grease is likely to collect in the exhaust trunks and may easily be set alight by sparks from the galley range or by flames from a *boil-over* of cooking fat.

Steam pipes are lagged to conserve the heat in the pipes, to protect adjacent surfaces and fittings from the heat, and to prevent inflammable materials (e.g. oil) which may fall on the pipes, from catching fire. Any damage to the lagging of steam pipes should be reported at once, and combustible materials should not be stowed near them.

Spontaneous combustion. This is a dangerous source of heat which causes fire. Chemical action such as that which occurs between oil and the fibres of cotton can easily generate sufficient heat to cause a fire.

Smoking. The cause of numerous fires has been smoking; and failure to observe the smoking regulations, or to see that cigarettes, pipes or matches are properly extinguished, may result in a fire just as damaging as one caused by enemy action. Cigarette ends should never be thrown out of scuttles or over the side; they may fall into boats or lighters lying alongside, or be blown back by the wind and set fire to something on deck.

Sparks. Fires can be started by sparks from incinerators and galley funnels, so it is important to keep the funnels swept clean.

Sparking of electrical apparatus and shorting of electric leads also cause dangerous generation of heat, and great care must be exercised in the maintenance and use of such equipment, particular attention being paid to wandering leads and temporary connections.

Oxygen

Where air is present there must be oxygen, and it is impossible to eliminate it. Keeping watertight doors and hatches closed when not in use, however, prevents the spreading of fire as well as flooding, but in fire it is as important to close the doors and openings above the waterline as it is to close those below it. The control of ventilation in the vicinity of a fire is most important.

PRINCIPLES OF FIREFIGHTING

Once a fire has started it will probably spread very rapidly if unchecked, and one of the first principles of firefighting is to tackle a fire immediately it is discovered with whatever means are at hand. Many a potentially dangerous fire has been extinguished at its start by the resolute initiative of one man alone; it must be remembered, however, that a fire may quickly get beyond the control of the man or men in the vicinity. At the same time as a fire is tackled, warning of its outbreak must be given by shouting 'FIRE' and by informing the Officer of the Watch and any other responsible person by telephone or messenger. This will not only ensure speedy assistance, but will also ensure that the necessary precautions are taken to prevent the fire from spreading.

The firefighter's objective is to remove from the fire one or more of the elements upon which combustion depends; he must therefore strive to *starve* inflammable material, *cool* the material and its surroundings to below their ignition temperature, or *smother* the fire by preventing air, and therefore oxygen, from reaching it.

Starving

Starving the fire is effected by removing inflammable materials from the vicinity of the fire and cutting off all liquid fuel supplies in the area. For example, if a fire is being fed by oil flowing from a fractured oil pipe, the shutting of the appropriate oil valve is an essential precaution.

Cooling

Cooling is effected by water, which should if possible be applied to the burning material and not the flames. When the flames have died out it is essential thoroughly to cool everything that was burning, and its surroundings, to prevent it from reigniting. It must be remembered, however, that although an unlimited supply of sea water is usually available to a ship for firefighting, its excessive use may endanger the ship for the reasons given below.

1. Water is heavy, and, if used in sufficient quantities, may cause the ship to heel or even capsize.
2. All water used at the fire will eventually have to be pumped out of the ship.
3. Liquid fuels are lighter than water and will float on its surface, and under certain conditions the excessive use of water may therefore cause burning fuel to overflow from the tanks and so spread the fire.
4. Sea water is particularly harmful to electrical equipment and its use on such equipment should therefore be avoided if possible.
5. It is dangerous to direct a jet of sea water at live electrical apparatus owing to the danger of an electric shock; the danger of a shock with fresh water is not nearly so great.

6. Though water will prevent explosives from catching fire it will not necessarily stop them burning once they are alight, because explosives contain their own oxygen.
7. Water applied to some substances produces inflammable gases; an example is the production of acetylene gas when water makes contact with the calcium carbide contained in some smoke floats, sea markers and lifebuoy lights.
8. If water makes contact with certain lightweight metals when they are burning it decomposes them and accelerates their burning; this applies to magnesium alloys, which are as widely used in the construction of aircraft as are aluminium alloys.

All ship firefighting appliances are therefore designed not only to use water effectively, but to use it sparingly.

To cool everything adjacent to a burning compartment is very important. A compartment of a ship is like a metal box (fig. 5–2); it has four sides, a top,

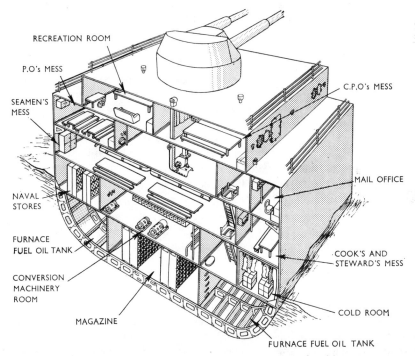

RECREATION ROOM

P.O's MESS

SEAMEN'S MESS

C.P.O's MESS

MAIL OFFICE

NAVAL STORES

FURNACE FUEL OIL TANK

CONVERSION MACHINERY ROOM

COOK'S AND STEWARD'S MESS

MAGAZINE

COLD ROOM

FURNACE FUEL OIL TANK

FIG. 5–2. Typical layout of compartments of a ship

and a bottom, all of which will become heated if fire breaks out in it, and this heating may spread the fire. The deck, deckhead and bulkheads in adjacent compartments must therefore be cooled by spraying them with water, but it must be used sparingly.

Smothering

The object of smothering a fire is to prevent oxygen reaching it; smothering alone may extinguish it, but other methods will often have to be used as well.

Smothering includes the use of steam, carbon dioxide, or CB/Freon, all of which displace oxygen and so have a smothering effect; and of foam, which floats on the gasoline or oil, blanketing the surface and separating the fuel from the air.

Wherever practicable, ventilation in the vicinity of a fire should be shut down, but if there is a large amount of smoke it may be necessary to leave an outlet open so that it can escape. It is possible to extinguish a fire of burning inflammable liquids by sealing the compartment in which it is situated. It may not be possible to effect a complete seal, but as long as there are no openings low down through which air can reach the seat of the fire this method has been found successful; it is essential, however, to keep adjacent compartments and structures cool with water-spray.

Reignition

Once a fire has been extinguished there is always a danger of it lighting up again, particularly if it was extinguished by smothering.

Smoke

Unless the fire is attacked in its very early stages the compartment will be filled with smoke and it will be almost impossible to see the actual seat of the fire. If the firefighter approaches the fire by crawling or crouching he will be able to breathe the clearer air near the deck and see the seat of the fire more easily, and by keeping low down he will also find the heat given off by the fire much less intense. Smoke can be driven off by a wide curtain of spray from a jet/spray nozzle, *provided that the smoke is driven towards an outlet*. When driving smoke in this way it will also be found that fresh air can be breathed by keeping the face close behind the nozzle.

It must be remembered that fire often gives off poisonous gases, and that as it always uses oxygen rapidly there may be insufficient air for breathing. If smoke and fumes are dense breathing apparatus must be worn.

Protective clothing

The firefighter should always be completely clothed, and his face and hands must also be covered for protection against the heat. Additional protection is afforded if the clothing is first damped and, when possible, kept damp by spray, provided that wet clothing is not worn too long. Fearnought suits and anti-flash hoods and gauntlets are supplied for fire parties, and the manning of the branch pipes at the fire should be taken over as soon as possible by men fully clothed with this gear.

Cover

Attacking the fire from low down is a relief from exposure to the heat, and, for further protection, advantage should also be taken of any bulkheads or lockers.

PORTABLE FIREFIGHTING APPLIANCES

Four types of hand extinguishers are provided in H.M. ships:

1. Two-gallon water (painted red)
2. Two-gallon foam (painted pale cream)
3. $2\frac{1}{2}$-lb CO_2 (painted black) for fires in electrical apparatus operating at voltages higher than normal ship voltages, e.g. wireless, radar and sonar equipment.
4. Dry chemical powder extinguishers (painted light French blue).

Two-gallon water extinguisher (fig. 5-3)

This consists of a container holding *fresh* water, into which is placed a steel cylinder charged with carbon dioxide (CO_2) under pressure. The screwed head of the cylinder carries a piercer, which can be forced down by striking the knob on the top; this punctures a disc in the top of the CO_2 charge, thus releasing the gas which creates a pressure in the outer container and forces the water out through the rubber discharge hose.

CO₂ CHARGE

1. REMOVE PROTECTIVE CAP
2. GRASP NOZZLE
3. STRIKE KNOB
4. KEEP UPRIGHT

FIG. 5-3. Two-gallon water extinguisher

To recharge, remove the screwed head and the spent charge. Refill the outer container with *fresh* water, fit a new charge and replace the head, screwing the head down as tightly as possible *by hand*. This operation is so simple and speedy that, with only two extinguishers and a constant supply of fresh water and charges, it can be continued indefinitely and without interruption.

Very little maintenance is necessary. To check the carbon dioxide charge remove it and shake it up and down; if the pressure has dropped a tell-tale device inside will rattle and a fresh charge should be substituted. When charges are at the correct pressure no rattle should be heard when they are shaken.

Two-gallon foam extinguisher (fig. 5–4)

This extinguisher produces a chemical foam by mixing two liquids which react with one another, and it should not be confused with the foam units mentioned in Volume II. It consists of an outer cylinder containing a solution of bicarbonate of soda and a stabilising substance, and an inner cylinder

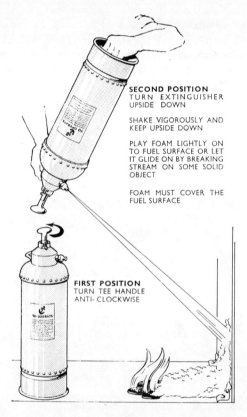

SECOND POSITION
TURN EXTINGUISHER
UPSIDE DOWN

SHAKE VIGOROUSLY AND
KEEP UPSIDE DOWN

PLAY FOAM LIGHTLY ON
TO FUEL SURFACE OR LET
IT GLIDE ON BY BREAKING
STREAM ON SOME SOLID
OBJECT

FOAM MUST COVER THE
FUEL SURFACE

FIRST POSITION
TURN TEE HANDLE
ANTI-CLOCKWISE

FIG. 5–4. Two-gallon foam extinguisher

containing a solution of aluminium sulphate. These liquids are prevented from mixing or spilling before operation by being sealed with two rubber valves coupled together. When the operator releases the 'T' handle in the cap the sealing valves are lifted; then, when the extinguisher is turned upside down and shaken, the liquids mix and form foam, which is discharged from the nozzle.

Recharging this extinguisher is a tedious operation. The refills are supplied in powder form, in yellow and blue tins for the outer and inner cylinders respectively, and complete instructions for the refilling operation are printed on the tins. When the cylinders have been recharged and replaced the cap should be screwed on, with the 'T' handle in the released or open position. When the cap is firmly screwed down the 'T' handle is pressed down and locked in the closed position.

These extinguishers should be inspected and the liquids tested every six months, because the chemicals deteriorate with time. This is done by dipping out specified quantities with special measures supplied. The foam resulting from mixing these liquids should nearly fill a half-pint measure; if it does not, the extinguisher should be recharged. These extinguishers should be kept under cover and preferably in temperatures not lower than 15°C (59°F).

$2\frac{1}{2}$-lb CO_2 extinguisher (fig. 5–5)

This extinguisher is operated by aiming the discharge horn at the base of the fire, removing the safety pin and squeezing the spring-loaded trigger. It is recharged by changing to a fresh cylinder, and this should be done even if the cylinder is only partly discharged. It releases 21 cu. ft of CO_2 in about half a minute.

FIG. 5–5. $2\frac{1}{2}$-lb CO_2 extinguisher

FIG. 5–6. Dry chemical powder extinguisher P12

Dry chemical powder extinguisher P12 (fig. 5–6)

These extinguishers are for use against fires in aircraft or helicopters on flight decks of aircraft carriers or in the vicinity of the helicopter landing area in smaller ships. The extinguisher consists of a container holding 30 lb of dry chemical powder which is discharged by the use of a small cylinder of CO_2 fitted externally to the container. Recharging of the container and replacement of the CO_2 cylinder are quite simple operations.

FIREFIGHTING INSTALLATIONS

Firemain system

This is the system of piping by which sea water under pressure is supplied to all parts of the ship. It is easily distinguished from other pipe systems because it is painted bright red throughout. Pumps situated between decks supply the sea water under pressure, and the system is usually divided by stop valves into several sections, each with its own pumps, so that if one section is damaged the remainder of the system can still be used (fig. 5–7). Modern aircraft carriers have also a completely independent flight deck firemain with its own pumps.

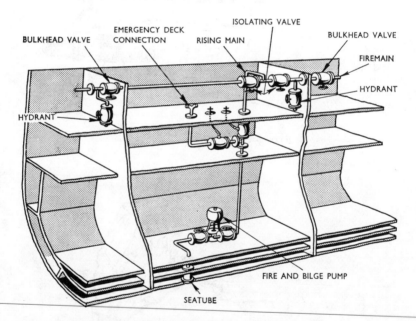

FIG. 5–7. Typical section of a ship's firemain

When firefighting, only a limited number of hoses can be used on one section, otherwise the capacity of the pumps will be exceeded and the pressure in the hoses becomes insufficient for their jets to reach the fire. As a rough guide not more than three hoses should be used on any one section. Extra pumps can be started, or other sections of the firemain be isolated, to boost the supply to the section in use.

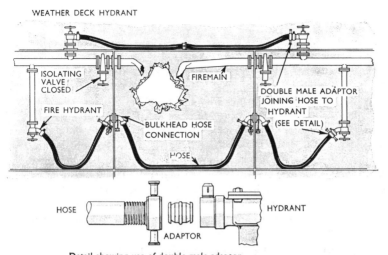

Detail showing use of double male adaptor.

FIG. 5–8. Damaged firemain section replaced by hose

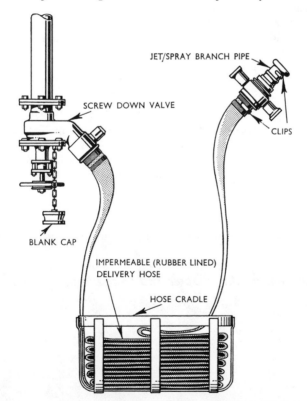

FIG. 5–9. Typical arrangement of hose stowage at hydrant

If one section of the firemain is damaged a temporary supply of water can be obtained by shutting the isolating stop valves in that section, and then connecting the hydrants on either side of the section by hose (fig. 5–8).

Hydrants (fig. 5–9). These branches from the main firemain system are fitted with valves and hose connections, and are to be found around the weather decks and in almost every main compartment of the ship. Hydrants are fitted with a female coupling containing a rubber washer.

Hoses. Impermeable delivery hoses are supplied for, and should be kept connected to, every hydrant throughout the ship, ready for instant use. The brass couplings at their ends must not be dropped, dragged along the deck, or knocked about. The coupling at one end of the hose is male and that at the other end is female; the male coupling should always be connected to the hydrant, and the female end of the hose taken to the fire. The joints in the coupling are made watertight with rubber washers, which must be inspected regularly and maintained in good order. Although not so easily damaged as canvas hoses, these hoses require care, and the following points in regard to their treatment should always be observed:

1. Hoses (and couplings) should not be painted.
2. Hoses should not be washed with strong soda.
3. Hoses should not be left faked for too long without opening them out for inspection.
4. Oil or grease should not be spilt on them.
5. They should be thoroughly dried before stowing, otherwise they will rot in their stowage.
6. Fire hoses should not be used for washing decks.
7. To expel the water from a hose it should not be walked upon along the deck, but should be underrun at shoulder height.
8. Hoses should be faked in their stowages ready for running out (fig. 5–9).

Nozzles. Three types of nozzles (branchpipes) are supplied to H.M. ships, namely spray-jet, jet-spray and 'oilfyre'. Spray-jets are for general purposes and produce a spray adjustable from a wide cone to a hollow jet. Jet-sprays are stowed at fireposts and certain other positions; they produce a jet or spray of more water than the spray-jet, and can be shut off completely by turning a sleeve on the nozzle. 'Oilfyre' nozzles are supplied chiefly for spaces such as boiler rooms where oil fires are likely to occur. They produce only a spray.

Nozzles must be protected from damage, and they must never be used as hammers or levers.

Questions on this chapter will be found in Appendix 2.

PART II

SEAMANSHIP

CHAPTER 6

Rope and its Usage

In this chapter are described the various types of rope with which a seaman works, and the manner in which he uses them. Rope of any kind can be described as belonging to one of three main types:

Cordage made of vegetable fibres,
Cordage made of man-made fibres, and
Steel wire rope.

The chapter has been divided into seven sections, headed as follows:

Construction and characteristics of vegetable fibre cordage
Construction and characteristics of man-made fibre cordage
Construction and characteristics of wire rope
Handling of vegetable fibre cordage
Handling of man-made fibre cordage
Handling of wire rope
Handling hawsers.

CONSTRUCTION AND CHARACTERISTICS OF VEGETABLE FIBRE CORDAGE

Construction and types

Though it is not necessary to go deeply into the process of ropemaking, an elementary knowledge of its principles is desirable.

Ropes are made from vegetable fibres each of which is only between two and four feet long, and the first process is to comb these fibres out in a long, even ribbon, as shown in an exaggerated form in fig. 6–1. The ribbons are then

FIG. 6–1. Fibres of a rope

twisted up into yarns, and the twist given binds the fibres firmly together so that they hold by friction when the yarn is subjected to strain. The shorter the length of the fibres the harder this twist must be to give the necessary strength to the yarn. This process is known as 'spinning', and the yarns are said to be spun left- or right-handed, according to the direction of twist. Next, a certain number of yarns are twisted together to form strands which, at the Admiralty Ropery, Chatham, are usually 150 fathoms in length when completed. The number and size of the yarns required to make each strand depends on the size of the rope it is intended to make. This stage is known as 'twisting the strands', and again, the twist can be left- or right-handed.

Three or four strands are now made up into a left- or right-handed rope. This process is called 'laying' and is always carried out in the opposite direction to that used in the previous stage of twisting the strands; it is, moreover, distinct from the simple spin or twist and is twofold, in that:

1. the strands are twisted up together to form the rope, and
2. at the same time the strands are rotated individually in the direction of their original twist.

Were this not done, laying the strands together would tend to untwist the yarns in each strand.

As the rope is laid up its length contracts like a coiled spring, giving it a certain elasticity. The harder the twist given to the strands in laying, the shorter will be the resultant rope—in practice, three strands of 150 fathoms lay up into a rope about 120 fathoms in length—and a rope is said to be *hard-laid* or *soft-laid*. Three strands so laid up constitute a *hawser-laid* rope (fig. 6-2), which is the type of cordage most commonly used.

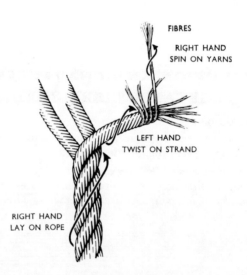

FIG. 6-2. Component parts of a right-handed hawser-laid rope

Four-stranded (rot-proofed manila or sisal) rope, laid up round a heart or centre made of the same material, is known as *shroud-laid* rope (fig. 6-3). It is somewhat weaker than three-stranded rope of a similar size, but is less liable to stretch. It is used for shrouds and stays of small craft and is supplied in coils of 120 fathoms.

Three hawser-laid ropes each of 120 fathoms, laid up together in the opposite direction to that of their own lay, will form a *cable-laid* rope, 100 fathoms in length (fig. 6-4). Such a rope is weaker than a hawser-laid rope of equal size, but by reason of its construction it is more elastic and is therefore used where elasticity is the chief requirement, as in towing. Furthermore, cable-laid rope, being more solid in construction, is more resistant to chafe and does not absorb water so readily as hawser-laid rope.

FIG. 6–3. Shroud-laid rope   FIG. 6–4. Cable-laid rope

Direction of the lay and description

In the Royal Navy hawser-laid rope is normally laid up right-handed; that is, the strands twist away from the eye in a right-handed spiral, as in fig. 6–2. The direction of the lay can also be seen at a glance when the rope is viewed from above, as illustrated in fig. 6–5 (i). In the rope trade, right-hand lay is

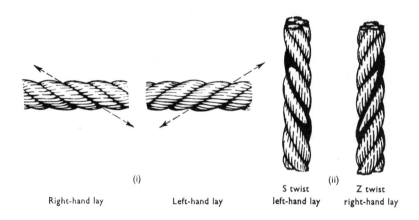

(i)

Right-hand lay   Left-hand lay

(ii)
S twist   Z twist
left-hand lay   right-hand lay

FIG. 6–5. Direction of the lay

described as *Z twist* and left-hand lay as *S twist*, the letters indicating the direction of the lay when the rope is viewed from above (fig. 6–5 (ii)). In a normal right-handed rope the fibres are spun right-handed to form yarns; the yarns are twisted left-handed into strands; and the strands are laid up right-handed into rope.

Left-handed ropes, in which each component is made in exactly the opposite direction, are found in commercial practice; but the only left-handed cordage supplied to the Royal Navy—and that in very small quantities—is hammock lashing and marline.

In the Royal Navy cordage is described by reference to the circumference of the rope measured in inches and to the material from which it is made—for example, 4½-inch manila. In some countries, and commercially in Great Britain, cordage is sometimes measured by its diameter. The size of a strand is that of the rope from which it was taken; thus a 2-inch strand is one taken from a 2-inch rope. The length of a rope is measured in fathoms.

General characteristics

The strands tend to unlay unless the end of the rope is whipped (i.e. firmly bound) with twine.

The rope will stretch under load, but may be expected to regain its normal length when slack, provided that the load applied is well within the breaking strength of the rope; a greater load, however, even if it does not part the rope, will cause a permanent extension in its length and thereby render it unfit for service. The older and more worn the rope, the less elasticity it will possess and the weaker it will become. Rope under load will tend to twist in the opposite direction to that of its lay and thereby tend to unlay itself, but it should regain its normal form when slack.

When wet, rope will usually shrink in length in proportion to the amount by which it swells in diameter, but it will recover its original length when dry and after use. Rope which is continually subjected to heat and damp—when in the tropics, for example—will lose its elasticity and strength sooner than rope used under normal conditions of temperature and humidity.

MATERIALS USED

The ropes supplied to the Royal Navy are made from various kinds of vegetable fibre which may differ in strength, weight, flexibility, hardness or resistance to wear, elasticity, resistance to weather, or behaviour when wet. The fibre selected, therefore, depends on the use for which the rope is intended.

When made of *manila* or *sisal*, the fibres of the rope are treated with a rot-proofing solution during the first stage of rope-making, when the fibres are being combed into ribbons. Rot-proofing neither weakens the rope nor increases its weight, but makes it watertight to the extent that, when wet, it absorbs hardly any water and is nearly as light and as easily handled as when it is dry.*

To assist in distinguishing the different types of cordage a coloured jute yarn known as a *rogue's yarn* is woven into the strands of each type of rope manufactured at the Admiralty Ropery. A rogue's yarn is also used in commercially manufactured rope to indicate the type of fibre, its quality, and perhaps the particular manufacturer.

Manila rope

This rope is made from the fibre of the *abacá* plant, which is grown extensively in the Philippine Islands and shipped from the port of Manila (whence its name), and also in Central America, Sumatra and Borneo. When mature the abacá plant, which grows to a height of from 10 to 30 ft, is felled and the fibre from the leaf sheaths is stripped off. The quality of the finished rope depends

---

* Rot-proofing was discontinued in 1963, because rot-proofed cordage has deteriorated in hot and humid conditions.

upon the thorough cleaning of the fibre during this stripping process. When new and untreated it is deep golden-brown in colour. The rope is flexible, durable, strong, and stands up well to wear and weather. It is impervious to salt water, and so it is very suitable for slings, falls, berthing hawsers and tow-ropes. Manila hawser-laid rope is supplied to the Royal Navy in coils of 120 fathoms, and it is marked with one red rogue's yarn in each of two strands. Manila cable-laid rope is supplied in coils of 100 fathoms.

Commercially manufactured manila ropes over 2 inches in circumference and complying with the specification of the British Standards Institution are identified as follows:

Grade I, 'Special', one black rogue's yarn in three strands;
Grade II, 'Standard', one black rogue's yarn in two strands;
Grade III, 'Merchant', one black rogue's yarn in one strand.

Sisal rope

This rope is made from the leaves of the *Agave sisalana* plant, which is a member of the cactus family. It is grown in Kenya, Tanganyika, Haiti and Java and, when new and untreated, is hairy and of a pale straw colour. New sisal rope is as strong as second-grade manila, but it is less flexible, durable and resistant to wear and weather. It should therefore be examined frequently for signs of deterioration. Because it is not so reliable as manila it is not used for boats' falls, slings or for any purpose where the parting of the rope may endanger life. Sisal hawser-laid rope is supplied to the Royal Navy in coils of 120 fathoms; it is marked with one yellow rogue's yarn in each of two strands.

Commercially manufactured sisal rope over 2 inches in circumference and complying with the specification of the British Standards Institution is identified with one red rogue's yarn in one strand.

Hemp rope

This rope is made from the fibres of the stems of the hemp plant which is grown in many parts of the world, but notably in Italy, Russia, China, U.S.A., New Zealand, St. Helena and India. New Zealand and St. Helena hemps are not true hemps like Italian, but produce hard fibres similar to those of sisal. Italian hemp is the strongest vegetable fibre used in rope-making. Indian hemp is not reliable for cordage. American hemp is about equal to European hemp, but is not used by the Admiralty.

Hemp is very much softer than the other fibres described above. The quality varies greatly with the soil in which it is grown, and for purposes of Admiralty specification it is graded for quality in the order Italian, European, New Zealand and St. Helena, and Indian. New and untreated hemp rope is hard, smooth, pale grey in colour and of a lighter shade than manila but darker than sisal. It is marked with a red rogue's yarn in each strand.

Hemp is heavier than manila and the best quality is stronger than the manila supplied to the Royal Navy. Its wearing qualities are about the same as those of manila, but it is far more flexible. It is used in the Royal Navy only for small lines and small stuff.

Coir rope

This rope is made from the fibres in the husks of coconuts grown in Ceylon. It is very hairy, and brown in colour. A coir rope is the weakest of all cordage, but it has the advantage of being so light that it floats on water. It is flexible and very springy, but soon rots if stowed away wet, and does not stand up well to chafe or weather. Coir rope is half the weight and one-fifth the strength of manila or sisal of equal size. It is supplied to the Royal Navy in coils of 120 fathoms, and is marked with one yellow rogue's yarn in one strand.

Special kinds of rope

Apart from the ropes which have been described above and *small stuff*, which is described later, the following special kinds of rope are used in the Royal Navy and at sea generally.

Boltrope. This is made from rot-proofed sisal, hemp, or one of the man-made fibres described in the next section of this chapter, in sizes from half-an-inch to six inches. Boltrope is soft-laid, is supplied in coils of 120 fathoms, and is used for edging sails and awnings. Weights and breaking strengths can be taken as being the same as those of cordage of similar size, material and normal lay.

Hammock lashing. This is made from sisal laid up left-handed because when used for lashing up with a marline hitch it is less likely to unlay than a right-handed rope. It is supplied in coils of 120 fathoms.

Stage lashing. This is made from rot-proofed sisal or European hemp, and Italian hemp toppings are also sometimes used. It is soft-laid, supplied in coils of 120 fathoms, and used for securing staging *which has already been slung by other means*. On no account must stage lashing be used for paint ship stages. Although, according to specification, stage lashing is equal in strength to normal European hemp rope, it is not reliable cordage and must not be used for running gear, hoisting or slinging.

Braided and plaited cordage. This includes log line, which is made up of a number of white hemp or man-made fibre yarns plaited together. It is very flexible and will not kink or untwist. It is used exclusively for towed logs.

Man-made braided cordage is also used where flexibility, strength and durability are needed, such as in safety nets of carriers and in signal halyards.

NOTE. Rot-proofed sisal signal halyard (being replaced by man-made cordage) is soft-laid, with one-quarter to one-third of the yarns in each strand reverse-spun (left-handed).

Hand lead line. This is also made from rot-proofed sisal and is soft-laid so that it will stretch very little. It is supplied in coils of 120 fathoms.

Junk. This consists of condemned cordage of four-inch size and above.

Rounding. This is condemned cordage of under four inches in size. Junk and rounding are supplied for lashings and other securings where the use of good rope is not necessary.

Oakum. This is made from tow, or from condemned cordage picked to pieces. It is used for caulking seams in wooden decks and in the sides of wood-built vessels and boats.

Small stuff

All cordage under half-an-inch in size is called 'small stuff'. This includes twines, spunyarn and houseline, lines, and marline and nettlestuff. Details of small stuff supplied to the Royal Navy, together with some additional stuff used in the Merchant Navy, are given below. Weight, breaking strength and methods of supply will be found in Volume II.

Twines. A twine consists of a number of yarns twisted or laid to produce a balanced twisted structure of continuous length. Roping twine is made from flax or Italian hemp, and is used for whipping medium-sized rope ends and for sewing boltrope to sails, awnings and other canvas gear. Seaming twine is also made from flax or Italian hemp and is used by the sailmaker for sewing canvas and other heavy fabrics. It varies from extra fine to extra coarse. Seine twine is a coarse twine made from European hemp which is used in the construction of seine fishing nets.

Spunyarn and Houseline. Spunyarn consists of from two to ten yarns twisted (spun) together, and may be made from any type of vegetable fibre or from yarns unlaid from any kind of old rope. The largest type likely to be encountered in the Royal Navy has only six yarns. It is normally twisted up left-handed, but if made from yarns from a left-handed rope the spunyarn will be right-handed. It may be rot-proofed and is used for servings, seizings, stops or any small work. Spunyarn is not a reliable cordage and has no specific strength. It is marked by a single yellow rogue's yarn throughout its length.

Houseline differs from small three-yarn spunyarn only in that it is made of rather more reliable material and has a specified breaking strength. It is made from three yarns of Italian or European hemp, and is used for general purposes. It is not now supplied to the Royal Navy.

Lines. Lines are small ropes made of threads twisted into strands which are then laid up into the line. The thread is a slender cord made from two or more yarns or man-made filaments twisted together.

White line is made from hemp and it is supplied in skeins of 20 fathoms and measured by weight; the classification '2½-lb line', for example, indicates that 20 fathoms weighs 2½ lb. White line ranges from ½ lb to 4 lb per 20 fathom length.

Fishing lines are similar to white line, but vary in length. They are classified as albacore, cod, mackerel and whiting line, and diminish in size in that order. Whiting line differs from the others in that it is made from fine flax seaming twine.

Hambro line can be made from Italian or European hemp. It is a small three-stranded line of normal right-hand lay, which may be tarred and usually presents a polished appearance. It is used for general lashings and seizing. It is not now supplied to the Royal Navy.

Round line differs from hambro line only in that it has a left-hand lay. It is not now supplied to the Royal Navy.

Marline and Nettlestuff. Marline is made from European, New Zealand or St. Helena hemp, and consists of two yarns laid up left-handed. It is used for marling down, small stops and similar work. As with hammock lashing, its left-hand lay makes it suitable for use with the marline hitch. It may be rot-proofed or natural.

Nettlestuff is made from New Zealand and St. Helena hemp. It consists of two or three yarns, reverse-spun (left-handed), and laid up together right-handed. It was once used for making hammock clews.

Care and maintenance

Natural fibre used in ropemaking has not a permanent elastic limit within which it can be worked indefinitely. Therefore no attempt should be made to put a heavy strain on a rope which has been well used or on a rope which has once been loaded to near breaking-point. The life of a rope depends on the amount it is used under strain, because the fibres tend to slip a small amount under each load in spite of the twist given during manufacture.

Ropes contract when wet, and a belayed rope must be slackened off before it is dangerously strained. On the other hand, advantage may be taken of this contraction for tightening lashings by wetting the rope. Never stow rope away while it is wet; if this is unavoidable the rope should be brought out and dried at the first opportunity. Boats' falls, which are stowed on reels, often have to be reeled up wet and are then very liable to rot. They should not be turned end-for-end without first being carefully inspected throughout their whole length.

Although any rope in good condition can be confidently expected to bear its full working load with ease, allowance for wear must be made in assessing the strength of used rope, particularly when it has been subjected to hard conditions. Before estimating the strength of such a rope it should be examined for damage, rot and fatigue. Serious damage can be seen when the strands are distorted and bear unequal strains, or when the rope becomes *opened*. Slack-jawed or opened rope usually results from hauling by hand, when there is a tendency to unlay it near the end. Examples of opened rope are often found in the last few fathoms of boats' falls, and those affected portions must always be cut off before the falls are turned end-for-end; failure to do so has been the frequent cause of accidents.

Loss of strength caused by external chafe can be estimated from the proportion of damaged yarns in a strand. To assist in this estimation it should be accepted that Admiralty manila and sisal have, very approximately, $C^2 \times 3$ yarns per strand, C being the circumference of the rope.

Rot can be detected by opening out the strands and examining their inner surfaces. Should the exposed fibres be healthy and strong, all is well; if they are powdery, discoloured, weak, or can be plucked out, rot exists and the rope should be condemned.

Fatigue will most probably show itself in a reduction of the circumference of the rope below its specified size. This indicates that the rope has stretched under a heavy load and has failed to return to its normal condition. A rope which has been so stretched has lost a considerable proportion of its initial tensile strength and should therefore be used with great caution.

If a rope is showing no signs of damage, rot or fatigue, it is unlikely to be much below its full strength, but some consideration must be given to its age and those occasions when its fibres may have been weakened or their grip on each other lessened. Such weakening may have been caused by any or all of the following:

Constant stretching under heavy loads
Stowing away wet
Subjection to extremes of heat and damp, as in the tropics
External friction round bollards or through fairleads
Internal friction due to bending round sheaves of blocks.

If short lengths of yarns can be taken which are representative of the used portion of the rope they may be tested for tensile strength and thus give an indication of the deterioration which has taken place. It is necessary, however, to know the actual or specified breaking strength of the yarns.

The only really reliable method by which the strength of the rope may be determined is to test a sample of the worst part of the rope to destruction. Sample lengths are taken for testing to destruction of all ropes manufactured commercially and at the Admiralty Ropery. Appearance, stretch and reduction in size are all important, but it is not possible to lay down rules which can be applied to determine the degree of deterioration in tensile strength which has occurred by these means. This has always been left to the judgement of experienced seamen or ropemen.

Manufacture

Not only does the twist imparted to a rope during manufacture give it elasticity and enable its fibres to hold together by mutual friction, but it also packs the material firmly, thereby helping to keep out moisture and giving the rope a hard surface against wear and tear. Twisting the fibres, yarns and strands in opposite directions also helps to counter any tendency of the rope to unlay. Rope which is given a hard twist in manufacture (hard-laid rope) loses in flexibility and strength but gains in elasticity and firmness. Soft-laid rope, on the other hand, is very flexible, and stretches less, but is more easily damaged by chafe. Rope used for general purposes is given a medium twist; but for edging sails, awnings and other canvas, where flexibility and minimum stretch are the first considerations, soft-laid boltrope is used.

The distance along the rope between any two points on the same strands is known as the *jaw* of the rope, and gives a measure of the hardness of the lay; the shorter the jaw the harder the lay. A similar result can be obtained from the *angle of the lay*, which is the angle between the line of the strands and that of the rope; the greater the angle the harder the lay. A rope in which the lay has become slack, perhaps even showing a gap between the strands, is known as *slack-jawed* or *opened*.

Twisting the fibres to form the yarn is essential to enable them to hold together, but it reduces the strength of the individual fibres, and, within limits, the lighter the twist the greater is the strength of the yarn. On the other hand, bad material in a rope may be disguised by reducing the angle of lay; so that, although it may pass the necessary test when new, it will probably fail afterwards under normal working conditions.

All vegetable fibre cordage supplied to the Royal Navy is manufactured at the Admiralty Ropery at Chatham, with the exception of log line and the majority of small stuff, which is made by commercial firms to Admiralty specification.

Strength

Tables in Volume II give the Admiralty specifications for weight and breaking strength of different types and sizes of cordage, but it must always be remembered that the breaking strengths given are those of *new* rope, and that these will decrease as the rope wears. A table giving details of small stuff is also included. Standard specifications for all rope are laid down by the British Standards Institution, London, but cordage will not necessarily comply with them unless a certificate to that effect is given by the manufacturers. Full details concerning cordage purchased from any reputable firm can be obtained from the manufacturers, and any information regarding Standard specification can be supplied on application to the British Standards Institution.

A rough method of finding the breaking strength of manila, hemp or sisal cordage is to square its circumference (in inches) and divide by 3, the answer being in tons. This allows for a good margin of safety for all types of cordage except coir. The safe working load is found by dividing the breaking strength by 6. Example for 3-inch cordage:

$$\textit{Breaking strength} \qquad\qquad \textit{Working load}$$

$$\frac{(3)^2}{3} = 3 \text{ tons} \qquad\qquad \frac{3}{6} = \tfrac{1}{2} \text{ ton}$$

A nearer approximation to the specific breaking strengths of new cordage is found by dividing the square of its circumference by 2·5 for ropes of size up to 6 inches, and by 2·6 for ropes of size above 6 inches.

To estimate the strength of rope which is well worn but in good condition, apply the formula as for new rope, but use the actual and not the nominal circumference.

CONSTRUCTION AND CHARACTERISTICS OF MAN-MADE FIBRE CORDAGE

In 1948 man-made fibre ropes became available commercially in Great Britain and are now firmly established throughout the world. Nylon, Terylene, Polypropylene and Polyethylene are such fibres, but they are by no means a substitute for natural fibre ropes. They have, however, characteristics of their own which in many instances are superior to those of natural fibres: at times these ropes can do a job which their natural fibre equivalents cannot handle at all. Man-made fibre rope is more expensive than natural fibre rope, but it has usually a longer life and may well be more economical in the long run.

It is not intended here to describe the chemical process of manufacture but to outline broadly the main characteristics of man-made fibre ropes, their advantages and limitations, how they are best used and handled, the precautions which should be taken when handling them, maintenance, and a general comparison with their natural fibre counterparts.

Polypropylene and Polyethylene are still in the development and experimental stage (1963), but they will undoubtedly be introduced into the Royal Navy at some future date because they will float.

Construction

Each strand consists of a sufficient number of equal-sized continuous yarns to produce a rope which conforms to the particulars set forth in the tables in Volume II. The finished hawser-laid rope consists of three strands, each uniform and well laid and as free as practicable from defects in preparation of yarn, strand and finishing.

Certain man-made fibre ropes require heat treatment during manufacture to set the lay and to obtain dimensional stability.

Some ropes of plaited construction should be used instead of hawser-laid ropes for single whips where there is a tendency to unlay.

Qualities

Some of the qualities which have helped the swing towards the use of man-made fibre ropes are:

Breaking strength and stretch. Nylon and Terylene rope is approximately three times and nearly twice as strong respectively as a natural fibre rope of the same size. Nylon rope will extend to 45 per cent and Terylene rope 38 per cent of its length before parting.

Shock resistance. The basic yarn extends 12 to 16 per cent before breaking. Nylon rope, used within its safe working load, will stretch 30 per cent of its length and has excellent powers of recovery after extension. Terylene rope, used within its safe working load, will stretch only 15 per cent of its own length and also has excellent powers of recovery. Terylene and manila ropes of the same size, used within their respective safe working loads, will stretch approximately the same amount. This extension and recovery in man-made fibre rope results in tremendous capacity for shock absorption and prevents the sudden build-up of a high peak load.

Wet strength. A thoroughly saturated Nylon rope retains 90 to 95 per cent of its tensile strength. As the rope becomes wet and its breaking strength falls, the extension increases so that the rope's shock resistance remains almost constant. The strength of Terylene rope is not affected when wet. When man-made fibre ropes are wet and under strain they emit a steamlike water vapour. This can be expected when working within the safe working load.

Lightness in weight. The specific gravities of the basic yarns are as follows: Nylon 1·14, Terylene 1·38, Polypropylene 0·91 and Polyethylene 0·95; whereas manila and sisal are both about 1·5. Therefore man-made yarns are the lightest available for rope-making. (Coir rope is not considered in this comparison.)

Immunity to temperature change. Nylon and Terylene ropes perform well in hot, dry conditions; but care should be taken to avoid excessive friction, since the yarn of Nylon melts at 250°C and Terylene at 260°C. At the other extreme, they are virtually unaffected by 80° of frost.

Immunity to chemical attack. Man-made fibre rope is unharmed by many chemicals such as crude oil, diesel oil, marine fuel oil and distillate oil. It is resistant to attack by alkalies, but may be affected by acids. If man-made fibre rope is to be given the same care as natural fibre rope, it should not be allowed to come into contact with any harmful agent.

Immunity to rot. Man-made fibre rope is proof against attack by moulds, bacteria and insects. It can be stored for long periods without fear of deterioration and can be stowed away wet without danger of rotting.

Limitations

Sunlight. All man-made fibre ropes lose strength when exposed to strong sunlight for long periods, but the loss is not enough to reach significant proportions. Even so, when not being used it should be stowed away or covered over.

Friction. Man-made fibre rope under strain and upon surging may develop glazed areas where it has worked against capstan, bollard or cleat surfaces. This glazing may be caused by the removal of paint from metal surfaces or the fusing of the fibres by heat generated from excessive friction. In either case the strength of the rope may be impaired and it must be carefully surveyed before it is used again. If the glazed area is extensive, and no other rope is at hand, the damaged length should be cut out and the parts of the rope short-spliced together.

Uses

Nylon and Terylene ropes are used in the Royal Navy when there is a requirement for heavy duty, long life, safety and ease of handling. A few instances are given below:

1. Ocean-going tugs are supplied with 10-inch Nylon towing hawsers because shock absorption and elasticity are the main requirements.
2. Harbour tugs are fitted with 5-inch Terylene towing hawsers because Terylene has greater ability to absorb shock loads than natural fibre, and Nylon stretches too much.
3. Aircraft carrier crash barrier nets are made from a soft-laid Nylon rope so that the net can stretch and absorb the shock loading as the aircraft is brought to a standstill.
4. Survey ships', some frigates' and destroyers' boats' falls—Terylene.
5. Aircraft carriers', submarines' and many other ships' berthing hawsers—Nylon.
6. Seaboat anti-shock slings—Nylon.
7. Some ship's dan-buoy mooring pendants—Nylon.
8. Awning tackles and some awning lacings—Nylon.
9. Outhauls for replenishment rigs of Armament Supply ships—Nylon.
10. Hurricane hawsers—Nylon.
11. Lower boom boatropes—Nylon.
12. Signal halyards—plaited Terylene.
13. Log lines—plaited Terylene.
14. Cargo nets—Nylon webbing.
15. Ships' towing hawsers—Nylon.

The use of man-made fibre materials is on the increase and within a few years most natural fibre ropes may be replaced by man-made fibre ropes, and canvas awnings, natural fibre boltrope and other awning fittings may also be replaced by man-made fibre materials.

Maintenance of man-made fibre rope

If Nylon and Terylene rope is properly handled and looked after by following the safe precautions for natural fibre rope it will give reliable and long service. Cordage allowances will decrease and the problem of carrying large reserves will be solved.

CONSTRUCTION AND CHARACTERISTICS OF WIRE ROPE

Construction

A wire rope is constructed of a number of small wires which extend continuously throughout its entire length; these wires are twisted into strands, and the strands themselves are laid up to form the rope. With the exception of certain special types (e.g. minesweeping ropes, and ropes of purchases), all wire ropes used at sea consist of six strands; the wires forming a strand are twisted left-handed around a jute or wire *core*, and the strands forming the rope are laid up right-handed around a hemp or jute *heart*. The hemp or jute heart has two functions:

1. It acts as a cushion into which the strands bed, allowing them to take up their natural position as the rope is bent or subjected to strain.
2. It absorbs the linseed oil or other lubricant with which the rope should periodically be dressed, so that as the rope is stretched or flexed the oil is squeezed between the wires, thus lubricating them and reducing the friction between them.

FIG. 6–6. Construction of a wire rope

A wire rope can be made flexible in one of two ways:

1. By replacing the centre wires of each strand with a large core of jute or hemp, in which case strength is sacrificed to flexibility.
2. By making up each strand with a large number of small-gauge wires round a wire core, in which case the full strength is retained.

Types

Ropes used at sea are manufactured on the foregoing principles, and those supplied to the Royal Navy fall into the four following groups. The hemp or jute hearts and cores have been omitted from the illustrations for clarity.

Steel wire rope (S.W.R.) (fig. 6–7). This is used for standing rigging such as shrouds and funnel guys, and so is not required to be flexible. Its strands are made up of a small number of large gauge wires wound round a steel wire or jute core, and the strands themselves are made up round a hemp or jute heart.

6 STRANDS   6 STRANDS
7 WIRES EACH (6–1)   19 WIRES EACH (12–6–1)

FIG. 6–7. Steel wire rope

Flexible Steel wire rope (F.S.W.R.) (fig. 6–8). This is used for running rigging, hawsers and other ropes in which flexibility is needed. To make it flexible necessitates sacrificing a certain proportion of its strength, and each strand consists of a number of medium gauge wires wound round a large jute core; the strands themselves are made up round a hemp or jute heart.

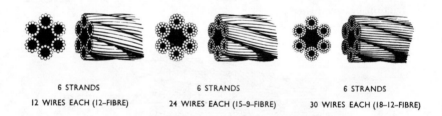

6 STRANDS   6 STRANDS   6 STRANDS
12 WIRES EACH (12–FIBRE)   24 WIRES EACH (15–9–FIBRE)   30 WIRES EACH (18–12–FIBRE)

FIG. 6–8. Flexible steel wire rope

Extra Special Flexible Steel wire rope (E.S.F.S.W.R.) (fig. 6–9). This is used where strength and flexibility are both essential. The strands are constructed of large numbers of small gauge wires which are made of higher quality steel than are those used for the other two groups. (The term 'extra special' refers more to the quality of the steel than to the flexibility of the rope.) The strands are made up round a hemp or jute heart.

Flexible Mild Steel wire rope (F.M.S.W.R.). This is supplied in small sizes only ($\frac{3}{16}$-in. to $1\frac{1}{4}$-in.), and used for such purposes as seizing and serving. It differs from the foregoing groups in that it is made of pliable mild steel, is much weaker, and of different construction. The smaller sizes consist of a single strand only, and the larger ($\frac{1}{2}$-in. and above) are made up of four strands.

Other wires. In addition to these main groups there are specially constructed wire ropes for equipment such as mine moorings and sweeps, crane purchases, boats' falls and sounding machines. Flexible copper wire rope is supplied in sizes from ⅜ to 1½-in. for ridge ropes and jackstays of bridge awnings, where

6 STRANDS
37 WIRES EACH (18–12–6–1)

6 STRANDS
61 WIRES EACH (24–18–12–6–1)

FIG. 6–9. Extra special flexible steel wire rope

steel wire would affect a magnetic compass. Aluminium alloy wire rope covered with P.V.C. for guardrails is being introduced into the Service (1962), and will gradually replace F.S.W.R.

Description

In the Royal Navy wire rope is described by initials denoting the type of the rope (e.g. S.W.R., F.S.W.R., E.S.F.S.W.R.), preceded by the circumference of the rope measured in inches, and followed by bracketed figures representing the number of strands in the rope and the number of wires in a strand, thus: 3-inch S.W.R. (6×7), or 3-inch F.S.W.R. (6×12), or 3-inch E.S.F.S.W.R. (6×37).

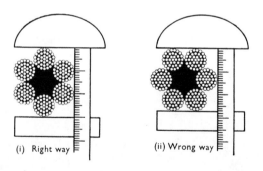

(i) Right way

(ii) Wrong way

FIG. 6–10. How to measure the diameter

Measurement

In the Merchant Navy and foreign navies, the size of wire rope may be measured by its diameter. When determining the size of a wire rope in this way it should be measured, at any point throughout its length, across its

TABLE OF COMPARISON BETWEEN ROPES

Wire Rope	Manila Rope	Nylon Rope
Strength and Weight From 4 to 7 times as strong as manila of equal size, and from $1\frac{1}{2}$ to 2 times the strength of manila of equal weight.	About the same as sisal of equal size, and five times stronger and twice the weight of coir of equal size.	About 3 times as strong as manila of equal size. Slightly lighter in weight than manila and sisal, and about $\frac{1}{12}$ the weight of wire rope of equal size. (Terylene has approximately 65 per cent the strength of Nylon.)
Elasticity For practical purposes it is not elastic.	When used within its Safe Working Load approximately 15 per cent of its length.	When used within its Safe Working Load approximately 30 per cent of its length, and, before parting, nearly 50 per cent of its length. (Terylene approximately 15 per cent of its length.)
Loss of Strength when Wet None. But prolonged immersion will corrode the wire rapidly, with a corresponding reduction in strength.	Approximately 45 per cent when saturated.	5 to 10 per cent when saturated. (Terylene rope is unaffected.)
Shock Absorption None, because of its lack of elasticity.	Fair. Suddenly applied loads tend to destroy the common friction of the individual fibres.	Extension and ultimate recovery to its original length result in tremendous capacity for shock absorption and prevent the sudden build-up of a high peak load.
Flexibility Much less than that of fibre cordage.	Fairly good when dry, but poor when saturated.	Good at all times.
Resistance to Rot and Mildew Very good if properly maintained and lubricated.	Poor.	Complete.
Anticipated Life Long if used with care and properly maintained, but slightly less than that of man-made fibre rope.	Manila is $\frac{3}{10}$ and sisal is $\frac{1}{4}$ that of Nylon.	Longer-lived than wire and much longer-lived than natural fibre rope if properly handled. (Terylene has a life $\frac{9}{10}$ that of Nylon.)

NOTES:

(i) Like all cordage, wire rope of normal lay will tend to twist in the opposite direction to that of its lay when under stress.

(ii) General remarks on wire rope, and information of a more advanced nature covering other types of wire rope, will be found in Volume II.

largest diameter (fig. 6–10). The following table shows a comparison between the circumference and diameter of different sizes of rope:

Circum-ference		Diameter		Circum-ference		Diameter		Circum-ference		Diameter	
in.	mm	in.	mm	in.	mm	in.	mm	in.	mm	in.	mm
1	25	$\frac{5}{16}$	8	3	76	$\frac{15}{16}$	24	5	127	$1\frac{15}{16}$	40
$1\frac{1}{2}$	38	$\frac{15}{32}$	12	$3\frac{1}{2}$	89	$1\frac{1}{8}$	28	$5\frac{1}{2}$	140	$1\frac{3}{4}$	44
2	51	$\frac{5}{8}$	16	4	102	$1\frac{5}{16}$	32	6	152	$1\frac{7}{8}$	48
$2\frac{1}{2}$	63	$\frac{13}{16}$	20	$4\frac{1}{2}$	114	$1\frac{7}{16}$	36	$6\frac{1}{2}$	165	$2\frac{1}{16}$	52

The lengths of wire ropes are measured in fathoms; they are issued in coils whose lengths vary with the type and size of the rope; usually the smaller the size of the rope the greater is the length of a coil. The following list gives a general indication of the lengths of coils of various types of wire ropes:

S.W.R. for standing rigging—150 and 200 fathoms.

F.S.W.R. for hawsers and running rigging—100, 150, 250, 300 and 360 fathoms.

E.S.F.S.W.R.—100, 150, 250, 300 and 500 fathoms.

Greater detail of the lengths will be found in Volume II.

Strength

The breaking strength of wire rope differs in each type. It may be calculated approximately in tons by multiplying the square of the circumference by the figure indicated below:

F.S.W.R. up to and including 4½-inch   2
F.S.W.R. above 4½-inch   2·5
S.W.R.   2·75
E.S.F.S.W.R.   3·6

The safe working load of wire rope is one-sixth of its breaking strength for standing rigging, cranes, hawsers and general-purpose wires, one-eighth for running rigging and slings, and one-twelfth for lifts and hoists. A table giving all factors of safety will be found in Volume II.

HANDLING OF VEGETABLE FIBRE CORDAGE

Elementary rules

Four lessons which a seaman must learn before he handles a rope are explained below.

The seaman's knife. The seaman should regard his knife as his best friend and should carry it with him wherever he goes; without it he is like a ship-wright without his tools. The knife should be worn on a lanyard round the waist and stowed in the back pocket of the trousers.

The seaman's knife is a tool and not a weapon; the end of the blade should be rounded, not pointed, and the blade should be sufficiently deep and thick to cut without bending. The edge of the blade should be sharpened like a chisel to avoid wearing away the thickness and strength of the blade, and the hinge should be kept lightly oiled.

Safety of tools. Whenever a seaman works aloft, or over the side, he must secure whatever tools he may be using with a lanyard secured to a part of the rigging or passed round his body. This is a commonsense precaution for avoiding possible injury to men working below him, or loss of the tools over the side.

Rope ends. When a rope is cut its ends should at once be whipped to prevent it unlaying and thus rendering a fathom or more of the rope useless. An unwhipped rope's end is the trade mark of the land-lubber. The different methods of whipping and permanent finishes for rope ends are given in Chapter 7.

Coiling down ropes. A heaving line, or any line or rope which is being hauled in, should be coiled either in the hand or on the deck *as it is hauled aboard.* This is an elementary, seamanlike precaution to ensure that the line or rope is immediately ready for further use.

Terms used when handling ropes (fig. 6–11)

The following terms are used to define the different parts of ropes and tackles when in use:

Bight. The middle part of a rope between its two ends, or between two points of suspension. A rope is said to *hang in a bight* when hanging slackly between two points.

Standing part. That part of a rope which is made fast to a mast, deck, block of a tackle, or other fitting, in contrast to the hauling or running parts.

Hauling part. That part of a rope or a tackle which is hauled upon.

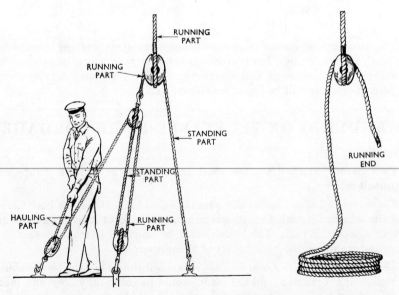

FIG. 6–11. Parts of a rope or fall

Running part. That part of a rope or tackle which runs through the blocks.

Fall. The rope of a tackle.

Running end. That part of a length of rope which first runs out from a coil, fake or reel, or through a block or fairlead.

PREPARING ROPES FOR USE

Coiling and uncoiling

A rope laid out straight will have no tendency to twist or turn either way, whether its lay be left- or right-handed, and from this position it can be stowed on a reel or coiled down. When stowed on a reel, or hauled off it, a rope will not develop any twists or turns in its length. When coiling down, however, the part of the rope remaining uncoiled will be given one twist or turn as each loop in the coil is formed.

When coiling down a rope the end should be kept free to allow the uncoiled length to rotate and thus keep it free from becoming snarled up with kinks or turns. Similarly, a rope which is run off a coil will acquire a twist or turn for every loop in the coil, but if the end is kept free the rope will usually free itself of these turns when hauled out straight. One method of avoiding these turns, should the end of the rope not be free, is to turn the coil round while coiling down the rope, thus turning the coil into a reel. Another method, as when coiling direct from a reel, is to allow as long a length as possible between reel and coil; this length will absorb the turns until the end of the rope is free from the reel, and so can be freed of its turns. Similarly, when coiling down a rope which is led through a block—as in a boat's fall, for example—the coil should not be made too near the block, otherwise a slight check may cause a kink to develop in the rope as it is running through and thus choke the luff of the block.

Coiling down (fig. 6-12)

Cordage is very resilient and will absorb a number of turns in its length without becoming snarled if the length is sufficient and the turns correspond

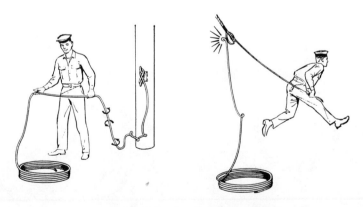

FIG. 6-12. Mistakes in coiling down

with the lay of the rope; if the turns are against the lay, however, it will quickly become snarled. For this reason rope of right-hand lay is always coiled down right-handed, and rope of left-hand lay is always coiled down left-handed.

To coil a rope for running (fig. 6-13)

Lay the rope as straight as possible along the deck; begin coiling it down close to where the standing part is made fast, and lay each loop flat upon the one below it until the bare end is reached. The size of the loops should be as

(i)   (ii)   (iii)

FIG. 6-13. To coil a rope for running

large as stowage space permits. The running part is now underneath the coil, so turn the coil over and the rope should then run out freely when required. Remember that the running part or end should always be on the top of any coil.

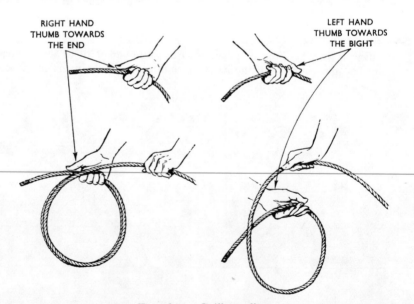

RIGHT HAND THUMB TOWARDS THE END   LEFT HAND THUMB TOWARDS THE BIGHT

FIG. 6-14. Coiling a line

To coil a small line in the hand (right-hand lay) (fig. 6–14)

When coiling in the right hand the rope should be held with the right thumb pointing towards the end; and when coiling in the left hand the left thumb should point towards the bight. The coil will then form correctly.

To thoroughfoot a rope

This is the most effective way of taking a large number of turns out of a rope. First determine whether the turns it is required to remove are left- or right-handed. Then, to remove left-hand turns, coil down left-handed, dip the end through the coil and haul the coil out straight. To remove right-hand turns, coil right-handed and proceed as before. If the bight of the rope is badly snarled, thoroughfoot the end for only a few fathoms at a time, repeating this operation as often as necessary.

'Thoroughfooting' also describes the method of joining two ropes by their soft eyes (fig. 6–15). The eye of rope A is passed through the eye of rope B, and the

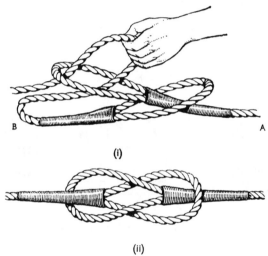

(i)

(ii)

FIG. 6–15. Thoroughfooting

bight of B is then hauled through the eye of A, thus joining the ropes by their eyes. This method is not used for joining two ropes temporarily, because it may take some time to unhitch them.

To fake* down a rope (fig. 6–16)

A rope which may have to be paid out quickly should be faked down in as long fakes as stowage space allows; falls, for example, must be faked from the bight to the end. When faked a rope does not acquire as many turns as when coiled, and it will therefore run out with less chance of becoming snarled. Care should be taken that each bight at the end of a fake is laid under that immediately preceding it to ensure a clear run.

---

* A fake is one of the turns of a rope when stowed or coiled. The term 'flake' has been used incorrectly in the past.

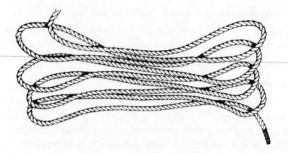

FIG. 6–16. Faking a rope

To cheese down (fig. 6–17)

When a neat stow is required for a short end of rope, such as a ladder check line or the cordage tail of an awning tackle fall, it may be *cheesed down*. This method should never be used when the rope will be required to render quickly through a block.

FIG. 6–17. Cheesing down a rope

Belaying

When a rope will have to be cast off while still under strain it cannot be secured with a bend or a hitch, except perhaps a slipping one. It is therefore belayed to a fitting made for the purpose, such as a cleat, staghorn or bollard. The action of belaying consists of taking sufficient turns round the fitting to hold the rope by friction when it takes the strain. Generally speaking, four complete turns should be sufficient, but the number of turns may have to be increased according to the degree of friction existing between rope and fitting. A wet and slippery rope or bollard, or a smooth cleat or staghorn and a well-worn rope, may require extra turns.

To belay a rope to a cleat or staghorn. Take initial turns as shown in fig. 6–18 and 6–19, then continue with figure-of-eight turns round the horns of the cleat or staghorn as many times as are required. It will be seen that when the figure-of-eight turns are removed the rope is ready to be checked under control. A rope belayed to a cleat or a staghorn must be ready for casting off at a moment's notice; therefore the turns should not be completed with a half hitch, because this may jam them. Cleats are not suitable for belaying wire rope.

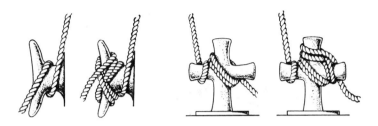

FIG. 6–18. Belaying a rope
to a cleat

FIG. 6–19. Belaying a boat's fall
to a staghorn

To hang a coil on a belaying pin or a cleat (figs. 6–20 and 6–21). Whenever possible a coil of rope should be hung up clear of the deck so as to keep the deck clear and the rope dry.

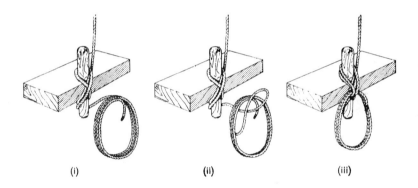

(i)　　　　　　　(ii)　　　　　　　(iii)

FIG. 6–20. Hanging a small coil on a belaying pin

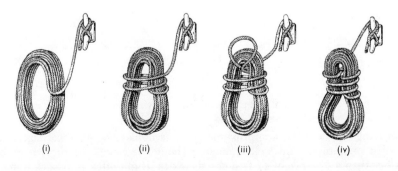

(i)　　　　(ii)　　　　(iii)　　　　(iv)

FIG. 6–21. Hanging a large coil on a cleat

Under-running

The bight of a rope, hawser or cable secured between two points is under-run to ensure that it is not foul of any object and is free to run if required. For example, a mooring rope is under-run for examination by hauling up its bight from the sea bed over the bows of a boat (fig. 6–22).

FIG. 6–22. Under-running a mooring rope

A tackle on the deck is under-run by separating its running parts to ensure that the fall is correctly rove and has no turns or kinks in it.

Throwing a heaving line (fig. 6–23)

As its name implies, a heaving line is a light flexible line that can be thrown. It is used as a *messenger* to pass hawsers from ship to shore, or vice versa. Old log line and signal halyard are very flexible and make excellent heaving lines.

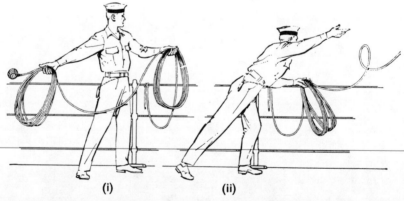

(i)   (ii)

FIG. 6–23. Throwing a heaving line

A heaving line consists of approximately 17 fathoms of $1\frac{1}{4}$-inch cordage, rot-proofed or natural, and well stretched; though it cannot be thrown much further than a distance of 12 fathoms the extra length often proves extremely useful. One end should be whipped and the other weighted with a *monkey's fist* (fig. 7–26) a small sand bag, or a heaving line knot (fig. 7–27). To weight the monkey's fist with a heavy nut, as is sometimes done, is dangerous and inexcusable.

To prepare a line for throwing it should be wetted, and from 12 to 13 fathoms should be coiled carefully in the left hand, using rather small coils. One-third of the line is taken in the right or throwing hand; the line is then thrown with the right arm straight, and it must be allowed to run out freely from the coil in the left hand. The most frequent cause of bad casts is failure to have this coil properly clear for running.

There is more than one method of heaving a line and most good throwers have their own variations. Some men take rather less than half the coil in the right hand and throw both halves together, letting go with the right hand before the left. This method is very effective but harder to learn, and to achieve a good throw by the first method is generally sufficient. Many seamen think they can heave a line further than they can; 70 feet is a good cast. Before heaving a line the standing end must be made fast (to the top guardrail, for example) with a clove hitch. Many a good throw has been rendered abortive and valuable time wasted through omitting to secure the standing end first. As soon as the heaving line has been caught the standing end should be bent to the hawser. Remember that a heaving line is only meant to take the strain of the weight of the hawser while it is being passed ashore or into the ship.

Handling new rope

Opening a new coil (fig. 6–24). A length of rope is supplied to a ship in a compact, machine-wound coil, bound with yarns or strands. To open up a new coil of rope below 6 inches in size a seaman should roll it over until the outside end of the rope is at the top and pointing directly at him. If the rope is of right-hand lay, he will then turn the coil over towards his left and lay it flat on its side; conversely, a coil of left-handed rope must be turned over to the right. The lashings are now cut and the inner end of the rope pulled out from the centre (fig. 6–24 (i)). The rope will then leave the coil correctly; counter-clockwise for a right-handed rope, and clockwise for a left-handed one. It can then be coiled down right- or left-handed according to the lay of the rope.

With rope of 6-inch size or larger the twisting involved in the preceding method is not acceptable and the coil must be unreeled in the opposite way to that in which it was made up. The coil should be placed on a turntable, or slung so that it can be revolved (fig. 6–24 (ii)). Cut the lashings and haul off from the outside.

To cut off a length of rope from a new coil. Rope used for general purposes is hauled from the coil, as previously described. Then the rope is whipped at each side of the position at which it is to be cut, to prevent the strands from flying apart, and then cut with a knife. Whenever a length of rope is cut off a coil, a label, on which should be clearly stated either the length cut off or the length remaining, should be attached to the coil.

A length of rope should never be cut unnecessarily. If too long for a temporary purpose it may be shortened by one of the methods described in the next chapter or it may be used on the bight, i.e. doubled.

(i) Opening a new coil of small rope

(ii) Opening a new coil of large rope

Fig. 6–24. Opening a new coil

Storage

Coils of new rope should be stowed clear of the deck, in a cool, well-ventilated, dry place, to allow the air to circulate freely around them. Used rope should be hung in loose coils if this is practicable. No cordage should be stowed in contact with bare ironwork, and if practicable it should be stowed clear of bulkheads. If cordage has to be stored in the open it should be protected from sunlight, because vegetable fibres are very susceptible to deterioration caused by the sun's rays.

Examination

Cordage made from vegetable fibres is very susceptible to rot from the effects of damp and mildew, and it is a wise precaution, particularly in the tropics, to examine new rope carefully before it is put into service. To examine a rope for signs of deterioration, open out the strands anywhere along its bight and look closely at their inner surfaces; if any dust or broken fibres fall out or can be rubbed off it is a sure sign of dry rot; if their inner surfaces are much darker than their outer surfaces it is a sign of dampness; and if there is a light grey film of dust on their inner surfaces it is a sign of mildew.

Rope which is suspect should never be tested by hanging a proof load on it, because, though it may pass the test without apparent failure, the load may be just sufficient to strain the fibres and disturb their grip on each other, and if this occurs the rope will probably part the next time it is used. It is more economical in the long run to discard rope which is suspect, particularly if it is intended to use it for hoisting.

HANDLING OF MAN-MADE FIBRE CORDAGE

Although the rules for handling vegetable fibre cordage generally apply to man-made fibre cordage, the properties and characteristics of the latter necessitate greater care in its handling. Here are a few hints that, if followed, will prevent misuse of the cordage and give the maximum advantage of use within the safety limits:

1. Do not uncoil a new rope by pulling the end up through the centre of the coil. Unreel it off a turntable.
2. When sets of ropes are to be used in parallel, such as boats' falls, do not pair man-made fibre rope with wire or manila.
3. Since hawser-laid rope is right-hand laid always coil it on bollards, capstans or reels in a clockwise direction.
4. When handling rope and coiling it down on deck, avoid coiling it in the same direction all the time, since this will tend to unbalance the lay.
5. Bollards, capstans, drum ends and other holding fittings used with man-made fibre rope should have smooth working surfaces to reduce abrasion and minimise surging of the rope under working conditions. Avoid bad leads and sharp metal edges. When handling hawsers take care that thimbles or other fittings do not chafe or cut the rope.

5*

6. When hawsers are used on capstans or drum ends for either heavy towing or impact loading, take six turns and two turns overlaying the last four turns. This will reduce the hazard of uncontrolled surges.

7. When securing a low freeboard vessel alongside, where the tide range is average, secure at half tide. No further handling should be required.

8. Hawser-laid Nylon hawsers tend to elongate around bollards when loaded. Use man-made fibre rope rackings. Do not use wire or natural fibre rope on the same bollard with Nylon or Terylene rope.

9. Use a man-made fibre rope stopper for holding man-made fibre hawsers under load. Do not use manila or chain.

10. Should man-made fibre rope become iced over, thaw it carefully at moderate temperature before stowing.

11. Should man-made fibre rope become slippery because of the accumulation of oil or grease, scrub it down with a mild solution of soap and fresh water. Isolated spots can be removed by the use of paraffin.

12. If the stretch of Nylon berthing hawsers becomes excessive, double them up by passing the bight, thereby halving the elongation under load. This will reduce the hazard of whipback, since the rope will usually part at the splice. This method is of use when drydocking and other close control work.

Precautions when handling man-made fibre rope

1. All man-made fibre rope stretches to nearly half its own length before parting, when the stretched rope immediately whips back directly along the line of pull, and will not curl about as does a wire after it parts. *A man must never stand in the direct line of pull when heavy loads are applied.*

2. Do not use a single part of hawser-laid rope for hauling or hoisting any load that is free to rotate.

3. Exercise extreme care when easing out Nylon or Terylene rope around bollards and cleats under heavy load. Because its coefficient of friction is lower than that of natural fibre rope it may slip when eased out and cause injury to personnel unfamiliar with its characteristics.

4. For control in easing out from a bollard, take two or three round turns before the figure-of-eight turns. Use of the round turns provides a better control when easing out or surging. Always stand well back from the bollards during these operations.

HANDLING OF WIRE ROPE

Wire rope is much less resilient, and therefore much less tractable, than cordage. It resists being bent, does not absorb turns readily, and is therefore much more liable to kinking and snarling, and tends to spring out of a coil, or off a drum or bollard. If handled correctly, however, it can be used for most of the purposes to which cordage is put, but bends and hitches cannot be made in it.

Kinking and crippling

Because of its construction and comparative lack of flexibility, wire rope requires more care in handling than cordage; if carelessly handled it may suffer serious damage through kinking and crippling.

Kinking (figs. 6–25 and 6–26). Any loop or turn in a wire rope can very easily be pulled into a kink, which permanently damages it. If a kink is seen to be about to develop it should be removed as indicated in fig. 6–26, and no attempt should be made to pull it out in the manner shown in fig. 6–25.

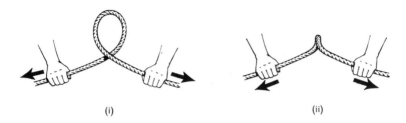

(i)   (ii)

FIG. 6–25. Wrong way to remove a kink in wire rope

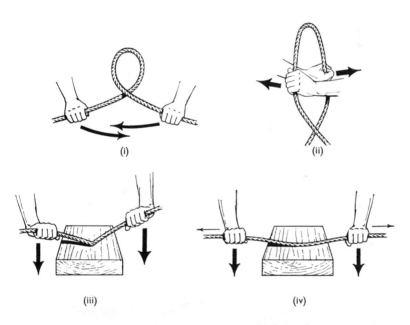

(i)   (ii)

(iii)   (iv)

FIG. 6–26. Right way to remove a kink in wire rope

Crippling (fig. 6–27). If a wire rope is bent at too acute an angle, or led over a sharp edge, it will be seriously damaged by distortion of its strands, which may result in a permanent kink or even in the rope parting. A rope so led is said to form a *bad nip*, and this results in it being *crippled*. (To *freshen the nip* is to veer or heave in a foot or two of a rope while it is under strain—a tow rope, for example—so as to bring a fresh portion of the rope to take the chafe where it passes through fairleads or around bollards.)

Most berthing wires leading from a ship to a jetty or other ship pass through *fairleads* near the ship's side. A fairlead (fig. 6–28) has rounded surfaces to give

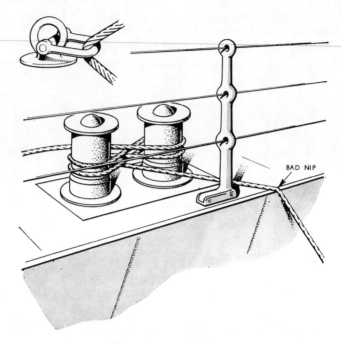

FIG. 6–27. Examples of bad nips (leads)

FIG. 6–28. Fairlead and Panama
plate

FIG. 6–29. A 'Frenchman'

the wire a fair lead. When a ship is berthed on a high jetty and there is some risk of the wire jumping out of the fairlead, a *Panama plate* is fitted to close the gap. This term originated in the Panama canal, where ships are hauled through the locks at varying heights.

To prevent crippling, a wire rope which will come under strain should never be led through a shackle or ringbolt to alter the direction of its lead. In addition, it should not be led round a bollard or drum of a diameter less than

4 times the circumference of the rope; and if it has to run through a block the diameter of the sheave should be at least 6 times the circumference of the rope.

Coiling and uncoiling

Wire rope, especially long lengths of it, should be stowed on reels, but where this is not practicable it must be coiled down. Wire rope is less able to absorb turns than fibre rope; when coiling down it is therefore all the more necessary to have the uncoiled portion free to revolve. Where this is impossible an alternative is to use left-handed loops, called *Frenchmen*, in the coil (fig. 6–29). These 'Frenchmen' serve to counteract the twists put in by coiling down right-handed.

'Frenchmen' are also necessary when coiling down a wire rope of which some portions have contracted a left-hand set (as will occur when a rope belayed left-handed round a bollard has been subjected to strain). Such portions will resist being coiled right-handed and each loop must be allowed to become a 'Frenchman'.

It is wise to stand clear when rope is being hauled off a coil containing 'Frenchmen', as such turns are very liable to jump up.

A coil of wire rope should always be well stopped to prevent the coils from springing out of place.

The best way to run out a coiled-down wire is shown in fig. 6–30.

FIG. 6–30. Running out a coiled-down wire

Handling of new rope

To unreel or uncoil a new rope. New wire ropes are supplied either in machine-wound coils or on cable drums (reels). They must be taken off the coils or drums in the correct manner, or kinks will quickly develop. A small coil can be rolled along the deck, but if space does not permit, or the rope is heavy, place the coil on a turntable and lash down two strong battens crosswise on the top of the coil (fig. 6–31). This will prevent the rope springing up over the top of the coil and kinking. Then cut the stops, and haul the rope off the coil as it rotates on the turntable.

COIL

TURNTABLE

FIG. 6–31. Uncoiling a new wire rope

To unreel the rope from a drum, pass a shaft through the drum and support the shaft at either end, thus allowing the drum to revolve; then cut the outer stops and unreel the rope off the drum (fig. 6–32). To coil down a small rope from a drum, upend the drum as shown in fig. 6–33, and lap the rope off the

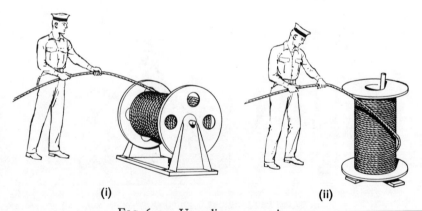

(i) (ii)

FIG. 6–32. Unreeling a new wire rope

top of the drum, lapping off each turn anti-clockwise. The twist put in the rope as each turn is lapped off is cancelled out automatically by coiling the rope down clockwise.

To cut off a length of wire rope. The rope should be very firmly whipped about one inch on each side of the position at which it is to be cut, then placed on the top of a bollard or similar hard surface, and the strands then cut with a hammer and cold chisel or with a wire-cutter.

Whenever a length of rope is cut off a coil or a drum, the coil or drum should be clearly labelled or marked, either with the length cut off or the length remaining.

FIG. 6–33. Lapping-off and coiling down a small wire rope

Making a temporary eye with bulldog grips

A temporary eye, either soft or thimble, can be made in wire rope by using bulldog grips, which are screwed clamps holding the two parts of the rope together. *It is most important that the grips should be fitted with the U-bolt over the tail end of the rope and the bridge on the standing part*, as shown in fig. 6–34.

FIG. 6–34. Making a temporary eye with bulldog grips

Bulldog grips are supplied in various sizes to fit each size of rope. Should the correct grip for a certain rope not be available the next largest size should be used. Three grips should be used on all ropes up to three inches in circumference, four grips on ropes over three inches and up to four inches in circumference, and five grips or more on ropes of over four inches circumference. Their spacing should be about three times the circumference of the rope. Grips are apt to mark or crush the rope, and both grips and rope should be frequently inspected for security and wear. Grips should not be used to join two wire ropes together.

HANDLING HAWSERS

As the name implies, a hawser was originally a heavy, vegetable fibre, cable-laid rope which was led through the hawsepipe for use in connection with the ship's anchors, or for towing. Nowadays the term is applied to any long length of heavy rope, cordage or wire, which is specially fitted and supplied to a ship

FIG. 6-35. Never stand within a bight or coil!

as part of her outfit and used for heavy duties such as towing, berthing and working ship.

Safety rules

Before working hawsers, the seaman should learn the simple rules for safety, which are illustrated in figs. 6–35 and 6–36 and briefly described below:

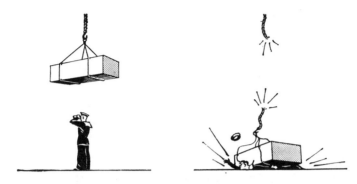

F I G. 6–36. Never stand underneath a hoist!

1. Look at the lead of the rope or hawser and determine which is the running end, the standing part, the hauling part, and which part forms a bight or a coil.
2. Never stand within a bight or a coil.
3. A wire which is being surged from bollards through a fairlead is liable to part at the fairlead. If this happens the parts may spring back and anyone standing between the fairlead and the bollards may be hurt.
4. A seaman always keeps a good lookout aloft and should seldom be caught unaware of what is happening above him. No seaman stands below an object which is being hoisted or lowered if he can avoid it. The warning cry to those below if something above them is about to be let fall, or may be accidentally falling, is '*Stand from under!*' or '*Under below!*'
5. Think out in advance where a rope will lead when it takes the strain. If likely to chafe anywhere, either shift it or use leading blocks to take it clear.
6. Always look out for chafe anywhere and take steps to prevent it, as it is a frequent cause of accidents.
7. Remember that a fibre rope which has been set up taut while dry will shrink when subjected to rain or dew. Unless the extra strain caused by the resulting shrinkage is relieved at once, it will pull the rope out of shape, and if thus repeatedly neglected the rope will eventually part.

Orders and terms used in handling hawsers, ropes and cables

In the course of his normal work the seaman uses the word *strain* as meaning the pull or tension on a rope (e.g. 'take the strain' and 'a rope under strain'), which is the sense given in the dictionary. In the mechanical sense, however, the term strain is applied to distortion of material resulting from force or stress applied to it, and this distinction must be remembered when dealing with mechanisms.

HEAVING

A heave	A pull on a rope or cable; a throw or cast with a rope.
To heave	To throw a rope, or to pull on a rope or cable either by hand or power.
Heave!	The order to give a strong pull together.
Heave in!	The order to heave in with the capstan.
Heave hearty!	An order for an extra strong pull by hand.
One, two, six, heave!	An order to men hauling on a rope to make them heave together, repeated as necessary.

HAULING

A haul	A pull on a rope by hand.
To haul	To pull by hand.
To haul hand over hand	To haul a rope in quickly with alternate hands.
Haul taut!	An order to take down the slack and take the strain.
Haul away!	An order to haul in steadily.
Avast hauling! and *Avast!*	Orders to stop hauling.
Hold fast!	An order to hold a rope under strain so as to keep it from moving.

HOISTING

A hoist	A system designed for lifting, or the load which is lifted.
To hoist	To lift.
Hoist away!	The order to haul away on a rope when hoisting something with it.
High enough!	The order to stop hoisting.
Marry!	The order to bring two ropes together side by side and handle them as one. Also a term used in splicing, meaning to butt two ropes' ends together with their respective strands interlocking.

LOWERING

Lower away!	The order to lower steadily.
Avast lowering!	An order to stop lowering.

GENERAL

Handsomely	Slowly, with care (e.g. 'lower handsomely').
Roundly	Smartly, rapidly.
Walk back!	An order to ease a rope back or out while keeping it in hand, or the order to pay back a rope or cable for a short distance when brought to the capstan.
Light to!	The order to fleet a rope back along the deck so as to provide enough slack for belaying it.
To veer	To pay or ease out a cable or hawser from the cable holder or capstan when these are connected to and controlled by their engines (veer on power); or to allow a cable to run out by its own weight or strain on the outboard end under control by the cable holder brake (veer on brake).

To check	To ease out a rope steadily by hand while keeping a strain on it.
To snub	Suddenly to restrain a rope or chain cable when it is running out.
To surge	To allow a hawser to ease out by its own weight or by the strain on the outboard end. A hawser slipping round the barrel of a capstan is said to surge whether the barrel is stopped or turning to heave in. Surging when the barrel is turning to veer is dangerous.
To render	A rope is said to render when it surges under strain round a bollard, cleat or staghorn.
Well! or *Enough!*	Orders to stop heaving, hoisting, hauling, lowering, checking, etc. *Enough!* is usually applied only to hoisting and lowering, and is preceded by *High* or *Low*, respectively.
To back up	To haul on the hauling part of a rope when passed round a bollard or similar fitting so that you assist the bollard to hold it. Also, to reinforce men already handling a rope.

Bending ropes to hawsers

To bend a heaving line to a berthing hawser (fig. 6–43). Secure the heaving line to the eye of the hawser with a long bowline. This will give the men hauling it a better grip as the bollard eye of the hawser comes to the fairlead or bollard and will enable the line to be slid clear as the eye is placed over the bollards.

To bend a messenger to a heavy hawser. A messenger is used instead of a heaving line to pass the heavier hawsers between ships, or ship and shore, as it is made of heavier stuff. It should be bent to the neck of the eye of the hawser with a rolling hitch, and firmly stopped to the crown of the eye. The eye of the hawser can then be hauled through a fairlead and the stop cut, leaving the eye free for shackling on or putting on to a slip. The rolling hitch should be well secured and stopped, and the stop on the eye should be firmly secured to prevent the hitch sliding over the shoulders of the eye (fig. 6–37).

FIG. 6–37. Rolling hitch and stop

Joining hawsers

Anchor shackle and grommet strop (figs. 6–38 and 6–39). Wire hawsers fitted with a hawser-eye are shackled together with an anchor shackle, which is a long shackle with a flush-ended bolt secured by a tapered pin and lead pellet

F IG. 6–38. Shackling wire hawsers together

through one of the lugs. A screw shackle, or one with a pin and forelock, should not be used, because the bolt is apt to shake loose when moved about the deck. If a shackle of suitable strength which will fit both eyes cannot be found, a doubled wire grommet strop can be used instead (fig. 6–39).

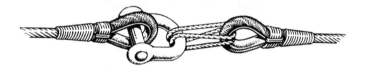

F IG. 6–39. Joining wire hawsers with a grommet strop

Securing a hawser to a bollard

Bollard strop (fig. 6–40). A wire hawser fitted with a hawser-eye is secured to a bollard with a bollard strop and an anchor shackle.

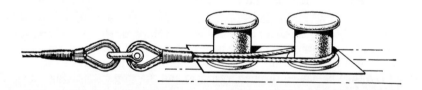

F IG. 6–40. Securing a wire hawser to a bollard with a bollard strop

Belaying

A fibre rope to a single bollard (fig. 6–41). Bring the rope to the bollard and belay it, as shown in the illustration. The first turn round the bollard must be as low down as possible, and overlapping or riding turns should be avoided.

A wire rope to a single bollard (fig. 6–42). Pass the rope round the bollard with sufficient turns to grip and then seize the end to the hauling part, as shown in the illustration. A good method of racking the end of a rope belayed to a single bollard is as follows (fig. 6–42 (ii), (iii) and (iv)):   •

1. Middle the racking underneath the rope.
2. Pass both parts of the racking over the end and under the rope.
3. Take a turn round the end.
4. Pass the seizing under the rope, and repeat 2 and 3 as often as required.
5. Separate the parts of the racking, bring them up each side of the cross, and secure them with a reef knot on the top.

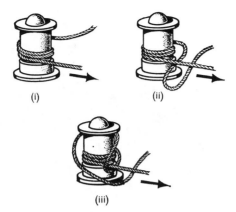

FIG. 6–41. Belaying a fibre rope to a single bollard

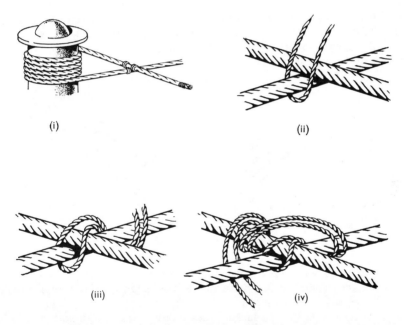

FIG. 6–42. Belaying a wire rope to a single bollard

Reasonably stout rope of at least $\frac{1}{2}$-in. size should be used for racking; spunyarn is not strong enough.

Two or more berthing hawsers over a single bollard (fig. 6–43). When two or more berthing hawsers have to be secured to the same bollard the eye of the second hawser must be passed up through the eye of the first before it is placed over the bollard; similarly, the eye of a third hawser must be passed up through the eyes of the first two; this enables the hawsers to be cast off the bollard in any order.

FIG. 6–43. Placing the eyes of two berthing hawsers on a single bollard

A hawser to twin bollards. Lead the hawser round the bollard farthest from the source of the strain, from outboard to inboard; then belay it with figure-of-eight turns as in fig. 6–44 (i). If the hawser is to be belayed for a full due the turns can be racked as follows (fig. 6–44 (ii)):

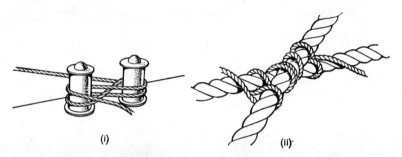

(i)   (ii)

FIG. 6–44. Belaying a berthing hawser to twin bollards

1. Rack together the two upper turns only.
2. Middle the racking and make an overhand knot round the cross of the two upper turns of the hawser.
3. With each part of the racking pass racking turns round both parts of the upper turns, working outwards from the cross.
4. When sufficient racking turns have been taken, knot both parts of the racking over the cross with an overhand knot.
5. Pass the ends in opposite directions down and round all the turns of the wire, haul the ends taut, and finish them off with a reef knot on the top.

A heavy hawser to twin bollards. When extra heavy strains are involved, as in towing operations where the load may be near the limit of strength of the bollards, it is advisable to belay the towing pendant as shown in fig. 6–45; this puts the strain on the bollard mounting in the most equable manner and obviates any tendency to rack the bollards together. The standing end can be

FIG. 6–45. Belaying a towing pendant to twin bollards

taken to a deck clench, as illustrated, or be belayed with figure-of-eight turns to another pair of bollards.

Handling hawsers under strain

To catch a turn on a single bollard (fig. 6–46). When a rope is under strain, catching an extra turn round a single bollard is difficult unless done correctly.

FIG. 6–46. Catching a turn on a single bollard

Careful attention should be paid to the position of the hands and fingers to prevent them being nipped, especially if the hawser should render.

To catch a turn round twin bollards. Fig. 6–47 shows how to catch turns with a hawser under strain round twin bollards. Note that the lead is first to the

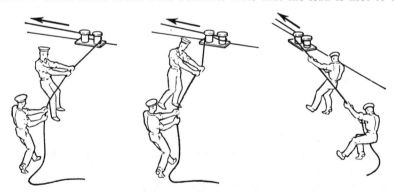

FIG. 6–47. Catching a turn round twin bollards

bollard farthest from the source of strain, and from outboard to inboard. Belaying turns of a hawser leading forward are taken right-handed on the starboard side of a ship, and left-handed on the port side.

To handle a heavy rope which is alternately slack and under strain. If space permits, it is best to keep one turn on the bollards and man the rope *before all* when hauling in the slack (fig. 6–48 (i)). As the slack comes in, one man (or

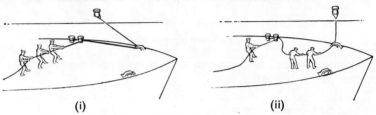

(i)   (ii)

FIG. 6–48. Handling a hawser which is alternately slack and under strain

two with a very large rope) can fleet it round the bollards, and at the same time be ready to back it up and take more turns when the strain comes on.

Backing up. When a seaman finds that the strain on a rope is becoming more than he can hold he instinctively takes a turn round the nearest bollard, cleat or other fixture, and then backs up the additional grip thus obtained with his own weight. If he expects a still heavier strain he takes as many additional turns round the fixture as are required to take the strain.

Paying out a heavy wire hawser (fig. 6–49). When paying out a heavy hawser it must be kept under control, otherwise the weight of its bight outboard may cause the hawser to take charge and run out. It should be faked in as long fleets as the deck space permits, and the bight of each fake should be secured. Each

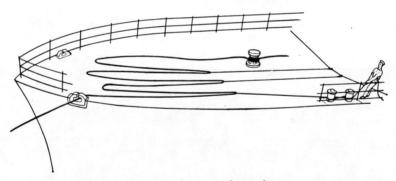

FIG. 6–49. Paying out a heavy hawser

bight should be eased out in turn by a light line surged round an adjacent pair of bollards, and a chain check stopper should be provided near the fairlead for use if required. When paying out, the bight should be neither too taut nor too slack, so as to keep to a minimum the effort required to haul it in. Theoretically, the minimum effort is required when the rope dips at an angle of about 52° to the horizontal, but for practical purposes this angle can be kept to between 35° and 70° (fig. 6–50).

Surging. Essential rules for surging are: to surge smoothly, not jerkily, and to keep sufficient control to be able to surge with the maximum safe strain on

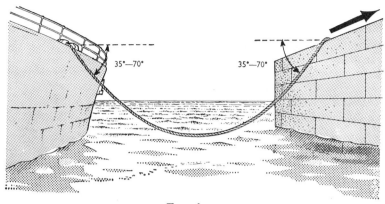

FIG. 6–50

the hawser. A hawser with too many turns round the bollard will not render round it smoothly and may therefore part, and with too few turns the hawser may take charge and run out. It should be remembered that catching an additional turn round a bollard is easier than taking one off.

When too many men back up a hawser they are apt to get in each other's way, with the result that efficient control of the hawser is lost. Success lies in taking a sufficient number of turns round the bollard to reduce the strain on the hauling part to manageable proportions. Generally speaking, two to three turns should suffice for surging under normal conditions, and up to three men should be sufficient for backing up. An expert seaman can handle a $3\frac{1}{2}$-in. wire rope by himself and keep it under complete control when surging by catching or removing turns as required.

The number of turns for surging will always depend upon the strain on the rope, the size of the rope and bollards and the resulting friction between them, and the number of men backing up on the hauling part. Under normal conditions when a man exerts a pull of 70 lb when backing up a wire, each turn round a bollard reduces the strain required on the hauling part to one-quarter of the load, so that one man will be able to hold:

> one-eighth of a ton with one turn,
> half a ton with two turns,
> two tons with three turns, and
> eight tons with four turns.

Seventy pounds is a very conservative estimate of the effort each man can apply; three men, by backing up, could easily part a 2-in. F.S.W. rope with three turns round a bollard, or a $3\frac{1}{2}$-in. F.S.W. rope with four turns; similarly, a 4-in. F.S.W. rope with five turns round a bollard could easily be parted when backed up by only one man. Applying this rule to surging, if three turns are taken round a bollard with a 3-in. F.S.W. rope and each of three men exerts a pull equal to half his weight, the rope should surge under a strain of 6 tons, which is about the limit of the working load of the rope.

It is emphasised that this rough rule applies only with normal conditions of friction between the rope and the bollard. With a greasy or wet rope, or a polished bollard, more turns or more men are required. Conversely, a rusty or dry rope, or a painted or rusty bollard, may increase the frictional grip of each turn by as much as four, or even eight, times.

Reeling a hawser under strain. A wire hawser which is reeled under strain on a winch (as when hauling in a target at high speed) will tend to unlay and thus develop a considerable number of turns which will be stored in the hawser. These turns will tend to snarl up the hawser when it is next unreeled unless a fair degree of tension is kept on it throughout the process of unreeling. The remedy lies in reducing the strain in the hawser as much as possible while reeling in.

Parting of hawsers. When a wire hawser is about to part it may emit a humming noise, or a high-pitched whine, as it reaches the limit of its strength. If the overload has been applied steadily the individual wires usually part first, then the strands will part one by one and the two ends of the parted hawser will usually 'lie dead'. If the overload has been applied suddenly there is a chance that all the strands will part simultaneously, in which case there is a possibility of the two ends springing back on their standing parts, with a consequent danger to anyone standing in the vicinity. If a berthing hawser parts it will probably part at the fairlead, or at the shoulder of the splice of its bollard eye, and it is therefore inadvisable for anyone to stand between the fairlead and the bollards when working hawsers.

Stoppers and stoppering

To belay a rope which is under strain the strain must be taken temporarily with a stopper. The type of stopper used depends on whether it is to hold a fibre or a wire rope, and on the strain it is required to take (fig. 6–51).

Cordage stopper. This is used for fibre hawsers only and consists of a length of cordage made fast to an eyeplate or other fixture. The stopper is laid alongside the hawser with its tail pointing towards the source of strain; the tail is half-hitched round the hawser *against* the lay, and then dogged round the hawser *with* the lay; the end is then held by hand or stopped to the hawser (i).

Chain stopper. This is used for wire hawsers only and is similar to a cordage stopper except that it consists of a length of chain. The half hitch is put on *with* the lay of the hawser, and the tail is dogged round *against* the lay (ii).

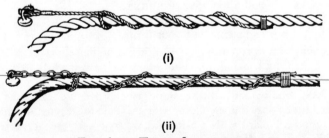

(i)

(ii)

FIG. 6–51. Types of rope stoppers

Fig. 6–52 shows an example of the use of a cordage or chain stopper. The hawser, which has been hove in by the capstan, is under strain, and it is desired to belay it to a pair of bollards. The stopper should be passed as close to the fairlead as possible, and as nearly as possible in the line between the fairlead and bollards, to avoid loss of slack as the hawser is transferred from the capstan to the bollards.

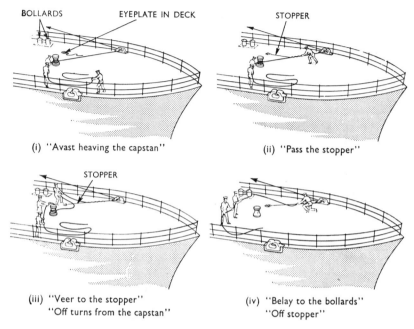

FIG. 6–52. Use of a stopper when berthing ship

Chain check stopper (fig. 6–53). This is different in nature and purpose from those already described, and is used to control the speed at which a wire hawser is being paid out. It is rove so that a pull on the tackle will jam the hawser against the eyeplate, thus operating as a brake and bringing it to rest.

If a heavy hawser is to be surged under strain it may be best to take two figure-of-eight turns with it round a pair of bollards, and rack it with a chain stopper by taking a round turn with it round the cross of the turns of the hawser, as shown in fig. 6–54. The standing end of the stopper is shackled to a

FIG. 6–53. A chain check stopper

bollard strop on one of the bollards and the hauling end is secured to a tackle.

FIG. 6–54. Racking a large hawser for surging round bollards

Carpenter's stopper (fig. 6–55). This is also used only on wire rope, and is for temporarily holding a rope which is under strain. It is a mechanical device consisting of a metal block made in the form of a thick-sided box, of which

(i) The stopper on a rope

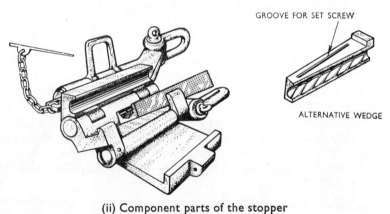

(ii) Component parts of the stopper

FIG. 6–55. A Carpenter's stopper

both ends are open and the top hinged to form a lid. The body of the box is made in two longitudinal halves, which are joined together at the bottom with a hinge so that it can be opened out for inserting the wire rope. Internally, one side of the box is parallel with, and the other inclined to, the lead of the rope, thus making the opening at one end wider than at the other. A groove, shaped to take the lay of the rope, is cut lengthways in the parallel side; and a wedge-piece, the inner side of which is similarly grooved to grip the opposite side of the rope, slides in against the inclined side. When the rope is inserted the lid is shut and clamped and the wedge-piece then pushed home as far as it will go, so that immediately any pull comes on the rope the wedge-piece is drawn hard into the block and jams the rope.

The stopper is attached by a chain bridle to a triangular link which is shackled to an eyeplate or other suitable fixture. Each stopper is supplied with two sizes of wedge-piece so that it can be used for two different sizes of rope; a 2-in. stopper, for example, can also be used for a $2\frac{1}{2}$-in. rope. The wedge-piece can be withdrawn and changed after slackening the set-screw securing it, which is inserted in the underside of the block.

BERTHING HAWSERS

Fig. 6–56 shows how berthing hawsers are used to secure a ship alongside a wall or a jetty.

Breast ropes

It will be seen that she has two breast ropes, marked 2 and 5, which are known respectively as the fore and after breast ropes. They are used to breast the ship bodily towards the jetty when coming alongside, and when belayed

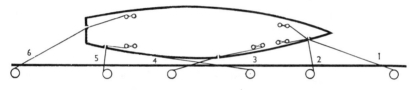

FIG. 6–56. Berthing hawsers

they limit her distance from the jetty. They are also used to hold a small ship upright against a jetty when she is resting on the bottom.

Springs

The hawsers marked 3 and 4 are known respectively as the fore spring and the after spring. Any spring which prevents the ship from moving back (aft) is known as a *back spring*, and one that prevents a ship from moving forward (ahead) is known as a *head spring*. When a ship is secured alongside, the head

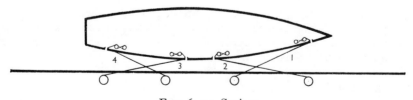

FIG. 6–57. Springs

and back springs prevent her from *surging* ahead or astern at her berth, and together they assist the breast ropes to keep her close alongside. For a large ship, or a ship berthed near a busy fairway where she is more liable to surge, or for any ship berthed in heavy weather, the springs may be duplicated as shown in fig. 6–57. These springs are then named as follows:

1. Fore head spring
2. Fore back spring
3. After head spring
4. After back spring.

Head and stern ropes

The hawsers marked 1 and 6 in fig. 6–56 are known respectively as the head rope and the stern rope. They assist the springs in preventing the ship from surging, and they are also used to adjust the position of the ship along the jetty, especially when she is going alongside.

Securing and casting off

When a ship goes alongside, the berthing hawsers required for working the ship to her berth will usually be a head rope, a stern rope, one head and one back spring, and perhaps two breast ropes. The order in which they will go out depends upon the circumstances, but each berthing hawser required for working the ship should be ready faked for running, with its bollard eye led out through the correct fairlead and stopped outboard to the top guardrail, where it will be ready for a heaving line to be bent to it by the time the ship is within heaving distance of the jetty. If the capstans are going to be used, it will probably be for breasting the ship in with the breast ropes, or for adjusting her distance along the jetty with the head and stern ropes.

When a ship is secured alongside in a tideway, particular attention must always be paid to her berthing hawsers as she rises and falls with the tide, and, whenever possible, the hawsers should be so belayed that each can be tended without disturbing another. A berthing hawser may be *doubled up* by a second hawser between ship and shore; such hawsers are usually *singled up* well before the ship is due to unberth so as not to delay the final stage of unberthing. A berthing hawser may also be *rove doubled* when there is nobody on shore to cast it off when the ship unberths; both ends of the hawser are made fast inboard.

When a ship leaves a jetty the number of berthing hawsers required will depend upon the circumstances, but normally the head and stern ropes and one head and one back spring should suffice. The head and stern ropes may have to be brought to the capstans and the springs may have to be surged.

When a ship is being warped by her berthing hawsers each hawser should be tended, and the hands tending them should be prepared to back up, surge, take down the slack, bring to the capstan, or belay them, as required. Smartness in handling hawsers is essential.

Off-fast moorings

At certain exposed berths a ship can haul herself just clear of the berth by using special off-fast or hauling-off moorings laid for this purpose. Each mooring consists of an anchor, a length of chain and a wire which is normally secured to one of the jetty bollards. On taking up her berth, a ship takes the ends of the wires, brings them through her outboard fairleads, and adjusts the tension in them according to the state of weather. When properly adjusted, the risk of damage to a ship alongside is much reduced.

On-fast moorings

At certain exposed berths, usually where the shore bollards or dolphins may not be strong enough to hold a ship in high winds, on-fast or holding-on moorings are provided. Each mooring consists of an anchor, a length of chain and a wire which is normally secured to one of the bollards. On taking up her berth, a ship takes the ends of the wires, brings them through her inboard fairleads (sometimes the chain as well) and secures them.

Precautions when berthed

Rat-guards. When a ship is berthed alongside, rat-guards should be clamped on each berthing hawser as soon as the ship is secured. Rat-guards are circular metal discs about 2 feet in diameter, and they prevent rats from climbing inboard along the berthing hawsers.

Propeller boards. These are boards on which is painted the word 'Propeller', and they are displayed in ships whose propellers project outboard from the side of the hull. They are shipped in brackets, facing outboard at upper deck level, over each propeller. They indicate to harbour craft the positions of the propellers and they should be shipped whenever the ship docks or berths alongside, or whenever she is manœuvred by tugs, or when other vessels are berthed alongside.

FITTING, SUPPLY AND MAINTENANCE OF HAWSERS

Length and fitting

In the Royal Navy vegetable fibre hawsers are supplied in coils of 120 fathoms and fitted with a point and becket at each end. With the exception of coir rope they are intended for use either as hawsers, messengers or as the falls of heavy purchases such as the deck-tackle which is used for weighing the anchors by hand. The point facilitates reeving through the blocks of purchases, and the becket enables the hawser to be tailed with a light line for ease in handling, as when reeving the hawser through an overhead block, for example. It is the practice to splice a bollard eye into one end of a fibre hawser if it is to be used as a berthing hawser.

Wire hawsers are supplied in lengths of 150 fathoms, fitted at each end with a hawser eye. A bollard strop made from wire rope of a smaller size is supplied for each wire hawser to enable its ends to be secured to bollards. An anchor shackle of the same strength as the hawser is supplied with each hawser for joining it to another hawser or to its bollard strop. Only anchor shackles whose bolts are secured with a pin and pellet are used for connecting hawsers; screw or pin and forelock shackles are not suitable for this purpose. Anchor shackles are provided because they are long enough in the clear to take the two hawser eyes, the ordinary joining shackle not being long enough for this purpose. The size in inches of the bollard strop and anchor shackle supplied for each size of wire hawser is given in the following table:

Hawser	Bollard strop	Anchor shackle
6½	5	2⅛
6	5	2
5½	4½	1¾
5	4½	1⅝
4½	3½	1⅜
4	3½	1¼
3½	3½	1⅛
3	2½	1
2½	2½	⅞

Berthing hawsers

These are usually of flexible, or extra special flexible, steel wire rope, but can be of fibre rope in small ships. They are supplied in coils of from 40 to 70 fathoms and are fitted with a bollard eye at each end. Six or seven berthing hawsers are usually supplied to each ship, the sizes of those supplied varying with her type and class. Nylon berthing hawsers are now being used in certain classes of ship, such as carriers, frigates and submarines. Eventually all berthing hawsers in the Fleet will be of Nylon.

Spring and hurricane hawsers

These are of manila or sisal and E.S.F.S.W. rope, and are made up in two ways as shown in fig. 6–58. They are used as berthing hawsers in heavy weather

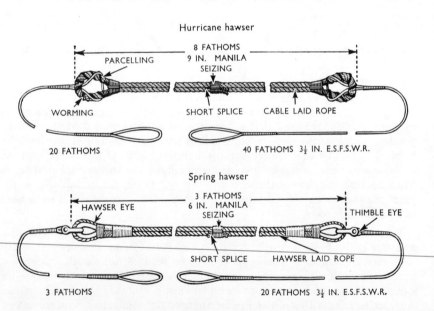

FIG. 6–58. Hurricane and spring hawsers

on account of their extra elasticity, and are also very suitable as emergency towing hawsers. The hurricane hawser is made up with cable-laid fibre rope, and the spring hawser with hawser-laid rope.

Ships' outfits

The number and types of hawsers supplied to a ship vary with her class and size. Some or all of the hawsers given in the following table may be provided in a carrier.

No.	Size and type	Length in fathoms	Special uses
I	6½-in. F.S.W.R.	150	Main towing hawser. Cable for laying out bower anchor.
I	5½-in. F.S.W.R.	150	Secondary towing hawser.
I	4½-in. F.S.W.R.	150	Cable spring for pointing ship.
2	3½-in. F.S.W.R.	150	General purposes.
I	2½-in. F.S.W.R.	150	Towing hawser for small targets.
4	4½-in. F.S.W.R.	70	Head and stern ropes for berthing.
4	4½-in. F.S.W.R.	60	Breasts and springs for berthing.
2	3½-in. F.S.W.R.	70	Berthing hawsers.
4	10-in. manila and 3½-in. E.S.F.S.W.R.	68	Hurricane hawsers.
I	8-in. Terylene	120	Picking-up rope or berthing rope.
3	6-in. Nylon	120	Messengers for main towing hawser or berthing ropes.
2	5-in. coir	120	Messengers for passing the 6-in. Nylon messengers.

Stowage

Fibre hawsers are usually stowed on simple reels, fitted overhead on a bulk-head or to a deck head. The drum and flanges of a hawser reel should be of skeleton framework construction to allow the air to circulate round the hawser and thus keep it dry. Both ends of the hawser should be stopped by their beckets to the framework of the flange. The reel should be secured by a lanyard, fitted on the flange, to prevent it rotating when the hawser is stowed.

Wire hawsers are stowed on heavy reels bolted to the deck; each reel is fitted with a pawl and ratchet, a hand band-brake and removable hand cranks (fig. 6–59 (i)). For reeling up (fig. 6–59 (ii), (iii) and (iv)), the eye on the first end of a large wire hawser is tailed with a short length of line. The eye should be inserted into the slot provided for it in the drum, and then be hauled inside as far as it will go and secured by this line; the neck of the eye is persuaded into the other part of the slot by a few light taps with a maul. The reel is then rotated while a steady strain is kept on the hawser and the turns are packed close with the maul. To obtain a neat stow it is most important that the first layer of turns should lie correctly, and this is best achieved by reeling the hawsers on the drum right-handed; if the first end is secured on the right of the reel, the hawser should be fed on from above and the reel be rotated as shown in fig. 6–59 (v). If the end is secured on the left of the reel, the rope should be fed on from below, as in fig. 6–59 (vi). The shape of the slot in the drum for the first end of the hawser automatically ensures conformity to the foregoing rules.

As the reel is rotated, layers will be formed alternately into right- and left-handed coils; if left thus reeled for a long time these turns may, in some degree, become set in the hawser.

6+M.S. I

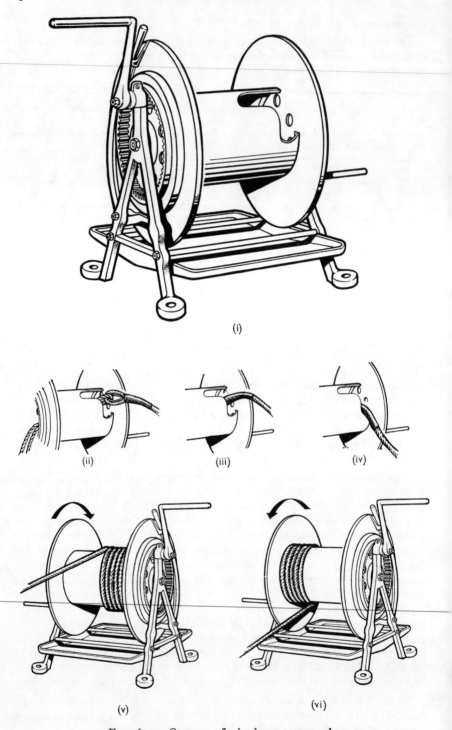

(i)

(ii)   (iii)   (iv)

(v)   (vi)

FIG. 6–59. Stowage of wire hawsers on reels

Maintenance of hawsers

Wire ropes intended for use on board ships are tinned or galvanised as a protection against rust. The smaller ropes are supplied in full-length coils, wrapped in sacking. They should be stored in a dry and well-ventilated place on battens to keep them clear of the deck and to allow the air to circulate freely around them.

Hawsers should be stowed on reels under a fitted cover whenever possible. While being reeled or otherwise stowed, the surface of a wire hawser should be washed with fresh water to free it of salt, dried with cloths, and then lightly smeared with an acid-free lubricant applied with a cloth pad. The best lubricants are boiled linseed oil, petroleum jelly, tallow or the proprietary brands supplied by the rope manufacturers. Care should be taken not to apply too much lubricant, otherwise the rope will be difficult to handle and will not provide sufficient friction to grip when brought to bollards or capstans.

Any broken wires protruding from the hawsers should be broken off as close as possible to the strands; and, if any portion of the hawser has been flattened, it should be carefully 'rounded up' by tapping it with a hammer or a maul.

Wire rope which has been allowed to become rusty should be well scrubbed with a wire brush to remove the rust, and then lubricated. Such rope, however, should be used with caution, as the rust shows that the galvanised protection has worn off and that the consequent corrosion may have considerably weakened the rope.

Wire hawsers not in constant use should be unreeled periodically, faked down on tarpaulins, and oiled overall with wads.

Wire hawsers are surveyed every six months, at the same time as the anchors and cables and rigging screws.

Questions on this chapter will be found in Appendix 2.

CHAPTER 7

Bends and Hitches and General Rope Work

Our forefathers devised various bends, hitches and knots as a means of making fast a rope so that it would hold under strain and yet be cast off easily when required. These must be learnt by every seaman before he can be of use to his ship.

This chapter is in two sections; the first deals with bends and hitches in common use in the Royal Navy; the second deals with general rope work, such as splicing cordage and wire, lashing, slinging, whipping, seizing and knotting in cordage. More advanced work in cordage and wire rope will be found in Volume II.

BENDS AND HITCHES

Strength of knotted ropes

All knots, bends and hitches reduce the strength of a rope in that portion of it where the knot, bend or hitch is made. This reduction varies from 40 to 60 per cent, and it should be borne in mind when putting a load on a knotted rope. If, for example, two 3-in. manila ropes were joined by a reef knot, the working load of the knotted ropes should be reduced from 13 hundredweight to $6\frac{1}{2}$ hundredweight.

Terms used (fig. 7-1)

The following terms are used when describing the formation of the various bends and hitches:

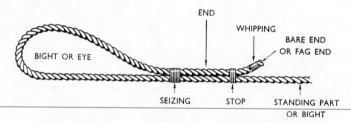

FIG. 7-1. Terms used in describing bends and hitches

Bight. The middle part of a length of rope. This term also refers to a loop of rope, and *to make a bight* is to form a loop.

End. The short length at either end of a rope, which may be formed into an eye, or used for making a bend or a hitch with which to secure it. The end of a rope is also that length of rope left over after making such an eye, bend or hitch. The *bare end*, or *fag end*, is the extreme end of a length of rope.

Standing part. The part of the bight of a rope which is nearest the eye, bend or hitch, in contrast to the end.

Stopping. A light fastening for temporarily holding in place a rope or any other object. It is not meant to bear any strain other than that required to keep the rope or other object in place.

Seizing. A seizing is used to fasten two ropes, or two parts of the same rope, securely together, to prevent them moving in relation to each other.

Whipping. The binding round the bare end of a rope for preventing the strands from unlaying.

Elements of bends and hitches

Most bends and hitches consist of a combination of two or more of the elements illustrated in fig. 7–2.

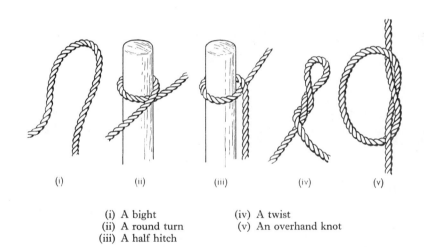

(i)	(ii)	(iii)	(iv)	(v)

(i) A bight   (iv) A twist
(ii) A round turn   (v) An overhand knot
(iii) A half hitch

FIG. 7–2. Elements of bends and hitches

Reef knot (fig. 7–3)

The reef knot consists of two overhand knots made consecutively, and is used as a common tie for bending together two ropes of approximately equal size. It is not liable to come undone when there is no strain on the knot, but it is not reliable if the ropes are of unequal size or very slippery unless the ends are seized back to their standing parts.

To form a reef knot care must be taken to cross the ends opposite ways each time they are knotted (i.e. right over left, then left over right, or vice versa), otherwise the result will be a *granny*, which will either slip or jam, depending upon whether it is made with or against the lay of the rope; a granny is also very liable to come undone where there is no strain on the knot, and for these reasons it is never used by seamen.

(i)   (ii)

FIG. 7–3. Reef knot

Figure-of-eight knot (fig. 7–4)

This knot is used to prevent a rope unreeving through an eye or a block. An overhand knot can also be used.

FIG. 7–4. Figure-of-eight knot

Marline spike hitch (fig. 7–5)

This hitch is for securing a marline spike, or similar object, into the bight of a line. Figure 7–5 (A) shows how it is used to haul taut a serving or lashing with a marline spike. It can also be used to secure a sling or the bight of a rope to a hook when the strain on both parts of the bight is approximately equal (fig. 7–5 (B)).

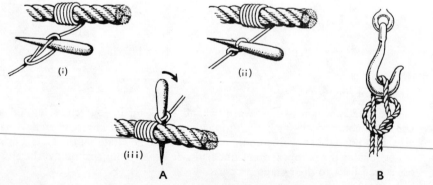

(i)   (ii)

(iii)

A   B

A—on a marline spike; B—on a hook

FIG. 7–5. Marline spike hitch

Marling hitch (fig. 7–6)

For lashing long bundles such as sails, hammocks and awnings. It will be seen from the illustration that in each hitch the end is passed down through the bight, thus jamming that part against the bundle and enabling the lashing to be hauled taut. The operation of binding together ropes or yarns by a succession of closely spaced marling hitches is known as *marling down*. Marling is usually begun with a timber hitch if no eye is spliced into the end of the lashing.

FIG. 7-6. Marling hitch

Timber hitch (fig. 7-7)

This hitch is used to secure a rope's end to a spar or bale.

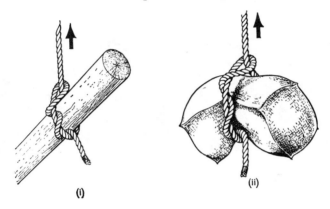

(i)

(ii)

FIG. 7-7. Timber hitch

Timber hitch and half hitch (fig. 7-8)

Used to tow, hoist or lower a spar. If the spar is tapered it should be towed or hoisted thick end first, with the timber hitch at the thin end and the half hitch at the thick end.

FIG. 7-8. Timber hitch and half hitch

Clove hitch (fig. 7-9)

A clove hitch is used to secure a rope to a spar, rail or similar fitting; also for many other purposes. It will slip along the spar or rail if subjected to a sideways pull. It can be made with the end or with the bight of the rope, as illustrated in Fig. 7-9 (a) and 7-9 (b) respectively.

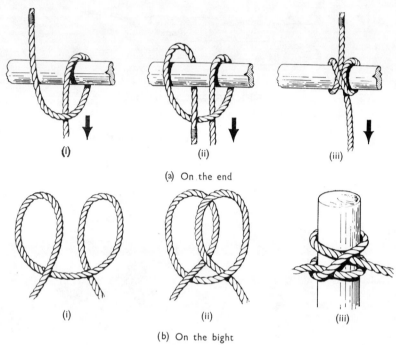

(a) On the end

(b) On the bight

FIG. 7-9. Clove hitch

Rolling hitch (fig. 7-10)

This hitch is also used for securing a rope to a spar when the pull is expected to be from one side or the other, and to another rope under strain. It is made by passing the end twice round the spar or rope, each turn crossing the standing part. A half hitch on the opposite side completes the hitch. Always pass the two turns on the side from which the pull is expected.

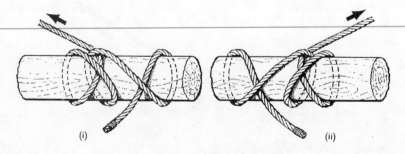

FIG. 7-10. Rolling hitch

Round turn and two half hitches (fig. 7–11)

This combination is used to secure a heavy load to a spar, ring or shackle such as the buoy shackle of a mooring buoy. It will never jam and can be cast off quickly. The end should be stopped to the standing part.

STOP

STOP

FIG. 7–11. Round turn and two half hitches

FIG. 7–12. Fisherman's bend

Fisherman's bend (fig. 7–12)

An alternative to a round turn and two half hitches, and normally used for bending a rope or hawser to the ring of an anchor. It is more suitable for a jerking pull, but will tend to jam and is not so easily cast off. The end should be stopped to the standing part.

Sheet bend or swab hitch (fig. 7–13)

This is used to secure a rope's end to a small eye, e.g. the lazy painter of a boat at the lower boom to the Jacob's ladder, or the hammock clew when the hammock is slung. It is also used to bend a small rope to a larger one. Originally used to secure a sheet to the clew of a sail. It will not slip and is easily let go.

FIG. 7–13. Sheet bend or swab hitch

FIG. 7–14. Double sheet bend

Double sheet bend (fig. 7–14)

A more secure method of accomplishing the same purpose as a single sheet bend. Used to secure a boat's painter to the eye of the lizard when at the lower, quarter or stern boom.

6*

Buntline hitch (fig. 7–15)

This hitch is a clove hitch on the standing part, and is used to secure a rope's end to a cringle or a small eye. It is more difficult to cast off than a sheet bend.

FIG. 7–15. Buntline hitch

Blackwall hitch (fig. 7–16)

A quick means of attaching a rope to a hook. It is used when the rope and hook are of equal size and is liable to slip if subjected to more than ordinary strain.

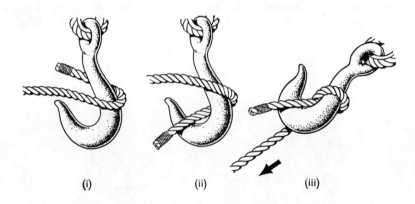

(i)   (ii)   (iii)

FIG. 7–16. Blackwall hitch

Double Blackwall hitch (fig. 7–17)

Used when the rope and hook are of unequal size. It is as secure as the midshipman's hitch (below).

Midshipman's hitch (fig. 7–18)

An alternative to the Blackwall hitch; it is preferred if the rope is at all greasy. It is made by first forming a Blackwall hitch and then taking the underneath part and placing it over the bill of the hook.

FIG. 7–17. Double Blackwall hitch

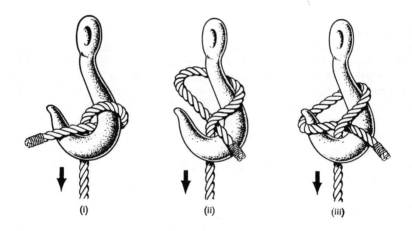

(i)   (ii)   (iii)

FIG. 7–18. Midshipman's hitch

Cat's-paw (fig. 7–19)
Used for shortening a cordage strop.

FIG. 7–19. Cat's-paw

Bowline (fig. 7–20)

This is the most useful knot for making temporary eyes in ropes of all sizes. It is used for bending a heaving line to a hawser, as a lifeline round a man's waist and for a great variety of similar purposes. Every seaman should be able to tie a bowline round his own waist with his eyes closed. The bowline is usually made in the following manner, which enables it to be formed while

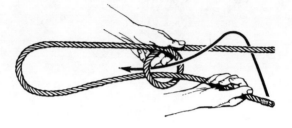

FIG. 7–20. Bowline

there is a strain on the rope: Take the end in the right hand and the standing part in the left. Place the end over the standing part and hold the cross thus formed between the index finger and thumb of the right hand, with the thumb underneath; the loop so formed becomes the bight of the bowline, and if required it can be formed round the body of the man making the knot. Then turn the wrist to the right, away from the body, and bring the end up through the loop so formed; this loop is sometimes called the *gooseneck*. Now hold the cross of the gooseneck in the left hand as shown in fig. 7–20, leaving the right hand free to manipulate the end, and complete the bowline by dipping the end under the standing part, bringing it up again, and passing it down through the gooseneck.

Running bowline (fig. 7–21)

Used to make a running eye in the end of a rope; it must never be placed round a man's body.

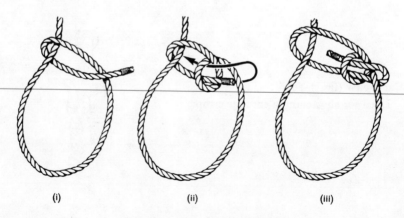

(i)   (ii)   (iii)

FIG. 7–21. Running bowline

Bowline on the bight (fig. 7–22)

As its name implies, this bowline is made on the bight, the first two operations in its formation being the same as for a simple bowline. It is used for lowering a man from aloft or over the ship's side, the short bight being placed under his arms and the long one under his buttocks.

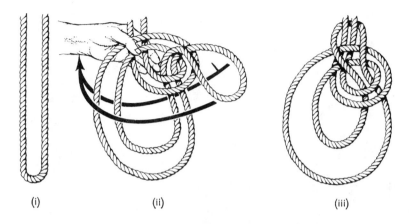

(i) (ii) (iii)

FIG. 7–22. Bowline on the bight

French bowline (fig. 7–23)

An alternative to the bowline on the bight and usually more suitable. It is made in a similar manner to a bowline, except that after the gooseneck has been formed and the end passed up through it the end is brought round and up through it again, so as to form a large bight which is passed under the man's armpits. The knot is then completed as for a simple bowline. The weight of the man sitting in the main bight keeps the arm bight taut, the knot lying roughly at his breast.

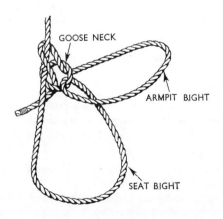

FIG. 7–23. French bowline

Slip knots (fig. 7–24)

The sheet bend, the bowline and the clove hitch are the three main knots which can be released quickly by using a bight instead of an end in the last phase of making them. Such slip knots will hold a steady strain fairly well, but cannot be trusted to stand a jerking pull.

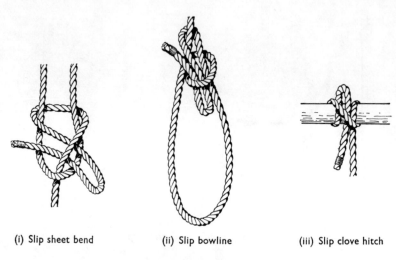

(i) Slip sheet bend   (ii) Slip bowline   (iii) Slip clove hitch

FIG. 7–24. Slip knots

Hawser bend (fig. 7–25)

The common method of joining two large hawsers together. The ends should be seized to their standing parts. Two bowlines can also be used for joining two hawsers.

FIG. 7–25. Hawser bend

Monkey's fist (fig. 7–26)

This is used to weight the end of a heaving line so that it will carry when thrown against the wind. In appearance it is very similar to a Turk's head (see Vol. II) and takes from 6 to 9 ft of line. It is made as follows:

1. Wind three turns round the hand.
2. Pass a second set of three turns across and round the first three, in the direction indicated by the arrows.
3. Pass a third three turns round and across the second three, but inside the first set and in the direction shown by the arrows; if the knot is correctly made the end will come out alongside the standing part.

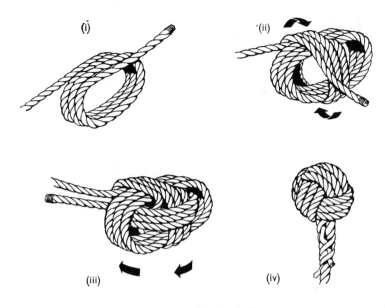

FIG. 7-26. Monkey's fist

4. To finish the knot, work all parts taut and splice the end into the standing part; alternatively, tie an overhand knot in the end and expend it by tucking it inside the monkey's fist, then work all parts taut as before.

Heaving line knot (fig. 7-27)

This knot is used as an alternative to the monkey's fist, and is quickly and easily made. Form a bight about 5 ft long at the end of the line. Start frapping the end round both parts of the bight at about 8 in. from the actual bend of the bight, and continue until it is all but expended. Then pass the end through the small loop left and haul on the standing part.

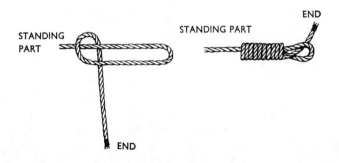

FIG. 7-27. Heaving line knot

(i)

(ii)

FIG. 7–28. Single carrick bend

Single carrick bend (fig. 7–28)

Used for joining two hawsers together when the join will have to pass round the capstan. The ends should be stopped to their standing parts. Make a cross in one end of rope with the fag end on top, then bring the other rope's end up through the bight of the first, over the cross, down between the standing part and fag end, and back and up through the bight on the *opposite* side to the first fag end.

Double carrick bend (fig. 7–29)

This is used when a more secure bend than the single carrick bend is required.

(i)

(ii)

FIG. 7–29. Double carrick bend

Middleman and butterfly knots (figs. 7–30 and 7–31)

These are mountaineer's knots, but are included here because they are useful to the seaman who is employed in land operations. They are used, when men are roped together to scale a cliff, for securing the middle man or men to the bight of the rope. An overhand knot is not used for this purpose because it causes a bad nip in the rope.

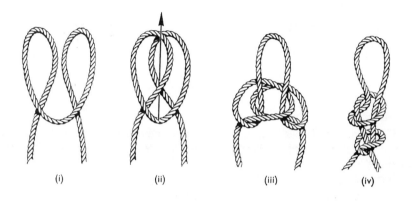

(i)   (ii)   (iii)   (iv)

FIG. 7–30. Middleman knot

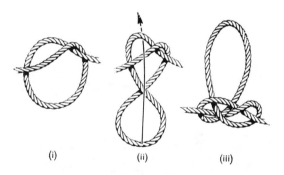

(i)   (ii)   (iii)

FIG. 7–31. Butterfly knot

Sheepshank (fig. 7–32)

This is used to shorten the bight of a rope temporarily without cutting it. The strain on the rope will usually prevent the sheepshank from slipping, but if necessary the loops can be stopped to the standing parts or secured with a toggle.

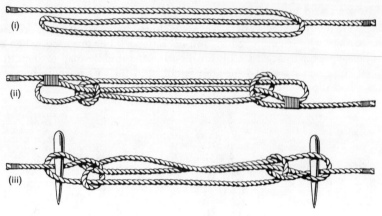

FIG. 7–32. Sheepshank

Chain shortening (fig. 7–33)

This series of hitches is for shortening the end of a rope; it looks very neat, and is useful when only a short length of rope can be handled at a time. It is made as follows:

1. Form a loop in the rope.
2. Pull the bight up through the loop, thus forming another loop.
3. Pull the bight through again, and repeat until the shortening is sufficient.
4. Secure the last loop, either with a toggle or by passing the end of the rope through it.

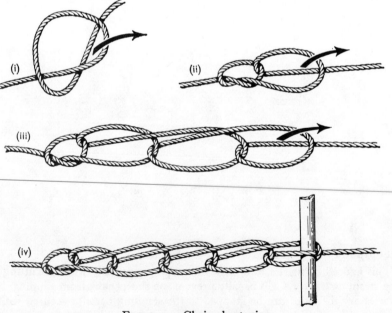

FIG. 7–33. Chain shortening

Fisherman's knots

Bending Nylon or gut to a hook (fig. 7–34). Reeve the end of the Nylon or gut through the eye, form a bight along the shank of the hook, then take several turns round the bight, starting from the eye and finishing through the end of the bight. Haul taut. This is very similar to the heaving line knot.

FIG. 7–34. Bending Nylon or gut to a hook

Joining Nylon or gut (fig. 7–35). Make a heaving line knot in the end of one length, then pass the other length through the bight before making a similar knot in it. Haul taut. The gut must be well soaked, and Nylon moistened, before they are manipulated.

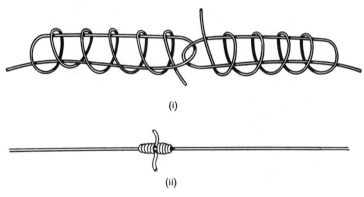

(i)

(ii)

FIG. 7–35. Joining Nylon or gut

Rose seizing (fig. 7–36)

This is used to secure an eye in a rope to a spar.

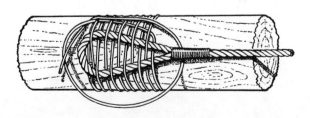

FIG. 7–36. Rose seizing

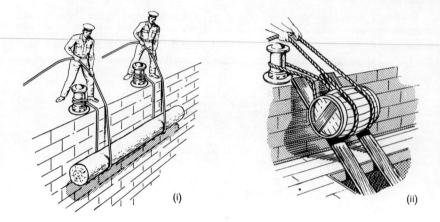

(i)

(ii)

FIG. 7-37. Parbuckling

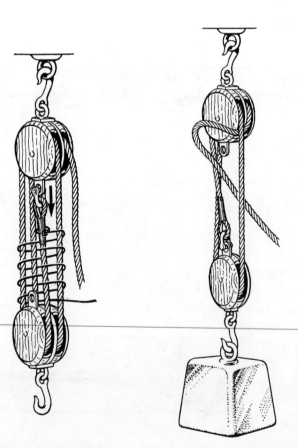

FIG. 7-38. Racking a tackle   FIG. 7-39. Choking the luff

Parbuckling (fig. 7–37)

This is used to haul up a drum, cask, heavy spar or similar object.

Racking (fig. 7–38)

This is used to hold a tackle temporarily while the fall is being belayed if the strain is too great for this to be done by holding opposite running parts, or the running and standing parts, together with the hands. The racking turns are passed with a short length of line, the end being held in the hand or secured round the parts. When a hawser, belayed round a single or double bollard, requires securing, the parts are racked as shown in figs. 6–42 and 6–44.

Choking the luff (fig. 7–39)

This method of holding a small tackle temporarily should only be used when no cleat is available and the load is light. It is bad for the rope.

(i)
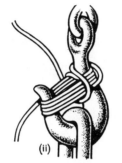
(ii)

(iii)

FIG. 7–40. Mousing a hook

Mousing (fig. 7–40)

A length of line or small wire rove between the point and shank of a hook to prevent unhooking. It is also used for keeping a pin, bolt or small bottle screw in position.

FIG. 7–41. Passing a shroud lanyard

Rigging lanyards (fig. 7–41)

These may be used to secure the lower ends of standing rigging to the shroud plates of sailing craft. Pass as many turns with the lanyard as are necessary (taking into account the strength of the lanyard and of the standing rigging); finish off with two half hitches around all parts below the thimble and tuck the end away.

Nippers (fig. 7–42)

A number of these are used as a temporary expedient to enable one hawser to hold or haul the other. A nipper should be one-third the size of the smaller hawser, and both its ends should be tended.

FIG. 7–42. Nipping two hawsers together

GENERAL ROPE WORK

Before a seaman can handle ropes and hawsers he must learn how to prevent a rope's end unlaying by whipping so that he can manufacture strops and lashings, and how to knot and splice cordage and how to splice wire. This section is divided into eleven parts which, when learnt in sequence, will prepare the seaman for the more advanced rope work described in Volume II.

WHIPPING

Common whipping (fig. 7–43)

Seaming or roping twine is used when the rope is not large, and small stuff is used when the rope is cumbersome and large. Place the end of the twine along the rope as in fig. 7–43 (i); pass turns of the twine over the rope against its lay, working towards the end of the rope, and haul each turn taut. Then lay the other end of the twine along the rope, as in fig. 7–43 (ii), and pass the remaining turns over it, taking the bight of twine over the end of the rope with each turn. When the bight becomes too small to pass over the end of the rope, haul this second end of the twine through the turns which you have passed over it until taut, thus completing the last turn round the rope, and cut off the end (figs. 7-43 (iii and iv)).

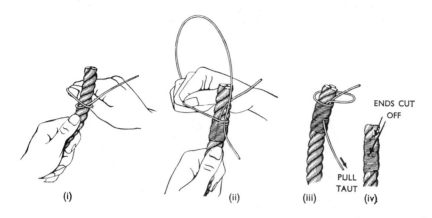

FIG. 7-43. Common whipping

An alternative finish, which can be used when the whipping is on the bight of the rope, is to take the last three or four turns loosely over one finger and pass the end back through them. The turns are worked taut, and the end hauled taut as above.

West Country whipping (fig. 7-44)

This is very useful when it is required to whip the bight of a rope. Middle the twine on the rope in the position required, pass the two ends round the rope in opposite directions and half-knot them on the other side; now bring the ends up and half-knot them again, and continue in this manner, making a half-knot every half-turn so that the half-knots lie alternately on opposite sides of the rope. Then finish off with a reef knot.

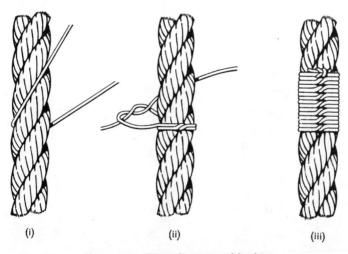

FIG. 7-44. West Country whipping

American whipping (fig. 7–45)

This is similar to the common whipping except that the first end of twine is left out clear between the first and second half of the turns. The two ends are secured together with a reef knot and cut off.

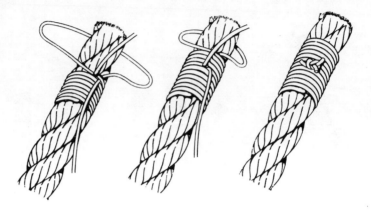

FIG. 7–45. American whipping

Sailmaker's whipping (fig. 7–46)

This whipping is the most secure: it will not work adrift under any circumstances, and is therefore used for reef points, awning stops, etc. Unlay the end of the rope for about 2 in. and hold it in the left hand, pointing upwards, with the middle strand furthest away. Now make a bight in the twine about 8 in. long and pass this bight over the middle strand only, with the two ends towards you. Then, with the bight of twine hanging several inches down the back of the rope and the ends pointing down in front, lay up the rope with the right hand. Leave the short end of twine where it is and, with the long end, pass the turns of the whipping, working towards the end of the rope against the lay.

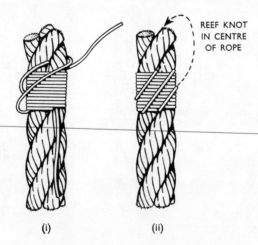

FIG. 7–46. Sailmaker's whipping

When sufficient turns are on take the bight of twine, pass it up outside the whipping, following the lay of the strand around which it was originally put, and pass it over that strand where the latter comes out at the end of the rope (fig. 7–46 (i)). Now haul on the short end so as to tighten the bight, then bring this end up outside the whipping, again following the lay of the rope, and then reef knot the two ends in the middle of the rope and out of sight (fig. 7–46 (ii)).

Whipping an end of man-made fibre cordage

A sailmaker's whipping should be used. As an added precaution against the strands unlaying, an American or common whipping should be placed at a distance from the end of the rope equal to approximately six times the circumference of the rope.

LASHING

Two crossed spars can be secured together either with a *square lashing* or a *diagonal lashing*. A square lashing is used when the spars are to be secured at right angles to each other, and the diagonal lashing when they are to be secured at an acute angle to each other.

Square lashing (fig. 7–47)

Make fast one end of the rope to one of the spars (preferably the smaller one) with a timber hitch and haul it taut. Then cross the spars with the smaller spar lying underneath. Bring the other end of the lashing up over the larger spar, down and under the smaller, up and over the larger, and so on until sufficient turns have been taken. To avoid riding turns, the turns on the larger spar should lie in succession outside those first applied, and those on the smaller spar should lie in succession inside those first applied. Finish by taking two or three *frapping* turns round the parts between the spars, and make fast with a clove hitch round all parts or round one of the spars.

FIG. 7–47. Square lashing

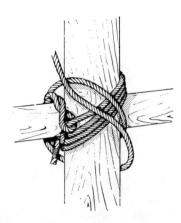

FIG. 7–48. Diagonal lashing

Diagonal lashing (fig. 7–48)

Make fast one end of the rope as for a square lashing, and pass as many turns as are required diagonally round both spars. Then bring the end up over one spar and take a few more turns across the opposite diagonal, finishing off as for a square lashing.

KNOTS

It is intended here to introduce the seaman to the two knots which form the basis of most other knots used in the Fleet—the crown knot and wall knot, and also to combinations of the two called the wall and crown knot and crown and wall knot. More advanced work in knots is described in Volume II.

Crown knot (fig. 7–49)

When finished, the crown knot leaves the three strands pointing back along the rope. It is used to begin a back splice and as a basis for more complicated knots, but seldom on its own. To form a crown, whip the rope at a distance from its end equal to three to four times its size. Then unlay the strands to the whipping, whip their ends and spread them out in the form of a star, with the centre strand furthest away from the body: and then (fig. 7–49) bring strand C to the front to form a loop (i); place strand A over C and behind B (ii); thread strand B through the loop of C (iii); pull all strands taut until knot is tidy and uniform (iv).

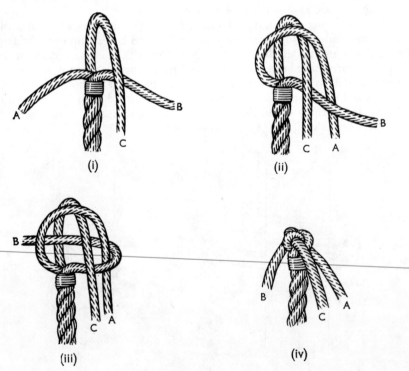

FIG. 7–49. Making a crown knot

Wall knot (fig. 7–50)

When finished, the wall knot leaves all three strands pointing in the original direction. It is, in fact, a crown knot turned upside down. Prepare the rope as for a crown: then take strand A and pass it under B; take strand B round A so as to enclose it, and pass it under C; take strand C round B so as to enclose it and bring it *up* through the bight *a*.

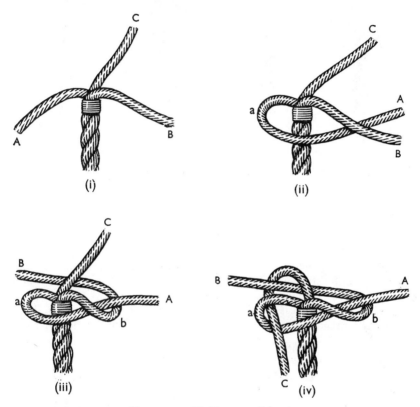

FIG. 7–50. Making a wall knot

If the wall is to be used by itself to prevent a rope unreeving, the strands should be whipped together where they emerge from the knot and the ends then be cut off.

Wall and crown knot

This can be used to prevent a rope such as a rudder lanyard from unreeving, and also to form the foundation for more advanced knots. The whipping is placed at a distance from the end equal to six times the circumference of the rope, the wall being formed first and the crown made on the top of it.

Crown and wall knot (fig. 7–51)

This differs from the wall and crown in that the crown is made first and the wall formed under it. It is used for finishing off the ends of seizings to prevent them from unreeving. The strands are unlaid right down to the turns of the seizings, against which the crown is formed as close as possible. The wall is then made under it and hauled taut, thus jamming the knot in tightly.

(i)   (ii)   (iii)   (iv)

FIG. 7–51. Making a crown and wall knot

SEIZINGS

Types of seizings

A seizing may be defined as being a method of fastening together two parts of rope sufficiently strongly to stand a required strain. Three standard seizings designed to meet certain specific requirements are employed in the Royal Navy. Although, on occasion, departure from them in detail may be made, they should be regarded as the basis for all-round work of this description.

Flat seizing. A light seizing for use when the strain on the two parts of rope is equal. It consists of one layer of approximately 11 round turns.

Round seizing. This is also used when the strains on the parts are equal, but it is stronger than a flat seizing. It consists of approximately 11 round turns and 10 riding turns; the number of riding turns is always one less than the number of round turns.

Racking seizing. When the strains on the parts of the rope are unequal or exerted in opposite directions a racking seizing is used. It is formed by passing one layer of racking turns, and then passing one of round turns so that they lie between the racking turns. The number of round turns is necessarily one less than the number of racking turns. Sufficient turns are taken for the length of the seizing to be equal to the circumference of the rope (i.e. for racking two 3-in. ropes an overall length of seizing of 3 in. is required).

Strength of seizings

For seizing cordage it is usual to use small stuff (2-lb line, codline, or nettlestuff, for example, depending upon the size of rope to be seized). When seizing wire ropes flexible mild steel wire is used.

The number of turns to be used for a seizing depends upon the strength of the seizing stuff and the strain to which the seizing will be subjected. For cordage, 11 and 21 turns have been recommended for flat and round seizings respectively, and a width of seizing equal to the circumference of the rope has been recommended for the racking seizing. These figures are based on a size of seizing stuff of about one-sixth of the size of the rope; e.g. codline would be required for seizing a three-inch sisal rope. Another method of assessing the number of turns for a racking seizing is to divide the breaking strength of the rope by one and a half times the breaking strength of the seizing stuff; 31 turns of codline would be required around two parts of a 4-in. sisal, for example.

Making up seizing stuff (fig. 7–52)

To make up left-hand twist spunyarn for a seizing or a service, wind it clockwise round the left hand with as many riding turns as are required, and finish with a clove hitch on the bight around the middle. Work with the first end which is drawn out through the opposite side of the coil, thus thorough-footing the spunyarn and making it easier to work with by taking the twist out of it. The turns in the coil are held in place by the clove hitch.

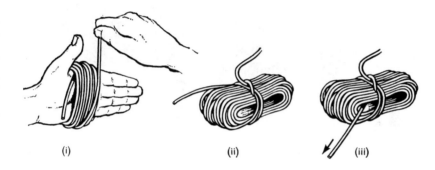

(i)   (ii)   (iii)

FIG. 7–52. Making up seizing stuff

Use of heaving mallet and Spanish windlass

When seizing heavy rope the turns must be hauled more than hand-taut, and for this purpose the following mechanical aids may be used:

Heaving mallet (fig. 7–53). The lower turns of a seizing can be tautened with a heaving mallet as follows:

1. Lay the mallet in the bight of the line, as shown in fig. 7–53 (i), and as close up to the work as possible.
2. Take a turn diagonally round the head of the mallet, bringing the end up the opposite side of the handle (ii).
3. Take half a turn round the handle, and take the end again behind the head (iii).
4. Jam the end between the head and the standing part, and bring it up over the handle, as indicated by the dotted line in (iii).
5. Place the head against the rope and heave, using the handle as a lever (iv).

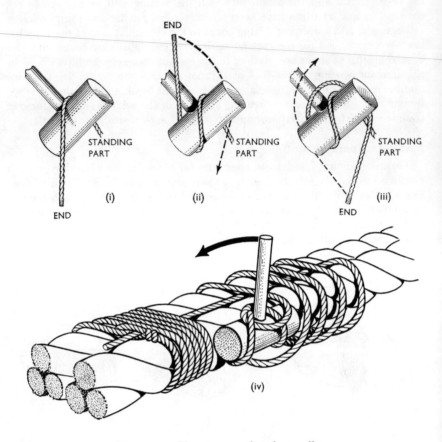

FIG. 7–53. How to use a heaving mallet

Spanish windlass (figs. 7–54 and 7–55). This also can be used for tautening the lower turns of a seizing. The windlass is formed by taking a turn with the line to be tautened round a suitable bar, and then turning the bar with a lever inserted through a bight of this line, as shown in fig. 7–54. A Spanish windlass can also be used to rack the two parts of rope together before putting on the seizing. For this purpose it is formed with a strand, well greased along its middle part, with a spike inserted at each end of the bar for use as levers, as shown in fig. 7–55.

Starting seizings

All seizings are begun by making a small eye in the end of the seizing stuff. Take the seizing round both parts and pass the end through the eye, taking care to keep this eye in the centre and clear of both parts of the rope (fig. 7–56 (i)).

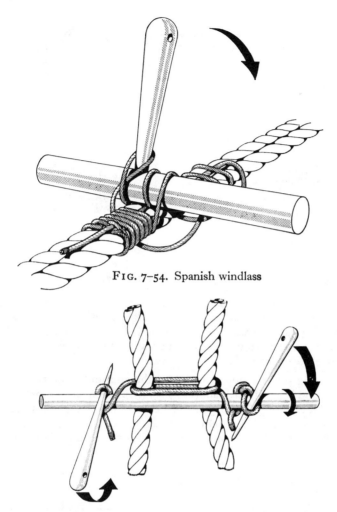

FIG. 7-54. Spanish windlass

FIG. 7-55. Racking two ropes with a Spanish windlass

To pass a flat seizing (fig. 7-56)

Having begun the seizing as described, take the round turns very loosely round both parts of the rope, then pass the end back, along and between the two parts of the rope, under the turns and through the eye of the seizing as in fig. 7-56 (ii). Then heave each turn taut and take a cross turn round the seizing between the two parts of rope, as in fig. 7-56 (iii). Now haul the seizing well taut and secure its end with a clove hitch, one part of the clove hitch being on each side of the round turn, as in fig. 7-56 (iv). Finally, unlay the seizing stuff and finish off with a crown and wall close up against the hitch, as in fig. 7-56 (v).

To pass a round seizing (fig. 7-57)

Having begun the seizing as previously described, take the same round turns as in the flat seizing, pass the end down between the parts, up through

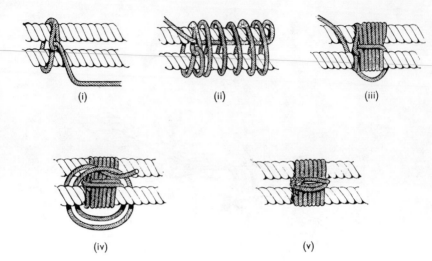

FIG. 7–56. Passing a flat seizing

the eye, and heave each turn taut with a heaving mallet or Spanish windlass as before (fig. 7–57 (i)). The end is now in the right position to begin passing the upper or riding turns, which will come exactly between the parts of the lower turns. The number of riding turns is one less than the number of lower turns, and they are hove taut by hand.

After passing the last riding turn, lead the end under the last turn of the lower turns and heave it hard taut (fig. 7–57 (ii)). Then take a cross turn round all parts of the seizing (fig. 7–57 (iii)), heave it well taut, and secure with a clove hitch each side of the round turn, as in the flat seizing (fig. 7–57 (iv)). To finish off, unlay the end of the seizing back to the clove hitch and make a crown and then a wall underneath it.

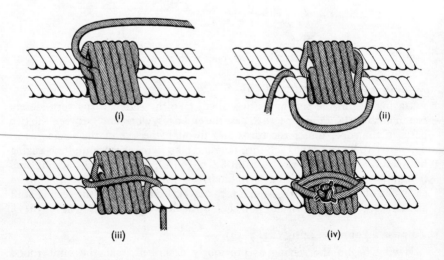

FIG. 7–57. Passing a round seizing

To pass a racking seizing (fig. 7–58)

Begin the seizing as already described. If the seizing slips when taken round both parts of rope, take the end round one part only and reeve it through the eye. Then dip the end between the two parts of rope and take a number of figure-of-eight turns round each part alternately, taking care to have the same number round each part and to leave room between each racking turn for the round turn which will come later (fig. 7–58 (i)). When the racking turns have been hove taut, dip the end under the last turn and pass the round turns back towards the eye, filling the spaces between the racking turns (fig. 7–58 (ii)). When the last round turn has been passed (see that there is one less than the racking turns), finish off the seizing with one round turn around the whole seizing and a clove hitch between the two parts of rope; then unlay the end and form a crown and a wall under it, as in the round seizing (fig. 7–57 (iv)).

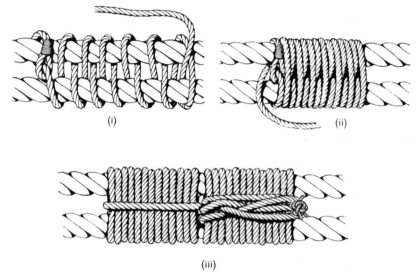

(i)

(ii)

(iii)

FIG. 7–58. Passing a racking seizing

If the seizing has a large number of turns it is finished off by passing a round turn round one half of the turns, and a round turn and clove hitch round the other half (fig. 7–58 (iii)), before making the crown and wall.

CORDAGE SPLICING

Every seaman worth his salt must be able to splice cordage. There is nothing difficult about it, and with practice splicing becomes a simple operation. It is a method of joining the ends of two ropes together, or of making an eye in the end of a rope, by interlocking the strands. Unless otherwise stated it should be accepted that all splices *reduce the strength of the rope by one-eighth.* The only tools needed are a fid, which is a pointed wooden spike made of lignum vitae or other hard wood, a heaving mallet for heaving tucks into place, and a sharp knife.

When reference is made in the text of this section to *the left* or *the right* of a rope the reader should imagine himself to be looking along the rope towards the end which is being handled.

Types of splices

Back splice. For finishing the end of a rope which is not required to be rove through a block; it prevents it from unlaying.

Eye splice. For making a permanent eye in the end of a rope.

Short splice. For joining two ropes.

Long splice. For joining two ropes which are required to pass through a block. A well-made long splice does not increase the diameter of the rope and should not reduce its strength.

Cut splice. For making a permanent eye in the bight of a rope.

Chain splice. For splicing a hemp tail into a chain which has to be led through a block or fairlead; the earrings and outhauls of awnings are examples. The chain splice is not more than two-thirds of the strength of the rope.

Flemish eye. An ornamental eye worked in the ends of gangway and other manropes.

The back splice, eye splice and short splice are described in this section; the remainder are described in Volume II.

Back splice (fig. 7–59)

Whip the rope at a distance from its end equal to five times the circumference of the rope, then unlay the strands to the whipping and whip the end of each strand. Make a crown knot (i), cut the whipping and then tuck each strand over one strand and under the next, to the left and against the lay of the rope, as shown in (ii). After each strand is tucked, pull the strands taut and tidy up this first tuck until each strand is uniform. Repeat this tucking twice more (iii). Always tuck to the left, using the next strand to the left.

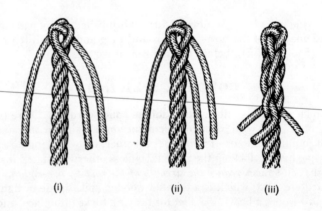

(i)   (ii)   (iii)

FIG. 7–59. Making a back splice

If the splice is to be served, as shown in fig. 7–60, taper it down after the third tuck, as follows:

1. Take one-third of the yarns out of each strand and tuck the remaining two-thirds once, as already described; though discarded, the thirds should not be cut off until the splice is completed.
2. Halve the reduced strands, then tuck one-half of each and leave the other.
3. Heave all parts taut, including the discarded ends, which should now be cut off.

FIG. 7–60. Tapering and serving a back splice

Eye splice (figs. 7–61 to 7–63)

Whip the rope at a distance from its end equal to five times the size of the rope, then unlay it to the whipping and whip the end of each strand. Mark the place intended for the crown of the eye, and bend the rope back from there so as to bring the unlaid strands alongside the place where the splice is to be made, with the left and middle strands lying on the top of the rope (fig. 7–61); the set of the splice will depend on selecting this middle strand correctly.

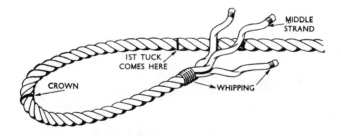

FIG. 7–61. The start of an eye splice

Now refer to fig. 7–62, in which the middle strand is marked A, the left-hand strand B, and the right-hand strand C, and make the splice as follows:

1. Tuck A, from right to left, under the nearest strand of the standing part.
2. Tuck B, from right to left, under the next strand of the standing part.

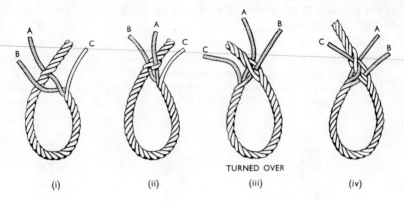

TURNED OVER

(i)   (ii)   (iii)   (iv)

FIG. 7–62. Making an eye splice

3. Now turn the rope right over so as to bring the remaining strand C on the top, and then tuck C from right to left under the unoccupied strand of the standing part. Care must be taken to retain the lay of the rope in the last strand tucked, as this enables it to lie closer.
4. Now, beginning with C, heave each strand taut with a heaving mallet. Then tuck all three strands a second and third time.
5. Finish off by tapering the splice or, if the appearance of the splice is of secondary importance or maximum strength is required, by dogging the ends by halving each of the three strands and whipping each half to its neighbour over the adjacent strand of the main rope, as shown in fig. 7–63 (i).

(i)

(ii)

(i) Dogged; (ii) tapered and served

FIG. 7–63. Eye splice finishes

Short splice (figs. 7–64 and 7–65)

The strands of each rope are tucked between the strands of the other rope against the lay, each strand being taken over the strand on its left, then under the next strand and emerging between this and the subsequent strand. In fig.

7–64 the ends of the ropes are lettered A and B, and their unlayed strands C, D and E, and F, G and H respectively. (Certain whippings and stops have been omitted to show the tucking of the strands more clearly.)

1. Whip each rope at a distance from its end equal to five times the size of the rope (this whipping has been omitted from rope A in the illustration).
2. Unlay the strands to the whipping and whip their ends (these whippings have also been omitted).
3. Marry the two ropes so that one strand of each lies between two strands of the other (fig. 7–64 (i)).
4. Having ensured a close marry, whip the strands strongly round the join to prevent them slipping, and stop ends C, D and E to rope B with a strong stop (whipping and stops have been omitted).

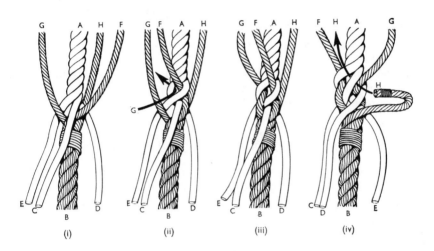

FIG. 7–64. Making a short splice

5. Cut the whipping on A.
6. Take F over C, under E, and bring it out between E and D (ii).
7. Take G over E, under D, and bring it out between D and C (ii and iii).
8. Take H over D, under C, and bring it out between C and E (iii).
9. Stop G, F, and H to A, cut the stop and whipping on B, and tuck C, D and E in a similar manner.
10. Heave all six strands equally taut with a heaving mallet.
11. Again tuck each strand over the strand on its left and under the next one, and then repeat this operation a third time.

If the splice is not to be served, finish it off by dogging the strands as shown in fig. 7–65.

Splicing man-made fibre cordage

Because of its smoothness and elasticity man-made fibre rope needs special care when it is spliced. The strands of the rope tend to unlay more readily than the strands of natural fibre rope, so firm whippings of either twine or tape must always be used. With ropes of 3-in. circumference and above each unlayed strand should be marled along its length.

F IG. 7–65. Finishing a short splice by dogging

The normal method of splicing is used and five full tucks should be made if the ends of the strands are to be finished off dog-knotted and whipped, using a dead fox (which is a yarn taken from the strand being worked) for the purpose; or four full tucks, one half tuck and one quarter tuck if the splice is tapered and served over. The serving should be put on tightly and the first three tucks left uncovered. During splicing care should be taken that:

1. Strands lifted for tucking under are not kinked.
2. Strands are not allowed to run forward but are pulled back as far as possible.
3. The rope is kept level the whole time and strands are only lifted high enough for the tuck to take place.
4. The rope itself is not allowed to kink.

WORMING, PARCELLING AND SERVING

A rope or part of a rope is wormed, parcelled and served for three reasons:

1. To protect its outer surface against wear from chafing.
2. To make its outer surface smoother, so as to prevent other ropes from chafing when led over it.
3. With a steel wire rope, to protect the hands of those using it from the sharp ends of wire projecting from any splice in it.

Worming, parcelling and serving is not necessarily watertight or damp-proof, and there is a danger that damp may rot a rope underneath its covering. Ropes so treated should therefore be inspected frequently for signs of deterioration.

Worming

This consists of filling in the spaces between the strands with lengths of spunyarn or small stuff laid along the lay of the rope, and its object is to make the rope smooth and round.

Parcelling

This consists of binding the rope with strips of tarred canvas. The strips should be from 2 to 3 inches wide and it is customary to bind them on in the direction of lay of the rope, working towards the eye. Each turn should overlap that preceding it by half the width of the strip, and the rope should first be well tallowed.

When parcelling and serving a stay throughout its whole length the parcelling should be worked upwards from the eye of the lower splice to the eye of the upper splice, as this affords the maximum obstruction to the entry of water.

Serving

This consists of binding a splice or a length of rope with close turns of spunyarn. Each turn is hove taut with a special serving mallet, which has a score in its head to fit the rope and a wooden handle about 15 inches long. A

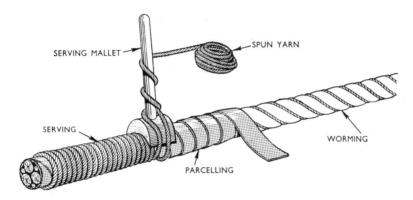

FIG. 7–66. Worming, parcelling and serving

service is always bound on in the opposite direction to the parcelling, so as to avoid bunching up the latter. It is therefore put on against the lay of the rope, which may be memorised thus:

> *Worm and parcel with the lay,*
> *Turn, and serve the other way.*

A service is begun as for a common whipping, and for an eye splice it is usual to work from the splice to the eye. The first few turns are put on by hand and hauled taut with a spike or heaving mallet. The serving mallet is then placed on the rope and the turns of the service are passed as follows:

> take a half-turn round the handle; then one turn round both the fore end of the head of the mallet and the rope; then dog the serving round the handle of the mallet.

Some mallets work better if a preliminary round turn is taken round the rope and after end of the head, and then followed by the turns described above.

To put on a service, stand with the rope on your left side while facing in the direction in which the turns are advancing. Then pass the ball of spunyarn round and round in step with the service. Having completed the required length of service, finish it off by passing the end back under the last four turns, haul all parts taut, and make a crown and wall.

NOTES:

(i) If serving over a restricted length of rope—up to an eye splice, for example— which does not allow the mallet to advance ahead of the last turns, the spunyarn should be brought to the mallet as follows:

> up over the cut in the fore end of the head; one quarter-turn round the handle; one turn round the rope and rear end of the head (taken in the direction of the service, i.e. against the lay of the rope); and then dogged round the handle.

(ii) Smear the rope or splice with tallow before beginning to serve, if it is not parcelled.

(iii) Services with flexible mild steel wire differ little from those with cordage.

PERMANENT FINISHES FOR ROPES' ENDS

The various permanent ways of preventing a rope's end from unlaying (fig. 7–67) are briefly described below. Detailed instructions for making the point, becket and hawser eye are given in Volume II.

Back splice (fig. 7–59)

A back splice has the disadvantage that it will not reeve through a block intended for the rope.

Point

This is the most efficient and most ornamental method of ending a rope which is intended to pass easily through a block or eye (e.g. a boat's painter).

Becket

This is a small loop fitted to the pointed end of a large fibre hawser, and is made from rope of about one-quarter the size of its hawser. It enables the hawser to be *tailed* with a line to facilitate handling it or reeving it through an overhead block.

Thimble eye

This is formed by fitting and splicing the end of the rope round a thimble, the splice holding the thimble in place. It is fitted in the ends of cordage and wire ropes which are intended to be used in conjunction with a joining shackle or other rigging fittings.

Hawser eye

This is an alternative to the thimble eye and just as efficient. The eye is first spliced larger than the thimble, and the thimble then fitted into the eye and secured in place by a strong seizing just below it; this enables a damaged thimble to be easily removed and replaced, merely by cutting the seizing and then renewing it.

Soft eye

This is a small eye spliced in the end of a rope. It can be converted to a hawser eye by inserting a thimble and seizing it into place.

Bollard eye

This is a large soft eye, 5 ft long from crown to splice, fitted in the ends of berthing hawsers so that they can be placed over bollards.

Knot

One of the knots used on the ends of manropes, rudder lanyards, etc., most of which are described in Volume II.

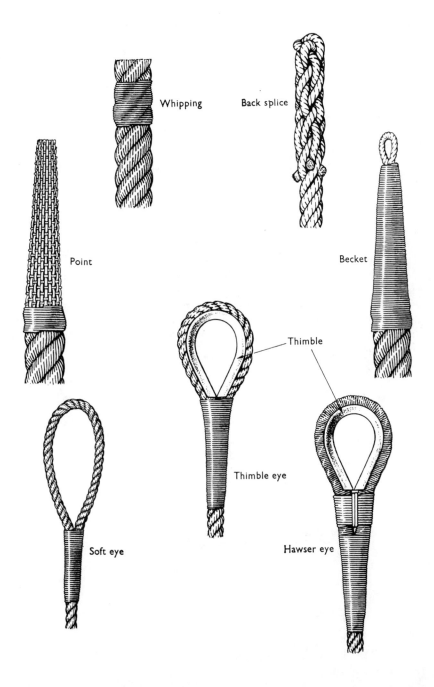

Whipping

Back splice

Point

Becket

Thimble

Soft eye

Thimble eye

Hawser eye

FIG. 7-67. Permanent finishes for ropes' ends

STROPS

A strop is a ring of cordage or wire rope, usually made in one of the following forms:

Common strop

This is made from a short length with its ends bent or spliced together. It is used to pass round a rope, spar, chain cable, etc., so as to provide an eye to take a hook or shackle.

Bale sling strop

This is similar in construction to the common strop but much longer. It is primarily intended as a sling for hoisting bales, but can be used for many other purposes.

Selvagee strop

This is used for the same purposes as the common strop, but has the virtue of being able to grip the spar or other object round which it is passed more strongly so that it will withstand a sideways pull. It is made of spunyarn and thus has no specified strength. To make a selvagee strop (fig. 7–68) fix two bolts, nails or hooks at a distance apart equal to the length of the strop required, and pass roundabout turns with a ball of spunyarn, taking care to have *every* turn well taut; when the strop is of the thickness required marl it down with a series of marling hitches.

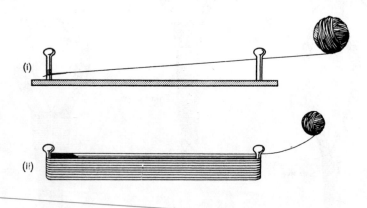

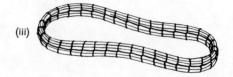

FIG. 7–68. Making a selvagee strop

Grommet strop

This may be long or short and differs from the common and bale sling strops only in its construction. It is formed of either one or two strands made up into a ring and laid up round their own parts. The grommet strop made from one or two strands of wire rope is the strongest type of strop used. It is extensively used for heavy work, such as laying chain moorings, lifting heavy weights, and joining two wire hawsers together. Its construction is described in Volume II.

To put a strop on a spar (fig. 7–69)

Use a common strop. If the pull is from one side so that a strong grip is required, use a selvagee strop in a similar manner.

FIG. 7–69. Putting a strop on a spar

To put a strop on a rope (fig. 7–70)

Middle a common or selvagee strop on the rope. Dog the bights opposite ways and hook the tackle on to both bights. A selvagee strop will hold on wire rope, but for a strong pull chain must be used. The chain can either be knotted into a strop and used as above, or be put on as a chain stopper as described in Chapter 6.

FIG. 7–70. Putting a strop on a rope

SLINGS AND SLINGING

When anything is to be hoisted, whether it is a single item or a collection of packages of stores, it is attached to the hook of the hoisting rope by means of a sling, which may be formed by a strop or consist of special fittings, such as those described in Volume II. Care must always be taken when using slings, as their misuse or over-loading is a frequent cause of accidents.

An important principle in slinging is illustrated in the three diagrams in fig. 7–71. These show an object weighing one ton slung in three different ways,

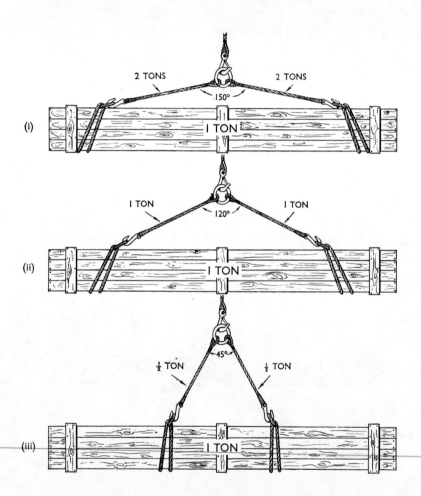

FIG. 7–71. Stresses in the legs of a sling

with the tension in each leg of the slings marked in each method. It will be seen that the greater the angle between the legs of the slings the greater is the tension they have to bear. For two-legged slings used in commercial practice the working load is laid down for various angles between 0° and 120°, and these slings are seldom, if ever, permitted to be used with the legs beyond this limiting angle of 120°. There are, however, occasions when an unavoidably large angle has to be accepted, and the seaman must then take care that his sling is strong enough to take the extra strain.

The same principle applies also to simple strops, as illustrated in fig. 7–72. In (i) the angles between the four legs of the strop are wide and each leg bears about 1½ times the weight of the case; in (ii) the angles between the four legs of the strop are small and each leg bears about half the weight of the case.

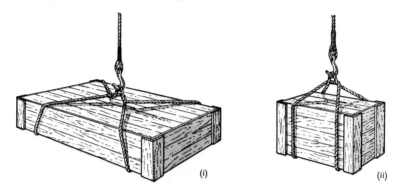

(i) Wrong way; (ii) right way

FIG. 7–72. Slinging a case by a strop

Weights should always be slung so that their centre of gravity is as low as possible, and the places where the slings are liable to be chafed, such as the sharp edges of packing cases, should be padded.

It is emphasised that lifting gear of any kind should never be used in a casual manner. Any lifting gear such as a sling should be examined before use to see that it is in a fit condition and of sufficient strength for the duty required of it.

To sling a cask

Horizontally. A butt sling or a bale sling can be used for slinging a cask. Place the cask on its bilge with its bung up. If using a butt sling, pass it round one end of the cask and through its own eye; then pass the tail round the other end of the cask, in the same direction as the standing part of the eye, and finish by clove-hitching the end to its own part (fig. 7–73 (i)). If using a bale sling, middle it under the cask and dip one bight through the other (ii).

Head up (fig. 7–73 (iii)). This method is used if the head of a cask is missing or damaged. Place the cask on its end, pass a rope under the cask, and with the ends make an overhand knot on the top of it; then open out the knot and slide the two halves down the sides to a quarter of the way down the cask; haul taut and finish off with a reef knot on the top.

Breaking bulk. This is the operation of removing the first cask from a tier. The cask must first be slightly lifted to make room for passing a sling around it. *Can hooks*, which fit under the chines (figs. 7–73 (iv) and (v)), are used for this purpose, but they should not be used to sling a cask, because if its chines are weak or damaged an accident will result.

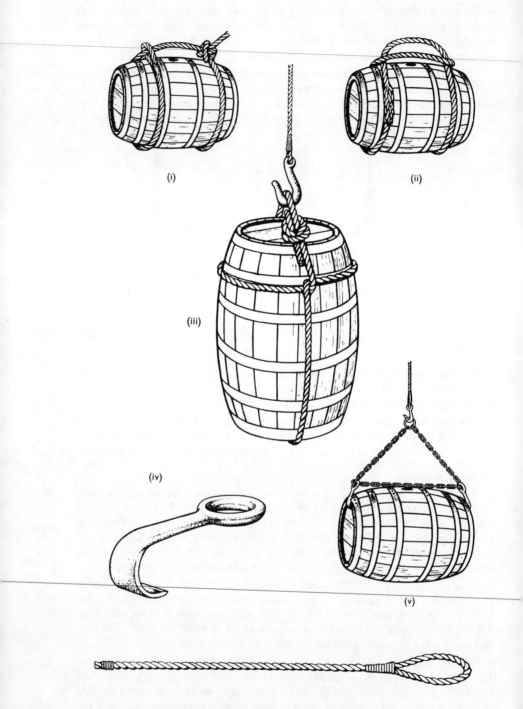

FIG. 7–73. Ways of slinging and lifting a cask

SPANS

A span is a length of rope, wire or chain made fast at two points so that a weight can be suspended on its bight. The three sketches in fig. 7–74 show three spans each supporting a weight of one ton, and it will be seen that, as when using slings, the greater the angle between the legs of the span the higher is the tension they have to bear.

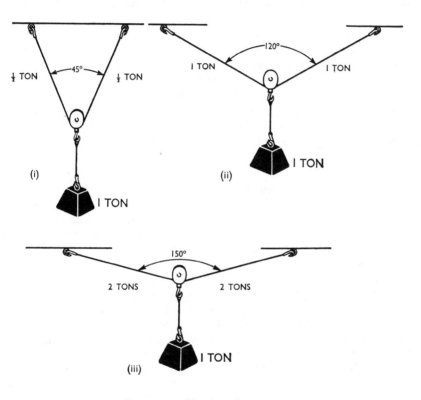

FIG. 7–74. Tensions in a span

The most common misuse of a span is exemplified when hooking a tackle on to a taut jackstay. This is a most reprehensible practice, as it results in a tension in the jackstay of from 10 to 15 times the force applied by the tackle. This power is legitimately used by the seaman, however, in *swigging off* on a fall of which the hauling part is made fast (as in a halyard or a tack tackle). He hauls on the fall at right-angles to its lead, thereby exerting great force, and then recovers the slack so obtained.

The foregoing paragraphs are intended to give the seaman a rough guide to the stresses set up in slings and spans. If required, these can be estimated accurately by methods described in Volume II.

WIRE SPLICING

Wire rope is spliced in roughly the same way as fibre rope; but, wire being much less tractable, greater skill is required and particular care must always be taken with whippings and seizings. In this section it is intended only to describe the eye splice, all other work in wire rope being described in Volume II.

It should be remembered that the bending of the wires during the process of splicing may injure their galvanised surface. When possible, splices should therefore be dipped in a preservative, such as mineral tar or tallow, before being wormed, parcelled and served.

Splicing reduces the strength of wire rope by approximately one-eighth, but a badly made splice will reduce it appreciably more. The less the strands are distorted and disturbed when tucking, the less will be their loss of strength; also the splice must be carefully tapered from its beginning at the eye down to the extreme ends of the last strands tucked.

There are several ways of making the first tuck of an eye splice, but there appears to be little to choose between them as regards their effect on the strength of the rope, and appearance is a matter of taste. The method of splicing described here is that which is used in the Royal Navy, and is called the Admiralty Service Splice.

A marline spike with a long tapered point should be used to open the strands; the correct way to use it is best demonstrated by an instructor, but proficiency will not come without practice. The spike should be inserted before each strand is tucked, and withdrawn after that tuck is complete. The tucking strand is passed through the rope in the same direction as, and beyond, the spike, and it is then pulled into place in the splice.

The twisting and pulling caused in tucking the strands tend to distort their natural set and must be reduced to a minimum. Distortion is greatest when the strands are inserted close to the point at which they emerge from the last tuck (i.e. with a short nip), and it will be found that the strands will usually go more kindly into place if the spike is introduced under the correct strand but some inches farther down the rope. The tucking strand should then be passed through, as already described, and hauled into place while working the spike back along the lay of the rope. The less the strands are distorted the neater and stronger will be the splice. In the Royal Navy all strands are tucked against the lay, as in cordage splicing.

When preparing wire for splicing the ends of the strands must always be firmly whipped before they are unlaid from the rope.

Tucking sequence

For wires up to and including 4-inch

1. One tuck with the core in each strand.
2. Two tucks after the core of each strand has been removed.
3. One tuck with two-thirds of each strand.
4. One tuck with half of each remaining strand.

For wires above 4-inch. A third tuck is made after the core of each strand has been removed. The gradual reduction in the size of each strand gives the splice its uniform taper.

To make an eye splice (fig. 7–75)

1. Put a stout whipping on the rope at a distance equal to one foot for every inch of the circumference of the wire; for example, for a 4-in. wire the whipping would be placed 4 ft from the rope's end. Whip the end of each strand, unlay the strands to the whipping, and cut out the heart of the rope that is exposed (i).
2. Form the size of eye required and stop the two parts of the wire firmly together to prevent movement during the tucking of the strands (stopping not shown).
3. Place three strands on one side of the wire and the remaining three on the opposite side of the wire (i).
   NOTE: For convenience in the following instructions the strands are numbered from 1 to 6, the top strand being No. 1 as shown in fig. 7–75 (i). The parts of the rope are distinguished by naming them the *standing part* and the *tucking end* (the terms are self-explanatory) and all references to the right and left apply only when looking down the rope from the crown of the eye.
4. When ready for splicing, place the eye so that the tucking end lies to the left of the standing part, as shown in (i), thus enabling No. 1 strand

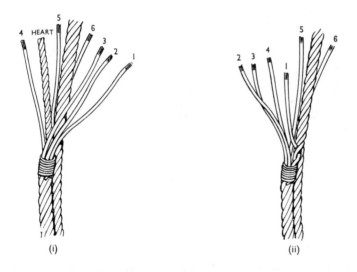

FIG. 7–75. Making an eye splice in wire (1)

to be inserted from the right-hand side and against the lay.
5. Tuck No. 1 strand under the strand immediately below it (ii).
6. Tuck Nos. 2, 3 and 4 under successive strands of the standing part, as shown in figs. 7–76 (i), (ii) and (iii).
7. Tuck No. 6 under the remaining two strands of the standing part (iv).
8. Finally, tuck No. 5 so that it emerges between the two strands under which No. 6 lies and after passing under one strand only, as shown in (v). This will result in the six strands emerging equidistantly around the standing

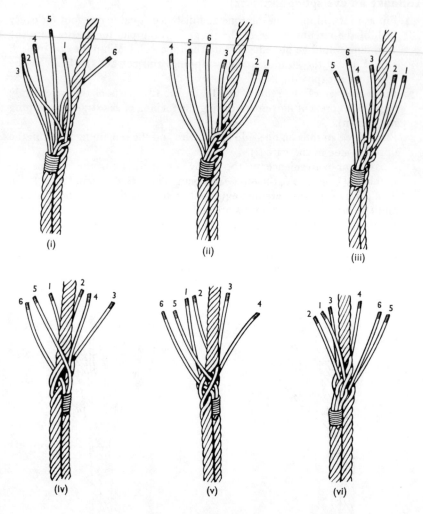

FIG. 7–76. Making an eye splice in wire (2)

part, the variation in the regular sequence of tucking being necessary for a locking tuck and to make a neat splice, as shown in (vi).

9. Now pull the strands down towards the crown of the eye, taking care not to cripple the wire, and place a seizing outside the tucks to prevent them easing back during the subsequent stages. Then, if the strand cores are jute or hemp, remove the whippings at the end of the strands, cut out the cores, and then replace the whippings.

10. Tuck these coreless strands in regular sequence again, twice for rope up to and including 4 inches in circumference, and three times for rope above 4 inches in circumference, not forgetting to place a seizing outside each series of tucks. Then take one-third of the wires out of each strand and

stop them back towards the crown of the eye. Tuck the remaining two-thirds once, and then stop back half the wires in each strand again. Tuck each of the one-third strands once, remove the seizings from each tuck, and then tap down all tucks with a mallet, starting from the first tuck and finishing off at the tail, to remove any slack and to round up the splice.

11. Then break off all ends, including those stopped back, by bending each separate wire to and fro; though broken off short, a small hook is thus formed in the end of each wire which will prevent it from drawing through the holding strand.

12. The splice is now wormed, parcelled and served by the method described earlier in this chapter.

Questions on this chapter will be found in Appendix 2.

CHAPTER 8

Rigging

RIGGING FITTINGS

Various fittings used with the standing and running rigging of a ship are illustrated in figs. 8–1, 8–2 and 8–3, and briefly described below. The strengths of these fittings are dealt with in Volume II.

SHACKLES

These are coupling links (fig. 8–1) used for joining ropes and chain together or to some fitting, and are usually made of wrought iron or mild steel. Those which are U-shaped are called *straight shackles*, and those which have curved sides are called *bow shackles*; a bow shackle is weaker than a straight shackle.

Parts of a shackle

The ends of a shackle are called the *lugs*, the space between them is called the *jaw*, and the part opposite the jaw is called the *crown*. The inside width or length of a shackle is called the *clear*; thus a shackle may be described as being 'long in the clear' or 'wide in the clear'. The jaw is closed by a removable *bolt* which passes through a hole in each lug, and a general-purpose shackle is usually named by the manner in which its bolt is secured in place.

Types of shackle

Screw shackle. The end of the bolt is screwed into one of the lugs, and the bolt may be fitted with a flange at its head. It should be moused.

Forelock shackle. The end of the bolt projects beyond one of the lugs, and a flat tapered split pin called a *forelock* is passed through a slot in the end of the bolt; the forelock may be attached to the shackle by a keep chain.

Feathered shackle. The bolt is made with two projections, called *feathers*, which fit into slots in the lugs called *featherways*; when the bolt is passed through the lugs it is locked in place by a half-turn so that the feathers and featherways are out of line with each other.

Joining shackle. A tapered hole is drilled through one of the lugs and the end of the bolt, and the bolt is secured in place by a similarly tapered pin being driven into this hole and held in place by a lead pellet hammered into the mouth of the hole over the head of the pin.

Clenched shackle. The end of the bolt is heated and then hammered over so that it cannot be removed, thus closing the shackle permanently.

Shackles for anchors and cables

Shackles used with the anchors and cables of a ship are specially named according to the purpose they serve.

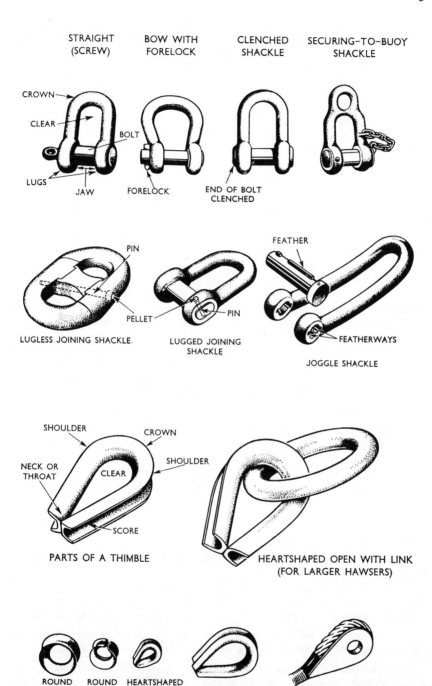

STRAIGHT (SCREW) BOW WITH FORELOCK CLENCHED SHACKLE SECURING-TO-BUOY SHACKLE

CROWN
CLEAR
BOLT
LUGS
JAW
FORELOCK
END OF BOLT CLENCHED

PIN
PELLET
LUGLESS JOINING SHACKLE.

PIN
LUGGED JOINING SHACKLE

FEATHER
FEATHERWAYS
JOGGLE SHACKLE

SHOULDER
CROWN
SHOULDER
NECK OR THROAT
CLEAR
SCORE
PARTS OF A THIMBLE

HEARTSHAPED OPEN WITH LINK
(FOR LARGER HAWSERS)

ROUND WELDED ROUND OPEN HEARTSHAPED OPEN FOR MACHINERY HEARTSHAPED OPEN SOLID THIMBLE

Fig. 8-1. Shackles and thimbles

Shackle of the anchor. This is also known as the 'anchor ring' and joins directly to the anchor shank. It is always considered to be part of the anchor.

Anchor shackle. This joins the cable to the ring of the anchor. It is longer in the clear than other shackles, and the ends of the bolt, which is secured by pin and pellet, are flush with the lugs. For this reason it is always used for joining two hawsers together.

Securing-to-buoy shackle. This is used to join the bridle (end of cable) to the buoy shackle. It is wide in the clear, and the bolt, which is secured by pin and pellet, is chained to the shackle so that it will not be lost if dropped during the process of shackling or unshackling.

Joining shackle. Used to join two lengths of cable together.

Joggle shackle. A long and slightly curved feathered shackle which is designed to fit over any link of the cable so that a wire rope may be shackled to it.

Towing shackle. A specially long shackle to take the end of a towing hawser and the tongue of a towing slip.

THIMBLES

Thimbles (fig. 8–1) are classified according to the circumference of rope for which they are intended and also their shapes. They are manufactured from mild steel, iron or gunmetal. When an eyesplice is formed at one end of a fibre or wire rope a thimble is inserted to take the chafe of a shackle or shackle bolt and also to support the eye formed in the rope. The support given by the thimble prevents a bad nip in the bight of the rope when under tension. Large thimbles are made from material of special section and bent to shape. Small thimbles of gunmetal and circular in shape are cast in one piece.

Thimbles are either round or heart-shaped and open or welded. The gap formed at the throat of an open thimble (except the engineers' or machinery type, which is too stiff) can be sprung open to allow the eye of a tackle hook or lug of a shackle to enter. Heart-shaped are preferable for thimble or hawser eyes, in both wire and fibre ropes, because the rope can be spliced close to the throat of the thimble.

Types of thimble

Round welded thimbles. Of mild steel, these are used for boom gear and in the edges and corners of awnings.

Round open thimbles. These are used when it is necessary to insert something in them; for example, the eye of the hook of a common stropped block is put in the thimble before the strop is made and the thimble seized into position.

Small gunmetal thimbles. For reefing cringles and corners of boats' sails, also for bridge awnings when there is a magnetic compass on the bridge.

Solid and machinery (engineers') thimbles. Designed to fit closely round a bolt or pin so that there is no movement and the thimble will not collapse under stress.

Machinery (engineers') heart-shaped thimbles. These are shorter and thicker than general-purpose heart-shaped thimbles.

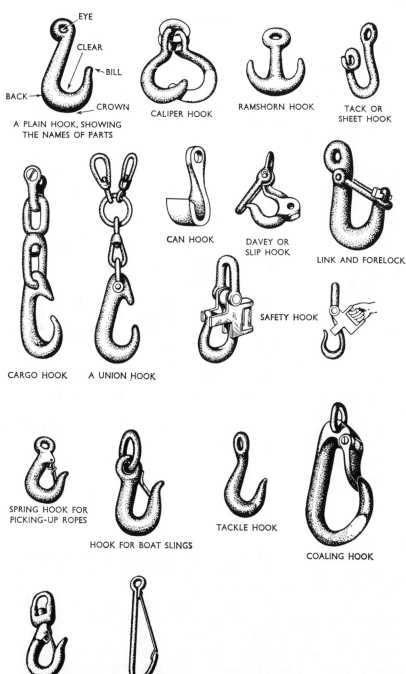

FIG. 8–2. Hooks

HOOKS

Hooks used at sea (fig. 8–2) are of many different designs and are usually made of galvanised mild steel. They are generally much weaker than shackles of similar size.

The point of a hook is called the *bill*, the body is called the *shank*, and the bottom the *crown*; the part of the shank opposite the bill is the *back*; the *jaw* is the space between the bill and the top of the shank, and the *clear* is the inside diameter of the crown.

Types of hook

Cargo hook and Union hook. These hooks are very similar and they are made large enough in the clear to take the four legs of a sling without jamming them against one another. The projection fitted to the upper part of the shank acts as a guard to prevent the bill catching accidentally in a hatch coaming or some projection in its wake. The union hook is designed to take two whips.

Ram's-horn hook. This hook keeps the parts of a sling separated, and thus entirely eliminates the possibility of their jamming together.

Caliper hook or Clip hook. Used instead of a shackle in the sailing gear of some Service boats and in the rigging of signal yards. Its advantage over a shackle is that it has no bolt to rust up or get lost, but it must always be moused with line or yarn to prevent it from becoming unhooked.

Sheet hooks and Tack hooks. These hooks are also used with sailing gear; the corkscrew-shaped bill acts as a mousing to prevent accidental unhooking.

Coaling hook. Similar to a cargo hook, but has a spring tongue to prevent the legs of a sling from slipping off.

Can hooks. Extensively used in commercial practice, but seldom in the Royal Navy, for slinging drums and lifting casks.

Tackle hooks. General-purpose hooks made either with the eye in line with the hook, or with a 'reversed eye', i.e. one at right-angles to the hook.

Swivel hook. This hook is fitted with one or more swivels which prevent any twist in the whip being transmitted to the hook; without such a fitting the load would spin as the whip takes the weight and this might cause the splice of the whip to draw.

Spring hook. This hook has a mousing device, in the form of a spring-operated tongue, which prevents it from unhooking. Some other hooks have a link and forelock, for the same purpose.

Safety hook. This hook has a handle fitted with cheeks which close the jaw of the hook when the handle falls in place. Some hooks have a mousing shackle to prevent the hook from catching an obstruction.

Davey or Slip hooks. Designed for slipping a load in mid-air, or for slipping the eye of a hawser under strain. In the former type an eye is forged at the back of the hook to which a tripping line is secured; when the line is hauled upon, it up-ends the hook. The latter type, which is used in many tugs, is hinged at the crown and moused with a link and forelock; when the link is knocked off the pull of the hawser opens the hook.

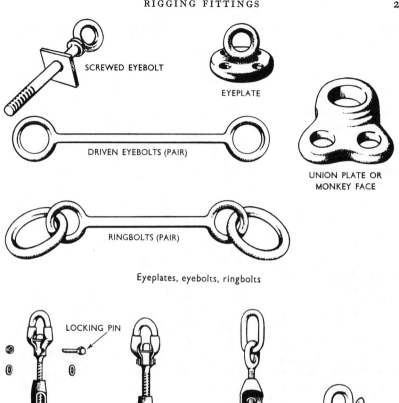

Eyeplates, eyebolts, ringbolts

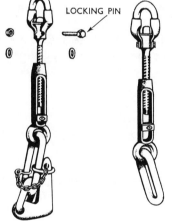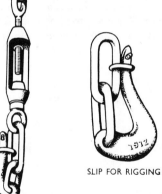

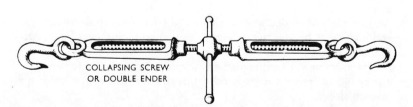

Rigging screws

FIG. 8-3. Rigging fittings

EYEPLATES, EYEBOLTS, DECK CLENCHES, RINGBOLTS AND UNION PLATES (fig. 8-3)

Eyeplates. These are of stamped steel and are used for securing an eye to a metal structure; they are either riveted or welded in place.

Eyebolts. Of wrought iron or mild steel, these are used for securing an eye to a wooden structure. They are of two types, the *screwed* type, which is by far the stronger of the two and in which the bolt is forced through a bored hole and held in place by a nut on its protruding end, and the *driven* type which is driven into the wood. Screwed eyebolts are supplied in pairs, and must be cut and threaded as required before use.

Deck clenches. Heavy metal fittings provided as anchorage points on the deck for standing rigging, hawsers or cables which may be subjected to heavy strains. They consist of a triangular piece of metal, which is bored with a hole to take the bolt of a shackle and fixed to a base plate which is clenched through the deck by four bolts in the same manner as a driven eyebolt. The base plates of the larger deck clenches are riveted to the deck plating or other structure.

Ringbolts. These are of wrought iron or mild steel and are used wherever it is required to fit a ring to a wooden structure, usually for making fast a rope. They consist of a screwed eyebolt with a ring or a link attached. Ringbolts are supplied in pairs, and must be cut and threaded as required before use.

Union plates. Triangular or square metal plates with a hole drilled at each corner. They are used as links for shackling the ends of three or four ropes or lengths of chain together; the triangular plates are usually known as *monkey faces* or *shamrock plates*.

RIGGING SCREWS (TURN-BUCKLES) AND RIGGING SLIP (fig. 8-3)

Rigging screws. Various kinds of rigging screws are used to *set up*, i.e. adjust for length or tension, any rigging equipment. They must not be confused with the turning-in screw, which is used to break-in a wire rope round a thimble and which is sometimes called a rigging screw. They are of the following types:

1. A screw fitting into an internally-threaded sleeve, with a swivel eye at the head of the screw and a standing eye on the sleeve.
2. A similar assembly, but with the swivel eye on the sleeve and the standing eye on the screw.
3. An internally-threaded sleeve with a right-handed screw taking into one end and a left-handed screw into the other, standing eyes being fitted at the head of each screw.
4. A central screw with a threaded sleeve taking on each end (one end having a left- and the other a right-handed thread) and with a standing eye fitted to each sleeve.

In (1) and (4) the length is adjusted by turning the screw (usually with a tommy bar) and in the others by turning the sleeve; after adjustment, simple locking devices are used to prevent the screw or sleeve from moving further.

Rigging screws in the Royal Navy comprise all four of these types, and they are known generally as *screws and slips*, *screws without slips*, or sometimes *bottle-screws*; type (4) is called a *double-ender*, or *collapsing screw*. Those issued for general purposes are of the first type described. In each type the screw is locked to the sleeve by a sliding block, and to the swivel eye at its head by a bolt taking into a slotted plate, as illustrated in fig. 8-3. In addition, screws of other types are issued for special purposes such as the adjustment of guardrails and davit guys. The collapsing screw is much more clumsy than the remainder, but can be designed with a longer travel. Bottle-screws are also used with the slips for securing an anchor in the hawse pipe.

Rigging slip. This is a quick-release link used for joining the end of a rope or a chain to a fitting when the end may have to be cast off frequently or rapidly.

BLOCKS

A block is a portable pulley, made of wood, metal, or wood and metal.

Parts of a block (fig. 8-4)

The main parts of a block are the *shell* or body; the *sheave* or wheel over which the rope runs; the *pin* on which the sheave turns; the *bush* or bearing between the sheave and the pin; and the eye, hook, strop or other fitting by which the block is secured in the required position.

The top of the block where the eye or hook is fitted is called the *crown*; the bottom of the block is the *arse* or *tail*; the sides of the shell are the *cheeks*, and the groove made in the cheeks of some blocks to take the strop is called the *score*; the opening between the sheave and shell through which the rope passes is the *swallow*; and the eye sometimes fitted at the tail is the *becket*.

Classification of blocks

Wooden blocks are classified by their size, which is their length from crown to tail measured round the shell; an ordinary wooden block will take a rope one-third of its size, so that a 9-inch block, for example, would be required for a 3-inch rope. Metal blocks are classified by the size of rope for which each is designed, which is marked on a plate affixed to one cheek. Blocks may have more than one sheave; a single block has one sheave, a double block two, a triple block three, and so on.

Types of block

Internal-bound (I.B.) block (fig. 8-4). This block has a shell partly of wood and partly of metal, and is the modern type of wooden block. The metal portion consists of a fork-shaped steel fitting, called the *binding*, which incorporates both the eye or hook and the becket when fitted; it also takes the pin of the sheave. The wooden portion, which is of elm, is really a fairing piece and takes no part of the load; it can be replaced on board if broken. External-bound blocks are used in commercial practice, but not in the Royal Navy.

Metal blocks (fig. 8-4). These blocks are supplied to the Royal Navy and are usually built up of steel plates and fittings. Like the I.B. blocks, their shells

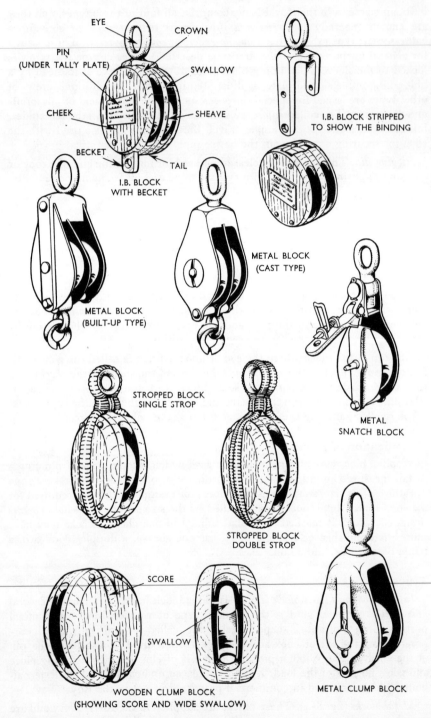

EYE

CROWN

PIN
(UNDER TALLY PLATE)

SWALLOW

CHEEK

SHEAVE

BECKET

TAIL

I.B. BLOCK
WITH BECKET

I.B. BLOCK STRIPPED
TO SHOW THE BINDING

METAL BLOCK
(CAST TYPE)

METAL BLOCK
(BUILT-UP TYPE)

STROPPED BLOCK
SINGLE STROP

METAL
SNATCH BLOCK

STROPPED BLOCK
DOUBLE STROP

SCORE

SWALLOW

WOODEN CLUMP BLOCK
(SHOWING SCORE AND WIDE SWALLOW)

METAL CLUMP BLOCK

FIG. 8–4. Blocks

have a binding which supplies the strength, but the cheeks, etc., are of light plating. The simplest pattern is the *gin block*, which consists of a binding carrying one large sheave, and a skeleton rope guard instead of cheeks. Some types of metal blocks, however, have their shells cast in one piece.

Metal blocks vary considerably in quality and finish, the better ones being manufactured for special purposes such as the upper blocks of boats' falls or the blocks of engineers' tackles. Some special-purpose blocks are made entirely of gunmetal or phosphor bronze, which do not corrode as easily as steel when exposed to weather and are not liable to cause sparks when working.

Snatch blocks (fig. 8–4). These are single blocks, either of metal or internal-bound, in which part of the shell is hinged to allow a bight of rope to be inserted into the swallow from one side. They should not be used when a solid block is suitable for the job. They should NEVER be used when the safety of life depends on them.

Common blocks. These blocks, which are slowly going out of service, have shells made entirely of elm. They are the old-fashioned type of wooden block, which is held in position by a strop passed round its shell and seized into a thimble-eye at the crown; the strop thus strengthens the shell and the block.

Clump block (fig. 8–4). This block can be of wood or metal and it has an exceptionally large swallow. The wooden clump block is made in a similar manner to the common block, but it will take a rope of half its own size; a 6-in. clump block, for example, will take a 3-in. rope. Wooden clump blocks are used on lower booms to support the bights of the boat ropes, and metal clump blocks are usually designed to take chain.

Fiddle blocks. These are double blocks, usually of metal, in which the sheaves are carried one above the other instead of side by side. Though not supplied in the Royal Navy, they are used in the Merchant Navy where a double block is required but where there is either insufficient lateral room for the normal type or where it is desired to separate the parts of the fall with which the block is rove.

Sheaves and bearings

The sheaves of all wooden blocks are of phosphor bronze, and those of metal blocks are either of phosphor bronze or mild steel. Phosphor bronze sheaves are the more expensive, but are desirable where the blocks are exposed to corrosion, as in boats' falls and engineers' tackles, or where sparking may be dangerous, as in ammunition hoists. The pins of all blocks are of steel.

The bearing between the sheaves and the pin may be of the plain, roller or self-lubricating type. In accordance with common engineering practice a mild steel sheave with a plain bearing has a small brass bush let into its centre to form the bearing, because steel bearing on steel is liable to seize. Roller bearings are fitted in a number of special metal blocks, including most of those used for boats' falls. Self-lubricating bearings have a perforated bronze bush next to the pin, the perforations being filled with a special lubricant. They are used in the Royal Navy for some derricks and in boat-hoisting machinery.

Means of attaching

Every block, except a stropped block, has a fitting at its crown by which to secure it where required. A list of such fittings is given below:

1. A standing eye in line with the sheave.
2. A standing eye at right-angles to the sheave (reversed).
3. A standing eye at right-angles to the sheave, with a free hook.
4. A swivel eye.
5. A swivel hook.
6. A swivel eye and a free hook.
7. A jaw in line with the sheave.
8. A jaw at right angles to the sheave.

NOTES

(i) A *jaw* is a fork-shaped fitting by which a block can be suspended and at the same time kept from turning; it is fitted to the upper blocks of some boats' falls.

(ii) All blocks fitted with a swivel at the crown are called *swivel blocks*.

(iii) As a general rule 1, 2 and 4 I.B. blocks have an oval eye for which a shackle is required, whereas similar metal blocks have a shackle permanently fixed in the eye.

Description

A block is fully described as follows:

1. Size (wooden blocks only).
2. Number of sheaves.
3. Type (I.B., common, steel, etc.), with details of sheaves sometimes included.
4. Size and type of rope (metal blocks only).
5. Means of attachment (standing eye, swivel hook, etc.).
6. Pattern number.

EXAMPLES

1. A 12-in., double I.B. block, fitted with swivel oval eye and becket, pattern 281.

2. A treble steel block with mild steel sheaves for 3-in. cordage, fitted with a standing eye reversed, free hook, becket and thimble, pattern 5124A.

Strength of blocks

The safe working loads of blocks are dealt with more fully in Volume II, but in general it can be said that an I.B., a metal, or a common block is stronger than the rope for which it is designed. A snatch block is about one-third of the strength of an I.B. block used for the same size of rope; a clump block is about one-quarter of the strength of such a block. Every block has its safe working load shown on a plate fixed to one cheek.

PURCHASES AND TACKLES

A purchase is a mechanical device by means of which an applied pull or force is increased; it may be a system of levers, a system of revolving drums or wheels geared to one another, or a combination of blocks or pulleys rove with rope or chain.

A tackle (pronounced 'taycle') is a purchase consisting of a rope rove through two or more blocks in such a way that any pull applied to its hauling part is increased by an amount depending upon the number of sheaves in the blocks and the manner in which the rope is rove through them.

Parts of a tackle (fig. 8–5)

The blocks of a tackle are termed the *standing block* and *moving block*; the rope rove through them is called the *fall*, which has its *standing, running* and *hauling* parts. The size of a tackle is described by the size of its fall; a 3-in. luff, for example, would be rove with a 3-in. fall.

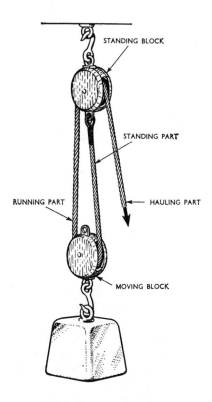

STANDING BLOCK

STANDING PART

RUNNING PART

HAULING PART

MOVING BLOCK

FIG. 8–5. Parts of a tackle

Mechanical advantage

The amount by which the pull on the hauling part is multiplied by the tackle is called its mechanical advantage (M.A.) and, if friction is disregarded, this is equal to the number of parts of the fall at the *moving* block. In fig. 8–6 for example, there are two parts at the moving block, therefore the mechanical advantage is two; in other words, a pull on the hauling part of 1 cwt would, if friction were disregarded, hold a weight of 2 cwt.

Friction, which occurs in the bearings of the sheaves and in the fall as it bends round the sheaves, reduces the mechanical advantage considerably; this loss through friction is explained on page 219.

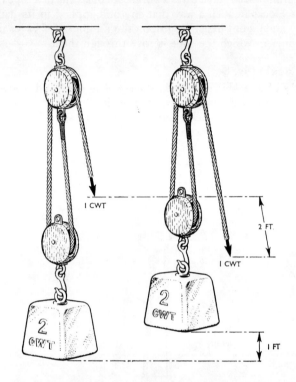

F IG. 8–6. Mechanical advantage and velocity ratio of a tackle

Velocity ratio

Mechanical advantage is gained only at the expense of the speed of working. In fig. 8–6, for example, the weight will only be raised one foot for every two feet of movement of the hauling part. The ratio between the distance moved by the hauling part and that moved by the moving block is known as the velocity ratio (V.R.) and is always equal to the number of parts of the fall at the *moving* block.

Reeving a tackle to advantage and to disadvantage

The number of parts at the moving block, and therefore the mechanical advantage, is always greater when the hauling part comes away from the moving block, and such a tackle is said to be *rove to advantage*. Conversely, a tackle in which the hauling part comes away from the standing block is said to

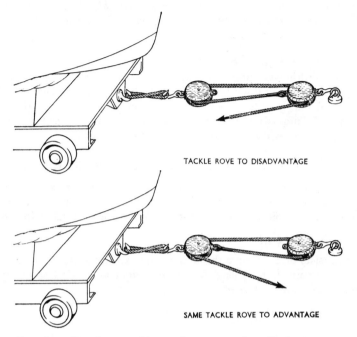

TACKLE ROVE TO DISADVANTAGE

SAME TACKLE ROVE TO ADVANTAGE

FIG. 8–7. Reeving a tackle to advantage and to disadvantage

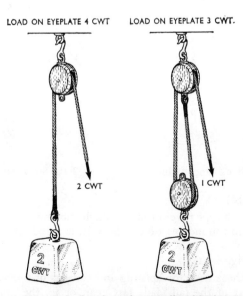

LOAD ON EYEPLATE 4 CWT   LOAD ON EYEPLATE 3 CWT.

2 CWT

I CWT

FIG. 8–8. Load on the standing block

8+M.S. I

be *rove to disadvantage* (see fig. 8–7). *Where practicable, therefore, rig a tackle so that the hauling part leads from the moving block, and make the block with the greater number of sheaves the moving block.*

Load on the standing block (fig. 8–8)

The load on the standing block, and therefore on the fitting to which it is attached, is dependant upon the mechanical advantage of the tackle used. This load is calculated by adding the pull required on the hauling part to the weight which is being moved; and so for a given weight the greater the mechanical advantage the less will be the load on the standing block.

EXAMPLES OF TACKLES AND PURCHASES

Examples of whips, tackles and purchases used at sea, together with their velocity ratios and mechanical advantages, are given below; in each the approximate loss of mechanical advantage due to friction has been taken into account.

Single whip (fig. 8–9)

This consists of a fall rove through a single standing block; no mechanical advantage is gained. It is used for hoisting light loads, and where speed of hoisting is an important factor.

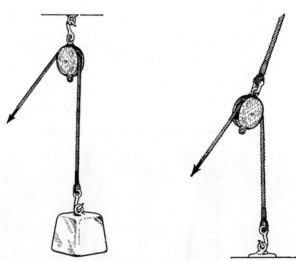

FIG. 8–9. Single whip   FIG. 8–10. Runner

Runner (fig. 8–10)

This consists of a rope rove through a single moving block. As there are two parts of the fall in the moving block, the V.R. is 2 and its M.A. is 1·82.

Double whip (fig. 8–11)

This is a purchase used for hoisting and consists of two single blocks with the standing part of the fall made fast near, or to, the upper block, and it cannot be rove to advantage. Its V.R. is 2 and its M.A. is 1·67.

Gun tackle (fig. 8–12)

This is the term usually applied to a purchase consisting of two single blocks, but which is not used for hoisting; it cannot then be called a double whip, as this term is applied only when it is used for hoisting. In the gun tackle the standing part of the fall is always made fast to one of the blocks. The name originates from the small tackle which was used to run out the old muzzle-loading gun carriages after they had recoiled. The V.R. is 3 if rove to advantage, and 2 if rove to disadvantage, and its M.A. is 2·5 and 1·67 respectively.

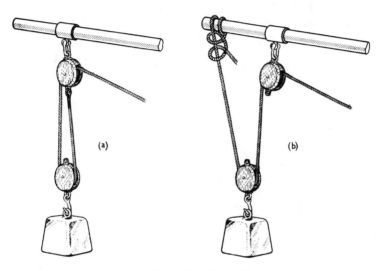

(a) (b)

FIG. 8–11. Double whip

FIG. 8–12. Gun tackle

Luff (fig. 8–13)

This is a purchase of 3 in. in size or greater. It consists of a double and a single block, with the standing part of the fall made fast to the single block. Its V.R. is 4 if rove to advantage, and 3 if rove to disadvantage, and its M.A. is 3·08 and 2·3 respectively.

Jigger

This is similar to a luff, but of from 2 in. to 2½ in. in size.

Handy billy

This is a small tackle of less than 2 in. in size; it is usually rove as a jigger, but can be rove as a small gun tackle.

FIG. 8–13. Luff

FIG. 8–14. Two-fold purchase

Two-fold purchase (fig. 8–14)

This consists of two double blocks and is a useful general-purpose tackle. Its V.R. is 5 if rove to advantage, and 4 if rove to disadvantage, and its M.A. is 3·57 and 2·26 respectively.

Three-fold purchase (fig. 8–15)

This consists of two treble blocks; its V.R. is 7 if rove to advantage, and 6 if rove to disadvantage, and its M.A. is 4·37 and 3·75 respectively. It is used mainly in boats' falls.

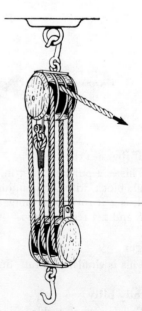

FIG. 8–15. Three-fold purchase

Tackles having more than three sheaves to a block, such as the four-fold, five-fold and six-fold purchases, are not provided as upper deck tackles because they are too cumbersome to handle efficiently and because the friction in their sheaves considerably reduces their gain in mechanical advantage. If additional mechanical advantage is required it is better to combine two simple tackles.

Luff upon luff (fig. 8–16)

This is a general term used to describe the combined use of two tackles in which the moving block on one is clapped on to the hauling part of the other; its mechanical advantage is the product of the mechanical advantage of each tackle. Fig. 8–16 shows two luffs rove to advantage and as a luff upon luff, whose V.R. $= 4 \times 4 = 16$; its M.A. is $9 \cdot 49$.

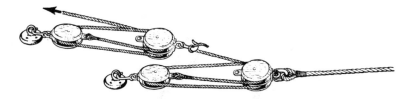

FIG. 8–16. Luff upon luff

Runner and tackle (fig. 8–17)

This is a tackle with its moving block made fast to the hauling part of a runner. The velocity ratio of the runner and tackle illustrated is $2 \times 4 = 8$, and the mechanical advantage is $1 \cdot 82 \times 3 \cdot 08 = 5 \cdot 61$.

Five-part or three-and-two tackle

This consists of one triple and one double block, the standing part being made fast to the double block. This tackle is found in H.M. ships and is sometimes used in boats' falls.

Dutchman's purchase (fig. 8–18)

This is a tackle used in reverse to take advantage of the velocity ratio of the tackle; an example of its use is to drive a light whip at a fast speed from a slow but powerful capstan. In the example illustrated in fig. 8–18, the whip would move a distance of 5 ft for every foot travelled by the moving block. When using a tackle in this manner the pull exerted by the capstan must be equal to the product of the weight to be hoisted and the velocity ratio of the tackle, plus the friction in the tackle and its leading blocks; in this case a pull of at least $5\frac{3}{5}$ times the weight to be hoisted. Make sure that the tackle and its pendant are strong enough for the job.

Friction in a tackle

When a tackle is being worked considerable friction is set up, both in the bearings of the blocks and within the fall as it bends round the sheaves. This friction accounts for the difference between the velocity ratio of the tackle and its mechanical advantage, as shown in the examples of tackles already described. The general approximate rule for estimating the amount of friction is to allow

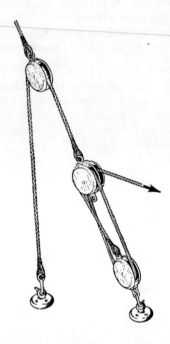

FIG. 8–17. Runner and tackle

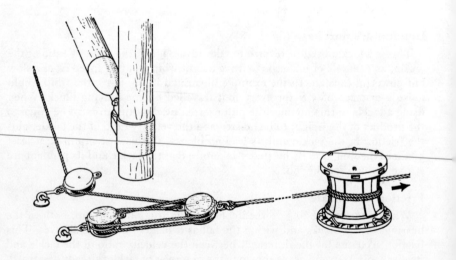

FIG. 8–18. Dutchman's purchase

from one-tenth to one-eighth of the weight to be hoisted for each sheave of the tackle according to whether the tackle is well made and in good condition or of poor quality and badly maintained.

To estimate the pull required on the hauling part of any tackle to hoist a given weight, divide the weight by the mechanical advantage of the tackle. Conversely, the weight which can be hoisted by a given pull on the hauling part of a tackle can be found by multiplying the pull by the mechanical advantage of the tackle.

When holding or lowering a load with a tackle, the friction will take part of the weight, and the force required on the hauling part is less than that required to hoist the load.

NOTES

(i) The above statements are approximate and no block is to be used for lifting loads greater than the safe working load shown on it unless special approval has been obtained.

(ii) The effects of friction in tackles and purchases are more fully described in Volume II.

MASTS AND SPARS

In merchant ships supports are needed for the derricks, and masts have developed in size, shape, number and strength according to the weights to be lifted and the number of holds. Nowadays the conventional mast is very much less in evidence. Masting for merchant ships generally is more in the form of a series of pairs of king-posts (or samson posts, or derrick posts) designed to function in connection purely with the cargo-handling facilities. The additional masting required for carrying steaming lights, signalling apparatus, radio aerials, etc. is readily met by the provision of light topmasts at the head of ordinary derrick masts, or on the cross bracing platform between the heads of king-posts. It is fairly common practice to erect a light polemast above the navigating bridge structure. The heavy masts and king-posts are of tubular steel construction with steel wire shrouds and stays as necessary, and provision is made for additional stays to be rigged when heavy lifts are undertaken. Steel vertical ladders are secured directly to the masts and derrick posts for access purposes. Bipod masts are fitted in some new merchant ships.

THE CONVENTIONAL MAST

This mast (fig. 8–19) is described here because most of the terms, although based on the sailing ship mast, are used today in sailing craft and to a lesser extent in modern power-driven ships.

Parts of a mast and mast fittings

A mast is made in either one or two pieces; if made in two pieces the lower one is called the *lowermast* and the upper the *topmast*; if made in one piece the mast is called a *polemast*, and if particularly tall the upper part is called the

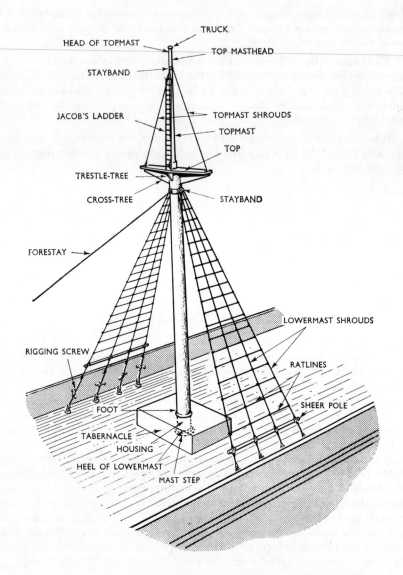

FIG. 8-19. The conventional mast

topmast and the lower part the lowermast. The top of a mast is called the *head* and the bottom is called the *heel*.

A mast is said to be *stepped*, i.e. supported, at the place where its heel rests. A polemast or a lowermast may be stepped on the ship's keelson, on one of her lower decks, or on her upper deck; a topmast is stepped at the head of its lowermast. Where a mast passes through a deck, the deck round the *mast-hole* is strengthened by girders and beams called *mast partners*, and the mast is secured in the hole by wedges. The mast-hole in the weather deck is made watertight by a canvas cover called the *mast coat*, which fits snugly round the mast and its hole.

The heel of a mast stepped on the upper deck is fitted into a box-like structure called a *tabernacle*, which supports the lower part of the mast. The masts of river-going vessels which are stepped in tabernacles may be hinged so that they can be canted aft or laid on deck when the vessels have to pass under low bridges. For the same purpose a topmast is fitted so that it can be lowered and secured alongside its lowermast, in which position it is said to be *housed*; but if it is sent right down on deck it is said to be *struck*.

A mast, whether a polemast, a lowermast or a topmast, is divided into three parts known as the *housing*, the *hounding* and the *masthead*. The housing of a lowermast is that part which extends from its heel to the upper deck or the top of its tabernacle; the housing of a topmast is that part which extends from its heel to the head of its lowermast. The hounding is that part which extends from the top of the housing to a position some distance below the head where the standing rigging is secured. The masthead extends from the top of the hounding to the head of the mast, that of a lowermast being called the *lower masthead*, and that of a topmast being called the *top masthead*. The lower part of the hounding of a lowermast just above the upper deck is called the *foot*. In a polemast there is neither a lower masthead nor a topmast housing, the part above the position to which the topmast rigging is secured being called simply the masthead.

Where a topmast is fitted the lower ends of its standing rigging may be secured to athwartship and fore-and-aft cross-pieces which are fitted to the lower masthead and called respectively *cross-trees* and *trestle-trees*; these are supported by brackets called *cheeks*, and over them is built a platform called a *top*.

On the head of a lowermast is fitted a band called the *mast cap*, to which is hinged a hoop called the *trunnion hoop* through which the foot of the topmast is stepped. At the upper end of the hounding of a mast is fitted a metal hoop called a *stayband*, which has a number of eyes to which the upper ends of the standing rigging are shackled. A wooden disc called a *truck* is fitted to the head of a topmast or a polemast; it is usually provided with one or two small sheaves to take signal halyards.

Wooden masts and yards are provided with lightning conductors consisting of copper strips running their entire length and connected to the steel hull of the ship; special contacts between mast and mast, and mast and yard, are provided where necessary.

Mast spars

A spar which is crossed horizontally athwart a mast is called a *yard*, and a spar projecting aft from a mainmast and cocked up at an angle of about 45 degrees with the mast is called a *gaff*; yards are used to carry signal halyards and wireless aerials, and a gaff is used for wearing an ensign. The booms fitted at the foot of most merchant ships' masts and used for working cargo are called *derricks*.

Some masts may be fitted with *spurs*, which are steel arms of varying sizes projecting horizontally from the mast and used for carrying signal halyards or

8*

the gantlines for hoisting oil navigation lights and other gear into place. Brackets are provided on the foremast and the mainmast at the prescribed height above the upper deck for carrying, respectively, the fore and main steaming lights.

Standing rigging

A mast, except one of the plated, tripod and lattice types, is stayed, i.e. supported in position by its standing rigging; this consists of *forestays* and *backstays* which support it in a fore-and-aft direction, and *shrouds* which support it athwartships. The component parts of standing rigging are named after the mast they support, e.g. *fore-topmast backstay*. The upper ends of the standing rigging are shackled to their stayband and the lower ends are fitted with rigging screws so that the rigging can be set up taut. Lowermast standing rigging is secured to the gunwales or the weather decks; topmast rigging may be secured either to the cross-trees and trestle-trees of its lowermast or to the weather decks.

Insulators are fitted in all standing wire rope rigging to prevent electrical interference with radio and radar installations. The positions of these insulators must not be altered, as they are correctly determined by technical officers of the Admiralty.

The shrouds of a lowermast are led each side to the gunwales; and, being led slightly abaft the mast as well as abreast it, they serve to some extent as backstays. The forestay of a fore-lowermast is usually led to the eyes of the ship, and its backstays (if fitted) are led abaft the shrouds each side to the gunwales. The forestay of a main-lowermast is usually led to a position on the upper deck well before the mast and on the midship line, and the backstay is led to the stern.

The topmast is a comparatively light spar and is therefore not so heavily stayed as the lowermast. The shrouds of a topmast usually serve the double purpose of shrouds and backstays, and are led to the ends of the cross-trees. If backstays are fitted they can be led either to the deck in the same way as those of the lowermast, or to the after end of the trestle-trees. If a forestay is fitted it can be led to the deck in the same way as that of the lowermast, or to the fore end of the trestle-trees.

After the shrouds and stays have been set up taut their rigging screws are locked, packed with grease, parcelled with canvas strips and fitted with laced canvas covers called *gaiters*.

When the ship rolls, or when a heavy weight is slung outboard from a mast derrick, the shrouds on one side may slacken owing to the mast working slightly. To support the upper ends of the rigging screws and keep them in their correct relative positions when this occurs a horizontal steel rod called a *sheerpole* is usually fitted; it is seized to each shroud just above its rigging screw, and this serves also to keep turns out of the shrouds when the rigging screws are being set up.

Above the sheerpole, at intervals of about 15 in., the shrouds may be joined by a number of light horizontal lines called *ratlines*; the shrouds then form a ladder, of which the ratlines are the rungs, for use when going aloft. The operation of fitting ratlines is known as *rattling down*, because originally it was begun at the masthead and continued downwards, but the modern practice is to rattle upwards from the sheerpole. In many ships no ratlines are fitted and the mast is then climbed by a Jacob's ladder leading up the mast, or by means of steel rungs fitted to the side of the mast and projecting slightly from it.

Running rigging

In the days of sail the running rigging of a full-rigged ship was very complex and included, for example, *halyards* for hoisting and lowering the yards and sails, *sheets* for trimming the sails, *braces* for slewing the yards and *lifts* for squaring them, together with the various tackles for working them. Nowadays the running rigging on a mast is comparatively simple and consists chiefly of signal *halyards* and *dressing lines*, which are described below, and the rigging required to work a mast derrick, which is described later.

Signal halyards. These are made of plaited Terylene and rove through sheaves in the truck or the masthead, or through gunmetal blocks on a yard, spur or gaff. Their ends are fitted with *Inglefield clips* which are specially designed to enable flags to be quickly bent on to the halyard. A signal halyard is named from the position at which it is rove, e.g. masthead halyard, and starboard yard-arm halyard.

Gantlines. These are made of cordage, of small-size wire rope or of chain, and are rove through blocks on the masts or funnels. They are used for hoisting gear aloft and can be kept permanently rigged, and as they often have to bear the weight of a man they must be inspected frequently. Examples of gantlines are *clothes lines*, which are used for hoisting washed clothes to dry, and the *mast rope* for hoisting a man or material to the masthead.

Dressing lines. These are used on ceremonial occasions for 'dressing ship', i.e. for hoisting flags bent at close intervals on lines which, in a two-masted ship, run from the stem to the fore-masthead, thence to the main-masthead and thence to the stern. They consist of wire rope lines to which the dressing flags are permanently bent, and are tailed with cordage whips for hoisting them into position. The foremost line is called the *fore-down*, the amidships line is called the *fore-to-main*, and the after one the *main-down*. Ships with a single mast are fitted with a fore-down and a main-down only.

SPARS

Yards

Most modern yards are firmly secured to the mast and do not need standing and running rigging to keep them squared off. But there are a few *slung* yards in service and one will be described briefly, because some of the terms are common to all yards.

A slung yard (fig. 8–20) is supported at its centre or *bunt* by a shackle called the *sling*, which joins the eye of an iron band round the yard, called the *parrel band*, to the eye of an iron band round the mast, called the *mast band*. The yard is kept horizontal by *lifts* and is kept from slewing by *braces*. The ends of the yard outside the braces and lifts are called the *yard-arms*, and the parts of the yard between the bunt and the yard-arms are called the *quarters*. The bunt of some slung yards may be kept close against the mast by a strop called a *parrel*, which is passed round the mast and secured to eyes welded to the parrel band.

A *jackstay* and *footropes* are rigged along the yard to provide, respectively, hand-hold and foot-hold for men working on it, but these are not fitted on smaller yards if the lifts are within reach from the mast. The footrope is supported at intervals by *stirrups*.

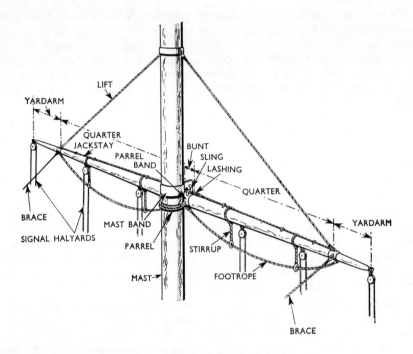

FIG. 8–20. A slung yard

Gaffs

A gaff in a sailing vessel is a wooden spar used to support the head of a four-sided fore-and-aft sail; it is therefore rigged with halyards for raising and lowering it, and its lower end is fitted with jaws which fit round the mast and thus allow it to slew sideways or be topped up or down. A gaff in a modern ship, however, is used only for wearing the ensign conspicuously, and is therefore rigged as a standing gaff in the manner described below and illustrated in fig. 8–21.

The lower end or *throat* of the gaff is fitted with an eyed metal sleeve called a *gooseneck*, which is bolted to a fork-shaped fitting pivoted at the upper end of the main-lowermast hounding; the gaff is thus supported at its throat by a joint which is hinged both horizontally and vertically. The gaff is also supported by a *standing topping lift* consisting of a pendant shackled to a *spider band* fitted round the middle of the gaff, the other end being shackled to a fitting on the after end of the main-lowermast trestle-trees; the length of the pendant is such that the gaff is held at an angle of about 45 degrees with the mast. The gaff is stayed from slewing sideways by two *vangs*, which are shackled to the spider band and brought down to each side of the after superstructure. To the upper end or *peak* of the gaff is fitted a gunmetal block through which is rove the peak halyard. In some ships with lattice masts the vangs and topping lift are steel struts welded to the lattice.

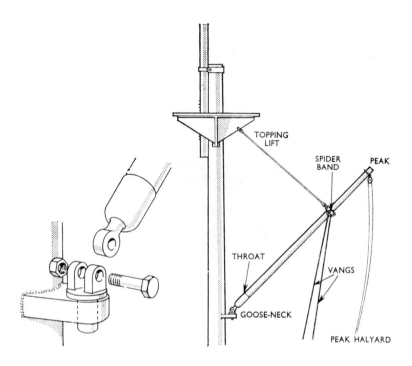

FIG. 8–21. A gaff and (inset) a gooseneck

WARSHIPS' MASTS

The conventional mast existed in warships, mainly for flag signalling purposes, until the First World War, when the need for increased arcs of gunfire and the need to house many gun control personnel above the gun smoke caused the introduction of *tripod* masts. The foremast supported a structure called the 'fore top', while the mainmast supported the main derrick, which was used for hoisting the boom boats. Both masts had topmasts and yards for signal halyards and wireless aerials.

During the Second World War both masts were used to carry radar aerials and the number of yards decreased as radio and daylight signalling lamps replaced flag signalling for communication. When the number of radar aerials increased, particularly in small ships, a *lattice* mast of lighter and stronger construction was introduced and wooden yards were replaced by fixed steel yards.

A later trend is for masts to be plated. This has the advantage not only of providing the extra strength to carry heavier and more complex aerials, but the space inside can be used for radar offices, etc.

FIG. 8–22. A lattice mast

Precautions when going aloft

Radio and radar aerials often carry very high voltages, and radar aerials are liable to move without warning. Permission must be obtained from the Officer of the Watch before any man goes aloft, or works near an aerial, and he must report when the work is completed. Before permission is granted, the necessary precautions are taken to ensure that all aerials are safe and cannot rotate.

DERRICKS AND WINCHES

Derricks

A derrick is a spar, made of wood or steel, rigged as a swinging boom and used for hoisting boats, stores, cargo, ammunition or gear in and out of a ship. It can be fitted to a mast or a kingpost, when it is called a *mast derrick*, or to the side of a ship's superstructure, when it is called a *screen derrick*. The lower end or *heel* is pivoted in a similar manner to that of the throat of a gaff, thus allowing the derrick to pivot both vertically and horizontally. The upper end or *head* is supported by a topping lift and stayed by guys. The load is hoisted or lowered by a whip or a purchase, which is rove through a block at the derrick head and a leading block at the heel and then taken to a winch.

The rig of a derrick varies considerably in detail according to the purpose for which it is provided, the weight it is designed to hoist, and the position in which it is fitted. A simple mast derrick as fitted in merchant ships is illustrated in fig. 8–23. The topping lift and guys are shackled to a spider band at the

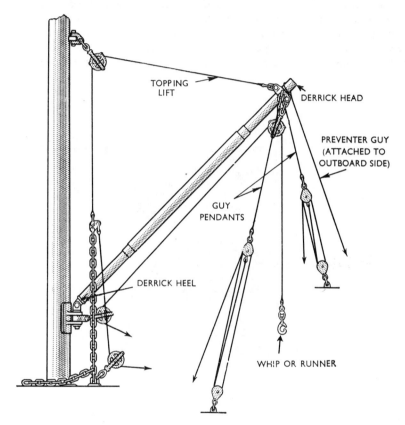

FIG. 8–23. A mast derrick

derrick head. The topping lift of a mast derrick is usually led to the masthead, and that of a screen derrick to a point on the superstructure directly above the heel of the derrick; the guys are led to positions on deck near the ship's side and well before and abaft the heel. Topping lifts are of two main kinds, *standing* and *working*. Guys usually take the form of short pendants tailed with tackles; two are usually fitted, but heavy derricks may be fitted with as many as four; some derricks are provided with standing guys called *preventer guys*, which are fitted to prevent the derrick from swinging too far in a certain direction.

Cargo derricks and methods of working them are described in more detail in Volume II.

Winches

A winch in its simplest form is a reel which can be turned in either direction by hand cranks. The mechanical advantage gained by this machine depends upon the diameter of the winch drum and the length of the crank arms: the smaller the drum and the longer the crank arm the greater will be the mechanical advantage, and this can be further increased by incorporating gearing between the cranks and the drum. The end of the winch rope is secured to one end of the drum, and the rope is wound on the drum as it is rotated; care should always be taken to ensure that the rope is wound on right across the drum, so that each new turn lies snugly against the last. Hand winches (fig. 8–24) are always provided with a pawl and ratchet wheel on the crank shaft to prevent the winch from taking charge if the load becomes too heavy to hold by hand; the pawl should always be engaged when the winch is used for hoisting.

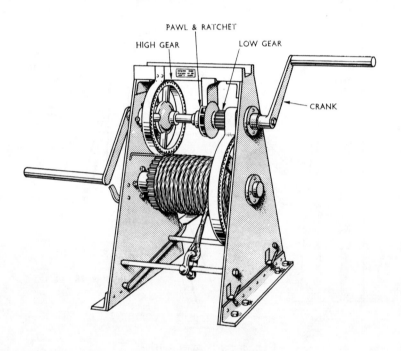

FIG. 8–24. A hand winch

Power-driven winches, which are mostly electrically-driven in modern merchant ships, differ widely in design. Various forms of drive, clutch and brake are fitted, depending on the use for which the winch is intended, e.g. cargo work, minesweeping. They are usually provided with two *warping drums* driven off the winch motor and fitted one on each side of the main drum; these are used for hauling ropes, hawsers and the running rigging of the derrick (fig. 8–25).

To bring a rope to a warping drum take two turns of the rope round the drum in the required direction and back up the hauling part as it comes off the drum; two turns should be sufficient for the rope to grip the drum, but if the load is heavy or the rope slips a third turn should be taken. As the rope passes round the drum the turns have a tendency to ride from the middle towards one end; this tendency is counteracted by the load on the rope forcing the turns down the curve to the narrowest part of the drum. To hold the rope stationary while the drum is heaving in, ease the pull on the hauling part sufficiently to

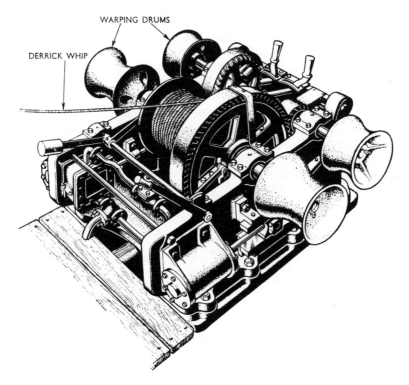

FIG. 8–25. A steam winch

allow the turns to slip, or *surge*, round the drum; when the drum is veering, however, do not surge the rope, because you may then lose control of it. Never allow riding turns to develop on a warping drum, because if this happens control of the rope is lost unless the drum is stopped.

BOOMS

Booms are fixed or swinging spars rigged horizontally from ships' masts or structures. Boat booms are rigged from the ship's side at the after end of the forecastle port and starboard, on the quarter port and starboard or right aft projecting aft. These booms are known respectively as *lower booms*, *quarter booms* and the *stern boom*.

In the days of sail the lower studding sail booms were rigged as boat booms, hence *lower boom*. The rigging of the lower boom is illustrated in fig. 8–26. Quarter booms have a similar rig, but are shorter. The stern boom is generally fitted as an alternative to the quarter booms. If it is secured by steel clamps to the quarter deck it has no guys. A life-line is rigged from the ensign staff stanchion.

Lizards, boatrope blocks and Jacob's ladders (fig. 8–26) are shackled to thimbles seized into wire grommets fitted round the booms. Boat's painters can be secured to the eyes at the ends of the lizards, lazy painters to the ladders; but heavy boats are secured to the wire strops at the end of boatropes. Boatropes provide a spring and take the snatch off the boom in a seaway. The heaviest boats should be secured to the boatrope that is closer to the spider band.

Booms are swung out and in by rigging runners or tackles to the eyes spliced into the guys. Eyes are provided at both ends of the boom for lifting it inboard. It is customary for the booms to be swung out as the anchor is let go, or by order on the pipe or bugle when securing to a buoy or jetty. Booms are fully rigged beforehand, except for boatropes, but the gear must not show outboard while the ship is under way.

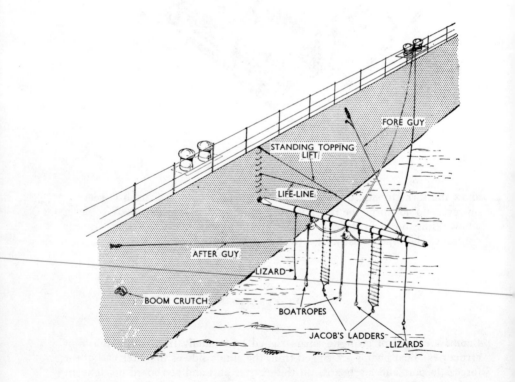

FIG. 8–26. A lower boom

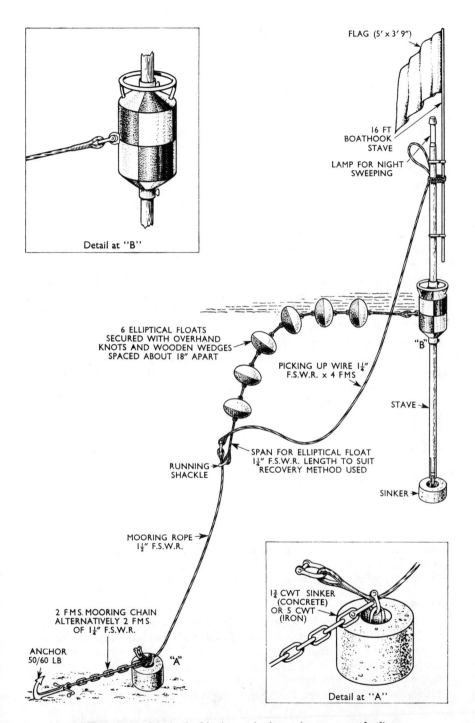

FLAG (5' x 3' 9")

16 FT
BOATHOOK
STAVE

LAMP FOR NIGHT
SWEEPING

Detail at "B"

6 ELLIPTICAL FLOATS
SECURED WITH OVERHAND
KNOTS AND WOODEN WEDGES
SPACED ABOUT 18" APART

PICKING UP WIRE 1¼"
F.S.W.R. x 4 FMS

"B"

STAVE

SPAN FOR ELLIPTICAL FLOAT
1¼" F.S.W.R. LENGTH TO SUIT
RECOVERY METHOD USED

RUNNING
SHACKLE

SINKER

MOORING ROPE
1½" F.S.W.R.

2 FMS. MOORING CHAIN
ALTERNATIVELY 2 FMS.
OF 1¼" F.S.W.R.

1¾ CWT SINKER
(CONCRETE)
OR 5 CWT
(IRON)

ANCHOR
50/60 LB

"A"

Detail at "A"

FIG. 8–27. Method of laying a danbuoy (*see text overleaf*)

DANBUOYS

Danbuoys are used extensively in minesweeping operations to mark out an area or channel as it is searched or cleared. They are part of each minesweeper's outfit, but can be used by any vessel for temporarily buoying a position. Full details of the methods of laying and lifting various types of danbuoy, and how they are rigged, are given in the *Minesweeping Manual*, but a short description of the standard danbuoy, and one method of lifting and laying it, are given here.

Standard danbuoy (fig. 8–27)

The standard danbuoy consists of a cylindrical can with a circular lifting becket, sloping top and a tube through the centre to take the danbuoy stave, which is clamped in position by two screw bolts, one at each end of the tube. Unmodified cans have 'jug handle' lifting beckets.

The danbuoy stave is fitted with a metal U-shaped bracket at the bottom for securing a $\frac{1}{2}$-cwt sinker, and a metal ferrule at the top for securing a lamp for night sweeping. A boathook stave is lashed or clamped to the top of the stave to carry a size 4 flag (which may have radar reflecting copper gauze stitched into it) or a radar reflector, which should be secured to the can with a line so that the reflector is not lost if the stave breaks.

Dan moorings. Mooring wires are supplied in lengths of 2, 5, 10, 20 and 50 fathoms of $1\frac{1}{4}$-in. F.S.W.R. with a thimble eye in each end. The weight of the mooring rope is supported by a number of metal elliptical floats (or *fishermen's pellets*) which are rove on their own wire span about 18 in. apart. The span is secured to the mooring rope with a running shackle and to the lug on the side of the can. Six floats are normally used, but more may be needed in deep water or strong tides.

The danbuoy is anchored to the bottom by a $1\frac{3}{4}$-cwt concrete (or 5-cwt iron) sinker backed by a 50/60-lb Admiralty pattern anchor on the end of two fathoms of chain.

Laying

Having assembled the buoy and mooring as shown in fig. 8–27, lash the buoy (flag foremost) outside the rails on the quarter. Place the sinker and anchor outside the rails abaft the buoy. Shortly before reaching the dropping position, stream the mooring rope, then throw the buoy clear of the ship's side. At the dropping position push the sinker and anchor over the side.

Lifting

The danbuoy is always approached head to wind and tide and the pellets are grappled from the forecastle or amidships with the ship stopped. The buoy is then hauled close and hoisted by a whip hooked to the lifting becket until the picking-up rope can be cut loose. A messenger is then hooked into the end of the picking-up rope, brought to a drum and the mooring rope hove in. The pellets are unshackled and the buoy brought inboard.

Questions on this chapter will be found in Appendix 2.

CHAPTER 9

Ships' Boats

This chapter is divided into five sections to describe the types and classes of ships' boats, their construction and equipment, rigs, stowages and methods of slinging and disengaging. A detailed description is given of the Montague whaler and 32 ft sloop-rigged cutter because, although being replaced at sea by the motor whaler, they are still used for training. Power boats (other than the motor whaler), the 27 ft surf boat and inflatable boats are described in Volume II.

A warship's boats are of several different types and are used on many different duties. All power boats have diesel engines to reduce the risk of fire. All warships' boats, except some boats used for a survey, are capable of floating with an adequate reserve of buoyancy should they become swamped. When in harbour a warship's boats are used for embarking, disembarking and transferring mail, stores, armed parties, working parties, fire parties, libertymen, passengers and visitors; also for mooring, laying out the ship's anchors, laying down buoys for salvage work, for training and for recreation such as regattas and picnics. They are supplemented by boats of the Port Auxiliary Service as necessary; these boats are shore-based and are not fitted for hoisting on board.

When at sea a warship's boats are used for rescue, as in man-overboard, for transferring men and stores to and from another ship, for boarding a ship with an armed boarding party, and for landing and embarking personnel and stores from beaches. For work on open beaches, special boats such as landing craft and surf boats are sometimes used; and special boats are also used for surveying, mine clearance, minehunting and other specific duties.

Merchant ships' boats are generally used only as lifeboats, their prime function being to save the lives of passengers and crew in the event of shipwreck or fire. Any transport facilities required by a merchant ship when in port but not berthed alongside are usually provided by special tenders and shore boats; but certain cruise ships and others trading to ports with limited facilities carry their own special launches, which are sometimes dual-purpose. In a few ships, recreational dinghies and painting punts are carried in addition to lifeboats.

TYPES AND CLASSES OF BOAT

Boats may be distinguished by their construction—open or decked—and by their means of propulsion—rowing, sailing or power.

Rowing and pulling boats

A rowing boat is an open boat (i.e. not decked in) and is propelled by oars in one of the ways illustrated in fig. 9–1. The parts of an oar and the methods by

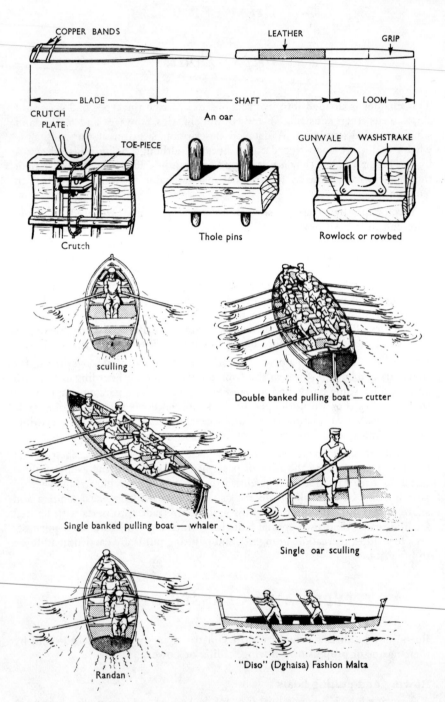

FIG. 9–1. Parts of an oar, methods of pivoting, and different ways of propelling rowing boats

which it is pivoted in a boat are also illustrated. In all methods of rowing the oar is pivoted at about one-third of its length from the grip, and is used as a lever by dipping the blade in the water and pulling or pushing on the loom, thus driving the boat through the water.

Sculling defines that method of rowing in which each member of the boat's crew mans a pair of oars, and also that in which a boat is propelled by manipulating a single oar over the stern; in this latter method the loom is worked from side to side in a figure-of-eight motion and the blade does not leave the water. Manipulation of a single oar pivoted on the gunwale by pulling or pushing on its loom is termed *rowing*. Vessels such as barges or lighters may be propelled by very long oars known as *sweeps*, which may either be pulled or pushed. In shallow waters boats, lighters and other small craft may be propelled by poles pushed on the bottom, this method being called *punting* or *quanting*.

In single-oared sculling, and in all methods of pushing on the loom of the oar, the crew stand up in the boat and the boat is propelled and steered by the manipulation of the oars alone. These methods are dangerous with an unskilled oarsman, because he may easily lose his balance and fall overboard or capsize the boat; they are therefore only used by skilled oarsmen and in calm weather.

Pulling. The normal method of rowing a boat is to sit facing aft and pull on the looms of the oars, the boat being steered by its rudder. In the Royal Navy all rowing boats are propelled by the normal method, rowing is called *pulling* and the boats are called *pulling boats*. If a pulling boat is equipped with masts and sails she is known in the Navy as a *pulling and sailing boat*.

Banks. Pulling boats may be *single-banked* or *double-banked*. In a single-banked boat there is one oarsman to each thwart and he sits on the side furthest from the blade of his oar. In a double-banked boat two oarsmen sit on each thwart and each oarsman pulls an oar on his own side. The term *bank* is also used in the sense that the oars of one side of a boat are known collectively as a 'bank of oars', and in the sense that when two men pull a single oar that oar is said to be 'double-banked'.

Types of pulling boat. A pulling boat is named according to her type, and this name may be prefixed by her length or the number of oars with which she is equipped. Examples are: the *dory*, a small flat-bottomed boat carried by fishing vessels; the *dinghy*, a small boat holding three or four people; the *skiff*, a similar small boat but used in inland waters; the 27 ft *Montague whaler*, and the 32 ft *cutter*, which are, respectively, single-banked and double-banked boats supplied for training in the Royal Navy.

Sailing boats

A sailing boat is a boat whose primary means of propulsion is by sail, but she may also be equipped for rowing or with some form of mechanical propulsion, in which case she is known as an *auxiliary sailing boat*. Sailing boats are usually wholly or partly decked-in. Ships do not normally carry sailing boats, but the 27 ft motor whaler may be rigged for sailing and some ships carry one or more 14 ft sailing dinghies in peacetime for recreational purposes.

Types of sailing boat. A sailing boat may be classified by her build, length, rig, tonnage, use and port of origin; for example, 6-metre yacht, Bermudian sloop, 5-ton yawl, sail training craft and Brixham trawler. Large fishing boats are generally known as *smacks*.

Power boats

Power boats are driven by internal combustion engines and are therefore known as 'motor boats'. They may be classified as *inboard* or *outboard* according to the position of the motor. They may also be classified according to speed (fast, medium speed or slow).

Hull form (fig. 9–2)

There are two main types of hull form, one where the athwartship sections are *round-bilge* and the other where they are *hard-chine*. The hard-chine boat planes at speed and is therefore faster than a round-bilge boat, but it has poor sea-keeping qualities. All warships' boats are round-bilged except fast motor boats.

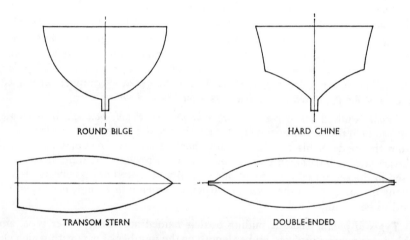

FIG. 9–2. Hull forms

All warships' boats except the whaler have a square *transom* stern. The whaler, which is only slightly fuller at the stern than at the bow, is *double-ended*.

CONSTRUCTION

Boat hulls are made of wood or glass-reinforced plastic (G.R.P.), or a combination of the two, or of rubber-proofed fabric.

WOODEN BOATS

Wooden boats (fig. 9–3) are either made of planks or plywood or a combination of the two. Planked boats may be *clinker*, *carvel* or *diagonal* (fore-and-aft or double). Plywood boats may be *cold-moulded* or *hot-moulded*.

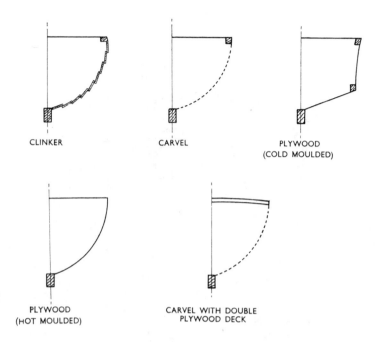

FIG. 9-3. Types of wood construction

Clinker build

In the clinker-built boat the planks run fore-and-aft, with the lower edge of one plank overlapping outboard the upper edge of the plank below it (fig. 9-4). The planks are fastened to the timbers of the boat and to each other by copper nails, which are clenched over washers called *roves*. A clinker-built boat is comparatively easy to repair, because a damaged plank may be removed and replaced without unduly disturbing the adjacent planks.

Carvel build

In a carvel-built boat the planks are placed edge to edge so that they are flush with one another (fig. 9-5); they may run fore-and-aft from end to end of the boat or rise diagonally from the keel to the gunwale at an angle of about 45°. In single-skinned carvel-built boats the planks run fore-and-aft and are fastened to the timbers of the boat by copper nails clenched over roves. The seams may be backed by a strip of wood called an *edge strip*, or be caulked with spun oakum or cotton. In double-skinned carvel-built boats the planks of the outer skin may run fore-and-aft and those of the inner skin diagonally, or the planks of both skins may run diagonally in opposite directions, crossing each other at right-angles (fig. 9-6). In both types a single thickness of oiled calico is spread over the inner skin to make it watertight and the two skins are clenched to each other and to the timbers of the boat.

The carvel build provides a more streamlined outer surface for the hull than the clinker build, but for single-skinned boats it is not so strong as the clinker build. The carvel double-diagonal build is the strongest form of construction

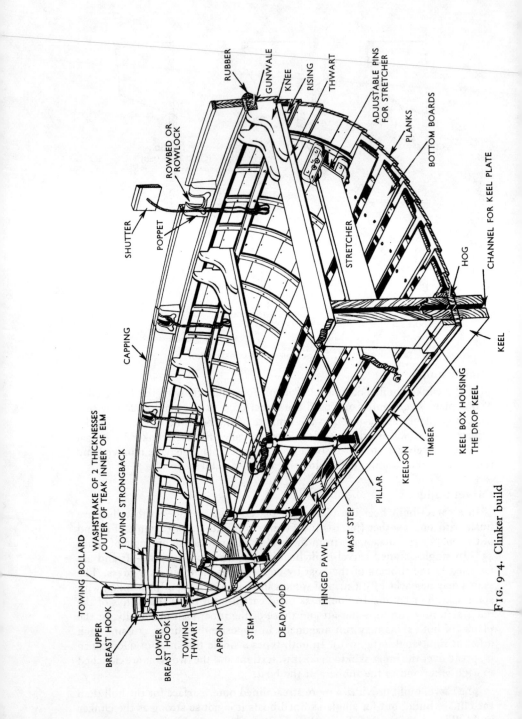

FIG. 9-4. Clinker build

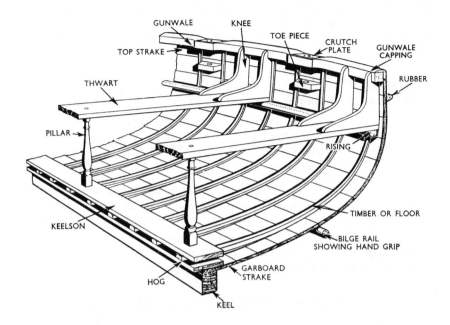

FIG. 9–5. Carvel build

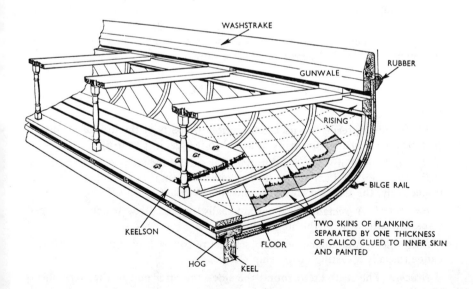

FIG. 9–6. Carvel double-diagonal build

for wooden boats, and its strength does not depend so much on the support of the timbers of the boat as in the clinker build or the single-skin carvel build; but it is difficult to repair if the inner skin has been holed. The largest ships' boats of wooden construction in the Royal Navy are of the carvel double-diagonal build.

Timbers used

The timbers used in the Royal Navy's wooden boats are the following:

African mahogany	Sitka spruce
Canada rock elm	Teak
English elm	Wych elm
English oak	

All timber is given preservative treatment before being worked into the boat, and the bottoms of boats operating in waters where damage from marine borers is likely to occur are sheathed with copper sheeting or Nylon fabric.

Fastenings

The fastenings of wooden boats are of copper or brass.

GLASS-REINFORCED PLASTIC BOATS

Glass-reinforced plastic boats are made of layers of glass fibre impregnated with polyester resin. A number of these layers form a laminate. The glass-reinforced plastic laminate is heavier than water; so low-density, closed-cell expanded plastic is incorporated. In some boats the expanded plastic material is inserted between two laminates; this is called *sandwich construction* and is used mainly in small boats as it gives adequate rigidity to the hull without recourse to framing. Most G.R.P. boats, however, have hulls of single laminate with frames and/or longitudinals of G.R.P. Wooden members are often incorporated as engine bearers and as a base for securing such items as rubbers and bilge rails. Typical constructions are shown in fig. 9–7.

PARTS OF A WOODEN BOAT

The hull

The following terms are used to describe the parts of the hull of a wooden boat and those fittings normally attached to it (figs. 9–4 to 9–9).

Apron. A piece of wood fitted to the after side of the stem and forward side of the stern post and extending throughout their length, to which are secured, respectively, the forward and after ends of the planks.

Backboard. A rectangular board, usually ornamented, which is shipped across the after side of the stern benches.

Badge block. A circular wooden block secured on each bow to take the boat's badge (usually a casting of the ship's crest).

Benches. The seats fitted round the sides and after end of the stern sheets (see *Stern sheets*).

Bilge. The space between the bottom of the boat and the floorboards.

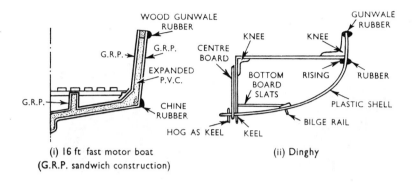

(i) 16 ft fast motor boat
(G.R.P. sandwich construction)

(ii) Dinghy

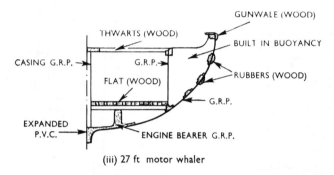

(iii) 27 ft motor whaler

FIG. 9–7. Glass-reinforced plastic boats—typical sections

Bilge rails. Lengths of wood fitted along the outside of the turn of the bilge to reduce rolling. The slots cut in them provide a hand-hold for the crew in the event of the boat capsizing.

Bilge stringers. Lengths of wood which run fore and aft over the timbers along the inside of the turn of each bilge. They strengthen the hull at the turn of the bilge and provide an anchorage for the outer edges of the floorboards.

Bottom boards. Slats of wood which form the curved flooring of the boat to protect the planking; they are secured to the timbers with eyes and wooden pins so that they can be removed if required.

Breasthook. A piece of wood of the thickness of the gunwale, either grown to shape or laminated, which is fitted to the curve of the gunwales in the eyes of the boat where they join the apron and so serves to strengthen the bows of the boat. In a double-ended boat a sternhook is also similarly fitted in the stern.

Buoyancy blocks. An expanded plastic material whose cells remain watertight. It is extremely light and replaces buoyancy tanks in smaller boats.

Buoyancy tanks. Copper or plastic tanks fitted in the bow and stern of some boats to increase their reserve of buoyancy.

Canopy. A wooden, fabric or glass-reinforced plastic covering, usually detachable, fitted over parts of a boat for the protection of passengers, crew and engine.

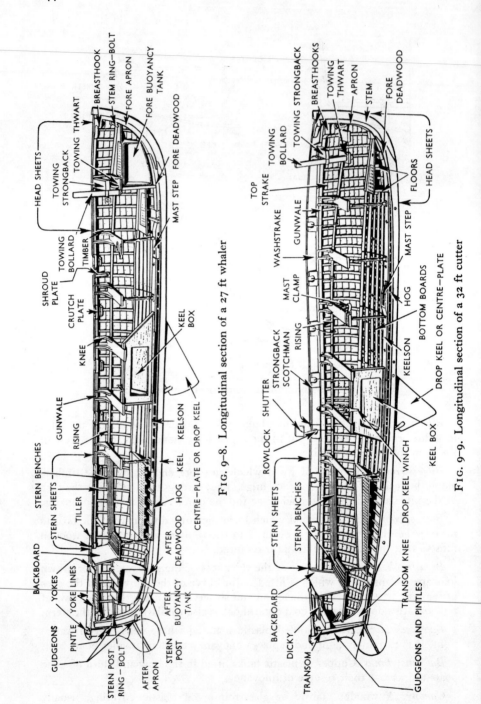

FIG. 9–8. Longitudinal section of a 27 ft whaler

FIG. 9–9. Longitudinal section of a 32 ft cutter

Capping. A strip of Canadian elm which is fitted to the top of the gunwale or washstrake to strengthen and protect it. At intervals it is pierced to take the plates for the crutches or thole pins, or cut away for the rowlocks. (See also *Washstrake* and *Rowlocks.*)

Carlings. These are strengthening pieces. For example, when a hatch through the deck of a boat cuts through a beam, longitudinal carlings are fitted.

Centre-plate or *drop keel.* A metal plate which can be lowered through a slot in the keel so that it projects below the boat and thus reduces her leeway when under sail. It is housed in a wooden casing known as the *keel-box* or *centre-plate trunk* the bottom of which is joined to the keel with a watertight joint. It is raised and lowered by a *centre-plate winch* or by hand.

Cleats. Pieces of wood or metal on which sheets or halyards are belayed. In Montague whalers *thumb cleats* are fitted at each end of the after thwart.

Coaming. This is the raised surrounding of a hatch to keep out water.

Counter. This is the overhanging part of the stern of a boat (or ship) above the waterline.

Crutches. In some single-banked boats these metal U-shaped fittings take the place of rowlocks. They fit into metal *crutch plates* in the gunwale and are always secured to the boat by a lanyard, but are unshipped whenever the oars are not in use except when the boat is prepared as a seaboat.

Deadwood. Pieces of timber at each end of the boat which join the aprons to the hog and to which the ends of the lower planks are fastened, thus strengthening the joints of the stem and the stern post with the keel.

Dickies. Small seats, sometimes known as *quarter seats*, fitted in some square-sterned boats in the angle made by the gunwale and transom, on which the coxswain sits when the boat is under oars.

Eyes. The foremost part of the boat just abaft the stem. (In ancient times an eye was painted on each side of the stem.)

Floors. Pieces of wood which extend athwart the bottom of the boat at the bows and stern; they serve to strengthen the bottom of the boat at her ends where the angle at which the timbers meet the keel is acute. They are also fitted athwartships to engine bearers to prevent the bearers from tipping.

Floorboards. Removable planks or gratings which form a horizontal platform over the bottom of the boat.

Footrail. A strip of wood fitted along the top of the gunwale of decked-in boats to protect the gunwale and provide a foothold.

Garboard strake. The line or strake of planks which runs next to, and each side of, the keel. The inner edges of these planks are let into a groove in the side of the keel, which is called the *rabbet* of the keel.

Gratings. In addition to the platforms (floorboards) they are used to cover certain other spaces in a boat, for example, the stern grating of a whaler abaft the backboard.

Gudgeons and pintle. The fittings by which the rudder is hung and pivoted to the stern post. The pintle is a vertical pin, and the gudgeons are horizontal eyebolts into which the pintle fits.

Gunwale. A stringer or length of wood of square cross-section which runs along the inside of the upper part of the top strake and on the top of the timbers. It strengthens the upper part of the hull. (See *Stringers* and *Top strake.*)

Head sheets. The platform, or the space, in the bows of the boat between the stem and the bow thwart.

Hog. A length of wood fitted to the upper part of the keel and extending between the fore and after deadwoods. With the keel and deadwoods it provides the anchorage for the inner edges of the garboard strakes and the lower ends of the timbers. It also serves to strengthen the keel.

Keel. A heavy length of wood of rectangular cross-section which forms the backbone of the boat; it runs along the fore-and-aft midship line and is joined to the foot of the stem and the foot of the stern post. The keel may be sheathed at its forward and after ends with metal strips to protect it when the boat grounds or is hauled up a beach, and in some boats it is slotted to take a centre-plate (drop keel).

Keelson. A length of wood fitted to the upper part of the hog and extending from the bows for about two-thirds of the length of the boat. It is secured to the hog and keel by through bolts or to the hog only by means of toggles and eyes; and sockets are cut in it to receive the mast step and the feet of the thwart pillars. The inboard edges of the floorboards are secured to it and the bottom boards scarfed under it.

Knees. Wooden fittings which secure the thwarts to the sides of the boat. They are now made of laminated wood (in older boats they are of wood grown to shape) and then fitted and bolted or clenched to the upper strakes and gunwale and to the upper side of the ends of the thwarts. In decked-in boats the knees are inverted, being then called *hanging knees* or *brackets*, and they secure the deck beams to the timbers and the sides of the boat.

Mast step, clamp and *pawl.* The foot of a boat's mast fits into a wood or metal slot in the keelson called the mast step. The mast is held to a thwart by a mast clamp (or clasp). In cutters the mast is clamped in a hinged iron clamp on the fore side of the third thwart, then raised so that the heel slides into its step in the keelson and is locked in position by a hinged mast pawl.

Number. All boats in the Royal Navy are given a number, which is carved in two places in the boat. In double-ended boats it is carved in the stem and the stern post; in transomed boats it is carved in the transom and in the hog just abaft the fore deadwood or just abaft the collision bulkhead. In power boats the first two figures of this number indicate the year in which the boat was built, but in pulling boats figures denoting the year are added. With the number are also carved the length of the boat, the abbreviated name of her original storing yard, and the Government broad arrow.

Pillars. Vertical supports for the thwarts; their heels are stepped in the keelson.

Pintle. See *Gudgeons and pintle.*

Planking. The general term for the wood forming the skin or skins of a boat, whether of clinker or carvel build.

Plug. A wooden bung or screwed metal plug which fits in a hole bored in one of the lower strakes for draining the boat when she is hoisted. The plug of a seaboat should be visible from the ship when she is hoisted at her davits so that it may be seen to be in place before she is lowered; a starboard seaboat, for example, will have its plug in one of the lower port strakes.

*Poppets.** The pieces of wood which support the rowlocks and the washstrake. They also form the backing for the *shutters* when they are shipped.

Quarter badges. A shaped slab of wood fitted on each quarter at the after end of the rubber for protecting the quarters of the boat from damage when lying alongside.

Ringbolts. These are fitted in the stem and stern to take the fore-and-aft legs of the slings when the boat is hoisted. The stem ringbolt also has the boat's painter shackled to it.

Risings. See *Stringers.*

Rowlocks or *rowbeds.* U-shaped spaces cut in the washstrake to take the shafts of the oars. They are sheathed with strips of brass.

Rubbers. Strips of wood extending from the stem to the stern post or transom, and fitted to the outside of the top strakes, level with or just below the gunwale. They protect and strengthen the top strakes.

Rudder. A wood or metal fitting which when turned to one side or the other alters the course of the boat. It is hung and pivoted on the stern post, and is also attached to the boat by a lanyard secured to a ringbolt so that it will not break adrift when unshipped. The rudder is operated either by a tiller or a yoke and yoke lines, which are fitted to its head.

Shutters.† Detachable portions of the washstrake in boats fitted with rowlocks. They are secured by lanyards to the risings.

Skeg. A stern casting fitted in some wooden power boats which supports the lower bearing of the rudder and through which the propeller shaft runs in a single screw boat.

Sling plates. Clenched through the keel near each end of a boat, these plates take the vertical legs of the slings when the boat is hoisted and therefore the weight of the boat.

Stem. The foremost vertical member of the hull, the lower end of which is scarfed to the keel. Its fore edge is usually protected with a strip of metal called the *stemband.*

Stern post. The aftermost vertical member of the hull, the lower end of which is joined to the keel. In boats with pointed sterns, the stern post is fitted with an apron to which the after ends of the planking are fastened. The stern post carries the rudder, which is hung from it by means of pintles and gudgeons.

---

* The term 'poppets' has, for many years, been used to describe shutters.

† Hitherto in the Service these have been called 'poppets'.

Stern sheets. The space or platform extending from the stroke thwart to the backboard, and round the sides and after end of which are built the stern benches.

Sternsom. This term is sometimes used for the after apron in a double-ended boat. (See *Apron.*)

Strakes. Lengths of planking which, in clinker- and carvel-built boats, extend parallel with each other from stem to stern.

Stretchers. Adjustable boards or wooden bars fitted athwart the bottom boards to provide footrests for the oarsmen.

Stringers. Lengths of wood extending fore-and-aft over the timbers, to which they are fastened and which they thus brace and support. The stringers which support the ends of the thwarts are called *risings*.

Tabernacle. A wooden frame, extending from the mast thwart to the mast step, which forms the housing of the mast.

Thwarts. Benches fitted athwart the boat on which the oarsmen sit. The foremost thwart is called the bow thwart, and the after thwart the stroke thwart; the intermediate thwarts are numbered consecutively from forward aft, the thwart next abaft the bow thwart being called No. 2 thwart. In cutters a spare thwart is provided which can be shipped across the stern benches abaft the stroke thwart.

Tiller. See *Rudder.*

Timbers. Curved pieces of wood which extend upward and outward from the keel at short intervals throughout its length and form what are virtually the ribs of the boat; the spacing between adjacent timbers is governed by the size and build of the boat. The planking is fastened to the outboard sides of the timbers and they may be braced inboard by stringers.

Top strake. The uppermost strake of a boat's planking, along the inside of which runs the gunwale.

Towing bollard. A stout post of timber by which a boat is towed, or by which she can ride when at anchor; it is stepped in the towing thwart in the head sheets, and clamped to a strongback shipped between the gunwales; the tow rope or anchor cable is belayed round it.

Transom. A board which is fitted to the after side of the stern post of a square-sterned boat and extends to each side of the boat; the after ends of the planking are fastened to it. A *false transom* in the form of a doubling is sometimes fitted over the transom to strengthen it.

Transom knee. A piece of wood, grown to shape, which is fitted between the stern post and the hog of a square-sterned boat to support the stern post and the transom. It takes the place of the stern post apron and the after deadwood, and in some boats is incorporated in the stern post.

Washstrake. An extra thick strake, fitted in some boats, which extends from stem to stern and is fixed to the top of the gunwale and the top strake. It may be cut at intervals to form rowlocks for the oars, or be fitted to take crutches.

Additional fittings for sailing

Belaying pins. Metal pins fitted through the thwarts to which the halyards of a sailing boat are belayed; sometimes called *thwart pins* when they project only below the thwart.

Bullseyes. Rings of wood, usually seized into a strop or tailed with a lanyard, through which running rigging such as sheets and brails are rove. These must not be confused with deadeyes.

Deadeyes. Round, flat blocks of wood with three holes used in the standing rigging of a sailing ship; sometimes called *monkey faces.*

Forestay shackle. In some boats a long shackle is bolted through the top of the stem to take the forestay and the foresail tack hook.

Horse. A curved bar of metal, fitted along the top of the transom, to which the after block of the mainsail sheet is shackled; the block travels from side to side of the horse when the boat is put about.

Main sheet eyeplates. These are fitted to the gunwale abreast the stern sheets on each side of a Montague whaler. The standing blocks of the main sheets are clipped to them.

Running hook. A hook fitted on each side of the bows of the boat to which the tack of the foresail is hooked when the boat is sailing before the wind.

Shroud plates. Plates screwed into the gunwale on either side of the mast for securing the lower ends of the shrouds.

Tack hook. This hook for the foresail tack in a Montague whaler is permanently fitted to the forestay shackle.

Thwart pins. See *Belaying pins.*

Additional equipment and fittings

Barricoes (pronounced 'breakers'). Small casks for drinking or ballast water, which are designated by the number of gallons they hold. Replaced by canned water in all boats.

Boat's cable. A length of manila rope or rigging chain by which the boat rides when at anchor. It is stowed either on a reel fitted beneath a thwart, or in a cable locker built into the headsheets.

Lazy painter. A 4-fathom length of 1-in. or 1½-in. cordage by means of which the boat can be hauled under the Jacob's ladder when made fast to a boom. The inboard end is secured to the stem ringbolt. The lazy painter should not be used for making the boat fast.

Lifeline. A line fitted along each rubber so that it hangs in bights outside the boat and thus affords a handhold to anyone being rescued from the water. It should not be confused with the lifelines on a boat's davits.

Painter. A length of stout cordage by which the boat is towed, or by which she rides when made fast to a boom. Its length should be 1½ times that of the boat, and its size varies with the size of the boat. One end is pointed; the other is spliced with a 2½- to 3½-ft soft eye into which are seized two thimbles, one at the throat and one at the crown, the two parts of the eye being then married and served over. The painter is shackled to the stem ringbolt.

Slings. A boat's slings provide the means whereby a boat is hoisted. They consist of two sets, the forward and after slings, each consisting of two legs of rigging chain or wire rope joined to a ring. The ends of the legs are shackled to sling-plates in the keel and hooked to the ringbolts in the stem or stern. Two *steadying spans* of chain or wire rope are joined to the ring of each sling and hooked to eyebolts fitted in the gunwales.

Stay shackle. In some boats a long shackle is bolted through the stem to take the forestay and the fore tack hook.

Sternfast. A length of cordage, usually shackled to the stern ringbolt, used for securing the stern when alongside.

Strongback. A heavy baulk of timber which can be shipped athwart the boat amidships, over the gunwales or wash strakes, with its ends projecting well beyond the rubbers. It is used when a heavy weight such as a bower anchor is slung below the boat for transportation. The gunwale or washstrake is strengthened in the wake of the strongback, which is secured to the sides of the boat and to the thwart below it by fitted metal shores; over the strongback is rove the sling for the weight.

Additional equipment in power boats

Drip tray. A metal tray under-running the engine so that oil leakage does not immediately spread to the bilges.

Engine bearers. Additional floor timbers on which the engine is bedded and secured.

Engine case. A wooden box-like structure encasing the engine.

Sterntube chock. An athwartship timber providing additional support for the stern tube between the engine and the stern gland.

SAILING RIGS

Sail and rigging terms

The parts of three-sided and four-sided sails are named in fig. 9–10. In fig. 9–11, which illustrates the rig of a 27 ft Montague whaler, the details shown are common to most fore-and-aft rigged boats. Additional information about boats, sails and rigging follows.

Backstay. A rope leading aft from the masthead to assist in preventing the mast from falling forward; its name is also derived from that of the mast it supports, e.g. 'fore-topmast backstay'.

Bending on the head or foot of a sail means to secure it to a spar by its earings and lacing.

Boltrope. The roping on the edge of a sail; it is always sewn on the side of the sail which will be to port when the sail is set. The luff of a sail is always roped, the leach seldom, and the foot usually only when laced to a boom; the sides of a sail can therefore always be identified during the day by sight, and at night by feeling them.

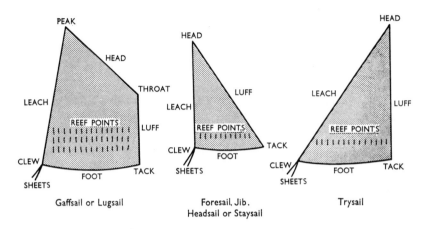

FIG. 9–10. Parts of a boat's sails

Boom. The spar to which the foot of any sail is bent.

Cringles. Eyes worked into the boltrope at the sides or corners of a sail and to which are bent or hooked the halyards, the sheets and the tack hook.

Earing. The lashing which secures the throat, peak, tack or clew of a sail to a spar.

Eyelets. The eyes worked into the head or foot of a sail for lacing it to a spar.

Foresail. The sail set immediately before the foremast, or immediately before the mainmast if there is no foremast.

Forestay. A rope leading forward from the masthead to assist in preventing the mast from falling aft; its name is derived from that of the mast which it supports, e.g. 'main topmast stay'.

Gaff sail. A four-sided sail the head of which is bent to a gaff.

Gaff topsail. A triangular sail set between a gaff and the masthead.

Genoa. A large triangular sail set in place of the foresail. Its clew reaches well abaft the mainmast.

Halyard. A rope by which a sail is hoisted and lowered. To *settle* a halyard is to ease it away.

Headsail. Any sail set before the foremast, or before the mainmast if there is no foremast.

Jib. Any headsail set before the foresail; if there are two they are called the *inner jib* and the *outer jib*, and if three the foremost one is called the *flying jib*.

Loose-footed sail. A sail that has no boom at its foot.

Lugsail. A four-sided sail the head of which is bent to a yard.

Mizzen. The sail set on the mizzen mast.

Reef. To reef a sail is to reduce the area it offers to the wind in order to prevent the boat from heeling over too far and getting swamped or capsizing. A loose-footed sail is reefed by gathering up its foot to the required line of reef-points and then stopping each pair together round the gathered-up foot with a reef knot. A boom-footed sail is reefed by settling its halyard until the required line of reef points can be stopped round the boom. *Taking down a reef* is putting a reef in a sail, and *shaking out a reef* is taking it out again. A sail is said to be *single-reefed*, *double-reefed* or *treble-reefed* according to the number of rows of reef-points used.

Reef-points. Short lengths of line secured to each side of a sail in pairs above its foot (fig. 9–10) and used for reefing it; a sail may have one, two or three rows of reef-points.

Running rigging. This comprises all the movable ropes, such as halyards and sheets.

Sheet. A rope bent to the clew of a sail by means of which the sail is trimmed as required; it is named after the sail to which it is bent, e.g. 'fore sheet'. To check a sheet is to ease it off so that the sail is eased out; to *aft* a sheet is to haul it in so that the clew of the sail is hauled aft; and to *let fly* a sheet is to let it run so that the sail flaps and the wind is spilled out of it.

Shrouds. Ropes leading from the masthead to the sides of the boat for supporting the mast athwartships. They also are named after the mast which they support, e.g. 'mizzen shrouds'.

Spinnaker. A large balloon-type sail with luff and leach of equal length which may be used in place of a foresail when the wind is abaft the beam.

Standing rigging. This comprises all the permanently fitted and secured ropes, such as the stays and shrouds.

Staysail. Any triangular sail whose luff is supported by a stay; its name is derived from that of the stay which supports it, e.g. 'main topmast staysail'.

Stormsails. Special sails for use in very strong winds instead of a boat's normal suit of sails; they are smaller and made of heavier canvas than the normal sails.

Trim. The trim of a sail refers to the angle between its mean plane and the fore-and-aft line of the boat, and is altered as necessary for the sail to receive the maximum wind pressure possible on the course to be steered. The sails are trimmed nearly at right-angles to the fore-and-aft line if the boat is sailing with the wind directly astern, but if she is sailing as close to the wind as possible they are trimmed nearly parallel with her fore-and-aft line.

Trysail. Any triangular sail (except the mizzen) which is set immediately abaft the foremast, or immediately abaft the mainmast if there is no foremast.

Yard and gaff. The head of a four-sided sail is bent to and supported by either a yard or a gaff; a yard crosses the mast, but a gaff has jaws at its throat which fit round the mast. The halyard of a gaff is bent to the gaff itself, but the halyard of a yard is bent to an iron hoop with a hook on it called a *traveller*, to which the yard is hooked by means of a strop.

The sailing rigs of a 27 ft whaler, a 32 ft cutter, a 14 ft R.N.S.A. dinghy and a 27 ft motor whaler will now be described.

27 ft whaler (fig. 9–11)

The mainmast is stepped in the keelson, held by an iron clamp to the second thwart, and stayed by two shrouds set up with lanyards to eyeplates in the gunwales and by a forestay of wire rope secured to the stay shackle on the stem. The mizzenmast passes through a specially fitted crosspiece and is stepped in the hog abaft the stern benches; it is not stayed. The boom of the mizzen can be triced up by a topping lift, and its heel is hinged to the mizzenmast.

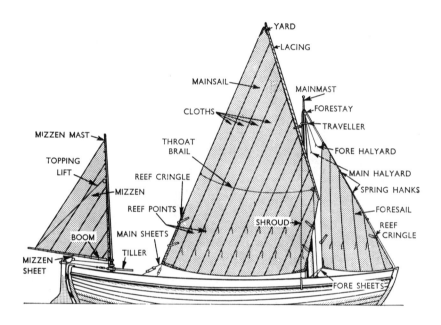

FIG. 9–11. Sailing rig of 27 ft whaler

The sails comprise a foresail, a standing-lug mainsail and a triangular mizzen the foot of which is laced to a boom; a trysail is also provided for use as a stormsail in place of the mainsail, or as a spinnaker for which a boom is provided for bearing out its foot. The foresail can be single-reefed and the mainsail double-reefed. The fore and main halyards are single whips rove through mast sheaves set up to thwart pins under the mast thwart; the fore halyard is of cordage and the main halyard is a wire rope pendant tailed with cordage. The main yard is hooked to a traveller shackled to the main halyard, and the tack of the mainsail is bowsed down by a tack tackle rove to the keelson. The luff of the foresail is clipped to the forestay by spring hanks. The mizzen is laced to its mast and boom. The fore sheets consist of a length of rope seized at its bight and secured to a clip hook which hooks into the clew; the main sheets consist of two double whips rove through bullseyes and joined by a clip hook to the clew, and the mizzen sheet is rove from the boom through a block or a bullseye on the stern post to a cleat on the mizzenmast. Lizard bullseyes made fast to the risings are provided as fairleads for the fore sheets, and eyeplates are provided in the stern sheets for the standing blocks of the main sheets. The mainsail is fitted with brails and provided with a spar for bearing out its foot when the boat is reaching or running.

32 ft cutter (fig. 9–12)

The rig illustrated is called sloop rig, this being the general term used for a boat rigged with a foresail and standing-lug mainsail. The mast is stepped, through a hinged iron hoop on the third thwart, into its step in the keelson where it is locked in place by a hinged pawl; it is stayed by two shrouds, two backstays (commonly called runners) and a forestay, all of wire rope. The

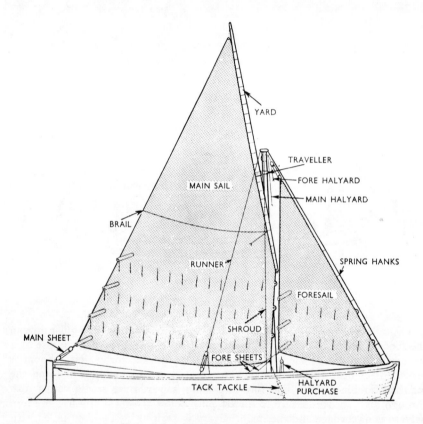

FIG. 9–12. Sailing rig of 32 ft cutter

heads of the shrouds, runners and forestay are shackled to a spider band at the masthead; the shrouds and forestay are set up by lanyards, the former to shroud plates inside the gunwales and the latter to the upper breasthook; the runners are set up, abaft the shrouds, by the runner tackles to shroud-plates and cleats inside the gunwales. The weather runner is always set up taut, and the lee runner eased to allow the sail to take up its natural belly.

The sails comprise a foresail, mainsail, trysail (which may be used as a spinnaker) and storm foresail. Spars are provided for bearing out the clews of the mainsail and spinnaker. The foresail can be double-reefed, and the mainsail treble-reefed.

The main halyard is a wire rope pendant rove through a mast sheave. One end is shackled to the traveller, and the other tailed with a double-whip; the standing block of the whip is shackled to a spider band on the mast just above the thwart, the hauling part being rove through a leading block on the same band and set up to a thwart pin under the fifth thwart. The tack of the mainsail is bowsed down by a tack tackle secured to an eyebolt in the keelson. The fore halyard is a double-whip, the standing block of which is shackled to the spider band at the masthead and the moving block to the head of the foresail.

The main sheet is a jigger, the single block of which is hooked to the clew of the mainsail with a tack hook, and the double block of which is hooked to the horse. The two fore sheets each consist of two parts, one sheet being rove on each side of the boat; the standing part of each is secured to the rising abaft the mast thwart, then led through a bullseye on the clew of the foresail and then aft through a lizard bullseye secured to the rising abaft the standing part.

The luff of the foresail is hanked to the forestay. A running hook is provided on the gunwale on each bow, to which the tack of the foresail is hooked when the boat is running before the wind. The mainsail is fitted with brails led through bullseyes on a strop at the throat of the yard.

14 ft R.N.S.A. sailing dinghy (fig. 9–13)

This boat is a modified version of the original Island Class 14 ft racing dinghy, strengthened for sea service and supplied to H.M. ships and establishments for instructional, recreational and general purposes. The hull is clinker-built and varnished. Because of its light construction this boat should be treated with great care, especially when being hoisted in and out and stowed, and it should not be left at the lower boom for longer than necessary and it must never be lifted by the sailing horse. The hull should be kept varnished, not painted. The boat is sufficiently robust for general duties of a light nature, but being designed primarily as a sailing boat she is not so good under oars as are the standard Service pulling boats; she will pull better if the drop keel is lowered a little.

Normal rig. The rig comprises a foresail and a gunter-mainsail, and being essentially part of the racing rig, with yacht quality gear, it should be given every care and attention. The forestay and the two shrouds are of wire rope and fitted with bottle screws and rigging slips. The fore halyard is a single whip rove through one sheave of a double block on a masthead pendant. The gaff is fitted with throat and peak halyards the throat halyard is shackled to the throat of the gaff, rove through a mast sheave and belayed to a pin in the mast thwart; the peak halyard is shackled to a span shackle running on a wire span fitted to the gaff, and is rove through a mast sheave and belayed to a pin in the mast thwart.

The heel of the gaff is fitted with a hinged traveller, which is secured by a parrel to the mast. The heel of the boom fits over a gooseneck pin hinged at the foot of the mast, thus enabling the sail to be reefed by revolving the boom so that it winds the foot of the sail around it; the heel is bowsed down by a lanyard

9*

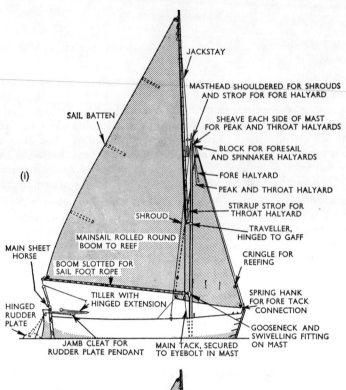

(i)

JACKSTAY

MASTHEAD SHOULDERED FOR SHROUDS
AND STROP FOR FORE HALYARD

SHEAVE EACH SIDE OF MAST
FOR PEAK AND THROAT HALYARDS

SAIL BATTEN

BLOCK FOR FORESAIL
AND SPINNAKER HALYARDS

FORE HALYARD

PEAK AND THROAT HALYARD

STIRRUP STROP FOR
THROAT HALYARD

SHROUD

TRAVELLER,
HINGED TO GAFF

MAINSAIL ROLLED ROUND
BOOM TO REEF

MAIN SHEET
HORSE

CRINGLE FOR
REEFING

BOOM SLOTTED FOR
SAIL FOOT ROPE

TILLER WITH
HINGED EXTENSION

SPRING HANK
FOR FORE TACK
CONNECTION

HINGED
RUDDER
PLATE

GOOSENECK AND
SWIVELLING FITTING
ON MAST

JAMB CLEAT FOR
RUDDER PLATE PENDANT

MAIN TACK, SECURED
TO EYEBOLT IN MAST

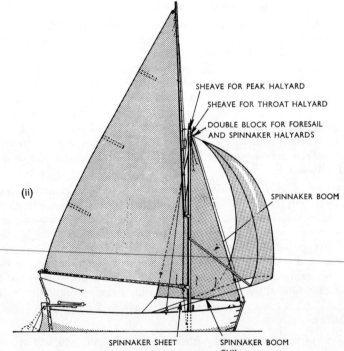

SHEAVE FOR PEAK HALYARD

SHEAVE FOR THROAT HALYARD

DOUBLE BLOCK FOR FORESAIL
AND SPINNAKER HALYARDS

(ii)

SPINNAKER BOOM

SPINNAKER SHEET

SPINNAKER BOOM
GUY

(i) Normal rig; (ii) racing rig

FIG. 9-13. 14 ft R.N.S.A. sailing dinghy

secured to an eyebolt near the heel of the mast, so that the boom is prevented from turning when the sail is reefed and kept in place on its gooseneck pin.

The luff of the foresail is hanked to the forestay; the fore sheets are rove through bullseyes in the sides of the boat and can be belayed on jamming cleats abaft the bullseyes. The head of the mainsail is laced to the gaff, and its footrope is secured in a slot in the boom; its curved leach is fitted with three wooden spreader battens. The main sheet is a jigger with its single block running on a horse fitted on the transom.

The rudder post is fitted with a hinged rudder plate to which is attached a pendant by which the plate can be raised when the boat is running free or in shallow water, and lowered when beating to windward. The tiller is fitted with a hinged extension piece to allow the helmsman to steer from amidships.

The drop keel is raised and lowered by a small winch fitted near the heel of the mast, the end of the winch rope being belayed to a cleat on the keel box.

The mainsail is reefed by settling the throat halyard, unhooking the lanyard and then rotating the boom so that it winds the sail around it, the luff being kept close to the heel and the leach hauled out so that the foot remains straight and uncreased. The boom is then secured by the lanyard.

Racing rig (fig. 9–13 (ii)). In addition to the normal rig a large foresail and a spinnaker are provided for racing. The spinnaker halyard is rove through the other sheave of the double block mentioned under the normal rig. When hoisted, the spinnaker is held by a 6-ft boom, spiked into the clew and forked round the mast. One of the spinnaker sheets acts as the boom guy; the other sheet fulfils its normal function.

27 ft MOTOR WHALER

This boat is primarily a power-driven seaboat, but it can be used for pulling and sailing, either for training or recreation. It replaces the 27 ft Montague whaler in H.M. ships. It is designed to give a relatively high performance under sail and must be used with discretion and skill.

The hull

The overall length is 27 ft 8½ in. and the maximum breadth 7 ft 0 in., giving a total carrying capacity of 23 persons. The lifting weight is 2½ tons (including a crew of 4). The hull is of double-skin mahogany construction, the inner laid diagonally and the outer fore and aft to give a combined thickness of ¾ in.

The foremost of the four thwarts is portable to provide more stowage space. The mast thwart is divided by the mast tabernacle.

The centre-plate is raised and lowered by a small hand winch situated at the top of the fore end of the centre-plate casing (keel box).

The rudder has a hinged plate extension controlled by a pendant. The plate should be raised when under power, in shallow water, or when running free under sail in slight or moderate sea conditions; it should be lowered when beating to windward or running in a heavy following sea.

Lightweight plastic buoyancy blocks are fitted under all the side benches and in the fore and after peaks.

Rowbeds are cut in the washstrake, two on each side, and fitted with shutters. A portable P.V.C.-coated Nylon fabric canopy can be fitted amidships.

Machinery

The engine is a horizontally-opposed, twin-cylinder, air-cooled diesel, with a rated B.H.P. of 11·5 at 1,500 rev/min. Boats are fitted with conventional gearbox and a fixed two-bladed propeller which can be lined up within the shadow of the sternpost when sailing. When the engine is run while the boat is at the davits, the stern bearing must first be lubricated by an internal grease gun at the coxswain's position.

When under sail the engine remains in the boat, and the exhaust outlet each side of the boat must be stopped with a wooden plug.

The maximum speed under normal load is $6\frac{1}{2}$ knots, at which an average fuel consumption of $\frac{1}{2}$ gallon per hour may be expected. The total capacity is 6 gallons.

Sailing rig

The rig is of gunter type, with a generous sail area. With an experienced crew of five or six the boat can be balanced by sitting out to windward, provided web straps are fitted around the thwarts. The material of the sails is Terylene of weight $7\frac{1}{2}$ oz per sq. yd except the spinnaker, which is of Nylon fabric of weight $1\frac{1}{2}$ oz per sq. yd and light blue in colour.

The spars consists of a mainmast, gunter yard, boom and spinnaker boom, all of sitka spruce. The mainmast is of hollow construction, and the gunter and main boom have a groove for the insertion of the luff and foot ropes. The mainmast is supplied complete with all standing and running rigging, which comprises: four shrouds; one forestay; two backstays each spliced through an eye of a block in a three-part hemp purchase; a foresail halyard of wire rope and a single whip hemp purchase, the latter shackled to an eye on the mast sleeve; a throat halyard of wire rope shackled to the heel of the gunter yard and passing through a masthead sheave to a block taking a single-whip hemp purchase, one end of which is shackled to the mast sleeve; and a hemp spinnaker halyard which is rove through a masthead block. All blocks are light-weight, laminated composition 'Tufnol' blocks. The gunter yard is supplied complete with a wire peak halyard for the mainsail and a hemp tail, also a burgee halyard.

Four sailbags are provided, one for each sail. The mainsail bag contains the mainsail, sheet, tackle, six reefing pendants and two sets (one set spare) of three sail battens. The foresail bag contains the foresail with the sheets and the tack strop. The genoa bag contains the genoa with sheets attached, and the spinnaker bag contains the spinnaker with sheets attached.

Method of rigging

Raising the mast. The mast is laid along the thwarts, with the trunnion arms above the tabernacle slots. The standing and running rig is sorted out. The head of the gunter yard is entered into the masthead clamp, and the traveller at the heel entered into the stop provided on the after side of the mast. The throat halyard is shackled to the traveller and the purchase temporarily secured

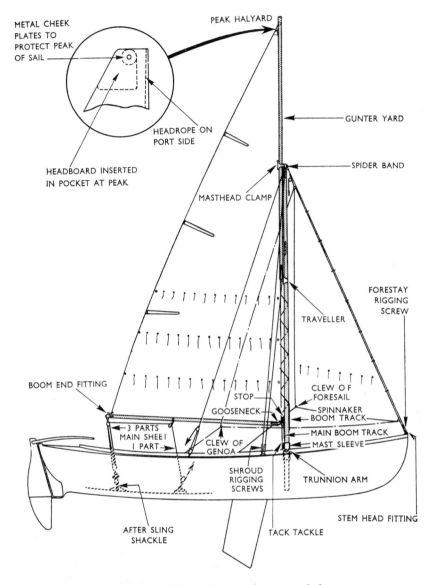

METAL CHEEK
PLATES TO
PROTECT PEAK
OF SAIL

PEAK HALYARD

GUNTER YARD

HEADROPE ON
PORT SIDE

SPIDER BAND

HEADBOARD INSERTED
IN POCKET AT PEAK

MASTHEAD CLAMP

FORESTAY
RIGGING
SCREW

TRAVELLER

BOOM END FITTING

CLEW OF
FORESAIL

STOP

GOOSENECK

SPINNAKER
BOOM TRACK

3 PARTS
MAIN SHEET
1 PART

MAIN BOOM TRACK

CLEW OF
GENOA

MAST SLEEVE

SHROUD
RIGGING
SCREWS

TRUNNION ARM

STEM HEAD FITTING

AFTER SLING
SHACKLE

TACK TACKLE

F IG. 9–14. Sailing rig of 27 ft motor whaler

round the mast and yard. The shrouds are now secured to the shroud plates. The backstays are secured but left slack.

The main tack tackle is used for raising the mast by securing it between the thimble of the forestay (allowing the bottle-screw to swing free) and the hole for the foresail tack in the stem head fitting. The mast and yard are lifted at the upper end, the trunnion arms being entered into the slots in the tabernacle and the strain taken on the main tack tackle as the mast is raised. The heel is entered into the mast step and the mast pawl lowered into position. The shrouds, backstays and forestay are now set taut and rigging screws moused. The fore, throat and spinnaker halyards are sorted out.

Fitting the boom. Insert the slide of the gooseneck fitting into the track on the after side of the mast, and close the gate at the bottom of the track; rig the tack tackle from the lower eye in the slide of the gooseneck fitting to the after eye on the mast sleeve. To set up the main sheet, shackle the single block to the long shackle in the sling-plate; shackle the double block to the eye in the end of the boom, with the hauling part leading forward to a single block secured about one-third of the way along the boom, thence down to a swivel block shackled to an eyeplate on the floor between the engine bearers, and then round a cleat on the side of the centre-plate casing.

Rigging the mainsail. To rig the mainsail, insert the three sail battens into their respective pockets in the leach of the sail. Thread the foot of the sail along the groove of the boom from forward to aft, securing the tack to the gooseneck fitting with the drop-nosed pin; pull out the foot of the sail and lash the clew to the top eye on the boom end fitting with a lanyard. Enter the head board of the mainsail into the groove of the gunter yard and shackle to the wire peak halyard. Hoist the sail by the hemp tail of the peak halyard and secure to the cleat at the heel of the yard, leaving most of this hemp tail free. Hoist the gunter yard with the throat halyard, taking care not to rip the sail in the mast-head clamp,* then lace the mainsail to the mast with the remaining hemp tail of the peak halyard. Haul down the throat halyard until the boom slide is well up the main boom track; make fast the halyard, haul down on the tack tackle and secure.

Rigging the foresail or genoa. The luff of the foresail or genoa is hanked to the forestay in the normal way and the tack strop shackled to the stem head fitting; the sheets are rove through their respective bullseyes and thence to their cleats. The head of the sail is shackled to the forestay halyard, hoisted, and made fast to a thwart pin.

Rigging the spinnaker. Lay the spinnaker in the fore end of the boat and pass one sheet round the forestay, making it fast in the boat. Enter the spring clip of the spinnaker boom fitting into the wire strop in the clew, and pass the other sheet aft and make it fast. Enter the other end of the spinnaker boom into the eye of the slide in the track on the fore side of the mast. Secure the Inglefield clip on the head of the spinnaker to the clip on the spinnaker halyard and hoist, making fast to a thwart pin.

The sheets are led aft outside the shrouds and backstays. The one which is on the same side as the spinnaker boom becomes the spinnaker guy and the other the spinnaker sheet. When the spinnaker is gybed, the spinnaker boom is shifted to the other bow and the guy becomes the sheet and the sheet becomes the guy.

Reefing. To reef the mainsail use two reefing pendants, inserting a long pendant upward through the aftermost reefing cheek on the boom, through the

---

* If the hemp tail is used as the luff lacing it will be found that it takes too long to settle the peak of the mainsail. It is recommended that the peak halyard be brought to the mast thwart straight from the gunter yard cleat, and that a separate lacing be fitted and used.

lower cringle on the leach of the sail and down through the opposite reefing cheek; the short reefing pendant is rove through the lower cringle on the luff of the sail and passed down round the gooseneck fitting. Slack away the luff lacing, haul taut on each of the pendants and ease out on the throat halyard. Make fast the two reefing pendants and tie each pair of reef points for the first reef under the boom. The procedure for the second and third reefs is the same. When shaking out a reef, it is essential to untie all the reef points of the reef before casting off the reefing pendants at the clew and tack, or the sail will be torn.

STOWAGE OF BOATS IN H.M. SHIPS

Boats are either hoisted at *davits*, from which they can be easily lowered at any time, or hoisted and lowered by crane and stowed in *crutches* on deck within the radius of the crane.

DAVITS

The four main types of davit in general use are described below:

Radial davit (fig. 9–15)

Each davit is pivoted at its heel so that it can rotate round its vertical axis. Each pair is stayed in position by fore and after guys, and a *span* set up between the davit heads; these must always be set up taut. A boat hoisted at these davits can be turned inboard by slipping the guys and turning first one davit and then the other inwards and inboard. After the boat is turned inboard it can be griped in to its spar or crutched down on deck.

Quadrantal type davit (fig. 9–16)

Each davit is hinged at its heel so that it can be canted outboard, or inboard to its stowage position. Each pair is stayed in the same manner as are the radial davits. When the davits are canted inboard the boat rests on keel chocks fitted on the davits, and no other stowage for the boat is provided.

Fixed or gantry type davit

This is a fixed bar projecting horizontally from the ship's side, and each pair may be stayed in a similar manner to radial davits. They may be fitted with traversing gear; this consists of a traveller, fitted with an inhaul and an out-haul, which runs on rollers along the davit and by means of which the boat can be run inboard along the davits to its stowage and there crutched down.

Gravity davit

Each davit consists of a 'cradle', which supports the boat, moving on rollers up or down an inclined track called a 'skid'. This skid is angled so that the cradle and boat will operate under gravity when the ship is heeled up to 30 degrees away from the side of the boat. These davits are fully described in Volume II.

DAVIT FITTINGS

The fittings of davits vary considerably according to the type of davit and the use to which it is put.

Radial davit (fig. 9–15)

This type of davit is used for boats and accommodation ladders. It has a locking pin at its heel by which it can be locked in either its outboard or its inboard position. It may be hinged at its heel so that it can be turned in and stowed flat on the deck when not in use. *Davit slips*, consisting of a rigging slip and bottle-screw, are fitted to each davit head, and the boat is slung on these when she is turned in or out or when her falls are renewed; if slung by her falls when being turned in or out she would foul them. A cleat for belaying the falls is fitted on the side of each davit, and a *standing lifeline* of the same size as the falls is fitted to each davit head.

When a seaboat is hoisted at radial davits they are provided with the extra fittings described below and illustrated in fig. 9–15. Each davit is fitted with a hinged bracket into which is clamped the *griping spar*. The boat is bowsed in to the spar by two *gripes* made of canvas-covered sword matting; these are rove from the head of each davit and then outside the boat to the heel of the opposite davit, where they are set up on a rigging slip by jiggers or lanyards; when set up by a jigger the moving block is fitted with a pendant which is rove through the thimble of the gripe and then put on the slip. A hammer for knocking off the slips of the gripes is secured by a lanyard to each davit. A *jackstay* with a lizard running on it is rigged from near each davit head to an eyeplate on the ship's side near the waterline; when the boat is hoisted or lowered these lizards are tended in the head and stern sheets to prevent the boat from swinging outwards if the ship is rolling. A staghorn bollard is fitted to the deck near the heel of each davit, to which the falls are belayed and from which the boat is lowered. Cordage *sea lifelines* (3-in. for cutters and $2\frac{1}{2}$-in. for whalers), one to each thwart except the bow and stroke thwarts, are slung from the davit span; they should be just long enough to reach the water when the ship is at light-load draught. If the freeboard of the ship is considerable the lifelines may be fitted at intervals of a few feet with standing Turk's heads to provide hand and foot holds for anyone having to man the boat or climb inboard after she has been lowered. A *jumping net* is rigged between the griping spar and the ship's deck to enable the crew to man the boat when she is hoisted at the davits.

Quadrantal davits (fig. 9–16)

These have fittings similar to those of radial davits, with the following exceptions. The davit is turned inboard and outboard by a worm engaged in a sleeved spindle and operated by a crank handle. When the davits are canted inboard the keel of the boat rests on chocks fitted on each davit; each chock is fitted with a locking clamp worked by a lever, and these clamps must be freed before the boat and the davits can be canted outboard. No griping spar is provided, but each davit is fitted with a *griping pad* against which the boat is bowsed by the gripes; the gripes must be slipped before the boat and the davits can be canted outboard. Davit slips are fitted for all boats. The davits are not hinged at their heels for close stowage, nor are they provided with locking pins. Staghorns are not usually provided, the boat being lowered from

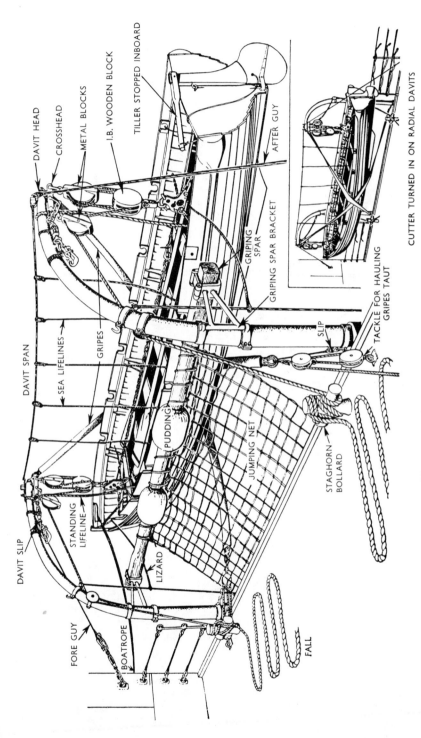

DAVIT HEAD

CROSSHEAD

METAL BLOCKS

I.B. WOODEN BLOCK

TILLER STOPPED INBOARD

AFTER GUY

GRIPING SPAR

GRIPING SPAR BRACKET

TACKLE FOR HAULING GRIPES TAUT

SLIP

DAVIT SPAN

SEA LIFELINES

GRIPES

PUDDING

JUMPING NET

STAGHORN BOLLARD

DAVIT SLIP

STANDING LIFELINE

LIZARD

FORE GUY

BOATROPE

FALL

CUTTER TURNED IN ON RADIAL DAVITS

FIG. 9–15. Cutter hoisted on radial davits

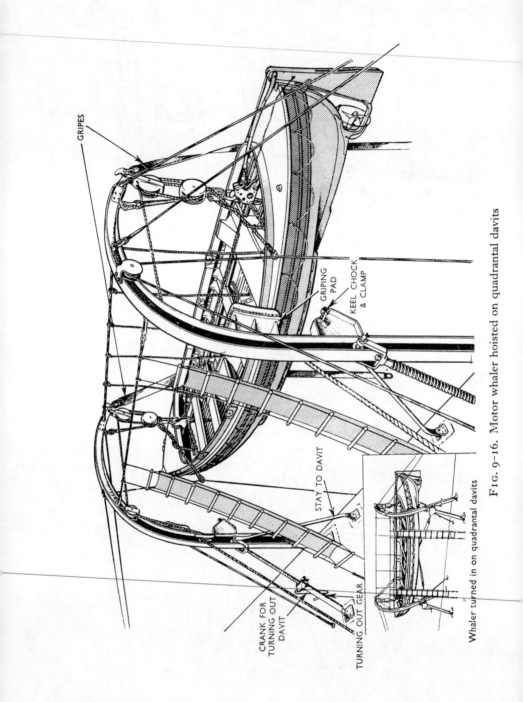

GRIPES

GRIPING
PAD

KEEL CHOCK
& CLAMP

STAY TO DAVIT

CRANK FOR
TURNING OUT
DAVIT

TURNING OUT GEAR

Whaler turned in on quadrantal davits

FIG. 9–16. Motor whaler hoisted on quadrantal davits

cleats fitted on the davits. Two Jacob's ladders are clipped to the inner davit span and secured on deck. These ladders have an extension, to be used when the boat is turned out.

With this type of davit it is important to ensure that when the davits are canted outboard the guys and span are set up so that the heads of the davits are in line with their heels, and that they are correctly stayed in this position.

Fixed or gantry type davits

These may be fitted with guys and a span and standing lifelines. When used for a seaboat, jackstays and lizards, sea lifelines, a griping spar or griping pads, and jumping nets or Jacob's ladders may also be rigged. Davit slips are provided for slinging the boat when the falls are unrove or renewed, and crutches are provided for the boat in its stowage position. The upper block of each fall is secured to a traveller which runs on rollers along the horizontal davit. The traveller is hauled in and out by an inhaul and outhaul which are brought to a winch worked by hand cranks. The falls are of E.S.F.S.W.R. and their hauling parts are brought to power-driven winches. As the boat is run out the winches must be veered, and as she is run in the slack of the falls must be taken down by the winches.

Turning-in a boat on radial davits

The boat is slung on the davit slips, the standing lifelines are passed inboard and manned, and the fore and after guys are slipped. The after davit is turned aft by hauling on its lifeline, and the foremost davit is turned aft by bowsing down on the span. The foremost davit is then turned inboard and then forward by hauling on its lifeline, and the bows of the boat are guided inboard and forward. The after davit is then turned inboard and the stern of the boat guided inboard, and the boat is then swung aft (see inset of fig. 9–15). The boat is turned out in the reverse manner.

Before turning-in a seaboat the gripes are slipped, the griping spar is unshipped and placed in the boat, and the spar brackets are housed. If the ship is rolling, frapping ropes to check the swing of the boat must be rove before the gripes are slipped. These are rove parbuckle fashion, from inboard and over and round the boat at her bows and quarters.

Reeving, fitting and maintenance of falls

Boats' falls, and the way they are fitted and rove, vary considerably. The purchase may be three-fold, fore-parted, two-fold or a luff. Some falls have two blocks, either fixed or swivelling, at each davit head to separate the hauling part from the running parts. The upper blocks are usually metal blocks, but the lower blocks should be I.B. wooden-cheeked blocks fitted with swivel-ring shackles so that the boat's slings can be hooked on to the ring shackles without first having to remove any turns in the falls. The pins of the swivel-ring shackles must always be moused with seizing wire.

The standing part of the fall is shackled to the davit head or spliced to the crown of one of the blocks so that the boat may be hoisted to two blocks. The way in which the falls are rove is determined by the hauling part from the throat of the upper block to the leading block on deck.

The size of a fall, which is determined by the weight of the boat and the type of purchase, varies from 2-in. to 4½-in. manila or man-made fibre rope. Wire rope falls are usually made of 2-in. E.S.F.S.W.R. The length of a fall depends upon the number of parts in the purchase, the height from the davit head to the waterline, and the length of run along the deck for the hauling part. Sea-boat's falls are marked with bunting so that they may be married to the marks and the boat hoisted clear of the water on an even keel. When the falls take the weight of a boat they may have a tendency to twist, especially when new; this may be overcome by passing a bar (anti-twister) between the parts of the falls.

After a boat is lowered at sea the falls should be recovered inboard. They should be handed outboard as the boat returns to the ship; the inboard parts or the standing part of each fall should be kept in hand until the boat is hooked on to ensure that the fall is clear for running. After a boat is lowered in harbour the falls should be rounded up, the lower blocks shackled to the heels of the davits, and the inboard ends reeled up or faked down.

A boat's falls should be carefully inspected at frequent intervals, and they should be renewed or turned end for end if their condition warrants it. The life of a boat's falls made of natural fibre cordage is considerably less in tropical than in temperate climates owing to heat, damp and the effects of the sun's rays. Before deciding to turn a fall end for end it should be carefully inspected for any signs of deterioration or wear, particularly the last few fathoms of the inboard end, which will become the most subject to wear when transposed. Any slack-jawed rope should be discarded.

CRUTCHES

A ship's boat is stowed in specially fitted crutches which support her bottom and bilges at two or more positions along her length. When a boat is stowed in her crutches they may entirely take her weight, but additional support should be provided by keel chocks placed where most required, usually where her beam is greatest or below her engines. The bearing surface of each crutch is shaped to fit the shape of the boat's hull at the position where it is intended to bear, and each is padded and covered with leather so that the whole of the bearing surface is in contact with the boat. It is important therefore to ensure that a boat is *pitched* (i.e. lowered on to her crutches) so that the crutches bear in their correct positions (which are usually marked by copper strips tacked to the keel or bottom planking of the boat), and that the crutches fit correctly. If a boat is incorrectly pitched she will lose her shape, spring a leak, or be stove in. A shipwright should be in attendance whenever a heavy boat is pitched.

Boat's crutches are usually portable. They are bolted to the deck, usually with vice-headed bolts, the holes for which are staggered so that the crutches cannot be replaced incorrectly. The crutches of boats not normally hoisted at davits are placed within the radius of the crane or derrick used for hoisting them, and such boats are known as *boom boats*. Some crutches may be hinged to stow on the deck when not in use. A small boat may be stowed in removable crutches within a larger boat; this is known as a *nested stowage*.

If no crutches are available a boat may be stowed temporarily in an upright position (see fig. 9–17) with her keel resting on wedge pieces, which should be

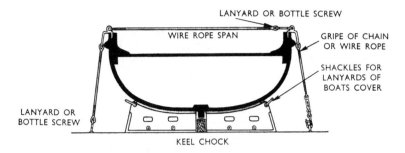

LANYARD OR BOTTLE SCREW

WIRE ROPE SPAN

GRIPE OF CHAIN OR WIRE ROPE

SHACKLES FOR LANYARDS OF BOATS COVER

LANYARD OR BOTTLE SCREW

KEEL CHOCK

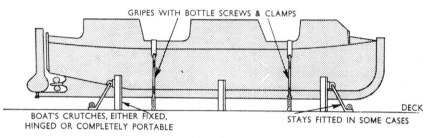

GRIPES WITH BOTTLE SCREWS & CLAMPS

BOAT'S CRUTCHES, EITHER FIXED, HINGED OR COMPLETELY PORTABLE

STAYS FITTED IN SOME CASES

DECK

Normal stowage

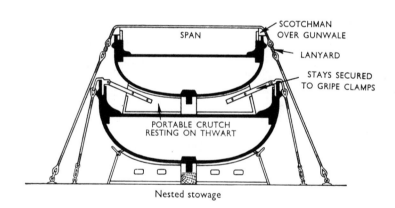

SPAN

SCOTCHMAN OVER GUNWALE

LANYARD

STAYS SECURED TO GRIPE CLAMPS

PORTABLE CRUTCH RESTING ON THWART

Nested stowage

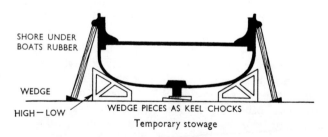

SHORE UNDER BOATS RUBBER

WEDGE

HIGH — LOW

WEDGE PIECES AS KEEL CHOCKS

Temporary stowage

FIG. 9–17. Stowage of boats in crutches

placed at the positions where her crutches would take; if these positions are not known the wedge pieces should be placed abreast the boat's bows and quarters, and amidships or below her engines, care being taken that the weight of the boat is evenly distributed between them. To keep the boat upright *high-lows* are placed on each side below her bilges; larger boats should also be supported by two or three shores on each side, lashed in position under her rubbers.

A boat is secured in her crutches by gripes of chain or of wire rope. Their upper ends are fitted with clamps which fit over the gunwale or washstrake, and their lower ends are fitted with lanyards or rigging screws, with which they are set up to eyeplates in the deck; the gripes must not be set up too taut, otherwise the shape of the boat may be distorted and the crutches may split the planking. In open boats a wire span is fitted between opposite clamps of the gripes and set up by a rigging screw or a lanyard. When a boat is crutched down her cover should be put on and secured by the lanyards to the shackles provided on the crutches. In hot climates it is particularly important that a boat should be covered during the day to preserve her structure from the heat of the sun. A small amount of water in the bilges will help to preserve the watertightness of the boat.

SLINGING AND DISENGAGING

Ships' boats are fitted with slings for hoisting at davits or by crane or derrick. These *boat's slings* are of chain when the boat is permanently hoisted at davits and consist of two sets, of which the after set is shown in fig. 9–18. Each boat has its own fitted slings.

When a boat is normally hoisted by crane or derrick the boat's slings are made of wire rope joined to rings to which the legs of a two-legged *bridle sling* are hooked (fig. 9–19 (i)), or the boat may be hoisted by a four-legged bridle sling shackled to four *gunwale sling-plates* (fig. 9–19 (ii)).

When a boat, normally hoisted at davits, is hoisted by crane, either a bridle sling with spreader is used, hooked into the boat's chain slings, or wire boat's slings and a bridle sling are used. The purpose of the spreader is to ensure a vertical lift at each set of boat's slings, otherwise an undue stress would be applied to the stem and stern ringbolts and the boat would be distorted. Spreaders are marked with the weights to which they have been tested, and it is important that a spreader of the correct length and strength be used.

The slings of a boat are fitted in the dockyards by experienced shipwrights so that the weight of the boat will be correctly distributed between the legs. The slings of boats hoisted at davits are carefully adjusted to conform to the span of the davits; a boat should therefore be hoisted by her own slings and at her own davits whenever practicable. When lowered, her slings should always remain in the boat. Much time will be saved when hoisting boom boats if a part of the forward leg or legs of bridle slings is painted a distinctive colour.

The various lifts of ship's boats are shown in figs. 9–20 and 9–21.

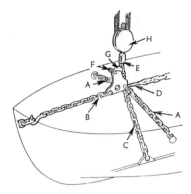

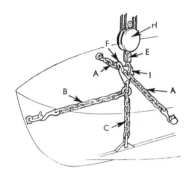

AFTER SLING OF A SEA BOAT

AFTER SLING OF A BOAT OTHER THAN A SEA BOAT

A   Steadying spans hooked to
     eyebolts in gunwales
B   After leg of sling hooked to
     after ringbolt
C   Lower leg of sling shackled to
     keel sling-plate
D   Wire pendant of fore-and-after
     (disengaging gear)

E   Swivel-ring shackle on lower
     block of fall
F   Shackle for davit slip
G   Robinson's disengaging hook
H   Lower block of fall
I   Robinson's common hook

FIG. 9–18. Slings of boats hoisted at davits

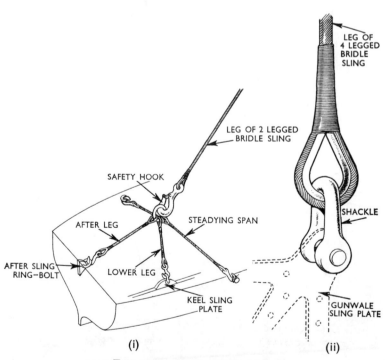

FIG. 9–19. Slings of boom boats

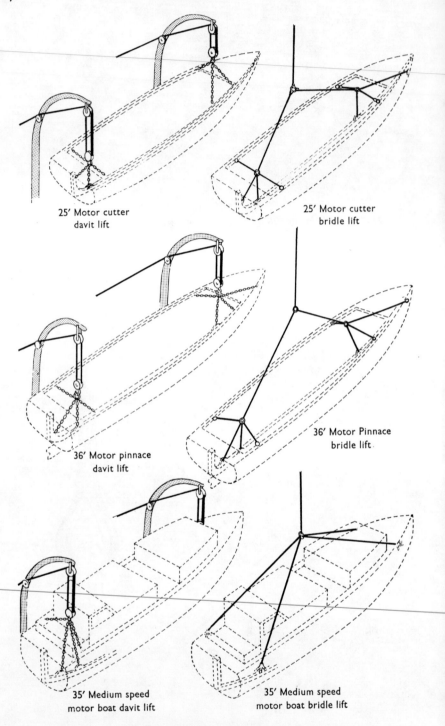

25' Motor cutter
davit lift

25' Motor cutter
bridle lift

36' Motor pinnace
davit lift

36' Motor Pinnace
bridle lift

35' Medium speed
motor boat davit lift

35' Medium speed
motor boat bridle lift

FIG. 9–20. Methods of slinging boats (1)

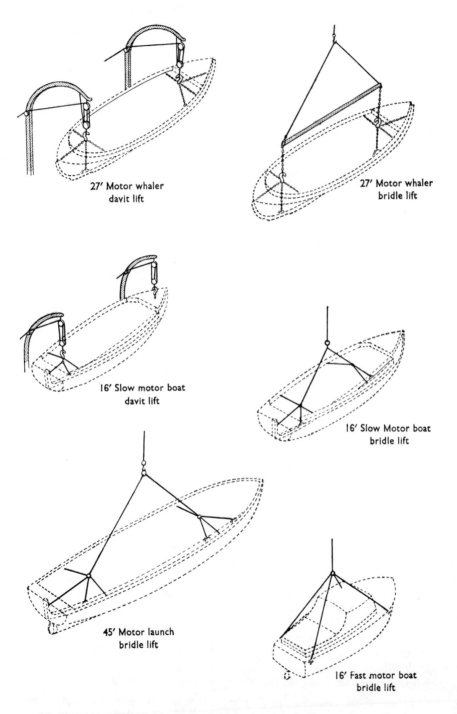

27' Motor whaler
davit lift

27' Motor whaler
bridle lift

16' Slow motor boat
davit lift

16' Slow Motor boat
bridle lift

45' Motor launch
bridle lift

16' Fast motor boat
bridle lift

FIG. 9–21. Methods of slinging boats (2)

DISENGAGING GEAR

There are two main types of disengaging gear—one which cannot be operated until the boat is completely waterborne and the weight is off the falls, and the other which is slipped whilst the boat is clear of the water. A combination of the two types, permitting airborne or waterborne release as desired, is also available. Merchant Navy boats are fitted with the first type, the design in general use being the *Mills release gear*; this design has the advantage of easy re-engagement and is fitted in R.N. survey boats and landing craft.

Warships' boats are fitted with the second type, the design used being *Robinson's disengaging gear*; one set is fitted to each seaboat and some ships carry a spare. The Robinson's gear consists of two tumbler hooks, to which are connected the legs of the slings and the steadying spans (fig. 9–22). The tumbler hook is held in place by a removable safety pin, and the releasing devices within the hooks are connected by a span called the *fore-and-after*. The fore-and-after is made up of two wire rope pendants which are connected by a chain; a bottle-screw slip is shackled to the after pendant and its tongue engages in one of the long links of the chain; the slip is operated by a releasing lever. When the boat is slung on the falls with the fore-and-after slack, the weight of the boat is on the safety pins and they cannot be removed from their hooks. When the fore-and-after is set up the weight of the boat is taken off the pins, which can then be removed, so that when the slip of the fore-and-after is released by its lever the two hooks are released simultaneously from the lower blocks of the falls.

A disengaging hook is illustrated in fig. 9–23, and its action is shown in fig. 9–24. Fig. 9–24 (i) shows the parts of the hook when it is set up ready for slipping, with the weight of the boat on the hook. The tumbler hook is pivoted between the two side plates, which are riveted together, and its tail is supported on the nose of the releasing lever, which is pivoted through its head. In this position the pull of the weight on the hook forces its tail down on to the nose of the releasing lever and so forces the heel of the releasing lever back against the safety pin, which is thus jammed in position. The hook is prevented from closing by the rivet A which bears on its tail, and the forward travel of the toe of the releasing lever is limited by the rivet B. The jaws of the hook are moused by the mousing link, which is pivoted at its foot and held in place by a spring (fig. 9–23). The turning outwards of the mousing link is limited by the rivet C, and its turning inward is limited by the toe of the releasing lever.

The end of the fore-and-after is connected to the tail of the releasing lever, and when the fore-and-after is taut the tail of the releasing lever is drawn forward slightly, taking the weight off the safety pin, which can then be removed from its hole. The hook is then held in place by the releasing lever and the fore-and-after. When the fore-and-after is slipped the releasing lever is free to turn on its pivot, so that it is turned backwards by the pressure of the tail of the tumbler hook on its nose (figs. 9–24 (ii) and (iii)). Eventually the tail of the hook slips off the nose of the releasing lever and the hook is up-ended, thus releasing the boat from the swivel-ring shackle on the fall.

To set up the hook for hooking on, it should first be turned to its forward position, and then the releasing lever should be moved to its forward position by hauling on the pendant of the fore-and-after, after which the safety pin should be inserted in its hole and moused.

The length of the fore-and-after is to a limited extent adjustable by means of

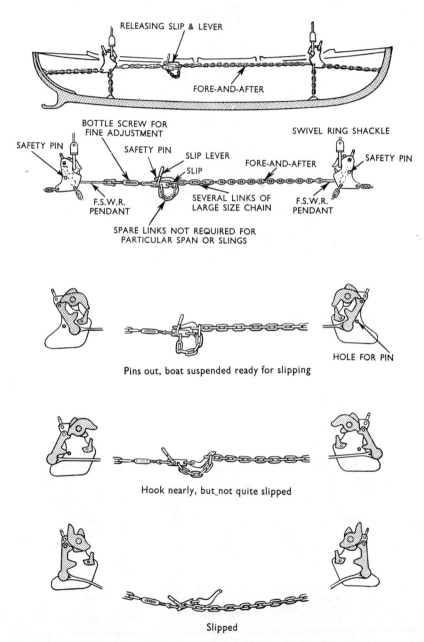

Pins out, boat suspended ready for slipping

Hook nearly, but not quite slipped

Slipped

FIG. 9–22. Operation of Robinson's disengaging gear

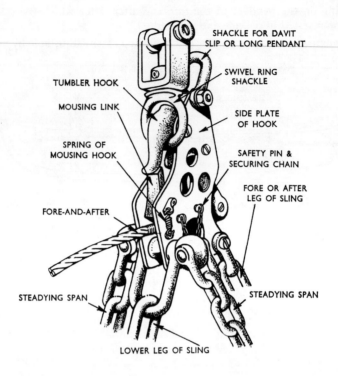

FIG. 9–23. Robinson's disengaging hook

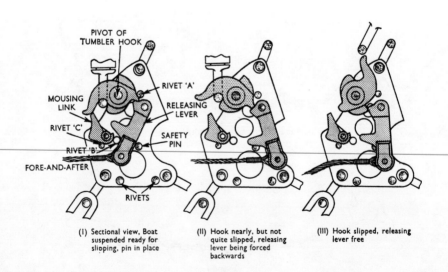

FIG. 9–24. Action of Robinson's disengaging hook

several links in the chain which are large enough to take over the tongue of the slip, so that the same fore-and-after can be used in several types of boat.

To set up the disengaging gear the hooks are first set up and then hooked on to the lower blocks of the falls, facing each other, and with the slip of the fore-and-after aft in the boat. The bottle-screw of the fore-and-after is then set to its maximum scope; the fore-and-after is then set up hand-taut by engaging the tongue of its slip in the most appropriate link of the chain, and is finally adjusted by screwing up the bottle-screw until the weight of the boat is taken off the safety pins.

Questions on this chapter will be found in Appendix 2.

CHAPTER 10

Boat Handling

LOWERING AND HOISTING BOATS IN HARBOUR

Many types of boats are in use in the Royal Navy and all require different methods for lowering and hoisting. To avoid detailing every drill it is intended here to give the drill only for the lowering and hoisting of the 27 ft motor whaler, when stowed at davits, and a general description of hoisting boats in and out by crane or derrick. Other davit boats follow this drill in general, but it is left to the individual ship to form its own drill for each davit boat other than the 27 ft motor whaler.

Whenever a boat is being manned, lowered or hoisted no one in her is allowed to be before the foremost fall or abaft the after fall; because, if one fall were to part, a man in either of these positions would be crushed between the other fall and the bow or stern of the boat. No one in the boat is allowed to place his hand on the falls, and everyone in the boat must hold on to a lifeline.

DRILL FOR LOWERING A 27 ft MOTOR WHALER FROM DAVITS IN HARBOUR

The crew consists of the coxswain, four seamen and one M.E. The lowerers may be forecastlemen (or other part of ship) or watch or part of watch.

Order	Action
'*Away Motor Whaler's crew, prepare your boat for lowering.*' '*Forecastlemen* (or other part-of-ship or watch, or part of the watch) *muster abreast the Motor Whaler's davits.*'	The crew fall in abreast their boat, are mustered by the coxswain, then man the boat. One seaman tends the foremost block, the coxswain tends the after block. The other seamen sit on their thwarts, and the M.E. sits by the engine.
	The lowerers, directed by the Petty Officer in charge, clear away around the davits, fake down the boat's falls for running, and man the falls inboard of the cleats or staghorns.
'*Ease back the slips.*'	The bowman and the coxswain unscrew the davit rigging slips until the weight of the boat is taken on the falls.
'*Off slips.*'	The bowman and the coxswain knock off the slips and screw the slip up into its shortened position. The crew man the lifelines.
'*Turns for lowering.*'	The lowerers remove the outer turns from the cleats or staghorns and back up the falls.

276

'Start the engine.'

The M.E. starts the engine, and reports to the coxswain when it is running correctly. The coxswain reports *'All ready in the boat, Sir.'*

'Start the falls.'

The falls are surged handsomely round the cleats or staghorns so that the boat is lowered slowly.

'Lower away.'

This is the next order given if all is well. The falls are surged roundly and without jerking so that the boat is lowered more rapidly, care being taken to keep the falls under perfect control and to keep the boat on an even keel.

'Handsomely foremost (or after) fall', or *'Avast lowering foremost (or after) fall.'*

If the boat is not being lowered on an even keel these orders may be given to correct her trim. When she is again on an even keel the order *'Lower away'* is given, the boat being again lowered at the normal speed by both falls.

'Light to.'

This order is given when the boat is water-borne. The lowerers let go the falls, remove the lowering turns from the cleats or stag-horns and overhaul the falls sufficiently to enable the bowman and coxswain to unhook the falls from the boat's slings, *the after fall being unhooked before the foremost fall.*

The falls are then recovered inboard by the lowerers, the lower blocks secured to the griping slips at the heels of the davits, the falls rounded up and their hauling parts flemished or faked down, or reeled up. The falls should not be crossed because, when being rounded up, they would be chafed on the cheeks of the steel upper blocks.

The lifelines are recovered inboard and cheesed down, and the boat proceeds to the gangway, boom or as ordered by the Officer of the Watch.

DRILL FOR HOISTING A 27 ft MOTOR WHALER AT DAVITS IN HARBOUR

Boats are normally hoisted by power, using boat-hoisting winches; but power may not always be available, so the seaman must know how to hoist a boat by hand. The following drill is a guide for hoisting a boat by hand; the orders would be slightly modified for power hoisting.

Order	*Action*
'*Away Motor Whaler's crew, prepare your boat for hoisting.*'	The whaler's crew man their boat, set up the forward and after slings, and move under the davits.
'*Topmen* (or other part-of-ship or watch, or part of watch) *reeve Motor Whaler's falls.*' (The falls are usually rove by the part-of-ship to which the boat is assigned.)	The part-of-ship hands cast off the lower blocks from the davit griping slips, take the turns off the cleats or staghorns, then over-haul the falls until the blocks are a foot or two clear of the water with the parts clear for running.
	The falls are rove through the necessary leading blocks and led clear along the deck.
	The whaler then hooks on. The bowman reports when he has hooked on forward, whereupon the coxswain hooks on aft and reports to the Officer or Petty Officer in charge '*Boat hooked on, Sir.*' Meanwhile spare hands in the boat climb inboard by the lifelines and stand by the falls.

While the boat is being hooked on, extra hands required to man the falls are piped to muster, e.g. '*Quarterdeckmen and forecastlemen up motor whaler.*' The hands man the falls evenly, with no one between the falls, and the Chief Boatswain's Mate, or the Petty Officer or Leading Hand in charge, reports '*Falls manned, Sir.*' The following orders, which should be repeated on the boatswain's call, are then given:

Order	*Action*
'*Haul taut singly.*'	The falls are hauled taut separately and all slack is taken down. Each man faces away from the davits, his arms spread and overlapping his neighbours'.
'*Marry.*'	The falls are brought together and gripped as one by the two lines of men.
'*Hoist away.*'	The hands run away with the falls and the boat is run up quickly and smoothly. When each man reaches the limit of available deck space, he doubles back and takes up the falls again.
'*Walk.*'	This order is given when the boat is nearing the davit heads. The hands break into a walk and walk the boat up the last foot or two.
'*High enough.*'	This order is given as the boat's falls are nearly two blocks. The hands stop hauling, but keep their weight on the falls.
'*Separate the falls.*'	The falls are separated from each other and the men in each line keep their weight on the falls. The men turn and face the boat, backing up the fall with both hands in front of the body.

If the boat is not then horizontal at her davits the order 'Midship fall, hoist' or 'Shipside fall, hoist' is given, and the men on the fall indicated hoist away on their fall until the boat is on an even keel and the order 'High enough' is given.

Order	Action
'*On slips.*'	The bowman and coxswain pass the tongues of their slips *down* and *through* the shackle provided on the boat's slings, and secure the tongue with the link and pin of the slip. The bowman reports to the coxswain '*Forward slip on*' and the coxswain then reports '*Both slips on, Sir.*'
'*Ease to the slips.*'	The hands keep the falls in hand and walk towards the davits until the slips take the weight of the boat and the falls slacken.
'*Light to.*'	A bight of about two fathoms of each of the slack falls is lighted towards the davits and the remainder let go. The hands positioned at the davits pass the bights over the davit sheaves, haul taut, belay them to the davit cleats or to the staghorns on deck, and report '*Foremost* (or *after*) *fall belayed, Sir.*'

The falls are then unrove from the leading blocks and coiled down or reeled up. The crew square off their boat on an even keel, coil down the lifelines, clean her and see that she is shipshape and man-of-war fashion.

NOTE. At all times when a boat is to be lowered or hoisted adequate lines must be provided forward and aft to control the fore-and-aft movement of the boat until she is either ready to move off or is clear of the water.

Some whalers, when being hoisted at davits, are not hung from the davit head by davit slips, but are temporarily held by the davit lifelines. When the boat's falls are nearly two blocks and the order 'High enough' is given, the following orders would then apply:

Order	Action
'*Pass the lifelines.*'	The bowman and coxswain pass the bights of their lifelines under the boat's slings diagonally, over the davit head, haul taut, pass the bight again over the davit head, under the slings and dog the end round all parts and back it up. On completion the bowman reports to the coxswain '*All fast forward*', and the coxswain then reports '*All fast in the boat, Sir.*'
'*Ease to the lifelines.*'	The hands keep the falls in hand and walk towards the davits until the lifelines take the weight of the boat and the falls slacken.

The falls are belayed as described previously and the lifelines eased until the falls have the weight of the boat. The lifelines are then cast off and coiled down in the boat.

HOISTING BOATS IN AND OUT BY CRANE OR DERRICK

Hoisting out

A boom boat must be hoisted out of her crutches with as much care as she is pitched in them, otherwise she may easily be damaged. The purchase of the crane or derrick should exactly plumb the ring of the sling when the weight of the boat is evenly distributed between its legs. For a light boat in calm weather only two steadying lines are necessary, one made fast to her bows and the other to her stern, but a heavy boat should have a steadying line made fast to each bow and quarter. *No one should ever be in a boat when she is slung inboard*; when hoisting her out, the crew should man her when she is slung over the side, and when hoisting her in they should step out of the boat on to the deck as she reaches deck level.

Hoisting in

As soon as the boat comes alongside under the purchase of the crane or derrick, head and stern lines should be passed into her and made fast; they should be led from well before and well abaft the boat, and tended. When the boat is level with the deck two more steadying lines may be made fast to her bows and stern if necessary.

PULLING

This section introduces the seaman to boat pulling. It contains instructions on how to check the boat's gear, how to instruct in boat pulling, the orders to expect after manning the boat, and pulling drill whilst under way.

CHECKING THE EQUIPMENT OF A PULLING BOAT

Before taking away a pulling boat her coxswain should see that all her equipment is correct. The more important points requiring his attention are given below.

Plug. This should be securely inserted in its hole.

Oars. There should be a full complement and one spare; it is particularly important that a dinghy equipped with only one pair of sculls should carry a spare oar. In double-banked boats, bow and stroke oars should be placed along the middle of the thwarts and the remainder on their respective sides, with their looms aft and all squared off; in single-banked boats the blades should be aft, and only the bow oar should be placed amidships, with its blade forward.

Crutches (single-banked boats, except motor whalers). There should be a full complement and one spare, and each should be secured by its lanyard to the boat. The lanyard may be spliced to the eye at the end of the shank, but this necessitates reeving the lanyard through the socket and toe-piece before shipping the crutch. A better method is to have the lanyard spliced round the groove at the shoulders of the crutch and secured to the rising midway between two sockets; the crutch can then easily be moved from one socket to another, or from one side of the boat to the other.

Shutters (double-banked boats and motor whalers). There should be one for each rowlock and its lanyard should be secured to the rising of the boat.

Stretchers. One should be fitted in place for each thwart.

Rudder. This should be shipped and its lanyard secured to the after ringbolt.

Tiller or Yoke. This should be shipped and secured with its split pin.

Painter. This should be shackled to the stem ringbolt.

Towing bollard. If portable, this should be in the boat together with its clamp and pin.

Slings, Baler, Bucket, Anchor, Cable, Boat's bag, Spare tiller, Lazy painter, Sternfast, Fenders and two Boat-hooks should all be stowed in the boat.

Special gear. In addition, any of the following special stores and fittings may have to be taken away on certain occasions: Lantern and candles, sea anchor, boat's compass, ensign and pennant staves, drinking water in sealed cans, strongback, spare thwart (32 ft cutters only), lifebuoy and lifejackets.

Boat's distress box and boat's bag

Distress box. This box can either be portable or a fixture in the boat. Its contents of pyrotechnics are for use when the boat requires to attract attention in an emergency. The contents of the box vary and depend to a large extent upon the station on which the ship is serving. For example, in the Far East a green light may denote the presence of sharks, yet in home waters it may denote something entirely different. In making up the outfit the Boat Officer should be guided both by current Admiralty Fleet Orders and Local Station Orders.

Boat's bag. This is a canvas bag made up in the ship. It contains sufficient equipment to repair a damaged hull, torn sails or other damage to fittings and boat. The items described below should always be stowed in the boat's bag when the boat is run under normal conditions. However, Service boats are sometimes detached for prolonged periods, and when this occurs it is necessary to increase both the items and the quantity of the contents of the boat's bag and, in some cases, to split the contents into two bags, the bags then being named the Boat's bag and the Carpenter's bag. It is left to the ship's Boat Officer to decide.

Contents of boat's bag. Spunyarn; tallow; palm and needle; marline spike; roping or seaming twine; beeswax; hand axe; a 1-lb hammer; cold chisel; tommy bar; punch; adjustable spanner; spare boat's plug (if the boat is so fitted); spare crutch (single-banked pulling boats only); box of matches in a watertight tin; electric torch; *Minor Landing Craft and Boat's Signal Book* (B.R.98(3)) in a protective cover; pair of hand semaphore flags; hand answering pennant; ensign and pennant in a protective wallet; boat's lead and line; 8 sq. ft of canvas; 3 copper tingles, squares varying from 6 in. to 12 in. in size, with nail holes punched round the edges; 2 sq. ft of fearnought; quarter pound of $\frac{5}{8}$-in. copper tacks; two beechwood wedges; a 1-in. wood chisel and a punch for copper tacks.

NOTE. Instructions for carrying out temporary repairs to the hulls of boats are given in Volume II.

INSTRUCTION IN BOAT PULLING

The following notes on instruction in boat pulling are given as a general guide to instructors. The principles of pulling are applicable to any type of boat, but there are certain minor differences in drill for single- and double-banked boats. It is important to stress at the beginning that when the blade of an oar is placed vertically in the water and the loom is pulled, the blade is gripped by the water and the boat is levered forward by the rowlock or crutch. The more efficient the design of blade, the better the grip on the water.

Manning the boat

It is assumed that the boat is alongside a ship or landing place and manned by two boat keepers. The crew should be detailed for their thwarts before manning the boat: in a Montague whaler the bowman, No. 3 and stroke, pull starboard oars and sit on the port side of their thwarts; the remainder pull port oars and sit on the starboard side of their thwarts. On the order 'Man the boat' the bowman and stroke relieve the boat keepers of their boat-hooks and hold the boat alongside while standing, respectively, in the head and stern sheets, and the remainder sit on their appointed thwarts. The crew should be taught to step (not jump) on to the thwarts or benches and thence to the bottom boards; they should also be taught to avoid stepping on the gunwale, to move carefully in the boat, and to step over the thwarts and not jump from thwart to thwart. The crutches should be unshipped, the fenders out and the oars squared off in their proper positions.

Each oarsman should sit squarely and upright on his thwart, with the after edge of the thwart where his buttocks meet his thigh muscles. His stretcher should be adjusted so that when his feet are resting on it his knees are slightly bent; his heels should be together and his toes turned outwards at an angle of 45°. The oar should be held with the hands from twelve to eighteen inches apart. The grip on the oar should be firm but light, with the fingers over the oar, the thumb underneath, and the inner wrist slightly arched. Both elbows should be close to the sides of the body and the back should be straight. This is the position of 'Oars'.

Initial training (fig. 10–1)

First stage. At the order 'Oars forward' each man bends forward from the hips, keeping his arms and back straight, until his trunk is between 30° and 40° from the vertical. In this position the oars should be at an angle of about 30° from the fore-and-aft line of the boat, with the blades about a couple of inches off the water and slightly over the vertical (fig. 10–1, positions 9, 10 and 1).

At the order 'Catch and pull through' each man lowers the blade of his oar into the water by raising his hands a few inches; he then pulls the loom by driving his feet against the stretcher and, while keeping his arms and back straight, swinging his trunk backwards until it is about 10° to 20° beyond the vertical (positions 2, 3 and 4). The end of the stroke is made, with the trunk still in this position, by bending the elbows and pulling the loom of the oar in to the chest with the arm and shoulder muscles, which should bring the blade

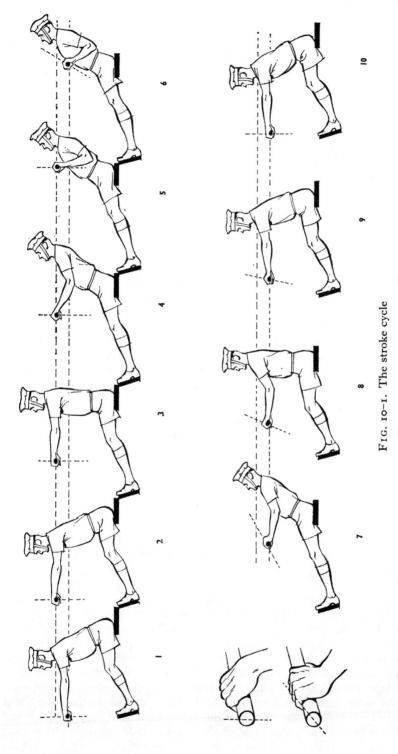

Fig. 10–1. The stroke cycle

of the oar just clear of the water at an angle of 45° with the vertical (position 5). These four stages are continuous.

At the order 'Oars' the recovery is made by dropping the hands a few inches to bring the oar to the horizontal, and dropping the wrists to feather the oar so that its blade is horizontal. The arms are then thrust forward and the trunk is swung upright by the stomach muscles until the position of 'oars' is again reached, this movement being helped by pulling with the legs against the straps which hold the feet to the stretcher (positions 6, 7 and 8).

This sequence is continued until all the crew are proficient in handling their oars.

Attention should be paid at this and subsequent stages to the following points. The crew should reach well aft when in the 'oars forward' position, but their buttocks should not leave the thwarts. The catch should be made exactly together, with as much weight as possible on the looms of the oars, and the arms should be kept straight throughout the stroke until the trunk has reached its backward position; if this is done correctly the oars will come home easily at the end of the stroke. The trunk should swing backwards and forwards in the fore-and-aft line, and the elbows should be kept close to the sides at the end of each stroke. The back should always be kept straight; this ensures that the full weight of the body is applied to the loom of the oar and also allows the man to breathe correctly. The trunk should not be allowed to fall too far back at the end of the stroke, because this puts an undue strain on the stomach muscles and encourages the fault of pulling the trunk up to the oar. At the end of the stroke the hands must be dropped before the wrists to ensure that the blade is clear of the water before it is feathered. At the start of the recovery the hands should lead the body and not follow it.

Second stage. The next stage of training is to blend the 'oars forward', the 'catch and pull through' and the 'recovery' into an even, rhythmic motion, without sacrificing the force of the catch, the drive of the pull through and the speed of recovery.

At this and subsequent stages attention should be paid to the following points. In the 'oars forward' position the shoulders should be kept braced back, and the arms and wrists should be rigid when the catch is made. At the moment of the catch and throughout the greater part of the stroke the legs should exert a powerful drive against the stretcher. The crew should begin and end each stroke together and any raggedness should be checked. There is no harm in allowing a crew to time the catch by glancing at the blades of the oars if in so doing the head is kept erect and facing aft. Any tendency to roll or turn the head should be checked, because this will upset the balance of the body and the rhythm of the stroke. The crew should time the end of the stroke by the click of the oars shifting in the crutches. There should be no pause at the moment before the catch, and the catch should not be started before the blade is in the water. If the blade enters the water with a splash it is a sign that the catch has started too early, which is a frequent cause of *catching a crab*. The blade should leave the water cleanly at the end of the stroke, leaving a swirl in the water. If spray is thrown aft by the blade as it leaves the water the stroke has been finished too early and the hands have been dropped too soon. If a feathery sheet of water runs off the blade as it leaves the water the oar has been feathered too early by dropping the wrists before the hands; this also is a frequent cause of catching a crab. If a man catches a crab by feathering too early he should not attempt to force the blade out of the water, but should allow the oar to swing fore-and-aft in the crutch before recovering it, or lift the oar out of the rowlock before it jams.

Third stage. In the final stage of initial training the pause between strokes at the 'oars' position is progressively reduced until each stroke is blended imperceptibly with the next. At this stage particular attention should be paid to the timing of the catch and the recovery, and to the rhythm of the stroke cycle. Tendencies towards over-rigidity and overstrain should be checked and the easy application of force at the right moment encouraged. The three stages of training should not be hurried; each stage of the stroke cycle should be thoroughly mastered before it is blended with the others.

Hints to instructors

General hints

1. Patience in dealing with faults is essential.
2. Insist on strict attention by all members of the crew.
3. Where possible, faults should be demonstrated practically.
4. The cause of a fault may be obscure; the instructor should be able to distinguish between cause and effect, and to trace a fault to its source.
5. The faults of each member of the crew should be corrected individually, and not by remarks addressed to the crew as a whole.
6. Ensure that faults are not caused by defective or ill-fitting equipment.

Faults to guard against

1. Using the biceps instead of the shoulder muscles to end a stroke; this results in the elbows sticking out from the sides.
2. Faulty grasp of the looms; this is the cause of many faults.
3. Over-reaching with the shoulders at the start of a stroke, instead of having them braced back.
4. Meeting the oar and rowing deep at the finish; usually both are caused by ending the stroke with the arms alone.
5. Screwing to one side during the stroke, due to the oarsman using one arm or leg more than the other.
6. Feathering under water, which is due to a faulty grasp, or to slurring into one the two motions of dropping the hands and turning the wrists at the end of the stroke.
7. Uneven swing forward, due to a sluggish or early recovery, or to the misuse of the correct muscles in recovering.
8. Faulty timing, which may be caused by rushing the forward swing, recovering too early or too late, under- or over-reaching at the start of the stroke, or watching the blade of the oar at the recovery.
9. Not rowing the stroke home; this may be due to a weak catch, a weak drive, an early recovery, or over-reaching at the start of the stroke.
10. Swinging across the boat when coming forward, due to not sitting squarely, or to leaning too much on the loom; the cause of leaning too much on the loom may be incorrect balance or positioning of the oar in the rowlock or crutch.

11. Fouling the water while swinging forward; this may be caused by the stretcher being too close to the thwart, or by the hands not having been dropped far enough, or shot out from the chest quickly enough, on recovery.
12. Bending the arms too soon, due to lack of drive with the leg and back muscles at the start of the stroke.
13. Clipping the water, due to faulty grasp of the loom at the start of the stroke, thus allowing the blade to enter the water at an incorrect angle.
14. Rowing deep, due to slicing the blade into the water at the start of the stroke, the cause of which may be a faulty grasp or a late recovery.

Pulling orders

When a pulling boat is under way any order to the oarsmen except 'Hold water' is obeyed on completing one full stroke after the order is given. All such orders should be given at the moment when the blades of the oars are in the water.

On obeying a pulling order the crew take their time by the stroke oarsman, who is usually the next senior rating to the coxswain. (In the absence of the coxswain the stroke oarsman takes charge of the boat; in double-banked boats he pulls the starboard stroke oar.) When 'port' or 'starboard' is included in a pulling order, it refers to the bank of oars on the port or starboard side of the boat, respectively.

Before saluting by tossing or laying on the oars, the cautions 'Stand-by to toss oars' or 'Stand-by for oars' should be given.

'*Ship your oars.*' This is the order to place the oars in the rowlocks or crutches in readiness for pulling.

'*Toss your oars.*' This is the order to bring the oars smartly to a vertical position, with the looms resting on the bottom boards and the blades fore-and-aft; it is not given in single-banked boats.

'*Shove off.*' This is the order to shove the boat off with the looms of the oars from the ship or landing place alongside which she is lying, or from the bottom if the boat is grounded.

'*Oars down.*' In double-banked boats when the oars are tossed, this is the order to bring them down into their rowlocks ready for pulling, i.e. with the oars horizontal, at right-angles to the fore-and-aft line, and blades horizontal.

'*Give way together.*' This is the order to start pulling, and it is obeyed together by the whole crew. If only one bank of oars is required to give way, the order 'Give way starboard' or 'Give way port' is given.

'*Oars.*' This is an order to cease pulling. At this order the crew sit squarely and upright on their thwarts, with their oars horizontal and at right-angles to the fore-and-aft line of the boat and with the blades feathered, i.e. parallel with the water. The order 'Lay on your oars' allows the crew to relax from the position of 'Oars'; they may then either rest on the looms of their oars or lay in their oars athwart the boat with the grips under the gunwale. This order is also given to alert the crew before ordering 'Give way together.'

'*Hold water.*' This is the order to reduce or stop the way of the boat by holding the oars at right-angles to the fore-and-aft line of the boat and with their blades in the water; it should be obeyed as soon as it is given. If required to hold water with one bank of oars only, the order 'Hold water' is followed by 'starboard' or 'port'.

'*Back together.*' This is the order to back water together by pushing on the looms of the oars instead of pulling. If only one bank of oars is required to back water the order 'Back starboard' or 'Back port' is given.

'*Stroke together.*' This is the order for all to give one stroke together. If only one bank of oars is to give a stroke the order 'Stroke port' or 'Stroke starboard' is given.

'*Easy all.*' This is the order to pull less vigorously, so that the speed of the boat will be reduced. If the boat is being turned the order 'Easy port' or 'Easy starboard' may be given. To resume normal pulling the order 'Give way together' is given.

'*Mind your oars.*' This is a warning to the crew to keep the blades of their oars clear of some obstruction. If the warning concerns only one bank of oars the order 'Mind your starboard oars' or 'Mind your port oars' is given.

'*Eyes in the boat.*' This is an order to the crew to keep their gaze from wandering abroad, and to pay attention to their duties.

'*Bow.*' This is the order to the bowman of a single-banked boat to boat his oar and be ready to fend off the bows of the boat with his boat-hook. In double-banked boats the order is 'Bows', and in obeying it the bowmen first toss their oars and 'kiss' the blades together before boating them.

'*Way enough.*' This is the order which, when given in a single-banked boat, requires the oarsmen to pull one more stroke, pass the looms of their oars over their heads and to boat the oars. In the motor whaler the oar is lifted out of its rowlock before passing the loom over the head. In a double-banked boat the oars are tossed after one more stroke, the stroke oarsman calling out 'Oars up!' If the oars are not to be boated or tossed, the order 'Oars' is given.

'*Boat your oars.*' This is the order to unship the oars from the rowlocks or crutches and lay them fore-and-aft in the boat on their respective sides.

PULLING DRILL

Getting under way in a Montague whaler

At the order 'Shove off' the bowman shoves off the bows of the boat and lays in his boat-hook, the stroke oarsman lays in his boat-hook and fender and springs the boat ahead, then both sit down on their thwarts; Nos. 2, 3 and 4 lay in the fenders on their respective sides. At the order 'Ship your oars' Nos. 2 and 4 ship the crutches and oars of No. 3 and Stroke, while Stroke and No. 3 ship the crutches and oars of Nos. 4 and 2, and the bowman ships his own crutch and oar. At the order 'Oars' each man grasps the loom of his oar and brings the oar to the athwartships position, with the oar and blade horizontal.

Going alongside in a Montague whaler

When the boat is within about 50 yards of the accommodation ladder or landing place the order 'Bow' is given. At this order the bowman lays in his oar athwartships, unships it and boats it amidships with the blade forward;

10*

unships his crutch; then stands in the head sheets facing forward and holding the boat-hook vertically. At the same time Nos. 2, 3 and 4 and Stroke put out the fenders on their respective sides. At the order 'Way enough' the crew pull one more stroke; then, taking their time from Stroke who raises one hand, they allow their oars to swing fore-and-aft in the crutches and then fleet their looms forward. Stroke and No. 3 boat the oars of Nos. 4 and 2 and unship their crutches, and Nos. 2 and 4 boat the oars of No. 3 and Stroke and unship their crutches. Stroke then stands up ready to check the way of the boat as she goes alongside, using his boat-hook or a manrope. Bow holds the boat alongside with his boat-hook or the boatrope. Nos. 3 and 4 square off the oars on their respective sides.

Getting under way in a cutter

The two bowmen and the inner stroke oarsman stand in the head and stern sheets, respectively, and hold the boat alongside. The remainder of the crew sit on their thwarts and the coxswain sits on the dickie abaft the backboard. At the order 'Point your oars' the remainder of the crew unship the shutters from their rowlocks, take their oars by the looms and place the blades on the wash-strake. The order 'Toss your oars' is then given. At the order 'Shove off' the bowmen shove off and Stroke springs the boat ahead. The order 'Fenders in' is then given, followed by the order 'Oars down', when the oars are lowered gently into their rowlocks so that the blades do not touch the water. 'Give way together' is then ordered.

These orders are given in rapid sequence and are executed by the crew in precise unison. The stroke oarsman, having laid in his boat-hook and sprung the boat ahead, gets in his fender, ships his oar and picks up the stroke. The bowmen, after shoving off, get in their fenders, toss their oars, kiss the blades before shipping them, and then pick up the stroke.

Going alongside in a cutter

When the boat is within 50 yards or so of her destination the order 'Fenders out' is given, followed by the order 'Bows'. At this order the bowmen toss their oars, kiss the blades together and then lay them in amidships, passing the looms aft between the midship oarsmen; they then stand in the head sheets facing forward with their boat-hooks vertical, ready to fend off the bows. Then the order 'Way enough' is given and the boat's crew toss their oars, taking their time from the starboard Stroke, who calls out 'Oars up'. The inner Stroke boats his oar and stands up in the stern sheets facing outboard, with his boat-hook vertical, ready to fend off the boat or check her way.

When there is insufficient height alongside for the oars to remain tossed, the order 'Toss and boat your oars' is given after the order 'Way enough'. The oars are tossed and held vertically for an instant, after which they are laid in together.

Oars are never tossed when going alongside a vessel under way or going alongside a ship at anchor in a heavy sea or swell, because the blades of the oars may catch under some projection or the platform of the accommodation ladder, and drive the looms through the bottom of the boat as she rises to sea or swell. Under such conditions the order 'Way enough, boat your oars' is given, and the oars are lifted out of their rowlocks, the blades swung forward in a horizontal arc, and, as the oars are boated, the looms are fleeted aft. When leaving a vessel under these conditions the oars are first pointed forward over the gunwale and then swung outboard in a horizontal arc and shipped in their rowlocks.

SAILING

Few landsmen realise that sailing a boat requires skill, practice and experience. It is possible now to buy a boat, take it to the coast, launch it and sail away without passing any test of skill and without any knowledge of the regulations to prevent collision.

The sea is a dangerous element, taking its annual toll of those who disregard the most elementary precautions when they set out upon it.

Those who cannot swim must always wear lifejackets. **Those who can swim must wear lifejackets in small sailing boats.**

The inexperienced should not sail in unfrequented waters, where an accident may be unobserved. **If you do capsize, try to remain with your boat.**

Learn the Rules for preventing collisions before you sail. **It may be too late to learn them afterwards.**

TERMS USED IN SAILING

In directing the steering of a sailing vessel the tiller is referred to as the helm, and in directing its movement reference is made to the weather or lee side of the vessel, i.e. to the upper or lower side, respectively; thus, at the order 'Up helm' the tiller is moved towards the weather or upper side of the boat, and at the order 'Down helm' it is moved towards the lee or lower side. When the helm is put up the bows will pay off from the wind, and when put down the bows will turn towards the wind; the order 'Bear up'* has the same meaning and effect as 'Up helm'. A boat is said to carry *weather helm* if, with the helm amidships, she tends to fly up into the wind; and she is said to carry *lee helm* if, with the helm amidships, she tends to pay off from the wind.

Close-hauled. A boat is close-hauled or sailing *by* or *on the wind*, when her sheets are hauled close aft and all her sails are drawing and she is sailing as close as possible to the direction from which the wind is blowing with advantage in working to windward. The actual angle for any particular boat depends upon her type and rig. Service boats, other than sail-training yachts, motor whalers and sailing dinghies, will not sail closer than about $4\frac{1}{2}$ points (50°) off the wind.

Full and by. This is sailing as near to the wind as possible while keeping the sails full.

---

* 'Bear up' has always been considered a bad term, as it is liable to confusion.

Sailing free. A boat is sailing free whenever her sails are filled and she is not sailing close-hauled, i.e. when sailing so that she is free to manœuvre on either side of her course without having to go about.

Reaching. A boat is reaching when she is sailing free with the wind abeam or before the beam, but is not sailing close-hauled. She is on a *close reach* or *fetching* when she is nearly close-hauled, and on a *broad reach* when the wind is abeam; and she is said to have a *soldier's wind* if she can sail to her destination on one reach and return from it on the other.

Running. A boat is running when she is sailing with the wind abaft the beam.

Port and starboard tacks. A boat is on the *port tack* when she is close-hauled with the wind on her port side, and on the *starboard tack* when she is close-hauled with the wind on her starboard side.

Tacking or *going about.* A boat *tacks* or *goes about* when she changes from one tack to the other by altering course into the wind and then away from it on the opposite tack. A boat is tacking or going about from the moment she is beyond head to wind until she has borne away; if beating to windward, to a close-hauled course; if not beating to windward, to the course on which her mainsail has filled. The order 'Ready about' is the warning given to the crew to stand by to tack. When the helm is put down the order 'Helm's a lee' or 'Lee ho' is given.

'Let draw.' This is the order to let go the weather sheet after tacking (or after it has been hauled to windward) and to haul aft the lee sheet.

Beating. When the destination of a sailing boat lies directly up wind she beats to windward by sailing close-hauled in a series of alternate tacks.

Gybing. A boat running before the wind and wishing to alter to a course which necessitates putting the stern of the boat through the wind, is said to *gybe*. A boat begins to gybe at the moment when, with the wind aft, the foot of her mainsail crosses her centre line and completes the gybe when the mainsail has filled on the other side.

Bearing away. This is altering course away from the wind until the boat is on her new course or begins to gybe.

Wearing. This is the term used to describe the action of altering course passing the stern through the wind. It is now virtually the same as gybing. In the past it meant keeping the sails under control (e.g. by brailing up or topping up), whereas gybing meant allowing the sails to move across out of control.

Running by the lee. A boat is running by the lee when she is running with her mainsail set on the windward side; she is then very liable to gybe, which is dangerous in strong winds.

Brought by the lee. A boat which is running before the wind is said to be brought by the lee when the wind suddenly changes from one quarter to the other; this often happens in squally weather owing to a shift of wind, but may also be due to a sudden yaw caused by bad steering.

To luff. This is altering course to bring the boat's head closer to the wind.

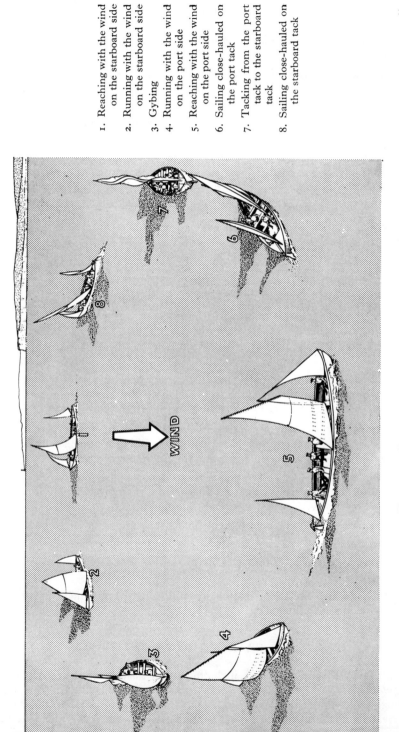

1. Reaching with the wind on the starboard side
2. Running with the wind on the starboard side
3. Gybing
4. Running with the wind on the port side
5. Reaching with the wind on the port side
6. Sailing close-hauled on the port tack
7. Tacking from the port tack to the starboard tack
8. Sailing close-hauled on the starboard tack

FIG. 10–2. Sailing terms

Luffing. A racing term which means to alter course towards the wind until the boat is head to wind.

To miss stays. A boat misses stays when she fails to go about from one tack to another and pays off on her original tack. If a boat misses stays frequently she would *wear* round to the other tack.

In irons. A boat is in irons when she fails to go about from one tack to the other and lies head to wind unable to pay off on either tack.

'*Keep away.*' An order to the helmsman to allow the bows to pay off from the wind; it is used instead of 'bear away' when the movement required is not so drastic.

'*No higher.*' An order to the helmsman to steer no closer to the wind.

'*Nothing off.*' An order to the helmsman not to allow the bows to pay off any further from the wind.

To weather. A boat weathers an object by passing to windward of it.

Flat aft. The sails of a boat are said to be flat aft when they are sheeted home as tautly as possible.

To back a sail. A sail is said to be backed when it is trimmed to catch the wind on what would normally be its lee side. This tends to stop the boat's headway, to drive her astern or, if in irons, to assist the boat to pay off on its new tack.

Flat aback. A boat is said to be taken flat aback when, owing to a sudden shift of wind or alteration of course, the wind suddenly fills the sails on their wrong side and so reduces the boat's speed or gives her sternway.

Heave to. A vessel may *heave to* because she wishes to stop or because the weather is too bad to continue on her course. A sailing boat is usually *hove to* as close to the wind as possible carrying the minimum canvas.

To hug the wind. This is to sail as close to it as possible. *To pinch* means to hug the wind too closely so that the sails are not properly filled and the boat therefore loses way.

To shorten sail. To take in sail by reducing the number or by reefing.

To set sail or *make sail.* To hoist the sails and get under way.

To goosewing. To set alternate sails to starboard and port when running before the wind.

The wind's eye. This refers to the actual direction from which the wind is blowing at any given moment.

SAILING RULES

To prevent collisions all vessels, including sailing boats, obey the *International Regulations for Preventing Collision at Sea* (usually called The Rule of the Road), though these may be modified by local regulations in narrow channels, harbours or rivers. No one is fit to be in charge of a boat, however small, unless he can apply the Regulations automatically. A summary of these regulations is given in Chapter 18, and the complete regulations are given in Volume II.

Racing. When racing, a boat may be required to comply with the *International Yacht Racing Union Rules* in addition to the Rule of the Road.

CONDUCT OF SAILING BOATS' CREWS

The way in which Service boats' crews conduct themselves whilst sailing can reflect credit or discredit upon the Royal Navy.

The crews of all sailing boats and yachts should always be dressed alike, perform their tasks quickly and smartly, and never shout or skylark.

When sailing open Service boats, but not racing, crews should comply in general with the following instructions:

When under way the crew should be used to balance the boat; for example, when beating to windward, or reaching, the position of the crew should be adjusted so as to keep the boat as nearly as possible upright, and the bowman should always keep a good lookout ahead and to leeward.

No one should move about the boat except when necessary, and then only quietly and carefully. No one should stand on the thwarts, or climb the rigging or the mast; if fouled gear aloft cannot be cleared with a boat-hook when standing on the bottom boards the sails and mast should be lowered to clear it.

Sheets should always be kept in hand (not belayed). Oars should never be shipped or used when under sail, except that in emergency the bow oars may be used to help to put the boat about. All running rigging should always be kept clear, the ends being neatly coiled and stowed so that the ropes will run freely when required.

It is bad seamanship to drift about in a flat calm with sails set because the slatting of the sails and the swinging of the spars chafes the gear; when the wind falls the sails should be furled, the masts lowered, the oars shipped and the boat pulled to her destination.

THEORY OF SAILING

To sail a boat intelligently a helmsman must possess an elementary knowledge of the theory of sailing and know how the wind acts on the sails to drive the boat ahead. The action of the force of the wind on the sail of a boat beating to windward is shown diagramatically in fig. 10–3. The sail acts as an airfoil, producing a large *lift* force AD at right-angles to the sail and a smaller *drag* force AC along the sail. The resultant force AB may be resolved into AF driving the boat along its course into the wind and a force AE at right-angles to this course.

The larger component AE acting on the sail tends to heel the boat over, but this tendency is largely overcome by the inherent stability of the boat and by positioning her crew to windward. The component AE would also tend to drive the boat to leeward, but is balanced by underwater hydrodynamic forces on the hull and keel, the course being inclined at a small angle to the fore-and-aft line of the boat. The smaller component AF, which is employed in propelling the boat ahead, is assisted by the shape of the boat's hull, which offers the least resistance to the water when the boat is moving on a course which is ahead or almost ahead.

If now the course of the boat is altered to bring the wind abeam, and if the trim of the sails is not altered, the lateral force tending to heel the boat over and drive her to leeward will be appreciably greater than that shown in fig. 10–3 and she will probably be blown over on her beam ends. If the sheets are

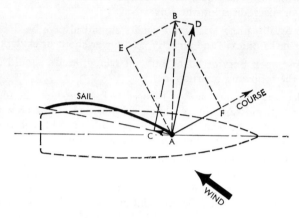

FIG. 10–3. Action of wind on the sails of a boat (1)

checked so that the sail takes up the position shown in fig. 10–4 the lateral component of the wind's force *AE* will be reduced, while the propelling component *AF* will be increased and the boat will move faster ahead than when the wind was on the bow.

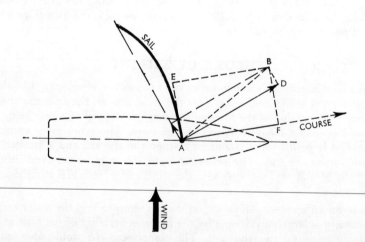

FIG. 10–4. Action of wind on the sails of a boat (2)

If this line of reasoning were carried a step further (by altering the course of the boat to bring the wind aft and by trimming the sails to the most effective angle with the wind), it would appear that the boat would move ahead still faster because of the further increase in the forward propelling component and the consequent reduction in the lateral component. This is not so, however, because so far we have only considered the effect of a steady wind on a boat at rest, whereas, in fact, her speed must be taken into account in order to determine the effective power of a wind to drive the boat ahead. If, for example, a boat is running at, say, 4 knots before a true wind of 10 knots (as in fig. 10–5 (i)),

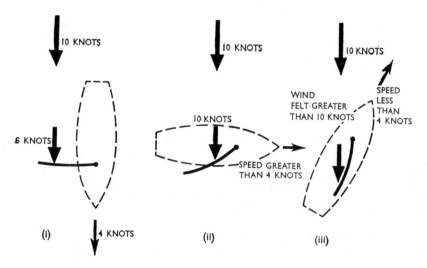

FIG. 10–5. Action of wind on the sails of a boat (3)

the effective wind acting on her sails to drive her ahead is only 6 knots. When the wind is abeam (as in fig. 10–5 (ii)) the effective wind is 10 knots, and though not all of it is employed in driving the boat ahead it will usually give the boat a greater speed than 4 knots. When the wind is on the bow (as in fig. 10–5 (iii)), although the effective wind is greater than 10 knots, its forward driving component is so reduced that the boat's speed will be much less than 4 knots.

A boat's speed is therefore greatest when she is reaching and least when she is sailing by the wind; and when running she will sail faster with the wind on the quarter than with the wind right aft. Though these deductions are dependent upon the shape of the boat, they are true of most modern sailing craft and, generally speaking, of all Service boats.

When the angle between the plane of the sails and the direction of the wind becomes less than what is known as the *critical angle* the sails will no longer hold the wind and its forward driving power will be lost. This critical angle differs with the rig and shape of the boat, and no two boats are exactly alike in this respect. In general it can be said that few Service boats will sail closer than $4\frac{1}{2}$ points (50°) from the wind, but when deciding the course to steer in order to weather an object an addition must be made to this $4\frac{1}{2}$ points to compensate for any leeway when beating or reaching. As a very rough guide, a boat should be able to weather an object on the opposite tack if she goes about when it bears about 3 points abaft the beam, but no hard and fast rule can be laid down because so much depends upon the skill of the helmsman, the set and trim of the sails, the trim of the boat, the strength of the wind and the state of the sea.

PRACTICE OF SAILING

The relationship between the pivoting point of the boat and the centre of pressure of the sail area, how to trim the boat to the best advantage, how best to set the sails, and how to trim them when beating, tacking, reaching, running or gybing are described below under their various headings.

Pivoting point (fig. 10–6)

Imagine the boat to be pivoted about a fixed and vertical pivot at some point along her keel, and floating broadside-on to a steadily flowing current; if then she shows no tendency to swing in line with the current she will be balanced about her pivoting point. If, however, she is now trimmed deeper by the bows or the stern she will present a larger area of her hull to the current before or abaft her pivot, respectively, so that she will be swung into line with the current unless the pivot is moved forward or aft to preserve her balance.

Now imagine a strong breeze blowing in the same direction as that in which the current is flowing; if the areas of the boat's freeboard before and abaft her pivot are unequal she will be swung by the wind in line with wind and current unless the pivot is shifted forward or aft the required distance to keep her balanced.

From these examples it will be seen that the pivoting point of a boat changes its position in accordance with her trim.

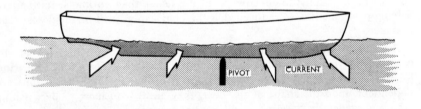

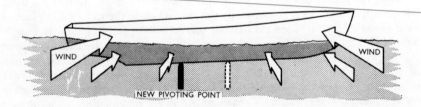

Fig. 10–6. Pivoting point of a boat

Centre of effort of sail area (fig. 10–7)

The centre of effort of any one sail is that point at which the driving force may be presumed to act (points A and B). This point will shift according to the trim of the sail and the angle between the plane of the sail and the direction of the wind. By combining the centres of effort of each sail, the centre of effort (C. of E.) of the total sail area can be obtained at X.

The centre of a boat's lateral resistance (C.L.R.) is at some point below the waterline and in line with her pivoting point (Y in fig. 10–7). It will shift as the trim of the boat alters in the same manner as does the pivoting point.

In a well-designed vessel the centre of effort of the sails should be as nearly as possible over her centre of lateral resistance, but, because both are continually changing their positions with the trim of the sails and of the boat, this cannot actually be achieved. If the centre of effort is abaft the centre of lateral resistance (as illustrated in fig. 10–7) the boat will tend to come up into the wind, and if before it she will tend to pay off from the wind. These tendencies can be countered by using the rudder, altering the trim of the boat, or altering the trim of the sails, and in practice all three are used continuously as the boat beats, reaches or runs.

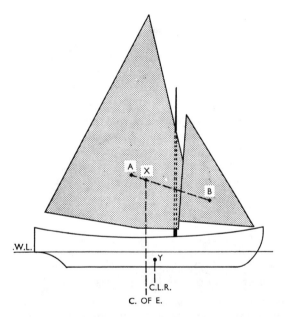

FIG. 10–7. Centre of effort of sail area and centre of lateral resistance

Use of rudder

A boat which tends to luff when the helm is amidships is said to carry *weather helm*, and a boat which tends to pay off is said to carry *lee helm*. The rudders of some Service boats do not project below the keel, and the more the boat heels over in a strong breeze the less the rudder is immersed and the less effective it therefore becomes. A boat carrying lee helm is therefore in danger of broaching-to and capsizing in a squall, because when she heels over to the wind her rudder is unable to counter her tendency to pay off broadside on to the wind. On the other hand, if a boat carrying weather helm is hit by a squall she comes up into the wind and so spills the wind from her sails. It is therefore always advisable in a Service boat to carry a certain amount of weather helm; but the speed of a boat carrying any helm will be reduced by the resistance of the rudder to the flow of water past it.

To give maximum effect to the rudder the crew should sit well to windward when beating or reaching so that the boat will heel to leeward as little as possible, and the boat may also be trimmed slightly by the stern by moving the crew further aft.

When altering course or going about, the helm should be eased over gently so as to *sail the boat round*; if it is suddenly put over, or if too much helm is used, the rudder will take the way off the boat and she will probably fail to answer her helm.

Trim of boat

The trim of a boat has a great effect on her sailing qualities and seaworthiness. Beating, reaching or running, light or strong winds, calm or rough seas, and deep or light loading, each require an adjustment of trim, and this adjustment is effected by shifting her ballast which, in a Service boat, is her crew. Generally speaking, a boat should be trimmed as nearly on an even keel as possible; if she needs much trimming to make her sail well, there is something wrong with the shape of her hull, her rig, or the disposition of the weights in her. The best trim for any given circumstances can be found only by experience, and the following remarks are given only as a general guide.

Passengers and stores should not be carried in the ends of the boat, because they would then so reduce the buoyancy of her bows and stern that she would not rise with the waves: she would therefore probably ship water over the bows when beating or reaching, or be pooped by a following sea when running; and excessive weight in the ends of a boat will also make her sluggish in answering her helm. When a boat is beating or reaching, undue weight in the bows will make her luff up, and undue weight in the stern will make her pay off. When a boat is running, undue weight in the bows will make her luff and may cause her to broach to and capsize. When beating or reaching, weather helm can therefore be corrected by trimming the boat by the stern, and lee helm by trimming her by the head. When running, a boat tends to bury her bows, and this should be corrected by trimming her by the stern.

If a boat pitches heavily in a head sea she may require trimming by the head to steady her and prevent her paying off; trimming her by the head will also lessen the chance of missing stays when going about.

Set of the sails

The set of a boat's sails is almost as important as their trim, and the chief factor in setting any sail is that its luff should always be set up taut.

In a standing lugsail the position of the strop on the yard is all-important. It should be placed at about one-third of the length of the yard from its throat, but exactly the best position can be found only by trial and error; by moving it towards the throat the yard will set higher and closer to the mast, but if it is moved too near the throat the downward pull of the tack tackle will give insufficient leverage on the yard to keep the leach taut. When the correct position of the strop is found it should be secured in place by thumb-pieces screwed to the yard on each side of the strop. When the yard is hoisted and the tack tackle set up a crease will be formed between the throat and the clew, but it will disappear when the sail is filled. When hoisted, the foot of the sail should be just clear of the gunwale or washstrake.

The correct lead of the fore sheets is also important. There should be a sufficiently wide gap between the leach of the foresail and the luff of the mainsail to allow the wind to flow freely between them, as shown in fig. 10–8 (i). In fig. 10–8 (ii) the foresail is not sheeted sufficiently far outboard. Fig. 10–8 (iii) shows the lead of a long-footed foresail, such as the genoa jib, which is particularly effective when reaching or beating in light winds.

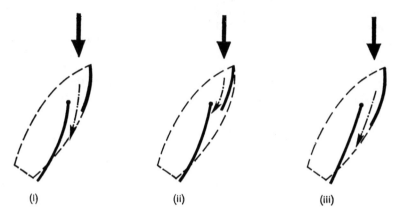

(i) (ii) (iii)

FIG. 10–8. Lead of fore sheets

If the sheets are led too far aft the foot of the sail will be too taut and the leach too slack, and if led too far forward the leach will be too taut and the foot too slack. When correctly led, a projection of the line of the sheet across the sail should approximately bisect the angle of the clew, and the pull of the sheet should tend to tauten the leach rather than the foot.

Most sails are cut to set in a slight curve or camber, whose greatest depth is usually just abaft the luff. Where a mainsail is bent to a boom the set of the foot can be altered by adjusting the clew lashing and the foot lacing. The sail should be allowed its full curvature when on a reach, but should be set fairly flat when beating.

Trimming the sails

The strength and direction of even a steady wind are continuously altering, and the art of sailing a boat lies mainly in paying constant attention to their slightest change and then altering course or trimming the sails to meet it.

Beating

The sheets should be hauled well aft and the boat steered as close to the wind as she will go without the luff of her foresail lifting. If the sheets are hauled too flat aft the sails will not hold the wind and the boat will lose way; the sails can be set flatter in a high wind than in a light wind, but they can also be set flatter in calm water than in rough water. When sailing on a wind the luffs of the sails should be just not lifting or shivering; to achieve this, first trim the sails correctly, then ease the helm down until the luffs start to lift, then ease the helm up until they are again steady, and keep the boat on that course.

Going about

Before going about from one tack to the other the boat should be paid off a little so as to gather enough way to enable her to fore-reach through the wind; the helm should then be eased gently down and the boat *sailed* through the wind on to the other tack. As the helm is put down the main sheet should be hauled aft and the fore sheet checked slightly, and as the bows pass through the eye of the wind the foresail should be backed by hauling aft the windward fore sheet, and the main sheet should be checked; this helps the boat to cast on the other tack. As soon as it is certain that the bows will pay off on the new tack the order 'Let draw, aft main sheet' should be given, the lee fore sheet and the main sheet being hauled aft at the order. If, as the bows come up to the eye of the wind, it appears unlikely that the boat will go about, the crew should immediately be fleeted aft to the old weather quarter (thus lightening the bows) and the foot of the foresail should be held out towards the old lee bow; if the boat then gathers sternway the helm should be reversed and the main sheet checked. When clawing off a lee shore, or when missing stays might be serious, an oar should always be kept ready to pull the bows round if required; this is the only occasion when oars may be used while under sail, because the lee oar may be caught in the water through the heeling of the boat, and may then split her gunwale or even capsize her.

Reaching

Keep the boat on as even a keel as possible by distributing the crew to windward evenly between the head and stern sheets, and trim the boat to carry a little weather helm. Check the sheets until the luffs of sails start to lift, then haul them in a little so that the sails are well filled. Lee or weather helm is best corrected by trimming the boat, but usually either can be corrected by trimming the sails; to correct lee helm haul aft the main sheet and check the fore sheet, and to correct weather helm check the main sheet and haul aft the fore sheet.

In a light wind bear out the foot of a loose-footed sail, as illustrated in fig. 10–9 (ii), so that the wind will fill it; if the clew of the foresail is hauled too far aft by its sheet there will be insufficient space for the wind to flow freely between it and the mainsail and it will not draw correctly (fig. 10–9 (i)).

Running

When running in a cutter or Montague whaler shift the fore tack to the running-hook, and, if rigged with loose-footed sails, bear their feet out at the clews with bearing-out spars.

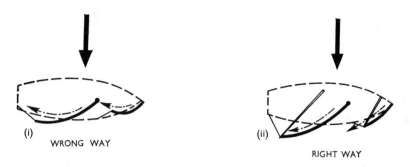

F IG. 10–9. Trim of sails when reaching

The sails should be set so that their plane is at right-angles to the direction of the wind (fig. 10–10). If the boat is running nearly dead before the wind the sails may be goosewinged; but running dead before a strong wind and a following sea should be avoided whenever possible, because the boat tends to yaw uncontrollably and may gybe, broach to and capsize. If your destination lies directly down wind it is better to steer for it on a zigzag course so as to keep the wind well on the quarter; no time will be lost by sailing the extra distance involved because the boat will sail faster with the wind on her quarter than with the wind right aft.

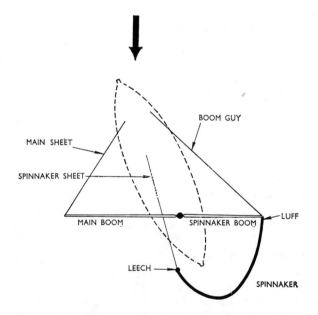

F IG. 10–10. Trim of sails when running—motor whaler

If a boat is rigged with a mizzen it should be furled when running before a strong wind, because if set it will make her yaw. If necessary to shorten sail the mainsail should be furled in preference to the foresail. A boat carrying too much sail when running will be sluggish to handle, and drive down into the water so that she tends to bury her bows; should any such tendency occur, sail should immediately be shortened or she may drive under.

When running before a strong wind and heavy sea, stream a drogue to prevent the boat from riding on the crest of a wave; this will also steady her and keep her from yawing. If a drogue is not available, stream a long bight of the boat's cable, or bend a line to an oar, a small sail, or a grating, and tow it astern. Do not forget to use the crew to trim the boat by the stern.

Gybing

A boat which is on a broad reach or running and alters course, thereby passing the stern through the wind, is *gybing*. The helm should be eased up gently and the sheets checked until just before the wind is right aft, then the mainsail should be brailed up if it is loose-footed and the fore sheet be hauled aft. As soon as the wind is on the other side, the mainsail should be set and the fore sheet checked; as the mainsail then fills on the new tack the boat will tend to luff up, and the helmsman should remember that if this is not met by bearing up the helm the boat may broach to. In a light wind it is not necessary to brail up, but the main sheet should be hauled aft roundly just before the wind is right aft, and checked roundly as soon as the wind is on the other side of the sail. With a boom-mainsail the main sheet should be hauled aft as the helm is eased up, and checked roundly as soon as the wind is on the other side of the sail. It is essential to avoid gybing heavily in a vessel rigged with a boom-mainsail, because the weight of the boom swinging across out of control may carry away the shrouds or backstays. However, when gybing a small dinghy it is sometimes necessary to let the boom swing across without shortening in the sheets because, being light in weight and draught, she may come roundly into the wind and more than likely capsize.

In boats rigged with backstays the lee runner must be set up taut as the helm is eased up and the main sheet hauled aft, otherwise this runner, which is now the weather runner, will not stay the mast when the mainsail gybes and the mast may go by the board.

Heavy weather. In heavy weather it is not good seamanship to gybe, because the helmsman has least control over the boat at the moment of gybing. It is far safer, and often quicker, to harden in on the sheets, ease the helm down and tack through the wind, checking the sheets as the boat pays off until she is running or reaching on her new course. Many famous yachts have been dismasted when trying to gybe in heavy wind and sea.

Handling in rough weather

When struck by a squall the sheets, particularly the fore sheet, should at once be let fly or roundly checked, and the helm should then be eased down to luff the boat up and so spill the wind out of her sails; the sheets can then be hauled aft and the boat paid off as necessary to continue on the original course.

Reefing. A reef should be taken down as soon as the boat begins to get *wet*, i.e. when water begins to splash over the lee gunwale. To take down a reef in a boat with a loose-footed mainsail the boat should be luffed up sufficiently to spill the wind from her sails, and the halyards should then be settled and the tack hooks and sheets shifted to the reef cringles. The foot of the sail should be gathered up, not rolled, and then be stopped by passing the reef points tautly round it. (A roll forms the neatest reef, but it catches any water and holds it.) A reef is shaken out by luffing the boat as before, and then unbending the reef points, settling the halyards and shifting the tack hooks and sheets to their proper cringles.

Capsizing. If a Service sailing boat capsizes or is swamped the crew should always remain with the boat, because she will remain floating, even though awash, and have a sufficient reserve of buoyancy to support her crew. Her sails must be lowered or cut away *immediately*, otherwise the wind will catch under the sail each time the boat begins to right herself and capsize her again. Then her standing and running rigging should be cut or cast off, her drop keel raised, and her sails, spars and rigging hauled clear. Her mast should then be un-shipped and lashed to the sails and spars, and be allowed to float clear of the boat but secured to her by a line, otherwise the mast may hole the boat as it is washed about.

Whenever possible, a swamped sailing boat should be unrigged and the mast unshipped before she is taken in tow.

Effect and use of centre-plate (drop keel)

The chief effect of a centre-plate is to reduce the leeway made by a boat when beating or reaching, but it also has other effects which are not commonly realised. In a small boat such as a dinghy the plate may weigh nearly as much as the hull, and when lowered it lowers the centre of gravity of the boat and thus has a stabilising effect; but in larger boats the plate is light in com-parison with the hull and the stabilising effect of its weight is therefore negligible.

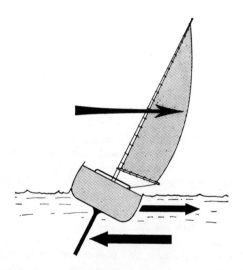

FIG. 10-11. Capsizing effect of a centre-plate in a squall

When the plate is lowered the resistance offered by the water to its surface reduces any tendency of the boat to roll, but when the boat is under sail and making leeway this lateral resistance will produce a capsizing moment, as illustrated in fig. 10–11. This moment is not appreciable under normal conditions of beating and reaching, but may become dangerous if the boat is blown broadside to leeward by a sudden squall, or if she yaws badly or broaches to when running.

The extent to which the plate should be lowered under the various conditions of sailing depends largely upon the type of the boat and can be found only by experience, but as a general guide it can be said that it should be fully lowered when beating, lowered half-way when reaching, and fully raised when running. The centre-plate should, of course, always be raised if there is any chance of the boat grounding, because if it hits the bottom not only might it be bent, which might prevent its being raised, but it might also either capsize the boat or split her open.

Getting under way

Before getting under way consider the weather conditions. If it is blowing hard take at least a full crew, and do not hesitate to take down one or more reefs before making sail. When under way it is much easier to shake out a reef than to take one down.

Before leaving the boom or ladder see that the sails are on the outboard side of the boat, the sheets are rove correctly, and the halyards and all other running rigging clear for running.

To get under way spring the boat ahead and cast her on the required tack, if necessary by backing the foresail to windward or bearing out the mizzen boom (if fitted) to leeward; from a ladder the boat is sprung ahead on the boatrope, and from the boom by passing the lizard aft and hauling on it. Then hoist the foresail, and as it draws set the mainsail and sheet it home. Trim the boat and the sails and see that all is shipshape (fenders in, no ropes' ends outboard, running rigging coiled down or in hand, and the crew properly positioned).

Coming alongside

Into wind. Always go alongside head to wind, if possible. Approach the ladder (or landing place) on a reach and steer for the ladder or just ahead of it. Remember that a heavily-laden boat will fore-reach (i.e. carry her way) much farther than a lightly-laden one. Give the order 'Down foresail' in plenty of time for the bowman to get out his boat-hook and fend off the bows, and, at the same time, order the fenders out. Haul aft the main sheet as you ease the helm down and brail up or lower mainsail just before the boat reaches the ladder; if the boat is likely to overshoot the ladder the sternsheetsman should be ready to check her with the check-line thrown from the lower ladder platform. An experienced coxswain should be able to bring his boat to rest with her stern sheets exactly alongside the gangway ladder without bumping it or having to check her way with the check-line, by putting the helm hard down at exactly the right moment; putting the helm hard over acts as a powerful brake in taking all way off the boat and preventing her from fore-reaching.

Down wind. If it is not possible to go alongside head to wind, have a drogue ready to check the way of the boat, and approach under shortened sail. A drogue can be fashioned from a bucket on a stout line streamed over the stern. Sail can be shortened by checking the sheets and spilling some of the wind from the sails, or settling the main halyard, or brailing up the mainsail and running in on the foresail; the latter is the most effective and must always be done with a following wind. In gaff-mainsail boats sail can be shortened by settling the peak halyard, thus *scandalising the mainsail*, but in a strong wind and with a heavily-laden boat it is best to lower the sails and proceed alongside under oars.

Heaving-to

A boat is hove-to in order to keep her as nearly stationary as possible; this is done by backing the foresail, sheeting aft the mainsail or mizzen, putting the helm down and adjusting the trim of the sails. The direction in relation to the wind in which a boat will best remain hove-to depends largely upon her free-board and the sails she can set. A Montague whaler will lie comfortably hove-to beam-on to the wind under her foresail and mizzen only. A cutter is difficult to heave-to because of the different areas of her foresail and mainsail and their consequent turning effect on the boat about her pivoting point; she lies best when hove-to under her foresail and storm trysail, with the boat trimmed as necessary to balance her against the wind.

Man overboard

If a man falls overboard from a boat under sail, at once throw out a life-jacket, oar, grating or anything that floats; then detail one of your crew to keep his eyes on the man, and get boat-hooks and lines ready for grappling him. If you are beating, or on a reach, wear your boat round so as to bring her to leeward of the man, whence you can approach him close-hauled and then luff up alongside him (fig. 10–12); your crew will then be able to get hold of him while the boat is stopped or only moving slowly, and he will not be dragged out of their hands.

If you are running you must run on for a short distance, then sail close-hauled, then go about so that you will come up just to leeward of the man and so be able to luff up alongside him (fig. 10–13).

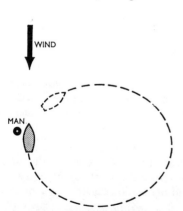

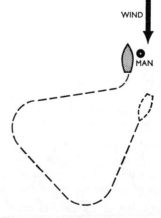

FIG. 10–12. Man overboard when beating or reaching

FIG. 10–13. Man overboard when running

SEABOATS

One or two of the boats slung on davits are kept ready for lowering at a moment's notice when at sea, one on each side of the ship if she is provided with two seaboats. A seaboat is used for rescuing any man who may fall overboard, communicating with another ship or the shore, recovering practice torpedoes, or for any other occasion when a boat is required at short notice at sea.

In order that it may be available at immediate notice the seaboat is kept turned out unless at quadrantal or gravity davits. The right gear must be in the boat, and it must be fully secured (griped in) at the davits against the rolling or pitching of the ship. The coxswain of a boat detailed for seaboat is responsible for securing and equipping her as a seaboat before the ship puts to sea, and the coxswain of the seaboat's crew of each watch is responsible that the boat is kept correctly secured, equipped and ready for immediate use until the ship returns to harbour. A full crew and the necessary number of lowerers are detailed from each watch or part of watch on deck, and throughout their duty watch they stand by in the vicinity of the boat to man her immediately the order is given by the Officer of the Watch. The crew and lowerers are mustered by the coxswain when leaving or entering harbour and at the beginning of each watch, and the boat is inspected by the coxswain at the same time. If all is correct the coxswain then reports to the Officer of the Watch: 'Seaboat's crew and lowerers of the watch correct, Sir; boat off the pins; falls clear for running; boat clear of water and plug in (if fitted).'

Unless the weather is too bad, the seaboat's crew and lowerers are ordered to 'Man the port (or starboard) seaboat for exercise' once in each night watch. Only one crew, with lowerers, are detailed whether there are one or two seaboats prepared. The coxswain should inspect his boat during his watch if there is a likelihood of anything being amiss. If the boat requires draining or pumping he must first ask the Officer of the Watch's permission to do so, and he must report again when it is done.

It may be desirable to settle the after fall of a seaboat to drain her quickly (when plug is fitted). This should only be done in fair weather and the boat re-hoisted and griped immediately afterwards.

Lifeboat. At sea during working hours the seaboat's crew is permitted to work part-of-ship, but not between decks. If the seaboat is required for an emergency, such as 'Man overboard', the pipe 'Away lifeboat's crew' is made, whereupon the boat is manned by any officer, seaman or other rating qualified to carry out the duties of a boat's crew, spare hands acting as lowerers.

Aircraft rescue. When it is known that a ship is likely to operate with a carrier, all ratings likely to be coxswains of seaboats should be sent to the carrier for instruction on the types of aircraft carried, the methods of entry, the positions of the crew and the dangers of, and precautions against, ejector seats.

In addition to its normal crew the seaboat should carry an L.S.B.A., a medical bag, a Neil Robertson stretcher and a Damage Control floodlight. In cold weather one of the crew should be wearing an immersion suit.

When a modern aircraft ditches it sinks rapidly and a boat or helicopter must reach it immediately. Therefore the seaboat must be fully manned and turned out by the time the carrier turns into wind for flying on or off.

SECURING A SEABOAT FOR SEA

When securing a seaboat for sea the following points should be noted:

1. The boat should be hoisted close up to the davit head and the falls should be belayed to the staghorns or davit cleats, or reeled on to the davit winches. The hauling parts of cordage falls should be reeled up on their own reels.

2. The disengaging gear, which should have previously been overhauled and oiled, should be set up and tested for tautness.

3. The griping spar (if fitted) should be clamped securely in its brackets and a jumping net or Jacob's ladder be rove between it and the deck edge. The gripes should be shackled to the davit heads and well set up round the boat so that she is firmly bowsed in to her griping spar or her griping pads. The commanders (i.e. hammers) for slipping the slips of the gripes should be secured to the heels of the davits by lanyards or placed in the brackets provided.

4. The guys and span should be correctly set up, and the davits be locked in position if fitted with locking pins. The lizards should be rove on the sea jackstays, and the jackstays should be either secured to the davit heads or rove through sheaves on the davit and set up on deck and the lower ends secured to eyeplates in the ship's side. (Unless in harbour and a boat is available, the jackstays will have to be secured at the waterline by lowering a hand over the side in a boatswain's chair, but this is a dangerous practice and should be avoided if possible.) The lizards should be lightly stopped in the head and stern sheets of the boat; *on no account should they be hitched to the lower block of the falls, because if there is any sideways stress on the lower blocks when the boat is slipped the hooks may not disengage correctly.* Jackstays are not usually fitted in ships with a low freeboard.

5. The sea lifelines should be rigged on the davit span and lightly stopped in position, and with the davit lifelines should be coiled down on the thwarts and clear for running.

6. An inflatable lifejacket for each member of the crew and one spare should be stowed in the boat in accessible positions.

7. The rudder and tiller should be shipped, and the tiller stopped over towards the ship's side by a split yarn; the rudder and tiller are then in their correct position to steer the boat out from the ship's side when the boat is slipped. A strong pull on the tiller should carry away the stop.

8. Crutches should be shipped (or the shutters unshipped) and their lanyards should be secured in the boat.

9. The oars and boat-hooks should be lightly stopped to prevent them rolling about, and the stretchers should be correctly fitted in place.

10. Bottom boards and gratings should be secured, except those in the wake of the slings which should be removed from the boat and stowed inboard.

11. The boat should be dry and the plug (if fitted) in place.

12. A boatrope of the same size as, or slightly larger than, the boat's anchor cable, with a long eye spliced in one end, should be rove from a position in the ship well forward and be secured in the boat in the following manner: the eye is led over the inner bow, under the foremost thwart and up abaft it, and is secured by passing the towing bollard or a similar billet of wood through it and then laying the bollard across the two foremost thwarts (fig. 10–14). A lanyard long enough to reach from the deck to the waterline may be spliced into the boatrope a few fathoms from its eye so that it can be recovered after it has been slipped from the boat. The purposes of the boatrope are:

(i) To keep the boat heading in the same direction as the ship and thus prevent her from broaching-to if the after fall fails to release when the boat is slipped.

(ii) To haul the boat ahead if she is slipped with the ship stopped, thus giving her sufficient steerage way to sheer out from the ship's side.

(iii) To tow the boat alongside the ship.

(iv) To haul the boat forward under the bows when the ship is coming to a buoy or going alongside, if the boat is not under power.

(v) To haul the boat forward under her davits when she is approaching to hook on in a seaway.

(vi) To hold the boat under her davits while she is being hooked on.

(vii) With the help of a sternfast secured aft in the boat, to prevent the boat from surging as she is being hoisted or lowered in a seaway.

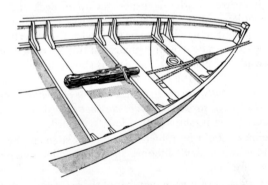

FIG. 10–14. Securing the boatrope in a seaboat

Gear. The following gear should be stowed in the boat, clear of the slings and the feet of the crew: anchor and cable, boat's bag, compass, lantern and candles, bailer and/or bucket, distress signal box, tins of emergency rations and fresh water. The boat's sailing gear (if she is a pulling and sailing boat) should not be put in the boat, but kept ready at hand to be put in if needed.

DRILL FOR LOWERING A SEABOAT

For seaboat drill to be carried out efficiently in all ships of the Fleet a standard sequence of orders must be adhered to. The drill described below is that for lowering a 27 ft Motor Whaler from quadrantal davits; the gripes have been slipped, the davits turned out and the davit slips, if fitted, knocked off. Usually the seaboat on the lee side is ordered to be manned. In a rough sea oil may be used to lessen the breaking of the waves, and a sternfast may be secured to a suitable fitting aft in the boat; the sternfast and boatrope are manned and tended inboard to prevent the boat surging fore and aft as she is lowered.

Order	Action
'*Away seaboat's crew, man the port* (or *starboard*) *seaboat.*' (If the seaboat is required for lifesaving the order will be '*Away lifeboat's crew. . . .*')	The crew man the seaboat at the rush, put on their lifejackets, position themselves by their respective thwarts, grasp their lifelines and await further orders. The coxswain and bowman unmouse the safety pins on the disengaging gear and then take the sea jack-stay lizards in hand. The M.E. makes sure that the exhaust is clear, and the shaft clear to rotate, then starts the engine. The lowerers, two experienced seamen to each fall with a leading seaman in charge, fake down the falls ready for running.
'*Turns for lowering.*'	The lowerers remove the outer turns from the davit cleats or staghorns. When the M.E. has started the engine and is satisfied that it is running properly he reports to the coxswain. The coxswain then reports to the Officer-in-Charge '*Seaboat ready for lowering, Sir.*'
'*Start the falls.*'	The falls are surged handsomely round the cleats or staghorns, so that the boat is lowered slowly.
'*Lower away.*'	This is the next order given if all is well. The falls are surged roundly and without jerking so that the boat is lowered more rapidly, care being taken to keep the falls under perfect control and to keep the boat on an even keel *at all times.* If the ship is rolling, the coxswain and bowman keep the boat from swinging outward by tending the lizards, if necessary taking a turn round a thwart or other strong point. Spare hands on deck lower rattan fenders between the boat and the ship's side.
'*Avast lowering.*'	This order is given when the boat is a foot or two clear of the water, or just clear of the wave crests. The lowerers stop lowering and back up the falls.

Order	*Action*
'*Out pins.*'	The bowman removes the safety pin from the forward disengaging gear and raises his hand to indicate to the coxswain that the pin is clear. At the same time the coxswain removes the safety pin from the after disengaging gear, then grasps the slip lever of the fore-and-after, removes its locking pin, raises his hand and then reports '*Pins out, Sir.*'
	At this stage the sea jackstay lizards should be in hand and not turned up in the boat—a member of the crew relieving the coxswain of the after lizard. The sternfast, if secured, should also be in hand.
'*Slip.*' (If the sea is rough or the ship is rolling, the order to slip is timed so that the boat will drop on the crest, and not in the trough, of an approaching wave.)	The coxswain slips the fore-and-after, the boat drops into the water, he grasps the tiller and parts its strop, and then orders the M.E. to go '*Half ahead*' on the engine. The lizards and sternfast are cast off, and the rest of the crew shove off hard from the ship's side if it is necessary to do so. The bowman slips the boatrope by order of the coxswain. (If there is no way on the ship the boat may have difficulty in sheering off; to help her in getting clear the boatrope should be manned inboard and the boat be hauled forward a short distance to give her sufficient way to sheer off.)

The falls and gripes are then hauled inboard; the falls are then rove for hoisting the boat on her return to the ship, and a sternfast is provided which should be of sufficient strength to withstand the shock of the boat surging forward. In calm weather the boatrope is stopped, at about a fathom from its eye, to the lower block of the foremost fall, but in rough weather it is made ready inboard with its tail ready to pass to the boat as soon as she is within reach. The scope of the boatrope and sternfast should be sufficient for them to be secured in the boat. The lizards are recovered by means of either a light line previously stopped to their eyes, or a boat-hook, and their ends stopped to the lower blocks of the falls.

DRILL FOR HOISTING A SEABOAT

While there are various reasons for employing different methods of hoisting a seaboat, such as power hoisting and advanced-design davits and gear, the majority of ships in the Fleet have cordage falls fitted and can hoist their boats either by power or by hand. The drill described below is for hoisting a Motor Whaler as a seaboat by cordage falls, by hand. It is assumed that the weather is bad enough to use Nylon anti-shock slings and the falls are already manned inboard.

A lee is formed by the ship, if possible; the 3-ft Nylon strops are spring-hooked to the swivel ring shackles of the lower blocks of the falls, which are then lowered over the side, care being taken to allow the right amount of scope and to tend the inboard parts to prevent them from twisting and the lower blocks from thoroughfooting themselves.

The steel wire pendants are shackled to the davit heads with a pin and forelock shackle, the other end being fitted with a spring hook. They are longer than the Nylon strops, which absorb the shock of the boat plunging up and down when alongside during the first stages of hoisting and keep the lower blocks of the falls clear of those hooking on. If these strops are not used, the boat's slings, the boat and the davits can be damaged.

When the boat is hoisted to two blocks the steel wire pendants are hooked to the top shackles of the disengaging gear and the falls walked back until the pendants take the weight of the boat. The Nylon strops are then removed, the falls overhauled and hooked to the hook of the disengaging gear; the weight is again taken on the falls and the boat hoisted to its proper position. The steel wire pendants are then removed and the boat secured as a seaboat.

Immediately the returning boat gets within reach, the boatrope and sternfast are passed to her and made fast in the bow and stern respectively. The hands inboard are ordered to 'Marry to your marks' and the falls are married with their strips of bunting in line with each other but allowing sufficient slack in the falls for hooking on. The bunting marks ensure that the boat is hoisted on an even keel. As the boat rises to a wave the foremost fall Nylon strop is hooked on, and immediately afterwards the after fall Nylon strop is hooked on; then the coxswain reports 'Hooked on, Sir.' The following orders are then given:

Order	Action
'Hoist away.'	The hands manning the falls run up the boat clear of the waves as quickly as possible. The boatrope and sternfast are manned inboard and tended to prevent the boat surging as she is hoisted. The coxswain and bowman tend their sea jackstay lizards. The M.E. cuts the engine. When the scope of the falls is short, surging may be reduced by crossing lifelines and manning them. Hands on deck man their fenders and follow up the boat as she is being hoisted.
'Avast hoisting.'	This order is given when the boat is high enough for the steel wire pendants to be hooked on. The hands manning the falls stop hoisting. The coxswain and bowman hook on their respective pendants to the upper shackles of the disengaging gear, both holding up one hand when the pendant hook is properly engaged. Two crew members relieve the coxswain and bowman of the lizards if the ship is rolling.
'Walk back to the pendants.'	The hands keep the falls in hand and walk back towards the davits until the pendants take the weight of the boat and the Nylon strops slacken, and continue to walk back as the coxswain and bowman remove the

Order	Action
	Nylon stops from the lower blocks of the falls and from the hooks of the disengaging gear. The coxswain and bowman then overhaul the falls until the lower block swivel ring shackles can be hooked directly to the hook of the disengaging gear.
' *Well.*'	The hands manning the falls stop walking back.
' *Hoist away handsomely.*'	The hands manning the falls walk away and continue to hoist up the boat. The coxswain and bowman, as soon as the weight of the boat is off the pendants, unhook them from the upper shackle of the disengaging gear and keep them clear from the parts of the falls as the boat is hoisted.
' *High enough.*'	This order is given when the boat's falls are nearly two blocks. The hands stop hauling, but keep their weight on the falls.

From this state the orders are the same as when hoisting a boat in harbour. After the falls are belayed the gripes are passed and set up, and the boat is secured for sea. If the boat is hoisted at quadrantal davits the davits are canted inboard before the gripes are passed, and the keel chocks are then clamped into position.

The falls are then reeled up and the boat squared off, after which the coxswain reports to the Officer of the Watch that his boat is secured for sea.

HINTS TO COXSWAINS OF SEABOATS

Getting away. You must get clear of the ship the moment your boat is slipped, so while the boat is being lowered warn your crew to stand by to shove off hard from the ship's side immediately she is slipped. If the boatrope is made fast in the boat ensure beforehand that it can be slipped easily, and give the order to slip it before the boat sheers too far out from the ship's side. Your bowman must be alert and know his duties.

Towing alongside. If you are to be towed alongside trim the boat a little by the stern so as to raise her bows, but station a man in the head sheets with his knife ready to cut or slip the boatrope in emergency. Keep from 10 to 15 ft away from the ship's side. The length of the boatrope should be adjusted inboard so that your boat rides with her forefoot on the crest of a wave of the ship's wash.

Signals. When away from your ship keep an eye on her for signals; on your outward passage one hand should be facing the ship to watch for flag, lamp or other signals. If you are to pick up a man or some other inconspicuous object, the ship will probably direct you to the position. The moment you sight the object keep your eye fixed on it until it is alongside.

Picking up a man. When going alongside a man, have a hand standing by at each end of the boat with a line ready to throw to him. If your boat is under oars do not boat them. Remember that your boat will drift to leeward faster than the man.

Returning. During your return to the ship have your slings and disengaging gear prepared for hooking on and ensure that the safety pins of the hooks are in place and moused. Your crew should be trained to prepare the gear with their eyes shut. When the hooks have been set up see they are tested by holding the slings up by the hooks.

Going alongside. When going alongside to hook on it is better to overshoot than undershoot the falls. If you overshoot, the boatrope can be recovered and secured, and the wind and sea will soon drop the boat astern under the falls; but if you undershoot, it will be difficult to haul the boat ahead even if the bowman has managed to grasp the after fall, and time will be wasted while the boatrope is passed and the boat hauled ahead on it. If the boatrope is thrown to you from the ship do not let your crew try to haul the boat up by it, but secure it and let the men in the ship do the hauling; they are better placed to do so. Do not be afraid to use the engine to keep the boat positioned under the davits until the boatrope and sternfast are secured.

Hooking on. When hooking on ensure that the foremost fall is hooked on first. The lower blocks are fitted with swivel ring shackles, so there is no need to take any turns out of the falls before hooking on. After hooking on and when not using anti-shock slings, the blocks should be held up while the slack of the falls is taken down, and the bowman and the coxswain should take any turns out of the falls by turning round the lower blocks; when the boat is being hoisted they should keep any turns from forming in the falls by means of a bar (anti-twister) passed between the parts.

Falls. Teach your men how to handle falls and never allow them to grasp the running parts. If the standing part is on the lower block, that part alone may be grasped if it is essential to do so. As the boat is being hoisted the rest of the crew should take their weight on the lifelines to lighten the boat.

HINTS TO COXSWAINS OF BOATS

It is an old Service saying that a ship is known by her boats; when away in a boat remember therefore that the reputation of your ship depends partly upon you.

Check the gear and equipment of your boat daily. This should be done when she is being scrubbed out, or before she is called away for the first trip of the day, or before she is lowered, or when you take over from your opposite number. Make good defects between trips; report any which you cannot make good to the Officer of the Watch and the Boat Officer. After the last trip of the day make sure that the boat is ready in all respects for the first trip of the following day.

Smartness in the boat

Ensure that your boat is manned smartly when called away. Always see that your crew are properly dressed in the correct rig and, if they are wearing caps, the chin stays are down. See that all gear is securely and neatly stowed.

In a pulling boat do not allow your crew to pull in a slovenly manner. Strict silence should always be maintained in a boat. The crew and passengers should not be allowed to stand up, except when necessary for carrying out their duties. Nobody should be allowed to place his arms or hands on the washstrakes or gunwales, expecially when the boat is alongside or about to go alongside.

Know your boat's pennants, and when away from your ship always keep a lookout for her recall or for any signals addressed to her. Memorise the salutes and marks of respect to be paid in boats, and other ceremonial drill in boats, all of which are given in Volume II. Do not cross the bows of your superiors.

Casting off

When casting off from an inner billet at the boom do not haul ahead, but drop your boat astern until she is clear of the outer boats; this is of particular importance in a tideway. If your boat is in the outer billet, spring her ahead on the lizard. Do not drop astern to the gangway, but bring the boat under oars, sail or power, from the boom to the accommodation ladder in the normal way. When getting under way ensure that all fenders are in and that no ropes' ends or bights are hanging over the sides of the boat.

Unhooking

When unhooking a boat from her falls always unhook the after fall before the foremost fall. If the foremost fall is unhooked first the boat may swing out, and in a strong tideway may broach-to. For the same reason, when hooking a boat to her falls the foremost fall should always be hooked on before the after fall.

Reporting for orders

Report personally to the Officer of the Watch for your orders and make sure that you understand them before leaving.

If you are sent to another ship with a message or letter, deliver it personally to the Officer of the Watch or the quartermaster. If you have to wait, lie off well clear on her quarter (unless permission is granted to make fast to the boom) and keep a sharp lookout for the signal or hail to return alongside (see fig. 10–15 for the code of gangway hand signals). Do not remain alongside an accommodation ladder unless expressly ordered to do so.

When under way

In setting your course make due allowance for leeway or the set of any current or tidal stream. Remember when proceeding up stream in a pulling boat that the current is usually weakest inshore. If your course lies beam-on to a heavy sea or swell it is better to steer a dog-leg course to windward than to steer the direct one. Keep a good lookout to windward in squally weather, and be prepared to make for shelter or the nearest ship should the need arise. Meet the wash of passing ships bows-on, and, in a pulling boat, warn your crew to mind their oars. Do not pass close under the bow or stern of a ship at anchor, and always give a wide berth to the bows of a ship anchored in a tideway. Be thoroughly conversant with the Rule of the Road.

FIG. 10–15. Code of gangway hand signals

Landing and going alongside

When going alongside a landing place, or a ship moored head and stern, always go alongside head to wind or tide, whichever is the stronger. When ordered to lie alongside a ship choose a position which is clear of scuppers or other discharge pipes. When going alongside a ship in a tideway avoid overshooting the accommodation ladder, because if you overshoot it your boat will very likely get jammed by the stream underneath the ladder. When alongside a ship in a tideway lead the gangway boatrope over the inner bow and secure it to the towing bollard, towing thwart, or bow cleat; then steer your boat and you will find that she will answer her helm just as if she were under way at slow speed (see Volume II).

When alongside a landing place do not allow the crew to leave the boat, and do not allow them to lounge about in the boat, smoke, or behave in any way likely to bring discredit on your ship or the Service. On returning to your ship report anything amiss in her appearance that you may have noticed while you were away.

Carrying passengers and stores

You should know the maximum number of persons and the maximum weight your boat is allowed to carry in calm weather; remember that these are maximum limits for *calm* weather, and that you must reduce them according to the conditions and sea which your boat will encounter. (See the table giving the carrying capacities of Service boats in Volume II.)

When embarking stores they should be placed as far as possible amidships and low down in the boat. If the centre of gravity of the stores is above the thwarts or gunwale the boat will be top-heavy and tender; if weights are placed right forward she will not rise to the waves and will be in danger of broaching-to, and if placed right aft she will be in danger of being pooped by a following sea. When loaded, your boat should have an even trim and no list, but when running before a heavy sea it is best to trim the boat slightly by the stern. If you are carrying top-weight alter course carefully, and if you are heavily loaded remember that the boat will carry her way for a much greater distance than when she is lightly loaded.

If you are sent to bring off unpackaged stores such as fresh meat or vegetables, see that you have a clean tarpaulin spread over the bottom of the boat to save both stores and boat from being fouled. When disembarking stores alongside a ship see that a net (save-all) is slung from the ship's side to the gunwale of your boat to catch any stores which may fall between the ship's side and the boat.

Carrying money. If you are sent to bring off the Supply Officer with money take a small buoy and buoy-rope with you. Before the money is embarked the bag containing it should be secured to the end of the buoy-rope, which should be long enough easily to reach the bottom at any point on your passage back to the ship; should any accident then occur the money can be recovered later by picking up the buoy and buoy-rope. When disembarking the money the buoy and buoy-rope should first be passed into the ship.

Anchoring

If you have to anchor see that the cable is correctly bent to the ring of the anchor and that the inboard end is secured to the boat. If of Admiralty pattern see that the anchor is correctly stocked with the forelock in place and moused. See that enough cable to reach the bottom is faked ready for running, and stream it before the anchor is cast overboard. When anchoring, have sternway on your boat to ensure that the cable is laid out along the bottom and that it will not foul the anchor. The length of cable by which you ride should be at least four times the depth of the water at high water, and, in a pulling boat, you should ride by your towing bollard by taking four turns of the cable round it and then seizing the inboard part to the outboard part. If the boat snatches at her cable in a heavy sea, pay out as much cable as possible. If she still snatches, and a 50-lb sinker or stone of similar weight is available, it may be secured by a lizard to the cable and allowed to run down the cable to the bottom on the end of a messenger; this will act as a spring on the cable and so reduce the tendency of the boat to snatch.

When anchoring on a rocky bottom, bend the cable to the crown of the anchor and stop the bight to the ring, so that if the anchor jams under a rock when being weighed the stop will part and allow the anchor to be hauled clear and weighed by its crown.

If the boat is to be left unattended at anchor off a rocky shore or a steeply shelving beach, shackle a block to the ring of the anchor, reeve the boat's cable through it, and to the cable bend a messenger of the same size as the cable. Drop the anchor in a position which will allow sufficient scope of cable for the boat to ride to it and yet swing clear of the shore or rocks. After disembarking make fast a stern rope on shore, allowing plenty of scope; then haul the boat seaward on the messenger until she has the correct scope of cable and make fast the messenger on shore.

Making fast to a boat boom

When ordered to make fast to the lower boom, secure to it in your proper berth; a pulling boat, being lighter than a power boat, is usually sent to the outer lizard. The painter should be rove through the eye of the lizard, then back through the thimble of the painter, and then be secured with a double sheet bend round both parts; the scope of the painter should be adjusted so that the boat rides easily without yawing or snatching in the prevailing wind, sea, and current or tidal stream; a fathom and a half is sufficient in calm weather. Secure the lazy painter to the Jacob's ladder with a single sheet bend and give it a greater scope than the painter.

Before ordering the boat's crew out of the boat see that:

1. All dirt inside or outside the boat is scrubbed or wiped off, particularly along the waterline.
2. Oars and boat-hooks are stowed on each side of the boat and secured by beckets to prevent them rolling about.
3. All movable gear is securely stowed.
4. In single-banked boats, the crutches are unshipped, stowed, and not left hanging by their lanyards.
5. In double-banked boats and motor whalers the shutters are shipped.
6. The tiller and rudder are unshipped.
7. The ensign is furled and the ensign staff unshipped.

Questions on this chapter will be found in Appendix 2.

CHAPTER 11

Anchors and Cables

An anchor is a hook, attached to a length of chain or rope called a cable, by which a ship or boat can be held temporarily to the sea bed in comparatively shallow water. The primitive anchor was a rock attached to a length of crude rope. Then, from about 400 B.C. until the days of Nelson, anchors made of iron and wood increased in size but changed little in design, whereas cable developed to the cable-laid hawsers that can be seen in H.M.S. *Victory*.

When iron and steel replaced wood in ship construction and sail gave way to steam, steel anchors of various designs were made, from which the modern anchor is derived, and iron and steel chain cable gradually developed into the very strong modern studded cable that has a strengthening stud in the centre of each link.

In this chapter the seaman will be introduced to the methods of securing a ship to the bottom, a modern anchor, wrought iron and forged steel chain cable and associated cable gear, the arrangements of anchors and cables in H.M. ships, and the sequence of events leading up to, and including, bringing a ship to single anchor and to a buoy. The table on page 330 gives the weights of anchors and the size and length of cables supplied to an aircraft carrier and a frigate. More advanced information on anchors, cables and anchor work is given in Volume II.

METHODS OF SECURING TO SEA BOTTOM

A ship can be secured to the sea bottom by means of her ground tackle, i.e. her anchors and cables, either with a single anchor or with two anchors, and in the latter case she is said to be *moored*. In ports and most large harbours a ship can also be secured to the bottom by unshackling one of her cables from its anchor and shackling the cable to a mooring buoy, which in turn is secured to the bottom by its own permanently-laid groundwork of mooring anchors and mooring chain.

Anchoring

Letting go a single anchor is the simplest method, and will be described more fully later in this chapter. If the anchor is of good design and sufficient cable is veered the ship will ride easily to her anchor in bad weather. The disadvantage of this method is that the ship takes up a lot of sea room when she swings round her anchor with the wind and tidal stream (fig. 11–1).

Mooring ship

The object of mooring with two anchors is usually to reduce the sea room required by the ship for swinging. The anchors are let go at some distance apart from each other and the ship is then secured midway between them so that she swings almost around her stem (fig. 11–2). In the Royal Navy this is known as *mooring ship*, though in earlier times it was more precisely called

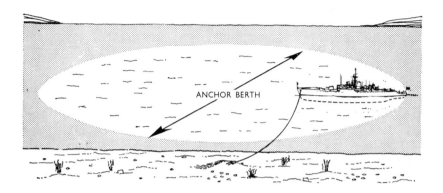

FIG. 11–1. A ship at single anchor

mooring a cable each way to distinguish it from other methods of anchoring with two anchors. A ship thus moored rides in safety if the directions of the wind and current and tidal stream lie approximately along the line of the anchors, but if she rides at a large angle to this line the cables form a taut span and the resulting heavy stress in them may cause the anchors to drag. The two anchors should therefore be let go in the line of the prevailing wind, current, or tidal stream, whichever is usually the stronger. When a ship lies across the line of her anchors, she is said to lie at *open hawse*.

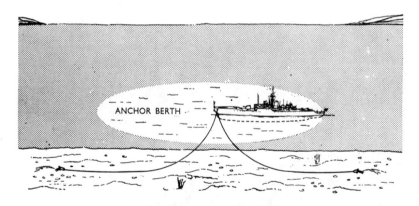

FIG. 11–2. A ship moored

To prevent turns forming in the cables as the ship swings with wind and tide, a *mooring swivel* is inserted between the cables and then veered outboard.

A ship may also be moored with the object of enabling her to ride out a gale with less likelihood of dragging her anchors. The anchors are then let go so that the ship lies with an angle between her cables of less than 20°; this helps to keep the ship from yawing and divides the weight of the ship between the two anchors. The mooring swivel is never used in this case.

If a ship is lying to a single anchor which starts to drag in bad weather, a second anchor, i.e. the other bower anchor, is lowered underfoot (beneath the stem) to reduce the yaw and stop the dragging. If this is unsuccessful the second anchor can be veered until both anchors hold.

Securing to a buoy

In harbours with inadequate space for anchoring it is usual for ships to secure to a permanent mooring. This consists of two or more anchors laid on the bottom and connected by heavy ground chains to a central ring which lies on the bottom (fig. 11–3). To the central ring is attached a single length of cable called the *buoy pendant*, the upper end of which passes through, and is supported by, a *mooring buoy*. To the upper end of the buoy pendant is fitted a large shackle known as the *buoy shackle* (usually called the *ring of the buoy*), to which the ship secures her own cable; a swivel is fitted in the buoy pendant to prevent it from becoming twisted as the ship swings. The purpose of the buoy is to keep the buoy shackle above the water when the moorings are not in use, but, for the sake of brevity, a ship riding to a permanent mooring is said to be *secured to a buoy*. The length of cable between the ship and the mooring buoy is called the *bridle*. A second bridle is frequently used.

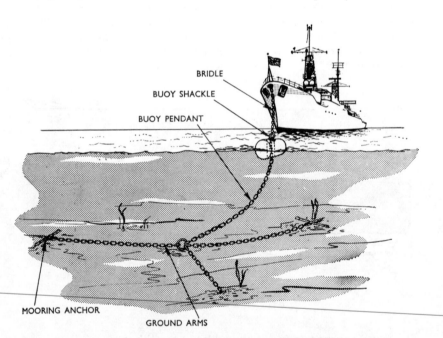

BRIDLE
BUOY SHACKLE
BUOY PENDANT
MOORING ANCHOR
GROUND ARMS

FIG. 11–3. A ship secured to a buoy

In naval ports permanent moorings may be of six classes numbered according to the maximum size of ship for which they are intended, a 1st class mooring being the heaviest. To the buoy shackles of the 1st and 2nd class moorings are usually attached two smaller links, called *reducing links*, to which smaller ships secure because their securing-to-buoy shackles are too small for the buoy shackle. (For a detailed description of permanent moorings see Volume III.)

Because of the good hold of their anchors and the heavy gear employed, permanent moorings usually afford the safest method of securing a ship. Although the anchors of these moorings are permanently bedded and have exceptionally heavy cables, they must be correctly laid in the first place and then inspected at regular intervals by the staff of the Dockyard Mooring Officer.

Parts of an anchor

Fig. 11–4 shows a modern anchor used in the Royal Navy. It should be noted that the flukes can move through an angle of 35° each side of the shank.

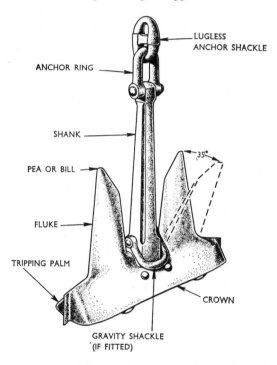

FIG. 11–4. Bower anchor, A.C. (Admiralty Cast) 14 type

Ship's anchors

Bower anchor. A ship's largest anchors are called her bower anchors. They are used for anchoring or mooring the ship and are stowed one on each bow in a hawsepipe.

Stream anchor. This anchor, which is used by some ships as a stern anchor, is stowed either in a stern hawsepipe or on deck under a suitable davit. A wire hawser with a swivel, shackled to the anchor, is used in place of a chain cable, and the anchor is weighed by the after winch or capstan, a carpenter's stopper being provided to hold the hawser.

Killick. Destroyers and frigates (including despatch vessels) need a light anchor or killick for general purposes. They are supplied with a 300-lb Danforth anchor, which is illustrated in Volume II. A small wire hawser is used as its cable.

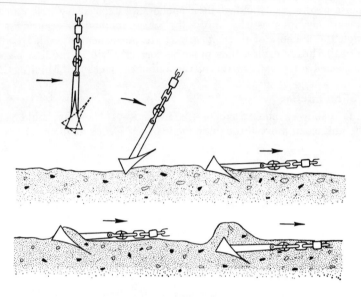

FIG. 11-5. How a modern anchor holds

How an anchor holds

Fig. 11-5 shows how an anchor beds itself in the bottom after it has been let go and the strain comes on the cable. The anchor lies flat on the bottom until the pull of the ship on the cable drags the anchor along the bottom; the tripping palms then tilt the flukes, which then dig themselves in. After a further amount of dragging the anchor embeds itself completely until it holds. For the anchor to maintain its hold the pull of the cable must always be horizontal where it leaves the sea bed.

Amount of cable. The cable must be long enough to ensure that a part of it near the anchor always remains in the sea bed. In firm ground, the anchor ring takes up a position just below the top of the sea bed and therefore the cable lies almost on the sea bed. The rest of the cable acts as a spring in preventing the anchor from being jerked when the ship is yawing from side to side or pitching. The amount of cable therefore depends on the depth of water, type of cable, length of stay, weather and, to a certain extent, the nature of the bottom. To ensure that the cable exerts a horizontal pull at the anchor it may be necessary to veer more forged steel cable than the larger, and therefore heavier, wrought iron cable. A rough rule for forged steel cable is: *Amount of cable to veer in shackles is twice the square root of the depth of water in fathoms.*

Both these types of cable will be described later. Further details of the ratio between length of cable and depth of water are given in Volumes II and III.

Nature of bottom and anchor design. The older-type anchors (e.g. Admiralty Standard Cast or Forged Head, Byer's, Hall's, etc.) will hold satisfactorily in firm sea beds such as clay, soft chalk, sand, sand/shingle and heavy mud, but will drag in softer sea beds such as soft mud, shingle and shell.

Improvements in the design of Admiralty anchors in recent years have resulted in obtaining satisfactory holds in any kind of sea bed, because these anchors embed themselves deeper in the softer grounds during the final period of drag before they hold.

No anchor, no matter how well designed, can be expected to hold on rock, except by a fluke; nor will it hold if fouled by some extraneous material picked up on the sea bed which prevents the anchor operating correctly.

Holding pull of anchor. The improvements in design mentioned above have increased the holding power of anchors from $2\frac{1}{2}$ to 10 times their own weight.

Breaking out an anchor

When the anchor is weighed the upward pull of the cable should break the flukes out of the bottom. If the flukes are very firmly bedded the cable can be held at short stay and the anchor broken out by using the main engines. If the flukes are caught in rock it may be necessary to weigh anchor by attaching a cable or wire hawser to the gravity shackle.

Chain cable

Anchor cable can vary in size, material and length, from the 20 fathoms of 2-in. manila of a small boat to the 518 fathoms of 3-in. chain cable of an aircraft carrier.

Studded chain cable is made in lengths of 15 and $7\frac{1}{2}$ fathoms, and these lengths are called respectively *shackles of cable* and *half-shackles of cable*. Before 1949 a shackle of cable supplied to the Royal Navy was $12\frac{1}{2}$ fathoms long, but now there are few ships so fitted.

A ship's bower cable is usually made up of four half-shackles of cable and a number of shackles of cable. The half-shackles are usually inserted in pairs, one at the outboard end next to the anchor, and the other midway between the outboard and inboard ends. This method of making up a bower cable in shackles and half-shackles enables the cable to be parted at the various points throughout its length when embarking and disembarking cable, or working cable during the operations described in Volume II.

Each shackle or half-shackle of cable is joined together with either a lugged or lugless joining shackle and the cable is secured to the anchor with an anchor shackle (all described in Chapter 8). Fig. 11–6 illustrates the ends of two shackles of cable joined together with a lugless joining shackle.

Ships of the fleet are normally supplied with forged steel cable, other ships with wrought iron cable. Size for size, forged steel chain cable is slightly heavier than wrought iron, but it is 40 per cent stronger, so that smaller cable for the same strength can be used and it is easier to handle.

The studs of 'Tayco' forged steel chain cable are formed as an integral part of the link, whereas in other forged steel chain cables the studs are closed in the links by pressure.

Associated cable gear

In the working of anchors and cables it is necessary to use many pieces of gear such as joining shackles, anchor shackles, slips of various types to hold the cable, hawsers, and other special shackles. Such gear is described in detail in

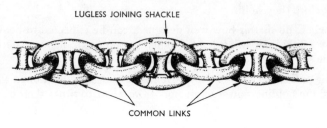

LUGLESS JOINING SHACKLE

COMMON LINKS

F I G. 11–6. Shackles of chain cable joined by a lugless joining shackle

Volume II. It is sufficient here to show a Blake slip (fig. 11–7) which consists of a length of chain, one end of which is secured to a deck clench and the other fitted with a slip. The slip fits across a link of the cable and the tongue of the slip is secured in place by a link and a pin.

DECK CLENCH   PIN   LINK   TONGUE

F I G. 11–7. A Blake slip

ARRANGEMENT OF ANCHORS AND CABLES

Cruiser

Fig. 11–8 shows a typical arrangement of the machinery and gear for working anchors and cables in a cruiser. The ship is seen riding to her port anchor. From the hawsepipe each cable leads aft to its *cable holder*, thence forward to its *navel pipe*, and down this pipe to its *cable locker*, which is situated in the bottom of the ship. On the centre line is the *capstan*, which is used primarily for working hawsers but can also be used for working cable should the necessity arise.

On the deck below the forecastle is the capstan engine, which can be made to revolve in either direction at varying speeds, its operation being controlled by a handwheel situated amidships abaft the cable holders. The capstan engine drives the spindles of the capstan and the cable holders by means of worm and rod gearing. The spindle of the capstan can be disconnected from the engine to enable the capstan to be worked by hand in ships provided with capstan bars.

Each cable holder can be connected to or disconnected from its spindle by a dog clutch, which is operated by revolving a plate on the head of the cable holder. Thus cable can be hove in or veered under power by connecting up its cable holder and setting the capstan engine in motion in the required direction; or cable can be allowed to run out freely by disconnecting its cable holder from its spindle. When both cables are being worked this arrangement enables both of them to be hove in or veered under power simultaneously; it also allows either cable to run out freely while the other is hove in or veered under power.

Each cable holder is fitted with a band brake, operated by a handwheel just abaft the cable holder. This brake controls the speed at which cable is allowed to run out when the cable holder is disconnected; it also holds the cable holder fast when the ship is riding at anchor or made fast to a buoy.

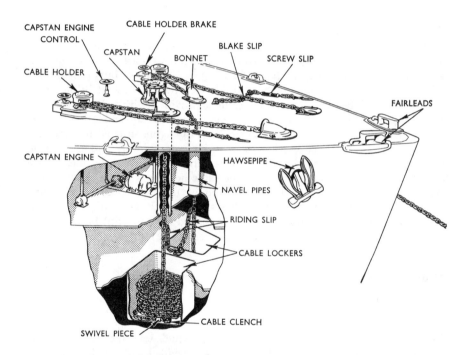

FIG. 11–8. Arrangement of anchors and cables in a cruiser

The cable can be stoppered (i.e. held temporarily) or secured by means of chain slips. Abaft each hawsepipe is a *screw slip*, used for heaving the anchor close home in its hawsepipe. Abaft each screw slip is a *Blake slip*, used for holding the cable temporarily while handling its inboard part, or as a *preventer*. At the top of each cable locker is a *riding slip*, which is put on the cable when the ship is at anchor or secured to a buoy, and acts as a preventer should the brake of the cable holder fail to hold the pull of the cable.

A removable *bonnet* is clamped over each navel pipe to prevent water from running down to the cable locker. Each cable is provided with two *swivel pieces*, one next to the anchor and one on the inboard end which is shackled to a *cable clench* at the bottom of the cable locker. The forecastle deck in the wake of each cable is strengthened and protected by a strip of steel plating called a *Scotchman.*

The ship rides by the cable holder brake, with the riding slip and Blake slip as preventers when anchored or secured to a buoy.

Carrier or depot ship

The arrangements are similar to those for a cruiser except that in older ships a *clump cathead*, which is a sheeve fitted at the deck edge, is provided on each bow for *catting* the anchor. When the ship is preparing to come to a buoy, one of the bower anchors is hung at the cathead, leaving room in the hawsepipe for the bridle. In new ships the trend is to fit large towing fairleads or a stem hawsepipe so that the clump cathead is not required.

Destroyer and frigate

Fig. 11–9 shows the general arrangement of cable gear for destroyers and frigates. In the stem is a stem hawsepipe through which the bridles are led when the ship makes fast to a buoy. Centre-line bollards or bitts (not shown) are sometimes provided for towing and for securing the second bridle when the ship is made fast to a buoy. Each cable is provided with a Blake slip and screw slip, and each is worked by a combined capstan and cable holder, which is driven by an electric or steam capstan engine situated on or under the forecastle deck. Each capstan is keyed to its spindle, and each cable holder can be connected to, or disconnected from, its capstan by means of a dog clutch. The method of operating the cable holders is similar to that in a cruiser. Some ships have *compressors* fitted in their bonnets which, when screwed down, nip a link of cable. Other ships, which have no compressors, are provided with an additional Blake slip (called a riding slip) between each cable holder and its navel pipe. The remainder of the cable gear is similar to that of a cruiser.

Minor warships

The forecastle arrangement in these vessels is shown in fig. 11–10. The capstans and cable holders are replaced by a *windlass*, which revolves on a horizontal shaft driven by a reversible steam or electric engine situated just abaft it on the forecastle deck. Two *gypsies*, which take the place of cable holders, are mounted on the shaft and each is provided with a band brake. As in a cable holder, each gypsy can be connected to, or disconnected from, the shaft by a clutch. *Warping drums*, which take the place of a capstan, are keyed and usually clutched, one to each end of the shaft and revolve with it. A *guillotine*, which is a deck fitting containing a hinged bar that can be dropped across a link of the cable outboard of the windlass, takes the place of a compressor. The ship rides by the windlass brake, with the guillotine and Blake slip as preventers, when anchored or secured to a buoy.

Merchant ships

A merchant ship's anchor and cable arrangements, except those of the large liners, are very similar to those of a minor warship equipped with a windlass.

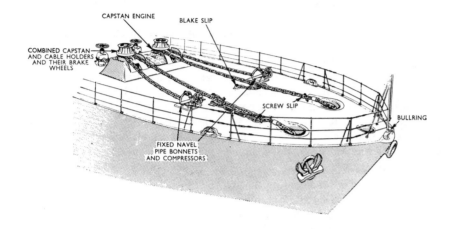

FIG. 11–9. Arrangement of anchors and cables in a destroyer

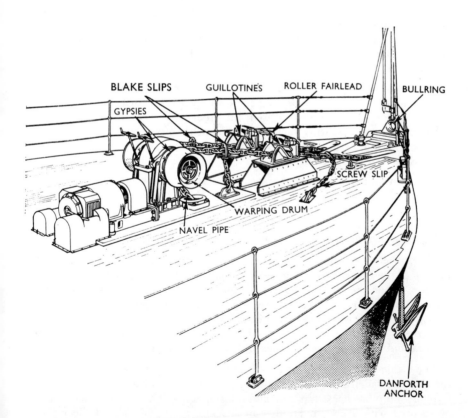

FIG. 11–10. Arrangement of anchors and cables in a minor warship

BRINGING A SHIP TO SINGLE ANCHOR

Before a ship anchors, the anchors and cables must be cleared of their sea lashings and prepared for letting go. The Captain studies the selected or allocated berth and decides which anchor to use and the amount of cable, taking into consideration the direction of the wind, the depth of water and the nature of the bottom. The Navigating Officer meanwhile has prepared an anchoring plan so that the ship's speed may be reduced and then the engines stopped in sufficient time. H.M. ships usually let go the anchor with slight headway so that the anchor is dropped in the exact position, and the cable is laid out in a bight clear of the anchor.

The cable party usually consists of the Cable Officer, the captain of the forecastle, the chief engineering mechanic or chief electrician, a shipwright, a communication rating and a number of experienced seamen on deck and in the cable locker. In a small ship, when tradesmen are not borne, their duties are taken by seamen under the direction of the captain of the forecastle.

Sea lashings are cast off all gear, anchor strops removed, bonnets (or their plates) taken off the navel pipes, riding slips taken off or compressors eased off, covers removed from the cable locker and the cable cleared away ready for running out. The anchor is then eased down the hawsepipe by unscrewing the screw slip until the cable is taut and the screw slip slack enough to be removed. The cable is then veered from the cable holder until its weight is taken on the Blake slip, the cable holder is then disconnected from its spindle. The anchor is now held only by the Blake slip and is ready for letting go.

H.M. ships always prepare both bower anchors and cables for immediate use when preparing to come to single anchor. If one anchor hangs (i.e. fails to move) when its Blake slip is released, the other anchor can be let go instead. When possible, the weather anchor (i.e. the anchor on the side from which the wind is blowing, or the tidal stream running) is always used so that the ship will swing clear of her cable.

The ship approaches the anchorage at slow speed, and usually heads into the wind or tidal stream. The cable locker party is cleared from the cable locker and one rating stands by to knock off the Blake slip while the shipwright mans the cable holder brake, the communication rating mans communications with the Bridge, and hands on the forecastle stand clear of the cable.

Shortly before reaching the berth the captain orders 'Stand by', whereupon the pin of the Blake slip is removed and the hammer raised ready to knock off the slip. When the captain orders 'Let go' the Blake slip is smartly knocked off and the anchor and cable run out freely until the shipwright is ordered to apply the brake. The engines are reversed at about the same time as the anchor is dropped, so that the ship is stopped by the time a few shackles of cable have run out and the cable has been laid out straight and taut.

The Cable Officer, when he is satisfied that the ship has got her cable (i.e. the ship has fallen back and is held by her anchor and cable), reports to the Captain 'Ship has her cable, Sir' and the Captain will then order the cable to be secured with a certain number of shackles out. The Cable Officer then heaves in or veers on power to comply with the order. The riding slip or compressor is put on, and the cable is veered until just before the riding slip or compressor takes the weight of the cable. The Blake slip is put on slack; the brake is screwed up hard, or with some cable holders put in the 'brake-to-brake' position and the cable holder disconnected from its spindle. The ship is now riding from the cable holder brake, with the Blake slip and the riding slip or compressor acting as preventers.

The other bower anchor is left in its prepared state for use if required (e.g. dropping the second anchor underfoot if the first anchor starts to drag). The forecastle is now squared up 'shipshape and man-of-war fashion' and the cable party secured.

BRINGING A SHIP TO A BUOY

To prepare a ship's cable that will form the bridle from the ship to the buoy, the cable must first be broken either at the first joining shackle if the ship is fitted with a stem hawsepipe or a bullring to take the bridle, or at the first half-shackle if the bridle is to be lead through the hawsepipe after the anchor has been catted. Fig. 11-3 illustrates a ship secured by a single bridle.

H.M. ships usually secure to a buoy with two bridles; that which is connected to the cable holder is called the *working bridle*, while the other is called the *standing bridle*. Only a single bridle will be described here.

The cable party is mustered on the forecastle and the anchors and cables are cleared away in the same manner as described for coming to single anchor. The anchor is veered and secured at the clump cathead, as described in Volume II, and the cable broken at the first half-shackle by removing the lugless joining shackle; or the cable is broken at the first joining shackle if the anchor is not catted. The cable holder is then veered and the cable lighted forward to the hawsepipe, towing fairlead or bullring, the cable party using cable hooks or a bullrope for the purpose. The securing-to-buoy shackle is then shackled to the end of the bridle and, just before the ship reaches the buoy, the cable is fed down the hawsepipe, fairlead or bullring until the end is approximately 6 ft clear of the water.

While the cable party is preparing the bridle the motor whaler/cutter is manned by its crew and two buoy jumpers, who carry the necessary tools for shackling the securing-to-buoy shackle to the buoy shackle. Then the boat is turned out and lowered to just above the waterline ready to slip when the order to do so is given by the Captain.

The cable party fake down a wire hawser called a *picking-up rope*, which is fitted with a strop and spring hook at its outboard end.

The ship approaches the buoy at slow speed, the boat is slipped and makes its way forward to receive a heaving line from the cable party on the forecastle, one end of which is bent to the end of the picking-up rope. The boat then proceeds to the buoy. The buoy jumpers, who must always wear lifejackets and leather shoes, jump on to the buoy, haul in the heaving line until they can pass the strop of the picking-up rope through the buoy shackle and hook it to the spring hook. The buoy jumpers now return to the boat, which stands off while the cable party bring the picking-up rope to the capstan and heave in.

When the ship is snug and close to the buoy and the picking-up rope taut, the buoy jumpers return to the buoy and secure the bridle either to the buoy shackle, or, if the ship is using a mooring designed for a larger ship, to one of the reducing links, with the securing-to-buoy shackle.

The buoy jumpers again leave the buoy while the cable party veers the picking-up rope until the bridle takes the strain and the picking-up rope becomes slack. The buoy jumpers remove the picking-up rope from the buoy shackle and the boat returns them to the ship.

The Cable Officer reports 'Shackled on' and then veers to the required scope. The Captain then orders 'Secure', and the cable is secured in the same manner as described when coming to a single anchor.

EXAMPLES OF ANCHOR AND CABLE OUTFITS

	Large Carrier	Frigate
Bower anchors	2 'Byers'	2 A.C. 14
Weight (each)	190 cwt	32 cwt
Size and type of cable	3-in. forged steel	1⅜-in. forged steel
Number of shackles	29 total, port and starboard	5 port
		5 starboard
Number of half-shackles	11 total, port and starboard	4 port
		4 starboard
Killick		1 Danforth 300-lb

Questions on this chapter will be found in Appendix 2.

PART III

SHIP ORGANISATION

CHAPTER 12

Elementary Organisation

Command

A man-of-war is commanded by an officer of the Seaman Branch who is known as the Commanding Officer or the Captain. He may be of any rank from Captain to Lieutenant, depending upon the size and type of the ship he commands.

Next in importance to the Captain is the Executive Officer, who may be of any rank from Commander to Sub-Lieutenant. He is specially appointed to carry out executive duties in the ship, and he is responsible to the Captain for the fighting efficiency of the ship, the general organisation and routine of the ship's company, and the discipline, morale and welfare of everyone on board her. In ships where the Executive Officer is of Commander's rank he is known as the Commander; otherwise he is known as the First Lieutenant. In ships where the Executive Officer is a Commander the officer of the Seaman Branch next in seniority to him is known as the First Lieutenant.

In the event of the death or incapacity of the Captain the command of the ship devolves upon the senior surviving officer of the Seaman Branch. In the temporary absence on leave or duty of the Captain the command of the ship for the time being is vested in the senior officer of the Seaman Branch on board.

Departments

The men who man a warship are known collectively as her *ship's company*, and for administrative purposes the ship's company is divided into *departments* which correspond with the various branches of the Service. The senior officer of each department is known as the *Head* of his department, and he is responsible to the Captain for the efficiency of his department and the work it carries out.

Watches

A continuous watch must be kept in a ship, both day and night and at sea or in harbour, to ensure her safety and to ensure her readiness for any duty she may be called upon to perform. A proportion of her complement of officers and men must therefore always be on watch, either actively engaged or standing-by at immediate notice. The number of officers and men on watch depends upon the type of ship, whether she is at sea or in harbour, and the duties on which she is engaged. In order to provide a continuous watch to suit every occasion, and to allow adequate periods for the rest and recreation of the men, a ship's company is divided into watches and parts of watches, in each of which there are sufficient men of the various branches, and with the necessary technical qualifications, to carry out any duty which the watch, or part of a watch, may be called upon to perform.

333

Watch systems

In the Royal Navy there are two types of watch organisation, known respectively as the *two-watch* and the *three-watch* systems. In either system each watch is divided into two parts, and in large ships each part may be divided into two *sub-divisions*. A part of a watch, or a sub-division, is the smallest body of men that is used to work or fight the ship.

The men off watch carry out their general ship's duties during working hours in accordance with the routine in force at the time. Whether the seamen work in two or three watches depends upon the type of ship and the arrangement of her armament, and they may be changed from the one to the other according to the duties she has to carry out. The Engineering Department usually work in three watches, except when steaming at full power for prolonged periods; other departments usually conform to the system adopted for the seamen.

Two-watch system. In the two-watch system the men are equally divided into the *starboard watch* and the *port watch*, and each watch is equally divided into the *first part* and the *second part*. With this system the men can be worked *watch-and-watch*, i.e. alternate watches on duty at sea, or one day on and the the next day off in harbour; or in four watches, that is one watch on duty out of four watches at sea, or one day on and three days off in harbour. In general ship work, and for manning the armament in wartime, this system provides for three-quarters, a half, or a quarter of the ship's company to be used at any time (fig. 12–1).

Three-watch system. In the three-watch system, the men are divided into *Red*, *White* and *Blue* watches, and each watch may be divided into its first and second parts. With this system the men can be worked in three watches, i.e. one watch on duty out of three watches at sea, or one day on and two days off in harbour. The system provides for two-thirds, one-third or one-sixth of the ship's company to be used for any work or duty required.

Organisation for work

For cleaning, maintenance and general shipwork the seamen of a ship can be organised in two ways:

Traditional or Part-of-ship system. This originated in the days of sail. The upper deck is divided into a number of parts according to the type and size of the ship. There can be four parts—Forecastle (F.X.), Foretop (F.T.), Maintop (M.T.) and Quarterdeck (A.X.); three parts by combining the tops (T); and two parts by omitting the tops. Seamen petty officers and men of each watch are divided equally between the parts of ship and they are then known as forecastlemen, topmen, etc.

Fig. 12–1 shows the division of a ship's company into parts-of-ship and starboard and port watches, and it will be seen that each part-of-ship is composed of approximately equal numbers from each part of the watch. Care is taken that each part-of-ship and each part of a watch contains an equal number of men of each different rate and qualification, and that they are equally balanced as regards seniority and experience. Each part-of-ship is under the charge of petty officers (one to each watch) known as the First and Second *Captain of the Top*.

Functional system. The seamen are organised according to their branches. For example, the crew of the forward gun or turret forms the basis of the forecastle party for working cable. Cleaning, maintenance and general shipwork are carried out in the vicinity of the armament that is manned, and sleeping accommodation is allocated nearby.

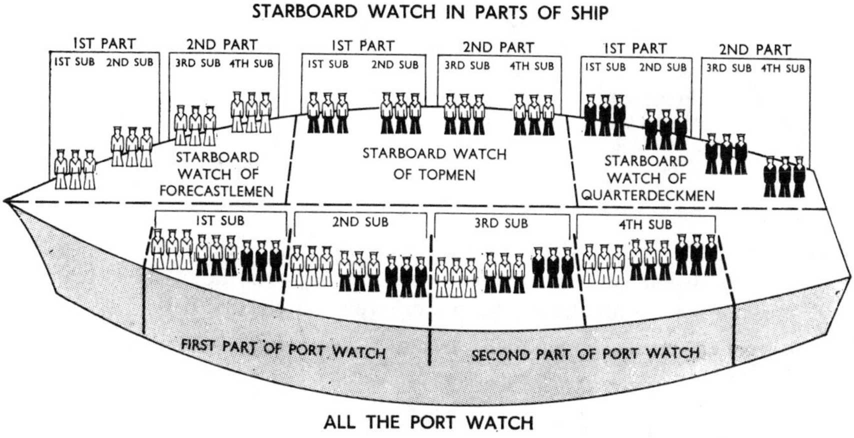

FIG. 12-1. Division of a ship's company

Divisions

For general administrative and welfare purposes, the whole ship's company is divided into a number of *divisions*, which correspond with the departments of the ship (e.g. Supply Division, Communication Division). The number of seamen in a ship is usually too large for them to be grouped in a single division, and they may therefore be divided into divisions which correspond with their parts-of-ship, watches or departments. The Engineering Department is also too numerous to be grouped in a single division, so the ratings are usually divided into four divisions, one for artificers and mechanicians and the remaining three for stoker mechanics, one division for each watch.

The main principle of the divisional system is that each division is composed of a body of men who normally work and mess together and who therefore know each other well. Each division is under the charge of an officer of the department concerned, who is responsible for the administration, training, instruction, advancement, welfare and general efficiency of everyone in it.

ROUTINE

Time and watches

The seaman uses the 24-hour clock and his day is divided into seven periods called watches. The day starts at midnight and the time is recorded in four figures, of which the first two denote the hour and the last two the minutes.

The following table shows the difference in the recording of time by civil and naval methods.

Name of Watch	Duration in Naval time	Duration in Civil time
Middle	0000 to 0400	midnight to 4 a.m.
Morning	0400 to 0800	4 a.m. to 8 a.m.
Forenoon	0800 to 1230	8 a.m. to 12.30 p.m.
Afternoon	1230 to 1600	12.30 p.m. to 4 p.m.
First Dog	1600 to 1800	4 p.m. to 6 p.m.
Last Dog	1800 to 2000	6 p.m. to 8 p.m.
First	2000 to 2400	8 p.m. to midnight.

The purpose of dividing the period between 1600 and 2000 into the two *dog watches* is to provide an odd number of watches in the 24-hour day so that the port and starboard watches will keep a different watch each day.

The seaman, unlike the civilian, does not speak of the morning, afternoon and evening, but of the morning, forenoon, afternoon and dog watches.

Striking the ship's bell

The time is indicated by striking the hours and half-hours on the ship's bell throughout each watch, except in silent hours and during church services, in accordance with the table below; the time thus indicated is called *one bell, two bells*, etc., according to the number of times the bell has been struck:

first half-hour	1 bell	second hour and a half	5 bells
first hour	2 bells	third hour	6 bells
first hour and a half	3 bells	third hour and a half	7 bells
second hour	4 bells	fourth hour	8 bells

This sequence is repeated in each watch, with the exception of the last dog watch: seven bells, for example, can therefore indicate 0330, 0730, 1130, 1530 or 2330, and so when quoting the time by this method the name of the watch is added; 1130, for example, is described as *seven bells in the forenoon*. Time in the last dog watch is marked as follows: 1830 by one bell, 1900 by two bells, 1930 by three bells and 2000 by eight bells.

Except for marking the time the ship's bell is struck only when the ship is at anchor in a fog or bad visibility, or in some ships to sound the general alarm in the event of fire or other emergency. The fog signal is the rapid ringing of the bell for about five seconds every minute. For a general alarm the bell is rung rapidly for considerably longer than five seconds, and this is usually followed by a bugle call or a *pipe* indicating the nature of the emergency and giving orders for dealing with it. The general alarm is only sounded by order of the Commanding Officer.

Silent hours

This term denotes the period of the night watches, between the times of *pipe down* and calling the hands, when it is customary not to mark the time by the ship's bell in order to avoid unnecessarily disturbing the watch below and the day-men. During the silent hours at sea the watch next on deck is sometimes called by the words '*All the (named) watch*', the call being made much less loudly than in daytime. At five or ten minutes to the hour for relieving the watches the bell may be struck once, softly, as a signal for the relieving watch to muster, this strike being called *little-one-bell*.

Daily harbour and sea routines

Normal everyday life in a ship is regulated in accordance with a time-table known as the *routine*. This routine must cover the general activities of the ship and her crew wherever she may be, and so there are a *harbour routine* and a *sea routine* for both weekdays and Sundays, and these differ for home and foreign stations, and for winter and summer. Although these routines must vary considerably with the type of ship and the station on which she is serving, the principles on which all routines are based are governed by the *Queen's Regulations and Admiralty Instructions*, and there are therefore certain main features which are common to all.

The day is divided into three main periods; the first *before* 0800, the second *from* 0800 *to* 1600 and the third *from* 1600 *to* 2300. In the first period the hands are called, secure their bunks and have breakfast. The second period, which covers the forenoon and afternoon watches, is devoted to the cleaning, maintenance and repair of the ship and her armament and equipment, and to the training and instruction of her crew. In the third period facilities are given to the crew for leisure, and for recreation and shore leave if in harbour, and the ship and her equipment are prepared for the night.

In the tropics it is usual to start the day's work earlier and *pipe down* when the hands go to dinner.

Make-and-mend

Originally known as *make and mend clothes* and still piped in this way, this was a half-holiday set aside weekly (usually on Wednesday) for the ship's company in which to repair and replace their kit. In those days few articles of clothing were supplied from store and most were usually made by the men themselves. Nowadays make-and-mends are usually granted on every Saturday when circumstances permit; and, in addition, when the ship is in harbour an extra make-and-mend may occasionally be granted for organised recreation and sports.

Guard and steerage

The steerage used to be right aft by the rudder head, and near or around this flat were berthed the officers, who, together with the guard and any passengers, were allowed to lie in later than the remainder of the hands and were roused by the call '*Up guard and steerage hammocks*'. Nowadays 'guard and steerage usually applies to middle watchmen.

INTERNAL COMMUNICATIONS

Piping and the boatswain's call

Piping is a naval method of passing orders and information, and every seaman should know how to use a *boatswain's call* and how to pipe an order. Orders thus passed are known as *pipes*.

The use of the boatswain's call in English ships can be traced back with certainty to the days of the Crusades, A.D. 1248. In former days it was worn in English ships and fleets as an honoured badge of rank, probably because it had always been used for passing orders. As long ago as 1485 it was worn as the badge of office of the Lord High Admiral of England, and by his successors in office up to 1562. Thereafter it was used throughout the English fleets for passing all orders, and since about 1671 it has always been known as the boatswain's call. Nowadays the boatswain's call and chain are the badge of office of the Chief Boatswain's Mate, quartermasters and boatswain's mates and junior seamen qualified. The expression *to pipe* means, generally, to make the sound of the boatswain's call and to give the spoken order which may qualify it. Some pipes, however, are orders in themselves and do not require any verbal addition.

A boatswain's call (fig. 12-2) can be tuned by scraping away and enlarging the wind edge of the hole in the *buoy*, until it will sound if the mouth of the *gun* is held directly into a moderate wind.

The boatswain's call is held in the right hand between the index finger and thumb, the latter being on or near the *shackle* (fig. 12-3). The side of the buoy rests against the palm of the hand, and the fingers close over the gun and buoy hole in such a position as to be able to throttle the exit of air from the buoy to the desired amount. Care must be taken that the fingers do not touch the edge of the hole in the buoy, or of the hole in the end of the gun, otherwise all sound will be completely choked.

A great variety of notes and tones may be obtained with the boatswain's call by manipulating the fingers and varying the breath blown into the mouth of the gun, but certain notes and tones are only used in piping in the Royal Navy, and these, together with the method of producing them, are described below.

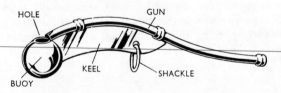

FIG. 12-2. The boatswain's call

There are two main notes, the *low* and the *high*, and there are three tones; these tones are the *plain*, marked on the chart (fig. 12-4) with a steady line, the *warble*, marked with a wavy line, and the *trill*, marked with an interrupted line. The plain low note is produced by blowing steadily into the mouth of the gun with the hole of the buoy unobstructed by the fingers. The plain high note is produced by throttling the exit of air from the hole of the buoy; this is done by closing the fingers around the buoy, taking care not to touch the edges of the hole or the end of the gun. Intermediate notes can be obtained by throttling to a greater or less degree.

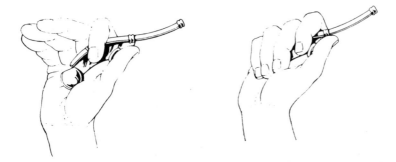

FIG. 12–3. How to hold the boatswain's call

The warble is produced by blowing in a series of jerks, which results in a warble similar to that of a canary. The trill is produced by vibrating the tongue while blowing, as in rolling the letter 'R'.

The chart shows the various *pipes* used in the Royal Navy today. The figures at the top of each diagram represent seconds of time. The nature, continuity and tone of the notes are indicated by the various lines, and the degree of their slope indicates the speed of ascent or descent of the notes.

Pipes

Except for Nos. 3, 4, 12 and 13 in fig. 12–4, the pipes are an order in themselves and require no verbal addition; e.g. it is incorrect and superfluous to follow the pipe for dinner by the words 'Hands to dinner'.

The *Still* is used to call all hands to attention as a mark of respect, or to order silence on any occasion, or to stop all work in the vicinity in order to prevent an accident. It is followed at the required interval by the *Carry on*, and, in the last example, usually not until verbal orders have been given to remedy what was wrong.

The *Hail* was formerly used to call all boatswain's mates, but is used nowadays to attract the attention of a particular person in an unobtrusive manner, the coxswain of a boat, a member of the gangway staff or the Officer of the Day, for example.

No. 4 pipe precedes any broadcast order; it draws attention to the order. It also precedes the calling away of any boat's crew, except that of the barge (for which No. 13 pipe is used). With the exception of the barge, the crew and not the boat is referred to when piping, examples of the relevant pipes being 'Aw-a-a-y first motor boat's crew', and 'Awa-a-a-y barge'.

No. 12 pipe precedes the calling of the hands and is followed by the order 'Lash up and stow'. In practice it is customary considerably to amplify this

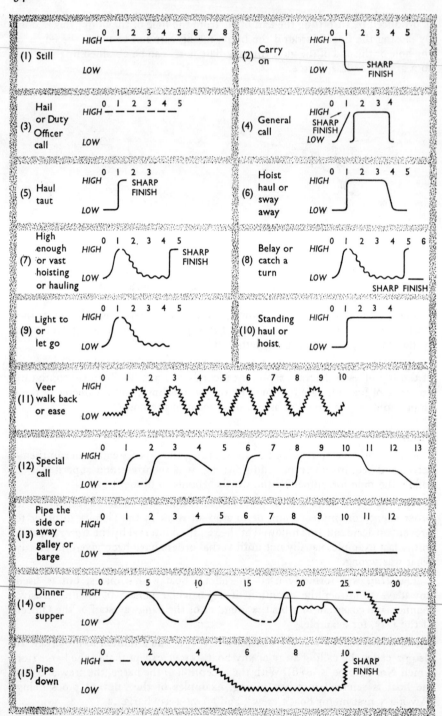

FIG. 12–4. Piping chart

pipe, a typical example being: 'Heave out! Heave out! Heave out! Show a leg! Show a leg! Lash and carry! Lash and carry! Rise and shine! Rise and shine! Heave out, lash up and stow! Heave out, lash up and stow! Heave out, lash up and stow!'; and this may be followed by a short description of any adverse weather, such as 'Gale and rain' or 'Ice and snow', to warn those below to put on suitable clothing.

When calling the watch at night the pipe is not used but merely the words 'A-a-a-ll the (named) watch', given in a low but clear voice and repeated once.

Out-of-routine orders or information of general interest to the ship's company are preceded by the words 'D'ye hear there!'; for example, 'D'ye hear there! The last mail will close at noon today.'

A pipe and its accompanying order are not repeated; the words 'hurry up the crew' may be used when a boat is urgently required; but the words 'at the double' should not be used, because everyone is expected to obey an order immediately. In general, piping is reserved for passing orders and information of importance; it should not be used for trivial matters or for purposes which could be served equally well by using a messenger or telephone.

Items of the daily routine are rarely piped nowadays, but a time check is normally broadcast before the start of the day's work.

Bugle calls

The more important routine orders are passed by the bugle in ships which carry a bugler. Most of these bugle calls are an order in themselves and require no qualification by pipe; so that if, for example, 'both watches for exercise' are required to muster in the usual place (on the forecastle), the bugle call 'Both watches for exercise' should not be followed by another order, as 'Both watches for exercise fall in on the forecastle'. If the watches are required to muster in an unaccustomed place, e.g. on the quarter-deck, the bugle call is followed by the order 'Muster on the quarterdeck'. It is the duty of all hands to learn and recognise the standard bugle calls and pipes.

RULES

The following rules should be observed when using a telephone, voicepipe, broadcaster, loud-hailer or other similar method of communication:

1. Make up your mind what you are going to say before you say it.
2. Read to yourself any written message before passing it verbally.
3. Speak clearly and deliberately.
4. Spell proper names by the phonetic alphabet if there can be any doubt about their correct reception.
5. Transmit important groups of numbers singly and phonetically.
6. Always make your message as brief as possible.

THE PHONETIC ALPHABET

Letters

A	Alfa	J	Juliett	S	Sierra
B	Bravo	K	Kilo	T	Tango
C	Charlie	L	Lima	U	Uniform
D	Delta	M	Mike	V	Victor
E	Echo	N	November	W	Whiskey
F	Foxtrot	O	Oscar	X	Xray
G	Golf	P	Papa	Y	Yankee
H	Hotel	Q	Quebec	Z	Zulu
I	India	R	Romeo		

Numbers

0	ZERO	5	FI-YIV
1	WUN	6	SIX
2	TOO	7	SE-VEN
3	THUH-REE	8	ATE
4	FO-WER	9	NI-NER

METHODS

The principal means of conveying orders and information within a ship or establishment are by Messenger, Telephone, Voicepipe and Broadcast.

Messenger

A messenger should know all the officers and senior ratings by name or title, and he should know his way round the ship.

He should deliver his messages as quickly as possible, by the shortest route. When delivering a message he has right of way anywhere; for example, he should not hesitate to enter the quarters of a senior officer when he has a message for him.

When given an important verbal message the messenger may be ordered to repeat it back as a means of checking that he will deliver it correctly. If a messenger does not clearly understand the message he is to deliver, he must at once ask for it to be repeated: a smart 'getaway' will in no way redound to his credit when he is reported for delivering it incorrectly; an incorrect message may have serious results in naval life.

On receiving a written message the messenger must make sure that he understands to whom it is to be delivered, and whether or not he is to bring back a reply.

On first approaching an officer a messenger should address him by his official title, or by his rank and name, e.g. 'Commander (E), Sir', or 'Lieutenant Jones, Sir'; he should wait until the officer is ready to receive the message, then deliver it, and then wait for a reply, an acknowledgement or his dismissal, before carrying on.

If for any reason a messenger is unable to deliver his message, he must immediately report the fact to the originator of the message.

Telephone

The telephone is a delicate instrument and should always be handled and replaced with care. Rules for using it are given below.

1. Speak directly into and close to the mouthpiece.
2. When calling, ask whenever possible for the number required, and not for the person.
3. When connected, state who you are and with whom you wish to speak—*do not say 'Hullo'*.
4. When replying, state who you are and from where you are speaking—*do not say 'Hullo'*.
5. When replying, identify the caller before continuing the conversation.
6. When using a shore circuit, make sure you are connected with the right person before discussing any Service matter.
7. Remember that a telephone system is never safe from eavesdroppers, so do not discuss confidential matters over it.
8. If you are disconnected in the middle of a conversation it is the responsibility of the caller to re-establish conversation; the person called should wait for half a minute before abandoning the call and replacing his receiver.
9. To transfer a call to another number on the same exchange recall the operator by depressing the receiver rest at intervals of about two seconds.
10. Wait at least a quarter of a minute before making a fresh call.

Voicepipe

The rules for using a voicepipe are as follows:

1. To make a call press the call push (if provided).
2. Speak loudly and directly into the mouthpiece.
3. When calling, first state the name of the position you wish to speak to and then the name of the position from which you are speaking; when answering, first state the position from which you are speaking, and then the position to which you are speaking.

Broadcast system

It is just as important in a warship to relay orders to all parts of the ship quickly and efficiently as it is for its crew to be a highly-trained and well-knit unit.

In former days orders were relayed throughout the ship by call-boys, each with a boatswain's call. This slow method meant that the crew received directions and orders long after they had been originated. As ships became more complicated and internally sub-divided, a system of broadcasting was needed so that every man in the ship might receive information from loudspeakers at precisely the same instant. This is called the General Broadcast system, in which orders can be given through a control box microphone and received from loudspeakers situated at positions throughout the ship. Control boxes are usually positioned on the bridge, at the steering position, near the quarterdeck, and in any other place where it is operationally necessary.

Each control box can be switched to transmit to selected sections within the ship; it can also give the General Warning (which is a series of low notes alternating with equal periods of silence) or the General Alarm (which is a series of long, low notes alternating with short periods of silence in the ratio of 3:1).

However, it soon became apparent that there was also a need for separate sectional broadcast systems for Machinery, Armament, and (in carriers) Flight Deck and Hangars. Each of these sections has its own problems and therefore needs to have immediate and direct control. Each section broadcast system is, in fact, a part of the General Broadcast system which can be 'locked out' from it and controlled from its own section box. This 'locking out' is necessary because engineering department ratings on watch are not concerned with the hoisting of a boat but with the orders between various machinery spaces, and the seaman has no need to know what is happening in the hangars or on the flight deck of a carrier if he is cleaning out his messdeck; and during Armament exercises the gunnery or TAS ratings need to hear only the armament orders and not the calling away of a boat.

Nevertheless, the General Broadcast system can make known to each section, by means of a section call, that the section is required to listen to an urgent general broadcast message. In each General Broadcast control box there are lights which indicate when a section is 'in use', and that particular section will not receive a general broadcast unless it is told to listen in.

The General Broadcast 'warning' or 'alarm' signals given from any control box take priority over all section broadcasts and will automatically cut in to a section broadcast even if the section is 'in use' or 'locked out'. This priority is not given over the Armament section broadcast, because the armament positions would probably be manned and the section 'in use' for armament control.

The Flight Deck and Hangars section broadcast system is basically the same as the Machinery section broadcast, but it has its own 'alert' and 'alarm' signals for use within the section. These signals are the same as the General 'warning' and 'alarm', but are of a distinctly higher pitch and can break into a normal General Broadcast. The 'alert' and 'alarm' signals of this section can only be overridden by the General Broadcast 'warning' and 'alarm' signals.

Destroyers and frigates have only the low note 'alarm' signal.

Every General Broadcast and Section Broadcast system mutes the S.R.E. (ships recreational broadcast system) when the press-to-speak (P.T.S.) switch in a control or section box is made.

Microphones. There are various types of microphones in use, including hand, bracket, or desk; switched or unswitched; watertight or non-watertight. They can be mounted as extending, universal bracket, bracket, or chest bracket; or with a flexible metallic tubing on a desk.

How to speak into a microphone. Place the mouth at a distance of about one inch from the mouth of the microphone, and at an angle of about 45°; speak slowly, at an even and normal level, with clear articulation. Where a shaped mouthpiece is provided, the face should be in contact with it and the voice level lowered.

Bugle calls. These should be sounded at about 6 ft, and never less than 3 ft, from the microphone.

Pipes. These should be made with the boatswain's call about 6 in. from the microphone.

Control and Section boxes. Instructions on how to operate these boxes are given on the inside of each box cover. The cover is hinged to open downwards, and as the cover is lowered the microphone is extended, as shown in fig. 12–5.

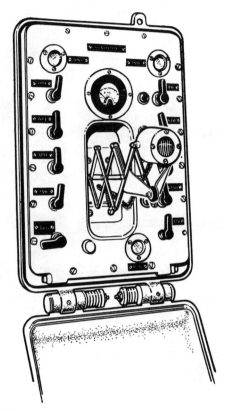

FIG. 12–5. General Broadcast control box

Questions on this chapter will be found in Appendix 2.

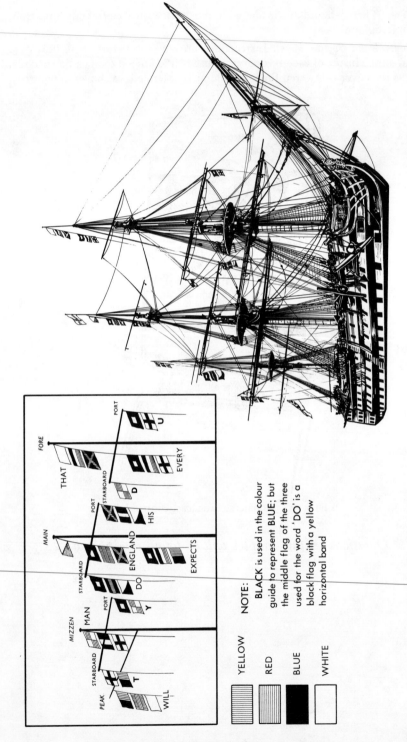

FIG. 13-1. H.M.S. *Victory* flying the famous signal made by Lord Nelson at Trafalgar

CHAPTER 13

Naval Communications

Communications are the means whereby command is exercised. Orders and information must be passed rapidly, accurately and, where possible, securely, between ships, aircraft and shore headquarters and establishments. An efficient system of communications is vital for the fighting efficiency of a modern fleet.

Historical background

The history of naval signalling goes back many hundreds of years, but the methods of signalling used today are nearly all of much more recent origin. Until the Napoleonic wars signalling was mostly performed by means of sail movements, the firing of guns and the display of flags in various positions to convey different meanings, the codes used having been privately compiled and printed and being limited both in scope and use.

In 1780 Admiral Kempenfelt devised a code (subsequently revised and elaborated by Lord Howe in 1790), consisting of numeral flags and a small number of special flags and pennants, by which several hundreds of different signals could be made. This code was basically the same as that used by Lieutenant Pasco to make Nelson's famous signal at Trafalgar (fig. 13-1), but the significations of the flags had been changed owing to the capture of the signal book by the French in 1804. A revised signal code containing much more detail was produced as the result of research by Admiral Home Popham, who for a number of years had devoted much of his time to this subject.

Semaphore signalling was adopted in 1795 from a system devised by the Reverend Lord George Murray, which at first consisted of a screen containing six shutters which could be operated to give numerous combinations. This system was used by the Admiralty for communicating with the Nore and Portsmouth Commands, the signals being relayed by a chain of signal stations situated within sight of each other on convenient hills. It was extended later to Plymouth, and an improved semaphore was adopted which was devised by Sir Home Popham in 1816 and consisted of two movable arms lit by lanterns at night and operated so as to form different angles. It is claimed that in clear weather a signal could be transmitted by this system from London to Portsmouth in ten minutes, although it had to pass through ten different stations in transit. These land stations were finally closed down in 1848, after the invention of the electric telegraph, but the system is commemorated to this day by many of the original sites of these stations being known locally as 'Telegraph Hill'.

The Morse code, so named after its American inventor Samuel Morse, revolutionised signalling on land with the introduction of the *electro-magnetic recording telegraph*. The use of this instrument was first demonstrated by the transmission of a message over a line from Baltimore to Washington on May 24th, 1844. The wide possibilities of this system were quickly recognised, and in 1865, as a result of experiments and trials carried out by Captain Philip

Colomb, R.N., and Captain Bolton of the 12th Regiment, the Royal Navy adopted the *flashing system* in which shutters and flags were used by day and lamps by night for transmitting signals in the Morse code.

Visual signalling held complete sway afloat until 1905, when wireless telegraphy emerged from its early experimental stage into practical use and further development. The revolution in naval communications brought about by the advent of wireless can be easily appreciated when it is realised that before 1905 a naval unit, when at sea and outside visual range, was entirely cut off from all outside communication except by despatch vessel.

The world-wide naval organisation and control achieved in recent years, and particularly during the Second World War (1939–1945), was made possible only by the communications network which was perfected as a result of the rapid progress in the development of wireless and other signalling systems.

Defence against nuclear attack in modern warfare frequently requires ships to operate in widely dispersed formations. Because of this, communication tends to be increasingly carried out by wireless. But visual signalling, particularly by directional light, still remains a vital part of naval communications because it is much less likely to be intercepted by the enemy than wireless.

SYSTEMS OF COMMUNICATION AND THEIR USES

The various systems of communication are complementary to each other, and although in certain circumstances one particular system may be quicker or more suitable than another, all are organised so that together they provide a network of communications to meet the varied requirements of the whole Naval Service. A message on its transmission route between originator and final addressee may therefore be *handled* by one, several or all of the following systems; and to enable the most efficient use to be made of them a number of transmission and signal codes have been devised, of which the more commonly used are mentioned later in this chapter.

Messenger

The transmission of messages by messenger, despatch rider, helicopter or despatch boat service, is very secure and fairly rapid. In naval ports a hand message organisation is used extensively between ships and shore authorities.

Mail

This system is used for the transmission of non-urgent messages. Messages may be sent by either surface or air mail and are then known as *postagrams* or *airgrams*. The messages are prepared for despatch by the Communications department, handed to the secretariat for transmission by the appropriate route, and on reaching their destination are given to the Communications department for distribution.

Sound

This is the means of communication which uses sound waves and includes siren, foghorn and whistle; the Morse code is normally used. Sound signalling is a cumbersome method and its use is restricted to emergencies when visual communication is impracticable (as in fog).

Underwater communications. Sound waves can be transmitted through water by using sonar sets employing the Morse code; this is known as *supersonic telegraphy* (SST). Underwater telephones provide a means of making either SST or voice transmissions through water. These methods are used with submarines.

Visual signalling (VS)

This embraces signalling by panels, pyrotechnics, coloured lights, flashing light, semaphore and flags.

Pyrotechnics and panels. These are used mainly as an emergency means of communication and for identification purposes.

Coloured lights. These may be displayed in accordance with a pre-arranged code to convey information, or for identification purposes.

Flashing light. This is a means of transmitting the international Morse code characters by light. A *directional* light is used to communicate with a single ship, and a *non-directional* light with several ships. It is a most suitable method of passing messages between ships in close company by day or night.

Semaphore

This provides a rapid means for passing messages over short distances during daylight.

Semaphore code. The different semaphore signs are made by moving one or two handflags so that they form various angles with the perpendicular. It is essential that each angle be formed correctly, as good communication depends upon accuracy in this respect.

Alphabet and special signs. The alphabet and the special signs used are shown in fig. 13–7. It will be noticed that the letters follow round in succeeding circles, differing from each other by angles of 45 degrees. The simplest method of memorising the signs is to take them in a series of circles, thus:

1st circle	A to G (single arm signs)
2nd circle	H to N (omitting J)
3rd circle	O to S
4th circle	T, U, Y
5th circle	Numeral sign, J and V
to complete	W, X and Z

It should be noted that there are no special signs for numerals, which are always spelt out. The numeral sign is used to indicate that the numerals that follow are to be recorded as digits.

Transmitting. When transmitting to another station the sender must always stand in a conspicuous position and choose a plain, light-coloured background, the best example of which is a skyline. It is better to transmit slowly and accurately; undue hurry in forming the letters will only result in bad transmission and mistakes.

The *direction sign* (J) shows from which side the letters are to be read. It is sometimes necessary to transmit to stations both in front of and behind the operator.

The signs for *long break* ($\overline{\text{BT}}$), *full stop* (AAA), and *repeat* ($\overline{\text{IMI}}$) are used in a similar manner to those of the Morse code.

Flag signalling

This involves the use of flags and pennants displayed from halyards and is employed by ships and shore stations. It is limited to daylight use and to comparatively short distances.

Construction of flag codes. The flags and pennants used in naval signalling comprise:

Alphabetical flags	the same design and colour as the
Numeral pennants	International code (fig. 13–5)
Substitutes	

Numeral flags	
Special flags	of special design and used by the Royal,
Special pennants	Commonwealth and Allied Navies (fig. 13–6)
Fourth substitute	

Each flag and pennant is allocated a meaning. This may vary with the circumstances in which it is hoisted (i.e. at sea or in harbour). In addition, two or more flags may form a group, which is also allocated a meaning. A flag signal may therefore consist of:

1. A single flag or pennant.
2. A combination of flags and/or pennants in one hoist.
3. Several hoists flying simultaneously, which are read in their relative sequence.
4. Several *displays*, each of one or more hoists, the displays being hoisted consecutively.

In certain cases additional meanings may be conveyed by hoisting a flag signal *at the dip*, i.e. at a position three-quarters of the full distance up the halyard. A flag signal is answered by hoisting at the dip either the same signal or the answer pennant. As soon as the signal is understood this answer is then hoisted *close up*, i.e. to the full extent of halyard. The signal is then ready to be executed. To execute a signal it is normally hauled down, but in some cases a flag signal is executed when it is dipped; when this is the case it appears in the meaning of the signal.

This combination of flags, together with their different meanings, is known as a *signal code*. Two codes are in use in the Allied Navies: the Naval code (used by warships) and the International code (used by merchant ships and between warships and merchant ships).

Line communications (L.T.)

These employ a physical path such as a wire or cable between terminals.

Radio communications

These employ radio waves between transmitter and receiver. Both line and radio communications travel at approximately the speed of light (186,000 miles per second), and comprise telegraphy, telephony, facsimile and television.

Telegraphy. The systems employed apply equally to both line and radio communications, and use some agreed code between sender and recipient.

Automatic telegraphy (A.T.). This forms the basis of Naval World Wide Communication, whereby messages are transmitted and received automatically at high speeds (about 60 w.p.m.) by means of telegraphic typewriters and perforated tapes. The radio system employed is known as *radio teletype* (RATT).

Morse telegraphy. When used with radio, this is commonly known as *wireless telegraphy* (W/T), and is still widely used in the Merchant Navy, but is steadily being replaced in the Allied Navies by A.T.

Telephony. This is a system for the transmission of speech by line or radio. The most common form of line telephony is the *telephone* (PN).

Radio telephony (Voice or R/T). This is mainly used for short-range communications between ships, aircraft and shore stations. Systems are being developed which will ultimately provide world-wide voice communications.

Facsimile. This is a means of sending still pictures recorded in a permanent form by either line or radio. It is used extensively for newspaper pictures and in the Navy for receiving weather maps from meteorological stations.

Television (TV). Domestic television is a familiar feature of modern living, but at present its naval use is limited to internal transmission of entertainment programmes in aircraft carriers, and for underwater detection in salvage operations.

THE MORSE CODE

The principal methods used for transmission of messages by the Morse code are:

1. Sound
2. Flashing light
3. Telegraphy
4. Line telegraphy.

Construction of the Morse code

Symbols of the Morse code are expressed by an arrangement of dots and dashes, as shown below. A dot is used as the unit of duration. A dash is equal to three units (or dots). The space between each dot or dash is one unit; between special characters three units; and between words seven units.

ALPHABET

A ● ▬	J ● ▬ ▬ ▬	R ● ▬ ●
B ▬ ● ● ●	K ▬ ● ▬	S ● ● ●
C ▬ ● ▬ ●	L ● ▬ ● ●	T ▬
D ▬ ● ●	M ▬ ▬	U ● ● ▬
E ●	N ▬ ●	V ● ● ● ▬
F ● ● ▬ ●	O ▬ ▬ ▬	W ● ▬ ▬
G ▬ ▬ ●	P ● ▬ ▬ ●	X ▬ ● ● ▬
H ● ● ● ●	Q ▬ ▬ ● ▬	Y ▬ ● ▬ ▬
I ● ●		Z ▬ ▬ ● ●

NUMERALS

1	• ▬ ▬ ▬ ▬	6	▬ • • • •
2	• • ▬ ▬ ▬	7	▬ ▬ • • •
3	• • • ▬ ▬	8	▬ ▬ ▬ • •
4	• • • • ▬	9	▬ ▬ ▬ ▬ •
5	• • • • •	0	▬ ▬ ▬ ▬ ▬

SPECIAL CHARACTERS

The bar over two or more letters indicates that they are to be transmitted as a single character.

$\overline{AA}$	• ▬ • ▬	Unknown station call.
$\overline{AR}$	• ▬ • ▬ •	End of transmission sign used when no receipt is required.
$\overline{BT}$	▬ • • • ▬	Long break. Precedes and follows the text portion of a message.
EEEEEEEE	• • • • • • • •	Error. A succession of eight or more Es means 'Erase the portion of the message just transmitted; the corrected portion will follow': or, if followed by $\overline{AR}$, means 'Cancel this message'.
$\overline{IMI}$	• • ▬ ▬ • •	Repeat. Made by the recipient, to the originator. If made alone it means 'Repeat all of your last transmission'. If the sign is followed by the letters AA (all after), AB (all before), WA (word after) or WB (word before) followed by a word, then it means 'Repeat only that portion of the message so indicated'. It is used by the originator to precede the second transmission of the whole, or a portion, of the message.
K	▬ • ▬	'Invitation to transmit' or 'This is the end of my transmission to you and a response is necessary'.
R	• ▬ •	Received; means 'I have received your last transmission'.
AAA	• ▬ • ▬ • ▬	Period. A full stop in plain language.

These are only some of the special signs used when transmitting in the Morse code; others are given in Communication publications.

COMMUNICATION PUBLICATIONS

A large number of publications is used in the Communications Department. These include callsign books, signal books and codes, cryptographic publications and procedure instructions.

Callsigns

Various types of callsigns are used in naval signalling. The more common are discussed below.

International callsigns. These are listed in a publication known as the 'Berne List', so named because it was compiled as the result of an international convention held at Berne in Switzerland. Every ship, both merchant and naval, is allocated a 4-letter callsign, also known as her 'Signal Letters', which is used in both visual and radio signalling. Signal Letters of British ships are also published in B.R.70, *Signal Letters of British Ships.*

Visual callsigns. These are allocated to all Allied naval vessels and consist of an alphabetical flag indicating the type of vessel, together with two or more numeral pennants which indicate her number in the Visual Callsign book. This callsign is also painted on a ship's side and stern, and is referred to as her hull number. Their use is restricted to visual signalling. A ship's visual callsign is commonly referred to as her *pennants* and every seaman must be able to recognise his ship's pennants, for example: D p⊖ p5 = DARING (destroyer).

Boats' visual callsigns. A boat's callsign consists of flag Quebec (type letter for boats) above a numbered pennant indicating the particular class of boat required. An individual boat of any class may be further identified by a numeral flag below. A boat belonging to another ship is identified by placing the ship's callsign below the boat's callsign.

Signal books and codes

Minor Landing Craft and Boat's Signal Book. This book, commonly known as the M.S.B., contains a simple code for use between ships, minor landing craft, boats of the Royal Navy, and naval signal stations. It contains sufficient information on procedure, callsigns, colours and meanings of flags, and common phrases which are allocated numeral groups, to allow the coxswain of a boat to communicate with other ships and small craft. The coxswain is responsible for keeping the book in good condition in a special painted canvas cover on which the name of the boat and the flags and pennants comprising the boat's visual callsign (which is also the *boat's recall*) are painted.

Allied Naval Signal Book. This book, which can be used with any means of communication, is designed for signalling between Allied naval ships. It contains the colours, meanings and usage of naval flags and pennants, together with the main signal vocabulary, which consists of operational and administrative signals arranged in two-letter groups.

The International Code. This code of signals is designed for use between ships of all countries, and so is printed in seven different languages: English, French, German, Italian, Japanese, Norwegian and Spanish. It is compiled in two volumes. Volume I, used for visual signalling only, is divided into the following main sections:

Single-letter groups
   Navigational and miscellaneous signals of an urgent nature.

Two-letter groups
   Other important signals, mainly those affecting safety or for use in emergency.

Three-letter groups
   The general code or *vocabulary*, giving the more common phrases in use at sea, and words for building up other phrases and sentences.

Four-letter groups

The *geographical section,* which gives the countries, places and landmarks, etc. bordering the navigable waters of the world, arranged alphabetically. All geographical groups begin with the letter 'A'.

When a warship hoists a signal from the International code, the code or answer flag (fig. 13–5) must also be hoisted, to avoid confusion with the Naval code.

Volume II, used for radio only, consists entirely of five-letter groups.

Cryptographic publications

These describe the various systems and cyphers used for disguising the contents and destinations of signals.

Procedures

To avoid misunderstanding and to achieve brevity, every message is made in a standard form and by means of a uniform method known collectively as procedure. Details of the various procedures used with the different systems of communications are laid down in Communication publications.

MESSAGE-HANDLING

Messages can be transmitted to any part of the world almost instantaneously by radio. To ensure that full use is made of these facilities it is important that the handling of messages at the place of origin, en route, and at the final destination is carried out rapidly. Messages may be delivered to, or distributed from, the message-handling centre (known in ships as the Main Signal Office (M.S.O.)) by hand, telephone, pneumatic tube or internal teleprinter (fig. 13–2).

FIG. 13–2. A main signal office

Correct *originating* and *drafting* of messages play an important part in rapid delivery by ensuring that messages are prepared in a concise and standard form. The originator is responsible for this and for indicating the required speed of handling of a message by using one of the *precedence* indicators listed below in descending order of urgency:

Precedence	Abbreviation
FLASH	Z
EMERGENCY	Y
OPERATIONAL IMMEDIATE	O
PRIORITY	P
ROUTINE	R
DEFERRED	M

In addition, every message is given one of the following *security classifications* by the originator, depending on the contents of the message:

TOP SECRET   RESTRICTED

SECRET   UNCLASSIFIED

CONFIDENTIAL

Top Secret messages are normally handled by officers throughout, and the remaining categories of messages are handled by ratings of the Communications department.

The contents of all messages of a security classification of Restricted and higher are never to be divulged to 'non-Service' persons. The classification Unclassified confers no degree of security; but this does not mean that the contents of an Unclassified message may be divulged to non-Service persons.

MESSAGE FORM

PRECEDENCE—ACTION O	PRECEDENCE—INFO P ~~DEFERRED~~	DATE—TIME—GROUP 141630Z	MESSAGE INSTRUCTIONS
FROM CinC PLYMOUTH			PREFIX GR

TO   LEANDER
      AJAX
      DIDO
			SECURITY CLASSIFICATION
			CONFIDENTIAL

			ORIGINATOR'S NUMBER (Not normally used in the R.N.)
INFO F 8			SPECIAL INSTRUCTIONS

PROCEED AND INVESTIGATE SUBMARINE CONTACT IN POSITION
50 15N 04 20W.

FOR OPRS USE	R	DATE	TIME	SYSTEM	OPERATOR	D	DATE	TIME	SYSTEM	OPERATOR	SIGNATURE *D. Hunt.*
											RANK COMMANDER.

FIG. 13–3. Naval message form

All the classifications mentioned above, with the exception of Unclassified, can be given additional security by the use of the prefix 'Exclusive'. This reduces to a minimum the number of persons who see the message, and is used extensively for messages concerning the private affairs of officers and ratings.

Preparation of messages

Fig. 13-3 gives an example of a message correctly drafted on a naval message form. The spaces outside the thick black lines are for use by the Communications staff.

Three copies of the message form are handed in to the M.S.O., where a date-time group is inserted. This, together with the name of the originator's ship, provides a reference for the message. The message is then prepared for dispatch and is transmitted in the following form:

Heading. This contains the callsign(s) of the station(s) being addressed, the precedence, security classification and address, including details of the stations concerned with the message.

Text. This contains the subject matter.

Ending. This contains the request for acknowledgement of receipt of the message and the end-of-message sign.

COMMUNICATIONS BRANCH ORGANISATION

The communications of a ship or naval station are under the control of a qualified Communications Officer or an officer appointed by the Captain to carry out this duty. The Branch comprises Tactical and Radio Communication ratings, whose skills and duties are listed below.

All Communications ratings are taught message-handling, also how to touch-type, to operate line and radio teleprinters, to operate radio telephone equipment and to code and decode messages.

Tactical Communication Operators

In addition, Tactical Operators are experienced in the transmission of messages by flags, semaphore and flashing light and are responsible for internal distribution of signals. At sea they are employed on the bridge or in the operations room as voice operators on manœuvring nets, on the flag deck manning visual means of communication, and in the Main Signal Office for the handling and distribution of messages.

The senior tactical rating, normally a Chief Communications Yeoman (CCY), is in charge of the Tactical Department. He also advises the Captain on manœuvring and ensures that he receives all signals.

Radio Communication Operators

Radio ratings are also taught to transmit and receive Morse at high speeds, and to operate all forms of radio equipment. At sea they are employed in preparing messages for transmission, and tuning and operating the radio equipment required for the various circuits which have been ordered.

The senior radio rating, normally a Chief Radio Supervisor (CRS), is in charge of the Radio Department.

FIG. 13–4. A bridge wireless office

Radio Communication Operators Special

These ratings serve in the Electronic Warfare (E.W.) section of the Communications Branch. They are specially trained in the operation of radio and radar detection and direction-finding equipment.

Questions on this chapter will be found in Appendix 2.

SIGNAL FLAGS
AND CODES

PENNANTS

PERSONAL FLAGS

ENSIGNS

CORRESPONDING
RANKS

Fig. 13-5

NAVAL AND INTERNATIONAL CODES–ALPHABETICAL FLAGS

The meanings given are those of the International Code only

A	ALFA		K	KILO	
		I HAVE A DIVER DOWN; KEEP WELL CLEAR AT SLOW SPEED			I WISH TO COMMUNICATE WITH YOU
B	BRAVO 	* I AM TAKING IN OR DISCHARGING OR CARRYING EXPLOSIVES	L	LIMA 	YOU SHOULD STOP YOUR VESSEL INSTANTLY
C	CHARLIE 	YES (AFFIRMATIVE)	M	MIKE 	MY VESSEL IS STOPPED AND MAKING NO WAY THROUGH THE WATER
D	DELTA 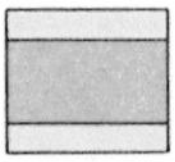	* KEEP CLEAR OF ME —I AM MANOEUVRING WITH DIFFICULTY	N	NOVEMBER 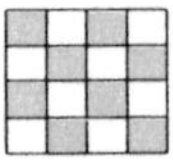	NO (NEGATIVE)
E	ECHO 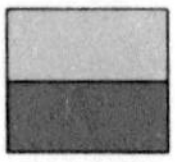	* I AM ALTERING MY COURSE TO STARBOARD	O	OSCAR 	MAN OVERBOARD
F	FOXTROT 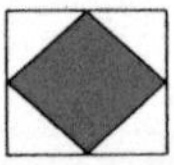	I AM DISABLED— COMMUNICATE WITH ME	P	PAPA 	In harbour : ALL PERSONS SHOULD REPORT ON BOARD AS THE VESSEL IS ABOUT TO PROCEED TO SEA
G	GOLF 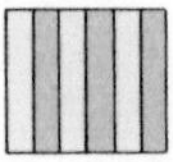	I REQUIRE A PILOT	Q	QUEBEC 	MY VESSEL IS HEALTHY, AND I REQUEST FREE PRATIQUE
H	HOTEL 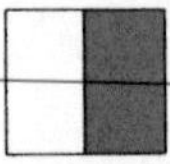	* I HAVE A PILOT ON BOARD	R	ROMEO 	
I	INDIA 	* I AM ALTERING MY COURSE TO PORT	S	SIERRA 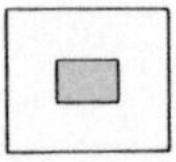	* MY ENGINES ARE GOING ASTERN
J	JULIETT 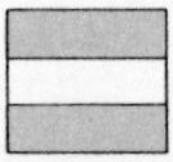	I AM ON FIRE AND HAVE DANGEROUS CARGO ON BOARD KEEP WELL CLEAR OF ME	T	TANGO 	* KEEP CLEAR OF ME, I AM ENGAGED IN PAIR TRAWLING

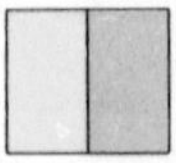

NOTE :- These single-letter signals may be made by any method of signalling : but signals of letters marked ✻ when made by sound may only be made in compliance with the requirements of the International Regulations for Preventing Collisions at Sea, Rules 15 and 28.

Fig. 13-5 (cont.)

NAVAL AND INTERNATIONAL CODES (CONTINUED)

ALPHABETICAL FLAGS AND SUBSTITUTES		NUMERAL PENNANTS	
U UNIFORM	YOU ARE RUNNING INTO DANGER	ONE	
V VICTOR	I REQUIRE ASSISTANCE	TWO	USED ON ALL OCCASIONS WHEN IT IS REQUIRED TO REPRESENT NUMBERS IN FLAG SIGNALLING
W WHISKEY 	I REQUIRE MEDICAL ASSISTANCE	THREE 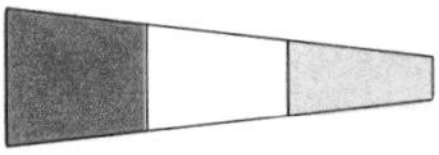	
X XRAY 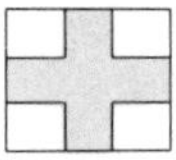	STOP CARRYING OUT YOUR INTENTIONS AND WATCH FOR MY SIGNALS	FOUR 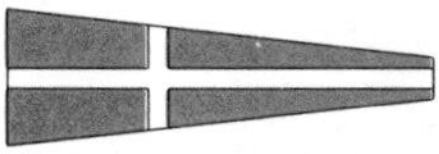	
Y YANKEE 	I AM DRAGGING MY ANCHOR	FIVE 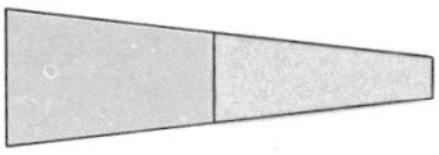	
Z ZULU 	I REQUIRE A TUG	SIX 	
1st SUBSTITUTE 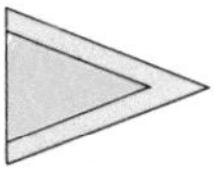	Used to repeat the first flag or pennant in the same hoist	SEVEN 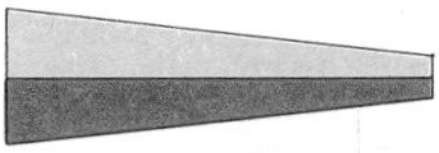	
2nd SUBSTITUTE 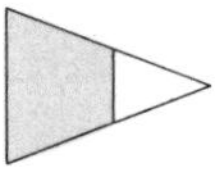	Used to repeat the second flag or pennant in same hoist	EIGHT 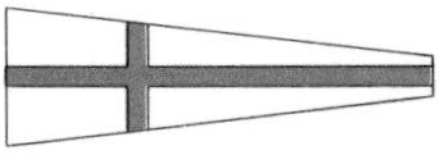	
3rd SUBSTITUTE 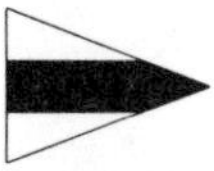	Used to repeat the third flag or pennant in same hoist	NINE 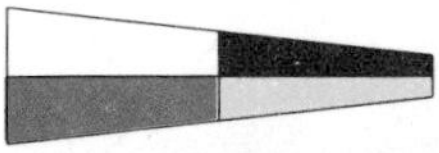	
CODE AND ANSWER 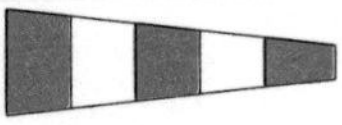	Used to acknowledge a signal. Also flown by a warship when making a flag signal from the International Code to distinguish it from the Naval Code	ZERO 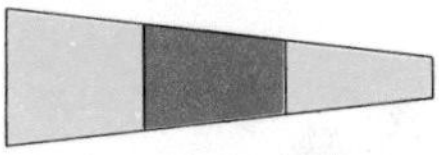	

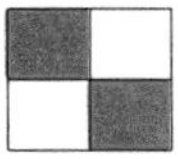

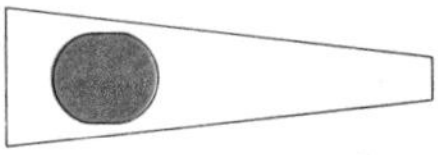

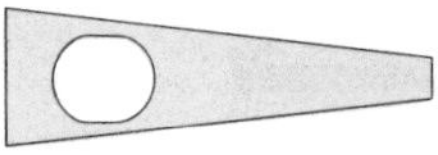

Fig. 13-6

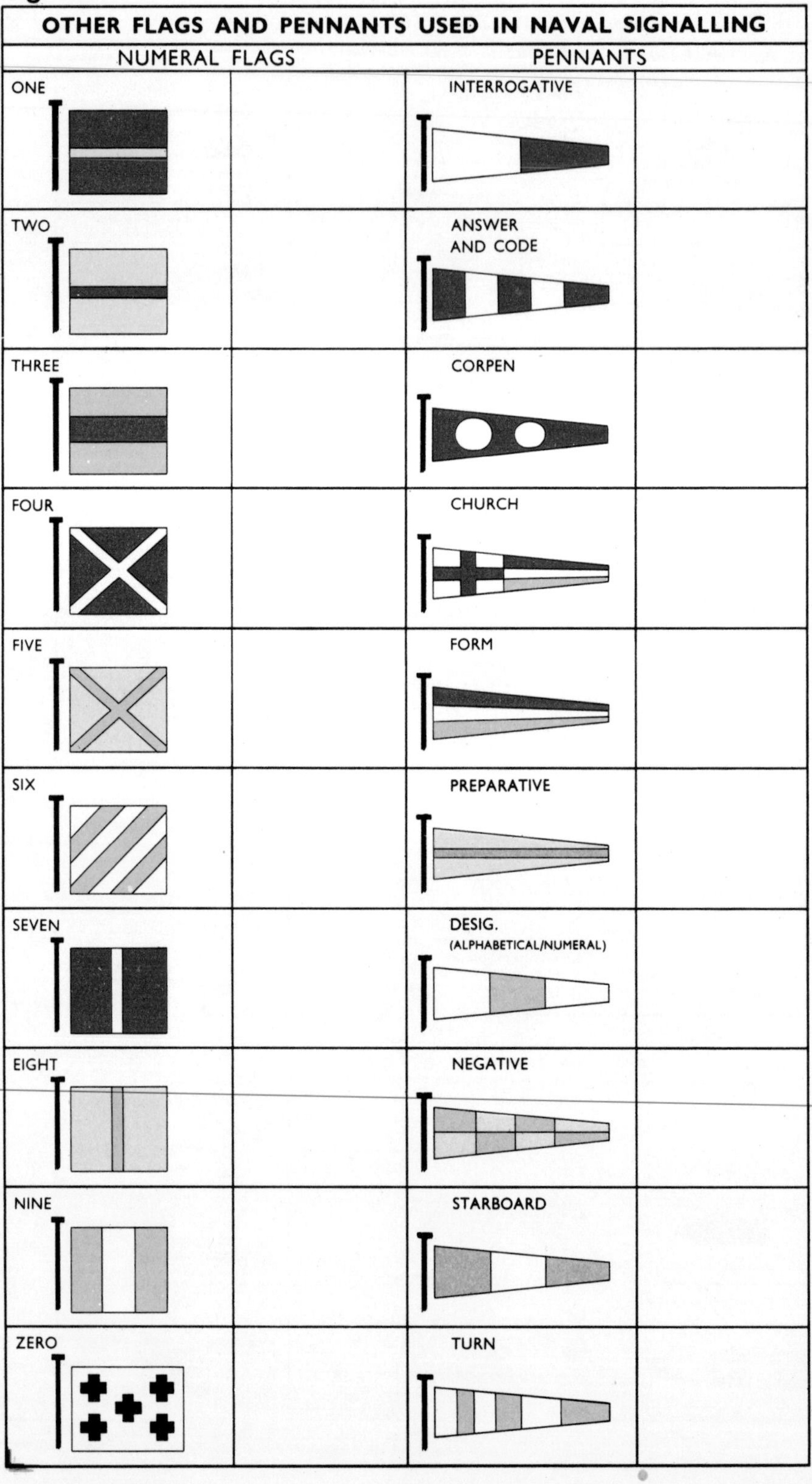

OTHER FLAGS AND PENNANTS USED IN NAVAL SIGNALLING

NUMERAL FLAGS		PENNANTS	
ONE		INTERROGATIVE	
TWO		ANSWER AND CODE	
THREE		CORPEN	
FOUR		CHURCH	
FIVE		FORM	
SIX		PREPARATIVE	
SEVEN		DESIG. (ALPHABETICAL/NUMERAL)	
EIGHT		NEGATIVE	
NINE		STARBOARD	
ZERO		TURN	

Fig. 13-6 (cont.)

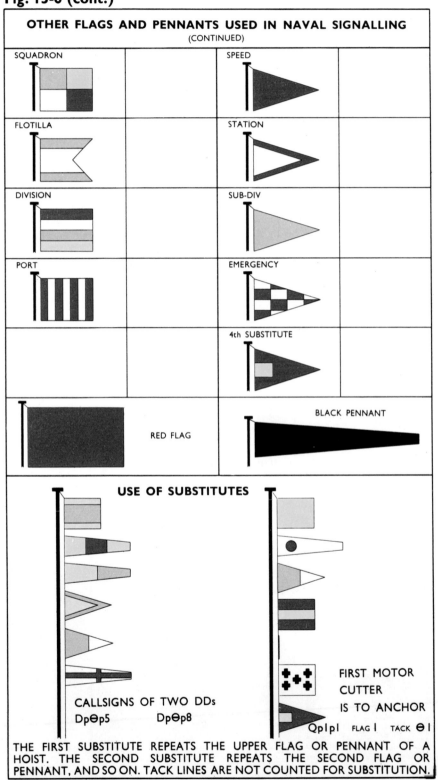

OTHER FLAGS AND PENNANTS USED IN NAVAL SIGNALLING
(CONTINUED)

SQUADRON

SPEED

FLOTILLA

STATION

DIVISION

SUB-DIV

PORT

EMERGENCY

4th SUBSTITUTE

RED FLAG

BLACK PENNANT

USE OF SUBSTITUTES

CALLSIGNS OF TWO DDs

DpΘp5   DpΘp8

FIRST MOTOR CUTTER IS TO ANCHOR

Qplpl   FLAG l   TACK Θl

THE FIRST SUBSTITUTE REPEATS THE UPPER FLAG OR PENNANT OF A HOIST. THE SECOND SUBSTITUTE REPEATS THE SECOND FLAG OR PENNANT, AND SO ON. TACK LINES ARE NOT COUNTED FOR SUBSTITUTION.

Fig. 13-7   SEMAPHORE CODE

A	B	C and Answer sign	D	E
F	G	H	I	J and Direction sign
K	L	M	N	O
P	Q	R	S	T
U and Attention sign*	V	W	X	Y
Z	ERROR SIGN Succession of E's	BREAK SIGN	NUMERAL SIGN	DIRECTION SIGN Back view

*ARMS WAVED UP AND DOWN

Fig. 14-1   ROYAL STANDARD AND DISTINGUISHING FLAGS

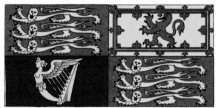

THE ROYAL STANDARD

GOVERNORS-GENERAL
OF COMMONWEALTHS
(NAME OF COMMONWEALTH IS SHOWN ON SCROLL)

GOVERNORS, LIEUTENANT-GOVERNORS,
HIGH COMMISSIONERS AND OTHER OFFICERS
ADMINISTERING A GOVERNMENT
(THE BADGE OF COLONY. PROTECTORATE
OR TERRITORY IS SHOWN WITHIN GARLAND)

DIPLOMATIC OFFICERS ON SHORE
AND AFLOAT
e.g. AMBASSADORS, MINISTERS
PLENIPOTENTIARY, AND CHARGÉS D'AFFAIRES

CONSULAR OFFICERS AFLOAT
e.g. CONSULS GENERAL, CONSULS
AND CONSULAR AGENTS

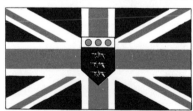

THE ARMY COUNCIL

MEMBERS OF THE AIR COUNCIL
INSPECTOR GENERAL OF
THE ROYAL AIR FORCE

UNIFIED COMMANDERS-IN-CHIEF

Fig. 14-2   ENSIGNS

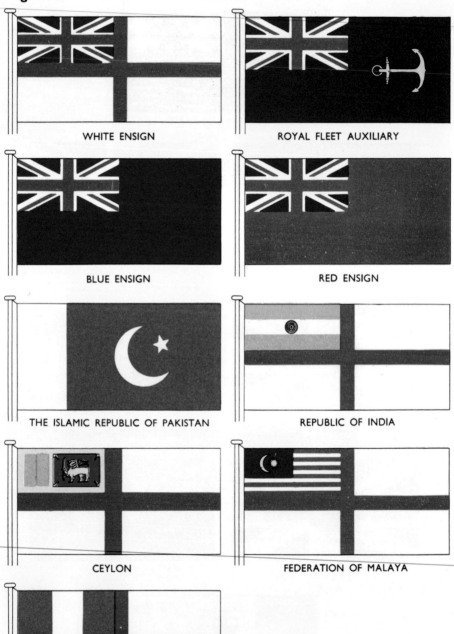

WHITE ENSIGN

ROYAL FLEET AUXILIARY

BLUE ENSIGN

RED ENSIGN

THE ISLAMIC REPUBLIC OF PAKISTAN

REPUBLIC OF INDIA

CEYLON

FEDERATION OF MALAYA

FEDERATION OF NIGERIA

Fig. 14-3 DISTINGUISHING AND SPECIAL FLAGS

QUEEN'S HARBOUR MASTER

FLAGS FOR ROYAL MARINE OFFICERS FOR USE WHEN AFLOAT
IN SMALL BOATS OR FOR USE IN MINIATURE ON MOTOR CARS

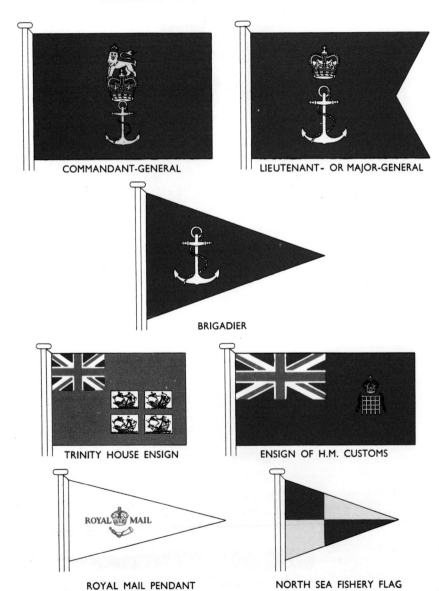

COMMANDANT-GENERAL

LIEUTENANT- OR MAJOR-GENERAL

BRIGADIER

TRINITY HOUSE ENSIGN

ENSIGN OF H.M. CUSTOMS

ROYAL MAIL PENDANT

NORTH SEA FISHERY FLAG

Fig. 14-4   DISTINGUISHING FLAGS OF THE ROYAL NAVY AND
ROYAL FLEET AUXILIARY

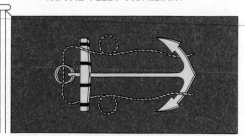

LORD HIGH ADMIRAL'S OR ADMIRALTY FLAG
THE FIRST LORD OF THE ADMIRALTY USES THE ADMIRALTY FLAG AS A CAR FLAG.

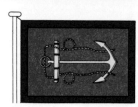

CAR FLAG OF CIVIL MEMBERS OF THE BOARD OF ADMIRALTY

THE FLAG OF AN ADMIRAL OF THE FLEET IS A UNION FLAG FLOWN AT THE MAIN

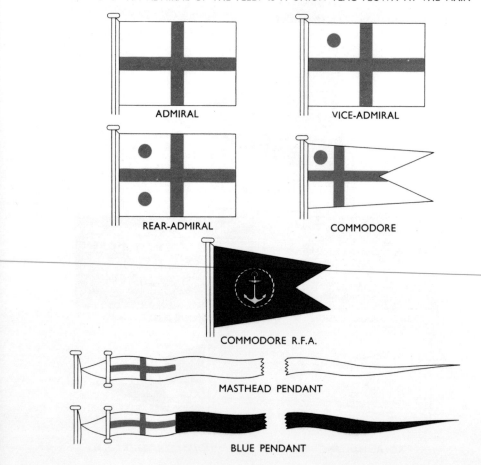

| ADMIRAL | VICE-ADMIRAL |
| REAR-ADMIRAL | COMMODORE |

COMMODORE R.F.A.

MASTHEAD PENDANT

BLUE PENDANT

Fig. 14-5 CORRESPONDING RANKS

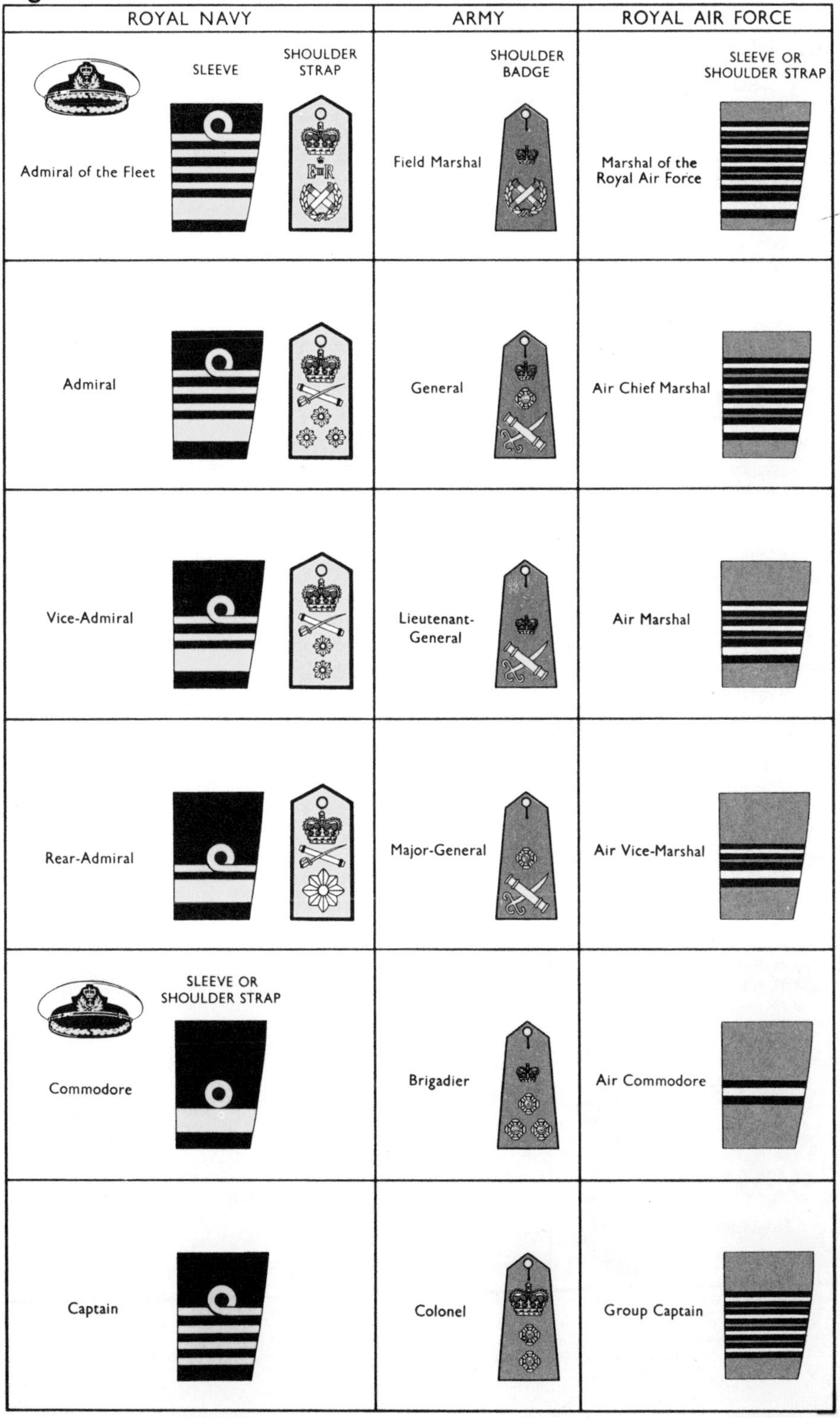

ROYAL NAVY			ARMY	ROYAL AIR FORCE
	SLEEVE	SHOULDER STRAP	SHOULDER BADGE	SLEEVE OR SHOULDER STRAP
Admiral of the Fleet			Field Marshal	Marshal of the Royal Air Force
Admiral			General	Air Chief Marshal
Vice-Admiral			Lieutenant-General	Air Marshal
Rear-Admiral			Major-General	Air Vice-Marshal
Commodore	SLEEVE OR SHOULDER STRAP		Brigadier	Air Commodore
Captain			Colonel	Group Captain

C.B.H

Fig. 14-5 (cont.)

CORRESPONDING RANKS (Cont.)

ROYAL NAVY		ARMY	ROYAL AIR FORCE	
	SLEEVE OR SHOULDER STRAP	SHOULDER BADGE		SLEEVE OR SHOULDER STRAP
 Commander		* Lieutenant-Colonel	 Wing Commander	
 Lieutenant-Commander		* Major	 Squadron Leader	
Lieutenant		* Captain	 Flight Lieutenant	
Sub-Lieutenant Acting Sub-Lieutenant (BUT JUNIOR TO MILITARY AND AIR FORCE RANKS)		* Lieutenant	 Flying Officer	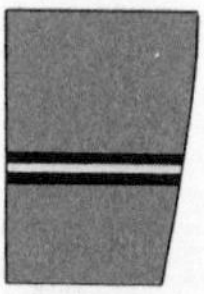
Midshipman (BOTH JUNIOR TO MILITARY AND AIR FORCE RANKS) Naval Cadet	 	* Second Lieutenant	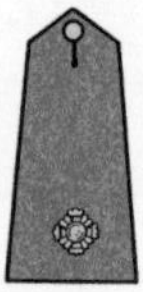 Pilot Officer Acting Pilot Officer (BUT JUNIOR TO SECOND LIEUTENANT)	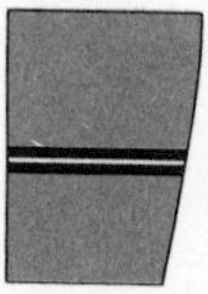

*ROYAL MARINE OFFICERS OF THESE RANKS, WHEN AFLOAT, HAVE A HIGHER EQUIVALENT RANK, E.G. A MAJOR RANKS WITH A COMMANDER

CHAPTER 14

Naval Ceremonial

TYPES OF FLAGS

Standard

This is a flag which depicts the armorial bearings of the person entitled to wear it. The Sovereign and certain members of the Royal Family have personal standards, which are flown to denote their actual presence in any ship or place, whether in residence or on a visit.

Colours

This is a general term describing any flag which is flown to denote the nationality of a ship, of a body of people, or of a place. Examples of colours are the ensigns and jacks worn by ships, the Union Flag of the United Kingdom and the colours of regiments. Except in the normal course of routine, colours are only lowered to denote respect, courtesy, mourning or surrender.

Distinguishing flags

These are flags of special designs which are authorised by the Sovereign to be worn by individuals to denote their rank, command, office or authority, and their display is governed by special rules. They are flown only during the period of office of the individual and denote the presence of the person in a ship or place.

The naval authorities authorised to wear distinguishing flags are the Board of Admiralty, the Naval Boards of the Commonwealth, flag officers and certain commodores.

Other authorities authorised to wear distinguishing flags include Governors-General, Governors, High Commissioners, Lieutenant-Governors and certain other officers who administer a government, H.M. Diplomatic Servants, the Army and Air Councils, General and Air Officers who command stations, Consuls-General, Consuls and Consular Agents.

Signal flags and pennants

These are specially designed in colour and shape to be distinguishable from each other at a distance. They are hoisted, singly or in greater numbers, to indicate orders or messages which are interpreted by means of signal codes.

Special flags or pendants

These may be flown in ships to indicate the duties on which they are engaged, for example, the Royal Mail pendant.

NOTE: Colours, standards and distinguishing flags are said to be *worn* by ships and by individuals, and they may also be said to be *flown* in a ship or at a place. Other types of flag are only described as being *flown*, never as *worn*.

THE UNION FLAG

The original national flag of England and Wales was the banner of St George (which is embodied in the White Ensign). By royal proclamation dated 12th April 1606, when the three countries were united under one Sovereign, the banner of St Andrew, representing Scotland, was united with the banner of St George. By royal proclamation dated 1st January 1801, the St Patrick's Cross, representing Ireland, was incorporated with the Union Flag, which thus represented the union of the four countries; and from this date the Union Flag has been the national emblem of the United Kingdom. It is always flown with the broader diagonal band of white uppermost in the hoist and the narrower diagonal band of white uppermost in the fly.

The Union Flag is generally flown on shore to indicate the British nationality of a subject or place, or to celebrate an event; it is also flown at the headquarters of army units and in certain specific circumstances, e.g. at the House of Commons when Parliament is sitting.

Afloat, the wearing of the Union Flag on the jackstaff denotes a ship of the Royal Navy, and it is not allowed to be worn by any other ships. When the Sovereign is embarked the Union Flag is also worn at the masthead, together with the Royal Standard and Admiralty Flag. The Union Flag is also worn at the main masthead by an Admiral of the Fleet, and is flown at the peak (or at the yard-arm if there is no gaff) to denote that a Court Martial is being held.

ENSIGNS

Ensigns are colours which are worn chiefly by ships. Naval ensigns are only worn on shore by naval establishments, by certain marine establishments belonging to public offices, and by certain recognised marine societies and yacht clubs when expressly authorised to do so under warrant issued by the Admiralty. Such authority is issued in respect of the vessel, society, or club, and not of the owner, representative or member of any such vessel, society or club, and therefore no person has the right to wear a naval ensign ashore or anywhere except in the actual vessel or place authorised by the warrant; nor are naval ensigns allowed to be borne in processions or parades outside naval establishments without the express permission of the Admiralty or, if abroad, of the local naval Commander-in-Chief.

The three ensigns authorised to be worn by British ships are the Red, White and Blue Ensigns, and it is both interesting and instructive to trace the origin of the regulations governing their wearing.

Up to and including the Tudor period the national colour for English ships was the St George's Cross. The Red Ensign as the national colour for British ships other than warships appears to have been introduced about 1700, and thereafter was commonly worn by them.

From early in the 17th century the fleets of the Royal Navy were divided into Red, White and Blue Squadrons, and by the middle of that century the ships of each of these squadrons were distinguished by wearing, respectively, the Red, White and Blue Ensigns. In 1864 this system was discontinued and, by Acts of Parliament of 1864 and 1865, the White Ensign was authorised to be worn by all ships of the Royal Navy, the Red Ensign by merchant ships, and the Blue Ensign by ships belonging to public offices and by ships of the colonial navies. From that time this general allocation of ensigns has remained in force, but has been altered in detail from time to time by subsequent Acts of Parliament. The reasons for the choice of this allocation are obscure. In the Royal Navy the seniority of the commanders of the three squadrons was in the order Red, White and Blue. The senior or Red Ensign was probably allotted to the merchant navy as it had been their colours since 1700.

The White Ensign was probably allotted to the Royal Navy because ships had sailed under these colours in battle since 1800, including the battle of Trafalgar. The reason for wearing the White Ensign in battle in preference to the Red or Blue was to avoid the risk of confusion of the two latter with the French 'tricolour'. A similar confusion, between the White Ensign and the German Ensign, arose in the First World War (1914–1918), and so H.M. ships then sometimes wore as their colours the Union Flag, Blue Ensign or Red Ensign, in addition to the White Ensign.

The White Ensign

All H.M. ships in commission wear the White Ensign. It is worn at the ensign staff when in harbour; it is also worn at the ensign staff at sea whenever possible, but in bad weather, or when cleared for action, or during war, it is worn at the peak of the gaff on the mainmast, or on a suitable staff mounted in the after part of the ship. In action, ships wear at least two ensigns in a conspicuous position. All shore establishments commanded by a commissioned officer wear a White Ensign at the peak of their flagstaff. It is also flown in H.M. ships on the occasion of their launching.

Vessels of the Royal Yacht Squadron are allowed by Admiralty warrant to wear the White Ensign as their colours, and Trinity House vessels may wear the White Ensign at the masthead when H.M. ships are dressed overall.

Ships of the Royal Canadian Navy, Royal Australian Navy and Royal New Zealand Navy wear the White Ensign. Ships of the navies of other Commonwealth countries wear ensigns of special design, some of which are shown in fig. 14–2.

The Blue Ensign

By Admiralty warrant British merchant ships may wear the Blue Ensign, plain and undefaced, if they are commanded by a retired officer of the Royal Navy, or by an officer of any of the Naval Reserves provided that the crew includes a certain number of officers and men of any of the Naval Reserves.

Royal Fleet Auxiliaries, ships under charter to the Admiralty and certain naval yachts wear a Blue Ensign bearing a yellow anchor in the fly, and ships of certain public offices of the United Kingdom—H.M. Customs and H.M. Post Office, for example—wear a Blue Ensign bearing in the fly the badge of their office.

Ships belonging to, or under charter to, the Colonial Governments wear a Blue Ensign bearing in the fly the badge of their colony. The national flags of Australia and New Zealand are Blue Ensigns embodying their emblems.

Vessels of certain approved yacht clubs are allowed by Admiralty warrant to wear a Blue Ensign defaced by the badge of their club. A list of such approved yacht clubs is published in the Navy List.

The Red Ensign

With the exception of H.M. ships and ships allowed by warrant to wear a special ensign, all ships of the United Kingdom wear a Red Ensign plain and undefaced as their colours.

The national flag of Canada is a Red Ensign bearing in the fly the shield of the coat of arms of Canada, and, with the exception of H.M. Canadian ships and ships allowed by warrant to wear a special ensign, all Canadian ships wear the national flag of Canada as their colours.

Australian and New Zealand ships (other than H.M. Australian and New Zealand ships and ships allowed to wear a special ensign) wear as their colours Red Ensigns embodying their emblems.

Vessels of certain yacht clubs of the United Kingdom are authorised by Admiralty warrant to wear a Red Ensign embodying the badge of their club. A list of such yacht clubs appears in the Navy List. Other vessels wear the Red Ensign plain and undefaced.

It is emphasised that when an ensign is authorised to be worn by warrant it may be worn only by the vessel named in the warrant, and if the officer holding the warrant is in command at the time.

JACKS

'Jack' is the name given to the colours worn on a staff at the stem or on the bowsprit by ships or vessels at anchor or alongside. It is a smaller flag than the corresponding ensign and can be square or rectangular in shape.

Ships of the Royal Navy wear the Union Flag. Ships of the navies of Commonwealth countries wear either their national colours or, in some cases, a specially-designed naval jack. Merchant ships usually fly their house flag as their jack.

There is a historical reason for allocating the Union Flag as a jack to ships of the Royal Navy. In the days when a man-of-war and a merchant vessel looked very alike and both wore the same ensign, it was essential that one should be distinguished from the other in order to prevent masquerading under false colours for purpose of piracy, unlawful aggression or improper aggrandizement; and so the Union Flag was ordered to be worn only by H.M. ships of war.

In later days, though the differences in appearance between men-of-war and merchant ships became more obvious, the need in the interests of both the Royal and Merchant Navies to prevent attempts at masquerading was as great as ever, particularly in the less-frequented seas and ports of the world. The wearing of the Union Flag is therefore still reserved exclusively for H.M. ships, although its use is confined to wearing it as a jack in harbour, and at sea only when ships are dressed.

COMMISSIONING OR MASTHEAD PENDANT

This pendant, which is flown at the main masthead, is hoisted on the day when a warship commissions, and, except when the ship is wearing a Royal Standard or a naval distinguishing flag, it is never struck until the day on which the ship pays off. H.M. ships not in commission do not wear any colours, except that when undergoing trials before acceptance into H.M. Service they fly the Red Ensign.

Certain ships which are authorised by warrant to wear a Blue Ensign may be specially authorised to wear a blue masthead pendant. Such ships are usually those which are commanded by an officer of one of the Royal Naval Reserves of the United Kingdom or of one of its Commonwealths. Otherwise no British ships other than H.M. ships are allowed to wear masthead pendants.

THE QUEEN'S COLOUR

The Queen's Colour is a special White Ensign embodying the royal cypher, presented by the Sovereign to the principal Home Commands and Commands abroad and to the Britannia Royal Naval College, Dartmouth. The Royal Canadian Navy, Royal Australian Navy and Royal New Zealand Navy also hold Queen's Colours. It is never paraded on board ship or on foreign territory, and is paraded on shore only on the following ceremonial occasions:

1. By a guard of honour mounted for the Sovereign or a member of the Royal Family, or for the head of a foreign state.
2. At parades held to celebrate the birthday of the Sovereign.
3. On important ceremonial occasions abroad as ordered by the Admiralty or by Commanders-in-Chief.

The Queen's Colour is lowered only to royalty or heads of foreign states, or to their representatives.

When the Queen's Colour is carried uncased it is received with the highest marks of respect, i.e. with arms presented, officers saluting and bands playing the National Anthem.

At the discretion of the Commander-in-Chief or the Senior Naval Officer present, the White Ensign may be paraded abroad on important ceremonial occasions at which the parading of the Queen's Colour is not authorised.

DISTINGUISHING FLAGS

A distinguishing flag may be worn by a person so entitled, to denote his presence in a ship, boat, vehicle, place or establishment.

The Admiralty flag

This used to be the flag of the officer formerly known as the Lord High Admiral, and is now the flag of the 'Commissioners for executing the Office of the Lord High Admiral,' known generally as the *Board of Admiralty*. It is flown day and night over the Admiralty in London, and at the main masthead afloat when the Board is embarked in an official capacity (at least two Lords Commissioners, and in addition a secretary, constitute a *Board* for this purpose). It is also flown in H.M. ships on the occasion of their launching.

When the Sovereign is embarked, the Admiralty Flag (in addition to the jack and ensign) is worn at the fore masthead, or in some other suitable position, to denote that the Sovereign is the source from which are derived the powers of the Board of Admiralty. The Royal Standard is worn at the main masthead and the Union Flag at the mizzen masthead or other suitable position.

Flag Officer's flag

A Flag Officer is an admiral who is entitled to wear a flag of rank and command by virtue of the nature of his appointment, and his appropriate flag is worn by a ship or shore establishment by day and night throughout the period of his command. When his flag is shifted from one ship to another, or to a shore establishment, it is hoisted to its new position simultaneously with being hauled down from its former position.

Commodore's broad pendant

When a Commodore is entitled by virtue of his appointment to wear a broad pendant it is worn in the same way as is the flag of a Flag Officer.

OTHER SPECIAL FLAGS AND PENDANTS

Paying-off pendant

Since before the Napoleonic wars it has been the custom for H.M. ships to fly a paying-off pendant at the main truck when they leave their fleet to return to their home port to pay off. Custom ordains that the length of the pendant should equal the length of the ship if she leaves her station at the end of a normal period of foreign service. If, however, a commission has been extended, the length of the pendant is increased in proportion to the extra length of service (e.g. for a commission of 2 years extended to 2 years and 2 months the length of the pendant would be the length of the ship plus $\frac{1}{12}$th). It is similar to, and flown in place of, the masthead pendant, and is displayed by a ship from a foreign station when entering or leaving harbours during her passage home, and by a ship of the Home Fleet on leaving for and arriving at her home port. It is also the custom on all stations for a ship to fly this pendant on the Sunday preceding her departure, or, if already in her paying-off port, on the Sunday preceding the day on which she pays off.

Blue Peter

This flag is commonly flown by merchant ships to denote that they are about to sail, and it is the general recall for any passengers or crew who may be out of the ship. If used as the recall by H.M. ships it is sometimes accompanied by the Morse sound signal.

House flags

These flags are flown by merchant ships, usually at the main masthead, to denote the ownership of the vessel. Their general use dates from about 1840. They bear the device of the individual or company owning the ship, or to whom the ship is chartered, and they are flown when entering or leaving harbour or on meeting other ships, or as a jack when at anchor or alongside.

Royal Mail pendant

This is displayed by merchant ships which are under contract to H.M. Post Office and are actually carrying the Royal Mails. It is usually flown at the fore masthead or fore yard-arm when entering or leaving harbour.

Courtesy flags

It is the custom among merchant ships when entering a foreign port and during their stay in that port to fly the colours of that country at the fore masthead, and, when leaving, similarly to fly the colours of the country to which they are immediately bound. Care is taken not to give offence by flying colours which may be exclusively reserved for warships or for special purposes, or by displaying the colours of a country which may be at enmity with the country which the ship is leaving; for instance, the correct flag for a foreign merchant ship to fly when leaving for, or entering, a British port is the Red Ensign.

It is the custom of yachts to fly in the starboard rigging the flag of the country visited when entering harbour, during the stay and when leaving.

Fishery flag

This flag is worn by H.M. ships engaged in fishery protection duties in the North Sea.

WEARING OF COLOURS

At anchor or alongside

H.M. ships in commission, when at anchor or alongside in ports of the United Kingdom, hoist their colours (i.e. the ensign and jack) at 0800 from 25th March to 20th September inclusive, and at 0900 from 21st September to 24th March inclusive. Abroad colours are hoisted at 0800 or 0900 in accordance with the orders of the Commander-in-Chief of the station. Colours are always lowered at sunset, unless the Senior Officer present directs otherwise.

At sea

Except when dressed, H.M. ships at sea or under way in harbour wear only an ensign. In war it is worn day and night, but in peace it is worn only when there is sufficient light for it to be seen and may be hauled down when out of sight of land and of other ships. No ceremonial is carried out at the hoisting or lowering of the ensign at sea.

Naval shore establishments

Naval shore establishments wear the ensign only from 0800 or 0900 to sunset.

Boats

Boats belonging to H.M. ships or establishments wear ensigns only on certain occasions, which are described in Volume II.

Half-mast

Ensigns are worn at half-mast to indicate a death, usually on the day of the funeral only and from the time the body leaves the ship or place where it has been lying until the time when it is buried.

Ceremony of hoisting

When colours are hoisted in harbour, at either 0800 or 0900, a guard and band are paraded 15 minutes before the time of hoisting whenever weather or other circumstances permit. During this period the band plays martial music (a 'troop' or a 'march') and the guard is drawn up athwartships, facing the ensign staff. If the ship is in company she takes her time from the Senior Officer's ship, which hoists the *Preparative* five minutes before, and hauls it down at, the appointed time. A signalman, specially detailed for this purpose, then calls out the hour, which is then struck on the ship's bell and immediately followed by the bugler sounding the *Alert*, the guard presenting arms, and the band playing the National Anthem. All hands on deck or within sight or sound (except men fallen in, who are called to attention instead) face the ensign and come to the salute on the sounding of the Alert, and the ensign is then hoisted slowly up the ensign staff so that it is close up as the last note of the National Anthem is played. At the same time in ships the jack is hoisted close up on the jackstaff. After a suitable pause the bugler sounds the *Carry On* and everybody returns from the salute. The guard and band then march off.

During the ceremony, whenever circumstances permit, all work and noise cease. Power boats stop engines, pulling boats toss or lay on their oars, sailing boats let fly sheets, crews come to attention and coxswains salute. The Carry On is not sounded until the full ceremony is over, and all hands on deck remain at the salute until it is sounded.

A similar ceremony for hoisting the ensign is carried out in shore establishments.

Ceremony of lowering

The full ceremony of lowering the ensign and jack at sunset includes the parading of guards and bands and the beating of the *Tattoo* for 15 minutes before the appointed time, but this is only carried out on special occasions. The normal ceremony is similar to that for hoisting the colours, and the same marks of respect are paid, except that guards and bands are not paraded; the signalman calls out 'Sunset, Sir' at the correct time, and *Sunset* is sounded on the bugle instead of the *General Salute*. The Commander-in-Chief may order the sentries of each ship to fire a volley of musketry at the hour of sunset. (The origin of this was to ensure that the muskets were in working order.)

DRESSING AND ILLUMINATING SHIP

Dressing ship

The flying of flags to celebrate an occasion or an event is one of the oldest customs. At one period our ships on occasions of celebration used to display flags and trophies captured from the enemy. Until 1889 it was left to the junior captain of a fleet or squadron to draw up the order of flags to be worn when ships dressed with flags overall, but now full instructions in regard to dressing ship are laid down in the *V.S. Equipment Handbook*. Flags and pennants of the signal codes, disposed in as variegated and symmetrical a manner as possible, are used. Except for the masthead ensigns, national flags and ensigns are not included, because the order in which they were flown might possibly give offence.

Illuminating ship

Ships are illuminated by floodlighting or outline circuits on special occasions of ceremony or festivity.

Floodlighting. Most ships of the Royal Navy have floodlighting equipment. The ship's sides are floodlit by screened lamps fixed to booms projecting over the sides. The superstructures, funnels and masts are floodlit from the decks.

Outline circuits. Some ships have special lighting circuits with lamps at intervals of a few feet, rigged round the ship at upper and forecastle deck levels, along the waterline, up the masts and funnels and in the positions of the dressing lines, so that the outline of the ship is picked out by the lamps.

SALUTES AND MARKS OF RESPECT

Salutes and marks of respect are accorded in different ways, examples being: the hand salute, blowing of bugles, piping the side, parading of guards and bands, playing of national anthems and other musical salutes, lowering or dipping of colours, and the firing of guns.

The hand salute

The hand salute is the personal salute of officers and men.

SALUTES BY THE BUGLE

The General salute

This is a personal salute paid to rank. It is only sounded when no band is available to play the appropriate anthems or musical salutes.

The Alert

Sounded on the bugle, this is a mark of respect paid to the occasion or to rank, and, with certain exceptions, it is accorded only to persons who are specifically entitled to it. When a bugle is not available the *Still* is piped on the boatswain's call, or blown on a whistle, instead of sounding the *Alert*. The Alert is sounded on the following occasions:

1. At the hoisting and hauling down of colours.
2. Between the times of hoisting the colours and sunset, on the arrival or departure of royalty or of certain other persons specifically entitled to it.
3. Between the times of sunrise and sunset, in a man-of-war not under way, when a boat or tender passes which is wearing a standard of royalty or the flags or emblems of other persons entitled to it.
4. Between the times of sunrise and sunset, when a man-of-war in harbour or in an anchorage is passing or being passed by a flagship or a foreign man-of-war, provided that one of the ships is at anchor.

NOTE: Whenever the Alert is sounded all hands on deck stand to attention and face outboard until the Carry On is sounded (except at the hoisting and lowering of colours, when all hands on deck or nearby stand to attention, face the colours and salute—except men fallen in, who are called to attention instead—remaining at the salute until the Carry On is sounded).

Sunset

This is the salute sounded when the colours are hauled down at the end of the day.

First Post and Last Post

These originate from the days when the Tattoo was beaten ashore and afloat at the time of curfew, and sentries were posted for the night. On board H.M. ships nowadays the First Post is sounded at 2040 and the Last Post at 2100, but if sunset occurs after 2040 neither is usually sounded. The Last Post (followed by the Reveille) is also sounded at military funerals over the body in its last resting-place, as a farewell salute to the deceased.

GUN SALUTES

The firing of salutes in honour of a royal or other personage, or of a country, is a very old custom. In gun salutes in the Royal Navy an odd number of rounds is always fired, the firing of even numbers of rounds in former days being reserved for occasions of mourning. A salute is referred to as, for example, 'a salute of 21 guns', or a '21-gun salute', though nowadays only 3 or 4 guns may actually fire the 21 rounds.

It used to be the custom when at sea for the saluting ship to turn and head towards the ship being saluted. This originated in the days when ships were armed with broadside guns only and the salutes were fired with shotted rounds; by heading towards the other ship the salute could not be mistaken for an act of aggression. This custom, however, is not observed nowadays.

The Admiralty prohibition against firing salutes above Gravesend is said to date from an occasion when a shot fired during a salute by a man-of-war lying off Greenwich went unpleasantly close to Greenwich Palace, where Queen Elizabeth I was then residing.

The interval between the successive rounds in a salute is 5 seconds. Before stop-watches were invented the interval was timed by the repetition, by the Gunner, of the couplet 'If I wasn't a Gunner I wouldn't be here, number (two, three, etc.) gun, fire!', spoken deliberately.

SALUTES BETWEEN SHIPS

When one man-of-war passes another in harbour they exchange salutes. The nature of the salute depends upon the nationality of the ships, and upon the relative ranks or seniorities of their respective Flag Officers or Captains or any important personages in them; it may be made by parading guards and bands, by sounding the Alert on the bugle, or piping the Still. At sea the salutes are made and returned by pipe only.

When a merchant ship passes close to a man-of-war, either at sea or in harbour, she dips her ensign as an act of courtesy and recognition, and the man-of-war acknowledges it also by dipping her ensign. On no other occasion (except when they are half-masted) are the colours of H.M. ships lowered out of routine times. H.M. ships do not dip their ensigns to each other or to foreign men-of-war.

RECEPTION OF OFFICERS

When, in H.M. ships, accommodation ladders are rigged on both sides, officers of lieutenant's rank and above enter and leave the ship by the starboard gangway, and all other officers use the port gangway. In flagships three accommodation ladders may be rigged, one on each side aft and one amidships; the starboard after gangway is then reserved for Flag Officers, officers of Captain's rank, and Commanding Officers when flying their pendants.

All officers are saluted by the gangway staff, both on arrival and departure, and the Officer of the Watch salutes all officers of, and above, his own rank and acknowledges the salutes of his juniors. The rank or status of an officer arriving by boat in daylight hours may be indicated by a flag, pendant or plate flown or displayed prominently in the boat; these should be identified in sufficient time for the proper marks of respect to be paid to the officer on his arrival.

PIPING THE SIDE

Piping the side is a mark of respect which, in the Royal Navy, is reserved for the Sovereign, a member of the Royal Family of the rank of Captain and above when in naval uniform, the Board of Admiralty and Commonwealth Naval Boards, officers of Flag Rank and Commodores, Commanding Officers of H.M. seagoing ships and tenders in commission, other naval officers while carrying out certain specified duties, and for all foreign naval officers in uniform. A corpse when being brought on board or sent out of a ship is also piped. The side is piped between Colours and sunset, although foreign naval officers are piped at all hours. The side is not piped for Commanding Officers of naval shore establishments, nor is the side piped at any shore establishment.

This mark of respect owes its origin to the days when captains used to visit other ships when at sea. On such occasions the visiting captain was hoisted aboard from his boat in a chair slung on a whip rove from the lower yard-arm, to the accompaniment of the pipe of the boatswain giving orders to the men manning the whip.

SOME NAVAL CUSTOMS AND CEREMONIES

Official visits

On the arrival of one of H.M. ships in a British or foreign port a series of official visits is exchanged between the Flag or Commanding Officer of the ship and the various governmental, naval, military or civil authorities in the port. The extent of, and rules for, such visits are laid down in *Queen's Regulations and Admiralty Instructions*. Sometimes the visits may occupy several days.

Entering harbour

When one of H.M. ships enters harbour all harbour gear is provided and prepared beforehand; lower booms are rigged and stowed ready for getting out, accommodation ladders are shipped and prepared for lowering, awnings are provided and prepared for spreading, and boats are prepared for hoisting out; but such preparations should not mar the shipshape appearance of the ship. All hands remain fallen in at their stations for entering harbour until the last practicable moment, when the 'Extend' is sounded on the bugle, or piped. At this order only those hands required for the various evolutions fall out and run to their appropriate stations, to the lower booms, ladders, boats, awnings, etc. The 'G' blown on the bugle, or the 'Hoist Away' piped on the boatswain's call, is the executive order for getting out lower booms, lowering accommodation ladders, hoisting out the boats, spreading awnings, etc. The speed and efficiency with which these operations are carried out are an indication of the smartness of the ship. The 'G' is sounded as the anchor is let go when coming to single anchor, as the second anchor is let go when mooring, and as the bridle is shackled on when coming to a buoy.

Officer of the Guard

On the arrival in a British port of a foreign man-of-war, a merchantman or a yacht, it is customary for the Senior Officer to send the Officer of the Guard (as nominated by the Guard Ship) to visit her and offer her the usual courtesies and facilities of the port. On his return the Officer of the Guard writes out a report of the details of his visit.

Man and cheer ship

Manning and cheering ship as a collective mark of respect in honour of a person or of another ship is a very old custom. In the days of sail the yards and shrouds were manned as well as the decks, but nowadays only the decks are manned. Some examples of occasions on which this mark of honour is paid are: visits of the Sovereign to the Fleet; the entry into port of ships which have shared in a victory; the final departure of a ship from a foreign station on her way home to pay off.

Parades ashore

On all ceremonial occasions the Royal Navy, as the senior Service of the armed forces of the Crown, is accorded the position of honour, i.e. on the right of the line in review order and in the van in marching order. The naval marches are 'Heart of Oak' for the march past, and 'Nancy Lee' for the advance in review order.

Badges

The badge of the Royal Navy is the naval crown, which consists of a circlet surmounted by the sterns of four men-of-war, each with three poop lanterns, and four square sails each spread on a mast and yard and fully filled and sheeted home; the ships and sails being positioned alternately. This badge or the Royal Crown is often displayed on the trucks of the ensign and jack staffs.

Each ship has her own badge or crest, with a motto, which is allotted to her on commissioning, by permission of the Board of Admiralty, from the College of Heralds. This badge is displayed prominently on board and also on the bows of her boats.

Ships display their *battle honours*, and those of their predecessors of the same name, in some prominent position on board.

Trophies

Any trophies of war, presentation cups or plate, etc. belonging to the ship and her predecessors are displayed between decks. All such trophies or presentation plate are the property of the ship and are recorded in the Ship's Book. Whenever a ship is paid off or broken up the trophies are returned to the manning port of the ship, where they are kept until the ship re-commissions or a new ship of the same name is commissioned. In war the trophies may be landed for safe custody.

Ship's bell

The ship's bell always bears the name of the ship and the date of her launching. Unless it is damaged, the bell remains with the ship until she is sold or broken up, when it is either presented to some public body or offered for sale, preference being given to anyone who served in her.

Launching ceremony

The custom of breaking a bottle of wine over the stem of a ship when being launched originates from the old practice of toasting prosperity to the ship in a silver goblet of wine, which was then cast into the sea in order to prevent a toast of ill intent being drunk from the same cup. This practice proved too expensive and so was replaced in 1690 by the breaking of a bottle of wine over the stem. Another old custom which is still observed is to pray for Divine blessing on the ship and her company throughout her life.

Until 1811 the ceremony for H.M. ships was always performed by a royal personage or a Royal Dockyard Commissioner, but in that year the Prince Regent introduced the custom of allowing ladies to perform it. It is interesting to note that on one subsequent occasion a certain lady missed her aim with the bottle, which struck and injured a spectator who sued the Admiralty for damages, and this resulted in the Admiralty directing that in future the bottle should be secured to the ship by a lanyard.

Traditional customs

New Year's Day. It is the custom for the youngest member of the ship's company (officer or man) to 'ring out the Old Year and ring in the New' by striking 16 bells at midnight on New Year's Eve.

Splicing the main brace. The order 'splice the main brace' may be given by the Sovereign, or by members of the Royal Family, on occasions of inspections of, or visits to, H.M. ships or establishments; or it may be ordered by the Admiralty on special occasions of celebration or national rejoicing. This order authorises the issue of a tot of rum to all officers over the age of 20, and an extra tot to all men over the age of 20, with which to toast the Sovereign and the occasion. Those who prefer it, and all who are under 20 years of age, may be issued instead with a ration of lemonade. The term 'splicing the main brace,' which was well known in 1756, appears to owe its origin to the custom of issuing an extra ration of spirit on occasions of particularly arduous service or exposure, such as might be experienced in the days of sail when repairing or replacing the main brace, which was a very important and heavy part of the running rigging.

Crossing the Line. The unofficial ceremonies of 'initiating novices into the brotherhood of the seas and as subjects of His Oceanic Majesty King Neptune' are held in many ships when circumstances allow as they cross the equator. The ship is usually placed out of routine for the day and officers and men share impartially in the proceedings, which are made the occasion for much good-natured skylarking.

Garlands. When a member of the crew of a ship is married in the port in which the ship is lying it is the custom to hoist a garland of evergreens between the masts on the day of the ceremony.

It is also the custom to decorate the trucks and yard-arms with sprigs of holly on Christmas Day.

Whistling. Whistling is prohibited in H.M. ships, because the noise is apt to be confused with the piping of orders.

Acknowledgment of orders. The seaman acknowledges an order with the words 'Ay, Ay, Sir!', and should then immediately carry it out.

Questions on this chapter will be found in Appendix 2.

PART IV

SHIPHANDLING AND NAVIGATION

CHAPTER 15

Ships' Compasses

A compass is an instrument which points in a fixed horizontal direction. This direction is *true* north in the case of a gyro-compass and *magnetic* north for a magnetic compass. Before describing these two compasses it is necessary to establish a measure of direction on the Earth's surface.

Direction on the Earth's surface (fig. 15–1)

The ends of the axis about which the Earth rotates are known as the *geographical* or *true* North and South Poles. Any imaginary line which joins the

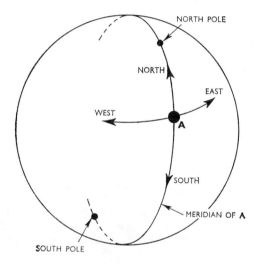

FIG. 15–1. Direction on the Earth's surface

geographical poles by the shortest route over the Earth's surface is called a *meridian*, and will run due north and south. Any such line passing through a place is known as the meridian of that place.

The Earth rotates counter-clockwise when viewed from above the North Pole. The direction of rotation is known as *eastward* and the opposite direction is known as *westward*. A line drawn due east or due west from any place is at right-angles to the meridian of that place.

If the direction of north from any place is known, then any other direction can be described by angular measurement relative to the direction of north. A man looking towards the North Pole is said to be facing due north; if he turns to his right through an angle of ninety degrees he will face due east; if he turns a further ninety degrees (180° in all), he will face due south; if he turns another ninety degrees to his right (270° in all) he will face due west; and by turning

375

yet another ninety degrees he will once more face due north. He will thus have
turned through 360° in a clockwise direction and will have faced in turn the
cardinal points of the compass, namely north (000°), east (090°), south (180°)
and west (270°).

Compass cards and their graduation

These cardinal points, and any intermediate directions, can be marked round
the edge of a circular card which, when mounted on a compass, is known as the
compass card. There are three methods by which a compass card is graduated
to indicate direction and these are described below.

Three-figure method. By this method the compass card is graduated in
degrees, clockwise from 000 (north) to 359, as illustrated in fig. 1–14. With this
method a direction is always described in terms of three figures; the direction
of north, for example, is described as *zero-zero-zero* and written 000°, and
the direction of east is called *zero-nine-zero* and written 090°. With this method
of graduation a direction can be described simply and accurately, and it is the
usual method used at sea.

Point method. This method is still used with some commercial magnetic
compasses. The compass card is graduated in 32 named *points*, as illustrated in
fig. 15–2. Of these, north, east, south and west form what are known as the

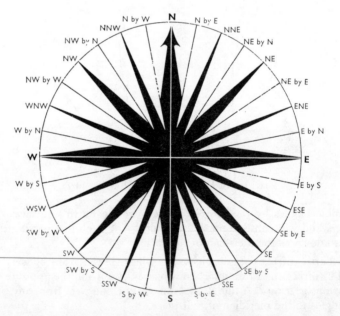

FIG. 15–2. A 'point' compass card

four *cardinal* points. By halving the right-angles between these cardinal points,
four other points are obtained, which are known as *intercardinal* points. These
are: north-east (N.E.), south-east (S.E.), south-west (S.W.) and north-west
(N.W.).

By halving the angles between the cardinal and intercardinal points a further series of points are obtained which are known as *intermediate* points. There are eight of these, and they are named from their nearest cardinal point thus: north-north-east (N.N.E.), east-north-east (E.N.E.), east-south-east (E.S.E.), south-south-east (S.S.E.), south-south-west (S.S.W.), west-south-west (W.S.W.), west-north-west (W.N.W.) and north-north-west (N.N.W.).

These cardinal, intercardinal and intermediate points together form the 16 points of the compass by which the seaman may describe direction in a general sense; a wind, for example, may be described as blowing from south-south-east.

The remaining sixteen points, obtained by halving the angles once more, are termed *by-points*, because they are named *by* their nearest cardinal or intercardinal points, thus: north-by-east (N. by E.), north-east-by-north (N.E. by N.), north-east-by-east (N.E. by E.), east-by-north (E. by N.) and so on through the second, third and fourth quarters of the compass.

The term *point* is also used to describe the angle between any two successive points of the compass, which is $11\frac{1}{4}$ degrees; 2 points thus equal an angle of $22\frac{1}{2}°$, 4 points an angle of 45°, 8 points an angle of 90° and 16 points an angle of 180°. This method of describing an angle or direction is usually used in a relative sense; the direction of an object may, for example, be described as *two points abaft the beam.*

Boxing the compass means naming the points of the compass in succession, clockwise, through the four quarters of the compass. The seaman, when boxing the compass, is required to name only the cardinal, intercardinal and intermediate points.

Quadrantal method. Another method by which the compass card is graduated is a combination of the three-figure and the point methods, and is known as the quadrantal method. This method is obsolete in the Royal Navy, but is still found on old magnetic compass cards. Here the four quarters or *quadrants* of the compass card are each graduated into ninety degrees, with zero at north and south and 90 at east and west. By this method the directions of the cardinal points are named simply north, east, south and west, while intermediate directions are named in degrees *from* north or south *towards* east or west. The direction of south-west, for example, would be described as *south forty-five west*, and written S.45°W.

Types of ship's compasses

Three types of compass are used at sea, namely the *gyro-compass*, the *magnetic compass* and the *gyro-magnetic compass*. All these compasses are capable of giving an accurate indication of direction provided they are properly installed and maintained.

The gyro-compass obtains its directive force from the rotation of the Earth and seeks true north. However, it is mechanically and electrically dependent upon the ship's power supplies and proper maintenance.

The magnetic compass obtains its directive force from the magnetic field of the Earth and therefore seeks magnetic north. It is independent of the ship's power supplies. However, its accuracy may be impaired by incorrect installation owing to magnetic effects introduced by the ship's structure and fittings, and it is for this reason that it has become increasingly difficult to instal a simple magnetic compass as the standard compass of a modern warship.

The gyro-magnetic compass combines the magnetic-north-seeking property of the magnetic compass with the stabilising property of a gyroscope and enables many desirable features of a magnetic compass to be utilised in modern ships. It is described in B.R.45(1), *Admiralty Manual of Navigation*, Vol. I.

THE GYRO-COMPASS

The gyro-compass functions on the principle that the axis of a perfectly balanced wheel which is spinning at high speed and suspended in gimbals so that it is free to turn or tilt will remain pointing in a fixed direction in space. By mechanical means such a wheel can be made to seek the direction of true north and remain pointing in that direction. If a compass card is mounted on the gimbals of the wheel so that its north-and-south line is in line with the axis of the wheel, the result will be a gyro-compass from which any direction can be ascertained.

A ship's gyro-compass is sited as near as possible to the roll and pitch centres of the ship to obtain the best performance. In order to allow it to settle, a ship's gyro-compass should be started about five hours before it is required. Modern warships of cruiser size and above are equipped with three gyro-compasses; smaller ships may be equipped with one or two.

By means of a system of electrical transmissions, a gyro-compass can operate *repeaters*, which are situated in various parts of the ship as required for navigational or other purposes. These repeaters consist of a compass card mounted in a bowl containing their operative mechanisms, and, with certain limitations, they will indicate the same direction as the gyro-compass by which they are operated. Each repeater is fitted with a switch by which it can be electrically connected to one or other of the gyro-compasses, and each is fitted with a mechanical device by which the compass card can be lined up with its gyro-compass.

It is important to ensure that the gyro-compasses and their repeaters are functioning correctly by frequently checking the readings of repeaters and gyro-compasses with each other or with some other indication of direction, such as a magnetic compass, an astronomical observation or known landmarks.

Failure of a gyro-compass or interruption of its power supply will be indicated by the *gyro alarm system*, in which electric bells are sounded and red lamps switched on in various positions such as the bridge, gyro room and the steering position.

Gyro error

A gyro-compass may function correctly, but at the same time register a small but constant error known as *gyro error*. All directions indicated by gyro-compass must be corrected for any gyro error before they can be recorded as true directions; conversely, all true directions must be corrected for gyro error to obtain gyro readings.

If the gyro-compass indicates a direction which is numerically larger than the true direction the error is described as *high*, and conversely a numerically smaller reading than the true direction is described as *low*. Simple rules for applying the gyro error are as follows:

When converting direction by compass to true direction: *subtract* the gyro error if *high*, and *add* the gyro error if *low*.

When converting true direction to direction by compass: *add* the gyro error if *high*, and *subtract* the gyro error if *low*.

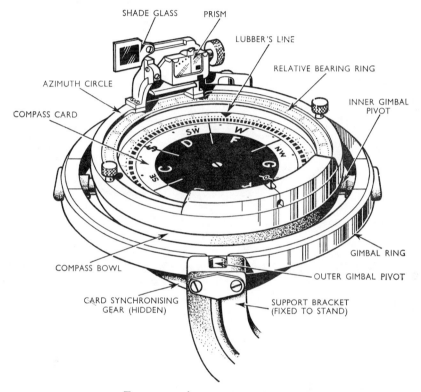

Fig. 15–3. A gyro-compass repeater

EXAMPLES

1. Ship's head by compass   218°
    gyro error   1°   high (subtract)
    true ship's head   217°

2. True course   057°
    gyro error   1°   high (add)
    compass course to steer   058°

3. Bearing by compass of an object 176°
    gyro error   1°   high (subtract)
    true bearing   175°

Types of gyro repeater

There are two main types of gyro repeater fitted in ships, namely 'bearing' repeaters and 'steering' repeaters.

Bearing repeaters. These are always mounted in gimbals and gimbal rings in order to maintain the repeater bowl and its compass card in a horizontal position when the ship pitches and rolls. They are mounted where a good view

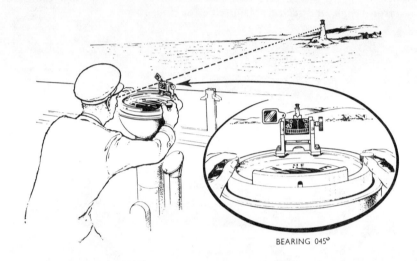

BEARING 045°

FIG. 15–4. Taking a bearing

of the horizon can be obtained on the compass platform, and in other positions from which the ship is conned. The direction of ship's head is indicated by a pointer, called the *lubber's line*, which is set in the direction of the fore-and-aft line of the ship. The repeater at the primary navigation position on the compass platform is mounted in a special stand and is known as the 'Pelorus'.

The bearing of an object can be obtained from a bearing repeater by sighting the object along an imaginary line joining the centre of the compass card to the object, and then reading the graduation on the edge of the card which is cut by the line of sight. This direction or bearing is known as the *compass bearing*.

To facilitate taking bearings, a bearing repeater can be fitted with a portable *azimuth circle* which can be rotated round the top of the bowl of the repeater. It is fitted with a 'V' sight and usually a prism whereby the bearing of the object indicated by the card is reflected, thus bringing the object and its bearing into line with the eye of the observer (fig. 15–4).

If the view of the horizon from a repeater is obstructed in any direction it is said to be *wooded* in that direction. The Pelorus of most ships is wooded, when looking aft, by funnels and superstructures; a bearing repeater, known as a *wing repeater*, is therefore fitted in each wing of the bridge, from which an unobstructed view can be obtained in the wooded directions of the Pelorus.

Steering repeaters. There are two types of steering repeater. One is similar to the bearing repeater except that it is not mounted in gimbals and can be fitted in any desired position. This type of repeater can be fitted with a *steering prism* or other device for magnifying a small arc of the repeater card on either side of ship's head to assist the helmsman. The other type of repeater, known as the *tape repeater*, is different in construction in that the compass card is represented by an endless tape mounted on rollers (fig. 15–5). The tape is viewed through a small window which allows up to about 15° on either side of the ship's head to be seen.

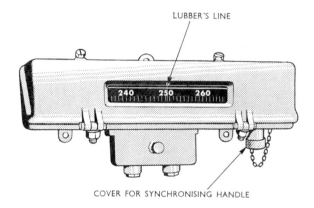

FIG. 15–5. A gyro-compass steering repeater

THE MAGNETIC COMPASS

Magnetism

Certain bodies (iron ores, lodestones, etc.) known as *natural magnets* possess the properties of attracting and repelling one another and of attracting pieces of iron and steel. These properties may be imparted to suitable pieces of steel, for instance, by rubbing them with a natural magnet, thus producing *artificial magnets*—a process known as 'magnetisation'. A compass needle is an instance of an artificial magnet. Both artificial and natural magnets, when suspended, will tend to set themselves pointing towards the north, since the Earth is known to be a large magnet.

Many substances may be magnetised to a greater or less degree; they are usually ferrous substances and commonly known as *magnetic materials*. Other substances, such as various non-metallic and non-ferrous materials, are extremely difficult, if not impossible, to magnetise, and are generally known as *non-magnetic materials*.

A magnet of elongated form will be found to have what are known as 'magnetic poles' near its extremities. The pole which sets towards north when the magnet is suspended is conventionally termed the 'red' pole, the other pole being the 'blue' pole. It is found that like poles repel one another, whereas unlike poles attract one another.

In the neighbourhood of a magnet there is a zone of magnetic influence known as the 'magnetic field', which may be represented, as in fig. 15–6, by lines of magnetic force emerging from a red pole and terminating in a blue pole. Other magnets or pieces of magnetic material in this magnetic field will tend to align themselves in the direction of the lines of force.

Substances may be magnetised by the following means:

1. Rubbing with a magnet
2. Hammering
3. Passing an electric current around the specimen
4. Allowing the specimen to remain in a powerful magnetic field.

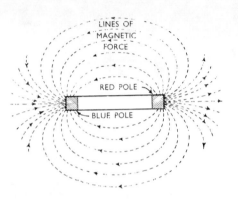

FIG. 15–6. Magnetic field of a magnet

Some substances, notably steel, tend to retain their magnetism for a very long period, and magnets produced from such a material are known as *permanent magnets*. Not only is this permanent magnetism retained, but it is difficult to produce and to remove unless strong magnetic fields are applied. On the other hand, certain other materials, such as soft iron, become magnetised very readily, even in a weak field, but they lose their magnetism as soon as the magnetic influence is removed. This type of magnetism is called *induced magnetism*.

Terrestrial magnetism

The fact that natural and artificial magnets, when suspended, will align themselves with their red poles pointing north suggests that the Earth itself possesses a magnetic field with a blue pole towards the north and a red pole towards the south; and it is this magnetic field which imparts directive properties to the magnetic compass.

The Earth as a magnet may be likened to a sphere with a small but immensely strong magnet near its centre. The lines of force from this magnet extend beyond the Earth's surface, emerging from a region in the neighbourhood of the south geographical pole and entering the Earth near the north geographical pole. Thus they are perpendicular to the Earth's surface where they leave and enter, and tangential to the Earth's surface in the approximate neighbourhood of the equator. Elsewhere, the lines of force are inclined to the horizontal plane, the amount of inclination being termed the *angle of dip*.

A magnetised needle, when freely suspended at its centre of gravity, will set itself along a line of force, with its red pole directed towards north. At the so-called magnetic equator, and there only, will the needle rest horizontally. Elsewhere the needle tilts red pole down in the northern hemisphere and blue pole down in the southern hemisphere. The *north* and *south magnetic poles*, where the lines of force enter and emerge, are identified as the regions where the suspended magnetised needle sets itself vertically.

A freely-suspended magnetised needle is a useless instrument as a compass—in the United Kingdom it would be inclined at $67\frac{1}{4}°$ to the horizontal—so means are adopted to make the magnet system of the compass pendulous, whereby the tilting tendency of the Earth's magnetism is counteracted by the bottom-heaviness of the magnet system. The needle then remains within two or three degrees of the horizontal wherever it may be situated. The direction in the horizontal plane taken up by such a needle is known as 'magnetic north' and defines the magnetic meridian of the particular site. The angle between magnetic north and true north is known as the *variation*.

Variation

Owing to the irregular pattern of the Earth's magnetic field, and to the fact that the true and magnetic poles are not coincident, the variation has differing values over the Earth's surface. These values are displayed on magnetic charts in the form of curves of equal variation, called *isogonals*. There is also a slow change in the general pattern of magnetic variation due to the change in the position of the magnetic pole. The value of the variation, and its yearly change, are shown on the compass roses of charts (fig. 15–7).

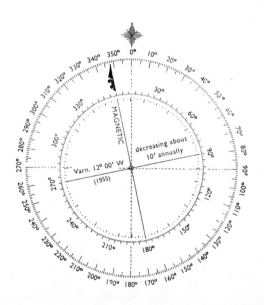

FIG. 15–7. Compass rose of a chart

If the direction of magnetic north from any place lies westward of true north the variation is said to be westerly, and if it lies eastward of true north the variation is said to be easterly. To convert a magnetic direction to a true direction, easterly variation is given a plus sign and westerly variation a minus sign; and to convert a true direction to a magnetic direction the signs are reversed. The following couplet provides a useful reminder for converting a true to a magnetic direction, and *vice versa*:

Variation east, magnetic least;

Variation west, magnetic best.

EXAMPLES (fig. 15–8)

Magnetic Direction	Variation	True Direction
Position A 130°M	20°W (−*magnetic best*)	110°
Position B 090°M	20°E (+*magnetic least*)	110°

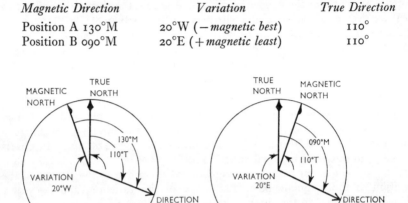

Direction at position A   Same direction at position B

FIG. 15–8. Examples of variation

Deviation

While an iron or steel ship is being built, she becomes magnetised from a number of causes, such as lying with her bows pointing almost to magnetic north—in which case she will acquire a red pole forward—and the hammering of her structure and the handling of her plates with a magnetic grab; so that by the time she is completed the 'hard' iron and steel in her hull and fittings will have acquired a considerable degree of permanent magnetism. This form of magnetism does not alter with change of course or with change of latitude; it may wear off to some extent as the ship settles down, but it eventually assumes a reasonably constant value.

On the other hand, any soft iron components will be magnetised by the Earth's magnetic field in a direction and to an amount depending on the direction and strength of the magnetic field. This is known as 'induced' magnetism and alters with course and latitude.

No two ships, even if they are of the same class and built alongside each other in the same port, will possess the same degree of magnetism. The magnetic properties of a ship inevitably affect the magnetic compass placed in her and the compass will point in a direction determined by the combination of the Earth's field and the ship's field. This direction is called *compass north*, and the angular difference between it and magnetic north is termed *deviation*. It will naturally vary with any changes in the ship's magnetic state, and will be different for various directions of the ship's head and these differences may be considerable. Fortunately, although these effects cannot be entirely eliminated, they can be sufficiently reduced by corrector magnets, soft iron spheres and the Flinders bar to enable the compass to be used for accurate navigation.

Electrical effects. Electric currents in the vicinity of a magnetic compass will cause deviations. The magnetic compasses of ships which have been *degaussed* (an electrical method of rendering a ship immune from magnetic mines) are fitted with special compensating coils. These *compass corrector coils* are energised from the degaussing system and are adjusted to produce an equal and opposite effect so that the degaussing system produces no deflection of the compass card when it is switched on.

Swinging ship

To eliminate the deviation of the magnetic compass as far as possible a ship is turned (or *swung*) through the points of the compass. During the process the deviation is reduced to a minimum by permanent magnets, soft iron spheres and the Flinders bar, and recorded on a *deviation card*. This process is known as *swinging ship for compass adjustment*.

Whenever possible the deviation of the compass is checked on individual courses by known transits or bearings of landmarks, or by astronomical observation.

Applying deviation

When applying deviation to convert a direction by magnetic compass to a magnetic direction, or *vice versa*, the following should always be borne in mind:

1. That the deviation to be applied is that for *the direction of the ship's head*.
2. That the deviation of one compass is different from that of another.

Deviation is applied in a similar manner to variation; that is, when converting a compass direction to a magnetic direction, easterly deviation is given a plus sign and westerly deviation a minus sign; and when converting a magnetic to a compass direction, the signs are reversed. The following couplet affords a useful reminder for applying deviation:

Deviation east, compass least;

Deviation west, compass best.

EXAMPLES

1. (fig. 15-9 (i))		2. (fig. 15-9 (ii))	
Ship's head or course, by compass	107°C	Bearing of an object, by compass	047°C
Deviation for 107°		Ship's head	202°C
(*compass least—add*)	3°E	Deviation for 202°	
Ship's head or course, magnetic	110°M	(*compass best—subtract*)	2°W
		Bearing of the object, magnetic	045°M

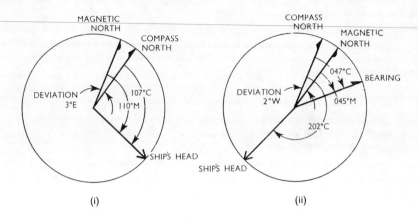

FIG. 15–9. Examples of deviation

Conversion of compass and magnetic directions to true directions

All charts are mapped in relation to true north and south, and therefore all courses are laid off and all bearings plotted as true directions. Directions obtained by magnetic compass have therefore to be corrected, first for deviation and then for variation, before they are marked on charts. Conversely, all true directions taken from a chart have to be converted, first to magnetic directions and then to compass directions, before they are applied to a magnetic compass. To avoid confusion between these different directions they are always recorded thus:

1. True directions, by three figures without a suffix, e.g. 210°.
2. Magnetic directions, by three figures with the suffix 'M', e.g. 042°M.
3. Magnetic compass directions, by three figures with the suffix 'C', e.g. 223°C.

The following examples show the method of converting compass to true directions and *vice versa.*

EXAMPLES

1. A ship is ordered to steer a course of 358°. What is the compass course to steer if the variation is 20°W?

True course	=	358°
Variation	=	20°W *(magnetic best—add)*
Magnetic course	=	018°M (378 – 360)
Deviation for N.N.E. (022½°)	=	3°E *(compass least—subtract)*
Course to steer		015°C

2. The bearing of a lighthouse taken from a ship steering 160°C is 002°C. What is the true bearing of the lighthouse if the variation is 7°E?

Compass bearing	=	002°C
Deviation for course S.S.E. (157½°)	=	3°W (*compass best—subtract*)
Magnetic bearing	=	359°M (362 − 3)
Variation	=	7°E (*magnetic least—add*)
True bearing of lighthouse	=	006° (366 − 360)

Magnetic compass binnacle (fig. 15–10)

A binnacle is the mounting in which the compass is normally gimballed and in which there usually are positions for the corrector magnets, Flinders bar and soft iron spheres.

It is important to remember that the functioning of a magnetic compass can be considerably influenced by any magnetic substance close to it. A magnetic compass is therefore housed in, and mounted on, non-magnetic materials such as brass, wood and copper; any magnetic materials such as steel and iron, or wires and cables carrying electric current, are kept as far away from it as practicable. For the same reason anyone using a magnetic compass—the Officer of the Watch or the helmsman, for example—first removes his knife, keys and any magnetic article he may have about him.

Magnetic compass

The compass bowl is mounted in a gimbal ring, which in turn is supported in the binnacle so that the lubber's line is set in the direction of the fore-and-aft line of the ship. Within the compass bowl there is the pivot upon which the card and magnet system is poised. The card is of mica and is mounted upon a float within which is the jewel bearing that rests on the pivot. Below the card and attached to the float are the magnetic needles. The bowl is closed above and below by glass cover plates and is provided with an expansion device to allow for volume changes in the liquid with which the bowl is completely filled. The liquid supports much of the weight of the magnet system, thereby reducing pivot friction, and damps out any tendency of the magnet system to oscillate. The liquid in the bowl is a mixture of alcohol and water, rendered unfit, and indeed dangerous, to drink. Leakage of the liquid will cause a bubble to appear in the bowl, which may be removed by inverting the bowl, removing the filling plug and topping up with distilled water. Dilatation of the expansion disc will ensure that no air bubbles remain. However, it is advisable to fit a new compass if bubbles appear in the liquid.

When used in a boat the compass should be placed with its lubber's line in the fore-and-aft line of the boat and as far as practicable from anything magnetic, such as the boat's engine.

Using a boat's compass. It should be remembered that the compass will not point to true north, because of the errors of variation and deviation; also that, quite apart from the effects of wind and current, the boat's return course will

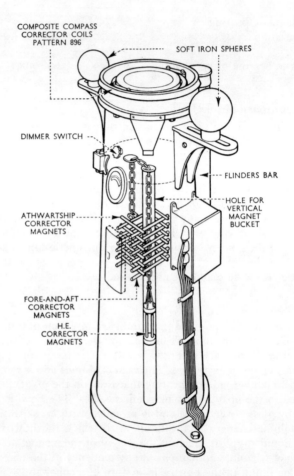

COMPOSITE COMPASS
CORRECTOR COILS
PATTERN 896

SOFT IRON SPHERES

DIMMER SWITCH

FLINDERS BAR

HOLE FOR
VERTICAL
MAGNET
BUCKET

ATHWARTSHIP
CORRECTOR
MAGNETS

FORE-AND-AFT
CORRECTOR
MAGNETS

H.E.
CORRECTOR
MAGNETS

FIG. 15–10. A magnetic compass binnacle

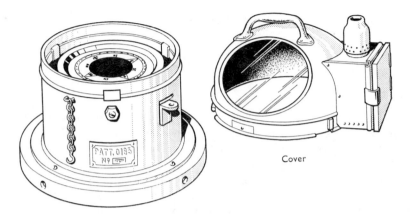

Cover

FIG. 15–11. A boat's compass

probably not be the exact opposite of her outward course, owing to the deviation of the compass. Whenever a course is steered by eye the corresponding compass course should therefore be noted and recorded, due allowance being made for the effect of any wind or current, so that in the event of fog or bad visibility a correct course may be steered by compass. The best way to take a bearing of an object from a boat is to point the boat at the object, taking care to have sufficient room to manœuvre.

Questions on this chapter will be found in Appendix 2.

CHAPTER 16

Conning and Steering

A captain manœuvres his ship by using her engines and her rudder(s). When under way and going ahead the ship's speed is determined by the number of revolutions of her propellers per minute, and her course is either altered or maintained by her rudder.

In a man-of-war the Captain, Officer of the Watch or Navigating Officer *cons* the ship by giving wheel or engine orders from the *compass platform* to the *steering position* (wheelhouse in small ships), where the quartermaster sees that they are applied, either by the helmsman to the steering wheel, for wheel orders, or by the telegraphsman to the *engine order and revolution telegraphs*, for engine orders. The engine and revolution orders are received in the engine room on *engine order repeaters* and applied to the engines by the watchkeepers.

In men-of-war the primary steering position in older small ships is usually one deck below the bridge, and in larger ships and modern small ships several decks below; first, because there is no room on the bridge for the personnel and equipment, and secondly to obtain a certain amount of protection.

In merchant ships the wheelhouse is usually on the bridge and easily accessible to the Master or Officer of the Watch, who can pass wheel orders direct to the quartermaster and handle the telegraphs themselves.

HOW A SHIP IS STEERED

One of the most important duties of a seaman is to be able to steer well, either by sight on the object ordered, or by compass. This ability can only be acquired by experience.

The movement of the steering wheel sets the steering mechanism in motion, which turns the rudder. When the ship is moving ahead the rudder turns the ship by swinging her stern away from, and her bows towards, the direction desired; it has the opposite effect when the ship is moving astern. When moving ahead the ship's head always pays off in the same direction as the top spokes of the wheel, so that if you wish the ship's head to go to port the top spokes of the wheel must be moved to the left. When moving astern the stern pays off in the same direction in which the top spokes of the wheel are moved.

Rudder angle

Within the limits of the movement of the rudder, the greater the angle between the rudder and the fore-and-aft line of the ship the quicker she will swing and the smaller will be her turning circle. A ship is usually designed to allow for a maximum rudder angle of 35 degrees each side of the *midships* position.

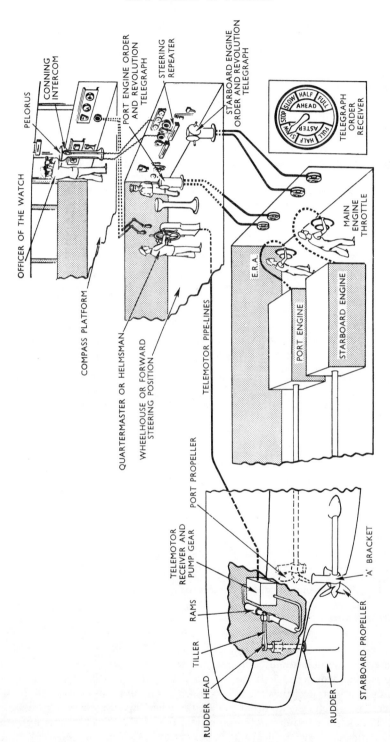

FIG. 16-1. How conning orders are obeyed

Putting on and taking off rudder

The wheel should always be turned steadily by its spokes, without using undue speed or force, until the required rudder angle has been put on. It should not be started or brought up suddenly, or the steering engine may be damaged. With *telemotor* steering gear the wheel should not be allowed to fly back to amidships too quickly. If there is any tendency for the wheel to jam, the fact should at once be reported. Any desired rudder angle can be put on up to the maximum of 35 degrees, when the wheel and rudder are each said to be *hard over* and there is a tendency for the steering mechanism to be strained or become jammed; and for normal purposes the largest rudder angle used is therefore 30 degrees. The amount of wheel required for any desired rudder angle is shown by a pointer, known as the *wheel indicator*, which is geared to the wheel and moves over a graduated scale situated in front of it.

STEERING ORDERS

It is most important that all steering orders should be given clearly and in the standard form. It is equally important that they should be acknowledged in the standard form and obeyed correctly and in orderly fashion.

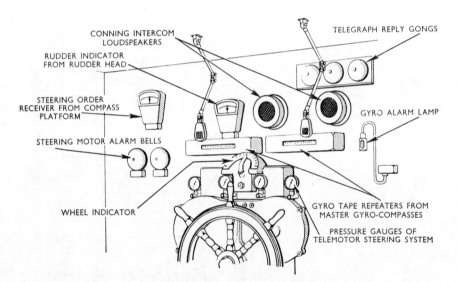

FIG. 16-2. Conning and steering instruments in the steering position

Altering course

Orders for an alteration of course always start with the direction and are immediately followed by the rudder angle, e.g. 'Starboard twenty'. This is repeated by the helmsman, who puts the wheel over until the desired rudder angle is obtained, when he reports 'Twenty of starboard wheel on, Sir'. As the ship's head approaches the new course the rate of swing may require to be reduced, in which case an order to ease the wheel may be given, e.g. 'Ease to ten'. The helmsman repeats the order and moves the wheel to port until the wheel indicator shows 10 degrees of starboard wheel, when he reports 'Ten of starboard wheel on, Sir'. When the ship's head is near her new course this wheel is taken off, and so the order 'Midships' is given, which should be repeated and obeyed by the helmsman as in previous cases. Shortly after this the swing may require to be countered and the order 'Port ten' would usually be given. The order is repeated and the rudder put over to the required angle, the helmsman reporting 'Ten of port wheel on, Sir'. When the ship's head is within a degree or two of the new course the order 'Midships' will be given.

If it is observed that the wheel has been put the wrong way, it is good practice for the Officer of the Watch to order 'Midships' before repeating the original order.

Steering by compass

When the helmsman is required to steer a course by compass the ship is conned as described above until her head is on the required course, when the order 'Steady' will be given. Immediately he hears this order the helmsman notes exactly which degree of the compass card coincides with the lubber's line, repeats the order and reports the course as indicated by his steering compass, e.g. 'Steady, course zero-five-seven, Sir'. If the ship's head pays off on either side of the new course immediately after the order 'Steady' is given, the helmsman moves his wheel in the direction required to return the ship to that course, and when her head is again on the correct course he makes his report 'Course, Sir, zero-five-seven.' The Officer of the Watch checks the reported course with the 'Pelorus' or the 'standard compass' and, if he is satisfied, he will say 'Very good' and the helmsman will continue to steer that course without further orders. If the helmsman's reported course is incorrect, or if his compass is registering deviation or a small gyro error, he will be ordered to steer another course, perhaps within a degree or two of his reported course, e.g. 'Steer zero-five-eight'. This order is repeated and the wheel moved accordingly, and when the ship's head is on the new course the report is made 'Course, Sir, zero-five-eight'. The helmsman then steers the ship on this course.

The following example shows the orders, replies and reports for an alteration of course from 008° to 306°:

Order	Reply	Report
'Midships' (see Note)	'Midships, Sir'	'Wheel's a'midships, Sir'
'Port thirty'	'Port thirty, Sir'	'Thirty of port wheel on, Sir'
'Ease to fifteen'	'Ease to fifteen, Sir'	'Fifteen of port wheel on, Sir'
'Midships'	'Midships, Sir'	'Wheel's a'midships, Sir'
'Starboard ten'	'Starboard ten, Sir'	'Ten of starboard wheel on, Sir'
'Midships'	'Midships, Sir'	'Wheel's a'midships, Sir'
'Steady'	'Steady, course three-zero-seven, Sir'	—
'Steer three-zero-six'	'Steer three-zero-six, Sir'	'Course, Sir, three-zero-six' (when the ship is on her course)

NOTE: Immediately before an alteration of course is made the order 'Midships' may be given. This serves the double purpose of ensuring that any rudder angle which may be on is taken off, and of warning the helmsman that an alteration of course is coming.

Steering by eye

In ships where the helmsman can see ahead from the steering position he may be required to steer on a ship ahead or on a distant object. If so, the ship will be steadied as nearly as possible on the desired course by conning, and, after the order 'Midships', the helmsman will be given such orders as 'Steady on the lighthouse', or 'Follow the next ahead'. In the former example he then steers the ship by keeping the lighthouse in line with the jackstaff and the centre of the wheel; in the latter he follows in the wake of the ship next ahead, keeping her masts and funnels in line dead ahead and turning astern of her in her wake if she alters course.

The helmsman should always be ready to revert to steering by compass as soon as this is indicated by the order 'Steady'.

HINTS ON STEERING

Use of the wheel

Remember that the 'lubber's line' is fixed in the fore-and-aft line of the ship and represents the ship's head, and that the compass card remains steady while the ship swings round it. The direction of the ship's head is read off the compass card against the lubber's line. To keep the ship on a given compass course the lubber's line must be kept constantly opposite the correct degree marked on the compass card. For example, if the lubber's line wanders off to the right the top spokes of the wheel must be turned to the left to bring it back into place.

When the wheel of a large ship is put over the ship does not begin to swing for some time. If, as sometimes occurs, the ship is swinging in the opposite direction at the time of putting the wheel over, she will take longer to answer the rudder than had she been steady. But when a large ship has begun to swing it takes a certain amount of opposite rudder to stop her again. It is important to lose no time in 'getting the feel' of the ship; she may show a tendency to assert a will of her own, and this tendency must be anticipated and forestalled.

The art of steering consists largely in watching the lubber's line very closely and putting the wheel over the instant the ship *starts* to swing off her course instead of waiting until she has actually swung off. The wheel must be eased again immediately the swing is checked, and opposite rudder used if she starts to swing in the opposite direction. The amount of rudder to be used depends upon the ship, her speed, and the weather, but *success lies largely in using as little as possible, and the higher the speed of the ship the less rudder she requires.*

Making good the course

In a seaway the ship cannot always be kept exactly on her course, but when she swings off it the helmsman should endeavour to swing her back an equal amount *to the other side.* He should not allow her to swing more to one side than the other, because the mean course steered will not be the correct one.

Carrying wheel

Unless wind and sea are right ahead, if the rudder of a ship is kept amidships she will usually wander off her course owing to the pressure of the wind on her superstructure or the force of the waves on either end of her hull. In most warships the ship's head tends to come up into the wind because the pivoting point is well forward; in some merchant ships, however, whose pivoting point lies further aft, it may tend to fall off to leeward. To counteract this tendency the helmsman has to apply a constant small amount of wheel.

ORDERS FOR HELMSMEN AND QUARTERMASTERS

A helmsman is always given orders as exactly as possible. He should not be ordered to steer more than five degrees either side of his reported course, any larger alterations being carried out by conning until the desired course is achieved.

On being relieved the helmsman must always turn over to his relief the course and the amount of wheel which the ship is carrying, e.g. 'Course zero-four-zero, ship carrying five degrees of port wheel.' The helmsman should never turn over to his relief during an alteration of course, but should wait until the ship is once more on a steady course.

The quartermaster is responsible for seeing that all wheel and engine orders are obeyed correctly. Whenever the ship is manœuvring (i.e. in confined waters, crowded shipping lanes, or in company with other ships) he should take the wheel himself. Before turning over the wheel to a helmsman he should first ask permission of the Officer of the Watch. When entering or leaving harbour the Chief Quartermaster (or coxswain in small ships) takes the wheel.

At the change of the watch the new quartermaster should report to the Officer of the Watch: 'Quartermaster relieved, Sir. Course (so and so), telegraphs at (so and so), revolutions (so and so), quartermaster (A.B. Blank) at the wheel.'

ORDERS FOR REGULATING THE SPEED AND MOVEMENT OF THE ENGINES

Telegraph orders

The wording of engine orders from the compass platform to the telegraphsmen has been standardised for the sake of uniformity and the avoidance of phonetic errors, such as confusion between the words 'port' and 'both'. The underlying principle is that the word 'engines' is *always* used in conjunction with the words 'both' or 'all', *but on no other occasion.* If it is seen that an engine has been put the wrong way, it is good practice for the Officer of the Watch to order 'Stop' before repeating the original order.

EXAMPLES

Two- and Four-shaft Ships

Revolutions seven-zero

Slow ahead port, half astern starboard

Stop starboard

Half ahead both engines

Revolutions one-one-zero

Three-shaft Ships

Revolutions seven-zero

Slow ahead port and centre, half astern starboard

Stop starboard

Half ahead all engines

Revolutions one-one-zero

The telegraphsmen should always repeat orders *word for word* before they transmit them to the engine room, and a further report should be made when they have been acknowledged by the engine-room staff.

EXAMPLE

Order	Reply	Report
'Stop both engines'	'Stop both engines, Sir'	'Both telegraphs repeated stop, Sir'
'Half ahead port'	'Half ahead port, Sir'	'Port telegraph repeated half ahead, Sir'

Engine order telegraphs

These spoken orders are transmitted electrically or mechanically to the engine room from the steering position by means of engine order telegraphs. These telegraphs are fitted in the primary steering position, one for each propeller shaft in single-, twin-, and triple-screw ships, and one for each pair of shafts in quadruple-screw ships; they are connected to their repeaters in the engine room electrically or by rod gearing.

The dial of each telegraph and repeater is graduated for the orders 'Full', 'Half' and 'Slow', for both 'Ahead' and 'Astern', and it is also graduated for 'Stop'. The order 'Stand-by' is sometimes included as well. When the hand-wheel or lever is turned to transmit an order, a pointer moves over the face of the dial indicating the order transmitted. In the mechanical type the handwheel has to be moved through one complete revolution for each step in the range of orders.

As each order is transmitted a bell rings in the engine room to draw attention to the order. The tones of these bells are different for port and starboard repeaters.

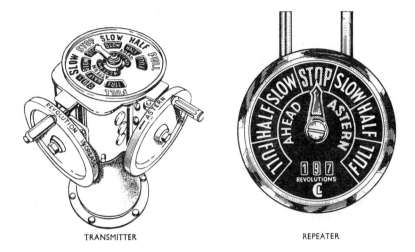

TRANSMITTER   REPEATER

FIG. 16-3. Combined engine order and revolution order telegraph

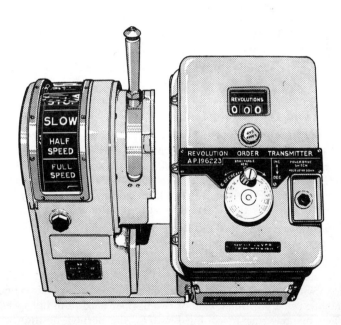

FIG. 16-4. Electric engine order and revolution order telegraph

Operation of reply gongs. Each change of engine order is acknowledged by the engine room by means of the engine order reply gong(s), using the following code:

Slow:	One ring
Half:	Two rings
Full:	Three rings
Stop:	Two double rings

A differently-toned gong is used for each shaft.

Revolution order telegraphs

A warship possesses a comparatively large range of speed which must be adjustable to within narrow limits (usually a quarter of a knot) to enable her to manœuvre in close company with other ships. Orders for her engines must therefore be qualified by the number of revolutions which correspond with the speed required. This is done by means of the *revolution order telegraph*, which transmits the number of revolutions required on each shaft to the engine room, where it is repeated on a *revolution order repeater*. The method of transmission is by handwheel and electric transmission or rod gearing, in steps of two revolutions at a time, one turn of the handwheel being required for each step. Whenever the revolutions are altered a warning bell with a different tone to that of the engine order telegraphs rings in the engine room. Revolution orders are acknowledged from the engine room by one or two strokes of the associated reply gong, which also has a different tone from the reply gongs of the telegraphs.

Alterations of revolution orders are only complied with when the appropriate engine telegraph is at 'Half'. There is, however, no objection to using a revolution order telegraph to warn the engine room what revolutions it is intended to use when the appropriate engine order telegraph is next put to 'Half'. This practice can be helpful and is recommended.

The engine and revolution order telegraphs are usually combined in one instrument, as shown in figs. 16–3 and 16–4.

In H.M. ships the revolutions per minute at which the engines are to be worked at the different speeds ordered are as follows:

Slow (ahead or astern). A pre-determined number of revolutions sufficient to give the ship steerage way—usually about 5 knots.

Half (ahead or astern). In two-shaft ships, fitted with only one revolution order telegraph, it is the number of revolutions ordered by the telegraph for whichever shaft is at 'Half ahead' or 'Half astern'. In other ships it is the revolutions ordered by the telegraph for the shaft or shafts concerned.

Full (ahead or astern). EMERGENCY—Maximum revolutions possible with the power available.

Merchant ships are seldom provided with revolution order telegraphs, because they do not normally travel in company and so their speed need not be adjustable to within narrow limits. They normally proceed at their economical speed, which is usually within a knot or two of their maximum full speed, and, except when manœuvring in confined waters, the normal position of their telegraphs while on passage is 'Full ahead'. 'Emergency full speed' (i.e.

speed employing the utmost power available) is indicated by moving the telegraphs from 'Full speed' to 'Stop' and back to 'Full speed' twice in quick succession.

CONNING AND STEERING POSITIONS, COMMUNICATIONS AND INSTRUMENTS

POSITIONS

Alternative positions from which the ship can be conned or steered are provided in all warships for use if the primary positions are put out of action. There are also alternative methods of steering for use if the main steering gear is damaged.

Bridge

The expression 'bridge' (of which the Admiral's bridge and compass platform are particular cases) refers to those positions in the upper portion of the bridge structure from which fleets, squadrons, groups of ships, or single ships are controlled and fought by the Admiral and/or Captain.

Admiral's bridge. The compartment designed for the use of the Admiral in controlling his fleet or squadron at sea.

Compass platform (*C.P.*). The compartment in the fore part of the bridge structure designed as the ship's primary conning position.

Pilotage position. The open position on the top deck of the bridge structure (in some ships with a closed compass platform from which the view is limited) provided to facilitate handling in confined waters, berthing, etc.

Emergency conning position (E.C.P.)

A position well separated from the compass platform from which the ship may be conned when the bridge is out of action. In cruisers it is in the after superstructure; in aircraft carriers there are two, one to port and one to starboard; in destroyers and frigates it is either amidships or aft, and if fitted with a wheel it is also called the 'emergency steering position'.

Forward steering position (F.S.P.)

The compartment designed as the primary steering position in cruisers and larger ships and in new-construction frigates.

Bow rudder steering position

The position from which the bow rudder is controlled in certain large ships. This position may be sited in the forward steering position.

Wheelhouse

The primary steering position in destroyers, older frigates and small craft.

Steam (or diesel) steering position

This is adjacent to the steam (or diesel) steering engine. If more than one position is fitted, they are known by their relative positions, e.g. port and starboard.

After steering position

This is the mechanical wheel for local control of power steering, fitted in a steering compartment aft. If more than one position is fitted, they are known by their relative positions, e.g. port and starboard.

Hand steering position

This is the space which contains the hand pump for operating the rudder gears by hand. In destroyers it is usually referred to as the *tiller flat*.

Emergency hand control steering position

The position at any of the power steering gear pumps where they are fitted with direct manual control for emergency use.

Tiller flat

This compartment in small ships contains both the after steering position and the hand steering position. The term is used in a collective location sense.

COMMUNICATIONS

The conning and steering positions are equipped with some or all of the following instruments and fittings, depending on the size of the ship.

Conning intercom (figs. 16–2 and 16–5)

This system of microphones and loud-speakers is the primary means of passing orders from the compass platform to the forward steering position. Orders from other conning positions are passed by telephone and 'steering order transmitters'. In ships with no voicepipes two independent systems are fitted.

Conning voicepipe

In some older ships this leads from the compass platform to the forward steering position, and is the secondary means by which conning orders are passed.

Emergency conning line

In ships with no voicepipe, this sound-powered telephone is the secondary means of passing conning orders.

Steering order transmitter and receiver (fig. 16–5)

These are electrically controlled instruments having a pointer which moves over a dial, marked in 5-degree steps up to 35 degrees, port and starboard, and with positions for the orders 'Midships' and 'Steady'. Transmitters are provided at the primary and emergency conning positions, and receivers are provided at all steering positions. Before steering orders are passed by these instruments the order 'Obey steering order receiver' is given by word of mouth, and when it is no longer required to pass the orders by this means the order 'Disregard steering order receiver' is given by word of mouth. In the

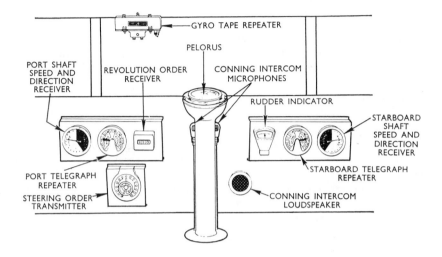

FIG. 16–5. Conning instruments on the bridge

event of a complete breakdown in other means of communication between conning and steering positions, the movement of the receiver pointer several times over its range is the order to obey the steering order receiver.

Wheel indicator (fig. 16–2)

This is provided in all steering positions to show the helmsman the amount the wheel has been turned. It consists of a pointer geared to the wheel mechanism, and moves round a scale marked in degrees from 0 to 35, both to port and to starboard.

Rudder indicator (figs. 16–2 and 16–5)

These indicators are fitted at all conning and steering positions, Machinery Control Room and Damage Control Headquarters. They are usually electrically-operated direct from the rudder head.

The rudder indicator should follow the wheel indicator; if it fails to register the same movement it means that the rudder is not lined up with the wheel, or that there is something wrong with the steering mechanism, and the fact must immediately be reported to the Officer of the Watch.

Telegraph repeaters (fig. 16–5)

These are situated on the compass platform, one for each set of main engines. They are electrically connected with the telegraphs and are operated as the telegraph orders are transmitted from the steering position.

Shaft speed and direction receivers (fig. 16–5)

These are situated on the compass platform, one for each set of main engines. They are electrically connected with the propeller shafts and indicate the direction in which, and speed at which, each shaft is turning.

Revolution telegraph repeat receivers (fig. 16–5)

These are situated on the compass platform, one for each revolution telegraph, to which they are electrically connected. They indicate the number of revolutions per minute to which the revolution telegraphs have been set.

Telephones

In nearly all men-of-war telephonic communication is fitted directly from the compass platform, the primary steering position and the alternative conning positions, to all engine rooms. In addition, there is usually a separate direct line from the compass platform to the usual engine control position. All these lines of communication are fitted with sound-powered telephones and manual call-ups, so that they are independent of outside power supply. In addition, communication with the engine rooms can be made through the main exchange and the DCHQ exchange.

STEERING GEAR IN H.M. SHIPS

Details of steering gear differ with the type and size of the ship, but it may be said that the gear is divided into two parts. The first part consists of the steering wheel and transmission system, whereby the motions of the wheel are transmitted to some after position in the ship; the second part is that which actually operates the rudder and whose movements are controlled by the first.

The telemotor or electric systems convey the movements of the wheel to the tiller flat or steering gear compartment, wherein is housed the electro-hydraulic gear which turns the rudder. The following is a very brief description of the whole system and it should be read in conjunction with the simplified diagram in fig. 16–6.

The telemotor system

When the wheel is turned to port, both pistons in the pedestal mounting of the wheel are moved upwards, thus putting pressure on the telemotor fluid (glycerine and distilled water) in the upper pipes. These pipes conduct the pressure to the 'receiver', which is situated in the tiller flat.

The receiver consists of two 'floating' cylinders which move backwards and forwards over four fixed and hollow pistons, to the heads of which are connected the four pipes from the steering pedestal. Each cylinder is divided into two separate compartments, and the cylinders are joined together by a crosshead. Any change in the pressure of fluid in the two sets of pipes will therefore cause the cylinders to move backwards or forwards. In this case, the pressure is being delivered to the forward compartment of each cylinder, and the two cylinders are moving aft. This movement is transmitted by means of a rod to a

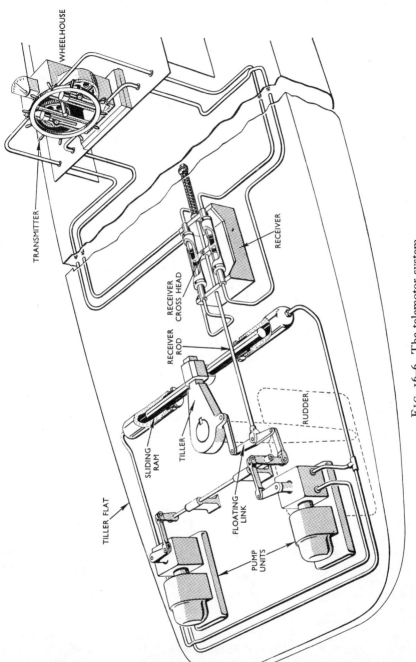

WHEELHOUSE

TRANSMITTER

RECEIVER

RECEIVER
CROSS HEAD

RECEIVER
ROD

SLIDING
RAM

TILLER

RUDDER

TILLER FLAT

FLOATING
LINK

PUMP
UNITS

FIG. 16-6. The telemotor system

'floating link', the inner end of which acts for the time being as its fulcrum because it is connected by a rocker-arm to the tiller-head. The movement of the receiver rod is therefore transmitted by the outer end of the floating link, through link gear, to the arm which operates the valves of the hydraulic pump units.

The pump units (Hele–Shaw or Williams–Janney) are electrically driven at constant speed. They are connected by fluid-filled pipes to the heads of two cylinders, in which works a sliding ram connected at its centre to the end of the tiller by means of a ball joint. Depending upon which way the arms of the valves are moved, the pumps will put pressure on the port cylinder or the starboard cylinder, thus causing the ram to move in the required direction.

In this case, pressure is applied to the port cylinder, causing the ram to move to starboard; and as the ram is connected to the end of the tiller, this moves the rudder-head clockwise, thus putting on port rudder. This movement would continue until the rudder was hard over were it not for the floating link connected to the tiller head. When the tiller begins to move, the fulcrum of this link is transferred to the end of the receiver rod, at its centre, and as the tiller head turns, the inner end of the link is moved aft and the outer end forward, thus centring the valves of the pump units. This equalises the pressure at either end of the sliding ram so that it stops moving, and the rudder thus comes to rest at the required angle.

The forward end of the receiver rod is attached to a spring which the movement of the rod subjects to compression or tension. The function of this spring is to centralise the receiver cylinders and thus return the rudder and steering wheel to their midships position when pressure is removed from the spokes of the steering wheel.

When the steering wheel is turned to starboard, the whole system functions in the reverse direction.

Precautions while steering. Move the wheel with a steady, even motion. On the top of the steering pedestal is the replenishing tank, and the fluid in this tank must not be allowed to fall below the glass gauge; the cock on the bottom of the tank must always be open when the steering gear is in use. Where the wheel tends to fly back to 'midships' of its own accord it must *not* be allowed to do so; it should always be eased back instead. Pressure gauges are fitted to the steering pedestal to enable the quartermaster to see what pressure there is in each side of the system. While the wheel is being turned the side in use must not be allowed to register a pressure of more than 600 lb per sq. in., which requires that the wheel should be turned gently. When the wheel is amidships the gauges should read zero; if for any reason they do not, the by-pass valve provided should be opened, which allows the pressure on both sides of the system to equalise, so bringing the rudder back amidships.

Electric steering system

A control console is fitted in the forward steering position. The movement of the steering wheel, which is part of the console, is transmitted electrically to a power unit in the steering gear compartment. The power unit controls the output of the electro-hydraulic gear which turns the rudder. Two separate systems are fitted in case of damage.

Automatic steering is incorporated in this system.

STEERING GEAR DEFECTS

It is not intended to attempt a detailed analysis of the many possible varieties of steering gear defect and breakdown. The most likely sources of failure are the following:

Wheel jam

This can happen with hand gears, and with chain or shafting control gears, because of some obstruction in the line of gears. In such a case it may take some time to locate and clear the obstruction, and it will be necessary to change to a different steering position.

It is most unusual for a wheel jam to occur with telemotor gear, but it can be caused by complete blockage of a telemotor pipe. This will be indicated by a high pressure on one transmitter gauge on the side of the damage. The hand by-pass valve on that pipe lead should be opened, after which it should be possible to continue steering with the remainder of the transmitter and the other pipe lead or leads.

It is possible, though unlikely, for a telemotor transmitter to jam in its gears. This can be recognised by a solid mechanical jam, with no excess pressure showing on any transmitter gauge. It is unlikely that anything can be done quickly to correct such a defect, and it will be necessary to change to another steering position. Before leaving a jammed telemotor transmitter, all its hand by-pass valves should be opened to free the locked hydraulic fluid, otherwise delay may be caused in the change-over.

Complete failure of telemotor system

This is very unlikely, but could be caused in action by damage which cuts or completely flattens all pairs of telemotor leads. It will be necessary to change to another steering position.

Complete failure of steering pump power

This is indicated by failure of the rudder to follow the wheel when the telemotor transmitter is free and its gauges show that the telemotor system is working correctly. It should also be indicated by the ringing of the steering pump alarm bells, unless power to them has also failed. It will be necessary to use emergency diesel or hand pump steering until power supplies are restored, or to steer by main engines.

Partial failure of steering power

In large modern ships with several sources of steering power (e.g. two turbine pumps and two motor pumps) special pressure gauges in the primary steering position will indicate if the primary (turbine) pump in use fails for any reason. There should be no failure of steering, because the secondary (motor) pump on that system should take over supply of steering power automatically. Under such circumstances the correct action is to change over to the other system so that a primary (turbine) pump is once again in use, with a secondary (motor) pump in immediate reserve. This change-over is effected by operation of a hand lever on the telemotor transmitter.

General

If the steering gear fails to operate correctly in any way, the quartermaster should at once inform the compass platform or other conning position in use. The Control Engine Room or Machinery Control Room should then be informed by telephone.

If the failure involves a change of steering positions it will be necessary to steer the ship by main engines in the interval, using drastic reductions of speed on one side or the other to counteract any swing.

CHANGE-OVER

Change-over of conning positions

It is probable that the first intimation to be received at the forward steering position that the compass platform has been put out of action will be an order by telephone, such as 'Emergency conning position in control; obey steering order receiver; man E.C.P. telephone'. The quartermaster should then arrange for a continuous watch on the emergency conning position telephone and obey all engine and wheel orders received from that position.

The forward position may, however, be the first to know of damage to the compass platform, in which case the quartermaster should immediately inform the E.C.P. and the engine room by telephone or messenger.

Change-over of steering positions

The quartermaster will probably be the first to notice any failure of the steering gear, by experiencing stiffness or jamming of the wheel, or seeing the rudder and wheel indicators get out of step, or by getting incorrect readings of the telemotor gauges, and he should immediately report any signs of failure to the Officer of the Watch. If the steering fails the ship will have to be steered by the main engines until an alternative method of steering is brought into use or the fault is made good. It may even be necessary to connect up one of the secondary steering arrangements and man one of the secondary steering positions. Until the ship is again under full steering control the 'not under command' daymark or lights should be hoisted.

As ships are differently equipped with alternative steering systems the procedure for their change-over may vary considerably, and the following example is given only to convey the sequence of reports, orders, and actions, which may be involved in such a change-over. The Captain's Orders should contain detailed instructions.

Q.M. to O.O.W.: 'Ship not steering, Sir', or 'Wheel jammed with ten degrees of port wheel on.'

O.O.W. to Q.M.: 'Man after steering position.'

O.O.W. to Engine Room: 'Steer by main engines. Steering gear break-down. Man after steering position.'

The quartermaster leaves the helmsman in charge of the telegraphsmen in the forward steering position. The ship is then steered by altering the revolutions of the main engines by orders from the compass platform.

In ships equipped with only one revolution transmitter it is the usual practice for one engine to be adjusted to revolutions ordered by the Officer of the Watch, and for the other engine to obey the revolution receiver. Both engines continue to obey their respective engine order telegraphs. When the quartermaster reaches the after steering position the procedure is continued as follows:

Q.M. to Helmsman: 'Q.M. closed up in after steering position.'
Helmsman to O.O.W.: 'Q.M. closed up in after steering position, Sir.'
Q.M. to Helmsman.: 'Check compasses.'

The quartermaster then checks his compass in the after steering position with the steering compass, and, if necessary, lines it up.

It should be noted that the forward steering position can be used to pass orders from, and to receive reports for, the compass platform; this relieves the Officer of the Watch of the necessity for handling a number of telephones and frees him to contend with the many problems confronting him in such an emergency.

The engineers investigate the failure and decide which of the alternative means of steering should be employed. When this has been decided, the quartermaster reports to the Officer of the Watch by telephone (from the after steering position to the compass platform) the details of the breakdown and which of the alternative methods of steering is to be employed. This may entail the quartermaster manning another position.

The engineers then connect up the secondary steering method selected, and the quartermaster reports as follows:

Q.M. to O.O.W.: 'Ready to steer from the after (or other) steering position.'

The Officer of the Watch then puts the change-over switch for the steering order transmitter (if fitted) to the required position, and orders a small alteration of rudder (say five degrees) by steering order transmitter to test the new system. This order is obeyed by the quartermaster at the after (or other) steering position. The rudder is then ordered amidships by steering order transmitter, and if the Officer of the Watch is satisfied the procedure continues as follows:

O.O.W. to Helmsman: 'Steer from after (or other) steering position.'
Helmsman to Engine Room and after (or other) steering position: 'Steer from after (or other) steering position.'

The Officer of the Watch then gives the required wheel orders by steering order transmitter. Subsequently, whenever the ship is steadied on a course the quartermaster reports the course by telephone to the helmsman, who repeats it to the Officer of the Watch. A continuous watch is maintained on the telephone between the forward and secondary steering positions.

Reverting to main steering

When the fault in the main steering gear has been repaired, the following procedure may be carried out to revert to steering from the forward steering position:

The engineers report to the Officer of the Watch that the main steering gear has been repaired.

O.O.W. to Helmsman: 'Revert to main steering. Steer by main engines. Wheel amidships.'

Helmsman to O.O.W.: 'Wheel amidships, Sir', and, when he has centred the wheel, 'Wheel's amidships, Sir.'

Helmsman to Engine Room and after (or other) steering position: 'Revert to main steering. Steer by main engines. Wheel amidships.'

The quartermaster at the after (or other) steering position then centres his wheel, which centres the rudder. The engineers disconnect the after (or other) steering position and connect up the main steering system to the forward steering position and, when all is ready, inform the helmsman. Meanwhile the ship is steered by main engines as before. As soon as the secondary steering position is disconnected, the quartermaster reports the fact by telephone to the helmsman, and, without further orders, returns to the forward steering position and resumes his duties there. The Officer of the Watch puts the change-over switch for the steering order transmitter to the forward steering position.

Helmsman to O.O.W.: 'After (or other) steering position disconnected. Ready to steer from forward steering position, Sir.'

The Officer of the Watch then tests the main steering system by a small alteration of course, and, when satisfied, resumes the normal procedure for steering the ship.

O.O.W. to Helmsman: 'Steer from forward steering position.'

Helmsman to Engine Room and after steering position: 'Steer from forward steering position.'

Questions on this chapter will be found in Appendix 2.

CHAPTER 17

Elementary Navigation

A ship can be navigated safely from one port to another by following a selected route on a *chart*; this is virtually a contour map of the sea bed and its surrounding coastline except that whereas a land map gives the heights of the land contours above sea level, a chart gives the depth of the bottom below sea level. This selected route takes into account the draught of the ship, so that there is always enough water under her bottom. The ship is steered along the route by her compass on courses obtained from the chart, and her progress along the route depends, naturally, on her speed.

Within sight of land the progress of the ship can be found by *fixing* her position by compass bearings of headlands, points and conspicuous buildings, and checked by *soundings*, i.e. comparing the depth of water obtained by the *lead* or echo sounding machine with that shown on the chart. Salient points are marked by *landmarks* such as lighthouses and beacons; shoals are marked by *seamarks* such as light-vessels and buoys. Lighthouses, light-vessels and some of the buoys are lit; and by using different colours and codes of flashes, these lights can be identified at night.

Within certain distances of the land and when in coastal waters in poor visibility, i.e. when no land is visible, a ship's position can be established by radio fixing aids such as radar, Decca, Loran and D/F.

When out of sight of land a ship's position can be ascertained by astronomical observations and calculations, using the sun, moon, planets and stars so that a safe landfall can be made.

This chapter will describe charts, buoyage, lights and hand sounding, which are a preliminary to the study of navigation in coastal waters described in Volume II. Full information on coastal navigation and radio fixing aids is given in B.R.45(1), *Admiralty Manual of Navigation*, Vol. I, and on astronomic navigation in B.R.45(2), *Admiralty Manual of Navigation*, Vol. II.

CHARTS

The level of the sea is constantly changing owing to the rise and fall of the tide, and this has to be taken into account when drawing a map or a chart. The heights marked on a map are heights above *mean sea level*, which is the average level of the surface of the sea calculated from observations taken over a long period of time. The depths shown on a chart are related to an arbitrary level of the sea called the *chart datum*, which is a low-water level below which the tide will seldom fall in the area covered by the chart. The depths indicated on a chart are therefore almost the minimum depths experienced, and the height of the tide must be added to them to obtain the estimated depth at any particular time. The actual depth obtained by sounding will therefore be greater than the charted depth by an amount equivalent to the height of the tide at the time (fig. 17-1).

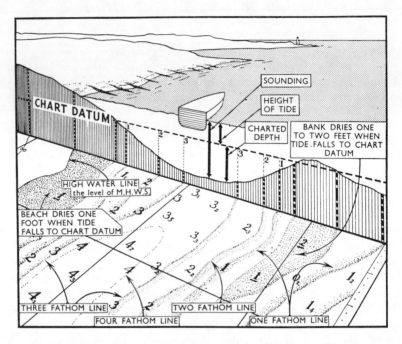

FIG. 17-1. Relation between charted depth and soundings

The depths shown on a chart are usually in fathoms, but where a depth is under eleven fathoms it is indicated in fathoms and feet; 8_5 on the chart would therefore represent a depth of 8 fathoms and 5 feet.

The height of a beach, bank, rock or other feature which is periodically covered and uncovered by the rise and fall of the tide is given in feet above the chart datum, the figure being underlined, e.g. 3, to distinguish it from a depth. For isolated reefs or rocks this height may be written *Dries three feet*, to distinguish it from a rock which is always covered.

The heights of all those features which are always uncovered, or only covered by exceptional tides, are given in relation to a level known as *mean high water springs* (M.H.W.S.), which is the mean level of the spring tides at that locality. The heights of these features are therefore indicated when nearly at their minimum.

The nature of the bottom is indicated on most charts by the initial letter, or a contraction, of the term describing its consistency; thus *Ck* is chalk, *Co* is coral, *Cy* is clay, *G* is gravel, *Gd* is ground, *M* is mud, *R* is rock, *S* is sand, *Sh* is shells, *Sn* is shingle and *St* is stones. Such knowledge of the nature of the bottom is required when anchoring a vessel.

There are various conventional markings and signs on a chart to indicate the different features of the shores and coasts which are of value and interest

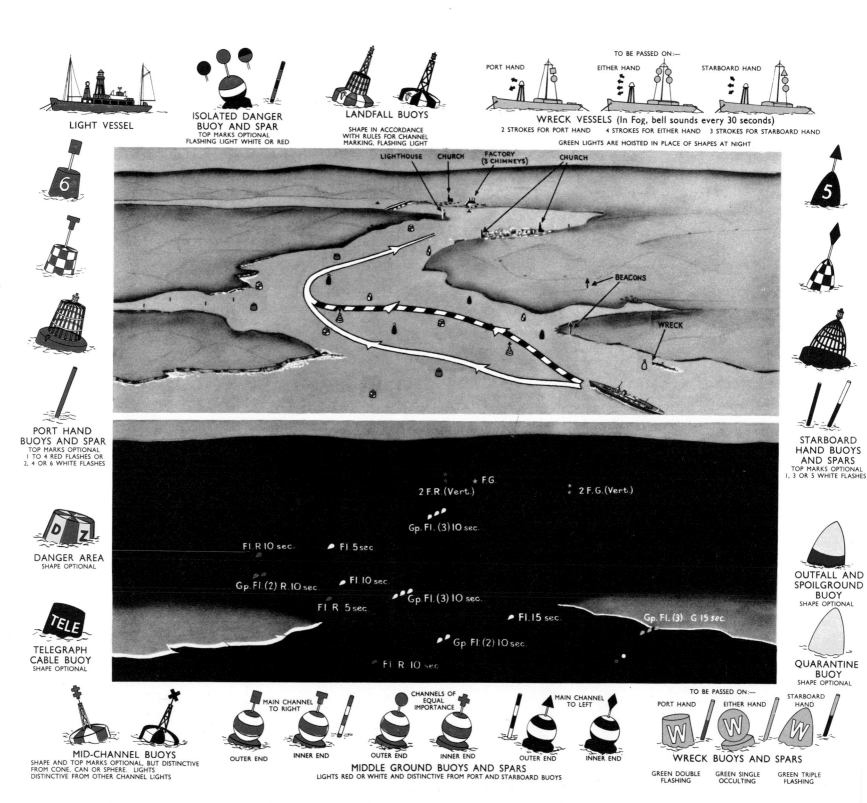

LIGHT VESSEL

ISOLATED DANGER BUOY AND SPAR
TOP MARKS OPTIONAL
FLASHING LIGHT WHITE OR RED

LANDFALL BUOYS
SHAPE IN ACCORDANCE
WITH RULES FOR CHANNEL
MARKING, FLASHING LIGHT

TO BE PASSED ON:—

PORT HAND   EITHER HAND   STARBOARD HAND

WRECK VESSELS (In Fog, bell sounds every 30 seconds)
2 STROKES FOR PORT HAND   4 STROKES FOR EITHER HAND   3 STROKES FOR STARBOARD HAND
GREEN LIGHTS ARE HOISTED IN PLACE OF SHAPES AT NIGHT

LIGHTHOUSE   CHURCH   FACTORY (3 CHIMNEYS)   CHURCH

BEACONS

WRECK

PORT HAND BUOYS AND SPAR
TOP MARKS OPTIONAL
1 TO 4 RED FLASHES OR
2, 4 OR 6 WHITE FLASHES

STARBOARD HAND BUOYS AND SPARS
TOP MARKS OPTIONAL
1, 3 OR 5 WHITE FLASHES

F.G.
2 F.R. (Vert.)   2 F.G. (Vert.)

Gp. Fl. (3) 10 sec.

Fl. R 10 sec.   Fl. 5 sec

DANGER AREA
SHAPE OPTIONAL

Gp. Fl. (2) R. 10 sec.   Fl. 10 sec.

Gp. Fl. (3) 10 sec.

Fl. R 5 sec.

Fl. 15 sec.   Gp. Fl. (3) G 15 sec.

OUTFALL AND SPOILGROUND BUOY
SHAPE OPTIONAL

Gp. Fl. (2) 10 sec.

TELEGRAPH CABLE BUOY
SHAPE OPTIONAL

Fl. R 10 sec.

QUARANTINE BUOY
SHAPE OPTIONAL

MID-CHANNEL BUOYS
SHAPE AND TOP MARKS OPTIONAL, BUT DISTINCTIVE
FROM CONE, CAN OR SPHERE. LIGHTS
DISTINCTIVE FROM OTHER CHANNEL LIGHTS

MAIN CHANNEL TO RIGHT

CHANNELS OF EQUAL IMPORTANCE

MAIN CHANNEL TO LEFT

OUTER END   INNER END   OUTER END   INNER END   OUTER END   INNER END

MIDDLE GROUND BUOYS AND SPARS
LIGHTS RED OR WHITE AND DISTINCTIVE FROM PORT AND STARBOARD BUOYS

TO BE PASSED ON:—

PORT HAND   EITHER HAND   STARBOARD HAND

WRECK BUOYS AND SPARS
GREEN DOUBLE FLASHING   GREEN SINGLE OCCULTING   GREEN TRIPLE FLASHING

Fig. 17.3   **Types of Buoys and Buoyage of Port Liberty**

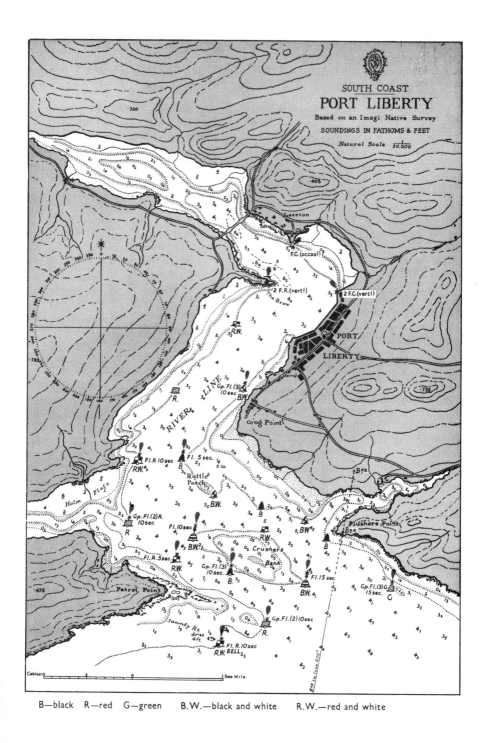

B—black R—red G—green   B.W.—black and white   R.W.—red and white

Fig. 17.2 **Chart of Port Liberty**

C.B.H. 0438 - Dd. 506021 - 50,000 - 8/72

to the seaman. The more common of these, together with the symbols used for buoys, beacons and other aids to navigation, are illustrated in Volume II.

BUOYAGE

Buoys are floating structures moored to the bottom, and are used to mark shoals, banks, rocks, wrecks or other dangers to navigation; they are also used to mark the edges of channels and fairways. The shape and colour of a buoy, also its *top-mark* when fitted, indicate its purpose, and they are made as distinctive as possible so that they can be easily recognised from a distance.

A buoy may be provided with a light to indicate its position in darkness, or with a bell or whistle to indicate its position in low visibility. Such a buoy is usually larger than an unlighted buoy and has a cage-work structure built up on the body of the buoy. Some buoys may also carry a radar reflector.

A buoy should not be used as a mark by which to fix the ship's position when other more reliable marks are available, because it is liable to drag from its position in bad weather and may be moved at short notice by the harbour authorities.

The types of buoys and marks used off the coasts of the British Isles are illustrated in fig. 17–2, which shows the entrance to an imaginary port ('Port Liberty') as viewed from seaward, and illustrates the method of buoyage. Opposite this illustration is a chart of the same port (fig. 17–3), and if this is compared with fig. 17–2 little difficulty should be experienced in understanding the system. The buoyage illustrated conforms with the *lateral system* and it may be encountered in all parts of the world; but many other systems of buoyage are used by foreign countries.

Starboard- and port-hand buoys

These define the respective sides of a channel or fairway, and they are also used to mark a rock or a shoal which may be passed only on one side.

The starboard hand of a channel or fairway is that side which is on your right hand when going with the main flood stream or when approaching a harbour, river or estuary from seaward; the port hand is that side which is then on your left hand. (The direction of the main flood stream around the British Isles is shown in fig. 17–4.) A ship should therefore leave a starboard-hand buoy on her starboard hand when entering a port or proceeding up a channel, and should leave it on her port hand when leaving the port or proceeding down a channel.

To differentiate a sequence or group of starboard- and port-hand buoys they may be lettered or numbered consecutively from seaward; when numbered, odd numbers only are used for starboard-hand buoys, and even numbers only for port-hand buoys.

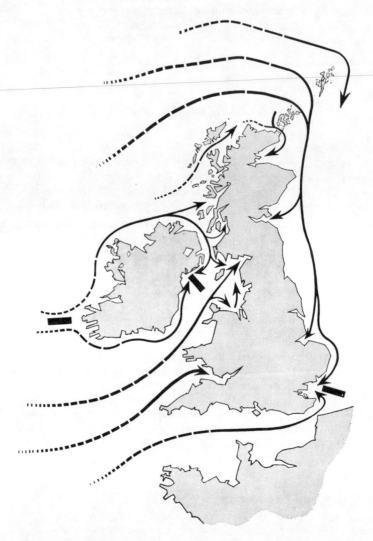

FIG. 17–4. Direction of the main flood stream round the British Isles

Middle-ground buoys

These mark the outer and inner ends of a shoal or other obstruction which lies in a channel and can be passed in safety on either side. Where the main traffic route passes on one side of the shoal and the secondary traffic route on the other, this fact is indicated by the top-mark of the buoy. Middle-ground buoys may also mark the junction of two or more channels.

Mid-channel buoys

These may be used to indicate the middle of a main deepwater channel or fairway, and, in conformity with the rule that a vessel should always keep to the right-hand side of a channel where it is used for two-way traffic, they should always be left on the port hand of a vessel whether she is going up or down channel.

Other buoys

Other buoys or marks used in coastal waters and harbours are described briefly below.

Quarantine. These mark the anchorage for shipping awaiting 'pratique' (i.e. permission from the port authorities for a ship to proceed to her allotted berth up-harbour).

Outfall and spoil ground. These mark the position where a sewage or other pipe discharges into the sea, and the discharging ground for dredgers and sullage lighters.

Telegraph cable. These mark the position of telegraph and other submarine cables in the vicinity of which anchoring is prohibited.

Danger area buoys. These mark areas allocated to naval and military authorities for purposes such as practice firing or bombing.

Danbuoys. At sea these may mark the limits of fishing grounds where submerged nets may be encountered, and also the limits of minesweeping areas.

Mooring. These are of many sizes and usually cylindrical in shape and may be found in any harbour or anchorage.

Landmarks and leading marks

Beacons and other conspicuous landmarks such as lighthouses, factory chimneys and church spires may provide marks for leading ships up a channel clear of navigational dangers, and are then termed *leading marks*.

Stakes close inshore may mark the limits of inshore fishing grounds, where submerged nets may be encountered.

Stakes, large branches of trees, or spars may mark the sides of the channel in small rivers.

Wreck-marking vessels and buoys

Wrecks which constitute a danger to shipping in the vicinity of channels or fairways may be marked by wreck-marking vessels or by wreck buoys. The side on which the wreck-marking vessel may be passed is indicated by shapes or lights hoisted at her yard-arm; the shape of the wreck buoy (either can, conical or spherical) indicates on which hand it should be left.

Landfall marks

Landfall marks such as light-ships or buoys with tall superstructures may be used to indicate the seaward approach to a harbour, river or estuary. Many such marks display their names painted conspicuously in white letters.

Light-ships

A light-ship is used instead of a light-buoy where it is necessary for the mark or light to be seen from a greater distance; unlike the light-buoy, its light is *watched* by the crew and is therefore more reliable. Light-ships are usually painted red or black, with their name painted in white letters on the hull, and they usually carry a *daymark* and their light on a mast or similar structure.

LIGHTS

A navigational mark such as a lighthouse, light-ship or buoy which exhibits a light during the hours of darkness is marked on a chart by a small purple splash of colour over the star or dot indicating its position.

The colour of a light may be white, red, green, blue, orange or violet, and it may show all round the horizon as one colour or may be split into sectors of different colours; also, the light may show over certain areas only, in which case a sector of some particular colour may indicate a fairway or an area of danger.

Characteristics

The nature of the beam exhibited by a light is known as its *characteristic*, of which there are four main types, namely: fixed, flashing, occulting and alternating. The letters in brackets are the abbreviations printed on charts.

Fixed (F.). A continuous steady light.

Flashing (Fl.). A light showing a single flash at regular intervals, the duration of light being always less than that of darkness.

Occulting (Occ.). A steady light with, at regular intervals, a sudden and total eclipse; the duration of darkness being always less than, or equal to, that of light.

Alternating (Alt.). A light which alternates the colour of its flashes.

Other lights may be a combination of two of the main types or a modification of a type:

Fixed and flashing (F.Fl.). A fixed light varied at regular intervals by a single flash of a relatively greater brilliance.

Group flashing (Gp.Fl.). A light showing, at regular intervals, a group of two or more flashes; both the flashes and the eclipses may be of unequal duration.

Group occulting (Gp.Occ.). A steady light with, at regular intervals, a group of two or more sudden eclipses. Both the periods of light and the eclipses may be of unequal duration, but the total duration of darkness is always less than, or equal to, that of light.

Fixed and group flashing (F.Gp.Fl.). A fixed light varied, at regular intervals, by a group of two or more flashes of relatively greater brilliance.

Quick flashing (Qk.Fl.). A light which flashes continuously at a rate of more than 60 times a minute.

Interrupted quick flashing (Int.Qk.Fl.). A light which flashes at a rate of more than 60 times a minute with, at regular intervals, a total eclipse.

Group interrupted quick flashing (Gp.Int.Qk.Fl.). A light which shows groups of quick flashes, as defined above, separated by relatively longer periods of total eclipse.

CHARACTER	ABBREVIATION	ILLUSTRATION
FIXED	F.W.	
OCCULTING	OCC.W.	
	OCC.W.	
FLASHING	FL.W.	
QUICK FLASHING	QK. FL.W.	
INTERRUPTED QUICK FLASHING	INT. QK. FL.W.	
GROUP INTERRUPTED QUICK FLASHING	GP. INT. QK. FL.(2)W.	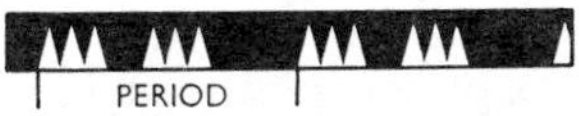
ALTERNATING	ALT. R. W. G.	
GROUP OCCULTING	GP. OCC.(2) W.	
	GP. OCC. (3 ÷ 4)W.	
GROUP FLASHING	GP. FL.(3)W.	
	GP. FL.(3÷2) W.	
	GP. FL.(AR.) W.	
FIXED AND FLASHING	F. FL.W.	
FIXED AND GROUP FLASHING	F. GP. FL.(2) W.	

FIG. 17-5. Diagrammatic examples of light characteristics

When the colour of a light is not given in the abbreviation on a chart, the light is white. Fig. 17–5, which is extracted from the *Admiralty List of Lights*, includes white as a colour in the abbreviations.

Period

The time shown on a chart or in the *Admiralty List of Lights* against the characteristic of a flashing light indicates the interval between the beginning of one flash and the beginning of the succeeding flash; for occulting, alternating, group flashing or group occulting lights the time shown indicates the interval of time occupied by one complete cycle. This interval is known as the *period* of the light.

Chart indications for lights

The distance at which a light can be seen in clear weather by an observer 15 ft above sea level is shown against most lights (but not against those of buoys), the visibility distance of the light depending upon its brilliance and its height above sea level. Most coastal lights in the British Isles and elsewhere are exhibited from sunset to sunrise, but a light marked **U** indicates that it is *unwatched* and that implicit reliance must therefore not be placed upon it. Buoys are, of course, always unwatched lights, although the symbol **U** is not marked against them on the charts.

Admiralty publications on lights

Details of all lights *except those of buoys and wreck-marking vessels* are contained in the *Admiralty List of Lights*, which is published annually in 12 volumes, each volume covering a certain area of the world. Full instructions for interpreting these lists are contained in the foreword to each volume. Details of light-buoys are given in the appropriate volume of the *Sailing Directions* and on the largest-scale chart of each area.

SOUNDING

A measurement of the depth of water is called a *sounding*. It is measured in feet or fathoms, or in a combination of both. A fathom measures 6 ft. Soundings are taken by a *lead and line*, as described in this chapter, or by echo sounding, as described in Volume II.

The simplest method of taking a sounding in shallow water is with a pole, and for this reason barge poles, the bearing-off spars of craft working in shallow waters and the boat-hook staves of ship's boats should be marked off in feet.

Boat's lead and line (fig. 17–6)

In less shallow water harbour craft and boats use a boat's lead and line for sounding. It consists of a weighted line marked at intervals along its length. The weight or *lead* is of leg-of-mutton shape and weighs 7 lb, and the *line* consists of 14 fathoms of 2½-lb line.

The first three fathoms of the line are marked respectively with 1, 2 and 3 strips of leather, and each of these fathoms is marked in feet by 1, 2, 3, 4 and 5 knots. Thereafter, up to 13 fathoms, the line is marked in the same way as a hand lead and line, which is described below.

When soundings are taken due allowance must be made for the speed of the boat through the water. This is done by heaving the lead ahead of the boat and reading off the sounding when the line is vertically up and down with the lead on the bottom; it must also be done when the boat is stationary but stemming a tidal stream.

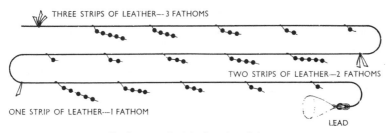

THREE STRIPS OF LEATHER—3 FATHOMS

TWO STRIPS OF LEATHER—2 FATHOMS

ONE STRIP OF LEATHER—1 FATHOM

LEAD

The feet in each of the first three fathoms
are marked by 1, 2, 3, 4 or 5 knots.

FIG. 17–6. Boat's lead and line

Hand lead and line (fig. 17–7)

This is used in ships not fitted with echo sounding for sounding to a depth of 20 fathoms, and at speeds not exceeding 10 knots; sounding is usually carried out by this method when entering or leaving harbours. The lead consists of a tapered bar of lead, weighing from 10 to 14 lb, to which is bent a 25-fathom length of $1\frac{1}{8}$-in. special lead line. The base of the lead is hollowed out to receive tallow, and the head is shaped into an eye through which is rove a hide becket. Placing tallow in the base of a lead is called *arming* it, and its purpose is to pick up a sample of the sea bed for examination if required.

The lead line has a long eye splice at one end and a back splice at the other. It is bent to the lead by reeving the eye splice through the hide becket and passing the lead through the eye.

Markings. The hand lead line is marked as follows:

2 fathoms	*two* strips of *leather*
3 fathoms	*three* strips of *leather*
5 fathoms	a piece of *white duck*
7 fathoms	a piece of *red bunting*
10 fathoms	a piece of *leather* with a *hole* in it
13 fathoms	a piece of *blue serge*
15 fathoms	a piece of *white duck*
17 fathoms	a piece of *red bunting*
20 fathoms	*two knots*

The three different materials, serge, duck and bunting, are used so that the markings can be distinguished from one another in the dark by the feel of their texture, either with the fingers or the lips.

When using a longer line than 25 fathoms successive tens of fathoms after 20 are marked by an additional knot, and every intervening 5 fathoms is marked by a single knot.

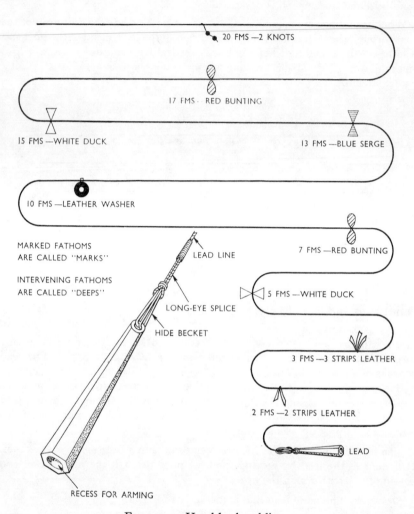

20 FMS —2 KNOTS

17 FMS · RED BUNTING

15 FMS —WHITE DUCK

13 FMS —BLUE SERGE

10 FMS —LEATHER WASHER

MARKED FATHOMS
ARE CALLED "MARKS"

INTERVENING FATHOMS
ARE CALLED "DEEPS"

LEAD LINE

7 FMS —RED BUNTING

LONG-EYE SPLICE

5 FMS —WHITE DUCK

HIDE BECKET

3 FMS —3 STRIPS LEATHER

2 FMS —2 STRIPS LEATHER

LEAD

RECESS FOR ARMING

FIG. 17-7. Hand lead and line

Marking the line

Before fitting a new lead line it should be stretched thoroughly by towing it astern, and it should then be accurately measured off and marked while wet. If it were marked when dry, it would be inaccurate in use because the line shortens when wet. The markings are measured from the end of the eye splice (thus giving a sounding 'the benefit of the lead') against previously marked-off lengths on the deck. Knots are made in mackerel line which, as with the material for the other marks, is tucked securely around two of the strands of the lead line.

Calling the soundings

The correct sounding is shown where the water level cuts the line when the line is up-and-down with the lead on the bottom, and the leadsman calls the sounding in accordance with the following practice:

Marks. All the fathom soundings which are marked, i.e. 2, 3, 5, 7, 10, 13, 15, 17, 20 fathoms (and 25, 30, 35, 40 fathoms, etc., when using a long line), are called *marks.*

Deeps. All the intervening fathoms, which are not marked, i.e. 4, 6, 8, 9, 11, 12, 14, 16, 18, 19, etc., are called *deeps.*

The leadsman therefore calls, for example, 'By the mark seven', and 'Deep nine'.

To assist in gauging the deeps they are sometimes indicated by a length of mackerel line tucked between the strands of the lead line. Fractions of fathoms are measured by the quarter and the half, i.e. 1 ft 6 in. and 3 ft respectively; and because of the possibility of confusion between the call of 'a quarter' and 'three-quarters' the latter is not used, but is called as a 'quarter less' the next highest mark or deep. Examples of the calls for fractions are:

'And a quarter six' for $6\frac{1}{4}$ fathoms
'And a half six' for $6\frac{1}{2}$ fathoms
'A quarter less seven' for $6\frac{3}{4}$ fathoms.

No bottom. If the lead does not reach the bottom, the leadsman calls 'no bottom at . . . fathoms'.

Heaving the lead

A leadsman sounds from the *chains.* In the days of sail he stood on the chainwale, which was a broad, thick plank projecting horizontally from the ship's side abreast a mast and over which the chain ends of the shrouds passed to give wider support for the mast. When masts were no longer stayed, hinged platforms were provided for the leadsmen.

Nowadays, in ships with echo sounding, the lead is seldom used except to provide the bridge with information of the movement of the ship over the bottom at the time of anchoring and weighing, and for sounding alongside or around a ship at anchor to ensure that there is enough water. Chains are no longer fitted and the lead cannot be hove. If a leadsman is required, he sounds from abreast the bridge.

Questions on this chapter will be found in Appendix 2.

CHAPTER 18

Elements of the Rule of the Road
(for Coxswains of Boats)

Ships sailing on the high seas have to abide by certain rules, otherwise there would be many collisions. These rules have been compiled by the leading maritime nations of the world and are called *The International Regulations for Preventing Collisions at Sea* or the 'Rule of the Road'. They provide for almost all occasions of two vessels approaching one another where risk of collision exists. They tell the seaman (in a section called 'The Steering and Sailing Rules') which vessel must give way, and describe the conditions under which he may expect the other vessel to keep clear of him.

They prescribe the means whereby vessels which are fully manœuvrable (i.e. normal power-driven or sailing ships) may be identified by night or in low visibility; also the means whereby vessels with no power (or limited power) or with limited manœuvrability (e.g. a ship towing another ship) may be distinguished by day or by night or in low visibility from those which are fully manœuvrable. By these means (i.e. the display of lights and shapes and the making of sound signals) the seaman may know instantly whether to expect another vessel to obey the Steering and Sailing Rules or whether she is unable to do so. They also include sound signals to be made by vessels in various circumstances, signals to be made by vessels in distress to attract attention or summon assistance, and precautions to be taken by all vessels.

This chapter will give the seaman the elements of the Rule of the Road, particularly the 'Steering and Sailing Rules', so that he may be able to handle a power-driven or sailing boat with safety.

The full regulations are given in B.R.45(1), *Admiralty Manual of Navigation*, Volume I, and in B.R.67(2), *Admiralty Manual of Seamanship*, Volume II.

Definitions

1. The word *vessel* includes every description of water craft (other than a seaplane on the water) used, or capable of being used, as a means of transportation on water.
2. The term *power-driven vessel* means any vessel propelled by machinery.
3. The term *sailing vessel* means any vessel which is propelled only by means of the wind and her sails. If a vessel is propelled by machinery and sails she is to be considered as a power-driven vessel.
4. The word *visible*, when applied to lights, means visible on a dark night with a clear atmosphere.
5. The term *short blast* means a blast of about one second's duration.
6. The term *prolonged blast* means a blast of from four to six seconds' duration.
7. The word *whistle* means whistle or siren.

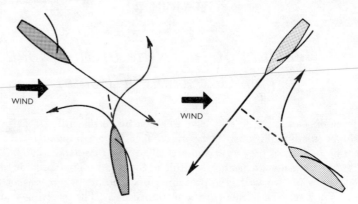

A vessel with the wind on the port side gives way
to a vessel with the wind on the starboard side.

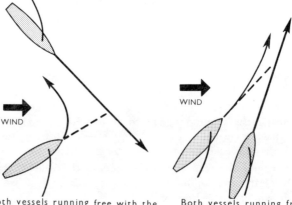

Both vessels running free with the
wind on opposite sides, the vessel
with the wind on her port side
gives way.

Both vessels running free with the
wind on the same side, the windward
vessel keeps out of the way of the
leeward vessel.

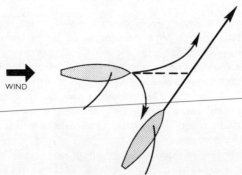

Two vessels with the wind on the same side,
the vessel to windward gives way.

FIG. 18–1. Examples of the sailing rules

8. A vessel is *under way* when she is not at anchor, or made fast to the shore, or aground. Thus a vessel may be described as 'under way, but stopped', or 'under way and making way'. All vessels under way are bound to obey the Steering and Sailing Rules unless they are *not under command*, i.e. unless they are unable to manœuvre for any reason.

Risk of collision

When two vessels appear to be on converging courses the possibility of collision depends upon their relative courses and speeds. The only certain way of determining whether risk of collision exists is to take a compass bearing of the other vessel. If the bearing does not alter, or alters only slightly, then risk of collision exists. If the bearing *draws forward* then the other vessel should pass ahead; if the bearing *draws aft* she should pass astern. If a compass is not available the relative bearing of the other vessel gives an indication of the risk of collision provided that your own vessel remains on a steady course.

RULES FOR SAILING VESSELS

These rules are related to the direction of the wind. Rule 17 of the 1960 International Regulations states:

(*a*) 'When two sailing vessels are approaching one another, so as to involve risk of collision, one of them shall keep out of the way of the other as follows:

(i) When each has the wind on a different side, the vessel which has the wind on the port side shall keep out of the way of the other.

(ii) When both have the wind on the same side, the vessel which is to windward shall keep out of the way of the vessel which is to leeward.

(*b*) For the purposes of this Rule the windward side shall be deemed to be the side opposite to that on which the mainsail is carried or, in the case of a square-rigged vessel, the side opposite to that on which the largest fore-and-aft sail is carried.'

Sailing vessels' lights (fig. 18–2)

When under way a sailing vessel shows a green light on her starboard side and a red light on her port side from right ahead to 2 points abaft the beam. She also carries a white light at the stern which shows from 2 points abaft the beam on one side, through the stern, to 2 points abaft the beam on the other side. (This is called the *overtaking light* because it indicates to another vessel that she is an overtaking vessel when this light can be seen.)

Sailing vessels' sound signals

In low visibility, day or night, sailing vessels under way make the following signals on the foghorn at intervals of not more than one minute:

one blast: vessel on the starboard tack
two blasts: vessel on the port tack
three blasts: vessel running with the wind abaft the beam.

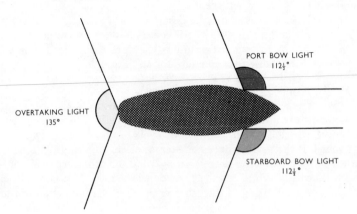

FIG. 18–2. A sailing vessel's lights

STEERING RULES

The rules for a power-driven vessel meeting another power-driven vessel depend upon the relative bearing of one ship from the other. The main principles upon which these rules are based are as follows:

1. When two vessels approach end-on, or nearly end-on, to one another, each must give way to the other by altering course to starboard.
2. In all circumstances where risk of collision exists one vessel holds her course and speed while the other gives way.
3. The vessel which is directed to give way does so by altering course, or reducing speed, or stopping, or going astern.
4. The vessel which is directed to give way should avoid crossing close ahead of the other vessel.
5. In a broad sense vessels keep to the right.
6. Every vessel, whether power-driven or sailing, overtaking any other shall keep out of the way of the overtaken vessel.
7. Vessels should always keep a proper lookout, exhibit the prescribed daymarks and lights, make the prescribed sound signals and be handled in a seamanlike manner with due caution and consideration for others, especially in conditions of low visibility.
8. If a collision appears probable each vessel must take whatever action is possible to avert it, even if such action involves a departure from the normal rules.

A power-driven vessel's lights (fig. 18–3)

When under way a power-driven vessel shows the bow lights and overtaking light in the same way as a sailing vessel. She also shows one or two white steaming lights (usually from her masts) according to her length, so that she may be identified as a power-driven vessel. Each steaming light shows over the combined arcs of the two bow lights. When there are two steaming lights the after light is the higher.

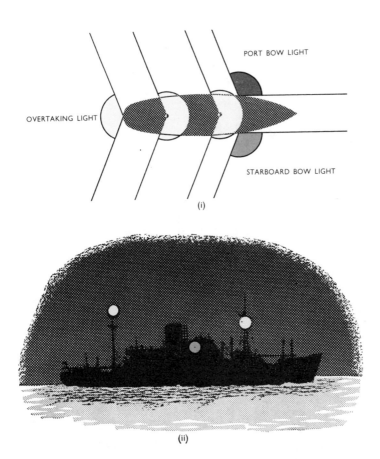

FIG. 18-3. A power-driven vessel's lights—(i) seen from above;
(ii) seen from her starboard beam (overtaking light not visible)

A power-driven vessel's sound signals

In sight. When vessels are in sight of one another, a power-driven vessel
under way and taking action to comply with the Steering Rules makes the
following signals:

> One short blast: 'I am altering my course to starboard'
> Two short blasts: 'I am altering my course to port'
> Three short blasts: 'My engines are going astern'

In fog, mist, etc. A power-driven vessel in fog, mist, falling snow, heavy
rainstorms or any other condition similarly restricting visibility, whether by
day or night, makes the following signals at intervals of not more than two
minutes:

> Making way through the water: one prolonged blast
> Under way but stopped: two prolonged blasts.

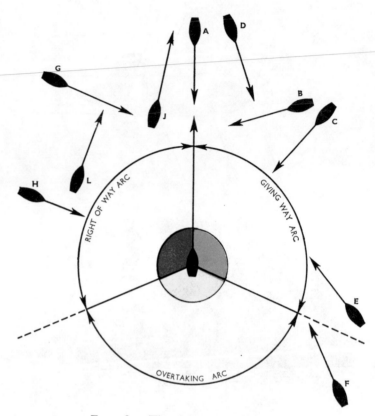

FIG. 18–4. The giving-way problem

The giving-way vessel

Divide the circle of your horizon into three arcs representing the arcs of visibility of the two bow lights and the overtaking light (fig. 18–4). Let us consider the case of each power-driven vessel in turn.

Ship A. Since A is approaching head-on (both bow lights and steaming light(s) visible at night) both ships take avoiding action by altering course to starboard.

Ship B. If B remains on a steady bearing (red light and steaming light(s) visible at night), own ship must give way by altering course to starboard and/or reducing speed, stopping or going astern.

Ship C. Provided that C maintains her present course and speed there is no risk of collision.

Ship D. On her present course (green light and steaming light(s) visible at night) ship D cannot collide with you and no action is required.

Ship E. If E remains on a steady bearing there is risk of collision. You can see her red light and steaming light(s) at night and she can see your green light and steaming light(s); therefore you must take avoiding action.

Ship F. This ship is an overtaking vessel (power-driven or sail), because she can see only your overtaking light; therefore she must keep clear of you. If this ship gains bearing, i.e. if she moves into the giving-way arc so that she can see your green light and steaming light(s), she is still an overtaking ship and must keep clear of you until she is finally past and clear ahead.

Ship G. This ship is on a collision course. You can see her green light and steaming light(s) and she can see your red light and steaming light(s); therefore she must take avoiding action and you must maintain your present course and speed.

Ship H. Provided that H maintains her present course and speed there is no risk of collision.

Ship J. If there is risk of collision by coming up on J at greater speed it is your duty to keep clear because you are an overtaking vessel and, at night, you would see only her overtaking light. Even though you may later see her green light and steaming light(s), you are still the overtaking vessel and must keep clear.

Ship L. This is the only situation in which there may be some doubt as to which ship has right of way. You are in a position that may be considered within the giving-way arc or the overtaking arc of ship L. At night you can determine your relative position because you can see either her bow and steaming light(s) or her overtaking light. By day it is not easy to judge your relative bearing from her. If there is any doubt at all it is prudent to assume that you are an overtaking vessel and to make an early and bold alteration of course.

Power-driven vessels' conduct

When obeying the Steering and Sailing Rules, the following points should be borne in mind.

1. If yours is the giving-way vessel, always give the other vessel as wide a berth as circumstances allow. It is bad seamanship and bad manners to pass close aboard another vessel.
2. If yours is the giving-way vessel your avoiding action should be made in such a manner as to leave no doubt of your intentions in the mind of the person in charge of the other vessel. You should therefore:
   - (*a*) take avoiding action in plenty of time;
   - (*b*) make a sufficiently large initial alteration of course for your intentions to be made clear;
   - (*c*) steady on your new course without undue yawing;
   - (*d*) make the appropriate sound signal.
3. When another vessel is approaching, steer as steady a course as possible and make allowances for the other vessel yawing. A vessel approaching nearly end-on, on an opposite course, may appear to be end-on now and again because she is yawing. Under such circumstances she should be treated as approaching end-on, and you should alter your course to starboard early and give her as wide a berth as practicable.
4. In a narrow channel keep to that side of the channel which is on your starboard hand.

POWER-DRIVEN VESSELS AND SAILING VESSELS

Power-driven vessels give way to sailing vessels except when the sailing vessel is overtaking. This obviously does not give the coxswain of a sailing boat the right to obstruct a large power-driven vessel in narrow channels, because the power-driven vessel is restricted in her movement.

Questions on this chapter will be found in Appendix 2.

APPENDIXES

APPENDIX 1

Glossary

Terms and expressions which have been explained in the text of this manual are not included here unless they have other meanings or interpretations. Slang terms, and proper terms with a slang version, are printed in *italics*. References to terms not included in this glossary may be found in the index of this volume, or in the indexes of Volumes II and III.

A.1—first-class, the best. The highest classification at Lloyds of a vessel's seaworthiness. (The letter refers to the hull and the number to the equipment.)

A.B.—able-bodied seaman. It denotes a man who is technically qualified and fit to carry out a seaman's duties, both aloft and on deck.

Adrift—absent, late for muster or an appointment.

AHOY!—the seaman's hail to call attention.

All at sea—confused, at a loss.

ALL STANDING—to bring up any thing or person all standing is to bring it or him to a sudden and unexpected stop.

AMAIN—suddenly.

Andrew Miller, or *the Andrew*—the Royal Navy. Andrew Miller was a zealous press-gang officer who impressed so many men into the King's Naval Service during the Napoleonic wars that he was said to own the Royal Navy.

ARISINGS—pieces of material or metal left over from a job which are of value. They are collected and may be sold, melted or made up again.

A'S AND A'S—alterations and additions to the structure, rigging and equipment of a warship.

ATHWART—across, as in 'athwart the hawse', 'athwart the tide'.

AWASH—level with the surface of the sea.

BAGGYWRINKLE—the service on standing or running rigging to prevent chafing where one rope crosses another. (See 'bolster' and 'scotchman'.)

BAR—a shoal or spit formed by the action of the tides at the mouth of a river or harbour.

Bare navy—members of a mess are said to live on 'bare navy' when they feed solely on Service rations.

BARE POLES—a sailing vessel is said to be under bare poles when she is underway and has no sails set.

BARGE—a cargo-carrying coastal sailing vessel. In the Royal Navy, the boat of a Flag Officer.

Barrack stanchion—a man who has served for a long period in a Naval barracks or shore establishment.

BARRATRY—fraudulent claim for compensation, as when a ship is deliberately wrecked or scuttled (which see) to obtain her insurance money.

BATTEN DOWN—to close all openings in the weather decks or superstructure of a ship, or to close all openings in one of her compartments.

Beach, on the beach—retired from sea service. (See *swallow the anchor*.)

BEAM ENDS—a ship is said to be on her beam ends when she is lying over on her side, with her beams and decks perpendicular. The expression is used colloquially to describe a precarious position.

BEAR A HAND—an order to hasten, or to do something smartly, quickly.

BELAY—colloquially, to countermand an order. (See *wash out*.)

BELOW THERE!—a hail from a man aloft to anyone below him.

BERTH—the allotted place or position for a ship or a man. 'To give a wide berth' is to keep well clear of anything. 'To shift berth' is to change position.

BETWEEN-DECKS—a general term applied to the space or the decks between the upper deck and the lowest deck of a ship.

Bilge—rubbish, nonsense.

BILL—a certificate or a written agreement, such as a 'Bill of Health', 'Bill of Lading', a 'Bill of Exchange'.

BITTER END—the inboard length of a ship's cable. (The cables of ships at anchor used to be belayed to specially fitted centre-line bollards called 'bitts'.)

BLEED—to drain a buoy of water. To *bleed the monkey*—to extract the contents of a rum barricoe by boring a small hole in it.

BLOCK-AND-BLOCK, TWO-BLOCKS—these terms describe the state of a tackle when its standing and moving blocks are hauled close together. Colloquially they are used to describe the position of two objects which are close together. (See 'chock-a-block'.)

BLOW THE GAFF—to divulge information you have learnt confidentially, to give away a secret. Its origin probably lies in a ship revealing her identity by hoisting her colours at the peak of her gaff.

BLUE-JACKET—a seaman of the Royal Navy (from the short blue jacket he used to wear).

BLUFF—a headland with a broad, perpendicular face. Hence, 'bluff-bowed'—a ship with broad, perpendicular bows.

BOARD (1)—the old name for the side of a ship, from which the following terms also are derived: 'to go aboard'—to enter a ship; 'to board'—to enter a ship by force or authority; 'boarders' or 'boarding party'—a body of men detailed to board a ship; 'inboard'—between the sides of the ship; 'outboard'—outside the ship; 'on board'—anywhere in the ship; 'to go by the board'—to fall over the ship's side; 'board and board'—alongside, side by side and touching; 'close aboard'—close to the ship's side; 'starboard'—the side on which the steering oar or 'steer-board' was formerly shipped (the right-hand side when in the ship or boat and facing forward);

'larboard'—the opposite side to starboard, over or through which the cargo was embarked or disembarked (originally spelt 'ladeboard').

(2)—the distance made good by a sailing vessel between two successive tacks when beating to windward.

BOBSTAY—properly the stay leading down from the nose of a sailing vessel's bowsprit to her stem near the waterline, but also applied to any stay used in a similar fashion. (See 'martingale'.)

BOLSTER—a pad or cushion of canvas or leather used to prevent chafe between ropes, or a piece of wood or metal used to give a fair lead to, or prevent a bad nip in, a rope. (See 'scotchman' and 'baggywrinkle'.)

Bone—to scrounge, pilfer or steal. (Derived from a boatswain of that name who served in the flagship of Admiral Cornwallis and was notorious for acquiring ship's stores from other ships to make good deficits or provide a surplus in his own ship. When the boatswain was leaving the ship the Admiral is said to have remarked, 'I trust, Mr. Bone, you will leave me my bower anchors'.)

BONNET—any small cover or hood, of canvas or metal, used to cover or protect a small fitting or opening.

BOOMKIN, BUMPKIN—a small boom.

BOOT-TOPPING—properly the operation of scraping marine growths from the waterline, but also the name for the painted band, four or more feet wide in a large ship, extending from stem to stern of the ship along her waterline; the paint is usually of a different colour from that of the sides and bottom, and is of a special composition designed to prevent the growth of marine organisms, which otherwise always form between wind and water.

Bottle—a reproof or admonishment (contracted from *a dose from the foretopman's bottle*, which was a cure for all evils).

BOTTOMRY—a system of pledging the hull of a ship as security for a loan.

BOUND (1)—restrained, tied, fettered, as in 'weather-bound', 'wind-bound', 'tide-bound', and 'iron-bound coast', used to describe a rocky and dangerous coast with no shelter.

(2)—ready to go to a destination, or on the way to a destination, as in 'outward bound', 'homeward bound'.

BOWSE—to haul on a rope; 'bowse down'—to tauten a rope or a lashing.

BREAK BULK—to start unloading a full hold.

Break surface—to wake up or come to life (has its origin in a submarine 'breaking surface' after being submerged).

Brick—a gun projectile or shell.

BRIGHT-WORK—polished metal fittings.

BROACH—to break into, or open for the first time, a cask, package or similar receptacle.

BROACH-TO—when applied to a vessel running before the sea, is to slew round inadvertently broadside-on in the trough of a wave.

BROKEN WATER—surf caused by breaking waves.

Bull a cask—to put a small quantity of water into an empty rum cask and leave it there until it becomes grog.

Bullocks—the name formerly given to men of the Royal Marine Artillery because of their magnificent physique. (See *jollies, turkeys, pongos* and *grabbies*.)

BULLROPE—a rope led from the ring of a buoy to the nose of the bowsprit of a sailing vessel, or to the stem head of a clipper-bowed ship, to prevent the buoy from bumping the bows at slack water.

BULLSEYE (1)—a light built into a bulkhead between adjacent compartments so that it illuminates both.

(2)—a thimble made of hard wood and usually inserted in the end of a lizard, or used as a small leading block. (See 'deadeye'.)

BUM-BOAT—a shore boat carrying fresh provisions or small merchandise for sale to ships in a harbour. 'Bum-boatman'—the owner of such a boat, or of her stock in trade.

Bundleman—a married man. (Originates from the days when men could buy ship's provisions for their families, and the married man could then be distinguished when going ashore by the bundle of provisions he carried.)

BUNT—the belly of a sail and the middle of a yard.

Bunts—a signalman (derived from bunting).

BURDEN—the carrying capacity of a merchant vessel. It is expressed either in tons weight or in tons of cubic capacity.

BUTT-END—the largest end of a spar, or any similarly shaped object.

Buzz—rumour. (See *galley-packet*.)

BY-AND-LARGE—under all conditions, generally speaking. (Derived from the sailing terms 'by the wind' meaning close-hauled, and 'sailing large' meaning running or sailing free.) (See 'large'.)

BY THE HEAD—a vessel trimmed more deeply forward than aft.

BY THE STERN—a vessel trimmed more deeply aft than forward.

Cag—to discuss, to argue.

CAMEL—a tank secured to the hull of a ship to provide her with extra buoyancy, used mainly in salvage work.

CANT—to incline from the perpendicular.

CAPFUL OF WIND—a puff of wind on a calm day, but of sufficient strength to fill a vessel's sails. (See 'catspaw'.)

CAPSIZE—to overturn, to turn bottom upwards.

CARRY AWAY—to break away, or to part.

CAST—to pay a vessel's head off on a course, or on a new tack.

CAT, CAT-O'-NINE-TAILS—a former instrument of punishment in the Navy. It was originally made of nine lengths of cord, with three knots at the end of each, spliced to a short length of thick rope to form a handle. *No room to swing a cat* means that there is insufficient space in which to wield a cat-o'-nine-tails.

CATSPAW—a light puff of wind on a calm day, just strong enough to ruffle the surface of the water; usually the forerunner of a sailing breeze.

CAULK—to drive oakum or other similar caulking material into the seams of planking to make them watertight; after caulking the seams are 'paid' by pouring molten pitch into them to preserve the caulking. Also, collo- quially, to lie down and snatch some sleep, which has its origin in the fact that a man who had just taken a *caulk* on a hot deck could be identified by the marks of pitch on his clothing.

Charlie Noble—the funnel of a galley or a stove when sheathed in brass and polished.

CHATHAM CHEST—a fund established by Queen Elizabeth I after the Armada for the care of wounded and infirm seamen. It was supported by contribu- tions from the men, which were kept in a special chest at Chatham. This chest is now in the National Maritime Museum, Greenwich.

Chats—Chatham.

Chippy chap—shipwright.

CHOCK-A-BLOCK—full up (from 'choking' the luff of a block). *Chock-a-block* and *chocker*—slang terms for bored or 'fed up'.

CHOKED—a block is said to be choked if its fall jams in the swallow. 'To choke the luff' is to choke the block of a tackle by leading the bight of the hauling part across the swallow of the block and jamming it between the swallow and the hauling parts, thus preventing the tackle from over- hauling.

CHOPPY SEA—a short, steep and usually confused sea.

CHOPS OF THE CHANNEL—the entrance to the English Channel (derived from 'chap' or 'chop', meaning jaws).

Chummy ships—ships whose respective officers and men are on particularly friendly terms.

CLAP ON—an order to man a fall or a halyard. To attach one tackle to another or to a rope.

CLENCH, CLINCH (1)—to join a rope to a fitting or to another rope by a half hitch with the end seized to its own part. This method was formerly used to join one end of a ship's hempen cable to her anchor, and the other end to the housing of her mainmast. A 'clench', nowadays, is a strong fitting securely attached to a deck or the hull structure, to which the end of a cable or hawser is shackled. A cable or rope is said to be 'out to a clinch' when it has all run out, or been paid out, but its end is secured inboard.
  (2)—to fasten two pieces of wood together by driving nails through both and turning their ends over (as in 'clinker'-, or 'clencher'-, built boats), or to hammer over the end of a bolt to prevent it from withdrawing from its hole (as in a 'clenched shackle').

CLEAN—to dress in the 'rig' (suit of clothing) ordered, or to change from night clothing or working rig into a clean rig.

CLEAR—good visibility, as in 'clear weather', or as in a 'clear sky', meaning that it is cloudless; free from shipping or obstructions, as in 'clear horizon' and 'clear channel'.

CLEAR—to free, the reverse of to foul (which see); to make free (a rope clear for running, to clear a block); to put in order, to tidy (to clear up decks); to pass an obstruction safely (to clear a point of land); to empty (to clear a hold or a lighter); to pay port or Customs dues and complete port formalities (to clear quarantine, or to clear Customs).

COASTER—a vessel which plies between the harbours of a particular coast or adjacent coasts, usually in pilotage waters and seldom out of sight of land.

A'COCK-BILL—an anchor is said to be a'cock-bill when it is hung up-and-down, ready for letting go. Yards are said to be a'cock-bill when they are topped at an angle with the horizontal. (See 'scandalise'.)

COME UP!—an order to slack off rope.

COME UP WITH A VESSEL—to overtake her.

COMPANION LADDER—a ladder or staircase leading from the poop or upper deck of a merchant ship to the saloon or main cabin.

COMPLAIN—a block is said to complain when its sheave squeaks.

Copper-bottomed—well found, reputable. (The bottoms of wooden ships were sheathed with copper to protect them from marine parasites; but, being very expensive, this was done only to ships whose owners were of substance and repute.)

CRAB—a small hand capstan.

CRACK ON—to set more sail, to increase speed.

CRANK—a ship is said to be crank when she heels readily to one side or the other and returns sluggishly to the upright. (See 'tender' and 'stiff'.)

CREEPER—grapnel (which see) used for sweeping or dragging for objects lost overboard. (See 'drag' and 'sweep'.)

CROWFOOT, CROW'S FOOT—three or more lines or small ropes radiating from the end of a whip or pendant, so that its support or pull is spread and divided between them. The lines are kept apart by an 'euphroe' (which see).

CROW'S NEST—a small shelter for the masthead lookout.

Crusher—a member of the ship's police.

CUDDY—the Master's cabin in sailing vessels, and the slang term for the Admiral's or Captain's cabin.

Cut and run—to escape or quit. (Derived from the days when a ship cut her hemp cable and left her anchor on the bottom to enable her to put to sea quickly in emergency; also, in similar circumstances, when she set her sails by cutting their gaskets, so unfurling them at the run.)

CUT-WATER—the stem of a ship. In sailing vessels with bluff bows it was a false stem.

CUT OF HER (or HIS) JIB—the general appearance of a ship or person.

DAVY JONES' LOCKER—bottom of the sea. The origin of the term is obscure, but it may have originated in a pirate of that name who made his prisoners walk the plank.

D.D.—the letters inserted in the ship's ledger against the name of a deceased officer or man to denote the closing of his account and signifying that he has been 'discharged dead'.

DEADEYE—a block of hardwood with one or more holes drilled in it to take a rope or ropes or the fall or a simple purchase; the earliest form of block. Now used for standing rigging only.

Dead marine—an empty bottle, which 'has done its duty and is ready to do it again'.

Dead men—stray ropes' ends hanging from aloft (see *Irish pendant* and *hanging Judas*).

DEEP (1)—a depression in the sea bed.

(2)—the fathoms on a lead line which are not marked, e.g. 'Deep six'.

DEMURRAGE—compensation paid to the owner of a vessel which has been delayed in port beyond the time agreed upon.

DERELICT—a ship afloat but abandoned by her crew.

DEVIL—in wooden ships a large seam near the gunwale. '*Between the devil and the deep sea*'—between the gunwale and the waterline; any precarious position.

Dhobeying—washing clothes (derived from the Indian word 'dhobey', a washerman).

DIP—to lower partially and temporarily. As slang this is used for disrating, forfeiting a good conduct badge, or failing an examination.

Ditch—the sea. '*To ditch*' is to throw overboard.

DITTY-BOX—a small wooden box which was issued to seamen as a receptacle for their small personal effects, but in 1938 was replaced by an attaché case.

DIVISION—two or more men-of-war of a squadron or a flotilla under one command. (See 'squadron' and 'flotilla'.)

Dodge Pompey—to evade doing a job of work.

DODGER—a canvas screen laced to guardrails to provide shelter from wind or spray. In the Royal Navy a slang term for a messdeck sweeper.

DOG—to twist a rope round a spar or another rope to obtain a grip of it.

Doggie—a midshipman detailed to attend on a senior officer.

DOG-VANE—a small wind-vane of bunting secured to the weather shrouds of a sailing vessel. (See 'wind-vane'.)

DONKEY—a prefix given to any small mechanical contrivance for saving labour, such as the 'donkey engine' used for working winches or small capstans and the 'sailmaker's donkey' or sewing machine.

DOREY—a flat-bottomed boat carried by fishing vessels.

DOWSE—to lower or slacken suddenly, to extinguish. '*Dowse the glim*'—to put out the light (see *glim*).

DRAG—to haul a grapnel (which see) or some similar instrument along the sea bed to recover something lost. (See 'sweep'.)

DRAW—a sail is said to draw when it is filled by the wind. A ship is said to draw so many feet (in draught). A ship is said to draw ahead of you if her position relative to yours advances, and to draw astern if it drops back.

DREDGE—to deepen a channel by excavating it.

Drip—to grumble or grouse.

DROWN—to drench or immerse. To drown a boat is to fill her with water by removing her plug, and is done to swell her planks and make her seams tight.

DUNNAGE—pieces of wood, matting, old rope, old canvas and other similar materials when used for raising cargo off the bottom of a hold, or packing it to keep it from shifting, or covering it to keep it dry.

EASY!—go or haul carefully, slowly, or less vigorously.

EDDY—a swirl in the water made by a fast-moving current passing over a rock or a hollow in the bottom; the swirl made by a current on the lee side of a rock or the buttress of a bridge, and the backwash of a current at the sides of a channel. Also a circular movement of the air.

END FOR END—to turn anything end for end is to reverse its position.

EUPHROE OR UVROE—a circular or oblong piece of wood, bored with holes and used to separate the parts of a crow's foot (which see).

FAG—to separate or tease out the strands of a rope ('fag-end' is the very end of anything).

FAIR—favourable, unobstructed, the reverse of 'foul' (which see); as in 'fair wind', 'fairlead' and 'fairway'.

Fairweather friend—one who is a friend only for so long as it suits his own ends.

FAKE—a coil in a coiled rope.

Fanny—a cylindrical mess tin holding about a gallon. (The introduction of tinned meat into the Navy was not popular and coincided approximately with the murder and dismemberment, in 1867, of a child called Fanny Adams. The tins in which the meat was packed were then used as mess utensils throughout the Service.)

FIDDLE—a bar of metal or wood holding a number of sheaves in line, and used chiefly for signal halyards or the halyards of wireless aerials. Also, battens fitted over a mess table to keep the mess traps in place in rough weather. *Working a fiddle* is to act dishonestly.

FIT OUT—to rig and provide a ship with her complete equipment of gear, stores and provisions.

Flannel—a term describing a long-winded or meaningless speech; also applied to nonsense or rubbish.

FLAT—a flat surface shoal or bank usually close inshore, which may or may not uncover at low water.

FLEET (1)—'The fleet' is a general name given to the Royal Navy as a whole; a fleet is a number of men-of-war under one overall command, and it can be sub-divided into squadrons, flotillas and divisions (which see).

(2)—shallow tidal waters, e.g. Benfleet, Purfleet.

(3)—the span or scope of a rope or tackle; the distance to which an object can be moved in one haul by a rope or tackle. 'To fleet' anything is to haul it along in a series of fleets, and to fleet a tackle is to overhaul a tackle which is block and block to its full scope. 'Fleet along', 'Fleet aft', 'Fleet forward', are orders to a body of men to move carefully in the required direction.

(4)—the area covered by a stage when painting a ship's side.

FLOTILLA—a number of small men-of-war under one command. Not used in the Fleet (1963).

FLOTSAM—floating cargo, stores or equipment, freed from a wreck or cast overboard to lighten a ship. It is the property of the owners, and if not claimed it becomes the property of the Crown. (See 'jetsam' and 'ligan'.)

FLYING DUTCHMAN—the ghost of a sailing vessel which is said to haunt the waters off the Cape of Good Hope. The sighting of it is supposed to portend disaster.

FORE-AND-AFT RIG (1)—a ship rigged with fore-and-aft sails only, as in a schooner.

(2)—a slang term for the dress of Royal Naval Chief Petty Officers, Petty Officers and of men not dressed as seamen. (See 'square rig'.)

FORE-FOOT—the lower end of the stem where it meets the keel.

FORE-PEAK—the compartment or space between decks in the bows of a ship.

FORESHORE—the beach below highwater mark.

FOUL—entangled, obstructed, or dirty.

Foul anchor—the badge of the Royal Navy, consisting of an Admiralty pattern anchor with a rope fouling its stock, shank and arms; it originated in the badge of Lord Howard of Effingham, who held office as Lord High Admiral in the reign of Queen Elizabeth I.

FOUNDER—to sink.

FRAP—to bind with lashing; to pass a rope round a sail or over an awning to keep it from breaking loose.

FREE—unobstructed, unencumbered, clear for running.

FRESHEN, or FRESHEN THE NIP—to shift the position at which a rope is being chafed (by a fairlead, for example), by paying it out or hauling it in a foot or so.

FULL DUE—to do anything 'for a full due' means to do it permanently, e.g. to secure a rope or a fitting 'for a full due'.

FURL—to fold up or roll up and stop a sail or an awning.

Gadget or *gilguy*—a small mechanical fitting or contrivance, a dodge or device.

GALLEY—a single-banked, six-oared pulling boat, properly called a 'gig', which was provided for the use of the captain of a ship.

Galley-packet—a rumour, usually unfounded (so-called because such rumours originated in the ship's galley or cook-house).

GANGWAY—any recognised entrance to, or passage way or traffic route within, a ship. Also used as an order or warning to make way.

GARLAND—a strop or rope sling round a mast or spar with which to lift or hoist it.

Gash—remnants of a meal; leavings and pickings.

GASKET—a stop used for lashing up a furled sail or awning.

GHOSTING—a sailing vessel or boat is said to be ghosting, or ghosting along, when she is making good way in a very light breeze.

GIG (see 'galley').

Gilguy (see *gadget*).

GINGERBREAD-WORK—the ornate gilt carving with which the sterns of former men-of-war were decorated. (The term is derived from the gingerbread sweetmeats formerly sold at fairs; they were made of treacle or honey and gilded over.)

GIRT or GIRDED—bound. A vessel is said to be girt when she is moored so tautly that she is prevented from swinging to wind or tide by fouling her cables as she swings round. Also said of a tug when she is inadvertently hauled broadside on her towrope, in which position she is powerless and must slip the tow or be capsized. To 'under-gird' is to bind the hull of a vessel with ropes or chains to strengthen it (see 'swift').

Glim—a light. (See 'dowse'.)

Gobbie—a coastguard. Until 1923 H.M. Coastguard Service was administered by the Admiralty and manned by pensioners of the Royal Navy, but in 1923 its administration was transferred to the Board of Trade, and in 1949 to the Ministry of Transport.

Goffer or *gopher*—a non-alcoholic fruit drink or mineral water.

Grabbies—soldiers. (See *pongos*.)

GRAIN—the line of water ahead of a vessel along which she will pass; the opposite to 'wake' (which see).

GRAPNEL—a small boat's anchor with three or four arms; used also for dragging, and for grappling a floating object. 'Grapnel-rope' is an old term for a boat's cable. (See 'drag', 'sweep' and 'creeper'.)

GREEN SEA—an unbroken wave. A vessel is said to be 'shipping it green' when unbroken water is driven aboard.

GROG—rum diluted with water; in the Royal Navy the regulation mixture is two parts of water to one of rum. A '*nor'-wester*' is a mixture of one part water to one of rum; the more northerly the direction the stronger the grog. Grog was introduced to the Fleet in 1740 by Admiral Vernon, who was known as 'Old Grog' because he habitually wore clothing made of material called grogram. (See 'tot'.)

Grog-blossom—a red nose or pimple.

GROUND SWELL—a heavy swell caused by a distant storm or by one that has passed; it may also be caused by a submarine earthquake.

Guzz—Devonport.

HALF-TIDE ROCK—a rock which uncovers at half-ebb.

Hanging Judas—a fall, whip or halyard which is not properly secured aloft, or not properly belayed, or hanging loose from aloft. (See *dead men* and *Irish pendants.*)

Hard tack—ship's biscuits, which used to be very hard and tough. (See *soft tack.*)

Harry Freeman—free of charge, a gift, or something obtained for nothing. The origin of this term is obscure.

HEADS—a ship's latrines. (The 'heads' of a sailing man-of-war were platforms on each side of the stem which were used as latrines by the men.)

HEAVER—a lever, handspike.

HOG OUT—to scrub out thoroughly. (A hog was a stiff brush used for scrubbing the ship's bottom.)

HOLIDAY—a gap left in a row or line; an unpainted patch in paintwork.

HOLYSTONES—blocks of sandstone that were used for scrubbing decks, so-called because their use entailed kneeling down. Medium-sized holystones were called *bibles*, and small ones *prayer books.*

Hook-rope party—a party of men detailed to give the decks a final clear-up just before an inspection.

HORSE LATITUDES—a belt of light and variable winds, between the Westerlies and the Trade Winds in the northern and southern hemispheres, in which sailing vessels were often becalmed for some time. The name had its origin in the middle of the nineteenth century, when numerous horses were transported from Europe to America and the West Indies, and the belt in the North Atlantic was often studded with dead horses.

HULK—a vessel condemned as unfit for sea service, and used in harbour for some purpose such as a store ship or an accommodation ship.

HULL A SHIP—to penetrate the hull of a ship with shot or shell.

In everybody's mess, but nobody's watch—a phrase applied to a plausible, work-shy man.

Irish pendants—rope yarns, or stray rope's ends hanging in the rigging, or flags with frayed flies. (See *dead men* and *hanging Judas.*)

JETSAM—sunken cargo which has been cast overboard to lighten a ship. If recovered it is the property of the owners, but if not claimed it is the property of the Crown. (See 'flotsam' and 'ligan'.)

JETTISON—to cast overboard.

Jew—a tailor.

Jollies—Royal Marines (see *bullocks* and *turkeys*).

Jonah—a bringer of bad luck.

Joss—luck (Chinese).

JUNK—old rope set aside for picking. (See 'rounding' and 'rumbo'.)

JURY—a prefix meaning temporary, as in 'jury-mast', for example, which is a mast specially made and rigged temporarily in place of a damaged one.

KEG—a small cask.

Ki—cocoa (the origin of this term is obscure).

KID—a small tub. (See 'spitkid'.)

KILLICK—a small anchor. A slang term used for a Leading Seaman, because the distinguishing badge he wears is an anchor.

LABOUR—a ship is said to labour when she pitches and rolls heavily in rough weather.

LANDFALL—first sight of land after a passage in the open sea.

LAND-LOCKED—surrounded by land.

LARGE—a ship is sailing large when she is sailing free with the wind abaft her beam; 'an offender at large' is one who is not under constraint. (See 'by and large'.)

LAY UP—to take a ship out of service. To twist the strands of a rope together.

LEAGUE—an obsolete sea measurement of distance equivalent to three nautical miles.

LEE-BOARD—a board lowered down into the water on the lee side of a sailing vessel to prevent her making lee-way when close-hauled or reaching.

LEE-SHORE—a shore towards which the wind is blowing.

LEE-TIDE—a tidal stream running in the same direction as the wind. (See 'weather-tide'.)

LET FLY—to let go instantly; usually applied to the sheets of a sailing vessel.

LET RUN—to let go a rope, chain or other flexible object so that it runs out of its own accord.

LIBERTY—leave of less than 24 hours.

LIGAN—sunken cargo or gear which has been cast overboard and buoyed. It is the property of the owners, but if unclaimed becomes the property of the Crown. (See 'flotsam' and 'jetsam'.)

Lights—an extension of the regulation time for 'lights out', which may be granted on certain occasions.

Lurk—to impose upon someone else's kindness, e.g. to persuade someone to take your trick or watch.

Lush up—to stand treat. *Lush* is sometimes used to mean abundant liquor, or, as an adjective, drunk.

MAKING—tides are said to be 'making' during the period between neaps and springs when their height progressively increases. (See 'take-off'.)

MANIFEST—an official inventory of all cargo carried by a merchant vessel.

MARTINGALE—a stay leading from the nose of the jib-boom of a sailing vessel to her stem; in some ships it is passed through the head of a dolphin striker to give it a better downward pull on the jib-boom. Any stay which prevents a boom, spar or strut from topping up is also called a martingale. (See 'bobstay'.)

MASTER—the captain of a merchant vessel.

MASTER-OF-THE-FLEET—The navigating officer appointed to the staff of a Commander-in-Chief of a fleet and charged with the navigation of the fleet as such.

Maties—dockyard workmen.

MESS TRAPS—food utensils for a naval officers' mess.

MESS UTENSILS—food utensils for a naval ratings' mess.

Money for old rope—something for nothing, simple.

MONKEY—a prefix meaning small, e.g. 'monkey's island', 'monkey jacket', 'monkey boom', 'monkey block'.

Mother Cary's chickens—small sea birds otherwise known as stormy petrels. (The origin of the term is legendary; it was well known among English seamen in the days of Captain Cook.)

MUFFLE—to muffle the oars is to parcel their looms with canvas where they pass through the rowlocks or crutches to prevent them from creaking.

MULCT—a fine imposed as a punishment; 'to mulct' is to fine.

Mundungus—rubbish (derived from the Spanish 'mondongo', meaning tripe).

Mungy—food (derived from the French 'manger', to eat).

MUZZLER—a gale blowing from right ahead.

NEAPED OR BENEAPED—a vessel which cannot leave harbour except at spring tides is said to be neaped; the term also describes a vessel grounded at the height of a spring tide which cannot be refloated until the next spring tide.

Neaters—neat rum.

Nicknames in general use afloat—'*Granny*' Anderson and Henderson; '*Dinger*' or '*Daisy*' Bell; '*Wiggy*' Bennet; '*Nigger*' Black; '*Ginger*' Casey; '*Nobby*' Clark; '*Jumper*' Collins or Short; '*Bandy*' Evans; '*Harry*' Freeman; '*Jimmy*' Green; '*Tosh*' Gilbert; '*Chats*' Harris; '*Cosher*' Hinds; '*Jerry*' King; '*Bogie*' Knight; '*Dodger*' Long; '*Pincher*' Martin; '*Dusty*' Miller; '*Pony*' Moore; '*Spud*' Murphy; '*Nosey*' Parker; '*Spike*' Sullivan; '*Buck*' Taylor; '*Hookey*' Walker; '*Sharkey*' Ward; '*Knocker*' White; '*Slinger*' Woods; '*Shiner*' Wright.

NIPPER—a stop or strop used temporarily to seize two ropes together.

NORTHERN LIGHTS—the 'Aurora Borealis', seen occasionally in the northern sky when in high latitudes at night. The similar 'Aurora Australis' or 'Southern lights' are seen in high southern latitudes.

Nor'-easter—the same as 'not entitled' (which see). (A north-easterly wind is an unpopular one, particularly in winter.)

Nor'-wester (see 'grog').

NOT ENTITLED—a report at a naval pay table signifying that a man is not due for any pay.

OFFING—that vaguely defined part of the sea which lies between the entrance to a harbour, or the shoal water of a coast, and the horizon.

Oppo—a friend in the same, or in another ship.

Opposite number—a man having the same station or duties as your own; e.g. the opposite number of a man in the port watch is the man in the starboard watch who carries out the same duties.

OVERHAUL (1)—to overtake.
      (2)—to examine carefully and repair where necessary.
      (3)—to haul the blocks of a tackle apart to the full scope of the fall.

PASS THE WORD—to relay an order or a summons.

PAY—to give a coating to a surface.

PAY A SEAM—to pour molten pitch into a seam.

PAY AWAY—to slacken a rope.

PAY OFF—to fall away from the wind. Also to place a ship out of commission (in former times the ship's company were then paid their wages and discharged).

PAY OUT—to ease out by hand.

PEAK: fore peak—the space immediately abaft the stem of a ship; after peak— the space immediately before her stern post. These spaces are often used in merchant ships for storage of fresh water in what are known as 'peak tanks.'

Perks—perquisites, i.e. allowance in cash or kind appertaining to a particular office or employment.

Pier-head jump—joining a ship just as she is about to sail.

PIPE DOWN—the last routine pipe of the day, after which silence is maintained throughout the messdecks until the hands are called. May also be given verbally as an order to stop talking, arguing or skylarking.

Plushers—the residue of the grog ration of a mess if the tots served out were of short measure, or if the ration served to the mess was over-measured.

Pompey—Portsmouth.

Pongo—soldier. (See *grabbies*.)

PORT—a square or rectangular hole cut in a ship's side as an entrance for embarking passengers or cargo, or for light and ventilation.

PREVENTER—any rope, chain or fitting backing up or limiting the movement of rigging, spars, cable, etc.

Private ship—any large ship other than a flagship, and commanded by an officer of Captain's rank.

PROUD—projecting from an otherwise flat surface, such as the head of a rivet which is not counter-sunk. The term is also applied to a wooden shore which is cut slightly longer than the space into which it is to fit, so that it has to be driven home when set up and so be jammed in place.

PUDDING—a rope fender, cylindrical in shape and sometimes with the ends tapered; generally used on the bows of tugs and harbour launches, also on the griping spar of radial davits.

Purser—the officer in a merchant ship responsible to the Master for the catering and accommodation of passengers. Formerly the officer in a ship of the Royal Navy charged with her provisions and clothing stores was called the purser.

Pusser (colloquial derivative of 'purser')—the Supply Officer of a man-of-war. '*Pusser's dip*'—a candle; '*pusser's dirk*'—a clasp knife; '*pusser's crabs*'—shoes; '*pusser's medal*'—a food stain on clothing.

Queen's hard bargain—a lazy, incompetent man.

Quiet number (see 'soft number').

Rabbit—any article made or converted from ship's stores for private use.

Raggie—friend or chum. Formerly seamen provided their own cleaning gear, and if two men shared their cleaning rags it was a sign of trust and friendship. '*To part brass rags*' is to dissolve a friendship.

Rake—to lean or incline from the perpendicular; to fire into a ship along her length. The term 'rakish' is applied to a ship with an appearance of force and speed.

Range—to lay out (usually applied to rope or cable).

Rattle—to be '*in the rattle*' is to be on the list of defaulters, or in the 'report'.

Refit—to repair, put in order, recondition.

Relief—the man who relieves another of his watch, trick or other specific duty.

Relieving tackles—tackles or ropes secured to the tiller of a vessel to assist her steering in a heavy sea.

Rigol—a curved metal fitting above a side scuttle to prevent water running down the ship's side from entering the scuttle.

Road, roadstead—an exposed or offshore anchorage.

Rockie—an officer or man of the Royal Naval Reserve.

Rogue's salute—the gun fired on the morning of the day appointed for a Court Martial.

Rogue's yarn—a coloured yarn laid up in a strand or strands of a fibre rope. It was formerly used to distinguish Service cordage from commercial cordage to prevent misappropriation of the former, but it is now used to distinguish one type of cordage, whether Service or commercial, from another. Service cordage, however, can still be distinguished from commercial cordage by the colour and the number of strands containing the rogue's yarn.

Rounding—condemned rope under 4 inches in size. Also any service on a rope or a spar. (See 'junk' and 'rumbo'.)

Round up—to haul together the two blocks of a tackle to a convenient scope for stowage.

Rumbo—condemned cordage. (See 'junk' and 'rounding'.)

Rumbo line—rope made from old rope, such as stage lashing.

Run (1)—the distance sailed (steamed) by a ship.
(2)—the note made in the ship's ledger against the name of a deserter. 'To run' is to desert.

Run down—to ram a vessel, either on purpose or by accident.

Runners—smugglers.

Scandalise—to settle the halyards of a gaff in order to spill the wind out of its sail (see 'a'cock-bill'). Yards are said to be 'scandalised' when they are not squared.

Scantlings—standard dimensions for the various parts of a ship's structure; they vary with the type or class of ship.

Scend—the scend of a sea is the vertical movement of its waves. A ship is said to scend when she rises and falls bodily on the crests and in the troughs of heavy seas; it is different from pitching, in which the bows and stern of a vessel are alternately raised and lowered. (See 'surge'.)

Scotchman—any piece of metal, wood, leather, canvas or other material used to prevent chafe or wear. (See 'baggywrinkle' and 'bolster'.)

Scran—food. A '*scran-bag*' was formerly used as a receptacle for the remains of a meal, but is now used as a stowage for personal gear, such as clothing which has been left lying about, until it is claimed by the owner; it is customary to pay a forfeit of a bar of soap for anything reclaimed.

Scud—low, fast-moving clouds. A sailing ship is sometimes said to be scudding before a gale when she is running before it.

Sculling—to leave something sculling is to leave it lying about or unattended.

Scupper—to sink, to founder (from water flooding aboard through the scuppers). '*I'm scuppered*'—an expression of defeat or resignation.

Scuttle—to cut a hole in a ship's bottom, or to open her seacocks, for the purpose of sinking her.

Sea-daddy—an experienced seaman detailed to instruct youngsters; sometimes applied to the officer in charge of the midshipmen.

Sea-lawyer—an argumentative man; one more given to questioning orders than readily obeying them, and to talking rather than working.

Sea-legs—a man is said to have 'got his sea-legs' when he can move about his ship without losing his balance when she rolls or pitches heavily.

Sewed (pronounced 'sued')—a ship is said to be sewed when she has been grounded on a falling tide, either intentionally or accidentally, and can only be refloated by the rising tide; the difference between the actual level of the water and the level to which it must rise to refloat her is the distance by which she is sewed. She can also be described as being sewed to a certain point, e.g. if the water was level with the bilge keel she would be 'sewed to the bilge keel'. The term is also used to describe the condition of a ship in this respect during the operations of docking and undocking in a dry dock. The term derives from the old verb 'to sew', meaning to drain.

Shake—to cast off fastenings; to take to pieces (a cask or a packing case, for example).

Sheer plan—a drawing showing the longitudinal cross-section of a vessel through her keel.

SHIP'S COMPANY—all the personnel of a man-of-war other than her officers. The synonymous term in the Merchant Navy is 'crew'.

SHIVER—to break in numerous pieces, to shatter.

SHIPSHAPE—seamanlike in appearance.

SHOT MAT—a heavy rope mat used to protect anything, especially the deck, from heavy weights dropped on it (originally to protect the deck in the event of cannon shot being dropped on it).

Shove in your oar—to break into a conversation; to interrupt or interfere.

SICK BAY—the ship's hospital.

SISTER SHIPS—ships built to the same design.

Skate—a man always in trouble or mischief.

SKIPPER—Master of a fishing vessel or of a small trading vessel. A rank in the Royal Naval Reserve.

SKULK—to avoid duty.

SLOPS—articles of uniform clothing made for the Crown and issued on repayment to officers and men of the Royal Navy.

Snob—a shoemaker.

SNOTTER—a strop supporting the heel of a swinging boom, derrick or sprit (which see). A rope or chain stopper used to hold the lifts of derricks. A type of rope or chain sling.

Snowball hitch (slippery hitch)—a hitch that will slip under strain.

SNUB—when applied to a rope or a cable, means to stop suddenly.

SNUG—properly secured; 'snugged down'—prepared to meet a gale.

Soft number—an easy job or duty; a sinecure.

Soft tack—bread. (See 'hard tack'.)

SPEAK—to communicate at sea with another vessel or a shore signal station by visual signalling.

SPELL—a period of continuous work, such as a 'spell at the pumps'; or a period of leisure, such as 'a spell on deck'. 'Spell ho!' is sometimes used as the call for a relief.

SPINDRIFT—spray blown from the crests of waves.

Spithead pheasant—the bluejacket's term for a kipper.

SPITKID—a small tub or other receptacle, placed on the decks during smoking hours, for cigarette ends, pipe dottles and waste paper.

SPLINTER MAT—a rope mat, with one side smooth and the other thrummed (or tufted), used for stopping small leaks in the hull of a vessel. (See 'thrums'.)

SPRING (1)—to split or crack. A 'spring' is a crack in a spar, and a sprung spar is one which is weakened by splits or by cracks. When a vessel makes water through straining her hull she is said to 'spring a leak'.

(2)—A spring is a hawser laid out to slew a vessel, or to point her in some required direction. 'To spring a boat ahead' is to haul her ahead on a guest-warp or a boatrope.

SPRING-PIPE—A short pipe running through bulwarks and used as a fairlead for hawsers.

SPRIT—a boom used for supporting and extending the mainsail of a sailing vessel; it extends from the tack to the peak, and its heel is supported by a 'snotter' (which see).

SPURNWATER—a wooden or metal beading, or low coaming, round the edges of decks or waterways to prevent wash-deck water spilling over the ship's side. The term is also applied to the breakwater on a ship's forecastle.

SQUADRON—a number of similar men-of-war under one command. (See 'division' and 'flotilla'.)

Square one's own yard arm—to put oneself in the right, usually with a superior, without regard for others; to observe the letter of the law (or of regulations or instructions) with the object of avoiding possible blame.

SQUARE RIG—the rig of a ship whose sails are set on yards athwart her masts. A slang term for the uniform of most ratings of the Royal Navy below the rate of petty officer. (See 'fore-and-aft rig'.)

Square yards (with anyone)—is to agree with him, or to enter into agreement with him.

SQUEEGEE—a form of broom with a rubber edge, used for sweeping water from a deck.

STAND—to sail in a certain widely defined direction, e.g. 'to stand in to the shore', 'to stand southward'.

STANDING—a term denoting anything fixed or permanent, e.g. 'standing rigging', 'standing guy', 'standing orders' and 'standing number' (i.e. a permanent job).

START—to move from rest, to loosen, to break out, or to allow to move from rest as in starting a boat's falls.

STATION (1)—a man's place or post for a specific duty, e.g. 'station for leaving harbour'; or the allotted position of a ship at sea with a fleet, squadron or flótilla. 'To station' is to allot a place or duty to a man or a ship.

(2)—an area of land and sea placed under the naval jurisdiction of a Commander-in-Chief, e.g. Home Station.

STAVE—to break in a plank or a stave, e.g. of a cask; 'to stave in'—to hole anything or break into it; 'stove in'—holed, e.g. the bows or side of a vessel which has been in collision.

STEVEDORE—strictly the person who contracts for the handling of cargo into or from a vessel. Now applied to men actually handling the cargo.

STIFF—very stable, the opposite of 'crank'. Such a ship will return quickly to the upright when heeled over. (See 'crank' and 'tender'.)

Stone frigate—a naval shore establishment.

THE STRAITS—the Straits of Gibraltar.

STRIKE (1)—A ship is said to strike when she hits the bottom. A ship on an ocean passage and approaching land is said to 'strike soundings' when she reaches water sufficiently shallow for taking soundings.

(2)—To lower from aloft; 'to strike the colours' is to haul them down in token of surrender. 'Strike down' is to lower anything into the hold of a ship or between decks.

STRIP TO A GANTLINE—to strip a ship of all her rigging, leaving one gantline rove to the masthead with which to begin refitting the rigging when required.

Strongers—a strong solution of soda and water used to dissolve dirt on decks.

SULLAGE—garbage, rubbish. 'Sullage lighter'—the lighter which, in some ports, is sent to ships to collect their sullage and so prevent the harbour from being fouled by jettisoning it. (See *gash*.)

SURGE—the lateral movement of a stationary vessel caused by a swell or the wash of a passing ship. (See 'scend'.)

Swallow the anchor—to retire from sea service.

SWASH-WAY—a channel across or between shoals or spits.

SWEAT—moisture on bulkheads, decks, deckheads and sides of a ship due to condensation.

SWEAT UP—to give an extra hard pull on a rope to take down every vestige of slack in it.

SWEEP—to drag the bight of a wire or chain along the bottom to locate or recover a sunken object. (See 'drag'.)

SWEEPER—In the Royal Navy, a man charged with the cleanliness of a compartment or a flat. (See *dodger*.)

SWEEPS—large oars used to propel lighters, barges and small sailing vessels.

SWIFT—to tauten, to bind, to stay; shrouds are swifted when the slack in them is taken down; a shaky vessel is swifted (or 'under girded') when her hull is bound round with hawsers or chains (see 'girt'); the outer ends of capstan bars are swifted to keep the bars shipped in the capstan-head.

SWIG OFF—to haul out on the bight of a taut rope at right-angles to its lead in order to take up the last few inches of slack in its span (usually applied to halyards and lashings).

Swing the lead—to avoid duty by feigning illness, to malinger. (See 'skulk'.)

TAFFRAIL—the top rail round the stern of a ship from quarter to quarter.

TAIL ON—to clap on to a rope. (See 'clap on'.)

TAKE CHARGE—an inanimate object, such as a rope or a cable, takes charge when it gets out of control and runs out by its own momentum.

TAKE OFF—the tides are said to be taking off when they decrease progressively between springs and neaps. (See 'making'.)

TAKE UP—to tauten, to absorb, to swell; to 'take up the slack' (of a rope or nut, for example); when a dry boat is placed in the water her planking will gradually take up and become tight; when applied to 'slops' (which see), it means to buy.

TAKEN ABACK—surprised; a sailing vessel is said to be taken aback when the wind strikes her sails on the wrong side.

TALLY—a label or the name of a person or an article. 'To tally'—to keep a record (of stores or cargo being embarked or disembarked, for example).

Tanky—the midshipman assisting the Navigating Officer; a seaman attached to the Supply department for special victualling duties, e.g. mixing grog.

Tar, or *Jack Tar*—name formerly applied to a seaman of the Royal Navy (from his tarpaulin hat and tarry trousers).

TARPAULIN—a heavy canvas cover, tarred or painted; usually used to cover hatches to make them watertight.

TELL-OFF—to detail men for work.

Tell that to the Marines—a seaman's repartee to an improbable story.

TENDER (1)—a small vessel employed to attend on a larger vessel, for duties such as ferrying, store-carrying or training. She is under the direct command of, and her accounts are kept by, her parent ship.
  (2)—a term applied to a ship having poor stability; one which rolls easily and recovers slowly, the same as 'crank' and the opposite of 'stiff' (which see).

THRUMS—short rope yarns forming the tufted surface of a mat (see 'splinter mat').

Ticklers—Service tobacco issued in tins. The term originated in the tinned jam which was first supplied to the Navy in 1908 by a manufacturer of the name of Tickler.

Tiddie-oggie—the bluejacket's term for a small flat meat pie of oval shape, called in the West Country a Cornish pasty.

Tiddley—neat, smart.

TIDE-RACE—a fast-moving, turbulent stretch of water, often with eddies and whirls in it, caused by a strong current meeting a tidal stream or a heavy sea or swell, or passing over a sharply uneven bottom.

TIDE-RODE—a vessel at anchor in tidal waters is said to be tide-rode when she is lying swung to the tidal stream rather than to the wind. (See 'wind-rode'.)

TIGHT—watertight.

TIMONOGUY—a guy fitted to a projecting fitting to prevent a rope from fouling it.

TOMBOLA—a game similar to a lottery played on board H.M. ships, another name for which is 'House'.

TOP-HAMPER—top-weight, i.e. any weight carried, either temporarily or permanently, above the upper deck; superstructures, masts, funnels and deck cargo are examples.

TOT—the ration of rum or grog issued to ratings of the Royal Navy.

TRIATIC STAY—a stay led from the head of the mainmast to the head of the foremast. It was formerly used for staying the mainmast.

TRICK—a short spell of special duty involving continuous work or alertness. Tricks are carried out in turn by men of the watch on deck, and their length depends upon the nature of the duty; lookouts do from half an hour to an hour, helmsmen one hour.

TRINITY HOUSE—a corporation which is the general authority for lighthouses on the coasts of England, Wales and the Channel Islands, and the pilotage authority for the London and Isle of Wight districts as well as 40 other ports in England and Wales. It was granted its first charter by Henry the Eighth, in 1518. Its members are elected from Master Mariners, the senior being known as 'Elder Brethren' and the junior as 'Younger Brethren'. As a private guild it administers certain charitable trusts for the relief of aged or distressed Master Mariners and their dependants.

Turkeys—the name formerly given to men of the Royal Marine Light Infantry because of the red tunics they wore. (See *jollies* and *bullocks*.)

TWO BLOCKS (see 'block-and-block').

Uckers—the sailor's name for the game of Ludo; a game of skill and chance played with counters and dice.

ULLAGE—the quantity a cask, case or tank lacks of being full.

ULOEING—a Chinese method of sculling with a single oar shipped over the stern of a boat. The oar is pivoted about a round-headed pin on the transom, and its loom is secured to the bottom of the boat by a martingale of rope or chain.

UNSTABLE—a ship is said to be unstable when she is top-heavy and so is unable to recover when heeled over by wind or sea. (See 'crank', 'stiff' and 'tender'.)

UVROE (see 'euphroe').

WAKE—the strip of water astern of a vessel through which she has passed. The opposite of 'grain' (which see).

WALL-SIDED—said of a ship with perpendicular sides and high freeboard.

Warm the bell—to act or arrive before the appointed time; to be early.

WARP—any rope or hawser used to haul a vessel from one position to another; 'to warp' is to move a vessel by this means. Also a lengthwise thread in the weave of canvas.

WASH—the disturbance in the water made by the movement of a vessel through it.

Wash out—to countermand an instruction or an order. (Derived from the days when signalmen recorded messages on a slate and expunged them before recording new ones.) (See 'belay'.)

WATER-LOGGED—a vessel is water-logged when she is full of water but still floating.

WEATHER-BOUND—unable to put to sea owing to the weather.

WEATHER-TIDE—a tidal stream flowing in the opposite direction to the wind. (See 'lee-tide'.)

WEEP—to leak slightly; a weeping cask, or joint in a pipe, for example.

Wet—stupid. *Wet as a scrubber*—extremely stupid.

WHARF—a lading-place for shipping.

WIND-RODE—a vessel at anchor in tidal waters is said to be wind-rode when she is swung to the wind rather than to the tidal stream. (See 'tide-rode'.)

WIND-VANE—a thin strip of metal mounted on a vertical pivot on the head of a mast, or other suitable place aloft, so that it will indicate the direction of the wind in relation to the ship's course and speed.

WINDSAIL—a ventilation trunk of canvas slung from aloft with its mouth set to catch the wind and its foot led below to the space to be ventilated.

WORK UP—to train the officers and ship's company of a newly-commissioned ship to an efficient state.

APPENDIX 2

Questions

Chapter 1. GENERAL SEA TERMS

1. A ship has two masts, a funnel and a bridge. The funnel is abaft the bridge, but before the after (or main) mast. A man is standing abreast the bridge and looking aft at a boat which is stowed amidships and to starboard between the mainmast and the funnel. Draw a plan of the ship and indicate the positions of these objects.
2. Two ships are steaming abreast of each other. The starboard-hand ship has a lighthouse abeam to starboard of her, while the other has a sailing vessel on her port quarter. Sketch the relative positions of the steam ships, sailing vessel and lighthouse.
3. A ship is steaming on a course of 045 degrees. A lighthouse bears 090 degrees from her. Sketch the relative position of the ship to the lighthouse, and indicate the direction of north.
4. A ship is sighted on a relative bearing of green 70, and a lighthouse bears red 140. Sketch the relative positions of the ship and the lighthouse.
5. What points of the compass are opposite to north-east and south-east?
6. Define the following terms: lift and launch; under way; adrift; sternway; ship's head; weather deck; lee side; to fleet.
7. The inclination of a ship on the port quarter is 20 degrees Right. Sketch the relative position and course of each ship to the other.
8. Make a sectional sketch of a ship showing her forecastle and her upper, main, lower and platform decks.
9. Draw a plan of a ship indicating the positions of her waist, forecastle, quarterdeck and boom boats.
10. Define the terms freeboard, camber, tumble home, sheer line, draught, bilge and flare.
11. What is the object of the Plimsoll mark and load lines?
12. What is the difference between displacement and gross tonnage?
13. What are the differences between a camber, a dry dock and a basin?
14. What are the purposes of a lock, a caisson, a patent slip and a slipway?
15. What are a trot, hard, warp, lighter, brow and pontoon?
16. How many feet are there in a fathom, and how many yards in a nautical mile?
17. What unit of speed is used at sea?

Chapter 2. TYPES OF SHIP

1. What is the distinction between the terms 'type' of ship and 'class' of ship?
2. Name the various types of warship.
3. Name the various types of merchant ship.

4. What are the main functions of each type of warship?
5. What are the main functions of each type of merchant vessel?
6. Sketch as many rigs of sailing craft as you can remember.

Chapter 3. DESIGN AND CONSTRUCTION OF WARSHIPS

1. Give the seaman's equivalent for the following civilian terms: room, floor, ceiling, inside wall, outside wall, trap-door, roof, stairs, upstairs, downstairs, cellar, window, steps, entrance, front door, banisters, railings, corridor, cupboard, ground floor, second floor, third floor, kitchen, rubbish, dustbin, tableware, drains?
2. How are a hatch, a door and a scuttle made watertight?
3. Should the edge of a hatch coaming be painted?
4. Before a hatch cover is opened what should you check?
5. How can you ascertain whether or not a compartment is flooded?
6. How is light prevented from showing through a side scuttle?
7. What are a remotely-controlled valve, and rod gearing? Why should gear never be secured or hung from them?
8. To whom would you report an electrical defect?
9. What care must be exercised when handling telephones?
10. What general precautions are necessary in regard to electrical equipment?
11. How would you clear dust and dirt from radio compartments?
12. Why is the risk of electric shock greater aboard ship than ashore?
13. Why should equipment such as electric irons and portable electric drills be repaired only by men of the Electrical Branch?
14. What is the object of watertight sub-division in a ship? Are the decks watertight?
15. Make a rough sketch of the longitudinal section of a man-of-war and indicate on it the following: engine room, boiler rooms, magazines and shell rooms, store rooms and living spaces.
16. How is a compartment ventilated? Why should the forced ventilation system not be tampered with by unauthorised persons?
17. What is the purpose of a punkah louvre?
18. How is a torpedo fired?
19. What compartments are protected by armour plating?
20. What is the difference between main machinery and auxiliary machinery?
21. What advantage does a ship fitted with diesel engines have over a ship fitted with steam turbines?
22. What provides the source of power in a nuclear-powered ship?
23. Name at least five living spaces.
24. For what periods is a man-of-war stored and provisioned?
25. Where are the following stowed: dry provisions, fresh meat and fresh vegetables?
26. Why is it necessary to economise in the use of fresh water in a ship? How is fresh water made from sea water?
27. How is electricity produced in a man-of-war?

28. Name at least two compartments which can be flooded direct from the sea by opening sea cocks in the ship's bottom.
29. How else can a compartment be flooded?
30. What is the firemain and how can it be identified?
31. For what other purposes is the firemain used?
32. How is flood water removed from a compartment?
33. What are the following: round down, arrester wires, safety nets, walkways, emergency barrier?
34. How is an aircraft brought to rest after landing on a flight deck?
35. What visible aids assist a pilot to land his aircraft safely?
36. How are aircraft launched from an aircraft carrier?
37. Explain the 1950 system of compartment identification.
38. Give an example of the markings of a door and a hatch.
39. What part of a ship's hull is called the 'entry'?
40. Where would you expect to find the thickest hull plating?
41. What are the following: bilge, strake, butt and seam?
42. Describe the following: frame, longitudinal, double bottoms and main structural bulkhead.
43. What are the functions of decks, beams and pillars?
44. What are the following: spurnwater, scuppers, gunwale, stringer, bulwarks, freeing ports and knee plates?
45. How does a submarine dive, and how does she maintain her required depth?

Chapter 4. SHIP SAFETY

1. What do the terms 'ship safety' and 'damage control' cover, and what are the main objects of damage control?
2. What knowledge must every person on board possess with regard to the ABCD organisation?
3. What is an ABCD section? Who deals with damage control in each section?
4. How many sections are there in a frigate?
5. What are the functions of the ABCD Headquarters? Do some ships have more than one headquarters position?
6. How would you in a cruiser communicate the discovery of a fire to a section base?
7. For what purpose would you use a telephone which is painted yellow?
8. How does ABCD Headquarters communicate with an electrical control position?
9. When may an Officer of the Watch control the ABCD organisation?
10. On what does the extent of the manning of damage control stations depend?
11. What are the responsibilities of the trained staff in H.Q.1?
12. At a section base who controls the section team, and which parties comprise the team?
13. When do men from one section work outside that section?
14. When would stations be manned only with skeleton teams?

15. If the stations are not manned who would then meet any damage control requirements?
16. How best can the spread of flooding, blast and fire be prevented?
17. What is the object of compartmentation in a man-of-war?
18. What are watertight integrity, and a citadel?
19. Give as many examples of watertight fittings as you can.
20. Why is it necessary for a ship to have a citadel?
21. How are the openings in the boundaries of citadels and gas-free spaces controlled?
22. Why is it necessary to have ventilation within compartments?
23. What principles are observed in the design and fitting of ventilation trunking with regard to water and gastight integrity?
24. How is the air in the citadel augmented by fresh air?
25. Why should the air pressure within the citadel be slightly more than the pressure elsewhere?
26. How is trunking which pierces a main watertight bulkhead made watertight?
27. How can slide valves be operated?
28. How can an unventilated compartment be ventilated?
29. Give the three watertight conditions and the two gastight conditions.
30. What is meant by risk markings?
31. If your ship is damaged and is flooding, what emergency order would you expect to be given, and how are the watertight fittings marked?
32. What is the red zone and who decides the extent of the openings within this zone?
33. What is the difference between the meaning of a red and a blue marking on a watertight fitting?
34. How would you know which fittings to close if a high degree of gastightness were ordered?
35. Name the seven control markings.
36. What are the basic principles of openings for control purposes?
37. What is the only occasion on which the user can exercise control over a fitting marked M?
38. Which are the only openings to bear two control marks?
39. What does the control mark R signify?
40. Which watertight condition would a ship be in during action?
41. An opening is marked Z. What is the colour of this marking?
42. Explain the meaning of B painted on a slide valve.
43. When may a door or hatch be opened in condition A?
44. How do you get into the citadel after the ship is contaminated with radioactive fall-out?
45. You see double black lines on a door; what do they mean?
46. How is an opening into the citadel marked?
47. What are the four uses of 'May be left open' discs?
48. Which disc would you display when you are required to visit a compartment once or twice a watch?
49. Which authority issues 'May be left open' discs?
50. Which gastight condition would a ship assume when an ABC attack is imminent?

51. When would you expect to find a third gastight condition, and how would the fittings be marked?
52. Explain the following conditions: YB, ZA, Y.
53. What is meant by 'states of readiness'?
54. What is meant by State 1?
55. What condition and state would a ship assume during exercises in peacetime? In action? When ABC attack is imminent?
56. Can a gastight condition be used alone? Explain your answer.
57. In what circumstances would a ship be when personnel had obeyed the order 'Assume State 3 condition Yankee Bravo'?
58. What markings would you expect to find on a main transverse bulkhead?
59. Where are drain pipes fitted?
60. What is an eductor and how does it work?
61. Why are main machinery and power supplies divided into self-contained units?
62. Where is damage control equipment stowed in a ship, and what does it consist of?
63. Why should damage control equipment never be tampered with?
64. Describe the emergency lantern. How does it work, and what should you (as an unauthorised person) never do?
65. What precautions are taken to ensure an adequate supply of stores on board?
66. What precautions would you take before entering an unventilated compartment? Should an anti-gas respirator be worn?
67. How would you protect yourself from the flash from an explosion?
68. If, in action, you are not employed at any time, what would you do? Why?
69. Why, in action, would you lie down athwartships with your feet pointing outboard?
70. What would you do if you saw a blinding flash in the sky?
71. What would you wear when tackling a fire in an enclosed compartment?
72. To whom would you report flooding or fire in your ship, both when at sea and when in harbour?
73. Can you find your way about your ship in the dark? You should be able to.
74. Where is your knife now, at this moment?
75. Why should locker doors be fastened?
76. What precautions should you take before locking up a store-room or compartment?
77. Tie a bowline round your waist, now, with your eyes shut.
78. What action would you take if you saw a rating reading by the light from an emergency lantern?
79. What dangers result from careless smoking?
80. How far can the following be seen on a dark, clear night: lighted match, lighted cigarette, unmasked torch?
81. What is the danger in wartime of the indiscriminate 'ditching' of 'gash'?
82. In war what personal equipment should you always wear, or keep handy for immediate use?
83. What precautions should you take when closing a watertight door or hatch?

84. Why should you never remove door clips for cleaning?
85. Would you paint over a tally?
86. How should you stow a fire hose?
87. What would you do if you saw an empty fire extinguisher?
88. When would you leave your place of duty?
89. What happens on the order 'Hands to emergency stations'?
90. Where is your lifejacket now?
91. When the order 'Abandon ship' is given, how would you leave the ship?
92. Why should you lash up your hammock tautly and stow it properly in a hammock netting?
93. When should a liferaft shove off from an abandoned ship?
94. If you are cast into the water from a sinking ship and are unable to reach a liferaft, what should you do?
95. How would you secure another man to prevent him from drifting away?
96. What is the result of frequent training in abandon ship drill?

Chapter 5. FIRE PRECAUTIONS

1. What three elements combined make a fire?
2. What are the three principal methods of extinguishing a fire?
3. How can most fires be prevented on board ship?
4. What constitutes one of the greatest fire dangers on board ship?
5. Name the most important precautions which must be observed during the embarkation of gasoline.
6. What action would you take on discovering an oil leak?
7. Where would you not stow timber?
8. Why should you not keep paint pots scattered about the ship?
9. Why should clothing and bedding be stowed properly?
10. Do you stow books and papers overhead near your sleeping billet?
11. Where would you find the regulations governing the safety of explosives and pyrotechnics?
12. How is fire prevented from originating from a very hot pipe?
13. What is the cause of spontaneous combustion?
14. Why should you never throw cigarette ends out of scuttles or over the side?
15. Why is the control of ventilation in the vicinity of a fire important?
16. What immediate action would you take on discovering a fire?
17. How would you starve a fire?
18. What are the points to remember when using sea water for firefighting?
19. Why should water not be used on electrical apparatus?
20. Why is it very important to cool everything adjacent to a burning compartment?
21. What is the object of smothering a fire?
22. What precaution would you take after extinguishing a fire?
23. Why should you approach a fire through smoke by crawling or crouching?
24. What precaution must you take if smoke and fumes are dense?
25. How should a firefighter be dressed?
26. Describe the operation of the four types of hand extinguishers supplied in the Royal Navy. Give examples of occasions when each should be used.

27. What is a firemain system?
28. How many hoses can be used simultaneously off a firemain section in normal circumstances? How can this number be increased?
29. How can a temporary supply of water be obtained if one section of the firemain is damaged?
30. What are hydrants, and where are they to be found?
31. What precautions should be taken in the care and maintenance of hoses?
32. Describe the three types of nozzle supplied to a man-of-war.

Chapter 6. ROPE AND ITS USAGE

Construction and characteristics of Vegetable Fibre cordage

1. What are vegetable fibres, yarns and strands? Describe how they form a rope.
2. How does a vegetable fibre rope hold together under stress?
3. Describe the process known as spinning.
4. Describe the process known as twisting.
5. How are strands made up into rope?
6. How long is a hawser-laid rope?
7. What is the difference between hawser-laid and shroud-laid rope?
8. What is cable-laid rope? What are its advantages and disadvantages when compared with hawser-laid rope?
9. Where would you expect to see cable-laid rope used?
10. What is the lay of a rope and how does it affect the rope's elasticity and strength?
11. How is the size of cordage measured in the Royal Navy?
12. How is the length of a rope measured?
13. What are the general characteristics of vegetable fibre cordage?
14. Is the resistance of vegetable fibre cordage to the effects of weather increased by rot-proofing?
15. From what materials is vegetable fibre cordage made, and how can the different types be distinguished at a glance?
16. What is a rogue's yarn?
17. On what depends the quality of manila rope?
18. Where would you expect to see manila cordage fitted?
19. What are the disadvantages of sisal cordage when compared with manila cordage?
20. In which country is the strongest type of hemp grown?
21. Describe coir rope. What is its main advantage over other vegetable fibre ropes?
22. What is boltrope, and where would you expect to see it fitted?
23. Where must you never use stage lashing?
24. For what purpose is log line used?
25. What are junk, rounding and oakum?
26. What is meant by small stuff? Name four types.
27. What is pound line? From which fibre is it made?
28. Which type of cordage is used when making up hammock clews?

29. Place cordage made of Italian hemp, sisal, manila and coir in their order of precedence in regard to their strength, weight, flexibility and wearing qualities.
30. Place the following types of cordage in their order of precedence in regard to strength: shroud-laid rope, hawser-laid rope, cable-laid rope, boltrope and stage lashing.
31. What is the difference in construction of signal halyard, log line and lead line?
32. For what purposes are the following small stuffs used: twine, mackerel line, marline and nettlestuff?
33. What happens to cordage when it becomes wet?
34. What must you never do to a rope when it is wet?
35. How can dampness affect cordage?
36. Why does a rope become slack-jawed?
37. Before deciding to turn a boat's fall end for end, what special features should be looked for?
38. Approximately how many yarns are there in each strand of manila and sisal?
39. How can rot be detected?
40. How would fatigue show itself in cordage?
41. What are the causes of fibre weakness?
42. What is the most reliable method to ascertain the strength of a rope?
43. What are the advantages and disadvantages of ropes which have a hard lay; a soft lay?
44. Where would you expect to see soft-laid cordage used?
45. What is the jaw of a rope, and the angle of lay? How are these related to the hardness of the lay?
46. How can bad material in a rope be disguised?
47. Where is cordage supplied to the Royal Navy manufactured?
48. Where can you find the Admiralty specifications for weight and breaking strength of cordage?
49. How would you roughly calculate the breaking strength of manila or sisal?
50. How would you find the safe working load of cordage?
51. What is the breaking strength and safe working load of 4-inch manila cordage?
52. How would you estimate the strength of rope which has been much used but is in good condition?

Construction and characteristics of Man-made Fibre cordage

53. Name the various types of man-made cordage.
54. How does man-made fibre cordage differ in construction from vegetable fibre cordage?
55. What does a hawser-laid rope tend to do when used as a single whip?
56. Compared with natural fibre cordage, how much stronger is Nylon and Terylene cordage?
57. Approximately how much will Nylon and Terylene cordage stretch before parting?
58. Used within their safe working loads, how much will Nylon and Terylene cordage stretch?

59. What is the advantage of shock absorption?
60. What effect does wetness have on Nylon and Terylene cordage?
61. When does man-made fibre cordage emit a steamlike vapour?
62. What is the specific gravity of the basic yarn of Nylon?
63. What effect does temperature change have on cordage?
64. What chemicals have no harming effect on man-made fibre cordage?
65. Can you stow away man-made fibre cordage when wet?
66. What are the limitations of this type of cordage?
67. How can friction impair the strength of a rope?
68. Give twelve instances where man-made fibre cordage is used?
69. What is the advantage, with regard to stowage space, in having a ship fitted out with man-made fibre cordage?

Construction and characteristics of Wire Rope

70. How is wire rope constructed?
71. How many strands are there in wire rope?
72. What are the functions of the jute or hemp heart?
73. How is a wire rope made flexible?
74. Describe the various types of wire rope used in the Royal Navy and the purposes for which they are used.
75. Explain '3-inch E.S.F.S.W.R. (6×37)'.
76. How is the size of wire rope measured?
77. How is the length of wire rope measured?
78. What is the length of a coil of steel wire rope?
79. What are the approximate formulae for calculating the breaking strength of different types of wire rope?
80. How do you find the safe working load of wire ropes?
81. What are the main differences between vegetable and man-made fibre and wire ropes?

Handling Vegetable Fibre cordage

82. What are the four elementary rules?
83. What is a bight of a rope?
84. Why should the end be kept free when coiling down a rope?
85. How should you coil down a rope which is led through a block?
86. What are the common coiling-down mistakes?
87. How is a right-hand laid rope coiled down?
88. How is a rope coiled for running?
89. When coiling a rope in the hand, which way should the thumb point?
90. What is meant by thoroughfooting a rope?
91. Describe what is meant by faking down a rope.
92. How is a rope cheesed down?
93. When should a rope never be cheesed down?
94. Demonstrate the methods of belaying to a cleat and to a staghorn. Why is it necessary for the first belaying turns to be taken correctly? Why should you never complete with a half hitch?
95. How are a small coil and a large coil stowed on a belaying pin or cleat?
96. What is meant by under-running?

97. What is a heaving line and how is it prepared for throwing?
98. Why should you always make fast the end of a heaving line before throwing it?
99. Describe the methods of opening up a new coil of rope.
100. How would you cut off a length of rope from a new coil?
101. How are coils of new rope stowed?
102. Why is it important to examine new rope before it is put into service?
103. What are the signs of dry rot in vegetable fibre cordage?
104. What would you do with a rope which is suspected of having dry rot?

Handling Man-made Fibre cordage

105. How is a coil of new rope uncoiled?
106. In which direction is rope belayed on bollards?
107. How can you avoid abrasion and chafe?
108. When towing, how is a hawser secured to a capstan?
109. Is there any advantage in securing alongside at half-tide?
110. How would you clean oil from a rope?
111. What is the greatest danger when a rope parts?
112. Where must you never stand when handling this type of cordage?
113. Why should you exercise extreme care when easing out rope round bollards?
114. How can greater control be gained when easing out from a bollard?
115. What material would you use when racking a rope?

Handling Wire Rope

116. How is a kink removed from wire rope?
117. What is a bad nip? How is wire rope crippled? How are kinks avoided when coiling wire rope?
118. What is meant by 'freshen the nip'?
119. What are a fairlead and a Panama plate?
120. When using wire rope, what is the minimum diameter of bollard or drum?
121. When using wire rope, what is the minimum diameter of a sheave?
122. What is a Frenchman, and where is it used?
123. How would you run out a coiled-down wire?
124. Why should not wire rope be run out from the top of a coil?
125. Describe the methods of opening up a new coil of wire rope.
126. How would you cut off a length of wire rope?
127. Demonstrate the use of bulldog grips. Can they be used for joining two wire ropes together?

Handling hawsers

128. What is a hawser and where is it used?
129. What are the safety rules? Name six of them.
130. Explain the following orders and terms: 'Heave!', to haul, 'Haul taut!', 'Hold fast!', to hoist, 'Marry!', 'Lower away!', 'Handsomely!', 'Roundly!', 'Light to!', 'Veer!', to snub, to surge, to render, to back up.
131. How would you bend a heaving line to the bollard eye of a berthing hawser, and a messenger to the hawser eye of a heavy hawser?

132. Describe two methods of joining hawsers together.
133. How is a hawser, fitted with a hawser eye, secured to a bollard?
134. How is a fibre rope belayed to a single bollard?
135. How is a wire hawser belayed to a single bollard, and why should the end be racked to the hauling part?
136. When securing two or more berthing hawsers to a single bollard, how should their bollard eyes be placed over the bollard, and what is the reason for this?
137. How are the turns of a wire hawser racked when belayed to twin bollards?
138. How is a towing hawser belayed to twin bollards?
139. Demonstrate how to catch a turn on a single bollard, and a turn round twin bollards.
140. How should a hawser be manned when hauling in the slack round bollards?
141. How is a heavy hawser controlled when being paid out?
142. Describe the essential rules for surging a hawser round a bollard.
143. What is the holding effect of three turns of a wire hawser round a bollard when backed up by one man?
144. What attention should always be given to a wire hawser under strain as it is being reeled up?
145. What indication does a wire hawser give as it reaches the limit of its strength?
146. Where should you not stand when working hawsers?
147. What is the difference between a cordage stopper, chain stopper, chain check stopper, and a Carpenter's stopper, and where would each be used?
148. When using a rope or chain stopper, how can a slackening of the hawser be avoided when it is belayed?
149. Why is a Carpenter's stopper supplied with two sizes of wedge-piece?
150. Name the berthing hawsers of a ship secured alongside a jetty.
151. What is meant by doubling-up and singling-up?
152. What are off-fast and on-fast moorings?
153. What precautions are taken when a ship is berthed alongside?
154. What is the length of a fibre hawser, and how is it fitted at each end?
155. What is the length of a wire hawser, and how is it fitted at each end?
156. What other gear is supplied for each wire hawser?
157. What is the purpose of a bollard strop?
158. What is the length of a berthing hawser, and how is it fitted at each end?
159. For what purpose are spring and hurricane hawsers used? Describe the difference between them.
160. What is the difference between a hawser, a berthing hawser and a hurricane hawser?
161. Name at least six types of hawser supplied to a carrier.
162. How are fibre hawsers stowed?
163. How is the end of a wire hawser secured to the spool of its reel?
164. Describe how a wire hawser is reeled up?
165. Why is acid harmful to wire rope? What lubricant would you use for a wire hawser?
166. When would a wire hawser be rounded up?
167. What does the presence of rust on a wire hawser indicate?
168. How often are wire hawsers surveyed?

17 + M.S. I

Chapter 7. BENDS AND HITCHES AND GENERAL ROPE WORK

Bends and hitches

1. Does a knot, bend or hitch in a rope reduce its strength? If so, by how much?
2. Which parts of a rope are called the fag end, standing part and bight?
3. How many elements can be used in bends and hitches? Name them.
4. Make the following knots, bends and hitches blindfold; and describe where you would use them: reef knot, clove hitch, round turn and two half hitches, fisherman's bend, double sheet bend, single carrick bend, buntline hitch, double Blackwall hitch, bowline, cat's-paw.
5. State which knots, bends or hitches you would use for the following purposes, and demonstrate each example named: lashing up a sail or awning; slinging a bale; hoisting or towing a spar; hitching a rope to a rail or spar; bending a fibre hawser to the ring of an anchor; making fast a boat's painter to a ringbolt; making fast a boat's painter to a lizard; bending a boat's lazy painter to a Jacob's ladder; bending a sheet to a sail; bending a rope to a cringle; lowering a man over the side; bending a heaving line to a berthing hawser; and bending two fibre hawsers together which (a) will not be passed round a capstan, and (b) will be passed round a capstan.
6. How can a rope be temporarily shortened?
7. How is the bight of a rope secured to a hook?
8. How are slip knots made?
9. What is a monkey's fist?
10. Demonstrate two mountaineer's knots and two fisherman's knots.
11. How is the eye of a rope secured to a spar?
12. What is parbuckling?
13. How can the strain be taken off the hauling part of a fall?
14. What is meant by choking the luff, and what is its disadvantage?
15. What is a mousing?
16. How can a hawser hold or haul another hawser?

General rope work

17. What other whippings are there besides the common whipping, and where would they be used?
18. What is the purpose of whipping a rope?
19. Which whipping is the most secure?
20. How would you whip the end of a man-made fibre rope?
21. Demonstrate how two spars are cross-lashed.
22. What is meant by taking frapping turns?
23. Demonstrate the following knots, and give instances where they would be used: crown knot; wall knot; wall and crown knot; crown and wall knot; heaving line knot.
24. What is a seizing?
25. What are the different types of seizing, and where could they be used?

26. Describe the relationship between the strength of the seizing stuff and the number of turns of a seizing.
27. What is the relation between the size of a seizing and the size of the rope on which it is used?
28. How is seizing stuff made up?
29. How is a heaving mallet used?
30. How is a Spanish windlass used?
31. What is the purpose of using a heaving mallet?
32. How is a seizing started?
33. How is each type of seizing finished off?
34. Does a splice reduce the strength of a rope, and if so by how much?
35. What tools can be used when splicing cordage?
36. Where would the following be used: long splice, cut splice, chain splice, Flemish eye?
37. Demonstrate your ability to make a back splice, an eye splice and a short splice. What are their purposes?
38. How is a splice finished off?
39. What is meant by tapering, dogging?
40. Why is it necessary to marl the strands of man-made fibre cordage before you start splicing?
41. What precautions should be taken during the splicing of man-made fibre cordage?
42. How many tucks are made when splicing man-made fibre cordage?
43. How is a splice in man-made fibre cordage finished off?
44. Why is a rope wormed, parcelled and served, and what precaution is necessary with a rope so fitted?
45. How is a rope wormed, parcelled and served?
46. How can water be prevented from entering a stay which is parcelled and served throughout its whole length?
47. How is a serving started and finished off?
48. Name eight permanent ways of preventing a rope's end from unlaying, and when would they be employed?
49. What is a selvagee strop and how is it made?
50. How would you put a strop on a spar? On a rope? What type of strop would you use for each?
51. What is the chief point to remember about the use of slings?
52. How is the tension in the legs of a sling increased or reduced?
53. How would you sling a cask horizontally?
54. What are the following: can hooks, butt sling, bale sling?
55. What is meant by breaking bulk?
56. What is a span, and how is the tension in a span increased or reduced?
57. What is meant by swigging off? How would you swig off on a fall?
58. Does a splice reduce the strength of a wire rope? If so, by how much?
59. Which method of wire splicing is used in the Royal Navy?
60. What is a marline spike?
61. Are the strands of a wire rope tucked with or against the lay when splicing?
62. What is the tucking sequence for wires up to, and including, 4-inch and for wires above 4-inch?
63. How much wire is allowed for tucking?

64. Describe how a wire rope is prepared before splicing an eye into it.
65. What is a locking tuck?
66. Describe how you splice an eye in wire rope.
67. How is a wire rope splice tapered off?
68. How would you remove the remaining wires of each strand after completing the taper?
69. How is a wire rope splice finished off?
70. Demonstrate your ability to make an eye splice in $1\frac{1}{2}$-inch F.S.W.R.

Chapter 8. RIGGING

Rigging fittings

1. For what purpose is a shackle used?
2. Describe the following shackles: straight shackle, bow shackle, screw shackle, forelock shackle, feathered shackle, joining shackle and clenched shackle.
3. Name the parts of a shackle.
4. What is meant by 'wide in the clear'?
5. Describe six shackles which are used for anchors and cables.
6. Why is a joggle shackle slightly curved?
7. For what purposes are thimbles used?
8. Describe the different types of thimbles.
9. Where would you expect to see a round welded thimble fitted?
10. Name the parts of a hook.
11. Which is the stronger, size for size, a hook or a shackle?
12. For what purposes are the following hooks used: cargo hook, ram's-horn hook, swivel hook and trip hook?
13. How many ways can a hook be moused?
14. Describe the following: eyeplate, eyebolt, deck clench, ringbolt and union plate. For what purposes are they used?
15. What is the difference between a rigging screw and a turning-in screw?
16. What different types of rigging screw are provided in the Royal Navy?
17. What is a rigging slip?
18. What is meant when a rigging screw is set up?
19. Give three examples where a rigging screw is used.
20. What is a block?
21. Name the parts of a block.
22. How is the size of a wooden block measured?
23. What size of ordinary wooden block would be required for a $2\frac{1}{2}$-inch rope?
24. What is the relation between the size of a metal block and the rope it is designed to take? How can you tell the size of a metal block?
25. Describe an I.B. block, metal block, gin block, snatch block, common block, clump block and fiddle block.
26. Where would you expect to see fitted a clump block, a snatch block?
27. Describe the sheaves and bearings of wooden and metal blocks.
28. What different means of attachment are fitted to blocks?
29. What is meant by the jaw of a block?
30. How is a block described? Give an example.

31. When should a snatch block never be used?
32. What is the difference in the strength between an I.B. block, a clump block and a snatch block?
33. How can you find the correct lifting load allowed for a block?

Purchases and tackles

34. What is a purchase?
35. What is a tackle?
36. Name the parts of a tackle.
37. What is meant by the terms 'mechanical advantage' and 'velocity ratio' when applied to a tackle?
38. What is meant by the terms 'reeving to advantage' and 'reeving to disadvantage'? Sketch an example of each.
39. When hoisting a given weight how can the load on the standing block be reduced?
40. Describe the following whips and tackles and state the mechanical advantage of each: single whip; double whip; gun tackle rove to advantage; luff rove to disadvantage; jigger; handy billy; two two-fold purchases (each rove to advantage) rigged luff upon luff.
41. Why is it more efficient to use more than one tackle than to increase the number of sheaves in a tackle?
42. Describe a Dutchman's purchase. When is it used?
43. What is the practical rule for finding the loss in the mechanical advantage of a tackle due to friction?
44. What is the loss due to friction in a two-fold purchase when used to hoist a weight of 1,000 lb?
45. How would you estimate the pull required on the hauling part of a tackle to hoist a given weight?

Masts and spars

46. For what purpose are masts fitted in merchant ships?
47. Name the parts of a conventional mast.
48. What are the following: tabernacle, mast coat, mast partners, stayband, truck, trunnion hoop, spur, Samson post and trestle-trees?
49. What are a yard, a gaff, a derrick?
50. How is a mast supported in position?
51. Why are insulators fitted in all standing rigging?
52. Who determines the positioning of insulators?
53. Describe how a topmast is fitted.
54. What are the following: sheerpole, gaiters, ratlines?
55. What are the following: hammock gantlines, dressing lines, Inglefield clips? What is the name of the dressing line which is rigged between the masts?
56. Name the parts of a yard.
57. Describe how a slung yard is rigged.
58. Describe how a gaff is rigged.
59. What are the advantages of a tripod mast and a lattice mast over a polemast?
60. Describe how a derrick is fitted and how it is rigged.

61. Is any mechanical advantage gained by a winch?
62. On what depends the amount of mechanical advantage gained by a winch?
63. What is the purpose of the pawl and ratchet on a winch?
64. What is a warping drum? How would you use it?
65. What would you do if you had allowed a riding turn to develop on a warping drum?
66. What is the term used when the warping drum is allowed to revolve within the turns of a rope?

Booms

67. With what boat booms is a large man-of-war equipped?
68. Describe a lower boom; what is its purpose, how is it fitted and how is it rigged?
69. What is a boatrope? When is it rove, what is its use and how is it rigged?
70. When are booms swung out into their harbour position?

Danbuoys

71. What is a danbuoy, and for what purpose is it used?
72. Describe how a standard danbuoy is rigged.
73. Describe the moorings of a danbuoy.
74. How would you lay a danbuoy?
75. How would you lift a danbuoy?

Chapter 9. SHIPS' BOATS

1. When a man-of-war is in harbour, for what tasks are her boats used?
2. When a man-of-war is at sea, for what tasks are her boats used?
3. For what purpose do merchant ships carry boats?
4. What different methods do you know of propelling a rowing boat?
5. How are pulling boats propelled in the Royal Navy?
6. What is a 'pulling and sailing boat'?
7. What is meant by single-banked, double-banked, bank of oars?
8. Name five types of pulling boat.
9. How are different types of sailing boat described?
10. What are the two main classes of power boat?

Construction

11. Name and describe the different methods of boat construction in general use.
12. What materials are used in boat-building?
13. What is the difference between a clinker-built boat and a carvel-built boat?
14. What is the strongest form of construction for wooden boats?
15. Name at least five kinds of timber used in the construction of wooden boats.
16. How is the bottom of a wooden boat protected from marine borers?
17. Describe the construction of boats made from glass-reinforced plastic.

18. Where, in a boat, are the following situated, and what is the purpose of each: apron, backboard, benches, bilge stringers, breasthook, buoyancy blocks, canopy, carlings, drop keel, crutches, dickie, floor, gudgeon and pintle, hog, keelson, knee, rubber, shutter, stringer, tabernacle, timber, transom and washstrake?

19. Where in a boat are the eyes, head sheets and stern sheets?

20. What is the purpose of each of the following items of a boat's fittings or equipment: bullseye, horse, running hook, lazy painter, sling-plate steadying span, strongback and engine case?

21. To what fittings in a boat are the boat's slings attached?

Sailing rigs

22. What are the following: boltrope, sheet, earing, genoa, jib, spinnaker?

23. Name the parts of a four-sided and of a three-sided sail.

24. What is the difference between a lug sail and a gaff sail?

25. What is the name of the sail set between a gaff and the masthead?

26. What are stormsails?

27. Give an example of a trysail and of a staysail.

28. What is the difference between a foresail and a jib? What is a headsail?

29. What are the terms for putting a reef in a sail and taking a reef out of a sail?

30. How is the mainmast of a 27 ft Montague whaler stayed?

31. What is the difference between standing rigging and running rigging?

32. Describe the rig of a Montague whaler.

33. What is the rig of a 32 ft cutter?

34. Describe the fore sheets of a 32 ft cutter.

35. How, in a 32 ft cutter, is the luff of the foresail secured to the forestay?

36. Describe the normal rig and the racing rig of a 14 ft R.N.S.A. sailing dinghy.

37. How, in a 14 ft dinghy, is the gaff secured to the mast?

38. Describe the rudder of a 14 ft dinghy.

39. Give a general description of a 27 ft motor whaler.

40. What precaution would you take with regard to the engine of a motor whaler before shoving off under sail?

41. Describe the sailing rig of a motor whaler.

42. How is the mast raised?

43. Describe how you would rig the mainsail.

44. Describe how you would rig the spinnaker.

45. What are the spinnaker sheet and the spinnaker guy?

46. Describe fully how the mainsail is reefed.

47. How is a reef shaken out?

Stowage of boats in H.M. ships

48. Describe the four main types of boat davits in general use.

49. What is the difference between the radial davit and the quadrantal davit?

50. What extra davit fittings are provided when a seaboat is hoisted at radial davits?

51. What are sea lifelines, griping spar, jumping net?

52. Describe the fittings of quadrantal davits.
53. On fixed or gantry-type davits how is the upper block of each fall secured?
54. How would you turn in a boat hoisted at radial davits?
55. How are the boat's falls rove in your ship, and what is the length and size of each fall?
56. How are the falls of a seaboat marked? Why?
57. How would you take out the twists in a boat's fall?
58. When are a boat's falls renewed or turned end for end?
59. When inspecting a boat's falls what details would you look for?
60. Why is it important to see that a boat is properly positioned in her crutches?
61. When is a boat pitched?
62. What are boats called which are normally stowed on crutches?
63. What are boom boats, nested stowage, high-lows?
64. Describe how you would stow a boat whose crutches are not available.
65. How is a boom boat secured in her crutches?
66. What precautions would you take with a boom boat in hot climates?

Slinging and disengaging

67. Describe the boat's slings of a boat permanently hoisted at davits.
68. What slings are used when hoisting a boom boat?
69. What are a bridle sling and a gunwale sling-plate?
70. How is a boat, normally hoisted at davits, hoisted by crane?
71. What is the purpose of a spreader?
72. With what is a spreader marked?
73. When are a boat's slings fitted, and who is responsible for fitting them?
74. When a boat is returned to store should her slings be returned with her?
75. What is a Robinson's common hook and where is it used?
76. Describe fully the operation of Robinson's disengaging gear.
77. Demonstrate your ability to set up the disengaging gear of a seaboat.
78. What are the fore-and-after, releasing lever, tumbler hook, safety pin, mousing link?

Chapter 10. BOAT HANDLING

Lowering and hoisting boats in harbour

1. Why is nobody allowed before the foremost fall, or abaft the after fall, when a boat is being hoisted or lowered?
2. Why do you think it is dangerous to place your hand on a boat's fall, and to place your hand or arm on the gunwale of a boat?
3. Who constitute the crew of a motor whaler?
4. Give the detailed sequence of orders and the action which follows when lowering a motor whaler from davits in harbour.
5. If a boat is not being lowered on an even keel, what order would you expect to be given?
6. After a boat has been lowered, why should you not cross the falls before rounding them up?

7. Give the detailed sequence of orders and the action which follows when preparing to hoist, and hoisting, a motor whaler by hand at davits in harbour.
8. When would you expect to be given the order 'Shipside fall, hoist'?
9. How are the davit slips passed and secured?
10. Demonstrate how you would pass a davit lifeline.
11. How is a boat prevented from moving fore and aft during the operation of lowering and hoisting?
12. What is the duty of the boat's crew after a boat has been hoisted?
13. Describe how a boom boat is hoisted out by crane or derrick.
14. Should the crew of a boom boat be in their boat when she is slung inboard?

Pulling

15. Before taking away a pulling boat what items of her equipment should be in the boat?
16. Name eight items of special gear you may require to carry.
17. How would you find out the contents of a boat's distress box?
18. What is a boat's bag, and what are its contents?
19. When would the contents of a boat's bag be split? What name is then given to each bag?
20. What is meant by 'catching a crab'? How can this be avoided?
21. What do the following orders mean: 'Shove off'; 'Oars down'; 'Give way together'; 'Oars'; 'Stroke together'; 'Easy all'; 'Eyes in the boat'; 'Bow'; 'Way enough'?
22. Describe the duties of the crew when getting under way in a Montague whaler.
23. Describe the duties of the crew when going alongside in a Montague whaler.
24. Describe getting under way and going alongside in a cutter.
25. When going alongside in a cutter how is the order 'Way enough' obeyed?
26. On what occasion are a cutter's oars boated without first being tossed? Why is this necessary?

Sailing

27. What are the differences between close-hauled, sailing free, reaching, running?
28. When is a boat on the starboard tack?
29. What is meant by tacking or going about?
30. When are the orders 'Ready about', 'Helm's a lee' given?
31. What do the following terms mean: up helm, down helm, lee helm, weather helm, to be in irons, to miss stays, to keep away, to luff, to bear away, to pinch and to let draw?
32. What is meant by gybing?
33. What is meant by wearing?
34. When is a boat said to be beating?
35. When is a boat said to be running by the lee, brought by the lee?
36. If your boat gets in irons what would you do?
37. What is meant by flat aback, hove to, hug the wind, goosewing, make sail?

17*

38. Where would you find the Sailing Rules?
39. Name at least seven points of conduct with which you should comply when under way in a sailing boat.
40. What is a boat's pivoting point and what governs its position?
41. Why is the trim of a sailing boat so important?
42. Why is it inadvisable for a boat to carry lee helm?
43. When loading your boat with stores how would you stow them, having regard to the trim and behaviour of the boat under sail?
44. How would you correct lee helm?
45. How would you correct weather helm?
46. How would you trim your boat when running, reaching and beating?
47. How can you lessen the chance of missing stays when going about?
48. Why is a correct lead for the fore sheets so important?
49. Should the pull of a sheet tend to tauten the leach rather than the foot of a foresail?
50. How should your sails be trimmed when beating in a light wind?
51. Describe how you would go about with regard to the trim of the sails and the movement of the helm.
52. If your boat is slack in stays (i.e. sluggish in going about) how would you guard against missing stays?
53. What is the only occasion on which you may use an oar while your sails are set?
54. Describe how you would trim your boat and trim your sails when on a reach.
55. Describe how you would trim your boat and trim your sails when running before the wind.
56. When would you use your bearing-out spars?
57. Why should you avoid running dead before the wind in a strong wind and following sea?
58. When running before a strong wind and heavy sea how can you steady your boat and prevent her from yawing?
59. Describe how you would trim your sails and alter your helm when gybing?
60. What points must you watch carefully during the moment of the gybe?
61. Is it good seamanship to gybe your boat in heavy weather? Give your reason.
62. What would you do if your boat were struck by a squall when reaching, running and beating?
63. When would you reef your sails, and how is this done in (a) a boat carrying a loose-footed mainsail and (b) a motor whaler?
64. When reefing, would you gather or roll the foot of the sail? Why?
65. If your boat capsizes what is the most important point to remember about the crew?
66. What would you do with the sails and rigging after capsizing?
67. What is the object of a centre-plate? In what position would you have it when running, reaching, beating and approaching shoal water?
68. Describe how you would get a sailing boat under way from alongside a ship's ladder, and from the lower boom.
69. Describe how you would go alongside the ladder of a ship head to wind.
70. Describe how you would go alongside down-wind.

71. What is meant by heaving-to? How would you accomplish this in a Montague whaler? In a cutter?
72. What would you do if one of your crew fell overboard when reaching or running?

Seaboats

73. What is a seaboat, and for what purpose is it used?
74. Who is responsible for manning the seaboat?
75. When is the seaboat inspected, and by whom; and how often are the crew and lowerers mustered?
76. What personnel constitute the seaboat's crew and lowerers?
77. How often during the night watches is the seaboat's crew exercised?
78. If the coxswain of the seaboat sees that the seaboat requires draining, what action does he take?
79. When do you expect to hear the pipe 'Away lifeboat's crew'? Who would man the boat?
80. Is any special training necessary for coxswains of seaboats when their ship is operating as plane guard?
81. Give twelve points on how you would rig and equip a seaboat.
82. As coxswain of a seaboat what details would you check when taking over your duties, and what report would you make?
83. Why should the lizards never be hitched to the lower blocks of the falls?
84. How would you secure the boatrope, and what are its uses?
85. Why is the tiller of a seaboat stopped towards the side of the boat next to the ship?
86. Give the detailed sequence of orders and the action which follows when lowering a motor whaler as a seaboat at sea.
87. When a boat is being lowered in a seaway how is she prevented from surging, and from swinging towards or away from the ship's side?
88. What action do the hands inboard take as soon as the seaboat is slipped?
89. For what purpose are Nylon anti-shock slings used? Where are they rigged and how are they fitted?
90. For what purpose are the steel wire pendants used? Where are they rigged and how are they fitted?
91. Explain the order 'Marry to your marks'. What does this order ensure?
92. Give the detailed sequence of orders and the action which follows when preparing to hoist, and when hoisting, a motor whaler as a seaboat by hand in rough weather.
93. What action does the coxswain of a seaboat take after his boat is secured?
94. Give eight hints to coxswains of seaboats.
95. Is there any need to take the turns out of a seaboat's fall before it is hooked on? Why? When and how would you take out the turns?

Hints to coxswains of boats

96. As coxswain of a boat, what navigational information would you ask for if ordered to go to a strange landing-place?
97. What signals should you always be able to identify when away in a boat?
98. What details of the boat's equipment would you check before getting under way?

99. Why should not a boat be hauled ahead from an inner billet when casting off from the lower boom in a tideway?
100. When a boat is unhooked from, or hooked on to, her falls, which fall is unhooked first, and which is hooked on first? Give the reason in each case.
101. Why should the bows of a ship anchored in a tideway be given a wide berth?
102. Describe how you would make your boat fast alongside a ship's ladder in a tideway.
103. Where would you find the table giving the maximum number of persons who may be carried in a cutter and a motor whaler (a) in calm weather and (b) in rough weather?
104. When loading your boat with stores, how would you stow them?
105. What precautions would you take if ordered to bring off money or a valuable package?
106. Describe how you would anchor your boat (a) on a sandy bottom in 2 fathoms, (b) on a rocky bottom in 3 fathoms, and (c) off a steeply shelving beach when the boat is to be left unattended.
107. If your boat is anchored in a rough sea and snatching at her cable, what would you do?
108. Describe how you would make your boat fast to a lower boom, and what details you would attend to before allowing the crew to leave her.
109. What details would you attend to after your boat is hoisted inboard?

Chapter 11. ANCHORS AND CABLES

1. What are the three principal methods by which a ship can be secured with ground tackle to the bottom? What are the advantages or disadvantages of each?
2. What is meant by mooring ship, mooring a cable each way, open hawse?
3. What are the following: mooring swivel, buoy pendant, mooring buoy, buoy shackle, securing-to-buoy shackle, reducing link?
4. Name the parts of an anchor.
5. What are a ship's largest anchors called and where are they stowed?
6. What is an anchor at the stern of a ship called?
7. What is a killick?
8. Describe how an anchor holds. Why should the pull on the cable, where it enters the sea bed, be horizontal?
9. What prevents an anchor from jerking when a ship yaws?
10. Describe the difference between the older type anchors and the improved type anchors, with regard to holding power.
11. What is meant by 'breaking out' an anchor?
12. What is the length of a shackle of cable?
13. How is a ship's bower cable usually made up?
14. What is a half-shackle of cable? In what positions are half-shackles inserted in the bower cable, and why is this so?
15. How are shackles of cable joined together?
16. What is the difference between a lugged joining shackle and a lugless joining shackle?

17. What are the two types of chain cable used in the Fleet, and what are the differences between them?
18. What is a Blake slip and where is it used?
19. Sketch roughly the anchor and cable arrangements of a cruiser.
20. For what are the following used: cable holder, cable locker, navel pipe, capstan, screw slip, riding slip, preventer, bonnet, deck clench, cable clench, Scotchman, clump cathead, compressor, windlass, gypsy, warping drum, guillotine, stem hawsepipe, bullring?
21. How are the capstan and cable-holders driven?
22. How are the ends of a ship's bower cable attached (*a*) to the anchor and (*b*) to the ship?
23. Describe how a minor warship rides when anchored or secured to a buoy.
24. Describe the cable party of a cruiser.
25. How does a cable party prepare an anchor for letting go?
26. Why are two anchors prepared for letting go when a ship intends to come to single anchor?
27. Which anchor is normally let go when coming to single anchor?
28. Describe the sequence of events when coming to single anchor, from the time the Captain of a ship orders 'Let go' until the cable party is secured.
29. Describe how the cable of a ship is prepared for securing to a mooring buoy.
30. Describe the following: working bridle, standing bridle, bullrope, cable hook, picking-up rope.
31. How is a picking-up rope secured to a buoy shackle?
32. What are buoy jumpers and when must they never remain on a buoy?
33. Describe how a ship approaches a mooring buoy and secures her cable to the buoy shackle.
34. With what outfit of anchors and cables is a carrier equipped?

Chapter 12. ELEMENTARY ORGANISATION

1. By whom is a man-of-war commanded?
2. What are the general responsibilities of the Executive Officer of a ship?
3. What is the Executive Officer of a ship called when he is under the rank of Commander?
4. Who assumes command of a ship in the event of the Captain being absent on leave?
5. What is a department in a ship?
6. Why is a ship's company organised in watches?
7. What is the difference between the two-watch system and the three-watch system?
8. Into how many parts is a watch divided and sub-divided?
9. What is a part-of-ship? Of how many watches is it composed?
10. What abbreviations are used for the forecastle, foretop, maintop and quarterdeck?
11. What is a Captain of the Top?
12. What is meant by the Functional system?
13. What is a division? What is the main principle of the divisional system? Name four divisions.

14. What time and watch system does the seaman follow?
15. How does the seaman describe the morning, afternoon, evening?
16. What times of day are indicated by striking five bells?
17. How many bells are struck to indicate half-past seven in the evening? In which watch would it be?
18. For what purposes is the ship's bell struck other than for marking the time of day?
19. When are more than eight bells struck?
20. What does the term 'silent hours' mean?
21. What is 'little one bell'?
22. Into what three main periods is a day divided?
23. What do you understand by Daily Harbour Routine?
24. What is a 'make and mend'?
25. What is the Guard and steerage?
26. What does the expression 'to pipe' mean?
27. Demonstrate how to hold a boatswain's call.
28. Pipe a high note, a low note, a warble and a trill.
29. Pipe the following: 'Still', 'Carry on', 'Hands to dinner', 'Hoist away', 'Pipe down', 'Up spirits'.
30. Which pipes require no verbal amplifications?
31. What is the 'Hail'?
32. How would you call away (a) the barge, and (b) the first motor boat?
33. How are the hands called in the morning?
34. How is a watch at night called?
35. When is the expression 'D'ye hear there!' used in piping?
36. For what is piping generally reserved?
37. When does a bugle call require amplification by pipe?
38. What are the six rules to be observed when using any of the methods of communication?
39. Recite the phonetic alphabet and numerals.
40. What are the four principal methods of communication within a ship?
41. As a messenger, describe your duties.
42. How would you deliver a verbal message to an officer?
43. Describe how you would use a telephone.
44. Can telephone conversations be overheard by others?
45. What are the rules for using a voicepipe?
46. Describe the General Broadcast system in your ship.
47. What is a control box?
48. Describe the General Warning and General Alarm. How and from where are these signals made?
49. Why is it necessary for a ship to have section broadcast systems?
50. Can the General Broadcast system cut in on all sectional broadcasts?
51. When is the S.R.E. automatically muted?
52. If a section is 'in use' how can that section receive a General Broadcast?
53. Where will you find the instructions on how to operate a Control or Section Box?
54. How many different types of microphone can you name?
55. Describe how you would speak into a microphone.

Chapter 13. NAVAL COMMUNICATIONS

1. What was the name of Nelson's signal officer?
2. What is the origin of the name Telegraph Hill?
3. Name the various means of communication used in the Royal Navy.
4. What methods of signalling are included under the term visual signalling?
5. Make the following by the semaphore code: S E A M A N S H I P 1 9 6 3.
6. How can you tell which way the sender of a semaphore signal is facing?
7. What flags and pennants are used in Naval signalling?
8. Describe the colours and shapes of the following flags: R O Y A L N A V Y. What is the name given to each of these letters?
9. How is a flag signal normally executed?
10. How can you tell whether a signal hoisted by a man-of-war is from the Naval or International Code?
11. What is Radio Teletype?
12. By what system can ships receive pictures of weather maps?
13. Write your name and number and, below each letter and figure, mark the equivalent symbol of the Morse code.
14. What is a callsign? What is the callsign of your ship? What is the callsign of your motor boat?
15. Where is a boat's signal book kept and how is it protected from wear and tear?
16. What is the difference between the terms 'precedence' and 'security'? Name the various precedence and security classifications.
17. You are away in your ship's motor boat and your engine breaks down. Draft out the signal you would make to your ship on your Aldis light, and write down how it would be received if you used the correct procedure.

Chapter 14. NAVAL CEREMONIAL

1. What general distinctions are there between standards, colours, distinguishing flags and signal flags?
2. Why are some flags 'flown' and why are some flags 'worn'?
3. When and by whom is the Union Flag worn afloat?
4. Which ships wear the White Ensign, and which wear the Blue and the Red Ensigns?
5. When is the White Ensign worn at the peak of the gaff on the mainmast?
6. What vessels other than men-of-war are permitted to wear the White Ensign?
7. When is the Jack (Union Flag) worn by H.M. ships?
8. Why do men-of-war wear a Jack?
9. When do H.M. ships wear a masthead pendant?
10. When would you expect to see a vessel wearing a blue masthead pendant?
11. What constitutes a suit of colours of one of H.M. ships in commission?
12. What is the Queen's Colour?
13. When is the Queen's Colour paraded ashore?
14. What is the only occasion when the Queen's Colour is lowered?

15. What is the Admiralty flag?
16. What distinguishing flag is worn by a Vice-Admiral? By a Commodore?
17. For what purpose are the following flags flown: paying-off pendant, blue Peter, house flag, courtesy flag?
18. Between what times are colours worn by H.M. ships in harbour?
19. When may the White Ensign be hauled down at sea?
20. When is the White Ensign worn by naval shore establishments?
21. When is an ensign worn at half-mast?
22. Describe the ceremonies attending the hoisting and lowering of colours in harbour.
23. What is meant by dressing ship and illuminating ship?
24. How are marks of respect accorded?
25. What are the following and in what circumstances are they used: 'Alert', 'Still', 'Last Post', 'Sunset'?
26. What are the salutes by the bugle?
27. On board a man-of-war, what would you do whenever the 'Alert' is sounded?
28. Is the number of rounds fired in a gun salute odd or even? Give the reason for your answer.
29. How does one man-of-war salute another?
30. In what manner may a merchant ship salute a man-of-war?
31. If a man-of-war has an accommodation ladder rigged on each side, by which ladder should a midshipman go aboard?
32. What is meant by piping the side, and whence does this originate?
33. Who should be piped over the side?
34. What preparations are made before a man-of-war enters harbour? Where are the hands situated?
35. Who is the Officer of the Guard and what are his duties?
36. State what you know about the following customs: manning and cheering ship, splicing the main brace, sounding the hour of midnight on New Year's Eve.
37. Name two naval marches. For what occasions are they played?
38. What is the badge of the Royal Navy and where is it displayed?
39. Why is a bottle of wine broken over the stem of a ship when she is being launched?
40. What do you know about 'crossing the line', and 'garlands'?
41. How do you acknowledge an order?
42. Why is whistling prohibited in H.M. ships?

Chapter 15. SHIPS' COMPASSES

1. What is a meridian?
2. In which direction does the Earth rotate, and what is this direction called?
3. What are the three methods of graduating a compass card?
4. What are the following: cardinal point, intercardinal point, intermediate point and by-point?
5. What is a point, and how many degrees does it represent?
6. Box the compass, omitting the by-points.

7. What are the angular equivalents in degrees of 2 points, 4 points, 6 points and 8 points?
8. If an object is said to lie two points before the beam, what is its bearing in degrees relative to the ship's head?
9. What are the three types of compass used at sea?
10. What are the chief differences between the types of compass and in what direction does each point?
11. What is the lubber's line, and to what does it point?

The gyro-compass

12. Whereabouts in a ship would you expect to find her gyro-compasses?
13. How long does a gyro-compass take to settle when started, i.e. before it can be used?
14. How would you check that a gyro repeater is functioning correctly?
15. How is the failure of a gyro-compass indicated?
16. What is gyro error, how is it recorded, and how is it applied to obtain a true direction?
17. What are gimbals, and what is their purpose?
18. What is a 'Pelorus' and where is it situated?
19. What is an azimuth circle, and what is its use?
20. What is a bearing repeater, and where is it situated?
21. What is a compass bearing, and how is this obtained?
22. When is a repeater said to be 'wooded'?
23. What are the differences between a bearing repeater and a tape repeater?
24. What is a steering prism?

The magnetic compass

25. What is the difference between magnetic and non-magnetic materials?
26. If two magnets are placed side by side, which ends tend to attract each other and which tend to repel each other?
27. What is a magnetic field, and what are lines of magnetic force?
28. How can the properties of magnetism be introduced into a magnetic substance?
29. What is the difference between permanent magnetism and induced magnetism?
30. How does the Earth's magnetism affect a pivoted magnetic needle?
31. Do the Earth's lines of magnetic force run directly between the North and South Magnetic Poles?
32. Why doesn't a compass needle (and card) tilt when the ship is in high latitudes?
33. What is variation? Is variation the same at all places on the Earth?
34. Does variation alter from year to year at any one place, and where is the variation at any place recorded?
35. What is the rule for applying variation to a magnetic direction in order to obtain a true direction, and vice versa?
36. The bearing of a lighthouse is 115° magnetic; if the variation at that place is 17°E., what is the true bearing of the lighthouse?
37. How does a ship acquire magnetic properties?

38. What is deviation?
39. Is the deviation the same for all the magnetic compasses in a particular ship?
40. Is the deviation for a particular compass the same for all directions of the ship's head?
41. Does electricity affect a magnetic compass?
42. Describe briefly how a ship's magnetic compasses are adjusted for deviation.
43. What is a deviation card?
44. What is the rule for applying deviation when converting a compass direction to a magnetic direction, and vice versa?
45. What is the compass course to steer if the magnetic course is 323° and the deviation for that direction is 3°W?
46. How are true, magnetic and compass directions recorded?
47. The bearing of a lighthouse from a ship steering 123°C is 358°C; what is the true bearing of the lighthouse if the variation is 3°W and the deviation for course 123°C is 4°E?
48. What precautions are necessary when using a magnetic compass?
49. What precautions would you take when using a boat's compass?

Chapter 16. CONNING AND STEERING

1. Describe how conning orders are given, repeated and obeyed?
2. What is the difference between a conning and a steering position?
3. Why should the wheel be turned steadily when putting on or taking off rudder?
4. What are the normal limits of the rudder angle?
5. What is the purpose of the wheel indicator?
6. What is the meaning of the following: 'Starboard fifteen'; 'What's your ship's head?'; 'Midships'; 'Steady'; and 'Course, Sir'?
7. The course ordered is 270 degrees and the ship's head is pointing 268 degrees. Which way do you put the wheel to bring the ship back to her proper course?
8. What is meant by 'making good' a course?
9. What is meant by 'carrying wheel'?
10. What information does a helmsman turn over to his relief?
11. For what is the quartermaster responsible?

Orders for regulating the speed and movement of the engines

12. What is the duty of a telegraphman?
13. Describe the purpose of an engine order telegraph, and a revolution order telegraph.
14. What is the correct repeat and report for the engine order 'Stop port and centre'?
15. What is the purpose of the reply gongs?
16. For a two-shafted man-of-war how many reply gongs are provided at the primary steering position?

17. At which position should the engine telegraph be set for the engine room to obey an alteration in revolutions?
18. What is meant by 'Full ahead'?

Conning and steering positions, communications and instruments

19. Describe the following: bridge, compass platform, pilotage position, emergency conning position, forward steering position, wheelhouse, after steering position, hand steering position and tiller flat.
20. Describe the purpose of the following: conning intercom, conning voice-pipe, emergency conning line, steering order transmitter and receiver, rudder indicator, telegraph repeaters, shaft speed and direction receivers and revolution telegraph repeat receivers.

Steering gear in H.M. ships

21. Give a general description of the telemotor steering system.
22. In a telemotor system, what is the purpose of the pressure gauges on the steering pedestal?
23. What precautions are necessary when operating the telemotor steering system?
24. Describe the following steering gear defects: wheel jam, complete failure of telemotor system, complete failure of steering pump power, and partial failure of steering power.
25. As quartermaster what would you do if the steering gear was not operating correctly?
26. What action does the quartermaster take in the event of a change-over of conning positions?
27. Describe the reports, orders and sequence of operations necessary to change-over from the primary steering position to the secondary steering position, and back to the primary position.
28. Who is left in charge of the steering position while the quartermaster is closed up in the secondary steering position?
29. How is a ship steered during a steering position change-over?
30. How are communications maintained between steering positions when both positions are manned?

Chapter 17. ELEMENTARY NAVIGATION

Charts

1. What is a chart, and what information does it give?
2. What is the chart datum of a chart?
3. To what level of the sea are the depths shown on a chart related?
4. What depth is recorded by a sounding?
5. How are depths shown on a chart?
6. If a bank or rock is uncovered at low water how is this indicated on a chart? Explain this indication.
7. If the height of a lighthouse is shown on a chart, to what level is the height referred?

8. Why is it important to know the nature of the bottom? How is this indicated on a chart? Give some examples.

Buoyage

9. For what purposes are buoys used?
10. How can you identify a buoy from a distance?
11. Why should you never use a buoy to fix the ship's position?
12. What is the lateral system of buoyage?
13. On what sides are the starboard and port hands of a channel?
14. Which side of a channel is indicated by port-hand buoys?
15. If no land is visible how would you tell on which side to pass a port-hand buoy?
16. When leaving harbour, on which side do you pass a starboard-hand buoy?
17. What markings identify a group of starboard-hand buoys?
18. What is the purpose of a middle-ground buoy? Sketch the various types of middle-ground buoys, with their topmarks.
19. On which side can you pass a middle-ground buoy?
20. What is the purpose of a mid-channel buoy, and on which hand should it be left? Sketch one.
21. What are leading marks?
22. How is the position of a wreck marked, and how is the side indicated on which it may be passed?
23. What is the purpose of a landfall buoy? Sketch one.
24. What is a light-ship? Is it more reliable than a buoy? Give the reason for your answer.

Lights

25. How is a light indicated on a chart?
26. What is meant by the characteristic of a light?
27. Describe, with the aid of sketches, the four main light characteristics.
28. Describe with the aid of sketches the following lights: F.Fl.; Gp.Fl(3); F.R.; Gp.Occ.(2); and Qk.Fl.
29. What is the 'period' of a light?
30. What does the symbol **U** indicate when shown against a light on a chart?
31. Where are details to be found of lighthouses, light-ships and light-buoys?

Sounding

32. How can a sounding be taken?
33. Describe a boat's lead and line. How is the line marked?
34. Describe how a sounding by a boat's lead and line is obtained.
35. Describe a hand lead and line. How is the line marked and of what cordage is it made?
36. How is the lead bent to a hand lead line?
37. For what purpose is a hide becket used?
38. What is meant by the term 'arming the lead' and what is its purpose?
39. How is a lead line stretched before marking off?
40. What is the difference between marks and deeps?

41. How would you call the following soundings: 11 fathoms, 17 fathoms, 5½ fathoms, 8¾ fathoms?
42. What do you call if you cannot obtain a sounding?
43. When a ship is under way but not making way, how do you tell whether she is drifting?

Chapter 18. ELEMENTS OF THE RULE OF THE ROAD

1. For what does the Rule of the Road provide?
2. What is meant by a vessel, a power-driven vessel, sailing vessel, visible, short blast, prolonged blast, whistle, not under command?
3. What is meant by the term 'risk of collision'. How is it determined?
4. What is meant by the terms 'steady', 'drawing forward' and 'drawing aft', when used in relation to the compass bearing of another vessel?
5. Define the following terms: under way, on the starboard tack, on the port tack and running free.
6. Two sailing vessels are approaching one another on a steady relative bearing; which of the vessels gives way under the following circumstances:

    (a) both close-hauled on opposite tacks?
    (b) one running free and the other close-hauled?
    (c) both running free?
    (d) both running free, one with the wind right aft?
    (e) both close-hauled on the same tack?

7. What lights are shown by a sailing vessel when under way?
8. What sound signals are made by a sailing vessel under way in low visibility when she is on the starboard tack, on the port tack and running free?
9. Two power-driven vessels are approaching one another on a steady relative bearing. Which of the vessels gives way under the following circumstances:

    (a) when each is approaching the other end-on or nearly end-on?
    (b) when not end-on, but each is two points before the other's beam?
    (c) when one is two points abaft the other's beam?
    (d) when one is more than two points abaft the other's beam?

10. What is the rule when a sailing vessel or a power-driven vessel is overtaking?
11. Risk of collision exists between your vessel and another, but your vessel has right of way; what should you not do under these circumstances?
12. When may the Steering and Sailing Rules be disregarded?
13. If yours is the vessel which has to take avoiding action, what points would you bear in mind when deciding what action to take and when to take it?
14. Does an auxiliary vessel sailing close-hauled give way to a sailing vessel running free?
15. What lights are shown by a power-driven vessel?
16. When a power-driven vessel is under way and is in sight of any other vessel what do the following sound signals made by her indicate: one short blast, two short blasts, three short blasts?

17. What sound signal does a power-driven vessel make in low visibility to show that she is (*a*) under way but stopped, (*b*) making way through the water?

18. By means of a sketch show the arcs of the horizon relative to a vessel which determine whether she should hold her course or give way to an approaching vessel.

19. Which side of a narrow channel must a power-driven vessel keep?

20. Does a power-driven vessel have to give way to a sailing vessel? Would this rule apply in a narrow channel?

INDEX